Ritual and Economy in East Asia
Archaeological Perspectives

UCLA COTSEN INSTITUTE OF ARCHAEOLOGY PRESS
Ideas, Debates, and Perspectives

Volume 1

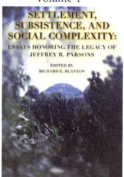

Settlement, Subsistence and Social Complexity: Essays Honoring the Legacy of Jeffrey R. Parsons
Edited by Richard E. Blanton

Volume 2

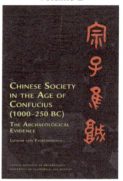

Chinese Society in the Age of Confucius (1000–250 BC): The Archaeological Evidence
By Lothar von Falkenhausen

Volume 3

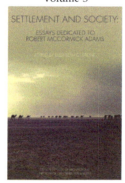

Settlement and Society: Essays Dedicated to Robert McCormick Adams
Edited by Elizabeth C. Stone

Volume 4

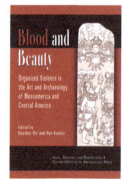

Blood and Beauty: Organized Violence in the Art and Archaeology of Mesoamerica and Central America
Edited by Heather Orr and Rex Koontz

Volume 5

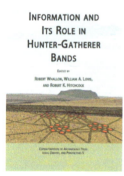

Information and Its Role in Hunter-Gatherer Bands,
Edited by Robert Whallon, William A. Lovis, and Robert K. Hitchcock

Volume 6

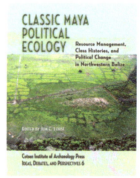

Classic Maya Political Ecology: Resource Management, Class Histories, and Political Change in Northwestern Belize
Edited by Jon C. Lohse

Volume 7

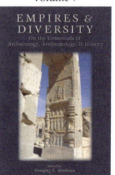

Empires & Diversity: On the Crossroads of Archaeology, Anthropology, & History
Edited by Gregory E. Areshian

Volume 8

Unmasking Ideology in Imperial and Colonial Archaeology
Edited by Bonnie Effros and Guolong Lai

Ritual and Economy in East Asia
Archaeological Perspectives

Edited by
Anke Hein, Rowan Flad, and Bryan K. Miller

Festschrift in Honor of
Lothar von Falkenhausen's 60th Birthday

Ideas, Debates, and Perspectives 9
UCLA COTSEN INSTITUTE OF ARCHAEOLOGY PRESS

THE COTSEN INSTITUTE OF ARCHAEOLOGY PRESS is the publishing unit of the Cotsen Institute of Archaeology at UCLA, a premier research organization dedicated to the creation, dissemination, and conservation of archaeological knowledge and heritage. It is home to both the Interdepartmental Archaeology Graduate Program and the UCLA/Getty Program in the Conservation of Cultural Heritage. The Cotsen Institute provides a forum for innovative faculty research, graduate education, and public programs at UCLA in an effort to positively impact the academic, local and global communities. Established in 1973, the Cotsen Institute is at the forefront of archaeological research, education, conservation and publication, and is an active contributor to interdisciplinary research at UCLA.

THE COTSEN INSTITUTE OF ARCHAEOLOGY PRESS specializes in producing high-quality academic volumes in nine different series, including *Monumenta Archaeologica, Monographs, World Heritage and Monuments, Cotsen Advanced Seminars,* and *Ideas, Debates, and Perspectives.* Through a generous endowment by Lloyd E. Cotsen, longtime Institute volunteer and benefactor, the Press makes the fruits of archaeological research accessible to scholars, professionals, students, and the general public. Our archaeological publications receive critical acclaim in both academic communities and the public at large.

THE COTSEN INSTITUTE OF ARCHAEOLOGY AT UCLA
Willeke Wendrich, Director
Aaron A. Burke, Editor-in-Chief
Randi Danforth, Publications Director
Deidre Brin, Digital Publications Director

EDITORIAL BOARD

Willeke Wendrich	Africa (Ex officio member)
Li Min	East Asia
John K. Papadopoulos	Mediterranean Basin
Gregson Schachner	North America–Southwest
Ellen J. Pearlstein	Conservation of Indigenous and Archaeological Materials
Richard G. Lesure	North America–Mesoamerica
Aaron A. Burke	West Asia–Near East
Randi Danforth	Ex officio member

Copyedited by Peg Goldstein
Designed by Sally Boylan

Library of Congress Cataloging-in-Publication Data

Names: Hein, Anke, editor, author. | Flad, Rowan K., editor, author. | Miller, Bryan Kristopher, editor, author. | Falkenhausen, Lothar von, honouree, writer of afterword.
Title: Ritual and economy in East Asia: archaeological perspectives : festschrift in honor of Lothar von Falkenhausen's 60th birthday / edited by Anke Hein, Rowan Flad, and Bryan K. Miller.
Description: Los Angeles : The Cotsen Institute of Archaeology Press, [2023] | Includes bibliographical references and index.
Identifiers: LCCN 2022056334 | ISBN 9781950446407 (hardback) | ISBN 9781950446414 (ebook)
Classification: LCC DS715 .R58 2023 | DDC 950--dc23/eng/20230109
LC record available at https://lccn.loc.gov/2022056334

Copyright ©2023 Regents of the University of California
All rights reserved. Printed in the United States of America

To Lothar von Falkenhausen in commemoration of his 60th birthday, from his students, colleagues, and friends

Lothar at the walled Neolithic site of Baodun, in Sichuan Province, July 23, 2005.
Photo by Rowan Flad.

Contents

Figures	vii
Tables	xiii
Preface: To Lothar *Li Shuicheng*	xv
Contributors	xvii
1 Introduction: Ritual and Economy in East Asian Archaeology *Rowan Flad and Anke Hein*	1

PART I: RITUAL ECONOMY

2 Uncovering Disguised Social Inequality: An Investigation of the Bronze Age Cemetery at Donghuishan *Wen Chenghao*	15
3 On the Margins of the Chinese World: The Bronze, Iron, and Gold of the Xi Rong at Majiayuan *Alain Thote*	35
4 Ritual Economies of Peripheral East Asia: Reflections on Mahan Mortuary Archaeology *Jack Davey*	59
5 State Regulations or Human Sentiment: The Disappearance of Funerary Figurines in Ninth Century Chang'an and Luoyang *Ye Wa*	81

PART II: RITUAL AND SACRIFICE

6 No Sacrifice Too Great: A Measured Speculation on the Motive behind the Great Sanxingdui Hoards *Richard Ehrich*	107
7 Raw Material Hoards, Ritual Deposits, or Disturbed Burials? Object Pits in the Mountains of Southwest China *Anke Hein*	121

8 The Zooarchaeology of Oracle Bone Divination in Northwest China   149
   Katherine Brunson, Li Zhipeng, Rowan Flad, Qiao Hong, and Wang Qianqian

9 Emergence of Chime-Bells and *Li-yue* in the Zhou Dynasty   167
   Kazuo Miyamoto

10 Consuming the Herds: Animal Sacrifice and Offerings of the Xiongnu   181
   Bryan K. Miller

PART III: TECHNOLOGY, COMMUNITY, INTERACTION

11 Long-Distance Influences and Local Adoption: Technological Innovation in
   Late Prehistoric Northwest China   199
   Rowan Flad

12 Organization of Copper Mining and Smelting along the Middle Yangzi River   225
   Shi Tao

13 Erlitou and Nanwa: Contextualizing White Ceramics in Early Bronze Age China   241
   Lee Hsiu-ping

14 Archaeology of Community: Changing Settlement Patterns from the Yingpanshan
   to the Shi'erqiao Period in Ancient Sichuan, China   261
   Lin Kuei-chen

15 China for Asia: Bencharong and Peranakan Porcelains in the Eighteenth and Nineteenth Centuries   283
   Ellen Hsieh

PART IV: OBJECTS AND MEANING

16 The Xi'an Kharoṣṭhī Inscription: A New Translation   297
   Minku Kim

17 Solidified *Qi* Clouds: Reconsideration of the Form and Name of *Boshan* Incense Burners   313
   Zhang Hanmo

18 "What Was the Nicest Thing You Ever Found?" An Essay on the Meaning of Objects   337
   Hans Barnard

Epilogue: The Number 60 and the Beginning of Everything   355
Willeke Wendrich

Afterword   365
Lothar von Falkenhausen

Index   373

Figures

Figure 1.1. Overview map showing the locations covered in each chapter
Figure 2.1. Location of the Donghuishan cemetery
Figure 2.2. Layout of the Donghuishan cemetery
Figure 2.3. Plot of correspondence analysis on grave goods from the Donghuishan cemetery with reference to age groups and sex
Figure 2.4. Plot of the confidence interval of the mean volume of graves in each tier of degree of completeness at the Donghuishan cemetery
Figure 2.5. Plot of the mean confidence interval of the number of grave goods in each tier of degree of completeness at the Donghuishan cemetery
Figure 2.6. Grave instances in the Donghuishan cemetery
Figure 3.1. Maps of sites mentioned in the text
Figure 3.2. Zhou bronze vessels
Figure 3.3. Bronzes and earthenware vessels from other sites
Figure 3.4. Bronzes, iron weapons, and silver torque
Figure 3.5. The deceased in Tomb 18, Majiayuan
Figure 3.6. Two earrings from princely tomb of Susa
Figure 4.1. Core sites mentioned in the text
Figure 4.2. Map of the Korean Peninsula and the supposed territorial extent of Mahan in the third century AD
Figure 4.3. Iron Age mortuary sites in western Korea frequently assigned to the Mahan culture
Figure 4.4. Site drawing of Tomb 2 from the Iksan Yŏngdŭng-dong cemetery
Figure 4.5. Cross-sectional diagram of the barrow tomb tradition of western Korea and the mounded tomb tradition of southern Korea
Figure 4.6. Distribution of cemeteries containing barrows, mounded tombs, or both
Figure 5.1. Map of site clusters mentioned in the text
Figure 5.2. Category I tomb figurines: tomb guardians and heavenly kings
Figure 5.3. Percentage of tombs with figurines in Chang'an from late sixth century to the late ninth century
Figure 5.4. Percentage of tombs with figurines in Luoyang from the mid- to late seventh century to the late ninth century
Figure 5.5. Category II tomb figurines: cavalry and honored guard
Figure 5.6. Category IV tomb figurines: animals
Figure 6.1. Map of sites mentioned in the text

Figure 6.2. Map of the Sanxingdui site
Figure 6.3. Bronze artifacts from Sanxingdui showing traces of burning and fragmentation
Figure 6.4. Levels of certainty in the case of the Sanxingdui hoards
Figure 7.1. Location of object deposits in Southwest China
Figure 7.2. Site locations in the Anning River valley by site type
Figure 7.3. Plan of object pits in the northern and southern part of Xichang Dayangdui; plan of Ka21; objects from pits; plan of Ka3
Figure 7.4. Plan of Dayangdui H1 and H2; objects from Pits H1 and H2 and Grave DM2
Figure 7.5. Objects from Puge Wadaluo H1; ceramics from Xichang Maliucun H1
Figure 7.6. Rubbings of the drum from Huili Luoluochong and bells from Huili Zhuanchangba
Figure 8.1. Map of sites mentioned in the text
Figure 8.2. Example of data collection protocols linked to descriptive variables in the online oracle bone database
Figure 8.3. Oracle bones from Huangniangniangtai and Donghuishan
Figure 8.4. Oracle bones from Qijiaping
Figure 8.5. Bone 374 in situ at the bottom of Huizuiwa Pit H2
Figure 9.1. Map of sites mentioned in the text
Figure 9.2. Nomenclature of *yongzhong* bells
Figure 9.3. Chronology of *nao* of northern China in the Late Shang Dynasty and Early Western Zhou Dynasty
Figure 9.4. Size variation of *nao* of northern China
Figure 9.5. Chronology of the *nao* bells of southern China
Figure 9.6. Classification of subtype attributes for *yongzhong* bells
Figure 9.7. Chronology of *yongzhong* of the Western Zhou Dynasty
Figure 10.1. Map of Xiongnu cemeteries mentioned in the text
Figure 10.2. Livestock offerings within the outer coffin versus those above the burial chamber, Grave 50, I'lmovaya pad', Russia
Figure 10.3. Common extremities and body portions of livestock in Xiongnu burials
Figure 10.4. Locations of Xiongnu cemeteries with livestock body portion offerings
Figure 10.5. Locations of Xiongnu cemeteries with livestock extremity offerings
Figure 10.6. Livestock offerings for Grave 7, Shombuuzyn-Belchir, Mongolia
Figure 10.7. Livestock offerings for Grave 16, Shombuuzyn-Blechir, Mongolia
Figure 10.8. Livestock offerings for Tomb 64, Takhiltyn-Khotgor, Mongolia
Figure 10.9. Schematic of the Xiongnu animal sacrificial process
Figure 11.1. Map of sites mentioned in the text
Figure 11.2. Qijia culture oracle bone (FCN4148) from 16GQ Trench 2 at Qijiaping
Figure 11.3. Rough distributions of cultural traditions in Northwest China
Figure 11.4. Maxianshan nephrite quarry location north of a tributary of the Dabi River; Maxianshan landscape; nephrite raw material at Maxianshan
Figure 12.1. Major sites and study area mentioned in the text
Figure 12.2. Distribution of ancient mining and smelting sites in the middle Yangzi River valleys
Figure 12.3. Mining galleries at Location 2, Orebody VII, at the Tonglüshan mine
Figure 12.4. Major sites in and around the Tonglüshan region mentioned in the text
Figure 12.5. Distribution of mining and smelting sites at the Tonglüshan preservation zone
Figure 12.6. Comparison of production-related remains at the Dalupu and Xiezidi sites
Figure 13.1. Map of site clusters mentioned in the text
Figure 13.2. White ceramic ritual vessels from Erlitou
Figure 13.3. Site map of Nanwa

Figure 13.4. Site map of Erlitou
Figure 13.5. *Doulixingqi*
Figure 13.6. *Longxingqi*
Figure 14.1. Neolithic sites on the upper Min River mentioned in the text
Figure 14.2. Neolithic sites on the eastern edge of Qinghai-Tibet Plateau
Figure 14.3. Ceramics of the first phase discovered at the Baodun site
Figure 14.4. Shi'erqiao site cluster in modern Chengdu City
Figure 14.5. Stone kneeling human figures discovered in Fangchijie, Meiyuan, and Sanxingdui
Figure 14.6. Pointed-bottomed vessels and jars with a ring foot discovered in the stone-slate burials at Yingpanshan
Figure 15.1. Locations discussed in this chapter
Figure 15.2. Examples of Bencharong porcelain at the Chao Sam Phraya Museum, Thailand
Figure 15.3. A Bencharong ware inlaid at the wall as part of the decoration (Wat Arun, Thailand)
Figure 15.4. Examples of Peranakan porcelain at the Pinang Peranakan Mansion, Malaysia
Figure 15.5. A sherd of Bencharong porcelain from the Mehan Garden site, the Philippines
Figure 15.6. Peranakan porcelain at the wall of Masjid Sunan Gunungjati, Indonesia
Figure 16.1. Map of sites mentioned in the text
Figure 16.2. Luoyang Kharoṣṭhī inscription (CKI 193), Stone A
Figure 16.3. Luoyang Kharoṣṭhī inscription (CKI 193), Stones B and C
Figure 16.4. Kharoṣṭhī Buddha (CKI 170)
Figure 16.5. Detail of Figure 16.4 (beginning of the inscription)
Figure 17.1. Map of sites mentioned in the text
Figure 17.2. *Boshan* incense burner excavated from the tomb of Liu Sheng
Figure 17.3. Queen Mother of the West and mushroom-shaped Mount Kunlun
Figure 17.4. Queen Mother of the West, King Father of the East, and hourglass-shaped, three-peaked Mount Kunlun
Figure 17.5. Triangle-shaped mountains
Figure 17.6. Mountain motif using curved lines
Figure 17.7. Mountain and salt well motifs
Figure 17.8. *Boshan* incense burner excavated from Dou Wan's tomb
Figure 17.9. Decorated tube with applied gold and silver and its unfolded design
Figure 17.10. Cloud clusters on the *qianqiu wansui yi zisun* embroidery compared to cloud patterns on the unfolded design on a gilt *boshan lu* cover
Figure 17.11. *Xunlu* with applied gold and silver from Maoling
Figure 18.1. Map of sites mentioned in the text
Figure 18.2. Google Ngram showing the occurrence of the words *thing(s)*, *meaning*, *object(s)*, *philosophy*, *anthropology*, and *archaeology*
Figure 18.3. Two statues of King Uthal of Hatra
Figure 18.4. Inscribed fossil of a mid-Eocene sea urchin *(Echinolampas africanus)*
Figure 18.5. Total ion current chromatogram of organic residue in the matrix of an ancient Greek unpainted angular kylix
Figure 18.6. Three gifts from Lothar von Falkenhausen to the author
Figure E.1. Map of places mentioned in the text
Figure E.2. Leather sandals found in the tomb of Pharaoh Tutankhamun
Figure E.3. Dichotomy of a landscape
Figure E.4. The Narmer Palette
Figure E.5. Tutankhamun's canopic chest with four canopic jars, protected by four goddesses
Figure E.6. The Ogdoad, from the Book of the Dead of Anhai

Tables

Table 2.1. Degrees of skeletal completeness at the Donghuishan cemetery

Table 2.2. Statistical indexes of grave volume according to degree of completeness at the Donghuishan cemetery

Table 2.3. Statistical indexes of the number of grave goods according to degree of completeness

Table 4.1. Summary of Mahan mortuary development

Table 4.2 Features of Mahan tombs

Table 4.3. Mahan tomb terminology

Table 6.1. Structural comparison of Pit 1 and Pit 2

Table 7.1. Deposits and chance finds from the Liangshan region

Table 8.1. Previously published oracle bones from sites in Gansu and Qinghai Provinces

Table 8.2. Oracle bones from Gansu and Qinghai Provinces examined by the OBEA project

Table 9.1. Combination of subtype attributes

Table 9.2. Collection of *yongzhong* found at graves of the Western Zhou Dynasty

Table 13.1 Sites with white ceramics in the Erlitou culture sphere

Table 13.2. Absolute and relative chronology of Erlitou and Nanwa

Table 13.3. Numerical data of white ceramics at Nanwa

Table 13.4. Numerical data of white ceramics at Erlitou

Table 14.1. Archaeological cultures prevailing on the Chengdu Plain and the Hengduan Mountains mentioned in the text

Table E.1. Examples of gendered dualities

Table E.2. Examples of geographic dualities

Table E.3. Examples of complementary dualities

Table E.4. Examples of triads

Table E.5. Organization in fours

Table A.1. Dedicatees of Festschriften to which Lothar von Falkenhausen has contributed

Table A.2. Partial list of UCLA professors in archaeology and related fields who are dedicatees of Festschriften

Preface: To Lothar

Li Shuicheng

1979–1981

A 20-year-old exchange student from West Germany quietly walked onto the Peking University campus. Young and shy, you lived in Building 26 with a roommate from Shaanxi from the class of 1978, and neither of us was quite used to the arrangement.

For the following two years, we often attended classes in the archaeology classroom in the eastern wing of the Humanities Building and viewed objects in the crowded and dimly lit artifact display room. Do you remember? Together we went to the Liulihe site in Fangshan and the Great Wall at Badaling. In the late autumn of 1980, along with other exchange students from various countries, you came with us to the Qianzhai site in Zhucheng, Shandong, and we excavated 5,000-year-old Dawenkou culture tombs. Although this excursion lasted but a short three days, during this ice-breaking time, we saw your unwavering efforts and hard work.

1990

In the midsummer, Beijing was unbearably hot and the air seemed to be humming with rage. Do you remember? Together with our other classmates of the '78 year, we gathered over a simple Korean barbecue at a restaurant on Qianmen Street, eating meat and mouthing off at each other, the sweat stinging our eyes and soaking our clothes. After dinner, we sat on the ground on the streets of Beijing, talking about the sadness of departing and the damned sun, attracting strange looks from passersby.

1999

In early spring, if I am not mistaken, you brought some of your students to trek through parts of Southwest China, measuring out Pujiang, Qionglai, and Zigong with our own feet, searching for ancient salt-making workshops. Do you remember? The boiling hot pot tested everybody's stomach. Along the Yangtze River, from Chongqing to Yichang, we saw the rare sight of the Baiheliang stone fish. The pointed-bottomed vessels of Ganjinggou and the stratigraphy of the Zhongba site excited everyone. We visited the once prosperous old salt town of Ningchang in Dashan County together, examining the derelict production sites, smelling the remnants of salt in the air, trying the simmering soup from White Deer Spring at Longjun Temple below Baoyuanshan, taking a boat down the Daning River to the Yangzi River—countless miles on densely packed roads giving us opportunity for endless reverie.

2009

You came to the campus of Peking University with your mother and family and celebrated your fiftieth birthday in the ancient capital of Beijing. I accompanied you and your family to the Sackler Archaeological Museum and listened to you hold forth on ancient Chinese relics and the history of China. We strolled under the shadow of the pagoda by the lake. Do you remember? The meeting had been agreed upon a year earlier at Xishan Puzhao Temple. On that day, you, Li Ling, and I went to the Futian cemetery to pay our respects to Wang Jing'an and our teacher Zou Heng. Afterward, we went to the Wan'an cemetery to lay flowers on the graves of Xia Nai, Zhu Dexi, and Qi Gong.

2019

You turned 60, and as the saying goes, "taoli tianxia 桃李天下" (you are a teacher with students everywhere), reaping your peaches and plums across the world. Teachers, students, and friends from all over the world gathered at UCLA to celebrate your birthday. I would like to take this opportunity to fondly remember our more than 40 years of friendship and cooperation. May you have happiness and health for many years to come!

Contributors

Hans Barnard
Cotsen Institute of Archaeology and Department of Near Eastern Languages and Cultures
University of California, Los Angeles

Katherine Brunson
Archaeology Program
Wesleyan University

Jack Davey
GW Institute for Korean Studies
George Washington University

Richard Ehrlich
School of Cultural Heritage
Northwest University

Rowan Flad
Department of Anthropology
Harvard University

Anke Hein
School of Archaeology
University of Oxford

Ellen Hsieh
Institute of Anthropology
National Tsing Hua University

Lee Hsiu-ping
Institute of History and Philology
Academia Sinica

Li Zhipeng
Institute of Archaeology
Chinese Academy of Social Sciences Institute of Archaeology

Bryan K. Miller
History of Art Department and Museum of Anthropological Archaeology
University of Michigan

Kazuo Miyamoto
Faculty of Humanities
Kyushu University

Shi Tao
School of Archaeology and Museology
Sichuan University

Alain Thote
École pratique des Hautes Études, 4ᵉ Section, Centre de recherches sur les Civilisations de l'Asie Orientale
Collège de France

Wang Qianqian
Qinghai Provincial Institute of Archaeology and Cultural Relics

Wen Chenghao
Institute of Archaeology
Chinese Academy of Social Sciences

Willeke Wendrich
Cotsen Institute of Archaeology and Department of Near Eastern Languages and Cultures
University of California, Los Angeles

Ye Wa
Cotsen Institute of Archaeology
University of California, Los Angeles

Zhang Hanmo
School of Chinese Classics
Renmin University of China

Chapter 1

Introduction
Ritual and Economy in East Asian Archaeology

Rowan Flad and Anke Hein

Ritual, economy, and the connections between them are topics interwoven throughout the work of Lothar von Falkenhausen, as most clearly reflected in the topics of his three most prominent monographs: *Suspended Music: Chime-Bells in the Culture of Bronze Age China* (Falkenhausen 1993), *Chinese Society in the Age of Confucius (1000–250 BC): The Archaeological Evidence* (Falkenhausen 2006 for the original English version and the Japanese translation, 2011 for the Korean translation, and 2017 for the Chinese translation), and the forthcoming *Economic Trends in Late Bronze Age China (1050–250 BC): The Archaeological Evidence* (preliminary title). These volumes reflect Falkenhausen's tremendous impact on the field of East Asian archaeology, an impact due not only to his comprehensive, erudite, and detailed treatment of the source materials and subject matters of concern but also to the fact that his work situates Bronze Age China squarely within a global discourse that interrogates the past to develop a deeper understanding of the nature of society, the relationships between individuals and institutions, and the fundamentals of the human condition.

Suspended Music, which was based on his PhD dissertation (1988), focused on ritual and its strong connection with music, an unsurprising topic given the author's strong musical talent and great love of music. The heart of that volume concerns reconstructing the music of bronze chime bells from the Shang and Zhou Dynasties and how tonal concepts and musical theory intertwined with political concepts that governed their creation and use. The book is not limited to music and politics, however. The very first chapter discusses socioeconomic issues; bronze production is the focus of another chapter. Altogether the book provides a discussion of the closely entangled relationship between ritual, politics, and technical aspects of bell creation and usage, and it effortlessly contributes to the field of musical theory.

The monograph *Chinese Society in the Age of Confucius* provides a social history of pre-Imperial China during the first millennium BCE. Von Falkenhausen produces a fresh analysis of archaeological evidence, particularly graves, as a window on elite and commoner society. Instead of allowing interpretation to be guided by textual narratives, his synthesis examines how a complementary and distinct view of ritual and society can be produced through careful attention to the material world within which people lived and acted. In particular, the book discusses the role of bronze vessels in ritual actions in both life and death, investigating what changes over time in these assemblages tell us about social and political structures. The work emphasizes the connection between ritual practices and social structures, discussing not only social stratification but also ethnicity, gender, and other forms of identity. It describes the Zhou lineage system as reflected in rituals and the way social structure and rituals changed during a ritual reform of the Middle/Late Western Zhou period (ca. ninth century BCE). The volume ends with a discussion of issues insufficiently explored in previous research on pre-Imperial China: demography, territorial expansion, military developments, and especially the economy. Economic topics, including trade, crafts, and agriculture, are fundamental components of society and are the center of his most recent monograph, in its final stages of publication when this volume was being produced.

This constant interweaving of ritual and economy in von Falkenhausen's work, sometimes emphasizing one and then the other, but always connecting the two, is at least partially a response to the preponderance of burial evidence in the archaeology of Bronze Age China. Ritual bronze vessels from burial contexts were particularly important in denoting rank, power, and also economic might. Producing these vessels required control over raw materials, manpower, symbolic representation, and technological know-how. Using them involved rituals through which individuals argued for and reinforced control over these economic levers. These rituals materialized social connections, social tensions, and social order, as did the various economic activities that were less directly implicated in the material culture of ritual.

On the occasion of Lothar von Falkenhausen's sixtieth birthday, June 6, 2019, dozens of students, colleagues, and other scholars influenced by his scholarship convened a conference and workshop titled The Art and Archaeology of Ritual and Economy in East Asia to further interrogate these themes and their connections. Participants presented and discussed a wide range of scholarship inspired by von Falkenhausen's work (Figure 1.1). In various ways, the scholarship explores different aspects of the nexus between ritual and economy, and participants shared a concern for clear terminology and explanation of underlying concepts. Accordingly, all contributions to this volume explicitly consider terminological and conceptual issues. Furthermore, several themes crosscut the contributions, and these themes reflect four issues central to the study of the relationships between ritual and economy not only in East Asia but in the ancient world more broadly. These issues give names to the four parts of this volume: "Ritual Economy," "Ritual and Sacrifice," "Technology, Community, Interaction," and "Objects and Meaning."

Each of these themes draws attention to the ways certain categories of social practice overlap with other categories. Accordingly, these themes aim to blur distinctions that, although sometimes heuristically useful, can obscure ontological overlaps and reify a notion that distinct spheres of social action are appropriate cross-culturally and transhistorically. In fact, as Michael Strevens (2020) recently discusses, the intellectual currents of the Enlightenment that promoted the privileging of empirical data and the consequential emergence of science in Western philosophical thought involved a partitioning of intellectual domains (for example, civil and spiritual) as well as spheres of expression (public and private). Other recent scholarship criticizes the assumption that domains of society can be neatly separated as independent units that constitute a composite whole (Asad 1993) and the Cartesian distinction between the natural and the cultural (Alberti and Bray 2009; de Castro 1998). The implication of much of this scholarship is that concepts that are sometimes framed as dichotomous, such as human and animal, social and natural, secular and sacred, structure and agency, and religion and economy, are categories that are better conceptualized as mutually constituted. The four central themes that cross-cut the contributions to this volume demonstrate the fluid boundaries between some such domains and reflect a set of concerns that are broadly considered in the study of art and archaeology in East Asia and beyond.

These dominant themes in the fields of art history and archaeology in East Asia pervade the work that von Falkenhausen has produced over the years. This is not an accident, given the significant impact he has had directing these fields and training a generation of scholars. We learn about the background for his influence from a personal preface by Li Shuicheng, one of Lothar's old classmates and friends from his study days in China, and then see the impact of his scholarship in the 18 essays that follow.

Ritual Economy

A number of the essays in this volume investigate the connections between a mutual constitution of sociopolitical structures, economy, and ritual. As one of us has elaborated elsewhere (Flad and Chen 2013:209), *rituals* are patterned, performative, distinctive formal acts that enable and solidify social bonds and reflect existing cultural principles (Bell 1997; Rappaport 1999; Valeri 1985). Rituals often manifest belief and notions of the sacred (see Insoll 2004; Kyriakidis 2007; Steadman 2009:23) and are central to the social identities of the participants (see Bell 1992, 1997). The *economy* might seem a domain that is even more clearly defined: "the way in which something is managed," with particular emphasis on the management of resources (*Oxford English Dictionary*). There has been considerable debate, however, over the degree to which economics are structured according to universally applicable considerations that can be formally modeled or whether there are substantive differences between the operational principles that underlie economies in different social contexts (Burling 1962; Dalton 1975; Firth 1965; Polanyi 1957; Wilk 1996). Much scholarship

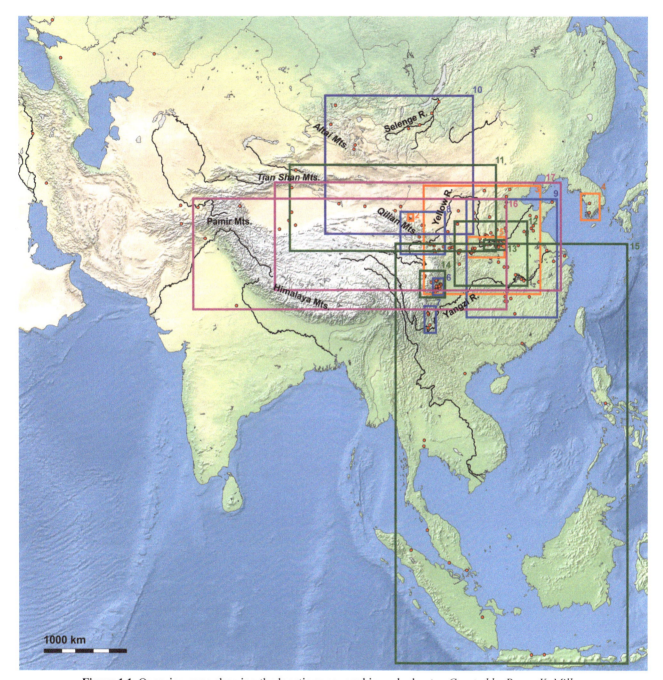

Figure 1.1. Overview map showing the locations covered in each chapter. *Created by Bryan K. Miller.*

on economics and economic anthropology has moved beyond this debate without fully resolving the underlying disagreements, but there is a shared recognition that the economy does not exist as a distinct domain that can be entirely separated from other aspects of social interactions. For example, the significance of economic concerns for political relationships is recognized by work on *political economy*, which broadly deals with the ways production and exchange are connected to laws, government, and custom and more specifically interrogates relations of power as manifest in the practice of managing resources (Earle 2000; Heyman 2013; Roseberry 1988; Woods 2000).

The concept of *ritual economy* ostensibly concerns both the economic aspects of ritual practices and the ritualized significance of economic practices (McAnany and Wells 2008; Miller 2015; Wells 2006; Wells and Davis-Salazar

2007). In one early consideration of these issues, Peter Metcalf (1981) considers the economy of ritual in burial practice in ethnographic Borneo to explain how occasions that involve different expenditures of resources and other variations can be thought of as equivalent. He argues that death rites can be best understood through an examination of economics, maintaining a rhetorical dichotomy between these domains even while recognizing their mutual constitution. More recently, scholars have pointed out that ritual economy is a concept that can be useful in the context of small-scale societies, where "ritual institutions can function to direct economic practices in the absence of hierarchical social divisions" (Miller 2015:124), implying that concerns often considered under the rubric of political economy remain important in the absence of formal political structures. We would furthermore suggest, building on the discussion in the previous section, that the tendency to assume that the domains of ritual, economy, and politics are meaningfully distinct needs rethinking. Several chapters in this volume consider the economic aspects of ritual practices, particularly burial rituals. They do not overly emphasize these concerns as separate domains but instead illustrate the inherent and pervasive connections between ritual and economy that are evident through this volume.

In his study of the second millennium BCE Donghuishan cemetery in Zhangye, Gansu, China, Wen Chenghao explicitly considers the concept of ritual economy, seeking to understand the socioeconomic dimensions of funerals that occurred in the Bronze Age community at this site. Following Metcalf (1981), Wen's investigation focuses on secondary burials at the site as a particularly useful phenomenon with which to examine provision and consumption in a ritualized context. Burial rituals were an occasion for mediating between economic inequality and a sense of community solidarity. He finds a relationship between evidence for secondary burial rituals and energy expenditure, explores other measurable aspects of the graves that illuminate the use of resources in the ritual process, and also describes how practices such as skull removal illustrate the significance of postmortem engagement with skeletons to the society at Donghuishan. This latter observation shows one way the ritual economy overlaps with the meaning of objects, a topic highlighted in the third section of this volume.

Also focusing on the region of Gansu Province in China but during the first millennium BCE, Alain Thote examines burial remains from the site of Majiayuan and other tombs associated with the Western Rong. Through a careful analysis of the material culture found in these tombs, Thote shows how the ritualized context of burials materialized the social and economic position of the Western Rong population between the steppe cultures to their north and west and the Central Plains communities associated with the Qin and Zhou to their east. Particularly important to the identity of the Western Rong was their engagement in craft-creative practices that reflect the social, cultural, and ideological significance of manufacture and thus embody the overlapping relationships between ritual and economic domains. (See recent extensive discussions of craft in Adamson 2021; Ingold 2013; Langlands 2018; Li 2021; Rizvi 2018.)

Jack Davey likewise examines mortuary contexts as a means to investigate overlapping concerns related to ritual and economy. His study problematizes the concept of the Mahan culture through a close consideration of the variability in the features associated with so-called Mahan burials on the Korean Peninsula. This variability indicates differences in ritual practices, the use of resources within those rituals, and processes of producing burials that together suggest heterogeneous identities. He concludes that the Mahan is a "process of becoming" produced in the context of contemporary and historical research. Although rooted in typological debates, Davey shows that an attention to ritual and economic practices is necessary to evaluate what was culturally meaningful to historical groups of individuals, and he challenges overdetermined efforts to assign coherent identities that have emerged primarily as a result of later historiographical discourse to communities in the past.

A fourth study of burial practices, by Ye Wa, examines social practices associated with funeral rituals, explicitly connecting changes in mourning processions during the Tang Dynasty (619–907 CE) to broad changes in the political economy of Tang society. As in the study by Davey, Ye follows von Falkenhausen in pointing to the need to critically examine the relationship between textual and material culture as sources of understanding about the past. Using these two sets of information in a complementary fashion, rather than privileging one over the other, Ye contextualizes changes in funeral practices by considering changes in the material culture found in graves in light of contemporary discourse on funeral practices and filial piety. This discourse is entwined with concerns about the economy of the state, and thus burial practices are necessarily connected to economic factors affecting the producers of burial goods and the practitioners who oversaw funeral rites. Her analysis indicates that the changes in Tang burial rituals, rather than being a reaction to political dynamics, as some have proposed, related to tensions between philosophical and economic concerns of the state on the one hand and individual concerns about filial piety on the other.

Ritual and Sacrifice

While the first section includes essays that examine the mutually constituted domains of ritual and economy in the contexts of burial practices, other studies examine ritualized practices more broadly in East Asian archaeological contexts. Some of these contributions focus on the significance of rituals, the sacrificial form of which famously constitutes one of the two foundations of the Chinese state: "The major affairs of the state are sacrifice and war" (国之大事, 在祀与戎, *Zuozhuan*, Cheng 13, Shisanjing zhushu, p. 1911). In that phrase, the term *si* 祀 is understood to mean ritual in a temple involving sacrifice, as in *jisi* 祭祀 (sacrifice), and more broadly has the connotation of worship or sacrifice to the ancestors. The Han Dynasty *Shuowen jiezi*, a dictionary dating to the first century CE, glosses the term *si* 祀 as "ji wuyi ye 祭无已也" (unceasing sacrificing). The latter term, *rong* 戎, in its earliest form is a combination of the characters for a weapon and armor or a shield, thus signifying warfare, but some scholars have pointed out that the significance here may also be understood to be "war sacrifices" (Shaughnessy 1996:159). As Rod Campbell has pointed out (2012:305), sacrifice (*jisi* 祭祀) is "usually subsumed under the broader category of li 礼" (ritual/propriety), an observation that illustrates that concepts in Chinese that relate to sacrifice and ritual and their intersection are numerous. Related terms include but are not limited to *si* 祀, *ji* 祭, *li* 礼, *xun* 殉 (to be buried with the dead), *xi* 牺 (using animals in sacrifice), *ci* 祠 (religious sacrifice/shrine), and other words for sacrifice, such as *zhao* 珧 and *yong* 禜. Not only are there large numbers of related terms, many of which were used at particular points in time throughout Chinese history and have roots in the Shang 商 and Zhou 周 periods (Li Yuan 2004), but the meaning of terms changed over time (Puett 2002) and were multiple. Si 祀, for example, meant the duration of a ritual cycle or a "round of sacrifice" (Smith 2010:21) in some oracle bone inscriptions and meant age, generation, or regnal year by the Tang Dynasty, as evidenced in the writing of Liu Zongyuan 柳宗元 (773–819 CE), if not earlier.

Sacrifice is a form of ritualized act that involves the giving up a subject to obtain some benefit (Carrasco 2013; Flad and Chen 2013:211; Hubert and Mauss 1964 [1898]; Valeri 1994). These concepts are obviously related through the process of ritualization and furthermore should be considered as categories whose constituent practices illustrate the problem of distinguishing ritual from other domains. Although some definitions of sacrifice and ritual rely on a distinction between sacred and profane, "a distinction between religious and secular distinctions or motivations is difficult and . . . fundamentally, historically flawed" (Campbell 2012:306; see also Bell 2007; Hesse et al. 2012), and sacrifices might be best understood as "ritualized practices combining offering and destruction" (Campbell 2012:306), typically involving performative violence "as a form of communication with a deity, gift giving, or expiation to a higher being" (Carrasco 2013:211).

Richard Ehrich considers one example of a sacrificial context in his discussion of pits filled with various jade, bronze, ceramic, gold, and ivory objects at the second millennium BCE site of Sanxingdui in the Chengdu Plain of Sichuan Province, China. He argues that these deposits result from a pattern of ritual practices that were crucial to placemaking at this site and were related to social processes intended to mitigate crises. Sacrifices, deposited in hoards, Ehrich argues, were one form of mediating with the supernatural and reinforcing the power of an elite stratum of society for the period during which Sanxingdui was a central place in this region.

Like Ehrich, Anke Hein also draws on analogous deposits in Europe to consider the nature of place-based sacrificial practices in Sichuan and wrestles with determining what terminology is most appropriate for categorizing such deposits. Her examples come from the mountainous Liangshan region of western Sichuan rather than the Chengdu Plain, and they date later than the Sanxingdui examples. Furthermore, rather than a default explanation focused on ritual and sacrifice, as is the case with the Sanxingdui deposits, the examples from western Sichuan have not always been recognized as part of a widely dispersed phenomenon. Hein argues that these are intentional deposits and that they fit into different categories, the understanding of which is enhanced by drawing on the more frequently discussed and interrogated examples from Europe.

Katherine Brunson and colleagues consider material evidence from ancient China of divination, a ritualized practice that is focused on mitigating uncertainty. The remains they present are oracle bones, a category of divination objects best known from inscribed examples from Late Shang (ca. 1250–1050 BCE) contexts from the urban center of Yinxu in Anyang, Henan, China. Those examples comprise the earliest corpus of writing from China and document the ritualized nature of much of this writing. Oracle bones are much more widely dispersed and have a long history of use, however, although most examples outside of Yinxu do not have inscriptions (see Flad 2008). Brunson and her colleagues are investigating this larger corpus through the lenses of zooarchaeology and technology, allowing chronological change and spatial variability in osteomantic divination in early China to be better understood.

Kazuo Miyamoto focuses on the dynamism of ritual from the Middle Western Zhou ritual reform (Rawson 1999) through the ritual restructuring of the Middle Springs and Autumns period, a topic that has been a particular focus of von Falkenhausen's research as well (Falkenhausen 2006). To trace this dynamism, Miyamoto considers the chronology of bells disposed of in burial contexts and in particular explores the relationship between *nao* bells of northern and southern China. With his close attention to chronology, he shows that changes in the ritual repertoire of northern China involved incorporation of southern forms and proposes that this process was part of a political and social incorporation of southern populations that used ritual practices as a means of creating harmony.

Drawing inspiration from Valerio Valeri (1994), Bryan Miller discusses the multiple dimensions of animal sacrifices recovered from Xiongnu graves dating to the period from about 200 BCE to 200 CE in Mongolia. Drawing on examples from two cemeteries that reflect broader patterns seen across the entirety of the Mongolian steppe, Miller shows that attention to the specific placement of animal parts in burial contexts reveals that animal sacrifices had multiple meanings in Xiongnu practices and that different portions of the same animals might have been employed in different ways with different significance at the same time. Accordingly, this Mongolian case study further demonstrates a nuanced perspective on the categories of ritual and sacrifice.

Technology, Community, Interaction

Other essays in this volume focus on topics typically considered to more closely align with the concerns of economy, including the nature of intercommunity and intracommunity contacts, exchange, and identity formation. These essays consider various scales of interaction and how different scales must be simultaneously examined to understand the nature of the social significance of economic practices. By examining the overlap among domains of production, consumption, use, exchange, and innovation, these essays show how scales of place and practice reflect on the interplay between ritual and economy.

The paper by Flad provides an exhaustive discussion of the nature of technology and argues that technological change must be considered as a process by which new or different ways of doing fit into existing practices. Taking a broad view of technology, including not only craft production but also subsistence practices and all other "practices interrelating transformation of material resources, abstract and practical knowledge, social and political relationships, and cultural beliefs" (Brezine 2011:82), Flad focuses in particular on the significance of different scales of distance in the processes by which innovation, appropriation, and adoption occur. In particular, he examines a case study of technological change in Northwest China associated with the emergence of the proto–Silk Road. Based on a discussion of evidence for subsistence, jade, and metal technology, he argues that selective adoption reflects a constant, localized process of evaluating the value of new ways of doing things in light of the costs necessarily associated with technological change. In prehistoric Northwest China in particular, old and newly introduced technologies (such as bronze metallurgy and new domesticates) were constantly being negotiated, with people weighing the costs and benefits of adopting or discarding one or the other. However, as Flad points out, these seemingly economic calculations were tied in with ritual practices and construction of value, making it crucial to discuss them together rather than seeing them as separate or even diametrically opposed elements. Technology and technological change, Flad argues, should always be considered through the mutually constitutive lenses of production processes, consumption, interaction, and community.

In his discussion of copper mining and smelting in the middle Yangzi River valley, Shi Tao focuses on the organization of resource extraction (in this case copper mining), taking a bottom-up approach by focusing on local labor organization in the middle Yangzi River rather than viewing the organization of resource extraction from the centers of Shang and Zhou rule in the Central Plains. While it was previously assumed that metallurgical work was centrally controlled, be it from the Central Plains or on a more local level, Shi argues that, at least prior to the Springs and Autumns period, mining was organized in a decentralized manner. This perspective pushes against the often still pervasive Central Plains–centric view of early dynastic China. While later periods saw a more centrally administered territory and maybe also production system, Shi's research draws attention to the fact that while different parts of what is now China became increasingly more interconnected in the search for and exploitation and working of metals, as well as distribution of the resultant products, many aspects of resource extraction and maybe also production were organized on a more local level based on local circumstances. Interestingly, recent research on the Terracotta Army of the first emperor suggests that such trends may have continued even into periods of strong centralized control, as seen in the early Chinese Empire (e.g., Bevan et al. 2018; Quinn et al. 2017).

While Shi discusses an early stage in production—resource extraction—Lee Hsiu-ping focuses on production–consumption relationships in the case of white pottery produced at a second millennium site called Nanwa. These ceramics may largely have been consumed at Erlitou, an important Early Bronze Age site in Henan, China. Like Shi, Lee argues against the narrative of strong central control of production, in this case during the Early Bronze Age and possibly later periods, emphasizing the agency of local producers and consumers alike. In his study, Lee is particularly concerned with the concept of interaction, in this case the small-scale interaction between two archaeological sites rather than the large- and medium-scale interregional or even continent-spanning types of contact that often receive most attention in archaeological research. By focusing on the smallest scale of interaction, Lee considers the agency of communities and even individual producers and consumers. He traces daily decisions made by both groups and how they shape patterns of production, consumption, and interaction between individuals, groups, and ultimately regions based on availability of resources, know-how, and the local demand for products.

Similarly, Lin Kuei-chen focuses on communities as a unit of analysis. For her, communities encompass several households but remain smaller than the medium- or large-scale units of region or state. Following Chang (1968), she argues that a community is the context for social interactions that form the background for material remains, making it an archaeologically meaningful unit. Changes in daily practices within communities then lead to large-scale cultural transformations, Lin argues, following Birch (2013). Lin's study examines production and a broad range of object consumption activities, in particular ritual. Her study focuses on the presence of both local-style and exotic goods in Neolithic and Bronze Age Sichuan, China, identifying evidence for increasingly more wide-ranging exchange and other forms of interaction. At the same time, increasingly consistent pottery types and frequent ceremonial and public activities may have served to strengthen community cohesion within and among settlements. Communities at these settlements were integrated by both production and ritual activities, areas that show considerable overlap, as seen in production modes for both ritual and daily needs. Places such as Sichuan, Lin argues, were not passive peripheries; their gradational participation in ritual systems helped them shape and strengthen community identities on the local level. They were engaged with urban centers elsewhere yet had their own self-contained economies supporting local ritual practices.

Ellen Hsieh identifies similar processes of construction of local social identities involving imported Chinese-made porcelains used mainly for ritual purposes in eighteenth and nineteenth century Southeast Asia. By focusing on Bencharong and Peranakan porcelain wares and the context of their usage and deposition, she traces overseas Chinese networks, identifying instances of creolization of practices and identities in Chinese and non-Chinese elements. She outlines entanglement among objects and people involved in their production, exchange, and use, leading, for instance, to Chinese double-happiness wedding plates appearing in an Islamic tomb. This paper thus makes a call for research into both unique occurrences and general patterns, connecting investigation into local developments with broader views of interregional networks and global trends.

Flad, Shi, Lee, Lin, and Hsieh thus all grapple with scales of analysis and the scale of networks, identities, and interactions, as well as their reflections in the material record, discussing patterns of exchange, production, and consumption in ritual and daily actions, providing a range of possible ways of approaching these issues.

Objects and Meaning

The papers in this section delve more deeply into terminological and conceptual concerns, combining textual, artistic, and archaeological evidence to explore ontological issues that focus on the meaning of objects. Although not explicitly framed in terms of the ontological turn that has become an increasingly significant part of archaeological discourse in the past decade (e.g., Alberti and Bray 2009; Alberti et al. 2011; Bauer 2019; Costa and Fausto 2010; Olsen et al. 2012; Olsen and Whitmore 2015; Preucel 2016), these articles illustrate ways that objects cannot be neatly categorized into distinct domains such as ritual and economy. It is through the lens of meaning attributed to objects that the connections between economic and ritual practices become most clearly manifest.

Minku Kim discusses a rare example of a Kharoṣṭhī inscription on the base of a gilt-bronze Buddha image found in Xi'an. He provides a new translation and argues, based on the terminology, phonology, and onomastics, that the text was produced by a person from Kroaina. Considering artistic and technological details of the statue itself, Kim confirms the previously suggested date of the mid- to late fourth century CE and points out various multicultural undercurrents. Additionally, he raises the potential that the old Chinese manufacturing technique of piece-mold casting may have been used rather than what he calls the "more international" lost-wax technique. His study thus shows the subtle interplay of technology, religion, ritual economy, and cross-cultural interaction that is characteristic for Buddhist practices and associated material culture. As this study skillfully shows, these complex connections are ideally understood in multi-method, multisource research combining methods from art history, history, archaeology, and linguistics.

Zhang Hanmo likewise combines textual and material evidence, considering the name, religious meaning, and material and artistic particularities of what in English are generally called *boshan* incense burners. Combining artistic evidence, information on ritual and religious meaning, and taxonomy, Zhang argues that these objects do not represent a mountain as usually assumed but instead depict flowing *qi* clouds. Additionally, he suggests that items that are referenced in texts as *boshan* burners were used to burn a specific fragrant grass called *boshan* and that the designs on such objects can vary, not needing to be mountains and often including clouds. This study thus cautions us not to take established terms for granted or let them guide our interpretation of objects. Instead we must be sensitive to the subtle interplay of form, design, meaning, function, and terminology. Terms like *boshan*, known from textual sources, may not neatly overlap with categories of objects created through art historical analysis. Taxonomic terms created for different purposes ultimately have different associated meanings.

The meaning of objects is also at the center of Hans Barnhard's contribution, though he is critical of focusing on objects with inscriptions. He argues that texts reflect only elite views and in turn may color the views of archaeologists. Barnhard points to the importance of objects not as individual treasures but as data that, in the aggregate, carry information. He admits difficulty transcending the attractiveness of special or beautiful objects, but he sees it as the duty of archaeologists to emphasize this information, and not the objects that embody it, to both themselves and the public. The importance of objects to archaeologists, he highlights, is facilitated by the fact that creation and use of objects connect functionality with meaning (building on, e.g., Gosden and Marshall 1999; Hodder 2012; Malafouris 2013).

Besides past meanings and functions, there is also the modern context in which ownership, preservation, and storage become an issue once an object has entered the archaeological realm. In this context, Barnhard discusses the role of museums, which have increasingly moved into the public realm, combining traditional roles of preserving objects and memories and creating narratives and a sense of community through research and education. This raises the question "Who owns the past?," which is often raised in relation to issues of repatriation from colonial contexts (e.g., Hicks 2020). Barnhard focuses more on the issue of authenticity in the context of restoration—that is, to what state an object with a complex history should be restored—and the use of copies and digital renderings (e.g., Brenna et al. 2019). Barnhard calls for a data-driven (rather than treasure-driven) holistic study of artifacts involving consultation with multiple stakeholders.

This last paper, therefore, in addition to elaborating the concerns with ritual, economy, and meaning that pervade the work of Lothar von Falkenhausen, also ties into his important engagement with international policies on heritage and antiquities. Serving on the Presidential Cultural Property Advisory Committee of the United States from 2012 to 2020 (Falkenhausen 2016), Falkenhausen was involved in discussions and recommendations concerning international agreements about the trade in antiquities. It is in realms such as this where scholarship on the meaning of past material culture and policies of the contemporary world come into most intimate connection. The meanings ascribed to objects position them firmly within social discourse that is situated in international trade and politics of identity, including the ritualized discourse that creates the imagined communities integral to the creation and maintenance of modern nation-states (Anderson 1991).

Conclusion

The volume concludes with an epilogue by Willeke Wendrich. Her essay also concerns meaning and ontology, focusing on value and meaning expressed in certain number systems, but her contribution relates to Lothar von Falkenhausen in a more personal manner. While she focuses mostly on the meaning of certain numbers within the context of ancient Egyptian society based on symbolism, textual references, and material manifestations evident in the archaeological record, she was motivated to reflect on the significance of numbers because of a number that holds particular importance in East Asian calendrical systems: 60. On the occasion of the sixtieth birthday of Lothar von Falkenhausen, nothing could be more apt than examining how numbers like 60 have culturally specific significance.

Adam Smith, one of von Falkenhausen's students, has explained the significance of the sexagenary cycle on which East Asian calendars are based and the connections of this cycle to ritual (2010). The textual evidence for this system extends as far back as the earliest writing in China and involves the combination of stem (*gan* 干) and branch (*zhi* 支) cycles of 10 and 12 graphs respectively. The 12-cycle stems are eventually associated with the 12 animals of the zodiac, and the return to a *jihai* 己亥 year of the pig in 2019 marked five cycles of 12 since the year of Lothar's birth. As Smith further points out, "The 10-cycle and 60-cycle also underlay the calendrical apparatus that was used to schedule sacrificial performances directed towards these same dead kin, a central religious preoccupation of elites and probably the early Chinese population more broadly during the late second millennium" (Smith 2010:2). Through the Shang and Zhou periods, the 60-cycle of days was an important feature of the ritualized calendrical system. By the Han, as represented on silk manuscripts buried in 168 BCE at Mawangdui, the 60-cycle was applied to the counting of years (Smith 2010:28), setting the stage for our celebration of Lothar in 2019.

It is fitting, given the influence he has had over so many people, that the scholars who converged in Los Angeles that June presented work with many overlapping themes. The sections into which we have arranged this volume were not preordained but instead reflect general trends and broad themes of importance in East Asian archaeology that resonate in many ways with the considerable corpus of Lothar's work. Each essay reflects on these connections and the ways his influence has shaped the work under discussion. The impact that has developed in this 60-cycle is something we can only hope will be repeated in the next.

Acknowledgments

We appreciate and acknowledge all participants in the conference associated with the celebration of the birthday that resulted in this volume, including those who presented papers and all the attendees, whose questions and discussions added immensely to the intellectual exchange. We would also like to express our thanks to the various funding agencies and individuals who supported the event financially, including the Luce Foundation, UCLA, the Cotsen Institute of Archaeology, the Chiang Ching-kuo Foundation, and Nancy Xu. For fund-raising and organizational help on the ground, we would like to express our thanks to Li Min, Yan Yunxiang, Lee Hui-shu, and Kirie Stromberg. We also want to recognize several individuals who provided useful feedback on various parts of this introductory essay, including Adam D. Smith and Roderick Campbell.

References

Adamson, Glenn
2021 *Craft: An American History*. New York: Bloomsbury.

Alberti, Benjamin, and Tamara L. Bray
2009 Animating Archaeology: Local Theories and Conceptually Open-Ended Methodologies. *Cambridge Archaeological Journal* 19(3):344–56.

Alberti, Benjamin, Severin Fowles, Martin Holbraad, Yvonne Marshall, and Christopher Witmore
2011 Worlds Otherwise: Archaeology, Anthropology, and Ontological Difference. *Current Anthropology* 52(6):896–912.

Anderson, Benedict
1991 *Imagined Communities: Reflections on the Origin and Spread of Nationalism*. London: Verso.

Asad, Talal
1993 The Construction of Religion as an Anthropological Category. In *Genealogies of Religion: Discipline and Reasons of Power in Christianity and Islam*, pp. 27–54. Baltimore: Johns Hopkins University Press.

Bauer, Alexander A.
2019 Itinerant Objects. *Annual Review of Anthropology* 48(1):335–52.

Bell, Catherine M.
1992 *Ritual Theory, Ritual Practice*. New York: Oxford University Press.
1997 *Ritual: Perspectives and Dimensions*. New York: Oxford University Press.
2007 *Teaching Ritual*. Oxford: Oxford University Press.

Bevan, Andrew, Xiuzhen Li, Zhen Zhao, Jianhua Huang, Stuart Laidlaw, Na Xi, Yin Xia, Shengtao Ma, and Marcos Martinon-Torres
2018 Ink Marks, Bronze Crossbows and Their Implications for the Qin Terracotta Army. *Heritage Science* 6(1):1–10.

Birch, Jennifer
2013 Between Villages and Cities: Settlement Aggregation in Cross-Cultural Perspective. In *From Prehistoric Villages to Cities: Settlement Aggregation and Community*, edited by Jennifer Birch, pp. 1–22. New York: Routledge, Taylor & Francis Group.

Brenna, Brita, Hans Dam Christensen, and Olav Hamran, eds.
2019 *Museums as Cultures of Copies: The Crafting of Artefacts and Authenticity*. Abingdon, UK: Routledge.

Brezine, Carrie J.
2011 Dress, Technology and Identity in Colonial Peru. PhD thesis, Department of Anthropology, Harvard University, Cambridge, MA.

Burling, Robbins
1962 Maximization Theories and the Study of Economic Anthropology. *American Anthropologist* 64:802–21.

Campbell, Roderick
2012 On Sacrifice: An Archaeology of Shang Sacrifice. In *Sacred Killing: The Archaeology of Sacrifice in the Ancient Near East*, edited by A. M. Porter and G. M. Schwartz, pp. 305–24. Winona Lake, IN: Eisenbrauns.

Carrasco, David
2013 Sacrifice/Human Sacrifice in Religious Traditions. In *The Oxford Handbook of Religion and Violence*, edited by M. Juergensmeyer, M. Kitts, and M. Jerryson, pp. 209–35. Oxford: Oxford University Press.

Chang, Kwang-chih
1968 *Early Chinese Civilization: Anthropological Perspectives.* Cambridge, MA: Harvard University Press.

Costa, Luiz, and Carlos Fausto
2010 The Return of the Animists. *Religion and Society* 1(1):89–109.

Dalton, George
1975 Karl Polanyi's Analysis of Long-Distance Trade and His Wider Paradigm. In *Ancient Civilization and Trade*, edited by J. A. Sabloff and C. C. Lamberg-Karlovsky, pp. 63–132. Albuquerque: University of New Mexico Press.

de Castro, Eduardo Viveiros
1998 Cosmological Deixis and Amerindian Perspectivism. *Journal of the Royal Anthropological Institute* 4(3):469–88.

Earle, Timothy K.
2000 Archaeology, Property, and Prehistory. *Annual Review of Anthropology* 29:39–60.

Falkenhausen, Lothar von
1988 Ritual Music in Bronze Age China: An Archaeological Perspective. PhD dissertation, Harvard University, Cambridge, MA.
1993 *Suspended Music: Chime Bells in the Culture of Bronze Age China.* Berkeley: University of California Press.
2006 *Chinese Society in the Age of Confucius (1000–250 BC): The Archaeological Evidence.* Los Angeles: Cotsen Institute of Archaeology Press. Reprinted in Korean in 2011 with translation by Simjae Hun 심재훈. Seoul: Sechang Publishing House 세창출판사. Reprinted in Chinese in 2017 with translation by Wu Changqing 吴长青, Wang Yi 王艺, and Shen Jiao 审校. Shanghai: Shanghai Guji Chubanshe.
2016 Trying to Do the Right Thing to Protect the World's Cultural Heritage: One Committee Member's Tale. In *Obama and Transnational American Studies*, edited by A. Hornung, pp. 375–90. Heidelberg: Universitätsverlag Winter.

Firth, Raymond W.
1965 *Primitive Polynesian Economy.* London: Routledge & Kegan Paul; Hamden, CT: Archon Books.

Flad, Rowan K.
2008 Divination and Power: A Multi-regional View of the Development of Oracle Bone Divination in Early China. *Current Anthropology* 49(3):403–37.

Flad, Rowan K., and Pochan Chen
2013 *Ancient Central China: Centers and Peripheries along the Yangzi River.* Cambridge: Cambridge University Press.

Gosden, Chris, and Yvonne Marshall
1999 The Cultural Biography of Objects. *World Archaeology* 31(2)169–78.

Hesse, Paula Brian Wapnish, and Jonathan Greer
2012 Scripts of Animal Sacrifice in Levantine Culture-History. In *Sacred Killing: The Archaeology of Sacrifice in the Ancient Near East*, edited by A. M. Porter and G. M. Schwartz, pp. 217–35. Winona Lake, IN: Eisenbrauns.

Heyman, Josiah McC.
2013 Political Economy. In *Handbook of Sociocultural Anthropology*, edited by J. G. Carrier and D. B. Gewertz, pp. 88–106. New York: Bloomsbury Academic.

Hicks, Dan
2020 *The British Museums: The Benin Bronzes, Colonial Violence and Cultural Restitution.* London: Pluto Press.

Hodder, Ian
2012 *Entangled: An Archaeology of the Relationships between Humans and Things.* Chichester: John Wiley and Sons.

Hubert, Henri, and Marcel Mauss
1964 [1898] *Sacrifice: Its Nature and Function.* Translated by W. D. Halls. Foreword by E. E. Evans-Pritchard. London: Cohen & West.

Ingold, Tim
2013 *Making: Anthropology, Archaeology, Art and Architecture.* New York: Routledge.

Insoll, Timothy
2004 *Archaeology, Ritual, Religion, Themes in Archaeology.* London: Routledge.

Kyriakidis, Evangelos, ed.
2007 *The Archaeology of Ritual.* Cotsen Advanced Seminars 3. Los Angeles: Cotsen Institute of Archaeology Press.

Langlands, Alex
2018 *Cræft: An Inquiry into the Origins and True Meaning of Traditional Crafts.* New York: W. W. Norton.

Li, Yung-ti
2021 *Kingly Crafts: The Archaeology of Craft Production in Late Shang China.* New York: Columbia University Press.

Li Yuan 劉源
2004 *Shang Zhou jizu li yanjiu* 商周祭祖禮研究

[Research on Sacrificial Ritual in the Shang and Zhou]. Beijing: Shangwu Yinshuguan 商務印書館.

Malafouris, Lambros
2013 *How Things Shape the Mind: A Theory of Material Engagement*. Cambridge: Massachusetts Institute of Technology Press.

McAnany, Patricia Ann, and E. Christian Wells
2008 *Dimensions of Ritual Economy, Research in Economic Anthropology*, Vol. 27. Bingley, UK: Emerald Group Publishing.

Metcalf, Peter
1981 Meaning and Materialism: The Ritual Economy of Death. *Man* 16(4):563–78.

Miller, G. Logan
2015 Ritual Economy and Craft Production in Small-Scale Societies: Evidence from Microwear Analysis of Hopewell Bladelets. *Journal of Anthropological Archaeology* 39:124–38.

Quinn, Patrick Sean, Shangxin Zhang, Yin Xia, and Xiuzhen Li
2017 Building the Terracotta Army: Ceramic Craft Technology and Organisation of Production at Qin Shihuang's Mausoleum Complex. *Antiquity* 91(358):966–79.

Olsen, Bjørnar, Michael Shanks, Timothy Webmoor, and Christopher Witmore
2012 *Archaeology: The Discipline of Things*. Berkeley: University of California Press.

Olsen, Bjørnar, and Christopher Witmore
2015 Archaeology, Symmetry and the Ontology of Things. A Response to Critics. *Archaeological Dialogues* 22(2):187–97.

Polanyi, Karl
1957 *The Great Transformation: The Political and Economic Origins of Our Time*. Boston: Beacon Press.

Preucel, Robert W.
2016 Pragmatic Archaeology and the Semiotic Mediation of Culture. *Semiotic Review* 4:1–8.

Puett, Michael J.
2002 *To Become a God: Cosmology, Sacrifice, and Self-divinization in Early China*. Cambridge, MA: Harvard University Asia Center for the Harvard-Yenching Institute.

Rappaport, Roy A.
1999 *Ritual and Religion in the Making of Humanity*. Cambridge Studies in Social and Cultural Anthropology 110. Cambridge: Cambridge University Press.

Rawson, Jessica
1999 Western Zhou Archaeology. In *The Cambridge History of Ancient China from the Origins of Civilization to 221 BC*, edited by Edward Shaughnessy, pp. 352–449. Cambridge: Cambridge University Press.

Rizvi, Uzma Z.
2018 *The Affect of Crafting: Third Millennium BCE Copper Arrowheads from Ganeshwar, Rajasthan*. Oxford: Archaeopress.

Roseberry, W.
1988 Political Economy. *Annual Review of Anthropology* 17:161–85.

Shaughnessy, Edward L.
1996 Military Histories of Early China. *Early China* 21:159–82.

Smith, Adam Daniel
2010 The Chinese Sexagenary Cycle and the Ritual Origins of the Calendar. In *Calendars and Years II: Astronomy and Time in the Ancient and Medieval World*, edited by John M. Steele, pp. 1–37. Oxford: Oxbow Books.

Steadman, Sharon R.
2009 *The Archaeology of Religion: Cultures and Their Beliefs in Worldwide Context*. Walnut Creek, CA: Left Coast Press.

Strevens, Michael
2020 *The Knowledge Machine: How Irrationality Created Modern Science*. New York: Liveright.

Valeri, Valerio
1985 *Kingship and Sacrifice: Ritual and Society in Ancient Hawaii*. Chicago: University of Chicago Press.
1994 Wild Victims: Hunting as Sacrifice and Sacrifice as Hunting in Huaulu. *History of Religions* 34(2):101–30.

Wells, E. Christian
2006 Mind and Religion: Psychological and Cognitive Foundations of Religiosity. *Antiquity* 80(309):734.

Wells, E. Christian, and Karla L. Davis-Salazar
2007 *Mesoamerican Ritual Economy: Archaeological and Ethnological Perspectives, Mesoamerican Worlds*. Boulder: University Press of Colorado.

Wilk, Richard R.
1996 *Economies and Cultures: Foundations of Economic Anthropology*. Boulder: Westview Press.

Woods, Ngaire, ed.
2000 *The Political Economy of Globalization*. New York: St. Martin's Press.

Part I

Ritual Economy

Chapter 2

Uncovering Disguised Social Inequality
An Investigation of the Bronze Age Cemetery at Donghuishan

Wen Chenghao

Mortuary practice is a primary focus of anthropological discourse. Analysis of burials by age, gender, vertical and horizontal social positions, personal identity, social classification, and other social personae of the deceased is fundamental to the archaeological investigation of early society (Binford 1971; Brown 1971). However, there has been a long debate on the correspondence between mortuary data and the social status of the deceased (Morris 1987; Parker Pearson 1999). As a result of the filter of funeral behavior, funeral goods do not always directly reflect but often exaggerate, mask, or even distort societal relationships as traditionally understood by archaeologists (Bloch 1971; Carr 1995; Parker Pearson 1999). The rationale behind mortuary evidence is that funeral practice, according to von Falkenhausen (2006a:75), is invariably replete with culturally determined worldviews and symbolic meanings and that mortuary data are at best a secondary outgrowth of a society's burial customs. Therefore a tomb, as von Falkenhausen (2006a:76) explicitly defines it, "is primarily the record of the instrumentalization of the deceased person by other members in the society for their own purpose."

I argue that the instrumentalization of burial rites can be explained by secondary burials. Characterized by postmortem rearrangement and redeposition of the corpse, secondary burials offer archaeologists more salient perspectives on identities, relationships, and conceptions of the world than primary burials (Kuijt 1996). If interring the dead can be simply perceived as spontaneous human behavior, then seemingly anomalous postmortem exhumation and reburying of the deceased must demand further explanations in terms of religious beliefs concerning death. Secondary burials resulting from intentional manipulation of the dead by the living and underlying ritual processes can be powerful agents for redefining, reaffirming, and renegotiating societal relationships between the bereaved and the deceased, as well as among living communities (Rakita and Buikstra 2005). Moreover, the economic dimension shall be considered to account for patterns in burial rites beyond religious and symbolic factors. Departing from conventional emphasis on the ritual contexts of economic processes (Rappaport 1968:410), I define "ritual economy" by stressing economic aspects of religious ritual—that is, provision and consumption throughout ritual processes. In many ethnographical contexts, the final form and scale of the materialization of ritual are essentially conditioned by the economic patterns of the living community (Hefner 1983; Metcalf 1981).

It is also necessary to point out that the current study is inspired by von Falkenhausen's theoretical emphasis on economic processes in archaeological interpretation. By means of his groundbreaking salt archaeology project in China, von Falkenhausen demonstrates the power of economic anthropology in interpreting conventional archaeological data (Falkenhausen 2006b:15). Methodologically, this study also owes a great intellectual debt to von Falkenhausen for his in-depth study of Chinese society in the first millennium BCE (Falkenhausen 2006a). His use of statistics and use of anthropological theory, which teases out underlying patterns behind mortuary data, greatly benefit the current study. Following, I apply such approaches to the study of secondary burials from Bronze Age Northwest China and aim to reach a nuanced understanding of social organization behind mortuary data.

Secondary Burial Rites and the Socioeconomic Dimensions of Funerals

As a specific kind of mortuary ritual, secondary burial is characterized by the intentional retrieving and reburial of human remains after a culturally determined time (Schroeder 2001). The study of secondary rites has attracted significant attention from anthropologists since a seminal study by Hertz (1960 [1907]) of the distinctive double funeral widely practiced by the Dayak tribes of Borneo. That observance comprises two rituals: the funeral, conducted immediately after death, and the concluding ceremony, which culminates in a grand feast celebrated after an interval of between eight months and five years and potentially even longer. Hertz analyzed the changing status of the body, the soul, and the living within each phase of the ritual process, simultaneously demonstrating parallels between binary concepts (the dead versus the living; the body versus the soul) imparted throughout the funerary rites.

According to Hertz's account, among the Dayak, the deceased is assumed to experience three successive phases of transformation: the separation of the soul from the living body, the transitional/liminal phase devoid of status and affiliation, and reaggregation in the afterworld, with new status as an ancestor. According to Dayak beliefs, the soul in its transitional stages is vengeful and thus dangerous to the bereaved. The soul will not rest peacefully until it has been successfully transported to the ancestral world, which is represented by the complete decomposition of the corpse. In the manner of the dead, the bereaved go through a tripartite process: initially, separation from the living community by a multitude of taboos; the transitional phase, during the mourning period, devoid of status; and upon the concluding ceremony, reunification with the living community. The same cultural pattern behind funerary rites had been observed and summarized by Van Gennep (1960 [1908]) under the classic concept of "rites of passage."

Along with its contribution to the symbolic analysis of death, Hertz's study also brought to the fore the intervening period between two burials in the case of secondary burial. Although he recognized this period as necessary to fulfill material prerequisites for the final ceremony (for example, economic preparation for the feast, acquisition of human heads, and decomposition of the corpse), he refuted Wilken (1884–1885) in his exclusion of socioeconomic factors when explaining the intervening period between the first and second funerals. Instead he argued that this postponement was necessary for local people to mentally recover from the shock of death on their "collective consciousness" (Hertz 1960 [1907]:32). His psychological thesis was criticized by Miles (1965) after he visited Borneo and made an ethnographic study of another branch of the Dayak tribe, the Ngadju-Dayak. By means of a detailed investigation of economic expenditures on the mortuary ritual of *tiwah*, Miles argued that secondary burial is a ceremony of conspicuous consumption. The length of the interlude between the first and secondary burials and the extravagance of the accompanying funerals, he concluded, were both determined by the economic resources of the bereaved family.

Based on his own field study of the same Dayak community in Borneo, Metcalf (1981) proposed similarly materialist explanations for the institutionalized postponement of *nulang* rites of secondary burial among members of this tribe. He attributed the flaw in Hertz's classic analysis to ignorance of alternative or abridged forms of funerals practiced by the Dayak and instead related the variety of double burial practices to economic factors. Metcalf demonstrated that availability of resources, rather than social status, helped determine the prescribed sequence of ritual ceremonies and led to alternative forms of ritual expression (Metcalf 1981:564). The time expended to complete the funeral rites would therefore be expected to vary along with the economic resources of bereaved relatives. Requiring more time than the wealthy to accumulate sufficient wealth to fund the entire ritual process, the poor would have anticipated a longer interim between the primary burial and the secondary burial or postmortem disturbance.

I argue that while preparing financially for such ceremonies, social debts may also be generated among community members as they negotiate ritual obligations and economic resources. The repayment of social debts would definitely energize the social interaction of reciprocity. Nonetheless, economic factors alone cannot explain the rationale underlying the sequence of rites in any given case. For example, only symbolic or religious factors can explain manipulating the remains of the dead in *nulang* rites, which include moving them from temporary storage to a final resting place, as Metcalf (1981:576) pointed out.

Economic activities permeate all aspects of social life. Funerary rites are no exception. As clearly shown by Goody (1962:44) in the case of the Lo-Dagga's funerary rites in Ghana, underlying the entire ritual process are economic factors: supply and consumption for the living. Food and drink provided for the bereaved nearby as well for mourners and visitors from afar are required for each phase of the rites of passage. Goody describes the ritual process as comprising four consecutive phases: the first phase is the burial ceremony; the second, third, and fourth phrases are the Diviner's Beer, the Bitter Funeral Beer, and the Cool Funeral Beer, respectively. As the names suggest, each phase includes a drink of grain porridge. The success of this ritual largely depends on the economic means of the bereaved.

The aforementioned ethnographic studies of secondary burials allow us to propose that in some societies, both the scale and extent of secondary burial practices that are culturally sanctioned are also directly related to the socioeconomic status of the bereaved. In an archaeological context, skeletal articulation can reflect the time span between death and secondary interment (Ubelaker 1974). Moreover, the completeness of the skeleton can represent the extent of postmortem disturbance, which in turn reflects the scale of ritual investment by the living. It should therefore be expected that the articulation and completeness of the skeleton relates to economic parameters or, in the words of Tainter (1978), the "energetic expenditure of mortuary practice"—for example, the volume of the grave and the expenditure on grave furniture. Whereas the well-to-do can prepare funerary rites so expeditiously that the corpse has yet to completely decompose, those of lesser means will take advantage of the time required for complete decomposition to prepare themselves for the secondary burial ceremony. If exhuming and retrieving the deceased's decomposed skeletal elements, which indicate a successfully transformation from ghost to ancestor and thus mark the end of funerary rites and the mental liberation of the living, are institutionalized in a ritual sequence, I argue that the following pattern of absent skeletal elements shall be observed in archaeological contexts: the well-to-do have a limited number of disarticulated elements to extract from the skeleton—primarily those that decompose in a short time period (usually a few weeks) after death, such as phalanges, skull, and sternum. The bereaved of lesser means, by contrast, require several months or even years to prepare for the secondary ceremony. The corpse will completely decompose after such a long interim. Therefore the number of extracted elements will be much greater than if the ceremony were prepared more expeditiously. In the following sections, I test these hypotheses against archaeological data from a site in Northwest China to begin to understand secondary burials commonly practiced in this region during the Bronze Age.

The Donghuishan Cemetery from the Perspective of Ritual Economy

The developmental trajectory of prehistory in the Hexi Corridor was initiated by the first settlers from central Gansu during the Late Majiayao period (2700–2500 BCE; Li 2001). During the Machang period (2300–1900 BCE), the Hexi Corridor was widely occupied by farming communities that practiced millet agriculture and also raised domestic animals such as pigs, dogs, cattle, and sheep/goats as meat sources (Li 1998). No later than the Late Machang phase (around 1900 BCE), crops first domesticated in Southwest Asia, such as wheat, barley, and oats, began to be introduced into the local diet (Atahan et al. 2011; Ma et al. 2014). Almost contemporary with those exotic crops was another innovative technology introduced into the Hexi Corridor from westerly neighbors: the metallurgy of copper and its alloys (Zhang et al. 1980). However, indisputable evidence of local metallurgical production did not surface in the Hexi Corridor until the Xichengyi culture (1880–1680 BCE; Gansusheng Wenwu et al. 2014, 2015). During the following Siba period (1780–1500 BCE), metallurgical production reached its peak, as indicated by abundant copper and bronze objects unearthed from the Huoshaogou cemetery (Gansusheng Bowuguan 1979).

The communities of the Siba culture mainly dwelled in oases along the northern piedmonts of the Qilian Mountains. Unearthed faunal and floral remains suggest that Siba communities practiced a mixed economy: millet-planting agriculture along with stockbreeding of cattle and sheep/goats. The percentage of agricultural cultivation and stockbreeding seems to vary in different regions according to climatic conditions. For example, pastoral animals like sheep/goats probably accounted for a larger part of daily life in the western part of the Hexi Corridor than in the eastern counterparts. Newly introduced crops such as wheat, barley, and oats had already been widely cultivated during the Siba period, even though millet still predominated the daily diet (Atahan et al. 2011).

As one of few officially excavated sites of the Siba culture, the Donghuishan cemetery contributes copious material culture for the understanding of the Early Bronze Age Hexi Corridor. It is located in the village of Liuba, Minle County, near an alluvial fan in the northern piedmont of the Qilian Mountains (Figures 2.1 and 2.2). Rescue excavations conducted by archaeologists in 1987 unearthed 249 tombs (Gansusheng and Jilin Daxue 1998), all concentrated in a rectangular plot measuring 35 by 15 m. By then, an irrigation canal had cut through the cemetery's central axis from north to south, seriously damaging its central section. An estimate of 300 tombs in the original cemetery would therefore be

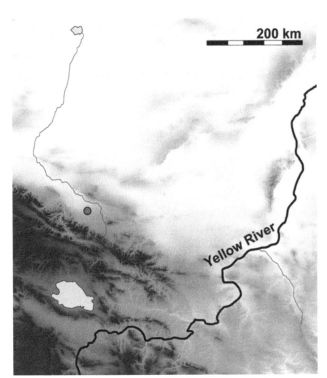

Figure 2.1. Location of the Donghuishan cemetery. *Created by Bryan K. Miller.*

realistic. One charcoal sample yielded a radiocarbon date of 3770 ± 145 BP (calibrated). New serial AMS dates based on carbonized crop seeds from cultural layers suggest a later range, from 1600 to 1400 BCE (Flad et al. 2010).

A high degree of homogeneity can be observed throughout the mortuary data at the Donghuishan cemetery: burial construction and orientation, position of the body, and assemblage of burial goods. Rectangular pit tombs represent the predominant form of burial (76.7%). These are followed by pit tombs with niches dug near the head or feet (22.9%). Pit tombs are on average 1.7 m long, 0.6 m wide, and 0.4 m deep. The estimate of grave volume is positively correlated to the quantity of grave goods according to Pearson's correlation test (p-value = 0.0026 < 0.05; coefficient of correlation is estimated at 0.22). The predominant orientation (88%) of tombs is NE–SW; only 10 percent are oriented NW–SE. Secondary burials or disturbed primary burials are common in all tombs (see Appendix A).

Due to the poor preservation of bodies in situ, only 150 of the 249 tombs can be described: 96 (38.6%) as single burials and 54 (21.7%) as including two or more individuals. There are 221 individuals who can be determined by age and/or sex. These include 91 male adults (41.2%) and 62 female adults (28.1%). The large number of skeletons of undetermined sex (68 individuals; 30.8%) prevents us from concluding that there was any great imbalance between sexes in the demographic structure. However, a bias against burying subadult individuals, especially infants or children (under 12 years old), can be clearly discerned in this cemetery: the 221 individuals include 178 adults (80.5%), 30 adolescents (13.6%), 11 children (5%), and two infants (0.9%). The population of infants and children is greatly underrepresented in this cemetery owing to alternative mortuary practices or a separate cemetery in which they were presumably buried. Similarly, the assemblage of grave goods shows no qualitative differentiation (Figure 2.3). Pottery vessels (632 total) comprise the primary burial goods. Only 62 tools and ornaments (stone, bone, and metal) are found in the 249 tombs. This extremely low number and diversity of grave goods renders the quantification of mortuary data ineffective in identifying social differentiation.

Nonetheless, the prevailing cases of disturbed burials in Donghuishan distinguishes the site from other cemeteries of the same period. Human remains from more than 218 tombs (87.6%) were disturbed to varying degrees, resulting in the dislocation of bodily parts from their original anatomical positions and even the absence of major components such as heads, femurs, and feet. Only 12 individuals represent primary burials with slight postmortem disturbance (including, in a few cases, the absence of phalanges). In some extreme circumstances, almost all human remains had been removed, with only undiagnosable fragments left in place.

According to the principles of corpse taphonomy (Duday et al. 2014), bodily parts to which relatively few connective tissues are attached (hands, distal parts of the feet, and cervical vertebrae) deteriorate relatively rapidly. The muscles between the scapulae and rib cage also putrefy quickly. By contrast, more tenacious joints such as the lumbar, lumbo-sacral vertebrae, sacroiliac, knee, ankle, tarsal, and metatarsal invariably require relatively more time to break down. The dislocation or detachment of specific skeletal elements can therefore indicate the length of time that has elapsed after death. Therefore, the more time that has elapsed after death or the decomposition of the corpse, the more skeletal elements will detach from the corpse and—if the extraction of bones is mandatory by those rites—the more bones will be extracted in secondary rites.

In the same vein, fewer bones can be extracted if postmortem exhumation quickly follows the decomposition of the corpse. Considering this, the completeness of the skeletons at Donghuishan can be divided into three tiers, from most disturbed to most complete (Table 2.1). It is straightforward that more time passed after death for one tier of degree of completeness than for the next highest tier. For example, a Degree I human skeleton was probably

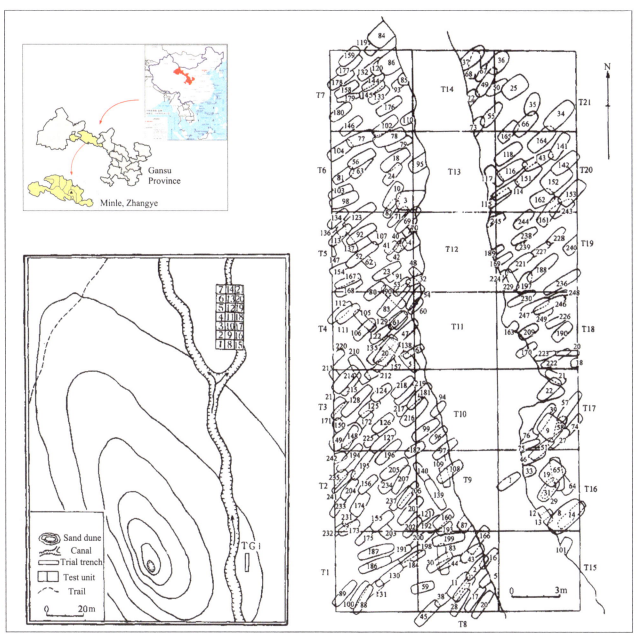

Figure 2.2. Layout of the Donghuishan cemetery.
Prepared by the author after Gansusheng and Jilin Daxue 1998: Figures 2 and 3.

disturbed after a longer period of time than a Degree II skeleton. If the gap between two funerals is conditioned by the socioeconomic status of the bereaved, as suggested by the above-mentioned ethnographic cases, one should expect that a lesser degree of completeness represents a lower socioeconomic status and vice versa. In the case of Donghuishan, socioeconomic status can also be measured by conventional parameters—for example, the volume of the grave, the quantity of grave goods, and the inclusion of rare goods. One might therefore expect a significant correlation between degrees of skeletal completeness and parameters of the socioeconomic status of the bereaved.

To eliminate the maximum degree of noise in statistical computations, I select only single burials (96 tombs) as my dataset. However, one would expect a positively or negatively skewed pattern of distribution if there were a positive/negative correlation between social status and degrees of disturbance. First I apply Spearman's rank correlation test

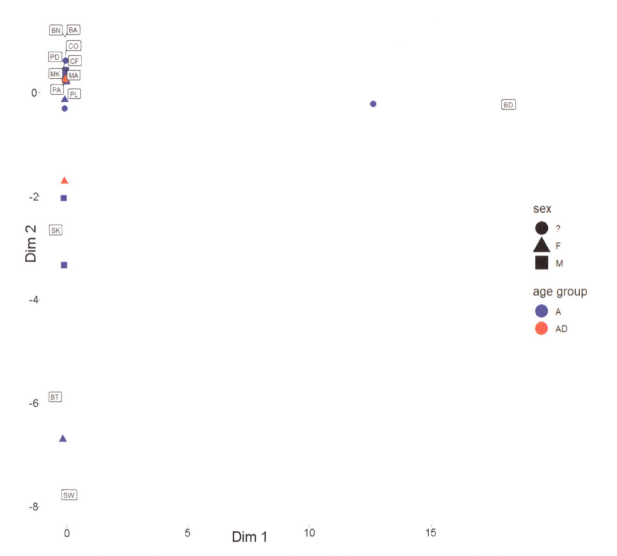

Figure 2.3. Plot of correspondence analysis on grave goods from the Donghuishan cemetery with reference to age groups (A: adults; AD: adolescents) and sex (?: undetermined; F: female; M: male). BA: bone awl; BN: bone needle; CO: cowrie; PD: perforated disk; CF: clay flute; MK: metal knife; MA: metal awl; PA: painted pottery; PL: plain pottery; SK: stone knife; BT: boar tusk; SW: spindle whorl; BD: bead. *Created by the author.*

using the software R to determine whether there are any correlations between the degree of completeness and other variables (for example, the total number of grave goods and the cubic volume of each grave), as the degree of completeness is measured in ordinal data. The results of this correlation test identify no significant correlation in either pair of variables. The estimate of the correlation coefficient (*rho*) between the degree of completeness and grave volume is low, 0.22 (p-value = 0.057 > 0.05). For the total number of grave goods, the estimate generates an even lower value, 0.17 (p-value = 0.11 > 0.05). To eliminate bias resulting from arbitrary classification of the degree of completeness, I also calculate the specific means of each variable with a 95% confidence interval (CI; Tables 2.2 and 2.3; Figures 2.4 and 2.5). There is a significant difference in the cubic measure of graves between Degree I and Degree II. However, the confidence interval of Degree III basically overlaps with the other two tiers and thus indicates no significant difference among them. The same situation can be observed in the number of grave goods in each tier. These statistics indicate significant correlations between the completeness of the skeleton, the cubic measure of the grave, and the number of grave goods. If disturbance of the deceased is a requisite stage of transforming the dead to an ancestor, one might argue that this funeral rite was universally practiced, regardless of grave goods or grave volume.

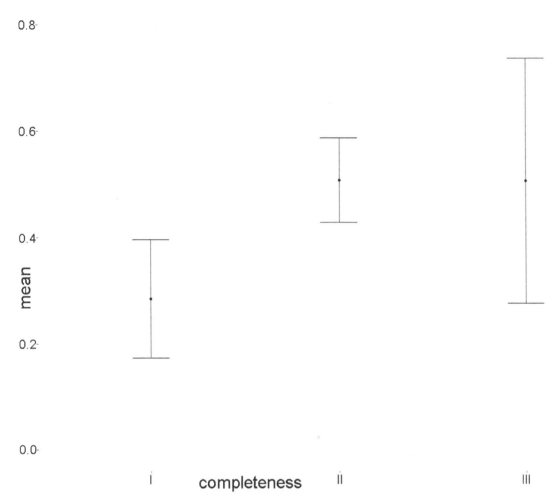

Figure 2.4. Plot of the confidence interval of the mean volume of graves in each tier of degree of completeness at the Donghuishan cemetery. *Created by the author.*

Together with the correlation test between degrees of completeness and other quantitative variables, one can determine whether the degree of completeness corresponds to certain age groups and sex or, in other words, whether disturbance of the deceased occurs preferentially with a certain age group or sex. First, results show that neither the distribution of sexes in each tier of completeness nor the distribution of age groups is skewed. The Pearson's chi-square correlation test also suggests insignificant correlation between the degree of completeness and the groups by age (p-value = $0.265 > 0.05$) and sex (p-value = $0.05004 > 0.05$). The same test is also applied to other categorical variables, such as orientation and burial facility. However, high p-values, 0.36 for orientation and 0.26 for burial facility, suggest that they are probably independent of each other.

A series of statistical tests suggests that the postmortem disturbance of the deceased as a funeral rite probably has no significant correlation with other mortuary variables, including age, sex, and orientation of the deceased; number of grave goods; or volume and other variables related to the grave. This disturbance was probably a universal funeral rite practiced by the Donghuishan community without consideration for the social status of the deceased. That is, the secondary burial could have been manipulated as the ritual means to eliminate social differences, if there were any, among the Donghuishan community.

In addition to hierarchical differences in the degree of completeness of the skeleton, one also finds close correspondence between grave volume and the first two tiers of completeness (Figure 2.5). Although the 95% confidence interval of the third degree generally overlaps with the first two tiers, statistics on the 10 single burials with the most complete skeletons in the entire cemetery yield a higher mean value in grave volume (0.57 m^3) than the average

Table 2.1. Degrees of skeletal completeness at the Donghuishan cemetery

Degree of Completeness	Description
I	The most disturbed; only one or no diagnosable components of human skeleton remain.
II	The human skeleton is disturbed; no more than six diagnosable components remain.
III	The human skeleton is disturbed, but at least half of body remains are complete.

Table 2.2. Statistical indexes of grave volume according to degree of completeness at the Donghuishan cemetery

Completeness	N	Median	Mean	SD	SE	Lower CI	Upper CI
I	20	0.207	0.284482	0.238395	0.053307	0.17291	0.396055
II	60	0.4405	0.50735	0.307433	0.039689	0.427932	0.586768
III	16	0.34	0.505895	0.432723	0.108181	0.275313	0.736478

Notes: N: number of samples; SD: standard deviation; SE: standard error; Lower CI: minimum value of the mean confidence interval; Upper CI: maximum value of the mean confidence interval.

Table 2.3. Statistical indexes of the number of grave goods according to degree of completeness

Completeness	N	Median	Mean	SD	SE	Lower CI	Upper CI
I	20	2	2.65	2.942877	0.658047	1.272691	4.027309
II	60	2.5	3.216667	3.30942	0.427244	2.361753	4.07158
III	16	4	4.8125	4.261748	1.065437	2.541575	7.083425

Notes: N: number of samples; SD: standard deviation; SE: standard error; Lower CI: minimum value of the mean confidence interval; Upper CI: maximum value of the mean confidence interval.

volume of all 96 single burials combined (0.47 m³). The average number of grave goods in these 10 single graves (6.1 items) is also larger than that in all single burials combined (3.4 items). These findings seemingly indicate a positive correlation between the completeness of the skeleton and energetic expenditure on the grave under certain circumstances.

Testing these conclusions against specific grave cases, we find the picture of correlation between different variables much more complex than initially suggested. A 35- to 40-year-old male buried in M18 represents the cemetery's most complete skeleton. All skeletal elements except the skull, right hand, and feet are anatomically articulated (Figure 2.6.1). The tomb pit in which it was discovered measures 2.2 m in length, 0.7 m in width, and 0.6 m in remaining depth. Its estimated volume of 0.924 m³ is much larger than the average volume (0.46 m³), median volume (0.38 m³), and upper quantile volume (0.55 m³) of all graves. A niche was dug into the eastern wall near the feet. The pattern of absent skeletal elements in this tomb conforms to previous hypotheses: skull and phalanges first decomposed after death and thus were probably retrieved in the secondary burial. Another tomb that supports this pattern is M127, which includes the largest number of grave goods (15 items) and accommodates an almost complete skeleton with only a few components dislocated or absent

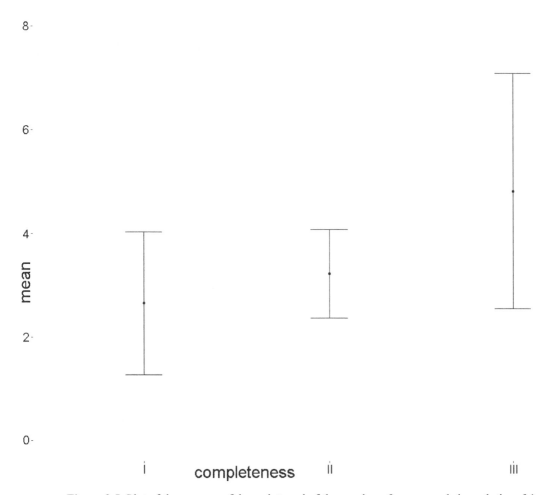

Figure 2.5. Plot of the mean confidence interval of the number of grave goods in each tier of degree of completeness at the Donghuishan cemetery. *Created by the author.*

(Figure 2.6.2). The grave volume (0.675 m³) is also above the upper quantile value of all tombs. The occupant of this tomb is an adult male about 50 years old. The skeleton is relatively less well preserved; only a few elements are missing. However, the pattern of absent skeletal elements does not support our hypothesis: aside from limbs, phalanges, and thoracic vertebrae, the connective tissues of which will decompose after death, the entire pelvis, which contains the most durable elements, such as the lumbo-sacral and sacroiliac joints, is also absent.

The skull, which is absent in most tombs, is preserved in M127. This abnormality might relate to the seniority of the occupant; even the most aged individuals in this cemetery did not outlive 55 years. M102 provides another good example (Figure 2.6.3). The skeleton of the deceased is well preserved. Missing elements, including the sternum, right carpals and phalanges, and both feet, also fit in the pattern of decomposition. However, the absence of limbs with more persistent tissues, such as the right humerus, left tibia, and fibula, indicates that postmortem disturbance occurred long after death. The much lower value than average (0.306 m³) grave volume and the lack of grave goods also suggest limited economic status of the bereaved.

By contrast, M24 seems to present a different picture. The occupant is an adult male about 40 years old. Parts of the skeleton above the pelvis were disturbed. Conforming to the pattern of decomposition as previously hypothesized, several elements, including the skull, right arm, scapula, cervical vertebra, and both hands, were absent (Figure 2.6.4). The exceptionally small volume of the tomb pit (0.34 m³) probably suggests limited economic means of the bereaved. This seems at odds with the good preservation of most elements of the skeleton, such as the pelvis and lower limbs. The amputation of the feet might,

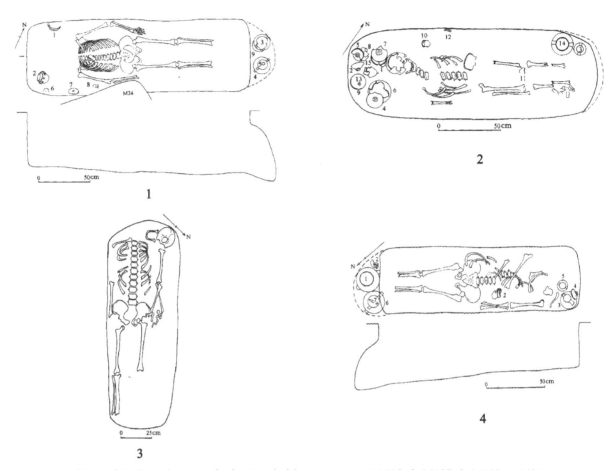

Figure 2.6. Grave instances in the Donghuishan cemetery: 1. M18; 2. M127; 3. M102; 4. M24.
Prepared by the author after Gansusheng and Jilin 1998:Figures 73, 86, 36, 75.

suggesting the unusual social status of the deceased at the time of death, might explain this contradiction. This special case suggests that aside from solely socioeconomic factors, philosophical-religious and other factors should also be considered in explaining mortuary patterns.

Presuming the treatment of that body—as with other mortuary variables, such as cubic volume of the grave and abundance of grave goods—may itself effectively and independently indicate the social status of the deceased in life, and that this treatment is further conditioned by ritual procedures, we then find that qualitatively universal rites produce quantitatively different treatments and thereby different degrees of completeness of the skeleton at the Donghuishan cemetery. It can therefore be inferred that the tension between members within a status hierarchy was probably disguised by the superficial homogeneity of mortuary practice. In ritual contexts, differences in degree of disturbance of the deceased are probably the means by which distinctions in socioeconomic status are manifested.

Discussion

Statistical tests indicate a correlation between the degree of disturbance of the human skeleton and the conventional parameters of energetic expenditure. But these relationships are not as significant as originally hypothesized. The analyses are compromised by many factors, including the small population available for testing. Data is limited to 96 tombs—all single burials and fewer than 50% of the total number excavated in the Donghuishan cemetery. Joint burials with two or more occupants are excluded from statistical computation owing to many uncontrollable variables. Similarly, it is too simplistic to classify tiers of completeness according to the specific number of remaining skeletal elements in each tomb; the arbitrary nature of this classification carries a degree of uncertainty. The low resolution of published data, however, does not allow for a much finer classification. Finally, inconsistent statistical results may relate to the complexity of ritual behavior and ritual procedures. Besides the disturbance of human skeletons, secondary burial rites—which were probably conducted more than once—also destroyed the original assemblage of grave goods. By contrast, grave volume was hardly affected by single disturbances. This probably explains why grave volume correlates with both the number of grave goods and the degree of completeness of the human skeleton, whereas the latter two parameters show no significant correlation with each other. Lastly, the randomness of ritual behavior could offset the structured nature of mortuary practice. Although burial rites are socially sanctioned and mandated, the scale, extent, and sequence of these rites are invariably conducted in distinctive ways.

Another noteworthy phenomenon is the absence and/or removal of skulls, which is omnipresent at Donghuishan. Only 14 skulls were uncovered among all 221 identifiable individuals excavated throughout the cemetery. The absence of skulls conforms to the pattern of decomposition after death: cervical vertebrae putrefy most quickly after death, leading to disarticulation of the skull. Nonetheless, this absence poses additional questions about the acquisition and recycling of the skulls of the dead, as well as about the social purpose and ritual meaning of these acts. More importantly, why were certain skeletal elements, apart from the skull, removed during secondary burial rites? Obviously, economic explanations alone cannot answer this question. The concept of "dividuality" of personality (Strathern 1988) might provide a potential perspective to help us understand the symbolic meanings of the human skeleton. However, further discussion of this topic would exceed the scope of this paper.

Conclusion

Mortuary remains, including human remains, possess the agency to reflect, mask, or even distort social organizations and relationships of the living. Secondary burial—like any form of postmortem manipulation of skeletal remains—presents a powerful means to (re)define, (re)shape, and maintain social relationships. Funerary rites, which are contingent on economic and material resources, provide an arena for a myriad of social interactions, whether interpersonal or intra/intercommunity. These include but are not limited to the destruction and reconstruction of social networks, as well as the inheritance and transformation of an individual's social role and status. Funerals therefore present social performances by which the living manipulate the dead for the former's well-being.

Although funerary rites are loaded with culturally defined worldviews and symbolic meanings, they must be eventually materialized by a living community. Building on this fact, investigating the economic dimension of ritual processes is not only legitimate but also productive, as suggested by the current study, in retrieving useful information about mortuary behavior and social organization from the taphonomical evidence of skeletons. The economic dimension provides a pragmatic but nonetheless insightful perspective on the rationale behind these rituals. An analysis from the perspective of ritual economy sheds new light on secondary burials commonly performed in the Donghuishan cemetery. This investigation proposes a correlation between the degree of completeness of the human skeleton and the socioeconomic status of the bereaved. To some extent, the completeness of the skeleton among secondary burials can therefore be used as an effective parameter to measure socioeconomic investment in the ritual. This conclusion may offer an alternative interpretation of the "secondary disturbed burials" in Neolithic and Bronze Age Northwest China (Chen 2006).

Analysis of secondary burials at the Donghuishan cemetery is a prerequisite to uncovering the economic inequality otherwise disguised by homogeneity in the mortuary material culture. As part of an essential sequence of funerary rites, the institutionalized postmortem disturbance may provide a ritual venue to fortify solidarity within the Donghuishan community by generating nonconsecutive periods of temporary equality, or "communitas" (Turner 1969). Variations in the form, scale, and extent of secondary ritual may reflect the differential responses of the Donghuishan community toward universal ritual obligations according to the socioeconomic status of members of the community. The few exceptions to this socioeconomic hypothesis remind us of the limitations of materialist explanations for secondary burials as well as the complexity of ritual behavior. In the future, philosophical-religious factors should certainly be given more attention in explaining mortuary patterns.

Acknowledgments

This paper presents part of my PhD dissertation. Many individuals—too many to name here—offered all sorts of support during my writing process. Appreciation from the bottom of my heart goes to you all. Thanks to Rowan Flad, Bryan Miller, and Anke Hein for reviewing and commenting on drafts of the paper. Many thanks to Kirie Stromberg and Elinor Pearlstein for their meticulous editing. Finally, I would like to thank Lothar von Falkenhausen for his inspiration, guidance, and encouragement for my PhD project.

References

Atahan, Pia, John Dodson, Xiaoqiang Li, Xinying Zhou, Songmei Hu, Fiona Bertuch, and Nan Sun
2011   Subsistence and the Isotopic Signature of Herding in the Bronze Age Hexi Corridor, NW Gansu, China. *Journal of Archaeological Science* 38(7):1747–53.

Binford, Lewis R.
1971 Mortuary Practices: Their Study and Their Potential. In *Approaches to the Social Dimensions of Mortuary Practices*, edited by J. A. Brown, pp. 6–29. Memoirs of the Society for American Archaeology 25. Washington, DC: Society for American Archaeology.

Bloch, Maurice
1971 *Placing the Dead: Tombs, Ancestral Villages, and Kinship Organization in Madagascar*. London: Seminar Press.

Brown, James A., ed.
1971 *Approaches to the Social Dimensions of Mortuary Practices*. Memoirs of the Society for American Archaeology 25. Washington, DC: Society for American Archaeology.

Carr, Christopher
1995 Mortuary Practices: Their Social, Philosophical Religious, Circumstantial, and Physical Determinants. *Journal of Archaeological Method and Theory* 2(2):105–200.

Chen Honghai 陳洪海
2006 Ganqing diqu shiqian wenhua zhong de erci raoluanzang bianxi 甘青地區史前文化中的二次擾亂葬辨析 [Critical Analysis of Secondarily Disturbed Burials among Prehistoric Cultures in the Gansu-Qinghai Region]. *Kaogu* 考古 1:54–68.

Duday, Henri, Françoise Le Mort, and Anne-Marie Tillier
2014 Archaeothanatology and Funeral Archaeology. Application to the Study of Primary Single Burials. *Anthropologie* 52(3):235–46.

Falkenhausen, Lothar von
2006a *Chinese Society in the Age of Confucius (1000–250 BC): The Archaeological Evidence*. Los Angeles: Cotsen Institute of Archaeology Press.
2006b Background and Purpose of the Project. In *Zhongguo yanye kaogu: Changjiang shangyou gudai yanye yu jingguan kaogu de chubu yanjiu (diyiji)* 中國鹽業考古—長江上游古代鹽業與景觀考古的初步研究（第一集）[Salt Archaeology in China: Ancient Salt Production and Landscape Archaeology in the Upper Yangzi Basin: Preliminary Studies, Vol. 1], edited by Li Shuicheng and Lothar von Falkenhausen, pp. 11–27. Beijing: Kexue Chubanshe.

Flad, Rowan, Li Shuicheng, Wu Xiaohong, and Zhao Zhijun
2010 Early Wheat in China: Results from New Studies at Donghuishan in the Hexi Corridor. *Holocene* 20(6):955–65.

Gansusheng Bowuguan 甘肅省博物館
1979 Gansusheng wenwu kaogu gongzuo sanshiniang 甘肅省文物考古工作三十年 [Thirty Years of Work in Archaeology and Cultural Relics in Gansu Province]. In *Wenwu Kaogu Gongzuo Sanshinian (1949–1979)* 文物考古工作三十年（1949–1979）[Thirty Years of Work in Archaeology and Cultural Relics, 1949–1979], edited by Wenwu Bianji Weiyuanhui, pp. 139–53. Beijing: Wenwu Chubanshe.

Gansusheng Wenwu Kaogu Yanjiusuo 甘肅省文物考古研究所, Beijing Keji Daxue Cailiao yu Yejinshi Yanjiusuo 北京科技大學材料與冶金史研究所, Zhongguo Shehui Kexueyuan Kaogu Yanjiusuo 中國社會科學院考古研究所, and Xibei Daxue Wenhua Yichan Xueyuan 西北大學文化遺產學院
2015 Gansu Zhangyeshi Xichengyi yizhi 2010 nian fajue jianbao 甘肅張掖市西城驛遺址2010年發掘簡報 [Brief Report on the 2010 Excavation at the Xichengyi Site in Zhangye City, Gansu]. *Kaogu* 考古 10:66–84.

Gansusheng Wenwu Kaogu Yanjiusuo 甘肅省文物考古研究所, Beijing Keji Daxue Yejin yu Cailiaoshi Yanjiusuo 北京科技大學冶金與材料史研究所, Zhongguo Shehui Kexueyuan Kaogu Yanjiusuo 中國社會科學院考古研究所, and Xibei Daxue Wenhua Yichan Xueyuan 西北大學文化遺產學院
2014 Gansu Zhangyeshi Xichengyi yizhi 甘肅張掖市西城驛遺址 [Xichengyi Site in Zhangye City, Gansu]. *Kaogu* 考古 7:3–17.

Gansusheng Wenwu Kaogu Yanjiusuo 甘肅省文物考古研究所 and Jilin Daxue Beifang Kaogu Yanjiushi 吉林大學北方考古研究室
1998 *Minle Donghuishan kaogu—Siba wenhua mudi de jieshi yu yanjiu* 民樂東灰山考古—四壩文化墓地的揭示與研究 [Archaeology at Donghuishan, Minle: Reveal and Study of Siba Culture Cemetery]. Beijing: Kexue Chubanshe.

Goodale, Jane C.
1985 Pig's Teeth and Skull Cycles: Both Sides of the Face of Humanity. *American Ethnologist* 12(2):228–44.

Goody, Jack
1962 *Death, Property and the Ancestors: A Study of the Mortuary Customs of the LoDagga of West Africa*. Stanford, CA: Stanford University Press.

Hefner, Robert W.
1983 The Problem of Preference: Economic and Ritual Change in Highlands Java. *Man* 18(4):669–89.

Hertz, Robert
1960 [1907] A Contribution to the Study of the Collective Representation of Death. Translated by R. and C. Needham. In *Death and the Right Hand*, edited by R. Hertz, pp. 29–76. Glencoe, IL: Free Press.

Kuijt, Ian
1996 Negotiating Equality through Ritual: A Consideration of Late Natufian and Prepottery Neolithic A Period Mortuary Practices. *Journal of Anthropological Archaeology* 15(4):313–36.

Li Shuicheng 李水城
1998 *Banshan yu Machang caitao yanjiu* 半山與馬廠彩陶研究 [Study of Banshan and Machang Painted Pottery]. Beijing: Beijing Daxue Chubanshe.
2001 Hexi diqu xinjian Majiayao wenhua yicun ji xiangguan wenti 河西地區新見馬家窯文化遺存及相關問題 [Newly Discovered Majiayao Culture Remains in the Hexi Corridor and Related Issues]. In *Su Bingqi yu dangdai Zhongguo kaoguxue* 蘇秉琦與當代中國考古學 [Su Bingqi and Contemporary Chinese Archaeology], edited by Su Bai 宿白, pp. 121–35. Beijing: Kexue Chubanshe.

Ma Mingming, Dong Guanghui, Emma Lightfoot, Wang Hui, Liu Xinyi, Jia Xin, K. R. Zhang, and Chen Fahu. 2014. Stable Isotope Analysis of Human and Faunal Remains in the Western Loess Plateau, Approximately 2000 Cal BC. *Archaeometry* 56(S1):237–55.

Metcalf, Peter
1981 Meaning and Materialism: The Ritual Economy of Death. *Man* 4:563–78.

Metcalf, Peter, and Richard Huntington
1991 *Celebrations of Death: The Anthropology of Mortuary Ritual*. Cambridge: Cambridge University Press.

Miles, Douglas
1965 Socioeconomic Aspects of Secondary Burial. *Oceania* 35(3):161–74.

Morris, Ian
1987 *Burial and Ancient Society: The Rise of the Greek City-State*. Cambridge: Cambridge University Press.

Parker Pearson, M.
1999 *The Archaeology of Death and Burial*. College Station: Texas A&M University Press.

Rakita, Gordon F. M., and Jane E. Buikstra
2005 Introduction. In *Interactions with the Dead: Perspectives on Mortuary Archaeology for the New Millennium*, edited by Gordon F. M. Rakita, Jane E. Buikstra, Lane A. Beck, and Sloan R. Williams, pp. 1–11. Gainesville: University Press of Florida.

Rappaport, Roy A.
1968 *Pigs for the Ancestors: Ritual in the Ecology of a New Guinea People*. New Haven, CT: Yale University Press.

Schroeder, Sissel
2001 Secondary Disposal of the Dead: Cross-cultural Codes. *World Cultures* 12(1):77–93.

Strathern, Marylin
1988 *The Gender of the Gift*. Berkeley: University of California Press.

Tainter, Joseph A.
1978 Mortuary Practices and the Study of Prehistoric Social Systems. In *Advances in Archaeological Method and Theory*, Vol. 1, edited by Michael B. Schiffer, pp. 105–41. New York: Academic Press.

Turner, Victor W.
1969 *The Ritual Process: Structure and Anti-structure*. London: Routledge.

Ubelaker, Douglas H.
1974 *Reconstruction of Demographic Profiles from Ossuary Skeletal Samples: A Case Study from the Tidewater Potomac*. Contributions to Anthropology 18. Washington, DC: Smithsonian Institution Press.

Van Gennep, Arnold
1960 [1908] *The Rites of Passage*. Translated by Monika B. Vizedom and Gabrielle L. Caffee. Chicago: University of Chicago Press.

Wilken, George A.
1884–1885 *Het animisme bij de volken van den Indischen Archipel*. Reprinted from *Indische Gids* 6:1:925–1001; 6:2:19–101; 7:1:13–59, 191–243. Amsterdam: De Bussy; Leiden: E. J. Brill.

Zhang Xuezheng 張學正, Zhang Pengchuan 張朋川, and Guo Deyong 郭德勇
1980 Tan Majiayao, Banshan, Machang leixing de fenqi he xianghu guanxi 談馬家窯、半山、馬廠類型的分期和相互關係 [Discussion of the Periodization of Majiayao, Banshan, Machang Type and Interrelationships]. In *Zhongguo kaogu xuehui diyici nianhui lunwenji (1979)* 中國考古學會第一次年會論文集（1979）[Proceeding of the First Annual Conference of Society for Chinese Archaeology], edited by Zhongguo Kaogu Xuehui 中國考古學會, pp. 50–71. Beijing: Wenwu Chubanshe.

Appendix A: Inventory of the Graves at the Donghuishan Cemetery

Tomb No.	Orientation	Tomb Construction	Length (m)	Width (m)	Depth (m)	Age	Sex	Grave Goods	Skeleton Completeness
1	NE–SW	pit	1.4	0.63	0.2	25–30	M	bone ornament 1	I
2	NE–SW	pit	1.85	0.6	0.25	?	M	pottery 4	II
3	E–W	pit	1.58	1.2	0.2	NA	NA	pottery 4	
4	NE–SW	pit	1.35	0.65	0.85	NA	NA	pottery 2, metal knife 1, bead 1	
5	NW–SE	pit	1.45	0.75	0.2	?/11–12	M + ?	pottery 1	
6	NE–SW	pit	1.6	0.55	0.3	NA	NA	pottery 6, spindle whorl 1	
7	NE–SW	pit	2.05	0.6	0.45	35–40/10	M + ?	pottery 3, stone knife 1	
8	NE–SW	pit	2.1	1.2	0.4	30–35/20–25	M + F	pottery 5	
9	NW–SE	pit	1.67	1.52	0.8	20/20	M + F	pottery 3	
10	NE–SW	pit + niche	1.9	0.85	0.5	NA	NA	pottery 11	II
11	NE–SW	pit	1.9	0.6	1.25	NA	NA		
12	NW–SE	pit	1.5	0.8	0.25	45/45–50/25–30	M + F + F	pottery 2	
13	NE–SW	pit	NA	0.75	0.35	NA	NA		
14	NE–SW	pit	1.8	0.5	0.25	?/16–17	M + F		
15	NE–SW	pit	0.9	0.55	1.37	NA	NA	pottery 2	
16	NW–SE	pit	1.5	0.45	0.9	NA	NA		
17	NE–SW	pit	1.95	0.7	1.35	NA	NA	pottery 3	
18	NE–SW	pit + niche	2.2	0.7	0.6	35–40	M	pottery 5, spindle whorl 1, stone knife 1, boar tusk 1	III
19	NE–SW	pit	1.5	1.4	0.53	30/?/15–16	M + M + F	pottery 7	
20	NE–SW	pit + niche	2	0.6	1.27	NA	NA	pottery 2	
21	NW–SE	pit	1.25	0.65	0.5	NA	NA	pottery 2, metal bracelet 1	
22	NE–SW	pit + niche	1.7	0.98	0.3	35/7	?	pottery 2, spindle whorl 1,	
23	NE–SW	pit + niche	2	0.56	0.9	NA	NA	pottery 5	
24	NE–SW	pit + niche	1.7	0.5	0.4	40	M	pottery 6	III
25	NE–SW	pit	1.7	1.25	0.4	25–30	M	pottery 4	II
26	NE–SW	pit	2	1	0.25	30	F	pottery 9, metal awl 1	II
27	NE–SW	pit	1.5	0.8	0.15	?	?		II
28	NE–SW	pit	1.9	0.65	0.35	?	?	pottery 4	II
29	NE–SW	pit	1.7	0.8	0.6	45/35–40/15/18			
30	NE–SW	pit	1.8	0.65	0.25			pottery 1	
31	NE–SW	pit + niche	1.55	0.55	0.2	50	M	pottery 7	II
32	NE–SW	pit	NA	0.4	0.8	NA	NA	pottery 1	
33	E–W	pit	NA	0.44	0.4	NA		pottery 2, perforated disk 1	
34	NE–SW	pit	2.15	1.1	0.45	25	M	metal earring 1	II
35	NE–SW	pit	1.8	1	0.5	25–30	M	pottery 6	II
36	NE–SW	pit	1.7	1.06	0.25	NA	NA	metal knife 1	
37	NE–SW	pit	1.65	1	0.35	17–18	?		I
38	NE–SW	pit	NA	0.6	0.35	NA	NA		
39	NE–SW	pit	2.15	0.7	0.2	NA	NA		
40	NE–SW	pit + niche	1	0.5	0.4	?	?		II

Tomb No.	Orientation	Tomb Construction	Length (m)	Width (m)	Depth (m)	Age	Sex	Grave Goods	Skeleton Completeness
41	NE–SW	pit + niche	0.9	0.6	0.35	?/40/40	? + M + F		
42	NE–SW	pit	1.05	0.45	0.55	NA	NA		
43	NE–SW	pit	1.75	0.65	0.25	NA	NA		
44	NE–SW	pit	1.8	0.4	0.2	NA	NA	pottery 1	
45	NE–SW	pit	1.8	0.65	0.4	35/19–20	F + F	pottery 3	
46	NE–SW	pit	1.55	1.15	0.4	?	?	pottery 3, bone awl 1	II
47	NE–SW	pit	1.9	0.7	0.3	?/17–18	? + ?	pottery 2	
48	NW–SE	pit	0.85	0.4	0.5	30–35	M	pottery 3	III
49	NE–SW	pit + niche	1.8	0.7	0.4	?	?	pottery 4	II
50	NE–SW	pit	1.8	0.65	0.2	NA	NA		
51	NE–SW	pit	1.8	0.6	0.3	?	?	pottery 1, metal earring 1	II
52	NE–SW	pit	2.2	0.5	0.5	25/20–25	M + F	spindle whorl 1	
53	NE–SW	pit	1.2	0.45	0.9	25	M		II
54	NE–SW	pit	1.6	0.6	0.4	45/?	M + ?	pottery 1	
55	NE–SW	pit	1.65	0.9	0.5	30–35	M	pottery 1	II
56	NE–SW	pit + niche	1.7	0.5	0.4	25	M		II
57	NE–SW	pit	2.3	0.7	0.35	NA	NA	pottery 3	
58	NE–SW	pit	1.5	0.75	0.15	NA	NA		
59	NE–SW	pit	1.75	0.75	0.37	40–45/17–18	M + F	pottery 9, stone knife 1	
60	NE–SW	pit	0.8	0.4	0.15	?	?		I
61	NE–SW	pit	1.7	0.65	0.2	35–40/8	M + ?	pottery 4	
62	NW-NE	pit	NA	0.4	0.35	13–14	F	pottery 3	III
63	NE–SW	pit	1.5	0.6	0.35	NA	NA		
64	NW–SE	pit	1.5	0.9	0.4	?/14–15	? + ?	pottery 1	
65	NW–SE	pit + niche	1.7	0.7	1.2	17/30/15/1/22/?	3M + 3?	pottery 14, cowrie shell 1, bone spreader 1	
66	NE–SW	pit	2	1.05	0.45	NA	NA	pottery 3	
67	NE–SW	pit	NA	NA	0.35	NA	NA	pottery 5	
68	NE–SW	pit + niche	1.85	0.65	0.7	12	?	pottery 4	II
69	NE–SW	pit	1.95	0.42	0.7	?/?	?		
70	NW–SE	pit	NA	0.5	0.7	30–35	F		II
71	NE–SW	pit + niche	1.9	0.55	0.8	30	M	pottery 3	II
72	NE–SW	pit	NA	0.75	0.5	25/?	M + M?		
73	NE–SW	pit	NA	1.15	0.4	40	M	pottery 2	I
74	NE–SW	pit	NA	0.6	0.15	?	M	pottery 4	I
75	NE–SW	pit	NA	0.53	0.3	NA	NA	metal knife 1	
76	NE–SW	pit	NA	0.75	0.12	NA	NA		
77	NE–SW	pit	1.6	0.5	0.25	40	M	pottery 4, cowrie shell 1	III
78	NE–SW	pit + niche	1.8	0.55	0.4	30	F	pottery 3	II
79	NE–SW	pit + wp	1.5	0.5	0.4	15	F	pottery 4, metal earring 1	II
80	NE–SW	pit + niche	1.5	0.45	0.4	20	?		I
81	NE–SW	pit + niche	1.3	0.4	0.4	20/15	? + F	pottery 6	

Appendix A: Inventory of the Graves at the Donghuishan Cemetery *(continued)*

Tomb No.	Orientation	Tomb Construction	Length (m)	Width (m)	Depth (m)	Age	Sex	Grave Goods	Skeleton Completeness
82	NE–SW	pit + niche	1.6	0.5	0.8	35	M	pottery 5	II
83	NE–SW	pit + niche	2.05	0.6	0.2	30/35/14	M + F + ?	pottery 7, spindle whorl 1	
84	NE–SW	pit	NA	1	0.2	NA	NA		
85	NE–SW	pit	NA	0.95	0.9	?	?	pottery 2	II
86	NE–SW	pit	NA	1.35	0.5	40/45/20/?/?	F + M + 3?	pottery 4	
87	NE–SW	pit	NA	0.9	0.4	25	?	pottery 3, bone needle 1	II
88	NE–SW	pit	1.8	0.6	0.45	?	?		II
89	NE–SW	pit	1.8	0.6	0.555	30/14	F + F	pottery 2	
90	NW–SE	pit + niche	2.05	0.65	0.4	35–40	F	pottery 10	II
91	NE–SW	pit + niche	NA	0.45	0.75	NA	NA	pottery 2	
92	NE–SW	pit + niche	1.95	0.75	1.1	20–25	F	pottery 9	III
93	NE–SW	pit	NA	0.6	0.6	NA	NA		
94	NE–SW	pit	1.25	0.5	0.15	17	F	pottery 6, spindle whorl 1	I
95	NE–SW	pit	NA	0.6	0.45	NA	NA	pottery 2	
96	NE–SW	pit	1.35	0.55	0.3	20/20	M + F	pottery 3, spindle whorl 1	
97	NE–SW	pit	1.9	0.75	0.25	45–50/20–25	M + F	pottery 8, stone knife 1, cowrie shell 1	
98	NE–SW	pit + niche	1.7	0.6	0.3	30–35/30	M + F	pottery 2	
99	NE–SW	pit	2.3	0.7	0.4	45/25	M + F	pottery 3, stone knife 1	
100	NE–SW	pit	1.8	0.5	0.45	17	F	pottery 8, stone knife 1	II
101	NE–SW	pit	NA	0.5	0.25	NA	NA	pottery 2, spindle whorl 1	
102	NE–SW	pit	1.7	0.6	0.3	40	M		III
103	NE–SW	pit	1.6	0.5	0.2	?	?		II
104	NE–SW	pit	1.8	0.5	0.9	25	M	pottery 2	II
105	NW–SE	pit	1.6	0.5	0.1	25	M	pottery 2	I
106	NE–SW	pit + niche	1.75	0.6	0.2	25–30	F	pottery 4	I
107	NW–SE	pit + niche	NA	0.75	0.5	NA	NA		
108	NE–SW	pit + niche	1.9	0.55	0.4	30–35/40	M + F	pottery 10, perforated disk 9	
109	NW–SE	pit	NA	0.6	0.3	25/25	M + F	pottery 1	
110	NE–SW	pit + niche	NA	0.6	0.6	NA	NA	pottery 3, spindle whorl 1	
111	NE–SW	pit + niche	1.75	0.55	0.2	?/25/15	M + F + ?	pottery 7, spindle whorl 1	
112	NE–SW	pit + niche	1.75	0.5	0.2	17	M		III
113	NE–SW	pit	1.8	0.45	0.7	NA	NA	pottery 1	
114	NE–SW	pit	1.8	0.5	0.35	NA	NA		
115	NE–SW	pit	NA	0.5	0.4	NA	NA		
116	NE–SW	pit	1.9	0.6	0.4	NA	NA	perforated disk 1, bone spreader 2	
117	NW–SE	pit	2.15	0.6	0.65	?	?	pottery 7	I
118	NE–SW	pit	1.9	0.65	0.5	NA	NA		
119	NE–SW	pit + niche	NA	0.5	0.4	NA	NA	pottery 1	
120	NE–SW	pit	NA	0.95	0.7	NA	NA	pottery 4	
121	NE–SW	pit	NA	0.65	0.4	?	?		I

Tomb No.	Orientation	Tomb Construction	Length (m)	Width (m)	Depth (m)	Age	Sex	Grave Goods	Skeleton Completeness
122	NE–SW	pit + niche	1.5	0.75	0.2	?/17	? + F	pottery 2, spindle whorl 1	
123	NE–SW	pit + niche	2.3	0.65	0.85	25	M	pottery 12	II
124	NE–SW	pit	1.3	0.7	0.3	40/20	M + F		
125	NE–SW	pit	1.6	0.6	0.3	NA	NA		
126	NE–SW	pit	1.4	0.8	0.35	NA	NA		
127	NE–SW	pit + niche	2	0.75	0.45	50	M	pottery 13, metal knife 1, perforated disk 1	III
128	NE–SW	pit	2.35	0.85	0.2	30	M	pottery 8	II
129	NE–SW	pit	1.2	0.7	0.15	25	M	pottery 1	II
130	NE–SW	pit	1.8	0.5	0.6	40	M	pottery 3	II
131	NE–SW	pit	NA	0.6	0.65	35	F	pottery 2	III
132	NE–SW	pit + niche	1.7	0.6	0.7	NA	NA	pottery 7	
133	NE–SW	pit + niche	1.63	0.6	0.65	35	M	pottery 3	I
134	NE–SW	pit	1.45	0.45	0.8	40	F		II
135	NE–SW	pit + niche	2.2	0.7	0.3	?/25/22	F + F + F	pottery 5, stone knife 1	
136	NW–SE	pit	NA	0.45	0.4	25	M		II
137	NW–SE	pit	1.15	0.55	0.5	NA	NA		
138	NW–SE	pit + niche	1.85	0.55	0.3	19	?	pottery 8	II
139	NW–SE	pit + niche	1.9	0.65	0.75	25/2/30	M + F + ?	pottery 13, spindle whorl 1	
140	NW–SE	pit	NA	0.55	0.35	45	F	pottery 5	II
141	NE–SW	pit	1.9	0.75	0.3	NA	NA		
142	NE–SW	pit	1.9	0.6	0.35	NA	NA		
143	NE–SW	pit	1.9	0.6	0.3	NA	NA		
144	NE–SW	pit	1.8	0.5	0.2	NA	NA	pottery 2	
145	NE–SW	pit + niche	1.8	0.4	0.4	NA	NA		
146	NE–SW	pit	NA	0.6	0.5	30–35/20	M + M	pottery 3	
147	NW–SE	pit	NA	0.45	0.85	NA	NA		
148	NE–SW	pit	1.7	0.55	0.25	35–40/20/8–9	M + F+?	pottery 5	
149	NE–SW	pit	2.25	1.12	0.75	NA	NA	pottery 2	
150	NW–SE	pit	NA	0.8	0.1	NA	NA		
151	NE–SW	pit	1.9	0.6	0.2	NA	NA		
152	NE–SW	pit	2	1.35	0.4	40	F	pottery 1	II
153	NE–SW	pit	2	0.8	0.5	NA	NA	pottery 1	
154	NE–SW	pit	NA	0.4	0.8	NA	NA	pottery 1	
155	NE–SW	pit	1.8	0.6	0.4	NA	NA		
156	NE–SW	pit	1.5	0.5	0.2	?	?	pottery 1, bead 1	II
157	NE–SW	pit + niche	1.55	0.5	0.27	10–11/15–16	? + F	pottery 10, metal knife 1	
158	NE–SW	pit + niche	1.8	0.5	0.4	35/20–25	M + F	pottery 6	
159	NE–SW	pit + niche	1.5	0.4	0.65	NA	NA	pottery 2	
160	NE–SW	pit	1.5	0.8	0.3	20–25/20–25	M + M	pottery 2	
161	NE–SW	pit	2	0.65	0.4	NA	NA		
162	NE–SW	pit	1.3	0.9	0.4	20	M		II
163	NE–SW	pit + niche	NA	0.6	0.3	30–35	M		I

Appendix A: Inventory of the Graves at the Donghuishan Cemetery *(continued)*

Tomb No.	Orientation	Tomb Construction	Length (m)	Width (m)	Depth (m)	Age	Sex	Grave Goods	Skeleton Completeness
164	NE–SW	pit	2	0.75	0.5	30–35	F	pottery 3	II
165	NE–SW	pit	1.8	0.6	0.4	NA	NA	pottery 1	
166	NE–SW	pit	1.9	0.5	0.45	45	M	pottery 6	II
167	NE–SW	pit + niche	1.8	0.47	0.6	30–35	M	pottery 3	III
168	NE–SW	pit + niche	2	0.65	0.65	40–45	M	pottery 3	II
169	NE–SW	pit	NA	0.55	0.5	NA	NA		
170	NE–SW	pit + niche	NA	0.5	0.3	30	F	pottery 6	III
171	NE–SW	pit	NA	0.7	0.2	NA	NA		
172	NE–SW	pit	NA	0.65	0.15	20–25	M	pottery 2	I
173	NE–SW	pit	1.7	0.4	0.3	35	M		I
174	NE–SW	pit	1.4	0.8	0.3	45	F	pottery 3	II
175	NE–SW	pit	NA	0.6	0.35	NA	NA		
176	NE–SW	pit	1.75	0.5	0.4	NA	NA	pottery 1	
177	NE–SW	pit + niche	1.9	0.45	0.3	NA	NA	pottery 2	
178	NE–SW	pit + niche	1.8	0.5	0.4	NA	NA	pottery 1	
179	NE–SW	pit	1.6	0.4	0.45	NA	NA		
180	NE–SW	pit + niche	1.6	0.5	0.6	NA	NA	pottery 9,	
181	NE–SW	pit	1.7	0.65	0.15	30	M	pottery 3, clay flute 1	II
182	NE–SW	pit	1.15	0.55	0.45	NA	NA	pottery 1	
183	S-N	pit	1.8	0.7	0.35	?	?		II
184	NE–SW	pit	1.9	0.55	0.35	NA	NA		
185	NE–SW	pit	NA	0.7	0.2	NA	NA	pottery 2	
186	NE–SW	pit	1.8	0.65	0.45	NA	NA		
187	NE–SW	pit	1.9	0.6	0.45	NA	NA	pottery 7	
188	NE–SW	pit + niche	2.35	0.5	0.55	?	?	pottery 12, clay flute 1	II
189	NE–SW	pit + niche	NA	0.6	0.5	NA	NA	pottery 4	
190	NE–SW	pit	1.5	0.65	0.2	20	F	pottery 10, stone knife 1	II
191	NE–SW	pit	NA	0.5	0.4	20	F	pottery 1	II
192	NE–SW	pit	NA	0.6	0.3	15	?		II
193	NE–SW	pit	NA	0.5	0.35	NA	NA		
194	NE–SW	pit	2.1	0.6	0.25	19–20	M	pottery 1, stone knife 1	II
195	NE–SW	pit	2.1	0.6	0.2	?	?	pottery 2	II
196	NE–SW	pit	1.9	0.5	0.1	?	?		I
197	NE–SW	pit	1.85	0.7	0.3	25–30	F	pottery 9	III
198	NE–SW	pit	1.9	0.5	0.35	NA	NA		
199	NE–SW	pit	2.15	0.57	0.3	?	?	pottery 8	I
200	NE–SW	pit	NA	0.65	0.4	?	F	pottery 3	II
201	NE–SW	pit	2	0.6	0.3	?/?	? + ?	pottery 4	
202	NE–SW	pit	2.1	0.6	0.3	?/14	? + ?	pottery 7	
203	NW–SE	pit	NA	0.8	0.4	NA	NA	pottery 1	
204	NE–SW	pit	1.5	0.5	0.2	NA	NA	pottery 1	
205	NE–SW	pit	2	0.65	0.4	30–35/?	? + ?	pottery 2, metal knife 1	
206	NE–SW	pit	2.1	0.6	0.3	?	F	pottery 2	II

Uncovering Disguised Social Inequality 33

Tomb No.	Orientation	Tomb Construction	Length (m)	Width (m)	Depth (m)	Age	Sex	Grave Goods	Skeleton Completeness
207	NE–SW	pit	1.8	0.6	0.3	35/2–3	M + ?	pottery 1	
208	E–W	pit	1.2	0.5	0.45	20–25/15	M + F	pottery 2	
209	NE–SW	pit + niche	1.5	0.6	0.3	25–30	F	pottery 8	III
210	NW–SE	pit	1.5	0.65	0.25	?	?		I
211	NE–SW	pit	NA	NA	0.1	NA	NA	pottery 1	
212	NE–SW	pit	NA	0.45	0.1	NA	NA		
213	NW–SE	pit	NA	0.4	0.1	20/20	M + F	pottery 3	
214	NE–SW	pit	1.95	0.6	0.25	20/?	M + ?		
215	NE–SW	pit	1.8	0.45	0.1	NA	NA	pottery 2, perforated disk 1	
216	NE–SW	pit	2.3	0.8	0.1	NA	NA		
217	NE–SW	pit	NA	0.55	0.1	NA	NA	pottery 1	
218	NE–SW	pit	1.65	0.55	0.1	50/40	M + F	pottery 2, metal knife 1	
219	NE–SW	pit	1.65	0.55	0.15			pottery 2	
220	NE–SW	pit	NA	0.65	0.3	?	?	pottery 5	I
221	NE–SW	pit	1.8	0.4	0.3	?/17	M + F	pottery 3	
222	NE–SW	pit	2.05	0.5	0.15	?	?		II
223	NE–SW	pit	1.6	0.4	0.2			pottery 2, gold earring 1	
224	NE–SW	pit + niche	NA	0.4	0.3			pottery 6	
225	NE–SW	pit	1.1	0.4	0.1	6	?		II
226	NE–SW	pit	1.4	0.4	0.2			pottery 5	
227	NE–SW	pit	NA	0.5	0.2				
228	NE–SW	pit	1.2	0.55	0.15				
229	NE–SW	pit + niche	1.6	0.55	0.5	40	F	pottery 2, spindle whorl 2	II
230	NE–SW	pit	1.9	0.5	0.15	20	?	pottery 7, stone knife 1	I
231	NE–SW	pit	NA	0.6	0.3	?/8	? + ?	pottery 1	
232	NE–SW	pit	NA	0.6	0.2	?	?		III
233	NE–SW	pit	NA	0.4	0.4	?	?		II
234	NE–SW	pit	NA	0.6	0.3	?	?	pottery 2	II
235	NE–SW	pit	NA	0.8	0.2	?	M		III
236	NE–SW	pit + niche	2	0.6	0.5	16–20	F	pottery 1	II
237	NE–SW	pit	2	0.6	0.4	40–45/50	M + F	pottery 2, perforated disk 1	
238	NE–SW	pit	1.9	0.55	0.4				
239	NE–SW	pit	NA	0.45	0.35				
240	NE–SW	pit	NA	0.8	0.7			pottery 4	
241	NE–SW	pit	2	0.55	0.4	?/50	M + F	pottery 4	
242	NE–SW	pit	NA	0.7	0.2				
243	NE–SW	pit	2.1	0.5	0.3			pottery 1	
244	NE–SW	pit + niche	1.4	0.65	0.55			pottery 1	
245	NE–SW	pit	NA	0.55	0.3				
246	NE–SW	pit + niche	2.05	0.5	0.25	30–35/35/5–6	F + M + ?	pottery 4, perforated disk 1	
247	NE–SW	pit	1.75	0.6	0.15				
248	NE–SW	pit	NA	0.4	0.1				
249	NW–SE	pit	NA	0.8	0.1	30/25–30	M + F	pottery 2	

Chapter 3

On the Margins of the Chinese World
The Bronze, Iron, and Gold of the Xi Rong at Majiayuan

Alain Thote

In 1996 Lothar von Falkenhausen published in the journal *Arts Asiatiques* a masterly article on Moutuo Tomb 1, Maoxian County 茂縣牟托, in Sichuan, about which a preliminary report had just been published (Falkenhausen 1996). He explained that the furnishings of this cist tomb and its three adjoining pits showed an unprecedented heterogeneity of character, for alongside locally made and Ba-Shu 巴蜀 objects were numerous Zhou bronzes of various origins, some coming from regions very distant from Moutuo. In his analysis of the origin and dating of the different pieces, he revealed the existence of a vast network of exchange. This discovery also raised the question of the routes by which these items had reached a region so far from their place of manufacture and so isolated. The site is located about 100 km from the Chengdu basin and connected to the latter only by a very deep valley. Von Falkenhausen's compelling study provided a better understanding of the complexity of the ancient cultures of Sichuan and their entanglement shortly before the kingdom of Qin invaded a large part of the area of this modern-day province.

Recent discoveries made in the eastern part of Gansu, at Majiayuan and in the surrounding area, seem to raise similar questions, but under quite different conditions and from a new perspective (Figure 3.1). In this article, I wish to show the ritual, economic, and technical implications of the finds of Majiayuan (Gansusheng 2013, 2014; Gansusheng and Zhangjiachuan 2008; Zaoqi and Zhangjiachuan 2009, 2010, 2012, 2018; Zhao 2018). Lothar has for some years focused his research on questions relating to the economy of the first millennium BCE, a subject that promises to be fascinating under his pen. Of a much more limited scope, my investigation focuses on the cultural origin and techniques of the burial goods associated with individuals buried in the third century BCE at Majiayuan and other cemeteries in the surrounding area. The paper's objective is to understand how such an accumulation of wealth could have come about, in which networks of exchange it was integrated, and what the technical and economic contribution of the community identified as the Xi Rong (Wang 2009), living in eastern Gansu, may have been. As early as the ninth century BCE, the Xi Rong 西戎 appeared as a population living west of the Zhou territory, whose epicenter was in the Wei valley in Shaanxi. Several wars between the Zhou and the Rong are recorded in historical texts, revealing the bellicose nature of their relationship and a form of instability on the western periphery of Zhou territory (Di Cosmo 1999:921–24). However, it is likely that history has retained only the milestones, wars, and military confrontations; neglected to consider exchanges and intermarriages; and underestimated the fact that a part of the Rong people lived within Zhou territory. Here we use the name Western Rong for convenience to refer to a group of people who lived on the western periphery of the Qin Kingdom in the fourth and third centuries BCE and whose material culture displays great wealth and pronounced distinctive features. Archaeological sources, up to the discovery of

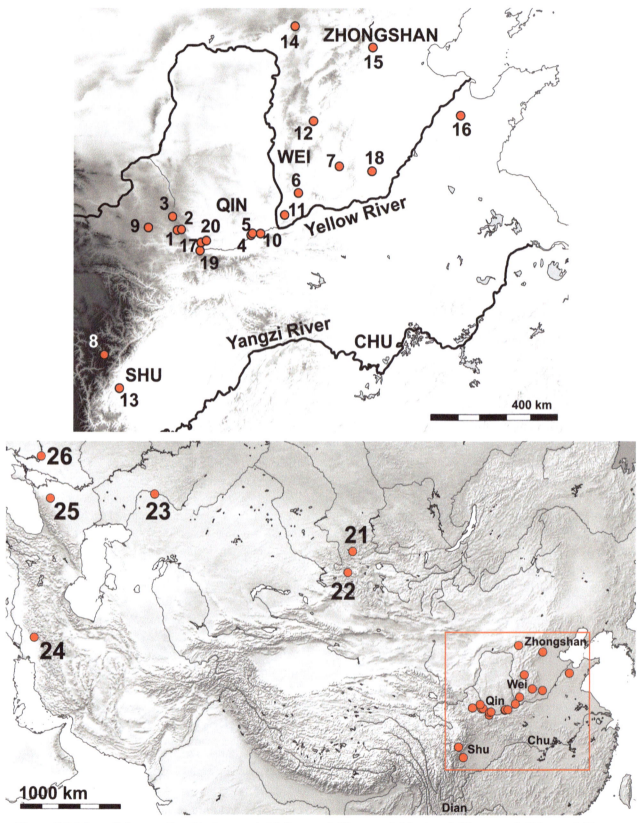

Figure 3.1. Maps of sites mentioned in the text. 1. Majiayuan; 2. Wangwa; 3. Liuping; 4. Xianyang; 5. Ta'erpo; 6. Houma Baidian; 7. Fenshuiling; 8. Moutuo; 9. Maojiaping; 10. Beikangcun; 11. Chengcun; 12. Jinshengcun; 13. Tongxincun; 14. Maoqinggou; 15. Mancheng; 16. Shangwang; 17. Rujiazhuang; 18. Liulige; 19. Yimencun; 20. Baoji; 21. Pazyryk; 22. Ak-Alakh; 23. Filippovka; 24. Susa; 25. Kelermes; 26. Tolstaya Mogila. *Created by Bryan K. Miller.*

the Majiayuan and East Gansu sites, suggested that Late Bronze Age inhabitants living on the margins of the Wei River system might correspond to people referred to as the Xi Rong in ancient texts (Falkenhausen 2006:227n31).

The Bronzes

Several tombs at Majiayuan contained a few bronze vessels—between one and eight (M18). Since most tombs were looted, the number of vessels certainly was higher initially. The vessels that remained belonged to two groups: a heterogeneous group of vessels of several different nonlocal types, and a group of vessels of a local style. The latter are tripods *li* 鬲 and *yan* 甗. To this group is added a *fu* pot 釜 (M1) and other small vessels.

The Ritual Vessels

There are seven *hu* 壺 of a long-lived type, widespread in Central China from the Late Zhou period to the Early Han period: one pair from Tomb 1, another pair from Tomb 16, and one specimen in each of the other three tombs (M4, M14, and M57). There are four *ding* 鼎 (M1, M3, M15, M19), a cocoon-shaped *jianxing hu* 繭形壺 vessel (M3), a pair of ovoid *dui* 敦 with grooved decoration (M18), a hemispherical *dui* (M18), a *yan* (M18), a large *pen* 盆 cup (M18), a *yi* 匜 pourer (M18), a *pan* 盤 basin (M23), and an ear-cup (M62).

Beverage Container *Hu* Vessels

The seven *hu* have roughly the same shape: a narrow neck widening to the opening, a bulging belly, and two *pushou* 鋪首, each of which has a movable ring. The lid, when present, is slightly domed and decorated with three fixed rings; at the top of the rings is a small spike. Type I is represented by four vessels (two in Tomb 1; one specimen each in Tombs 4 and 14), all resting on a fairly high ring base (Figure 3.2a; see Gansusheng 2014:116–19 [M1], 120–21 [M4]; Gansusheng and Zhangjiachuan 2008:12, 15, Figure 18, Figure 28.3; Zaoqi and Zhangjiachuan 2009:41, Figure 40, Figure 42.2 [M14]). Their surfaces are smooth and undecorated, underlined by three raised lines on the belly. Except for the ring base, these vessels correspond to a standard model from the Central Plains, as shown in the tomb of King Cuo of Zhongshan 中山䂂王, who died in 313 BCE (Hebeisheng 1995:1:124–25, 127, Figure 43-1). Type I became popular in Qin 秦 in the Late Warring States period and was made available in Qin in a variety of qualities, as shown in the furnishings of Tomb 32350 in Ta'erpo 塔爾坡 near Xianyang 咸陽, the only one containing bronze vessels in this graveyard: a *hu* and a *ding* of poor quality (Figure 3.3a; Xianyangshi 1998:52–55, 131, Figure 100.2). Close to Type I, Type II (two vessels, M16; see Zaoqi and Zhangjiachuan 2010:24–25, Figures 66, 68) is distinguished by its base, which is short and forms a ring with a straight edge, and by the presence of three bands slightly curved inward (Figure 3.2b). This model appears during the Warring States period, as evidenced by the Anyi Xiaguan *zhong* vessel 安邑下官'鍾, cast in the principality of Wei 魏 in the fourth to third century BCE (Shaanxisheng Xianyangshi 2002:45). As Types I and II are not very characterized, it is difficult to specify their dates of production. Type III comes from Tomb 57 at Majiayuan (Gansusheng 2014:124–25). It has the same shape as Type II but is ornamented with three registers of interlacing patterns of birds, whose beaks grasp the body of a dragon. According to excavations at bronze workshops in Baidian near Houma 侯馬白店 (Shanxi), this decoration was in use around 400 BCE, making it possible to date the vessel approximately and to attribute a Houma origin to it (Figure 3.3b; Shanxisheng 2012:244, Figure 225, Plate CXXIV.2).

Meat-Stewing *Ding* 鼎 Tripods

We can distinguish two *ding* types, which are nevertheless quite similar to each other. Both types have an oval profile. The cover follows the curvature of the belly and the bottom. In Type I (M1, M3, M4, M19), the feet are quite high and stand out well from the body of the vessel (Figure 3.2d).[1] This type, with the same rings on the lid, is represented by nine specimens in the west and east pits of the tomb of King Cuo of Zhongshan (Figure 3.3c; Hebeisheng 1995:1:111–14, 2:Plates LXXII.1–4, LXXIII.1–5). It appeared in Qin in the fourth century BCE and was in use until the late third century BCE, according to numerous specimens whose inscriptions give a precise date (Liu 2014:178ff.). Type II (M15) is quite similar to Type I, but its shape is hemispherical, its lateral handles are replaced by movable rings passed through a zoomorphic mask (*pushou*), and above all it differs from Type I by the presence of short feet located in the extension of the belly (Figure 3.2e). This rather rare type first developed in Houma in the first half of the fifth century BCE (Tomb 251 at Jinshengcun near Taiyuan [Shanxi]; see Shanxisheng and Taiyuanshi 1996:22, 23, 29, Figure 9, Plates XVIII and XIX) and was adopted in the fourth century BCE in the Central Plains, keeping a simple shape and a limited decoration. Several of them come from Changzhi County, including one from Tomb 35 at Fenshuiling 長治分水嶺 (fourth century BCE; Figure 3.3d), which is like that of Tomb 15 at Majiayuan (Shanxisheng et al. 2010:219–334 passim, Figures 90B.1 [M35], 91B.2 [M36], 101B.1 [M84], 102B.1 [M106], 112B.1 [M258]).

38 Alain Thote

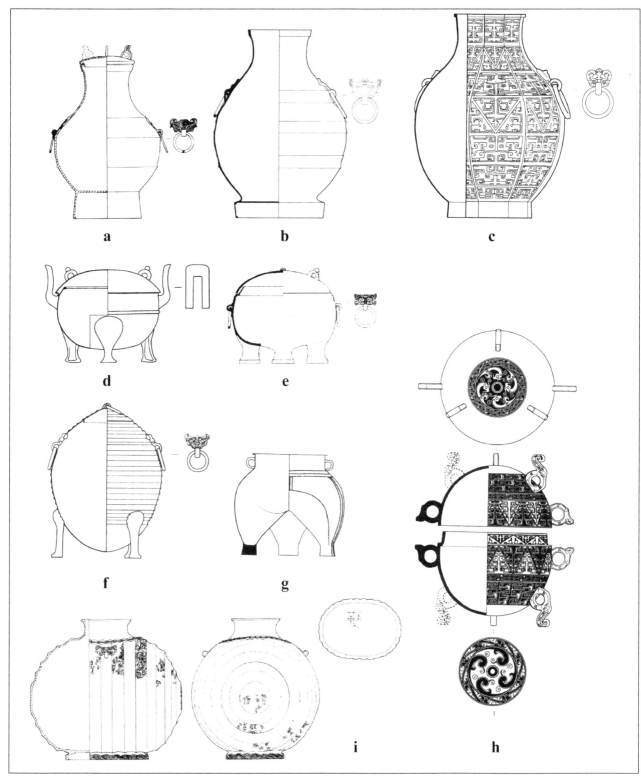

Figure 3.2. Zhou bronze vessels. a: Type I *hu*, height 27.4 cm (with lid), Tomb 1, Majiayuan, fourth to third c. BCE; b: Type II *hu*, height 30 cm, Tomb 16, Majiayuan, fourth to third c. BCE; c: decagonal *hu*, height 33 cm, Tomb 1, Wangwa, fifth c. BCE; d: Type I *ding*, height 15.1 cm, Tomb 19, Majiayuan, fourth to third c. BCE; e: Type II *ding*, height 15.6 cm, Tomb 15, Majiayuan, fifth c. BCE; f: oval *dui* (or *hu*?), height 24.5 cm, Tomb 18, Majiayuan, third c. BCE; g: *li* tripod, height 19.2 cm, Tomb 18, Majiayuan; h: *dui*, height 21.4 cm, fourth c. BCE, Tomb 18, Majiayuan; i: cocoon-shaped vessel, height 25.6 cm, Tomb 3, Majiayuan, third c. BCE. *Created by the author after Gansusheng 2012:29, Figure 3; Gansusheng and Zhangjiachuan 2008:Figures 28.3, 29; Zaoqi and Zhangjiachuan 2009:50, Figure 70.1; 2010:25, Figure 68; 2012:10, 14, Figures 16.1, 16.2, 16.4, 29.1.*

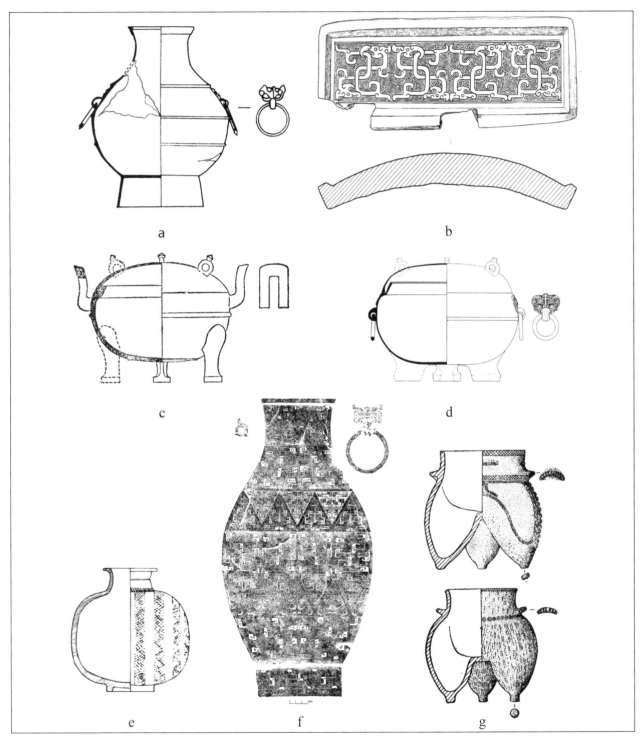

Figure 3.3. Bronzes and earthenware vessels from other sites. a: Type I *hu*, bronze, height 25.6 cm, Tomb 32350, Ta'erpo, Xianyang County (Shaanxi), fourth–third c. BCE; b. matrix, earthenware, length 18.4 cm, Pit H15, Baidian, near Houma (Shanxi), ca. 415–380 BCE; c: *ding* tripod, bronze, height 18.9 cm, Pingshan County (Hebei), tomb of King Cuo of Zhongshan, late fourth c. BCE (before 313 BCE); d: *ding* tripod, bronze, height 17.6 cm, Tomb 35, Fenshuiling, Changzhi County (Shanxi), fourth c. BCE; e: cocoon-shaped vessel, earthenware, height 21.4 cm, Tomb 6, Zaomiao, Tongchuan County (Shaanxi), fourth to early third c. BCE; f: *hu* vessel with inlay decoration, rubbing of the decoration, height 57.8 cm, Tomb 1, Liulige, Huixian County (Henan), ca. 400 BCE or earlier; g: Two *li* tripods, earthenware, height 23.6 cm and 32.4 cm, Tombs LM4 and LM12, Maojiaping, Gangu County (Gansu), Eastern Zhou. *Created by the author after Gansusheng 1987:390, Figures 23.1, 23.5; Guo 1959:Plate XCIX; Hebeisheng 1995:1:113, Figure 36.3; Shaanxisheng Kaogu Yanjiusuo 1986:Figure 4.15; Shanxisheng et al. 2010:Figure 90B.1; Shanxisheng 2012:Plate CXXIV.2; Xianyangshi 1998:131, Figure 100.2.*

Cocoon-Shaped *Hu* 繭形壺 (M3)

This vessel was unearthed from Tomb 3 at Majiayuan (Figure 3.2i). Its shape is quite rare in the bronze typology, as it is more often made of ceramic material with stamped or, later, painted decoration on its surface (Yang Zhefeng 2000). This *hu*, from excellent artisans, remains unique in its very round shape, its decoration, and the presence of a cast character, Yang 軮, under the base, perhaps the name of the foreman responsible for its manufacture. Terracotta cocoon-shaped *hu* were created in the Wei 渭 valley (Figure 3.3e). Teng Mingyu's (2003:37–40) detailed study of Qin material culture places their appearance during the mid–Warring States period, c. the fourth century BCE, in her ten-period chronology. The decoration of grooves, either vertical or horizontal, a characteristic feature of several bronzes produced by Qin workshops, is in fact a legacy of the Western Zhou foundries of the Wei valley.

Egg-Shaped *Dui* 敦 (M18)

An exceedingly rare pair of ovoid-shaped *dui* (called *hu* in the report) is decorated in a style close to the preceding vessel (Figure 3.2f). It seems that the use of horizontal or vertical grooves in these two vessels and in the previous cocoon-shaped *hu* was the mark of high-quality workshops that functioned in Qin in the fourth to third century BCE.[2]

Dui 敦 with Inlaid Decoration (M18)

While the hemispherical shape of this vessel, composed of two equal and perfectly symmetrical halves, is classical, its decoration stands out for its exceptional quality, as shown by the turquoise and red copper inlays preserved on its inner rim (Figure 3.2h). The only comparable example belongs to the Shanghai Museum (fourth century BCE) but has no known provenance (Zhongguo Qingtongqi 1998, no. 28). There is little doubt that both *dui* were made in close-by workshops working for a ruler's family. Their shape and decoration are similar, and the technique of inlaying wound-up copper wires to fill in the depressed areas of the surface, as described by Le Bas et al. (1996:124–27, 203–6), is the same. Their alternating triangular patterns in positive and negative are characteristic of the late fifth century BCE or later, a design attested mainly in Central China (Figure 3.3f). The decoration at the top of the Majiayuan *dui* formed by four spiral-shaped birds corresponds to an innovation from the late fourth century BCE. It is inspired by the fluid decoration developed in the art of lacquerware (Thote 2008). As a hypothesis, the workshop where the *dui* from Tomb 18 originated could be in present-day Henan.

Grain Steamer *Yan* 甗

In Tomb 18 at Majiayuan, two *yan* were discovered. One is local; the other has a peculiar shape. The lower part, which is usually a *li* tripod, has low feet that are barely marked. The body has a bulbous shape, a cylindrical neck, and a narrow opening. This vessel type seems to have been developed first in the Central Plains, more precisely in Henan (Zhongguo 1994:53–55, Figure 42). In the type's evolution, the feet diminished until they became nonexistent at the beginning of the Imperial period (Gansu and Beijing 1987:390). The vessel became gradually common to all the Zhou states. The *yan* from Tomb 18, therefore, could have been made either in Qin or in a workshop farther east in the Central Plains.

Other Vessels

As in the previous case of the *yan*, other vessels found in Majiayuan tombs are not very typical. Their shape is simple, and they are not characterized by any decoration. They are a *pen* cup 盆 and a pourer *yi* 匜 (M18), a *pan* basin (M23), and an ear-cup (M62).[3]

Finally, Tomb 1 at Wangwa, Qin'an County 秦安王洼, yielded a decagonal *hu* vessel with decoration in seven tiers (height 33 cm; Figure 3.2c). This *hu* is decorated with scrolls and triangles enhanced with turquoise inlays, in the same style as the *fanghu* in Tomb 1 at Liulige, Huixian County 輝縣琉璃閣 (Henan), which allows us to date it to the late fifth century BCE (Figure 3.3f). The two *hu* probably come from the same workshop or from a group of workshops attached to the ruling family of a state located in the Central Plains (Wei 魏?).

The above discussion shows that the Xi Rong placed Zhou ritual vessels in their burials, but in no tomb did these vessels form a coherent set according to Zhou prescriptions. Of 32 tombs, including Tomb 1 at Wangwan, only four contained a bronze *ding*. In five Majiayuan tombs, there was one *hu* (M4, M14, M57) or two *hu* (M1, M16) of rather common Late Eastern Zhou shape (small foot, round belly divided by three lines or strips, constricted neck, flaring opening), and in Tomb 3 was a cocoon-shaped *hu*. But in Tomb 18, from which the largest number of Zhou ritual vessels, eight to be precise, were unearthed, there were no *hu* wine vessels or any *ding* tripods. Yet the presence of at least one *ding*, and sometimes one *hu*, was of prime importance for the Qin neighbors of the Xi Rong. It could be argued that this lack of coherence in the ritual ensembles is due to the looting of several Majiayuan tombs. However, Tomb 18 was not plundered. Moreover, the *yi* pourer was not associated with a *pan* basin, even though a *pan* of the same style was discovered isolated in Tomb 23. The two vessels seem to have been made to fit together and may have been dissociated when they were buried. Tomb 18 contained two *yan* vessels; a Zhou ritual set usually had only one. All these facts suggest that the Zhou vessels placed by the Xi Rong in their tombs were gathered as a result of random relations or exchanges with neighbors, but certainly not because they had adopted Zhou customs. (On this point, consult Yang Jianhua and Linduff [2012:82], who reach a conclusion contrary to mine.)

Another important point must be emphasized here. The date of manufacture of the Zhou ritual vessels buried at Majiayuan and its region varies roughly between ca. 400 BCE or slightly earlier and the late third century BCE, over a period of about two centuries, while the tombs are dated approximately to the late third century BCE. Moreover, a majority of vessels undoubtedly come from Qin workshops (*hu* of Type I and Type II; cocoon-shaped *hu*), but the *hu* of Type III was produced in Houma, and the inlaid *dui* and the *hu* with pentagonal cross section come from a state workshop in Central China. In other words, given their varied origin, their uneven quality, and their dating, it is clear that many vessels passed through several hands before the Xi Rong took possession of them. They certainly were prestige goods for this population, no doubt acquired from their Qin neighbors as part of political or economic relations with them. Armin Selbitschka (2018:11–12), following Flad and Hruby in their analysis of specialized production (2007:9–11), developed seven useful criteria to define certain objects in the contents of a tomb as prestige goods: (1) relatively high production or acquisition costs (suggesting exclusiveness); (2) availability of raw materials; (3) labor intensity and technical expertise in production; (4) exoticism (nature of the object itself and provenance); (5) social restrictions; (6) special character in context of the tomb assemblage (nature of the object itself and its position in the tomb and in relation to the body); (7) heirloom. The Chinese ritual bronzes discovered in some Majiayuan tombs meet several of these criteria but not all. In particular, these bronzes had no equivalent in the culture of the Xi Rong (criterion 1) insofar as their artisans did not possess the expertise to cast them (criterion 3), as shown below. In imitation of their Chinese neighbors, only some individuals were buried with ritual bronzes, suggesting restrictions in their possession (criterion 6). Finally, analysis showed that many of the Zhou ritual bronzes were cast long before being deposited in the Majiayuan tombs, which could indicate that they had been owned for two or more generations by the families of the deceased (criterion 7). Without being "exotic," these bronzes may have been used by the Xi Rong "in imitation" of their Chinese neighbors but without following the strict rules of the Zhou. This too could indicate the prestige the vessels possessed in the eyes of the Xi Rong, who imitated the practices of the Qin elite while adapting them to their practices.

Bronze Vessels of Local Style

Next to the Zhou ritual vessels were seven bronzes cast in imitation of terracotta *li* and *yan* tripods: four *li* 鬲 (two specimens each in Tombs 14 and 18; Figure 3.2g) and three *yan* 甗, unearthed from Tombs 16, 18, and 19.[4] In addition, at least four tombs at Majiayuan (M2, M8, M20, M26) and Tomb 1 in Wangwa contained terracotta tripods.[5]

The bronze replications are faithful to their earthenware models. The earthenware *li* are characterized by a fairly high neck with one or two lateral handles (sometimes a tenon replaces the handle) and pouched-shaped legs that are far apart and sloped outward, with a small cylindrical end forming the base. Several *li* bear lines in relief that emphasize the shape of the feet, a decoration faithfully reproduced on the bronze *li* and *yan*. In addition, these tripods were widespread in the eastern region of Gansu (site of Maojiaping, Gangu County 甘肃甘谷毛家坪; Gansu and Beijing 1987:390 and Figure 3.3g) and in southwestern Shaanxi, the Wei valley, and its surroundings (Teng 2003:135–36). Moreover, their links with the earlier cultures of Lijiaya 李家崖 and Siwa 寺洼 have been established (Sun 2019). The relationship between earthenware and bronze *li* is even more interesting, since on the Chinese side, tripods made in such a close imitation of pottery are rare. The distinctive shape of the tripods from Majiayuan and its region has no equivalent in the Central Plains. The proximity between the bronze and terracotta tripods is so marked that one wonders if they were not cast locally.

In fact, it is easy to observe mold marks running on the surface of the bronze *li* from the base of the feet to the neck. Moreover, the handles on the neck are not aligned with the mold marks on the feet but positioned at a short distance. Together, these technical features indicate that the piece-mold casting technique specific to China (Bagley 1987:37–45; Fairbank 1962) was used to produce these *li* and *yan* tripods. Since vessels with these unique shapes and decoration are present in five tombs, unlike the ritual Zhou vessels, which are all different, one might infer that they were produced locally. However, this is most likely not the case for several reasons. First of all, vessels aside, all the bronze objects used by the Xi Rong are small, of simple shape, and mediocre in quality in general. They are steppe-like mirrors of about 6–7 cm in diameter,[6] protective elements added to axle caps (a specificity of their own), a linchpin representing the head of a Xi Rong,[7] pieces of harness (bridle holders, rings),[8] openwork plaques and animal-shaped ornaments for the decoration of wheels,[9] chariot fittings,[10] knives of steppe types,[11] crane-beaked hatchets (*hezuifu* 鹤嘴斧),[12] tips for ox horns,[13] and bells or clapper bells.[14] All these objects are quite different from Zhou bronzes in their shapes, small dimensions, sometimes mediocre casting, and often crude decoration. They either come from the steppes or follow the fashions, conventions, and decoration common to the steppe cultures with whom the Xi Rong had close ties. Many bronze burial objects from Majiayuan and Liuping are similar to burial pieces from the Yanglang 杨郎 culture (Wu En 2007:357–86), as Wu Xiaolong (2013) has noted. Moreover, there are also links between the sites of Maoqinggou 毛庆沟 (southern Inner Mongolia) and Liuping in the form and style of small bronze belt plaques.[15] Their mirrors, for example, while significantly different from those found in Xinjiang, are just as simple (Mei 2006:138–40). Among the bronze vessels discovered at Majiayuan there is no steppe-type cauldron (called *fu* 鍑 in Chinese). However, the distribution map of the finds, which covers a vast area stretching from eastern Siberia to the banks of the Dnieper, also shows the presence of steppe-type cauldrons in the region between eastern Gansu and Baoji (Li Gang 2011:209–34). The poor quality of the Majiayuan bronzes is also noticeable on three goblets (*zhi* 质) with slightly flaring or cylindrical bodies and measuring less than 8 cm high. One might suppose that these three goblets were cast locally.[16] The casting is defective, although they were made in simple bivalve molds.

The *li* and *yan* bronze tripods were markers of Xi Rong identity and were artifacts that required the highest level of craftsmanship. Nevertheless, when the Xi Rong made three-dimensional objects even of small size, they seem to have encountered technical difficulties.

To summarize, the Xi Rong, who were skilled in the use of gold, iron, and silver, encountered difficulties when producing bronze objects because they did not master the Chinese casting technique in complex segmented molds. Moreover, had they mastered this technique, would they have used it to cast only *li* and *yan* and not other shapes? It is reasonable to hypothesize that the *li* and *yan* cast in imitation of local ceramics were produced in Qin foundries for the Xi Rong. Indeed, it is known, thanks to the discovery of Beikangcun Tomb 34 北康村 near Xi'an (Shaanxi), that Qin workshops worked bronze or gold for non-Chinese people living on the margins of Zhou China (and also for people of Chinese culture) by conforming to the animal style of the steppes (Shaanxisheng Kaogu Yanjiusuo 2006:120–33, 202, 210; see also Liu 2012:289–91; Thote 2014:13–29).

Xi Rong Crafts and Techniques

Although the Xi Rong did not use the Chinese casting technique in segmented molds, they perfectly mastered several other metallurgical techniques, specific to them or that they shared with different steppe populations.

Iron

The Xi Rong wrought iron (Chen et al. 2014) whereas the Zhou cast iron (Wagner 1993). Majiayuan is one of the sites of the Zhou period with the greatest concentration and diversity of iron objects. Several tombs, if not all, contained iron weapons (daggers, swords, dagger-axes *ge* 戈, spearheads), knives, chariot fittings, pieces of harness (bits, frontlets, buckles), and ornaments. By contrast, hardly any weapons or chariot fittings were made of iron in Zhou China. Except for agricultural tools, Chinese metal artisans clearly preferred bronze to iron until the beginning of the empire. The use of iron in such high proportions by the Xi Rong for objects routinely cast in bronze in Central China is probably due to the existence of close links with human groups living in the Gansu Corridor and farther afield in present-day Xinjiang. We know today that iron metallurgy appeared in that part of Asia earlier than in Central China because of contacts with Inner Asia farther west. In addition, the gold and silver decoration of many iron objects unearthed at Majiayuan is made up of distinctive motifs. In this important use of iron, original motifs on iron objects manifest cultural traits vastly different from those of Qin.

Swords and Daggers

Iron swords, like the one in Tomb 61 (length 54.6 cm; Zaoqi and Zhangjiachuan 2018:18, 22, Figures 37, 51.9; see also Gansusheng and Qingshuixian 2014:57 [Liuping site]; Zaoqi and Zhangjiachuan 2010:15, 16, Figures 37, 38.4 [M8]), are about half the size of the Qin bronze swords of the late third century BCE. The 17 bronze swords found in Lintong Pit 1 臨潼 measure between 81 and 91 cm (Shaanxisheng Kaogu Yanjiusuo Shihuangling 1988:1:249–254).

The Xi Rong daggers followed several models. A dagger (partial length 21.7 cm) similar in shape to the sword from Tomb 61 (but its pommel has been lost) was found in Tomb 22 (Zaoqi and Zhangjiachuan 2018:23, Figure 52.7). Another model, from Tomb 23, consists of a blade with a diamond profile and a wooden handle attached to the front of the blade with two transverse pegs (M23MD cai:9; see Zaoqi and Zhangjiachuan 2018:15, 21, Figures 27, 50.15 [M23; total length 26.2 cm], 50.8 [M23; unknown length]).

The existence of iron swords and daggers that are distinct in shape from Zhou swords and daggers, and less efficient, is another feature of the Xi Rong culture. The Xi Rong preferred iron to bronze, probably because they had more experience in the use of that metal, as is confirmed to us by the case of the dagger-axes. They also may have had direct access to iron ore.

Dagger-Axes

The iron dagger-axes of Majiayuan imitate Chinese bronze *ge* but differ significantly from their Zhou models; they are simplified (Zaoqi and Zhangjiachuan 2018:15–21, Figures 28, 50.11 [M23]; see also Zaoqi and Zhangjiachuan 2009:48, 50, Figures 65, 70.8 [M12]; Zaoqi and Zhangjiachuan 2010:15–16, Figures 36, 38.3 [M8]). The specimen discovered in Tomb 23 has rare characters (Figure 3.4a). The tenon is in the extension of the blade, without any break in the profile, and the fanon is perfectly perpendicular to the tenon and blade. Moreover, the blade is short and narrower than the tenon in comparison with the classical Chinese dagger-axe. Finally, the end of the tenon has an unusual roundness, and the butt of the blade takes a triangular shape downward. This *ge* is not a copy of a Chinese dagger-axe of the third century BCE. It is modeled—though not exactly faithfully—on dagger-axes of more than two centuries earlier. In Jing Zhongwei's typology of *ge*, which is certainly the most complete, the closest model to the iron *ge* of Majiayuan M23 is his Type A, which comes in two versions, A-7 and A-8—one from Tomb 0003 in Chengcun, Linyi County 臨猗程村, and the other from Tomb 251 in Jinshengcun, near Taiyuan 太原金勝村 (Shanxi; six pieces; Figures 3.4b, 3.4c). Both versions, A-7 and A-8, are dated between the late sixth century BCE and the mid-fifth century BCE (Jing 2011:102–5; Shanxisheng and Taiyuanshi 1996:93, Figure 45.1–3; Zhongguo 2003:114–15, Figure 104.1). Other *ge* of the same shape, origin, and date come from the Fenshuiling cemetery, Changzhi County 長治分水嶺 (Shanxisheng et al. 2010:232, 240, 302, Figures 92.4 [Fenshuiling M10], 94C.1 [Fenshuiling M12], 104D.2 [Fenshuiling M126]). These three tombs are dated to the early phase of the Warring States period—that is, the fifth century BCE).

Tomb 23 had been almost completely looted, and the few artifacts unearthed were not distinctive enough to date it. While Tomb 23 is like other tombs from the third century BCE at Majiayuan, the presence of an iron *ge* made on a bronze model at least two centuries older from the workshops of the principality of Jin raises questions. Didn't the Xi Rong possess more efficient models to copy in the third century BCE? Was the iron *ge* an early weapon of the fifth century BCE? Zhou people did not produce iron *ge*. Li Jinghua, in his book on iron artifacts of early and medieval China, does not mention them (Li Jinghua 2007). The Xi Rong were most likely inspired by a bronze *ge* from Jin that came to them by chance from exchanges with their Qin neighbors. In the third century BCE, the classical bronze *ge* was particularly thin: both the blade and tenon tended to be extremely sharp (Figure 3.4d).[17] Several Majiayuan tombs contained bronze dagger-axe blades, all from the Zhou cultures of the Warring States period, but none of them correspond to Zhou *ge* of the time.

To sum up, most of the shapes of the bronze dagger-axes discovered at Majiayuan correspond to blades of the sixth to fifth century BCE, well before the time of their owners. In addition, Majiayuan's iron dagger-axes were made in imitation of bronze models that did not come from the workshops of their neighbors in Qin but from those made in Jin. Probably these models were seized by the Qin armies from their enemies and then exchanged with the Xi Rong through barter or given to the Xi Rong at a time when Qin warriors had long since stopped using these weapons in the Central Plains, probably because of their ineffectiveness by Qin standards.

Another iron *ge* deserves to be briefly considered, although it is broken (M12) (Figure 3-4e). It has the peculiarity of having a hook at the base of the butt. The hook is turned outward, probably to better fix the blade to the shaft. This peculiarity is exceptional, and I have observed it only on a single bronze dagger-axe blade from Shu 蜀 in the Sichuan basin (Sichuansheng 1998:241, Figure 47.3) (Figure 3.4f).

Gold and Silver Decoration

Among the wrought iron burial furnishings were objects whose decoration was made of gold, silver, and sometimes these two metals combined. Altogether, there are about 50 objects, most of them chariot fittings. Given the looting of the Majiayuan cemetery, it is likely that their number is grossly underestimated. These objects come from Tombs 1 (23 pieces), 3 (seven pieces), 14 (20 pieces), 16 (one piece), and 22 (one piece).

The association of gold and iron was developed in the material culture of the steppes from at least the seventh century BCE. The famous sword from Kurgan 1 at Kelermes (seventh century BCE) in the Kuban region near the Black Sea has an iron blade and a gold hilt, as well as a gold scabbard. It was accompanied by a very large ceremonial axe, also bimetallic, decorated with a series of animal motifs (deer, wild boar, ibex, and so on; Schiltz 1994:393–94; see also Metropolitan Museum 1975:3:Plate 7). And the iron daggers with gold handles, sometimes enriched with turquoise inlays, from Tomb 2 at Yimencun near Baoji 寶雞益門村 (Shaanxi) in the late sixth century BCE remind us that members of a non-Zhou elite with great wealth and relatively high status

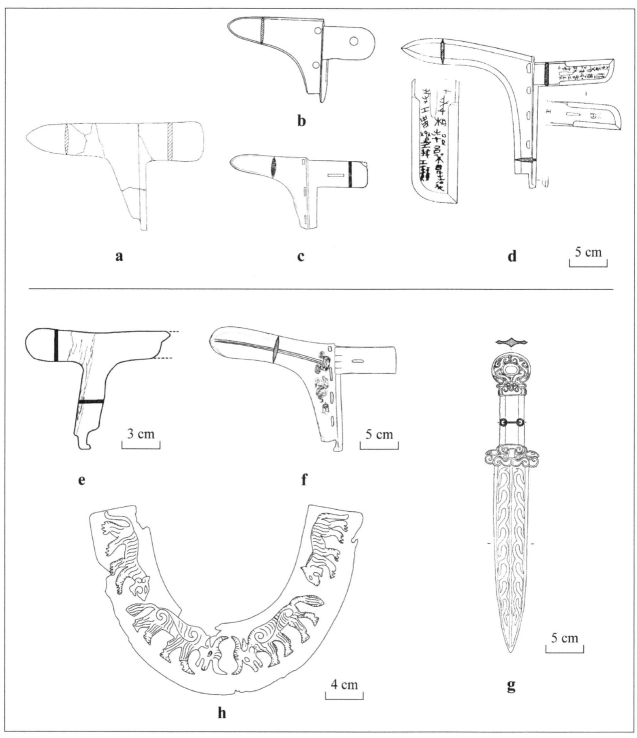

Figure 3.4. Bronzes, iron weapons, and silver torque. a: dagger-axe *ge* blade, wrought iron, length 22.7 cm, Tomb 23, Majiayuan, third c. BCE; b: dagger-axe *ge* blade, bronze, length 19 cm, Tomb 0003, Chengcun, Linyi County (Shanxi), late sixth–mid fifth c. BCE; c: dagger-axe *ge* blade (lower part broken), bronze, length 17.8 cm, Tomb 251, Jinshengcun, Taiyuan County (Shanxi), ca. 500–450 BCE; d: dagger-axe *ge* blade, bronze, length 26.8 cm, dated 244 BCE, Pit 1, Lintong (Shaanxi), tomb of the First Emperor; e: dagger-axe blade (broken), wrought iron, length ca. 11 cm, Tomb 12, Majiayuan, third c. BCE; f: dagger-axe blade, bronze, length 23.5 cm, Tomb 21-A, Tongxingcun, Yinjing County (Sichuan), third c. BCE; g: dagger; iron, gold, and silver; length 36.7 cm; Tomb 1; Mancheng (Hebei); ca. third c. BCE; h: torque decorated with bulls and tigers, silver, diameter 27 cm, third c. BCE. *Created by the author after Gansusheng 2014:201; Shaanxisheng Kaogu Yanjiusuo Shihuangling 1988:1:Figure 153.3; Shanxisheng and Taiyuanshi 1996:Figure 45.1; Sichuansheng 1998:Figure 47.3; Zaoqi and Zhangjiachuan 2009:50, Figure 70.8; 2018:21, Figure 50.11; Zhongguo 1980:1:Figure 72.5; 2003:241, Figure 104.1.*

were present in Qin, as shown by Lothar von Falkenhausen (2006:224–28). But the material culture associated with the deceased from Yimencun Tomb 2, even where gold or gold and iron objects are concerned, seems to be better integrated into sixth century BCE Chinese culture than the burial furnishings of the third century BCE Majiayuan site.

From a technical point of view, the Yimencun daggers are bimetallic, consisting of an iron blade and a gold handle. By contrast, the Majiayuan iron objects are plated with motifs cut out of thin gold and silver foils using a technique unknown in Zhou China and relatively little used in steppe cultures. The gold and silver cut foils seem to have been applied against the iron surface. Indeed, the Chinese technique of inlay decoration was different from what we see here. It consisted of gold, silver, or copper wires or small sheets affixed to cast-in recesses of the bronze or iron surface. It was first used in the sixth century BCE for inlaid inscriptions of gold and later, from the fifth century BCE on, for the decoration of bronze vessels. Chinese metal artisans started to decorate cast iron objects with gold and silver during the fourth century BCE. Inlaying gold and silver wires or small plates into iron also occurred among the Scythians. It is attested in the Urals on fourth century BCE objects from Kurgan 1 at Filippovka, situated to the north of the Caspian Sea (Shemakhanskaya 2009). At Majiayuan, it seems that only two iron objects were made using the technique of gold or silver wires or strips inlaid into recessed areas of their surfaces. They are a ring decorated with scrolls (M14) and probably the iron structure of a chariot box from Tomb 16 (Zaoqi and Zhangjiachuan 2009:42, Figure 49; Zhao 2018:46).

This unusual technique of gold- and/or silver-plated decoration is probably less complex than the Chinese inlay technique. It is not specific to the Xi Rong since it appears among the burial goods of several kurgans, including that of Filippovka, about 4,000 km as the crow flies, from the Majiayuan region. Filippovka is among the sites that delivered material with which the objects discovered at Majiayuan and its region are most resonant stylistically. Among these objects was a short sword of the Akinakès type (length about 55 cm), made of iron and decorated with wavy patterns cut out of gold foil (Aruz 2000:80–81). The sword is dated to the fifth to fourth century BCE. Another link with the steppes is given to us by S-shaped iron bit bars from Tomb 1 of Majiayuan (length 25 cm) (Gansusheng 2014:208–9). They are decorated at both ends with bird heads cut from gold leaf and plated on the surface of the iron. The S shape and bird decoration are reminiscent of wooden bars from a frozen tomb (kurgan) found at Ak-Alakh in the extreme south of the Altai, 15 km from the Chinese border, and dated to the fourth to third century BCE. At least four horses from a total of about nine were found with iron bits in their mouths. The wooden bars are carved in the style of Pazyryk wooden objects (Polosmak 1991:6–7, 1994:347–48).

It is noteworthy, but noted with due caution in view of the looting, that only four tombs at Majiayuan contained objects, in particular chariots, decorated using this technique. They are Tombs 1, 3, 14, and 16, which are among the wealthiest on the site. The motifs of all the iron objects decorated with gold and silver foil are either highly stylized animal heads or composed of triangle-shaped scrolls displayed head to tail. They have a relatively homogeneous style, different from the style in use in Qin and the Central Plains. The combination of iron, gold, and silver; the use of forging techniques for iron; the plating of fine cut foils; and the style of their decoration all argue in favor of creations made by Xi Rong artisans. These are not objects imported from the nomadic world. They are not objects coming from Zhou China. Moreover, one finds almost no comparable objects in the burial goods of the tombs of the Central Plains, with one noticeable exception: a dagger with a hilt and pommel in a silver alloy with gold inlays, with an iron blade decorated with flames cut from gold foil. This weapon comes from the tomb of Liu Sheng 劉勝, who died in 113 BCE (Tomb 1 of Mancheng 滿城, Hebei; Figure 3.4g; Rawson 2017:383; Zhongguo 1980:1:72, 2:Plate XIII.1). Although the dagger was discovered in a mid-Western Han tomb, it might be older.

Gold and Silver

The style of Majiayuan gold and silver objects deserves a thorough study to determine to which Central Asian cultures they relate. This search is not as easy as one might think, as several variants of animal styles have existed in the nomadic world, which stretches from southern Siberia to the Black Sea, and each variant evolved over time. Moreover, being essentially produced by nomadic populations, the objects circulated with humans, which caused many interactions between the different artistic foci.

The repertoire of zoomorphic motifs at Majiayuan is about the same as the appliqués made by the nomads in leather, bronze, gold, and other materials: tigers, ibexes, mouflons, deer, wild boars, wolves, horses, birds. Horses and wild boars are not particularly common, however. In addition, the mode of representation of quadrupeds is the same as in steppe art: the four legs of mammals are shown, whereas in traditional Chinese art, animals seen in profile are represented by a single front leg and a single hind leg (Figure 3.4h). At Majiayuan, certain animals, such as tigers and mouflons, appear to be winged (Gansusheng 2014:78–79 [mouflon], 72–73 [tiger]). But the wings are barely sketched compared to those of griffins. Moreover, according to a whimsical artistic convention of the animal style, interior scrolling marks joints and muscles of some wild animals (Figure 3.4h: the two horned animals; Bunker et al. 1997:no. 70; Francfort et al. 1990; Jacobson 1988:204–6). In addition, the tail of a feline is ended by a bird's head (Gansusheng 2014:38–39 [M14], 45 [M20]), and bird's heads are added to the corners of some plaques (Gansusheng 2014:46 [M15]). Finally, the representation of an animal twisting on itself—another characteristic feature of the animal style of the fourth–third century BCE—appears only on few objects unearthed at Majiayuan, in particular on a gold belt hook inlaid with carnelian and decorated with two wolves and with two scenes of predation showing a tiger devouring a deer (Gansusheng 2014:60–61). Both cervids and wolves have their bodies turned 180 degrees (M16). This mode of representation appears in several sites of the Altai, notably at Pazyryk (fourth–third century BCE) on tattoos from Barrow 2 (Rudenko 1970:111, Figures 53–54). Despite these stylistic similarities between the decoration of the belt hook and the materials from Pazyryk, most of the zoomorphic gold or silver foil motifs on the Majiayuan chariots have a style of their own, with the exception of a silver tiger depiction from Majiayuan Tomb 1, which forms a striking parallel to the deer figures in Kurgan 1 at Filippovka (Aruz 2000:72ff., catalog nos. 1–4; Gansusheng and Zhangjiachuan 2008:18, Figure 38. See also Gansusheng 2014:34–35).

Many chariot ornaments made of cut gold or silver foils are composed of volutes, foliage scrolls, and, more surprisingly, palmettes and half-palmette scrolls (Gansusheng 2014; Gansusheng and Qingshuixian 2014:passim; Gansusheng and Zhangjiachuan 2008; Zaoqi and Zhangjiachuan 2010). Volutes are common in Scythian art, especially in a slightly different but similar style in the gold objects of Kurgan 1 at Filippovka (fourth century BCE; Aruz 2000:nos. 1–4, 20–22, 25–29, 34, 39, 42, 52, 53, 69, 70, 73, 77, 78, 84–92). Furthermore, the palmette theme, which comes from Greece, is present in Pazyryk Barrow 3, dated to the first half of the third century BCE (Rudenko 1970:157–58, Figures 77–83). Rawson (2017:383–84) concludes judiciously, "The speed with which the Majiayuan peoples borrowed practices and motifs from the distant Altai contrasts with the resistance of the peoples of Central China to adopting these."

Silver

In Zhou China (as opposed to the steppes), few objects were made of silver, except for belt hooks from the late fourth century BCE onward. The silver set of vessels exhumed from Tomb 1 in Shangwang, near Linzi 臨淄商王 in Shandong (ca. 230 BCE), appears to be an exception (Ziboshi 1997). The shapes of the two silver goblets from Majiayuan are much simpler than the Shangwang vessels, which imitate bronze vessels. Their technique is also particular. The two edges of the leaf forming the goblet of Tomb 16 are soldered together. Those of the second "goblet" (as it is hollow, the silver leaf is supposed to have covered a wood or bamboo container) are "sewn" together with two parallel gold wires (M1), like bent wood. According to ethnographic studies, this mode of manufacture was a traditional technique used by nomadic people. It consisted of shaping a cylinder from the bark of a tree or a thin plank.[18] However, it is difficult to prove the existence of the bent wood technique among the steppe peoples because publications rarely indicate techniques used for the manufacture of wooden objects. They focus almost exclusively on metallurgical techniques. Nevertheless, bent wood is attested for the first time in China on lacquer objects from the kingdom of Qin in the late fourth century BC (Thote 2003). We can therefore ask whether the bent wood technique, which suddenly appeared in China, originated in the steppe cultures and was transmitted by people of the steppe to the artisans of Qin. In any case, it will be interesting to know the technique used for a cylindrical wooden container with cut-out gold and silver motifs found in Tomb 16 (height 17.8 cm; diameter 16 cm). So far, the first steppe objects made of birch bark come from slightly later sites in Inner Mongolia, the oldest from the Western Han (Nei Menggu 1994:375–77). The use of a silver leaf to transfer a cylindrical wooden container into metal reflects on the one hand the difficulties encountered by the Xi Rong when casting containers, even of the simplest kind, and on the other hand their preference for traditional objects used in daily life.

Several silver objects, always of small size, were made by the metal artisans of Majiayuan and Liuping: flat belt buckles, torques (Figure 3.4h), soles, animal-style ornaments cut from foils, earrings, and a bracelet. Whether it is by chance, or rather a sign of lesser wealth, the ornaments cut out of silver foils are numerous in Liuping while those in gold are nonexistent. Metallographic analyses made on 76 silver objects from Liuping reveal a very homogeneous composition for 74 of them, with an average silver content of 97.8%. The two exceptions (objects 1431 and 1434) are 90.9% and 73.4% silver, with an iron percentage of 6.1% and 7.9%, respectively (Chen et al. 2014:27–30). But these two objects do not differ stylistically from other objects with a composition in the middle range. It can therefore be estimated that they all have the same provenance. At the same time, their stylistic and technical proximity to comparable pieces at Majiayuan indicates that they were made by the Xi Rong for their own use.

Faience Beads

Faience is "a composite material whose body, made of a siliceous paste, is covered with a glaze" (Caubet and Pierret-Bonnefois 2005). At Majiayuan were discovered blue, blue-green, and purple beads, plus two conical stemmed beakers (M1, M19), a rare model in terms of shape and material in China. Analyses reveal that the beakers were made in China due to the presence of barium (Ba), in imitation of a model from Central Asia (Lam 2012). To date, the Majiayuan site represents the highest concentration of faience beads ever discovered at a Zhou site. Such a concentration cannot be the result of chance.

The eye beads were used as personal adornment. Of various types and colors, they were unearthed from at least three tombs (M6, M4, M18; Zaoqi and Zhangjiachuan 2009:30–31). The analyses carried out on two of them show that they come from the east coast of the Mediterranean (Lin et al. 2018:71–72).

The largest quantity of beads discovered at Majiayuan are tubular or round and unicolored. Three colors have been distinguished: *hanlan* 漢藍 (Chinese blue; $BaCuSi4O10$), *hanzi* 漢紫 (Chinese purple; $BaCuSi2O6$), and *qianbai* 鉛白 (lead white or ceruse). The names *hanlan* and *hanzi* distinguish their composition from that of glazed beads made in Egypt that contain calcium ($CaCuSi_4O_{10}$; Berke 2002). The first analyses of the Majiayuan glazed beads in the laboratory show that their composition includes barium instead of calcium, a specificity until the end of the Han period (Berke 2007). Therefore most of them were probably made locally. Only a small number would be of foreign origin. It must be noted that the production of pure Chinese blue and Chinese purple was the result of a complex process, requiring strict control of the amount of starting materials and a high temperature (about 1000°C) that had to be maintained for a certain time (Berke 2002:2485–86).

The considerable number of tubular and round beads from Majiayuan and the fact that so many beads of this kind have never been found at any other site of the Late Warring States period suggests a local production. One may conclude that the Xi Rong mastered the secret of producing the blue and purple synthetic pigments, known as Han blue and Han purple, and most likely traded those pigments with Qin. Indeed, analyses have identified Han purple among other colors (cinnabar, azurite, malachite) on the terracotta warriors of the First Emperor (Portal 2007:173–74).

Two points are worth mentioning here. First, Tomb 1A at Rujiazhuang, Baoji County 寶雞茹家莊 (Shaanxi), in the lineage cemetery of Yu 強, located in the western part of Shaanxi (ca. ninth century BCE), is the earliest site where large quantities of blue faience beads were discovered in China (Lu and Hu 1988:1:329–30). Probably these beads were introduced from far away (Brill et al. 1989; Lu and Hu 1988:1:646–50). Although that tradition has left little trace in the archaeological material in eastern Gansu and western Shaanxi from the Springs and Autumns period, faience beads like those from Rujiazhuang have been found in eastern Gansu (Berke 2007:23–24) and several Eastern Zhou sites of Central China, suggesting a diffusion from west to east (Li Hui 2014:160–62; Thote 1997:267–69). Second, at Majiayuan the beads were used in large numbers to create nets. They were strung in parallel rows to form a bicolor or tricolor armor, used mainly to decorate the deceased and part of the chariots (boxes and axles). Reconstructions have been proposed for the fishnet decoration of chariots (Zhao 2018:51–52, Figures 28, 29; Zhao and Ma 2020). On belts (M4, M16, M18) and necklaces (M18) strings of beads grouped together alternate with gold plaques (Gansusheng 2014:48–49). The use of faience bead nets is not attested anywhere else in China; it is by contrast common at Majiayuan. This mode of ornamentation for the chariots does not seem to be present in the steppe cultures of southern Siberia either, although faience beads are present in kurgans. In view of the huge number of beads for these specific uses at Majiayuan, and despite the time span of more than 600 years with the cemetery of Yu, one may suppose that a craft tradition of faience beads developed in eastern Gansu over several centuries, achieving spectacular results in the third century BCE.

Objects of Adornment

Personal adornment played a prominent role among nomadic peoples. At Majiayuan, although the Xi Rong seem to have been sedentary, they were strongly attached to nomadic traditions, as evidenced in the objects worn by their dead: necklaces, torques, belts, and earrings combining gold, silver, and semiprecious stones such as carnelian and turquoise. Only a few objects will be reviewed here to trace their origin.

The Gold Belt Plaques

Current publications do not yet provide a clear overview of the adornment of the deceased at Majiayuan. However, the photographic documentation offers additional details on some burials. The personal adornments from Tombs 4, 14, 16, and 18 (Tomb 16 had two or three belts for the deceased) appear on a few pictures in situ. On the belts, probably made of leather (or felt), were sewn gold plaques, arranged on the front part of the body, aligned next to one another. These plaques alternate with blue faience beads assembled on the belt.

The plaques were either cast in molds, which gave them a weight varying between about 19 and 157 g each, or were worked by stamping with a matrix or using repoussé techniques, which made them lighter, sometimes less than 1 g. In both cases, the manufacturing method allowed the identical reproduction of pieces. In the motifs and modes of representation, there are major differences between the two kinds. Interlaced dragons or snakes (M18), sometimes associated with birds (M16), prevail in the decoration of plaques cast in molds. On the plaques worked by repoussé, the decoration is based on wild boars fighting (M4), fighting birds (M14), or two mouflon heads nested one inside the other (M15).[19] Moreover, the way these animals are depicted corresponds to the animal style. The plaques of the first kind, of Chinese inspiration, were probably produced in Chinese workshops working on behalf of steppe populations living in contact with Qin (So and Bunker 1995; Thote 2014), whereas the plaques of the second kind were made by local artisans.

Gold Jewelry Inlaid with Carnelian and Turquoise

Among the objects discovered at Majiayuan are gold jewels, sometimes inlaid with turquoise, carnelian, or faience. I counted a dozen of them in five tombs (M4, M6, M14, M16, M25) likely to have come from the Persian world.[20] They are quite diverse in nature: earrings (M14, M25), pendants (M14), necklace elements (M6, M16), tubular beads (M14, M16), pointed beads (M14), a bracelet (M16), and a pendant (M4) described as a "small box" in spite of its tiny dimensions (height 3 cm, sides 1.5 x 0.8 cm).[21] The technique of the pendant combines granulation arranged in double rows and turquoise cloisonné in the shape of a cross against a field of carnelian. There are also inlays of faience beads. Each stone is framed by a gold wire. This cloisonné technique, with inlaid semiprecious stones in metal cells, was used in jewelry as early as the middle of the third millennium in Mesopotamia. It is attested on a ring discovered during the excavations of Tello (formerly Girsu) in Iraq in 1881, now in the collections of the Louvre (Département des antiquités orientales, AO277). Let us recall here that lapis came from Afghanistan and carnelian from the Indus River valley and that such objects already attested to the existence of very extensive trade networks from India to the Mediterranean. The granulation technique was widely used in antiquity. Analyses have revealed that, based on the composition of the solder, a tubular bead from Tomb 16, decorated with three to four evenly spaced granulations on its surface, might not have come from Persia or the Near East (Zaoqi and Zhangjiachuan 2009:79). However, its origin has not yet been determined.

The diversity of the material sources makes it difficult to trace the origin of each object. But carnelian and turquoise, or lapis lazuli, were present in the art of Achaemenid Persian goldsmiths in the fifth–fourth century BCE. And it is likely that two gold disks inlaid with carnelian and turquoise, belonging to the ornament of the deceased in Tomb 18 and placed on either side of his body, could be of such provenance or inspired by Achaemenid goldsmithing (Figure 3.5). One is round. The other one, smaller, is oval. They have different decoration but were produced in the same style. The cloisonné on the left side of the deceased, about 6 cm in diameter, consists of several concentric circles in which three carnelian and three turquoise scales alternate, each set in a cell delimited by a gold wire. In one circle the scales are arranged in a clockwise direction, whereas in another circle the scales are arranged in an anticlockwise direction (Gansusheng 2014:53; no photographs of these two pieces have been published). The composition of the oval plaque, about 4 cm wide, on the right side of the deceased, follows the same principle, but the scales are replaced by adjoining triangles, with alternating colors, red for carnelian and blue-green for turquoise. One cannot help but compare these plates with buttons and cloisonné earrings found in the Achaemenid tomb of Susa, Iran, dated between 350 and 332 BCE (Figure 3.6).[22] And the bracelet of Tomb 16 is ornamented with the same technique of polychrome cloisonné.

On the "box-shaped" pendant from Tomb 4, the cloisonné is associated with granulation, which also has a long history. That technique appeared in goldsmithing at the time of the royal tombs of Ur, in the middle of the third millennium BCE or even earlier. Then it spread throughout the Near East and Egypt, Cyprus, and Greece. But it was not until the third century BCE that this technique was evidenced in Central China, notably in Tomb 1 at Shangwang (Shandong; Ziboshi 1997:46, Figure 35). Gold beads with granulation can be related to several pieces of jewelry found in kurgans, including beads hanging from the tiara of the deceased from the kurgan of Tolstaia Moguila, fourth century BCE, located to the north of the Black Sea (Schiltz 1994:383, Figure 305).

Finally, a few necklace elements are composed of gold tubular beads soldered together in groups of five or six (Gansusheng 2014:48–49 [M18; see necklace]; Gansusheng and Qingshuixian 2014:147 [Liuping site]; Zaoqi and Zhangjiachuan 2009:30, Figure 9 [M6]; Zaoqi and Zhangjiachuan 2010:22, Figure 57 [M16]). Those in Tomb 16, numbering 15, adorned a chariot. Each is 5.7 cm wide and 3 to 3.7 cm high. The two in Tomb 6 consist of six tubes arranged in a fan-shaped pattern, with a row of granulation between two tubes. They are tiny pieces, 1.7

Figure 3.5. The deceased in Tomb 18, Majiayuan, in situ (lower part of his body).
Created by the author after Gansusheng 2014:53.

Figure 3.6. Pair of earrings, gold, lapis lazuli, turquoise, Susa Acropolis, Late Achemenid Period, ca 350 BCE, Musée du Louvre, Paris. (Sb2764, Sb2765). *Photo by the author and published with permission from the Agence photographique de la Réunion des Musées Nationaux et du Grand Palais.*

cm wide. These associations of joined gold tubular beads appeared during the third millennium, as evidenced by jewelry of the goddess Ishtar discovered in Mari, Syria, and dated to 2400 BCE, now in the Louvre Museum. One plaque of her personal adornment consists of nine adjoining tubes of the same kind as those found at Majiayuan, but the tubes of diminishing size form a triangle.

Majiayuan jewels are quite diverse either by their shapes, by the assembling of materials (gold, semiprecious stones, faience beads), or by their varied manufacturing techniques (gold hammering, granulation, repoussé, cloisonné). This disparate ensemble does not seem to have a unity of style likely to suggest coherent local production at Majiayuan. In addition, the gold plaques composed of five or six tubular beads soldered together, which could have originally been elements of necklaces for a goddess or a woman, were used in one case at Majiayuan (M16) to adorn a chariot. This change of use indicates that the gold plaques were probably acquired by the Xi Rong through barter.

Finally, the few comparisons made here show that a large part of the gold cloisonné objects inlaid with semiprecious stones, carnelian and turquoise, might have an Iranian or Near Eastern origin. If this conclusion is correct, these jewels would have been introduced into China through Central Asia from regions that had been dominated until 330 BCE by the Achaemenid. These artifacts meet several distinctive criteria corresponding to prestige goods (exoticism, technical expertise, rarity, use limited to a few deceased, position on the body) and originated so far away that they were probably traded indirectly through several intermediaries. All things considered, they were light and easy to transport. They testify to the long-distance exchanges, close contacts, and long-term relationships the Xi Rong had undoubtedly established with the populations of southern Siberia and perhaps even farther west.

In its largest territory, the Achaemenid Empire (ca. 558–330 BCE) extended from Thrace (Greece) to Bactria (present-day Afghanistan). After its conquest, Alexander's armies seized the entire eastern part of the ancient Persian Empire between 330 and 323 BCE, and a period of instability began, leading to the spread of its treasures. The presence of Achaemenid artifacts in several kurgans scattered between the Altai and the Black Sea (Brosseder 2015:14ff.) bear witness to these unsecure times. The Pazyryk site itself has yielded several objects revealing the existence of links between the Altai and the region formerly covered by the Achaemenid Empire, including a felt curtain (Barrow 5, 260–240 BCE), the border of a felt wall hanging (Barrow 1, fourth century BCE), and even a shabrack, part of which is made of Iranian cloth (Barrow 5; Francfort 2003; Schiltz 1994:277ff.). These links are also strongly attested in the material culture of nomadic tribes living in the Altai, not only in Pazyryk but also in numerous frozen tombs such as Berel's in Kazakhstan (Francfort et al. 2006). However, it should be noted that the gathering of so many Achaemenid and Near East jewels at such a distance from western Central Asia is uncommon. They bear evidence of the existence of strong long-distance relations and reliable trade networks.

Concluding Remarks

We started with evocation of the site of Moutuo, whose burial assemblage was composed of artifacts of various origins and led Lothar to explore the exchange networks of a community living on the margins of the Sichuan basin. At the beginning of my investigation, parallels appeared possible between Moutuo and Majiayuan. However, based on the analyses presented above, a rather different picture emerges. First, the wealth of each tomb at Majiayuan is out of proportion with Tomb 1 at Moutuo and its three adjacent pits. Second, the eastern part of Gansu was in the third century BCE in close proximity to its powerful neighbor, the state of Qin, whereas the Moutuo people lived in a mountainous, secluded area at a distance from Shu, and Shu itself was far from being organized on the model of the Zhou states before its conquest by Qin in the late fourth century BCE. Archaeologists identify the occupants of the Majiayuan tombs as belonging to a branch of the Xi Rong, based on historical geography, while the exact origin of the inhabitants of the Moutuo region is still subject to discussion.

Since the Majiayuan region was adjacent to the kingdom of Qin, one might think a priori that the cultural influence it received from Qin was strong, which apparently is not the case. The archaeological material found there is quite unusual. On the one hand, it testifies to powerful links with the distant cultures of the steppes. On the other hand, it presents original aspects, features unknown until now, undoubtedly proper to the Xi Rong, such as the unprecedented and unique decoration of chariots, probably made specifically for funerals. Finally, part of the burial assemblage is made up of prestige goods, of insignia luxury, coming from Central Asia or possibly from farther away. Objects of Chinese origin, however, are in the minority. Given this observation, the material culture of the site has been described as hybrid, due to the mixed composition of the funerary assemblage of each tomb. Wu Xiaolong writes, "The highly mixed culture at Majiayuan was not the static result of cultural encounters, simply reflecting the cultural exchanges, but was consciously created by social agents to negotiate power and status" (Wu 2013:131). It does not seem necessary to revisit here the question of hybridity. However, at Majiayuan, the proportion of Chinese funerary furnishings appears to be limited, probably not due solely to the fact that the tombs were looted but rather due to the ability of the Xi Rong to maintain their culture and probably an effort to keep up strong relations with steppe communities in the Altai.

Majiayuan is the southernmost site with a marked steppe character known so far in East Asia. And of all the archaeological sites located on the marches of what was to become the empire in 221 BCE, none appears at the same time geographically so close to the Chinese cultural sphere and presenting a culture so rich and well preserved, comparable in this respect to the flourishing culture of the kingdom of Dian 滇 before the Han conquest.

Moreover, the Majiayuan region certainly played an important role as a conveyor of ideas, techniques, forms, and objects from Central Asia and even farther afield, toward Sichuan and Dian. In Moutuo, for example, as well as in Dian civilization, conical bronze goblets have been found (Falkenhausen 1996:42); these evoke the shape of the faience goblets of Majiayuan. In addition, the steppe influence was felt on the art of both cultures, as demonstrated by Lothar for Moutuo and before him by Michèle Pirazzoli-t'Serstevens for Dian (Falkenhausen 1996:43ff.; Pirazzoli-t'Serstevens 1974:119–27). The Majiayuan cemetery now appears as a crucial site in the penetration of steppe cultures from Gansu to Sichuan and Yunnan. But what about the countries of Chinese culture?

In fact, in the Chinese states of the Late Warring States period, objects like those displayed by the Xi Rong in their tombs are few. It is only under the Han that the steppe influence began to be felt in a decisive way. Artifacts from the steppes are not only numerous in the tombs of the Han elite, but they were copied in various forms and were a major source of inspiration for Chinese artists working for kings of the Liu imperial family 劉 (Kost 2017:13–17) and individuals of the elite, such as in Mawangdui (Thote 2014:23–24). In the third century BCE, a few pieces of jewelry made of gold inlaid with carnelian, faience beads, and eye beads, possibly from western Central Asia, penetrated into China, but there was only a few gold or bronze plaques of the steppe type, and coming from the Majiayuan region were no glazed beads made with Han blue, Han purple, or white ceruse and almost no iron objects plated with gold or silver foil decoration. It is to be noted that lapis lazuli, of which present-day Afghanistan was the main source in antiquity, was exported in large quantities to Iran and the Near East but never to China. To date, no object of this material is known to have reached any Chinese site, even during the Han Dynasty.

Conversely, the Sinicization of the Xi Rong of Majiayuan appears to have been only partial. The way they were buried highlights their own customs and their attachment to traditions used in the distant regions of the Altai and farther afield: the importance of the adornment of the deceased, the objects and materials that enter into the composition of the adornment (gold, silver, semiprecious stones, glass beads), the presence of chariots inside the tombs (and not outside), and the numerous sacrifices of horses and cattle. Chinese ritual bronzes are part of the burial furnishings but appear above all as prestige goods whose accumulation was more important than their use in sacrifices like those of the Zhou. Nevertheless, the construction of the tombs did not follow the pattern of the kurgan but instead a pattern close to that of the Qin catacomb tombs (Falkenhausen 2004). The number of steps on the ramp was linked to the status of the deceased in a way similar to but different than the status marks used in Zhou burial traditions.

Wang Hui rightly suggested that Qin, to create a unified empire, needed to lean on its western flank to the Rong's territory and had to ensure peaceful trade relations with them. According to the archaeological material discovered at Majiayuan, animal husbandry was an activity of first necessity for the Xi Rong. In particular, horse sacrifices were attested in large numbers in all their tombs, which indicates the importance of equines in the local economy and suggests that the Xi Rong were certainly the providers of horses to Qin. In addition, they probably traded gold, silver, and eye beads from the Near East to Qin. They mastered many metallurgical techniques that did not require as much material organization as Chinese bronze foundries and used techniques unknown to their neighbors, such as tinning and the syntheses of blue and purple pigments.

It might also be appropriate to add perishable consumer goods, perhaps plants, which they may have brought into Qin but that left no material traces, at least in the state of our current knowledge. The wealth of this community, the preservation of its original culture can be explained only by trade relations useful to Qin on the one hand and the existence of well-established long-distance relations with the Altai on the other, but not solely by introducing luxury goods into Qin.

Indeed, the burial furnishings in the Majiayuan tombs suggest the existence of close trade ties with Qin. The Xi Rong acquired bronze *li* and *yan* imitating terracotta models from Qin foundries because these vessels were important cultural markers for their community. The Qin workshops cast gold plaques for the Xi Rong, perhaps in exchange for raw metals like gold and silver, or stones like carnelian and turquoise, which they brought to Qin. Their chariots are partly modeled on those of their Chinese neighbors: they have wheels with many spokes, between 24 and more than 30, whereas Central Asian chariots have fewer spokes. In addition, these chariots were lacquered, and during the Zhou period Qin had developed an important lacquer craft, which is often poorly recognized (Thote 2003). Yet their shapes differ from the chariots of the Central Plains, and especially their mode of construction is different, in some cases involving a wrought iron structure according to an original method of construction (Han 2014; Zhao and Ma 2020). These chariots are in a certain way representative of a hybrid culture.

With the discovery of the Majiayuan cemetery, we now have a better understanding of how trade routes were later established under the Han to foster trading networks forming the Silk Road. In the third century BCE, the Majiayuan site probably witnessed a special moment in the history of relations between the Chinese states and western regions. It reveals to what extent people, the Xi Rong in this case, played a preponderant role in these relations. Indeed, neither distance nor time were barriers to trade in antiquity. Rather, trade depended on the economic interests of the moment and especially on the capacity of people to undertake it.

Acknowledgments

I wish to express my deep gratitude for the comments and suggestions made by the two editors of this volume, Anke Hein and Rowan Flad, and by the anonymous reviewer. I would also like to thank Henri-Paul Francfort, director of research at CNRS, for his questions and comments following a talk I gave on the same issue to the Société Asiatique on January 17, 2020. Any errors that may remain are my own.

Notes

1 Type I: Gansusheng 2014:114 (M1), 115 (M4); Zaoqi and Zhangjiachuan 2012:14, Figure 29.1 (M19). The *ding* from Tomb 3 is not reproduced. Type II (M15): Zaoqi and Zhangjiachuan 2009:45, Figure 53.
2 See a related vessel close to the *dui* and probably of royal manufacture in Khayuthina 2013:76, catalog no. 52.
3 Zaoqi and Zhangjiachuan 2012:7, Figures 5 and 6 (*yi* 匜 pourer, *pen* 盆 large cup, M18); 2018:14, 19, Figures 26 (*pan* 盤 basin, M23), 42, 43 (*erbei* 耳杯, M62).
4 Zaoqi and Zhangjiachuan 2009:40, 41, Figures 39, 42.1 (*li*, M14); 2010:24, 25, Figures 63, 67.1 (*yan*, M16); 2012:8, 10, 12, Figures 7, 8 (*yan*, M18), 10, 11, 16.4 (*li*, M18), 20, 21 (*yan*, M19).
5 Gansusheng 2012:34, Figure 11 (Tomb 1 at Wangwa); Gansusheng and Zhangjiachuan 2008:16 (M2; not reproduced, just mentioned); Zaoqi and Zhangjiachuan 2010:15, 16, Figures 34, 38.1 (M8); 2012:17, Figure 41 (M20); 2018:16, Figure 30 (M26).
6 Gansusheng 2012:34, Figures 13, 14 (Tomb 2 at Wangwa); 2014:165 (M14, M15).
7 Locally cast axle caps: Gansusheng 2014:151 (M16), 152–53 (M3); Zaoqi and Zhangjiachuan 2018:13, Figure 16 (M25). Protective elements added to axle caps (specific to the Xi Rong culture): Gansusheng 2014:150 (M1); Zaoqi and Zhangjiachuan 2012:16, Figure 37 (M20); 2018:19, Figure 41 (M22). Linchpin in the shape of a Xi Rong head: Gansusheng 2014:148–49 (M4). Axle cap with casing-shaped protection: Gansusheng 2012:29, Figure 4.7 (Tomb 1 at Wangwa); 2014:159; Zaoqi and Zhangjiachuan 2010:10, Figure 16 (M5); 2012:13, Figure 26 (M19). Towbar cap: Gansusheng 2012:36, Figure 26 (Tomb 3 at Wangwa); Zaoqi and Zhangjiachuan 2010:24, Figure 64 (M16); 2018:13, Figure 17 (M25). Towbar ornament: Gansusheng 2012:36, Figure 25 (Tomb 3 at Wangwa). Draft beam fitting: Gansusheng 2012:36, Figure 24 (Tomb 3 at Wangwa).
8 Gansusheng 2014:162, 164 (M1, M3); Zaoqi and Zhangjiachuan 2009:28, 47, Figures 3 (M6), 63 (M12).
9 Gansusheng 2012:29, Figures 4.3, 4.4 (Tomb 1 at Wangwa); 2014:140–41 (M1), 142 (M10), 143–44 (M57), 146–47 (M1); Zaoqi and Zhangjiachuan 2008:21, Figure 49 (M3); 2010:9, Figures 14, 15 (M5).
10 Gansusheng 2014:144 (M1); Gansusheng and Zhangjiachuan 2008:20–21, Figures 44, 47, 48 (M1); Zaoqi and Zhangjiachuan 2009:28, Figure 3 (M6); 2010:14, Figure 30 (M7); 2012:13, Figures 22, 24, 25 (M19); 2018:11, 13, 14, Figures 13.6, 13.8, 13.11, 13.12 (M25, M60), 18, 25 (M25).
11 Gansusheng and Qingshuixian 2014:51–52, nos. 3 and 4 (Liuping site); Zaoqi and Zhangjiachuan 2009:47, 50, Figures 64, 70.7 (M12).
12 Gansusheng and Qingshuixian 2014:63, no. 18 (Liuping site).
13 Zaoqi and Zhangjiachuan 2009:42, Figure 43 (M14); 2012:13, Figure 23 (M19).
14 Gansusheng 2012:29, 34, Figures 4.2, 10 (Wangwa M1); Gansusheng and Zhangjiachuan 2008:20, 25, Figures 43, 64.1 (M1, two clapper bells).
15 See, e.g., Li Gang 2011:108–9 (peaks), 162–63, Figures 4.1–15.3, 15.4, 15.5, 15.7 (knives of steppe types); Wu En 2007:310–14 (openwork plaques and

animal-shaped ornaments from Maoqinggou 毛慶溝, Inner Mongolia), 369, 370, Figures 168.14 (knives of steppe types), 169.2 (clapper bells, Yanglang culture), 169.7 (protective elements added to axle caps, Yanglang 楊郎 culture, Ningxia). Many other examples are found in Höllmann et al. 1992.

16 Zaoqi and Zhangjiachuan 2010:18, Figures 43, 44 (M13); 2012:20, Figure 47 (M21).

17 The *ge* and *ji* blades (on the same model as the *ge* in Pit 1 of the tomb of the First Emperor correspond to the most advanced technology at the end of the third century BCE. See Shaanxisheng Kaogu Yanjiusuo Shihuangling 1988:1:256–59.

18 Leroi-Gourhan 1971 [1943]:236.

19 Gold plaques cast in molds: Gansusheng 2014:40–41 (M16, interlacing birds and snakes), 42–43, 53 (M18, fighting birds). Gold plaques made in repoussé (or by a stamping process): Gansusheng 2014:36–37 (M4, wild boars fighting), 38–39 (M14, feline devouring a goat), 44 (M14, reclining horse), 45 (M20, wolf devouring a stag), 46 (M15, heads of mouflons nested one inside the other, wolf devouring a stag). Cast gold belt hooks with Chinese decoration: Gansusheng 2014:54–55 (M14), 56–57 (M14, dragon interlace).

20 Personal communication from Henri-Paul Francfort, who directed me toward such an identification. I would like to express to him my deep gratitude.

21 Gold pendant inlaid with turquoise and carnelian (M4; Gansusheng and Shaanxisheng 2013:32, Figure 11); two gold plaques composed of six tubes separated by gold threads, with carnelian and turquoise inlays (M6; Zaoqi and Zhangjiachuan 2009:30, Figure 10); two fan-shaped gold plaques composed of six tubes, separated by a row of granulation (M6; Zaoqi and Zhangjiachuan 2009:30, Figure 9); several gold plaques composed of eight parallel tubes soldered together (M18; belonging to a necklace, they alternate with a series of blue earthenware beads and probably carnelian beads [Gansusheng 2014:48–49]); a pair of earrings composed of a gold ring and a pendant, including a faience bead between two half-carnelian beads and gold granulation elements (M14; Zaoqi and Zhangjiachuan 2009:37, 39, Figures 31, 37.3); tubular beads decorated with granulation arranged in triangle shapes (M14; Zaoqi and Zhangjiachuan 2009:42, Figure 45); a pointed bead terminated by granulation (M14; Zaoqi and Zhangjiachuan 2009:42, Figure 46); a pendant composed of carnelian, turquoise, and gold granulation beads (M14; Zaoqi and Zhangjiachuan 2009:42, Figure 47); a gold bracelet inlaid with carnelian and turquoise, associated with gold plaits (M16; Gansusheng 2014:62–63); a necklace element composed of gold tubes grouped by five (M16; Zaoqi and Zhangjiachuan 2010:22, Figure 57); an earring made of gold, granulation, turquoise, and carnelian (M25; Zaoqi and Zhangjiachuan 2018:13, Figure 15).

22 Tallon 1995:nos. 82, 242C. The scale-shaped partition reminds us of the treatment of some Achaemenid jewels from the Oxus treasure; cf. Curtis 2012:8, 50–52.

References

Aruz, Joan, ed.
2000   *The Golden Deer of Eurasia: Scythian and Sarmatian Treasures from the Russian Steppes: The State Hermitage, Saint Petersburg, and the Archaeological Museum, Ufa*. New York: Metropolitan Museum of Art and Yale University Press.

Bagley, Robert
1987   *Shang Ritual Bronzes in the Arthur M. Sackler Collections*. Cambridge, MA: Harvard University Press.

Berke, Heinz
2002   Chemistry in Ancient Times: The Development of Blue and Purple Pigments. *Angewandte Chemie International Edition* 41(14):2483–87.
2007   The Invention of Blue and Purple Pigments in Ancient Times. *Chemical Society Review* 36(1):15–30.

Brill, Robert H., Stephen Shap Chow Tong, and Zhang Fukang
1989   The Chemical Composition of a Faience Bead from China. *Journal of Glass Studies* 31:11–15.

Brosseder, Ursula
2015   A Study on the Complexity and Dynamics of Interaction and Exchange in Late Iron Age Eurasia. In *Complexity of Interaction along the Eurasian Steppe Zone in the First Millennium CE*, edited by Jan Bemmann and Michael Schmauder, pp. 199–332. Bonn: Rheinische Friedrich-Wilhelms-Universität Bonn.

Bunker, Emma, Trudy S. Kawami, Katheryn M. Linduff, and Wu En
1997   *Ancient Bronzes of the Eastern Eurasian Steppes from the Arthur M. Sackler Collections*. New York: Arthur M. Sackler Foundation.

Caubet, Annie, and Geneviève Pierrat-Bonnefois, eds.
2005   *Faïences de l'Antiquité: de l'Égypte à l'Iran*. Paris: Musée du Louvre Éditions.

Chase, W. T., and J. May Lee
1991 *Ancient Chinese Bronze Art: Casting the Precious Sacral Vessel*. New York: China House Gallery, China Institute in America.

Chen Jianli 陳建立, Zhang Zhouyu 張周瑜, Yang Junchang 楊軍昌, Hou Hongwei 侯紅偉, and Wang Hui 王輝
2014 Jin yin he duxi tongqi de zhizao gongyi yanjiu 金銀和鍍錫銅器的製作工藝研究 [Technical Study of the Manufacturing Process of Gold, Silver and Tinned Objects]. In *Qingshui Liuping* 清水劉坪 [Liuping, Qingshui], edited by Gansusheng Wenwu Kaogu Yanjiusuo 甘肅省文物考古研究所 and Qingshuixian Bowuguan 清水縣博物館, pp. 19–45. Beijing: Wenwu Chubanshe.

Curtis, John
2012 *The Oxus Treasure*. London: British Museum Press.

Di Cosmo, Nicola
1999 The Northern Frontier in Pre-imperial China. In *Cambridge History of Ancient China*, edited by Michael Loewe and Edward L. Shaughnessy, pp. 885–966. Cambridge: Cambridge University Press.

Fairbank, Wilma
1962 Piece-Mold Craftsmanship and Shang Bronze Design. *Archives of the Chinese Art Society of America* 16:8–15.

Falkenhausen, Lothar von
1996 The Moutuo Bronzes: New Perspectives on the Late Bronze Age in Sichuan. *Arts Asiatiques* 51:29–59.
2004 Mortuary Behavior in Pre-Imperial Qin. In *Religion and Chinese Society*, Vol. 1, edited by John Lagerwey, pp. 109–72. Hong Kong: Chinese University Press; Paris: École Française d'Extrême-Orient.
2006 *Chinese Society in the Age of Confucius (1000–250 BC): The Archaeological Evidence*. Los Angeles: Cotsen Institute of Archaeology Press.

Flad, Rowan K., and Zachary X. Hruby
2007 "Specialized" Production in Archaeological Contexts: Rethinking Specialization, the Social Value of Products, and the Practice of Production. In *Rethinking Craft Specialization in Complex Societies: Archaeological Analyses of the Social Meaning of Production*, edited by Zachary X. Hruby and Rowan K. Flad, pp. 1–19. Archaeological Papers of the American Anthropological Association 17. Berkeley: American Anthropological Association and University of California Press.

Francfort, Henri-Paul
2003 Archéologie de l'Asie intérieure de l'âge du Bronze à l'âge du Fer. École pratique des hautes études. Section des sciences historiques et philologiques. *Livret-Annuaire* 17:28–35.

Francfort, Henri-Paul, Daniel Klodzinski, and Georges Mascle
1990 Pétroglyphes archaïques du Ladakh et du Zanskar. *Arts Asiatiques* 45:5–27.

Francfort, Henri-Paul, Giancarlo Ligabue, and Zaimullah Samashev
2006 The Gold of the Griffin: Recent Excavation of a Frozen Tomb in Kazakhstan. In *The Golden Deer of Eurasia: Perspectives on the Steppe Nomads of the Ancient World*, edited by Joan Aruz, Ann Farkas, and Elisabetta Valtz Fino, pp. 114–27. New York: Metropolitan Museum of Art and Yale University Press.

Gansu Wenwu Gongzuodui 甘肃文物工作队 and Beijing Daxue Kaoguxi 北京大学考古系
1987 *Gansu Gangu Maojiaping yizhi fajue baogao* 甘肃甘谷毛家坪遗址发掘报告 [Excavation Report on the Site of Maojiaping, Gangu, Gansu]. *Kaogu xuebao* 考古學報 3:359–96.

Gansusheng Wenwu Kaogu Yanjiusuo 甘肃省文物考古研究所
2012 Gansu Qin'an Wangwa Zhanguo mudi 2009 nian fajue jianbao 甘肅秦安王洼戰國墓地2009年發掘簡報 [Preliminary Report on the Excavation of the Warring States Cemetery at Wangwa, Qin'an County, Gansu, in 2009]. *Wenwu* 文物 8:27–37.
2014 *Xi Rong yizhen: Majiayuan Zhanguo mudi chutu wenwu* 西戎遺珍：馬家塬戰國墓地出土文物 [Precious Remains of the Western Rong: Relics Excavated from the Warring States Cemetery at Majiayuan]. Beijing: Wenwu Chubanshe.

Gansusheng Wenwu Kaogu Yanjiusuo 甘肃省文物考古研究所 and Qingshuixian Bowuguan 清水縣博物館, eds.
2014 *Qingshui Liuping* 清水劉坪 [Liuping, Qingshui]. Beijing: Wenwu Chubanshe.

Gansusheng Wenwu Kaogu Yanjiusuo 甘肃省文物考古研究所 and Shaanxisheng Kaogu Yanjiuyuan 陝西省考古研究院
2013 Gansu Zhangjiachuanxian Majiayuan Zhanguo mudi M4 muguan shijianshi kaogu jianbao 甘肅張家川縣馬家塬戰國墓地M4墓棺實驗室考古

简报 [Preliminary Archaeological Report from Laboratory of the Coffin from Tomb 4 at the Warring States–Period Cemetery of Majiayuan, Zhangjiachuan County, Gansu]. *Kaogu* 考古 8:25–35.

Gansusheng Wenwu Kaogu Yanjiusuo 甘肅省文物考古研究所 and Zhangjiachuan Huizu Zizhixian Bowuguan 張家川回族自治縣博物館
2008 2006 niandu Gansu Zhangjiachuan Huizu zizhixian Majiayuan Zhanguo mudi fajue jianbao 2006年度甘肅張家川回族自治縣馬家塬戰國墓地發掘簡報 [Preliminary Report on the Excavations of the Warring States–Period Cemetery at Majiayuan, Zhangjiachuan Huizu Autonomous County, Gansu]. *Wenwu* 文物 9:4–28.

Guo Baojun 郭寶鈞
1959 *Shanbiaozhen yu Liulige* 山彪鎮與琉璃閣 [Shanbiaozhen and Liulige]. Beijing: Kexue Chubanshe.

Han Fei 韓飛, Wang Hui 王輝, and Ma Yanru 馬燕如
2014 Gansu Zhangjiachuan Majiayuan chutu chexiang ceban de shiyanshi kaogu qingli 甘肅張家川馬家塬出土車廂側板的實驗室考古清理 [The Archaeological Clearing in Laboratory of the Chariot Box Sides Unearthed at Majiayuan, Zhangjiachuan County in Gansu]. *Wenwu* 文物 6:39–43.

Hebeisheng Wenwu Yanjiusuo 河北省文物研究所
1995 *Cuomu: Zhanguo Zhongshan guo guowang zhi mu* 嚳墓: 戰國中山國國王之墓 [Cuo's Tomb: The Tomb of a Warring States–Period King of Zhongshan]. Beijing: Wenwu Chubanshe.

Höllmann, Thomas O., Georg Kossack, Karl Jettmar, and Guangjin Tian, eds.
1992 *Maoqinggou: Ein eisenzeitliches Gräberfeld in der Ordos-Region (Innere Mongolei)*. Mainz am Rhein: Ph. von Zabern.

Jacobson, Esther
1988 Beyond the Frontier: A Reconsideration of Cultural Interchange between China and the Early Nomads. *Early China* 13:201–40.

Jing Zhongwei 井中偉
2011 *Zaoqi Zhongguo qingtong ge, ji yanjiu* [Research on Early Bronze Dagger-Axes *Ge* and *Ji* from China] 早期中國青銅戈，戟研究. Beijing: Kexue Chubanshe.

Khayutina, Maria, ed.
2013 *Qin, l'empereur éternel et ses guerriers de terre cuite*. Zurich: NZZ Libro.

Kost, Catrin
2017 Heightened Receptivity: Steppe Objects and Steppe Influences in Royal Tombs of the Western Han Dynasty. *Journal of the American Oriental Society* 137(2):349–81.

Lam, Eileen Hau-ling
2012 The Possible Origins of the Jade Stem Beaker in China. *Arts Asiatiques* 67:35–46.

Le Bas, Antony, Noel Kennon, Ross Smith, and Noel Barnard
1996 Chinese Bronze Vessels with Copper Inlaid Décor and Pseudo-Copper Inlay of Ch'un-ch'iu and Chan-kuo Times. In *Ancient Chinese and Southeast Asian Bronze Age Cultures: The Proceedings of a Conference Held at the Edith and Joy London Foundation Property, Kioloa, NSW: 8–12 February, 1988: Conference Papers*, edited by John Bulbeck and Noel Barnard, pp. 123–58. Taipei: SMC Publishing.

Leroi-Gourhan, André
1971 [1943] *L'Homme et la matière*, Paris: Albin-Michel.

Li Gang 李剛
2011 *Zhongguo beifang qingtongqi de Ou-Ya caoyuan wenhua yinsu* 中國北方青銅器的歐亞草原文化因素 [Eurasian Steppe Cultural Elements in Northern Chinese Bronzes]. Beijing: Wenwu Chubanshe.

Li Jinghua 李京華
2007 *Zhongguo gudai tieqi yishu* 中國古代鐵器藝術 [The Skill of Iron Objects in Ancient China]. Beijing: Beijing Yanshan Chubanshe.

Li Hui 李會
2014 *Handaiqian de Zhongguo boli gongyi* 漢代前的中國玻璃工藝 [Chinese Glass Craftsmanship before the Han Period]. Wuhan: Huazhong Shifan Daxue Chubanshe.

Lin Yixian 林怡嫻, Zhou Guangji 周廣濟, Ian Freestone, and Thilo Rehren
2018 Zhangjiachuan Majiayuan Zhanguo mudi chutu boli yu xiangguan cailiao yanjiu 張家川馬家塬戰國墓地出土玻璃與相關材料研究 [Research on Glass and Related Materials Unearthed in the Warring States–Period Cemetery at Majiayuan, Zhangjiachuan]. *Wenwu* 文物 3:71–83.

Liu Yang
2014 Qin Ritual Bronze: Impact from the Central Plains and the South. In *Beyond the First Emperor's Mausoleum: New Perspectives on Qin Art*, edited by Liu Yang, pp. 158–89. Minneapolis: Minneapolis Institute of Arts.

Liu Yang, ed.
    2012. *China's Terracotta Warriors: The First Emperor's Legacy.* Minneapolis: Minneapolis Institute of Arts.

Lu Liancheng 盧連成 and Hu Zhisheng 胡智生
1988   *Baoji Yu guo mudi* 寶雞強國墓地 [The Cemetery of the Yu Polity at Baoji]. Beijing: Wenwu Chubanshe.

Mei Jianjun
2006   The Material Culture of the Iron Age Peoples in Xinjiang, Northwest China. In *The Golden Deer of Eurasia: Perspectives on the Steppe Nomads of the Ancient World*, edited by Joan Aruz, Ann Farkas, and Elisabetta Valtz Fino, pp. 132–45. New York: Metropolitan Museum of Art and Yale University Press.

Nei Menggu Wenwu Kaogu Yanjiusuo 內蒙古文物考古研究所
1994   Zhalainuo'er gu muqun 1986 nian qingli fajue baogao 扎賚諾爾古墓群1986年清理發掘報告 [Report on the Clearing and Excavations of an Ancient Group of Tombs at Zhalainuo'er, in 1986]. In *Nei Menggu wenwu kaogu wenji* 內蒙古文物考古文集, edited by Li Yiyou 李逸友, Wei Jian 魏堅, and Nei Menggu Wenwu Kaogu Yanjiusuo 內蒙古渭南無考古研究所, pp. 369–83. Beijing: Zhongguo Dabaike Quanshu Chubanshe.

Metropolitan Museum of Art and Los Angeles County Museum of Art, eds.
1975   *From the Land of the Scythians: Ancient Treasures from the Museums of the USSR, 3000 BC–100 BC.* New York: Metropolitan Museum of Art.

Pirazzoli-t'Serstevens, Michèle
1974   *La Civilisation du royaume de Dian à l'époque des Han, d'après le matériel exhumé à Shizhai shan (Yunnan).* Paris: École française d'Extrême-Orient.

Polosmak, N. V.
1994   The Ak-Alakh "Frozen Grave" Barrow. *Ancient Civilizations from Scythia to Siberia* 1(3):346–54.

Polosmak, Natalia
1991   Un nouveau kourgane à "tombe gelée" de l'Altaï (rapport préliminaire) [A "Frozen Tomb" (Kurgan) Recently Excavated in the Altai]. *Arts Asiatiques* 46:5–20.

Portal, Jane, ed.
2007   *The First Emperor.* London: British Museum Press.

Rawson, Jessica
2007   China and the Steppe: Reception and Resistance. *Antiquity* 91(356):375–88.

Rudenko, Sergei Ivanovich
1970   *Frozen Tombs of Siberia: The Pazyryk Burials of Iron Age Horsemen.* Berkeley: University of California Press.

Schiltz, Véronique
1994   *Les Scythes et les nomades des steppes: VIIIe siècle avant J.-C.-Ier siècle après J.-C.* Paris: Gallimard.

Selbitschka, Armin
2018   Genuine Prestige Goods in Mortuary Contexts: Emulation in Polychrome Silk and Byzantine Solidi from Northern China. *Asian Perspectives* 57(1):2–50.

Shaanxisheng Kaogu Yanjiusuo 陝西省考古研究所
1986   Shaanxi Tongchuan Zaomiao Qin mu fajue jianbao 陝西銅川棗廟秦墓發掘簡報 [Preliminary Report on the Qin Tombs at Zaomiao, Tongchuan, Shaanxi]. *Kaogu yu wenwu* 考古與文物 2:7–17.
2006   *Xi'an beijiao Qin mu* 西安北郊秦墓 [The Qin Tombs in the Northern Suburbs of Xi'an]. Xi'an: San Qin Chubanshe.

Shaanxisheng Kaogu Yanjiusuo Shihuangling Qin Yongkeng Kaogu Fajuedui 陝西省考古研究所始皇陵秦俑坑考古發掘隊
1988   *Qin Shihuang ling bingmayongkeng: yi hao keng fajue baogao 1974–1984* 秦始皇陵兵馬俑坑:一號坑發掘報告1974–1984 [Excavation Report on Pit 1 among the Soldier-and-Horse Figurine Pits at the Tomb of the First Emperor of Qin]. Beijing: Wenwu Chubanshe.

Shaanxisheng Xianyangshi Wenwuju 陝西省咸陽市文物局
2002   *Xianyang wenwu jinghua* 咸陽文物精華 [Splendors of Xianyang Relics]. Beijing: Wenwu Chubanshe.

Shanxisheng Kaogu Yanjiusuo 山西考古研究所
2012   *Houma Baidian zhutong yizhi* 侯馬白店鑄銅遺址 [The Baidian Bronze Foundry at Houma]. Beijing: Kexue Chubanshe.

Shanxisheng Kaogu Yanjiusuo 山西省考古研究所 and Taiyuanshi Wenwu Guanli Weiyuanhui 太原市文物管理委員會
1996   *Taiyuan Jin guo Zhao qing mu* 太原晉國趙卿墓 [A Zhao Minister's Tomb of the Jin Polity at Taiyuan]. Beijing: Wenwu Chubanshe.

Shanxisheng Kaogu Yanjiusuo 山西省考古研究所, Shanxi Bowuguan 陝西博物館, and Changzhishi Bowuguan 長治市博物館
2010 *Changzhi Fenshuiling Dong Zhou mudi* 長治分水嶺東周墓地 [The Eastern Zhou Cemetery at Fenshuiling, Changzhou]. Beijing: Wenwu Chubanshe.

Shemakhanskaya, Marina, Mikhail Treister, and Leonid Yablonsky
2009 The Technique of Gold Inlaid Decoration in the 5th–4th Centuries BC: Silver and Iron Finds from the Early Sarmatian Barrows of Filippovka, Southern Urals. *ArchéoSciences* 33:211–20.

Sichuansheng Wenwu Kaogu Yanjiusuo 四川省文物考古研究所 and Yingjing Yandao Gucheng Yizhi Bowuguan 滎經嚴道古城遺址博物館
1998 Yinjingxian Tongxincun Ba Shu chuanguanzang fajue baogao 滎經縣同心村船棺葬發掘報告 [Report on the Excavation of Boat-Coffin Burials of the Ba Shu Culture at Tongxincun, Yingjing County]. In *Sichuan kaogu baogaoji* 四川考古報告集, pp. 212–80. Beijing: Wenwu Chubanshe.

So, Jenny F., and Emma C. Bunker
1995 *Traders and Raiders on China's Northern Frontier*. Seattle: Arthur M. Sackler Gallery, Smithsonian Institution, and University of Washington Press.

Sun Zhanwei 孫戰偉
2019 Maojiaping B zu yicun zai renshi 毛家坪B組遺存再認識 [A Reappraisal of the B Group Vestiges at Maojiaping]. *Kaogu yu wenwu* 考古與文物 2:77–84.

Tallon, Françoise, ed.
1995 *Les pierres précieuses de l'Orient ancien des Sumériens aux Sassanides*. Paris: Éd. Réunion des Musées Nationaux.

Teng Mingyu 滕銘予
2003 *Qin wenhua: cong fengguo dao diguo de kaoguxue guancha* 秦文化: 從封國到帝國的考古學觀察 [The Qin Culture: Archaeological Examination from Principality to Empire]. Beijing: Xueyuan Chubanshe.

Thote, Alain
1997 Intercultural Contacts and Exchanges Illustrated by a Sixth Century BC Cemetery in Henan. *Hanxue yanjiu* (Taipei) 15.1(29):263–89.
2003 Lacquer Craftsmanship in the Qin and Chu Kingdoms: Two Contrasting Traditions (Late 4th to Late 3rd Century BC). *Journal of East Asian Archaeology* 5(1–4):336–74.
2008 Artists and Craftsmen in the Late Bronze Age of China (Eighth to Third Centuries BC): Art in Transition. *Proceedings of the British Academy* 154:201–41.
2014 Defining Qin Artistic Traditions: Heritage, Borrowing, and Innovation. In *Beyond the First Emperor's Mausoleum: New Perspectives on Qin Art*, edited by Liu Yang, pp. 13–29. Minneapolis: Minneapolis Institute of Arts.

Wagner, Donald B.
1993 *Iron and Steel in Ancient China*. Leiden: E. J. Brill.

Wang Hui 王輝
2009 Zhangjiachuan Majiayuan mudi xiangguan wenti chutan 張家川馬家塬墓地相關問題初探 [Preliminary Investigation of the Questions Concerning the Cemetery at Majiayuan, Zhangjiashan]. *Wenwu* 文物 10:70–77.

Wu'enyuesitu 烏恩岳斯圖 (Wu En)
2007 *Beifang caoyuan kaoguxue wenhua yanjiu: qingtong shidai zhi zaoqi tieqi shidai* 北方草原考古學文化研究:青銅時代至早期鐵器時代 [Research on the Archaeological Cultures of the Northern Steppes: From the Bronze Age to the Iron Age]. Beijing: Kexue chubanshe.

Wu Xiaolong
2013 Cultural Hybridity and Social Status: Elite Tombs on China's Northern Frontier during the Third Century BC. *Antiquity* 87:121–36.

Xianyangshi Wenwu Kaogu Yanjiusuo 咸陽市文物考古研究所
1998 *Ta'erpo Qin mu* 塔兒坡秦墓 [The Qin Tombs at Ta'erpo]. Xi'an: San Qin Chubanshe.

Yang Jianhua, and Kathryn M. Linduff
2012 A Contextual Explanation for "Foreign" or "Steppic" Factors Exhibited in Burials at the Majiayuan Cemetery and the Opening of the Tianshan Mountain Corridor. *Asian Archaeology* 1:73–84.

Yang Zhefeng 楊哲峰
2000 Jianxinghu de leixing, fenbu yu fenqi shitan 繭形壺的類型, 分佈與分期試探 [Typology of the Cocoon-Shaped *Hu* Vessels, Investigation into Their Geographical Distribution and Chronology]. *Wenwu* 文物 8:64–72.

Zaoqi Qin Wenhua Lianhe Kaogudui 早期秦文化聯合考古隊 and Zhangjiachuan Huizu Zizhiqu Bowuguan 張家川回族自治縣博物館
2009 Zhangjiachuan Majiayuan Zhanguo mudi 2007–2008 nian fajue jianbao 張家川馬家塬戰國墓地2007–2008年發掘簡報 [Preliminary Report

on Excavations of the Warring States–Period Cemetery at Majiayuan, Zhangjiachuan, in 2007–2008]. *Wenwu* 文物 10:25–51.

2010 Zhangjiachuan Majiayuan Zhanguo mudi 2008–2009 nian fajue jianbao 張家川馬家塬戰國墓地2008–2009年發掘簡報 [Preliminary Report on Excavations of the Warring States–Period Cemetery at Majiayuan, Zhangjiachuan, in 2008–2009]. *Wenwu* 文物 10:4–26.

2012 Zhangjiachuan Majiayuan Zhanguo mudi 2010–2011 nian fajue jianbao 張家川馬家塬戰國墓地2010–2011年發掘簡報 [Preliminary Report on Excavations of the Warring States–Period Cemetery at Majiayuan, Zhangjiachuan, in 2010–2011]. *Wenwu* 文物 8:4–26.

2018 Zhangjiachuan Majiayuan Zhanguo mudi 2012–2014 nian fajue jianbao 張家川馬家塬戰國墓地2012–2014年發掘簡報 [Preliminary Report on Excavations of the Warring States–Period Cemetery at Majiayuan, Zhangjiachuan, in 2012–2014]. *Wenwu* 文物 3:4–26.

Zhao Wucheng 趙吳成

2018 *Gansu Majiayuan Zhanguo mu mache de fuyuan (xu er)—Mache de sheji zhizao jiqiao ji niuche de gaizhuang yu sheji sixiang* 甘肅馬家塬戰國墓馬車的復原（續二）—馬車的設計製造技巧及牛車的改裝與設計思想 [Reconstitutions of the Chariots from the Warring States-Period Tombs at Majiayuan, Gansu (Section 2)—Design and Manufacturing Skills of the Horse Chariots, and Ox Cart Modifications and Design Concepts]. *Wenwu* 文物 6:44–57.

Zhao Wucheng 趙吳成 and Ma Yuhua 馬玉華

2020 *Zhanguo Rongren zaoche* 戰國戎人造車 [Chariots Manufactured by the Western Rong in the Warring States-Period]. Edited by Gansu sheng wenwu kaogu yanjiusuo 甘肅省文物考古研究所. Beijing: Wenwu Chubanshe.

Zhongguo Shehui Kexueyuan Kaogu Yanjiusuo 中國社會科學院考古研究所

1980 *Mancheng Han mu fajue baogao* 滿城漢墓發掘報告 [Excavation Report of the Han Tombs at Mancheng]. Beijing: Wenwu Chubanshe.

1994 Shaanxian Dong Zhou Qin Han mu 陝縣東周秦漢墓 [Eastern Zhou, Qin, and Han Tombs at Shaanxian]. Beijing: Kexue Chubanshe.

2003 *Linyi Chengcun mudi* 臨猗程村墓地 [The Cemetery at Chengcun, Linyi]. Beijing: Zhongguo Dabaike Quanshu Chubanshe.

Zhongguo Qingtongqi Quanji bianji weiyuanhui 中國青銅器全集編輯委員會

1998 *Zhongguo qingtongqi quanji di shi juan Dong Zhou (si)* 中國青銅器全集第十卷 東周（四）[Complete Collection of Chinese Bronzes, Vol. 10, Eastern Zhou, 4]. Beijing: Wenwu Chubanshe.

Ziboshi Bowuguan 淄博市博物館

1997 *Linzi Shangwang mudi* 臨淄商王墓地 [The Cemetery at Shangwang, Linzi]. Linzi: Qilu Shushe.

Chapter 4

Ritual Economies of Peripheral East Asia
Reflections on Mahan Mortuary Archaeology

Jack Davey

A major aim of Lothar von Falkenhausen's work has been to draw attention to and address a methodological imbalance in East Asian archaeology that has prioritized the historiographical tradition when interpreting material remains. As expressed in *Chinese Society in the Age of Confucius* (Falkenhausen 2006:19–24), his pragmatic approach takes existing textually dependent scholarship seriously but places the careful interpretation of local archaeological trajectories on an equal footing when modeling social development in early societies. Yet although von Falkenhausen's work often frontloads the archaeology, he is also sensitive to the arc of the Chinese archaeological tradition, not dismissing it or the value of prior historiographical research. Many of the papers in this volume use this foundation as a starting point, reflecting von Falkenhausen's impact on—and the potential of his approach to—Chinese archaeology. In the present paper, I apply the same principles to an archaeological case study in Korea, a region and a scholarly tradition deeply connected to but entirely distinct from China.

My concern is an Iron Age entity known as Mahan 馬韓, a protohistoric society deeply entangled in a long historical tradition and contemporary Korean identities, both national and regional. Mahan is a cultural designation for a number of polities or statelets on the Korean Peninsula that first appeared in Chinese sources of the third century. Most researchers place Mahan polities along the western edge of southern Korea, from the southern end of the early third century Daifang commandery 帶方郡 in Hwanghae Province (in present-day North Korea) to the Yŏngsan River valley in southwest Honam, at the southwestern tip of South Korea (Figures 4.1 and 4.2). Historians and archaeologists generally agree that Mahan's emergence from the first century BCE to the third century CE was pivotal in the formation of the first state-level or complex polities on the southern peninsula.[1] Additionally, as one of the Three Han[2] or Samhan 三韓 groups, Mahan forms the foundation for the historical lineages of later Korean polities, such as Silla 新羅 and Paekche 百濟, in the peninsula's domestic historiographical tradition.

Paralleling similar discussions in Chinese archaeology, researchers have been engaged in a protracted debate over how to distinguish Mahan in the material record and what makes Mahan groups distinct or different from other Iron Age polities in the region. While the utility of this research agenda can be critiqued on its own terms (see Falkenhausen 1993), it is particularly difficult to apply to Mahan. The archaeology of the supposed heartland of the culture is diverse and stubbornly resists coherent classification. This is especially true of the mortuary record, which presents a variety of tomb structures, construction materials, grave good types and placements, and treatments of the corpse that are hard to describe as a single sociocultural entity (Figure 4.3). Despite the best efforts of archaeologists, there is still no consensus as to what constitutes a "Mahan" tomb.

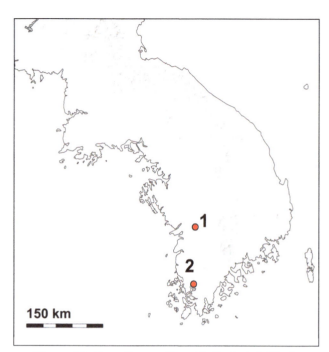

Figure 4.1. Core sites mentioned in the text. 1. Wanju Sangun-ni; 2. Naju Pannam. *Created by Bryan K. Miller.*

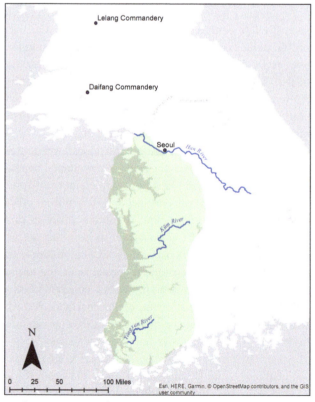

Figure 4.2. Map of the Korean Peninsula and the supposed territorial extent of Mahan (shaded area) in the third century AD. *Created by the author.*

While essentially a typological debate, at the root of this discussion is the question of what was culturally meaningful to groups in southwestern Korea and whether we can even use material remnants to reconstruct the dynamics of a once living sociopolitical entity. I offer here a preliminary review of the mortuary archaeology of southwestern Korea that questions the validity of Mahan as a classificatory term and advances a new methodology for reconciling a diverse mortuary record with more normalizing historical narratives.

The existence or nonexistence of Mahan is particularly consequential in the context of the later kingdoms and nations of Korea. Mahan has persisted as a dynastic ancestor in all subsequent Korean kingdoms and still forms an important, if sometimes subconscious, bedrock for contemporary South Korean national identity—even as Mahan remains the most poorly understood Samhan group and one of the most enigmatic entities in early Korean history. Unlike contemporaneous cultures like Chosŏn 朝鮮 and Koguryŏ 高句麗 and mythical rulers like Tan'gun 檀君 and Kija 箕子, whose importance to later dynasties has been examined in depth, Mahan's impact on later historiography has not been adequately interrogated (see Ch'oe 1980; Em 2004; Xu 2016). How do we at once engage with and account for larger discussions of heritage and identity derived from the historical tradition while also attempting to make sense of a complex material record that seems to resist these associations?

Mahan also offers an important check on Sino-centric models of culture contact and the centrality of China in the formation of states in so-called peripheral East Asia. Certain scholars (discussed more fully below) suggest that the culturally meaningful distinction of Mahan tombs is that their burial style was fundamentally different from that of Hàn China. Thus, unlike peninsular groups that adopted a version of the Central Plains wood-chambered mounded tomb, such as Chinhan 辰韓 and Pyŏnhan 弁韓, social change in Mahan seems to have been driven more by internal mechanisms and interactions with non-Chinese groups in the region.

I begin with a review of the Mahan concept in Korean historiography and how current usage of the term conflates several distinct phenomena: Mahan as a culturally and politically distinct entity in historical texts, Mahan as a dynastic ancestor for later Korean kingdoms, and Mahan as an archaeological descriptor for a diverse package of material culture in southwestern Korea. I then discuss the typological problems this conflation has generated for archaeologists and several innovative approaches within Korean archaeology to overcome these difficulties. My case study relationship to Wei Man Chaoxian (Wiman Chosŏn) 衛滿朝鮮 in northern Korea and its exiled leader named here the Marquis Chun (Zhun) 侯準; and dealings with the Lelang commandery 樂浪郡 (an administrative outpost of Hàn China, located near present-day Pyongyang in North Korea). The sections actually detailing Mahan culture and society are shorter still and filled with descriptions of Mahan households, sericulture, their (lack of) familiarity with Hàn Chinese ritual norms, and colorful description of customs that seem to have stuck in the memory of Chen Shou's informants.

It is difficult to make many concrete inferences about what exactly Mahan was based on this text, given its brevity and the contradictions to it preserved in the later *Hou Hànshu* 後漢書 version of the "Account of the Han" (see Ju Bo Don 2009). It likely reflects Hàn and Lelang's interactions with the Samhan groups most proximate to them and amenable to engaging with China. Mahan appears to refer in a general sense to people with a shared culture loosely organized into small, independent polities. Significantly, however, the *Sanguozhi*'s insistence that each Samhan culture was made up of discrete polities that were in turn made up of hierarchies of towns and ruling townships is different from descriptions of the Samhan's neighbors Okchŏ 沃沮 and Wa 倭. While it has been shown that Chinese accounts of peripheral groups tend toward normalizing narratives (Erickson et al. 2010), the Samhan appear to have been granted the distinction of being more politically complex than their closest peers.

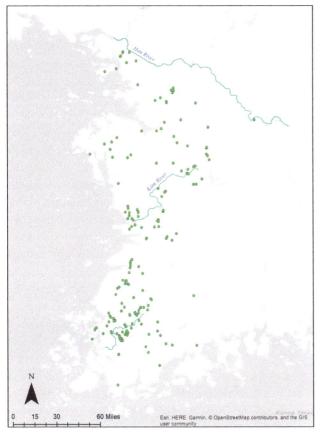

Figure 4.3. Iron Age mortuary sites in western Korea frequently assigned to the Mahan culture.
Created by the author.

It is not clear from the *Sanguozhi* if Mahan had any meaning as a designation for the Mahan groups themselves. The seventh century *Jinshu* 晉書, however, not only reaffirms the *Sanguozhi* characterization of Mahan but also suggests that the term was used by peninsular groups themselves. This text preserves a late third century record of Paekche being a part of Mahan as well as records of individual Mahan polities sending envoys to the Jin court (Fang Xuanling 1974). The fifth century *Songshu* 宋書 also mentions diplomatic contact with a "Muhan" (Mohan; 慕韓), which might be a variant transcription or scribal error for a southern peninsular group that used the Mahan name (Shen Yue 2018; see also Kwŏn Oyŏng 2015). Collectively, these records, if accurate, offer evidence that Mahan or Mohan was not just a term imposed by Chinese historians but a name that at least a few peninsular groups used as self-identification.

follows from these by breaking out of the historiographical paradigm of Mahan studies to look at important diagnostic features of tombs in southwestern Korea to determine how culturally cohesive the region actually was. I conclude that, when considered on its own terms, there is little evidence in either texts or this particular aspect of the archaeology for the existence of a coherent Mahan culture. However, when approached from the perspective of Mahan as a fluid process of becoming through time, the cultural designation becomes a very real product of historical sources, material culture, and the agency of local groups.

Mahan in Korean Historiography

The earliest usage of the term Mahan is as a designation for a distinct regional culture in Chinese historical sources. The earliest of these is found in the "Account of the Han" in the Dongyi zhuan 東夷傳 section of the third century *Sanguozhi* 三國志 by Chen Shou 陳壽 (chapter 30; see Byington 2009; Chen Shou 1959). The text is largely preoccupied with discussion of Mahan and other Samhan people's location, polity names, and leadership terms; their

These scattered mentions in Chinese sources constitute the entirety of information currently available on Mahan as a historical entity. Despite this, Mahan, Samhan, and other cultural entities also found themselves constantly recast in dynastic and privately compiled historical treatises of the Koryŏ 高麗 and Chosŏn 朝鮮 periods (spanning the tenth to the eighteenth century). As outlined by Stella Xu (2016), writers in these periods were overwhelmingly concerned with tracing a legitimate series of civilized antecedents in ancient history that not only connected the Korean Peninsula to the Chinese cultural tradition but also established Korea as a distinct (and in some senses coequal) entity in and of itself. While often using Chinese records like the *Jinshu* as sources,[3] the Mahan of Korean historiography loses much of its historical specificity as it became one of many dynastic ancestors claimed by successive peninsular regimes.

Many texts, like Iryŏn's 一然 *Samguk yusa* 三國遺事 (1281) and Kwŏn Kŭn's 權近 *Tongguk saryak* 東國史略 (1396), mention Mahan and the Samhan among many ancient groups that existed on the Korean Peninsula and contributed to the formation of a uniquely peninsular culture. Others, like Yi Sŭnghyu's 李承休 *Chewang ungi* 帝王韻記 (1287) and Hŏ Mok's (1595–1682) *Tongsa* 東事, presented Mahan and the Samhan as links in a chain of succession that connected Koryŏ and Chosŏn to the even more ancient kingdoms of Tan'gun Chosŏn and Kija Chosŏn.

Other texts placed Mahan and Samhan more centrally as a source of dynastic legitimacy. The most significant dynastic history of the ancient period written during the Koryŏ period, the *Samguk sagi* 三國史記 (1145), compiled by Kim Pusik 金富軾, incorporated Mahan into the lineage of the Three Kingdoms (traditionally 57 BCE to 668 CE). In the *Samguk sagi*'s Silla Annals, Mahan polities (or simply Mahan itself) are mentioned sporadically as a precursor to Paekche.[4] Mahan functions here as a stand-in for Paekche in early records where the use of the Paekche name would appear anachronistic (Best 2016). Most historians have a healthy distrust for the sparse and unreliable pre–fourth century records of the *Samguk sagi* (see Shultz 2004). Nevertheless, if we are to take them at face value and accept Kim Pusik's assertion that he was drawing on now-lost Silla sources, then we can say that the idea of Mahan as a distinct entity (or even an organized proto-state capable of mustering military attacks on Silla) was a plausible reality for Middle/Late Silla historians.

In the Chosŏn period, references to Mahan were used to bolster the ruling Yi Dynasty's image as a legitimate Confucian state in the vein of Ming China. Many histories positioned the Samhan as a direct successor or counterpart to Kija Chosŏn, the semi-mythical first Chinese-style state in Korea and linked to the venerable Shang Dynasty (1600 BCE to 1046 BCE) of the Chinese Bronze Age. Among these, Sŏ Kŏjŏng 徐居正 (1420–1488) and Yi Ik 李瀷 (1681–1763) explicitly identified Mahan as Kija Chosŏn's legitimate successor and steward of Confucian culture (see discussion in Xu 2016:64–65, 71–74).

What is perhaps more significant about Mahan and Samhan in this dynastic period is their gradual mutation into a designation for Korea as a whole. In the Koryŏ period, the name Samhan, as argued convincingly by Remco Breuker (2005), was used to designate (1) the Later Three Kingdoms (892–936) in Koryŏ history, (2) the ruling dynasty as a synonym for Koryŏ, and (3) the people of the Korean Peninsula as a whole. From this, Samhan became a supra-dynastic term for the peninsula in historical texts, geographical treatises, and poetry. The term was even inscribed on Koryŏ coinage. Mahan was not just a cultural designation for one area of the peninsula or a dynastic ancestor but was a component of Koryŏ's pluralistic identity and peninsular proto-nationalism (Breuker 2010). The names Samhan and Han persisted as shorthand for southern Korea in Chosŏn-period vernacular and popular literature (Choi 2015:347; Haboush 2016:49). Meiji Japan, in turn, used Samhan to refer to ancient Korea in justifications for its colonization of the peninsula (Schmid 2002).[5]

By modern times, Mahan and Samhan seem to have lost some of their significance as terms denoting a peninsular identity. Colonial-period Korean scholars from the ethnohistorical tradition, such as Sin Chaeho (1880–1936), reacting to the intellectual and political erosion of Korea's sovereignty in the early 1900s, marginalized Mahan and Samhan in the lineage of the Korean people. In his *Toksa Sillon* (Sin 1995), Sin traced Korean ethnicity through primarily northern dynasties like Ko Chosŏn, Koguryŏ, and Parhae 渤海 (see also Schmid 1997). Nevertheless, Han as a synonym for Korea continued to be used, particularly in South Korea, where the bulk of the Samhan groups were thought to have been physically located. South Korea preserves the character Han in both the formal title Republic of Korea (大韓民國, Taehan min'guk) and the more colloquial name Korea (韓國, Han'guk).

For the past several decades, however, Mahan and Samhan discourse has been the purview of historians and more recently archaeologists still engaged in the project of both situating Korea in East Asia and isolating a uniquely Korean culture. While these scholars use Mahan specifically to refer to the third century historical entity from Chinese sources, it has become difficult to disentangle the origins of the actual Mahan groups (if indeed they ever existed) from the nationalistic baggage the term has accrued over the centuries. Successive usages of Mahan have turned the term into an ambiguous signifier of ancient Korean culture rather than the coherent cultural entity it began as. In the following, I detail the implications of this for the mortuary archaeology of southwestern Korea.

Mahan Tombs in Korean Archaeology

Even without the ambiguous status of Mahan, the Iron Age archaeology of Korea's southwest (the supposed Mahan heartland) presents a number of specific methodological challenges. Mortuary diversity in this region during the Iron Age appeared relatively suddenly in the second century CE, growing out of a fairly uniform and long-lasting mortuary ritual tradition (Table 4.1). Prior to this, tombs in southern Korea as a whole seem to have developed along similar lines, albeit with some regional particularities. The stone-cist tombs of the Late Bronze Age gave way to simple pit tombs, which over time came to contain wood coffins on an increasingly regular basis.

Grave good inventories of this period were also typical of the Early Iron Age southern peninsula. Pit tombs contained unadorned earthenware vessels (in the Late Bronze Age Mumun style) and earthenware jars with distinctive clay rims (*chŏmt'odae t'ogi* 粘土帶土器). These are also found in habitation sites, but less commonly found black-burnished long-necked jars (*hŭkto* 黑陶) seem to have been a ceramic type restricted to mortuary treatments (see summaries in Choi 2008; KAS 2013:200–203). Metal objects are uncommon in pit tombs. Occasionally sets of bronze objects consisting of bells and clappers were found at sites along the western coastline, and individual tombs throughout southern Korea have yielded imported Warring States–style iron axes and slender objects usually classified as chisels (KAS 2013:197–99).

Diversity began to creep into the pit tomb tradition in the second century BCE, and by the second century CE (when we would expect to see Mahan groups in the southwest), tombs exhibited a wide array of features and configurations (see Table 4.2). Beginning in the first century CE, pit tombs were joined by larger, mounded variants, and by the second century CE, at least two different tomb types with distinctively shaped enclosing ditches had also emerged (Figure 4.4). Most of these ditches approximate a horseshoe shape, but round, square, trapezoidal, and U-shaped ditch tombs have also come to light. Certain regions have a preponderance of certain shapes over others, and some areas—like the Kŭm River region (the first major river system south of present-day Seoul)—contain an abundance of different tomb shapes. By the third century, the practice of burying multiple individuals in single burial mounds was also prevalent throughout southwestern Korea, but again with pronounced subregional and site-specific variations.

At this time in the far southwest, the Yŏngsan River region, a new form of mounded tomb appeared. It consisted of mounded burials surrounded by ditches featuring large jars placed in the tomb mound horizontally. In mounded tombs with multiple burials in Yŏngsan, we sometimes see tombs with a combination of wood coffin, jar, and wood-timbered burial chambers in a single tumulus.

With the evolution of different tomb styles, patterns of grave good deposition also changed. Overall, grave goods are less abundant than in the preceding pit tomb period and show more regional consistency than tomb construction. A new ceramic assemblage, often designated as "Mahan type," included globular jars (with variations that seem to have chronological significance, such as round or flat bottoms as well as unadorned or double rims) and top-heavy jars with ear- or lug-shaped handles. In more northern regions like Kyŏnggi, from the early third century onward, these jars seem to show adoption of aspects of the Lelang-style cord-pattern, beaten-pottery production method (Kim Kiok 2015).

Bronze production seems to have rapidly declined at this time, and a new locus of iron production appeared in the southeast, outside the western regions associated with Mahan. Despite a lack of production evidence, however, peninsula-produced iron objects, such as axes, sickles, ingots, knife blades, and arrows, have been found in tombs in all regions of southern Korea. There are also a few explicitly martial objects, such as decorated sword blades and spearheads. These are typically regarded as prestige goods related to a leader's ability to wage war with neighboring groups (Yi Hŭijun 2011; Yi T'aekku 2015).

In the mid-fourth century, a measure of uniformity appeared in the material culture of northwestern Korea. This is often linked by researchers to the supposed expansion of a newly emergent polity called Paekche, centered on Hansŏng in present-day Seoul (Kim Sŭngok 2011). This so-called Paekche material culture slowly spread southward into Mahan regions in the late fourth and fifth centuries. The last area to abandon earlier burial traditions linked to Mahan was the Yŏngsan River region, which retained its characteristic jar burial barrow tombs until the sixth century. The tradition of interring multiple burials over time in a single tumulus continued to be practiced here and nowhere else on the peninsula.

A frequent topic of interest for Mahan scholars is the emergence and dissemination of Paekche-style artifacts into the peninsula's southwest. This process began in the Kyŏnggi area around Seoul and other regions north of the Kŭm River. From the fourth to fifth century, along with the appearance of Paekche-style chamber tombs, we see the adoption of Hansŏng-period Paekche ceramics (*kyŏngjil* globular jars, wide- and straight-necked jars, black-burnished jars, raised dishes, and cups) and prestige goods like gilt bronze personal adornment. Farther south,

Table 4.1. Summary of Mahan mortuary development

Period	Mortuary Record	Major Tomb Types	Grave Goods
Late Bronze Age	Relatively consistent pit tombs in southern Korea as a whole. A relatively small number of pit tombs with ditches.	pit tombs, coffin tombs, ditch tombs	
Initial Mahan (third century BCE to first century CE)	Pit and coffin tomb tradition continues. Large mounded pit tombs develop and coexist with earlier traditions. Tombs begin to exhibit different shapes (square, horseshoe).	pit tombs, coffin tombs, large mounded pit tombs	attached rim pottery, iron agricultural tools, bronze bells and clappers
Early Mahan (first century to mid-third century)	Persistence of pit tomb tradition and appearance of ditch tombs with different burial chamber construction methods. Individual burials give way to clusters of tombs that share ditches or multiple burials within ditch enclosures. Central western Korea: large mounded pit tombs develop ditches and coexist with small pit tombs. Western coastline: appearance of barrow tombs with ditches. Shapes differ depending on the region (square, horseshoe, circular) Yŏngsan region: jar burial tradition first appears in the upper reaches of the Komak River and spreads to Koch'ang and Yŏnggwang.	pit tombs, coffin tombs, pit and coffin tombs with ditches, barrow tombs, jar burials	globular jars, two-handled jars, iron ring-pommel swords, spears, arrows, axes, sickles, ingots
Middle Mahan (mid-third century to mid-fourth century)	Horizontally expanded mounded tombs with multiple burials; many burials within ditch enclosures; barrow tombs extend into all regions. Appearance of burial chambers of piled stones. Kyŏnggi region: coexistence of pit tombs with ditches and barrow tombs. Single burials only. Square and rectangular ditches. Tombs with features linking them to burial practices of the Lelang commandery in Pyongyang. Central western Korea (Kŭm River region): barrow tombs near the coast; pit tombs with ditches more inland. Expansive horseshoe, square, and rectangular tombs made up of multiple burials. Yŏngsan region: distinctive, large-scale barrow tombs with multiple jar burials.	pit tombs, wood chamber tombs, pit and chamber tombs with ditches, barrow tombs, jar burials, individual burials, horizontally expanded multiple burials, multiple burials enclosed by a ditch	Similar to Early Mahan. Increasing divergence between barrow tombs (one or two ceramic vessels per tomb and small amounts of iron) and mounded tombs (large numbers of vessels and iron)

Table 4.1. Summary of Mahan mortuary development

Period	Mortuary Record	Major Tomb Types	Grave Goods
Late Mahan (mid-fourth century to mid-fifth century)	General decline of barrow tombs; appearance of Paekche-style stone-chambered tombs.	pit tombs, wood chamber tombs, jar burials, pit and chamber tombs with ditches, barrow tombs, Paekche stone-lined chamber tombs, vertically extended jar burial barrow tombs	globular jars, raised dishes, fan-necked jars, iron spearheads, sickles, swords, stirrups, cauldrons. Paekche prestige goods in the form of silver and gilt bronze headgear and personal adornment
	Kyŏnggi region: disappearance of barrow tombs and pit tombs with ditches. Paekche-style tombs dominate.		
	Central western Korea: barrow tombs persist in small numbers in Sŏsan and Wanju. Pit tombs with ditches are prevalent and seem to replace barrow tombs in many areas. In inland Ch'ungchŏng, Paekche-style stone-lined tombs appear.		
	Yŏngsan region: large-scale square barrow tombs expanded vertically by multigenerational burial practices. Persistence of jar burials.		
Final Mahan (mid-fifth century to early sixth century)	Barrow tombs persist only in Yŏngsan while pit tombs and Paekche stone-lined tombs are common in all other regions. Stone slab burial chambers are introduced. In the sixth century, barrow tombs in Yŏngsan also disappear.	Paekche stone-lined chamber tombs, wood chamber tombs, stone slab tombs, vertically extended jar burial barrow tombs	Paekche pottery and prestige objects

Note: The periodization used here follows Im Yŏngjin 1999.

Table 4.2. Features of Mahan tombs

Ditch	Burial Chamber Type	Burial Chamber Location	Mound	Tomb Location	Orientation	Burial Arrangement
No ditch	pit	above ground	no mound	coastal	east to west	single burial
Round	wood coffin	below ground	small	river valley	following terrain contours	conjoined ditch
Horseshoe	wood-timbered	in ditch	large	interior foothills		multiple burials in mound
U-shaped	wood chamber					multiple burials in mound and ditch
Square	jar					horizontally extended multiple burials
Trapezoidal	stone-lined					vertically extended multiple burials

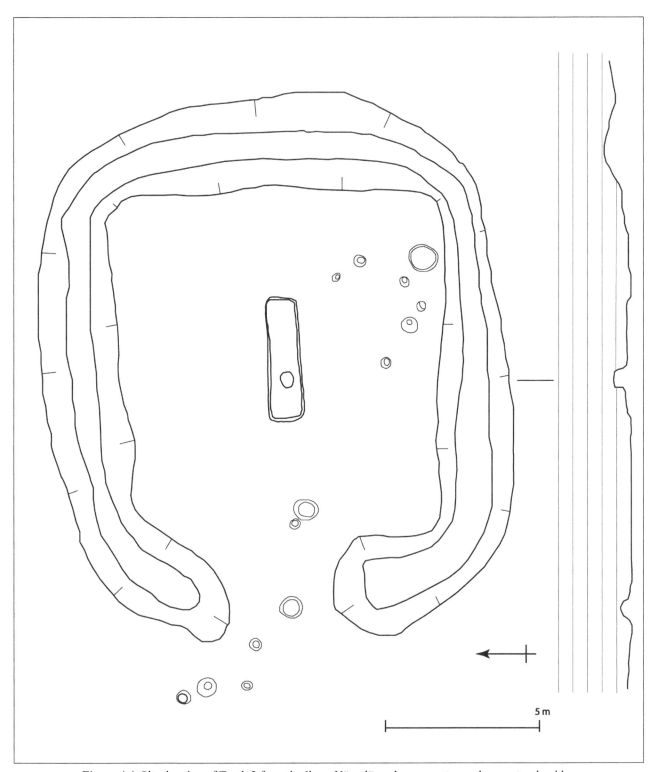

Figure 4.4. Site drawing of Tomb 2 from the Iksan Yŏngdŭng-dong cemetery, a barrow tomb with a horseshoe-shaped enclosing ditch. Redrawn from WUMPCI (2000). *Created by the author.*

in Ch'ungch'ŏng and Yŏngsan, Mahan pottery persisted, with regional variants including Yŏngsan-style double-rim globular jars, vessels with ear-shaped handles, and mounted dishes (see Kim Sŭngok 2011).

The problems of mortuary archaeology in Korea's southwest that emerge from this outline are a relatively sudden fluorescence of diverse practices that lasted for about 300 years (first century to the mid-fourth century), many subregional trends that are distinct from each other, and a comingling of diverse practices within single areas and even within individual cemeteries. Certain aspects of tombs appear to be unique, while others are derivative or inspired by practices in northern China. Other than the diversity itself, there are no clear material indicators or tomb attributes that can be definitively labeled as a coherent material culture. There are some pronounced regional differences in the Yŏngsan River area after the third century, but in other areas, like Kyŏnggi, and the Kŭm River basin, researchers are still grappling with a mishmash of burial chambers, ditch shapes, mound sizes, and construction techniques.

Despite this archaeological diversity, the historiographical orientation of Iron Age research has led to the a priori designation of the southwest as Mahan territory. This has, over time, generated a third usage of the name Mahan, as a material culture. Although habitation sites and dwelling features of this region have recently received attention (Hŏ China 2018; Pak Chiyŏng 2017), traditionally, the unique features of tombs in western Korea have been used to argue for the presence of a uniquely Mahan material culture.

Mahan seems to have become associated with these tombs beginning in the 1970s. Prior to this, there was no unified conception of Mahan archaeology in western Korea, and sites north of the Kŭm River were assigned to early Paekche (cf. Im Yŏngjin 2015). As historians turned to the Chinese *Sanguozhi* as a source of early history, Mahan emerged more and more as a subject of archaeological research. The focus initially was on the large jar burials of Yŏngsan and the pit tombs of Kyŏnggi and Chŏlla and their possible connection to early Paekche mounded tombs in Seoul, such as Karak-dong and Sŏkch'ŏn-dong (An Sŭngju 1985; Kim Wŏnyong 1973:195–98).

As detailed by Dennis Lee (2014, 2018), by the 1980s a consensus formed around the idea that Yŏngsan's distinctive third through sixth century mounded jar burials represented a Mahan burial tradition (Ch'oe Mongnyong 1986; Hwang Yonghon 1974; Yi Yŏngmun 1978). Somewhat later, Im Yŏngjin (1999) argued that these tombs were a kind of cultural island or remnant of Mahan culture, relatively untouched by Paekche until the sixth century, and that the traditional understanding of Paekche control of western Korea in this period needed to be rethought. Lee (2014:95) makes the trenchant criticism that assigning the label of Mahan to even the very distinctive tombs of Yŏngsan forces us into a paradigm that treats Mahan groups monolithically and for the Three Kingdoms period creates an automatic core–periphery relationship between Paekche and Mahan that occludes the true dynamics and diversity of the peninsula. I would add that the Mahan designation also creates an association between a unique and indigenous material culture tradition and a narrative of resistance and persistence in the face of conquest by the much more Sinitically oriented Paekche.

New excavations and new tomb discoveries elsewhere in western Korea during the 1990s revealed that variations of Yŏngsan's tomb traditions could be found in other regions (see summaries of research in the Kyŏnggi and Chŏnbuk regions in Cho Kayŏng 2015 and Pak Yŏngmin 2015, respectively). This produced a flurry of studies attempting to make sense of mounded ditch tombs with different shapes, burial chambers, and grave goods (see works collected in Ch'oe Wankyu 2006). In the absence of abundant grave goods unique to the region, these studies attempted a conceptual distinction between diverse second to sixth century tombs of western Korea and the pit and chamber tomb tradition still prominent in southeastern Korea and associated with Chinhan and Pyŏnhan.

The most influential of these was Yi Sŏngju's (2000) seminal study that divided Iron Age tombs of southern Korea into the barrow tomb tradition (*pun'gu myo* 墳丘墓) of western Korea and the mounded tomb tradition (*pongt'o myo* 封土墓) of the southeast. Using Japanese Yayoi tumuli as a starting point, Yi defined barrow tombs as stratified tumuli made up of successive burials and mounded tombs as subsurface single burials with a tumulus placed on top (Figure 4.5; Yi Sŏngju 2000:79). Mounded tombs were, according to Yi, imitative of the Chinese Central Plains tradition, while barrow tombs were a non-northern Chinese tradition that originated from Liaodong cairn burials of the Bronze Age and developed into the stone barrows of Koguryŏ before making their way down the western coast and spreading into the Chŏlla region and then the Japanese islands (86–91).

Yi's original study set out not to isolate barrows as a uniquely Mahan tradition but more to try to explain some of the fundamental differences between tombs in western and eastern Korea. Moreover, he offered a developmental model to explain how distinctive jar burials remained in use in Yŏngsan until the sixth century, long after the rest of the peninsula had adopted Paekche, Silla, or Kaya tomb forms showing clear influence from Warring States– and

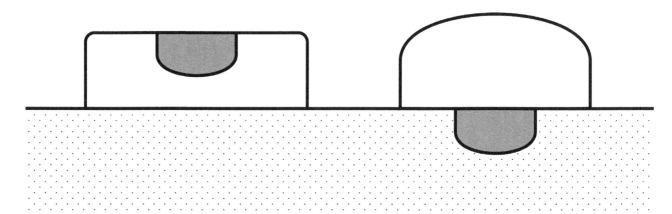

Figure 4.5. Cross-sectional diagram of the barrow tomb tradition (left) of western Korea and the mounded tomb tradition (right) of southern Korea. The primary distinction determined by Yi Sŏngju and expanded upon by Im Yŏngjin is the positioning of the burial chamber (shaded in gray) either inside or below the burial mound. *Created by the author.*

Hàn-style chamber tomb traditions. He made the theoretical distinction between a long-term tomb *tradition* that persisted for several centuries and short-term *transformations* that resulted in differential expression and experimentation in particular social contexts (Yi Sŏngju 2000:78). The diversity of barrow tombs could be explained as the result of a continuous tomb tradition within which various transformations were experimented with for social and ideological reasons. The variety of different mound shapes, surrounding ditches, and multiple-burial practices, in this context, were attempts to represent identity, emulate other groups, or assert particular social relationships (101–3).

From this foundation and an earlier Yŏngsan tomb study by Sŏng Nakchun (1983), Im Yŏngjin (2002) explicitly identified Yi's barrow tomb tradition as an archaeological marker for the historical Mahan culture. For Im, the defining feature of barrows was the fact that the burial chamber was dug into the tomb mound aboveground (*sŏn pun'gu hu maejang* 선분구후매장), in contrast to mounded tombs that featured burial chambers dug into the surface of the ground (*sŏn maejang hu pun'gu* 선매장후분구; Figure 4.5). This mode of burial, subsequently discovered in tombs not just in Yŏngsan but in western Korea generally, was for Im and others the defining characteristic of Mahan mortuary culture itself—a feature that went beyond regional and chronological differences and represented a fundamental cultural link over the entire Mahan region (see Im Yŏngjin et al. 2015). The variety of ditch shapes, multiple burials, and grave good assemblages in the region did not present a problem as long as the burial chambers in the tumuli conformed to the aboveground burial method found in barrow tombs.

Not all researchers are ready to equate the construction of barrow tombs to a cultural practice unique to Mahan, particularly since pit tombs of the mounded tomb tradition can be found in many areas of western Korea, particularly in central western Korea and areas just south of Seoul. In fact, the most prominent of these—the ditch mounded tomb (*chugu t'ogwang myo* 周溝土壙墓)—also feature ditches, may predate barrow tombs, and could have influenced barrow tomb development (Kwŏn Oyŏng 2015). Ch'oe Sŏngnak, a prominent critic of the barrow tomb concept and its association with Mahan culture, objects to the term as being both conceptually unclear and not useful when distinguishing Mahan tombs from other traditions (Ch'oe Sŏngnak 2007, 2018:162–74). He and other researchers point to the existence of ditches, multiple-burial practices, and distinctive burial features like jar coffins as better candidates for diagnostic Mahan cultural markers. There is still little consensus regarding even the correct terminology for these tombs, and excavators frequently coin a new descriptor for every variation on the mounded ditch tomb model they find or for the aspect of tomb construction they wish to emphasize (see Table 4.3).

Ongoing debates about the diagnostic features of Mahan mortuary archaeology underscore just how little archaeological coherency there is to work with in the region. This tomb variability also cross-cuts regional or chronological distinctions and does not seem to conform to differences in wealth, class, or any kind of kin affiliation. There was no agreement among Mahan groups, if indeed they existed, as to what constituted the "correct" way to bury a high-status individual; nor is there even agreement about whether different polities had a similar internal organizational structure. Additionally, the unexamined

Table 4.3. Mahan tomb terminology

Term		Romanized	Translation
封土墓		*pongt'o myo*	mounded tomb
	土壙墓	*t'ogwang myo*	pit tomb
	周溝土壙墓	*chugu t'ogwang myo*	pit tomb with ditch
	單純土壙墓	*tansun t'ogwang myo*	simple pit tomb
	木棺墓	*mokkwan myo*	wood coffin tomb
	木棺封土墓	*mokkwan pongt'o myo*	wood coffin mounded tomb
	木槨封土墓	*mokkwak pongt'o myo*	wood chamber mounded tomb
	甕棺封土墓	*onggwan pongt'o myo*	jar-coffin mounded tomb
	低封土墓	*chŏ pongt'o myo*	collapsed mounded tomb
	棺槨土壙墓	*kwan'gwak t'ogwang myo*	coffin or chamber pit tomb
墳丘墓		*pun'gu myo*	barrow tomb
	盛土墳丘墓	*sŏngt'o pun'gu myo*	piled-earth barrow tomb
	積石墳丘墓	*chŏksŏk pun'gu myo*	piled-stone barrow tomb
	葺石墳丘墓	*chûpsŏk pun'gu myo*	
	木棺墳丘墓	*mokkwan pun'gu myo*	wood coffin barrow tomb
	木槨墳丘墓	*mokkwak pun'gu myo*	wood chamber barrow tomb
	石室墳丘墓	*sŏksil pun'gu myo*	stone slab barrow tomb
	單純/複合墳丘墓	*tansun/pokhap pun'gu myo*	simple/complex barrow tomb
	低墳丘墓	*chŏ pongt'o myo*	collapsed barrow tomb
	墳丘式 古墳	*pun'gu sik kobun*	barrow-style tumulus
	墳丘墳	*pun'gu pun*	barrow tumulus
	墳丘形 土壙墓	*pun'gu hyŏng t'ogwang myo*	barrow-shaped pit tomb
甕棺墓		*onggwan myo*	jar burial
周溝墓		*chugu myo*	ditch tomb

application of the term Mahan to archaeology ignores the already multifarious historical and historiographical connotations of the term circulating within Korean ancient historical research. Interpretations that invest Mahan with more indigeneity and authenticity than other peninsular cultures of the time may therefore be a reflection of Mahan's historiographical positionality rather than anything intrinsic to the archaeology.

It is here that I draw on von Falkenhausen's approach to Chinese archaeology to intervene in this debate. In the following sections I outline the major features of tombs in western Korea that have been proposed as being distinctively Mahan. Rather than how they support or refute the idea of Mahan material culture, I am concerned with how they might be read with the aim of assessing the degree of cultural coherency within this territory and how they might have contributed to local regional identities. The focus here is on aspects of tomb construction that previous research has isolated as potentially meaningful for identity construction. As the summary above demonstrated, scholars have focused on aspects of tomb construction: mounds, ditch features, and barrow compounds made up of multiple burials. While there are some significant patterns of grave good distribution, the general sparseness of burial objects (usually one or two ceramic vessels per burial) and their similarity to objects found in southeastern Korea make it difficult to make meaningful generalizations in this context. Grave goods are discussed where relevant, but a full treatment of artifact placement and their role in the mortuary ritual will be reserved for a future and more thorough treatment. I begin, then, with a review of tomb construction features, their origins, and major arguments put forward regarding their significance before pursuing my own synthesis of the region's mortuary culture as a whole.

Features of Mortuary Archaeology in Western Korea
Barrows and Mounds

The first feature significant to so-called Mahan tombs is the overall construction of the tomb mound and the placement of the burial chamber within it. As discussed above, Yi Sŏngju used mound and burial chamber construction as the basis for his barrow versus mounded tomb distinction. Although he did not suggest this as a way to distinguish groups belonging to the Mahan culture per se, barrow tomb construction as defined by Yi has subsequently been designated as a uniquely Mahan mortuary tradition by Im Yŏngjin and other scholars (see Im Yŏngjin et al. 2015).

The two mound and chamber construction methods in evidence in Mahan territory isolated by Yi produce superficially similar mounded tombs in the landscape but seem to represent completely different burial paradigms. Mounded tombs are subsurface burials with a separate mound constructed over them, while barrow tombs are single aboveground features that combine mound and burial chamber.

There are clear ritual implications for each practice. Although mounded tombs seem to be an evolution of the pit tomb type of the Late Bronze Age seen all over the southern peninsula, the specific form of the mounded tomb of concern here seems to have a more direct connection to practices introduced into the region by Hàn China's administrative commanderies in northern Korea from the first century BCE to the second century CE (Yi Sŏngju 2000). Tomb types representing this burial construction method are numerous in Iron Age Korea. In Mahan regions, they are found primarily in the inland areas of western Korea corresponding to the Han River basin as well as the inner Kyŏnggi and Chŏlla provinces. Mounded tombs were also the primary burial practice of the Yŏngnam region (southeastern Korea and the supposed territory of Chinhan and Pyŏnhan) until the Three Kingdoms period. In Yŏngnam, the development of larger and more elaborate arrays of grave goods in mounded tombs suggests the adoption of aspects of Central Plains–style ritual feasting and offering practices (Yi Sŏngju 2014). The counterpart to these tombs in western Korea, the mounded pit tomb with surrounding ditch, is much sparser in terms of grave goods (Yi T'aekku 2015).

By contrast, in barrow tombs, interment of the corpse occurred after construction of the mound in the funeral process. It is a mode of burial that facilitates multiple-burial practices, as new burials can be added into the mound and the mound itself can be expanded over time to accommodate this. Barrows constructed in this fashion are most abundant in southwestern Korea, but examples have also been found along the entire length of the western coast, from Kyŏnggi in the north to Chŏllanam-do in the far south. The construction method, unlike that of mounded tombs, seems to have been wholly distinct from Central Plains–derived tomb structures. If anything, barrows bear a similarity to burial compounds in Japan, such as the Middle Yayoi burial mound at Yoshinogari in Kyushu or the rectangular tumuli of western Japan in the Late Yayoi (see discussion of these in Mizoguchi 2017:144–64). Im Yŏngjin (2016) also points to possible connections with the chambered pit tomb tradition (土墩墓) of the upper Yangtze River.

The appeal of declaring the barrow tomb to be a Mahan tradition is apparent; it is a distinctive tomb type wholly disconnected from the Hàn Chinese paradigm found throughout the region suggested by texts to be Mahan territory. But even if we are to assume that barrow tombs represent a cultural tradition wholly separate from practices in northern

China and elsewhere on the peninsula, it is unclear when and how barrows emerged in the region or how they relate to a cohesive Mahan culture, if any such thing existed. Fully formed barrows were in existence by the mid-second century CE in central western Korea at sites like Unyang-dong in Kimp'o (Kim Kiok 2010) and Yech'ŏn-dong in Sŏsan (PICP 2012), but the developmental predecessors of these tombs are difficult to ascertain. Scholars committed to the idea of barrows as a distinctively Mahan tradition point to ring-ditch tombs of the Late Bronze Age and Early Iron Age as early or proto-barrow tombs (Im Yŏngjin 2015). These are found in isolated pockets north of the Kŭm River region, such as the Poryŏng area, which is quite far from where the earliest confirmed barrow tombs have been found in abundance in southwestern Korea (Kwŏn Oyŏng 2015). If Bronze Age ring-ditch tombs are an earlier version of the barrow tomb, then it is unclear why they were abandoned in one area before reappearing in modified form much farther to the south several hundred years later. Given this, the barrow would seem to represent a fairly new burial paradigm that appeared at roughly the same time as mounded tombs connected to the northern Chinese tradition.

Another complicating factor is that, despite the conceptual utility of distinguishing barrows and mounds, it is often difficult to determine which paradigm individual tombs fall under. Contemporaneous barrows and mounds in central western Korea are generally found in coastal and inland regions, respectively. Yet in several areas, such as Sŏsan (south of Inch'ŏn and west of Ch'ungch'ŏng Province), aboveground and subsurface burial chamber traditions coexisted (Figure 4.6). Simple pit tombs have also been found at both barrow and mounded tomb sites. In the Kyŏnggi region, distinguishing between barrow tombs and the more common mounded burial traditions has proven difficult, as at many sites the tomb mound does not remain and both tomb types (as well as simple pit tombs) are found at the same sites (Cho Kayŏng 2015). There are also examples in Honam of what look to be barrow tombs where the initial burial was in fact dug belowground, similar to the way mounded tombs were constructed (KAS 2006; Kim Nakchung 2011). Others have argued that the differences between many observed barrows and mounded tombs may be overstated and better explained as a result of chronological, geographical, or status distinctions we have yet to isolate (Pak Sunbal 2000; Yi Namsŏk 2011).

Grave good assemblages do show some differentiation between barrow and mounded tombs. Mounded tomb cemeteries in the interior of North Chŏlla Province have conspicuously more ceramic vessels than contemporaneous barrow tombs along the coast (Yi T'aekku 2008). Globular

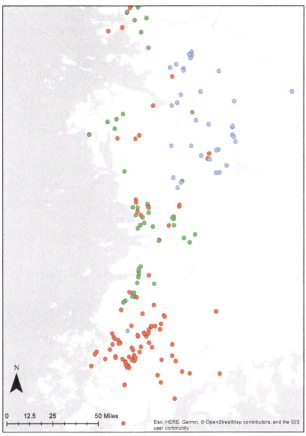

Figure 4.6. Distribution of cemeteries containing barrows (red), mounded tombs (blue), or both (green). *Created by the author.*

and high-necked jars are common to both, but mounded tombs are more likely to contain flat dishes that have been interpreted as evidence of the adoption of sacrificial offerings reminiscent of practices in the Central Plains of China (Yi Sŏngju 2014; Yi T'aekku 2015). Nevertheless, there are abundant examples of mounded tombs in Kyŏnggi and the Kŭm River region with grave good assemblages of one or two vessels identical to those found in mounded tombs (Cho Kayŏng 2015; Kim Sŭngok 2011). Metal objects are exceedingly rare in both tomb forms, but a small number of mounded tombs in central western Korea contain bronze belt hooks and bells (Kim Sŭngok 2011) that are similar to objects found in mounded tombs in coastal areas of the southeast associated with Pyŏnhan (KAS 2013).

There was also a considerable diversity of ways a barrow could be constructed, suggesting that, even if this was a coherent cultural practice, logistical practicalities and local conditions led to divergences on a micro-regional scale. Although he maintains the utility of the aboveground burial chamber as a marker of Mahan, Im Yŏngjin (2015) has also pointed to many of these divergences: there are barrows fashioned out of preexisting natural hillocks, those that seem to have been formed around a barrow around a jar or wood coffin burial chamber, and mounds with a 凹-shaped divot into which a burial chamber was installed. In sum, barrows are a unique practice in western Korea, but their diversity and relationship to the mounded tomb tradition argue against the idea that they should be taken as a coherent archaeological culture.

Surrounding Ditches

Further diversity can be seen in the ancillary feature shared by both barrows and mounded tombs: exterior surrounding ditches. These, along with other features, such as jar burial chambers and multiple burials within the same mound, were a common component of burials from the second century CE onward. For some, the presence of ditches is seen as a better ethnic marker for Mahan because it is shared by all tombs (both barrow and mounded tombs) in western Korea, from the Han River valley in Seoul to the Yŏngsan River region in the southwest (Ch'oe Sŏngnak 2018).

Nevertheless, this utility is undermined by the sheer inconsistency of ditch construction methods and resulting forms. Ditches seem to have had the practical utility of preventing tomb mound erosion, and their various shapes were the result of different logistical concerns resulting from the placement, topology, and micro-environmental contexts of each individual site and tomb (Yi Misŏn 2011). Horseshoe-shaped ditches that partially surrounded tomb mounds were relatively common from the mid-second century onward, but round, ovoid, square, and semicircular ditches were also widespread.

As with mound construction, there is also disagreement as to how the horseshoe-shaped ditches developed as a feature. Tombs with ditches do predate the Iron Age. Kim Kwŏnchung (2008) records 37 examples of wood or stone coffin or chamber tombs surrounded by a circular ditch at 11 Middle/Late Bronze Age sites. This is not enough to consider ditch tombs a common Bronze Age tomb type, but they have been found widely, including in Kangwŏn Province, central western Korea, and southern Yŏngnam. These do not really correspond to areas where Mahan barrow tombs are most common, and they are hard to link chronologically given the 400-year gap between the Bronze Age examples and the first mounded tombs associated with Iron Age barrows and mounded tombs.

The earliest ditch-bearing mounded tombs from the Iron Age date to around the first century BCE. These are perhaps related to the larger pit tombs of the mounded tomb tradition that appeared at this time, and Kwŏn Oyŏng (2015) suggests that early ditches were possibly an unintended result of scooping out nearby earth to construct larger mounds for these tombs. By the second century AD, however, the ditch seems to have become an intentional feature of tombs themselves. In Kwŏn's formulation, the presence of these early mounded tombs with ditches spurred barrow tomb burying groups to adopt a surrounding ditch feature as well.

Ditches emerge, then, as a widely adopted feature without clear ritual function or role in signaling cultural affiliation or identity. While the feature is common to the entire region associated with the Mahan of historical texts, its evolution indicates that it was initially an unintended result of tomb mound construction that had the utility of protecting burial features from erosion. Given this, it is difficult to interpret the micro-regional diversity of ditch forms as anything other than logistical conventions established in response to a variety of local environmental contexts. Nevertheless, the use of ditches also seems to be connected to the parallel development of another characteristic practice of southwestern Korea: the burial of multiple individuals in single barrow tombs.

Multiple-Burial Practices

The burial of multiple individuals in a single tomb has some precedence in Korean archaeology. Sacrificial burials in elaborate Three Kingdoms–era tombs associated with Kaya and Paekche are well documented (Yi and Kim 2011), and the eventual banning of the practice in sixth century Silla is preserved in the *Samguk sagi* (King Chijŭng, Year 3 [502], spring second month). Iron Age barrow tombs with multiple individuals in Korea's west, however, are better understood as tomb complexes resulting from successive interments over time rather than sacrifices. Multiple burial began in earnest in the third century and was retained until the fifth century, even in regions that were supposedly incorporated by Paekche. Given this, it is no surprise that the practice has been suggested to be reflective of a unique Mahan culture. Most prominently, Kim Nakchung (2009) argues that the practice is central to the development and evolution of Mahan barrow tombs, and Kim Sŭngok (2011) sees multiple burials as one of the three key elements of mounded burials associated with the culture.

Beginning in the mid-second century in central western Korea, barrow tombs at some sites began to change from distinct, single tombs to grouped tombs that shared a ditch. In barrow complexes of this kind containing a significant number of interments, there are often indications in the soil stratigraphy that the original enclosing ditch was extended and expanded horizontally to accommodate more individuals (see Pak Ch'anho 2019 for a recent overview).

By the third century, a version of the multiple burial could be found in all western regions of South Korea except the Han River area around Seoul. These early multiple-burial barrows contain fewer than four individuals. Usually, the initial central burial is surrounded by secondary interments or an additional burial is placed adjacent to an earlier grave (together in one mound or separated by a ditch). Representative sites containing burials of this kind include Hamp'yŏng Sunch'on (Ch'oe et al. 2001) and Koch'ang Namsan-ni (Kim et al. 2007).

To Kim Nakchung's (2009) assertion, the size and shape of the mound and ditch do seem to have developed symbiotically with the need to install additional burials. Horseshoe-shaped ditches became trapezoidal to accommodate more interments, and mounds expanded horizontally as more burials were added. At the same time, additional burials in the third century were influenced by the preexisting shape of the mound and placement of the ditch. At Ch'uk-dong in Kunsan (HCPRC 2006b), secondary jar burials have been found in ditches, and additional pit and coffin burials are often arranged parallel or perpendicular to the initial interment (HCPRC 2006a).

If barrow complexes of this kind seem like an ad hoc process of addition to existing single burial tombs, by the fourth century, interring many individuals in single barrows seems to have become a more purposeful ritual practice. Large barrows containing 10 or more individual burials have been found in the Kŭm and Yŏngsan River regions; they were constructed from the initial interment to facilitate the process of successive burials. In Yŏngsan, where these burial compounds persisted into the fifth century, burial mounds were expanded vertically with five to 10 additional burials, resulting in massive tumuli and tumuli complexes centered on the Pannam region south of Naju (Ch'oe Mongnyong 1988). Yŏngsan burials are also distinctive in terms of their massive double horizontal jar coffins within complex tumuli. This practice is thought to have emerged in the upper reaches of the Komak River in the third century and spread to Koch'ang, Yŏnggwang, and eventually Naju (Lee 2014). In barrow tombs with multiple burials in Yŏngsan, we often see a combination of wood coffin, jar, and wood-timbered burial chambers in a single tumulus (summarized in Ch'oe Sŏngnak 2018).

Grave good inventories of burials within barrow complexes reflect general patterns of burial offerings in Korea's west: one or two ceramic vessels occasionally found with iron objects. Yi T'aekku's (2015) survey of the Chŏnbuk region suggests a slight preponderance of martial objects like ring-pommel swords in initial central burials compared to the secondary burials that surround them. The latter are more likely to contain agricultural tools like axes and sickles. This changes dramatically in the late fifth and sixth centuries in Yŏngsan barrow complexes. Here, prestige goods reflecting contacts with Paekche, Silla, and Kaya in the form of gold and silver ornamentation, headgear, and equestrian equipment are found in the majority of burials (Ch'oe Sŏngnak 2018:235–68).

Despite their prevalence, multi-burial barrows cannot be considered a common or widespread practice anywhere but in Yŏngnam. As outlined recently by Pak Ch'anho (2019:10–36), in most regions, the single individual barrow or mounded tomb remained the dominant mode of burial, and even at sites with the practice in evidence, there are often many more single burials present. Even in Yŏngsan, only 30 out of the 50 barrow sites discovered contain distinctive massive tumuli containing 10 or more burials (Pak Ch'anho 2019:27).

Additionally, as with ditches, the sheer diversity of ways the multiple burial was expressed undermines the idea that it represents a singular cultural practice. Regional tomb construction methods seem predicated on local environmental factors and whether there was already a preference for locating tombs on slopes or summits of hills. In third century barrows, burials could be added to the central burial mound, placed in the enclosing ditch, or added to the edges of existing barrows, or separate barrows could be placed within the same ditch (Im Yŏngjin 2015:22–23). Even within the same tomb, burial chambers are often some combination of wood coffins, simple earthen pits, and jars. In the fourth and fifth centuries, stone chamber and stone slab burials reminiscent of Paekche practices are also present. Again, even in Yŏngsan, where the practice was relatively widespread and codified, multiple burials could take the form of lines of graves in a large trapezoidal mound (CNUM 2004), clusters of jar burials in a single square mound (DICP 2012), or other diverse forms.

In other regions there are significant tomb outliers at particular sites. Tomb 1 at Sangun-ni in Wanju, a massive barrow tomb, was found to contain 49 individual pit, coffin, and jar burials (JNUM 2010). Tomb 1 at Pungdŏng-ni in Koch'ang, meanwhile, is a large square barrow with five Paekche-style fifth century stone slab tombs in the center with two segregated clusters of stone chamber (eight graves) and jar burials (two graves; MPCRI 2012). Rather than a cultural practice common to a historical Mahan culture, multiple-burial tumuli reaffirm the lack of a regional consensus in mortuary traditions.

Beyond regional cultural cohesion, barrow complexes can speak to sociocultural affiliation and emerging distinctions on the smaller scale of villages or communities.

The gradual accumulation of burial clusters, first as an ad hoc process and later as a more formalized (in the case of Yŏngsan) practice, points on a general level to the solidifying of communities and the attachment of these communities to specific places. Simultaneously, the conscious placement of graves in relation to an initial burial in third century barrows at particular sites and the relative absence of certain objects from fourth century secondary burials (to say nothing of the massive fifth and sixth century Yŏngsan barrows containing exotic prestige goods) likely reflect increasingly complex and perhaps hierarchical intracommunity status distinctions that were asserted or challenged through the act of burial. Thus, though distinctive on the peninsula at this time, barrow complexes containing multiple interments do not get us closer to isolating a definitively Mahan culture.

Discussion

One could argue that the diverse tomb forms of western Korea as well as the unique mortuary practices of barrows and multi-person barrow compounds, and the ubiquity of ditch features, do constitute a distinct cultural horizon encompassing most of western Korea south of Seoul. Nevertheless, none of these aspects either collectively or individually provides convincing evidence of a distinct Mahan culture similar to the one described in early Chinese sources. If we move beyond Mahan, however, the array of mound and burial chamber configurations in the region do allow us to make some interesting cultural inferences. At least two distinctive burial types coexisted in western Korea, and there was also local variation within the barrow tradition. That much of this diversity can be pinpointed from the first century BCE through the second century CE suggests that the preexisting Bronze Age population began to interact with neighboring groups and was joined, over time, by incoming groups and influxes of diverse cultural traditions.

Similarly, the mere presence of ditches is not a good indicator of Mahan culture or even cultural unity, but it is interesting that the feature came to be associated with both tomb types in the region. They may have been a natural consequence of mound burial construction and subsequently adopted widely in barrow tomb practices or possibly a shared feature that persisted as tomb construction methods continued to diverge in coastal and inland areas. Despite their diversity and their practical function, they point, if not to cultural unity, certainly to shared practices and communication within the ritual space of the funeral.

It is also significant that the divergent burial paradigms and ditch shapes ultimately resulted in superficially similar enclosed mounded burials within the landscape. The primary differences are those that would be known only to the burying group or a single community: the interior structure of the tomb, the construction process, the type of burial chamber, and grave goods. This may have masked considerable local divergent practices and cultures and contributed to the *Sanguozhi*'s assumption of relative cultural unity in the region.

Despite these differences, general visual similarities among tomb mounds in the landscape and intercommunity interaction could have formed the basis for later cultural ties. Tomb ditches seem to have been an unintended result of an emphasis on constructing larger tomb mounds in the first century CE, and it is interesting that by the second century AD, the ditch was a prominent and deliberate feature of mounded tombs of both the barrow and mounded tomb burial traditions. Regardless of who first introduced the practice, the appearance and spread of ditches represent the selective adoption and sharing of a certain tomb attribute by different burying groups—an attribute that would have been visible in the landscape. Even as coastal and inland groups continued their mutually distinctive burial chamber construction methods, the ditch became a feature that reinforced a sense of shared culture.

Over time, the tomb itself became a focal or rallying point for identity and affiliation. What began as discrete burials changed over time to become shared ditch tombs, multiple burials within a single mound, and large-scale stratified barrows of many burials. Cemeteries themselves also became crowded and confusing. This is particularly pronounced in Yŏngsan, where the jar burial barrow tomb tradition produced large tombs containing many burials in distinctive clusters, such as those seen in the Pannam region. The various regional styles of barrow and mounded tombs in western Korea seem to have developed a symbiotic relationship with their local burying groups. The shared barrow burial tradition encouraged communities to maintain and revisit the same burial places for generations, and the tombs themselves became larger and more prominent as more burials were added over time. It is no surprise that in this context, distinctive regional traditions like those of the Yŏngsan persisted even as the geopolitical balance of the peninsula began to shift in the Three Kingdoms period.

Mortuary archaeology in western Korea therefore does not represent the sudden appearance and continuation of a distinct culture. Instead, funerary practices show how a culturally heterogeneous region gradually came to establish region-wide similarities in ritual behavior. The tombs themselves were equal participants in this process, with the unique features of barrow tombs encouraging the adoption of multiple-burial practices and the association of communities with distinctive monuments in the landscape.

Conclusions

Study of the mortuary archaeology of Korea's southwest has been preoccupied with finding a material culture correlate for Mahan—a discrete historical entity from Chinese sources of the third century, an entity subsequently laden with centuries of political baggage. This leads to friction among the three Mahan concepts circulating in ancient historical research: the historical Mahan of Chinese texts, historiographical Mahan in peninsular dynastic genealogies, and the so-called Mahan material culture of the Korean southwest. The above exercise suggests that, at least in the case of the mortuary record, attempts to find the archaeological expression of this unique culture would be difficult even if there were clear and consistent patterns among the many tomb forms of the region.

Despite this, the mortuary archaeology of western Korea at this time does point to a unique trajectory of sociopolitical development among peninsular groups, and the diverse array of barrow and mounded tombs constitutes an interesting archaeological phenomenon in its own right. To that end, I offer as a compromise a composite definition of Mahan that incorporates all connotations of the term: Mahan is the intersection of similarities in material culture built up and reinforced over several generations and the imposition of a cultural coherence by outside observers that later took root in Korean historiography. Like Chen Shou and other historians, contemporary researchers are just as complicit in the construction of Mahan through our desire to find cultural coherence within the noise of various distinct but intermingling material culture traditions.

Mortuary material is of course only one small aspect of the archaeological assemblage of western Korea, even if it has taken on an outsized importance within Iron Age research. The diversity of tombs can be usefully compared to other aspects of the archaeology of western Korea, such as the spread of iron metallurgy and distinctive stoneware ceramics, new developments in how craft production was organized, highly localized dwelling construction techniques, and sericulture. Ultimately, however, Mahan is not a coherent set of material correlates. It is not a thing we can isolate archaeologically and study. Instead, Mahan is a process of becoming, a process that began in the third century BCE and continues to this day.

Acknowledgments

I would like to thank the organizers of the workshop that led to this paper. I especially thank Anke Hein and Bryan Miller for their insightful comments on my earlier drafts. I undertook much of the research for this project as a research fellow at the Academy of Korean Studies in Seongnam, South Korea. An earlier version of this paper was presented at the George Washington Institute for Korean Studies (GWIKS) Korean Humanities Workshop.

Notes

1. There is no universally agreed-upon definition or set of criteria necessary for state-level complexity in archaeology, and the applicability of this sociopolitical concept to Korea has been challenged by historians (No Chungguk 1989; Yi Hyŏnhye 1984). Nevertheless, the Iron Age (ca. 300 BCE to 300 CE), of which Mahan is a part, is usually characterized as a liminal period that saw the appearance of the historical kingdoms of Silla, Paekche, and the Kaya groups. These kingdoms, or *kuk* 國, have been equated with the states of Childe's urban revolution and processual archaeology (associating them with the institutionalization of kingship, urbanism, massive public works, and a complex bureaucracy facilitating the distribution of resources among specialized producers; Choi and Rhee 2001; Kim Chŏngbae 2006). Contact with China (Pai 2000; Yi Hyŏnhye 1984), peer–polity interaction (Barnes 2001; Yi and Kim 2011), internal changes in the bases of political authority (Yi Hŭijun 2011), and the political economy of prestige good production (Yi Sŏngju 2009) have all been suggested as models for how southern Korean states or *kuk* came into existence.

2. In modern Korean, the *han* of Samhan and Mahan (韓) has the same pronunciation as the *han* of the Hàn Dynasty of China (漢). To avoid confusion, the name Han (without diacritic marks) is used for Samhan and Mahan groups, while Hàn (with diacritics) is used for Hàn China.

3. See, for instance, discussion of Chinhan in Silla historiography in McBride (2020:535)

4. The Paekche Annals themselves present a dynastic origin story that connects the kingdom much more strongly to Koguryŏ and Puyŏ rather than Mahan (see Best 2006).

5. A full treatment of the complex usages of Samhan and Mahan in Japanese historiography is beyond the scope of this paper. The terms appear in arenas as diverse as government, law, and the arts throughout the premodern period. Even in early historical texts like the Nihon Shoki, the name Han, often in connection with Paekche, can be found as a designation for those of mixed heritage (Lee 2018) or foreign subjects of the Yamato realm (Kanagawa 2019).

References

An Sŭngju 安承周
1985 Paekche t'ogwang myo ŭi yŏn'gu 백제 토광묘의 연구 [A Study of Paekche Pit Tombs]. *Paekche munhwa* 백제문화 16:5–32.

Barnes, Gina L.
2001 *State Formation in Korea: Historical and Archaeological Perspectives*. Surrey: Curzon Press.

Best, Jonathan W.
2006 *A History of the Early Korean Kingdom of Paekche: Together with an Annotated Translation of the Paekche Annals of the Samguk Sagi*. Cambridge, MA: Harvard University Press.
2016 The Silla Annals' Anachronistic Reference to Queen Himiko, the Wa Ruler of Yamatai. *Seoul Journal of Korean Studies* 29(1):93–114.

Breuker, Remco E.
2005 The Three in One, the One in Three: The Koryo Three Han as a Pre-Modern Nation. *Journal of Inner and East Asian Studies* 2(2):144–67.
2010 *Establishing a Pluralist Society in Medieval Korea, 918–1170: History, Ideology, and Identity in the Koryŏ Dynasty*. Leiden: Brill.

Byington, Mark E.
2009 The Account of the Han in the Sanguozhi: An Annotated Translation. In *Early Korea: The Samhan Period in Korean History*, Vol. 2, edited by Mark E. Byington, pp. 25–52. Cambridge, MA: Early Korea Project, Korea Institute, Harvard University.

Chen Shou 陳壽
1959 *Sanguozhi* 三國志. Beijing: Zhonghua Shuju.

Cho Kayŏng 조가영
2015 Kyŏnggi chiyŏk Mahan pun'gu myo sahoe ŭi yŏn'gu sŏnggwa wa kwaje 경기지역 마한 분구묘 사회의 연구성과와 과제 [Results and Questions in Research on Kyŏnggi Region Barrow Tomb Society]. In *Mahan pun'gu myo pigyo kŏmt'o* 마한 분구묘 비교 검토 [Comparative Examinations of Mahan Barrow Tombs], edited by Kwŏn Iji, pp. 65–97. Seoul: Hagyŏn Munhwasa 學研文化社.

Ch'oe Mongnyong 崔夢龍
1986 Kogohakchŏk ch'ŭngmyŏn esŏ pon Mahan 고고학적 측면에서 본 마한 [Mahan as Seen through Archaeology]. *Mahan Paekche munhwa* 9:5–15.
1988 Pannam-myŏn kobun'gun ŭi ŭiŭi 반남면 고분군의 의의 [Meaning of Tombs in Pannam Township]. In *Naju Pannam-myŏn kobun'gun: chonghap chosa pogosŏ* 羅州 潘南 古墳群: 綜合調查報告書, edited by Kim Chaeung, pp. 197–206. Kwangju: Kungnip Kwangju Pangmulgwan.

Ch'oe Sŏngnak 崔盛洛
2007 Pun'gu myo ŭi insik e taehan kŏmt'o 분구묘의 인식에 대한 검토 [On the Concept of Barrow Tombs]. *Han'guk kogo hakpo* 韓國考古學報 62:114–32.
2018 *Yŏngsan'gang yuyŏk kodae sahoe ŭi hyŏngsŏng kwajŏng yŏn'gu* 영산강유역 고대사회의 형성과정 연구 [Study on the Formation Process of Yŏngsan River Region Ancient Society]. Seoul: Churyosŏng.

Ch'oe Sŏngnak 崔盛洛, Pak Ch'ŏlwŏn 박철원, and Ch'oe Misuk 최미숙
2001 *Hamp'yŏng Sunch'on yujŏk* 함평 순촌유적 [The Site of Hamp'yŏng Sunch'on]. Mokp'o: Mokp'o Taehakkyo Pangmulgwan 목포대학교 박물관.

Ch'oe Wankyu 최완규
2006 Han'guk pun'gu myo charyo chip 韓國 墳丘墓 資料集 [Collected Resources for Korean Barrow Tombs]. In Pun'gu myo—pun'gu sik kobun ŭi sin charyo wa Paekche 墳丘墓—墳丘式古墳의 新資料와 百濟. *Chŏn'guk yŏksahak taehoe kogohak pu palp'yo chip* 제49회 전국역사학대회 고고학부 발표자료집 49.

Ch'oe, Yong-ho
1980 An Outline History of Korean Historiography. *Korean Studies* 4(1):1–27.

Choi, Gwan
2015 The Imjin Waeran in Korean and Japanese Literature. In *The East Asian War, 1592–1598: International Relations, Violence, and Memory*, edited by James B. Lewis, pp. 340–56. London: Routledge.

Choi, Jongtaik
2008 The Development of the Pottery Technologies of the Korean Peninsula and Their Relationship to Neighboring Regions. In *Early Korea: Reconsidering Early Korean History through Archaeology*, Vol. 1, edited by Mark E. Byington, pp. 157–98. Cambridge, MA: Early Korea Project, Korea Institute, Harvard University.

Choi, Mong-lyong, and Song-Nai Rhee
2001 Korean Archaeology for the 21st Century: From Prehistory to State Formation. *Seoul Journal of Korean Studies* 14:116–48.

Chŏnnam University Museum (CNUM) 全南大學校博物館
2004 Hamp'yŏng Yedŏng-ni Man'gach'on kobun'gun 咸平 禮德里 萬家村古墳群 [The Tomb Cluster at Hamp'yŏng Yedŏng-ni Man'gach'on]. Kwangju: Chŏnnam Taehakkyo Pangmulgwan 全南大學校博物館.

Daehan Institute of Cultural Properties (DICP) 대한문화재연구원
2012 Muan Tŏkam kobun'gun 무안 덕암고분군 [The Cemetery at Muan Tŏkam]. Chŏnnam: Taehan Munhwaje Yŏn'guwŏn 대한문화재연구원.

Em, Henry H.
2004 Minjok as a Modern and Democratic Construct: Sin Ch'aeho's Historiography. In *Colonial Modernity in Korea*, edited by Gi-Wook Shin and Michael Robinson, pp. 336–61. Cambridge, MA: Harvard University Asia Center.

Erickson, Susan N., Yi Sŏng-mi, and Michael Nylan
2010 The Archaeology of the Outlying Lands. In *China's Early Empires: A Re-appraisal*, edited by Michael Nylan, 135–68. Cambridge: Cambridge University Press.

Falkenhausen, Lothar von
1993 On the Historiographical Orientation of Chinese Archaeology. *Antiquity* 67(257):839–49.
2006 *Chinese Society in the Age of Confucius*. Los Angeles: Cotsen Institute of Archaeology Press.

Fang Xuanling 房玄齡
1974 *Jinshu* 晉書. Beijing: Zhonghua Shuju.

Haboush, JaHyun Kim
2016 *The Great East Asian War and the Birth of the Korean Nation*. New York: Columbia University Press.

Hŏ China 허진아
2018 Hosŏ-Honam chiyŏk saju sik chugŏji tŭngjang kwajŏng kwa hwaksan paegyŏng 호서-호남 지역 사주식주거지 등장 과정과 확산 배경 [Appearance and Spread of Four-Pillar Dwellings in the Hosŏ and Honam Regions]. *Han'guk kogo hakpo* 韓國考古學報 108:8–49.

Honam Cultural Property Research Center (HCPRC) 호남문화재연구원
2006a *Changhŭng Sangbangch'on B yujŏk* 長興 上芳村B遺跡 [The Site of Changhŭng Sangbanch'on B]. Chŏnju: Honam Munhwaje Yŏn'guwŏn 호남문화재연구원.
2006b *Kunsan Ch'uk-dong yujŏk* 群山 築洞遺跡 [The Site of Kunsan Ch'uk-dong]. Chŏnju: Honam Munhwaje Yŏn'guwŏn 호남문화재연구원.

Hwang Yonghon 黃龍渾
1974 *Yŏngam Naedong-ni onggwan myo chosa pogo* 靈岩 內洞里 甕棺墓 調査報告 [Report on the Survey of the Yŏngam Naedong-ni Jar Burials]. Seoul: Kyŏnghŭi Taehakkyo Pangmulgwan.

Im Yŏngjin 임영진
1999 Naju chiyŏk Mahan munhwa ŭi palchŏn 羅州地域 馬韓文化의 發展 [Development of Naju Region Mahan Culture]. In *Pokam-ni kobun'gun* 伏岩里古墳群, edited by Im Yŏngjin, Cho Chinsŏn, and Sŏ Hyŏnju, pp. 295–305. Naju: Chŏnnam Taehakkyo Pangmulgwan.
2002 Yŏngsan'gang yuyŏk kwŏn ŭi pun'gu myo wa kŭ chŏn'gae 영산강유역권의 분구묘와 그 전개 [Yŏngsan River Region Barrow Tombs and Their Spread]. *Honam kogo hakpo* 湖南考古學報 2002(16):79–99.
2015 Mahan pun'gu myo ŭi chosa: yŏn'gu sŏnggwa wa kwaje 마한 분구묘의 조사 - 연구 성과와 과제 [Investigation of Mahan Barrow Tombs: Research Results and Issues]. In *Mahan pun'gu myo pigyo kŏmt'o* 마한 분구묘 비교 검토, edited by Kwŏn Iji, pp. 13–49. Mahan yŏn'guwŏn ch'ongsŏ 마한연구원 총서 1. Seoul: Hakyŏn Munhwasa 學研文化社.

Im Yŏngjin 임영진, ed.
2016 *Mahan pun'gu myo ŭi kiwŏn kwa paljŏn* 마한 분구묘의 기원과 발전 [Origin and Development of Mahan Barrow Tombs]. Mahan yŏn'guwŏn ch'ongsŏ 마한연구원 총서 2. Seoul: Hakyŏn Munhwasa 學研文化社.

Im Yŏngjin 임영진, Kim Kiok 김기옥, Cho Kayŏng 조가영, Chŏng Haejun 정해준, Sŏ Hyŏnju 서현주, Yi T'aekku 이택구, Pak Yŏngmin 박영민, O. Tongsŏn 오동선, and Han Okmin 한옥민
2015 *Mahan pun'gu myo pigyo kŏmt'o* 마한 분구묘 비교 검토 [Comparative Examinations of Mahan Barrow Tombs]. Seoul: Hakyŏn Munhwasa 學研文化社.

Jeonbuk National University Museum (JNUM) 전북대학교박물관
2010 *Wanju Sangun-ni I-II-III* 완주 상운리 I-II-III. Chŏnju: Chŏnbuk Taehakkyo Pangmulgwan 전북대학교박물관.

Ju Bo Don
2009 Problems Concerning the Basic Historical Documents Related to the Samhan. In *Early Korea: The Samhan Period in Korean History*, Vol. 2, edited by Mark E. Byington, pp. 95–122. Cambridge, MA: Early Korea Project, Korea Institute, Harvard University.

Kanagawa, Nadia
2019 Making the Realm, Transforming the People: Foreign Subjects in Seventh- through Ninth-Century Japan. PhD dissertation, Department of History, University of Southern California, Los Angeles.

KAS (Korean Archaeological Society) 한국고고학회
2006 Pun'gu myo-pun'gu sik kobun ŭi sin charyo wa Paekche 분구묘-분구식고분의 신자료와 백제 [New Data on Barrow Tombs, Barrow-Type Tumuli and Paekche]. *Chŏn'guk yŏksahak taehŏe kogo hakbu palp'yo charyo chip* 전국역사학대회 고고학부 발표자료집 49.

KAS (Korean Archaeological Society) 한국고고학회, ed.
2013 *Han'guk kogohak kangŭi* 한국고고학 강의 [Survey of Korean Archaeology]. 2nd ed. Seoul: Sahoe P'yŏngnon 사회평론.

Kim Chŏngbae 金貞培
2006 *Han'guk kodaesa immun I: Han'guk munhwa ŭi kiwŏn kwa kukka hyŏngsŏng* 한국고대사 입문 I: 한국 문화의 기원과 국가형성 [Introduction to Korean Ancient History I: The Origins of Korean Culture and State Formation]. Seoul: Sinsŏwŏn 신서원.

Kim Chongmun 김종문, Kim Kyujŏng 김규정, and Yang Yŏngjun 양영주
2007 *Koch'ang Namsan-ni yujŏk* 고창 남산리유적 [The Site of Koch'ang Namsan-ni]. Chŏnbuk: Chŏnbuk munhwaje yŏn'guwŏn 전북문화재연구원.

Kim Kiok 김기옥
2010 Kimp'o Unyang-dong yujŏk pun'gu myo 김포 운양동 유적 분구묘 [Barrow Tombs at the Site of Kimp'o Unyang-dong]. *Paekche hakpo* 百濟學報 4:139–48.
2015 Kyŏnggi chiyŏk Mahan pun'gu myo ŭi kujo wa ch'ult'o yumul 경기지역 마한 분구묘의 구조와 출토유물 [Mahan Barrow Tomb Structure and Grave Goods in the Kyŏnggi Region]. In *Mahan pun'gu myo pigyo kŏmt'o* 마한 분구묘 비교 검토, edited by Kwŏn Iji, pp. 51–63. Seoul: Hakyŏn Munhwasa.

Kim Kwŏnchung 金權中
2008 Ch'ŏngdonggi sidae chugu myo ŭi palsaeng kwa pyŏnch'ŏn 青銅器時代 周溝墓의 發生과 變遷 [Appearance and Evolution of Bronze Age Ditch Tombs]. *Han'guk ch'ŏngdonggi hakpo* 韓國青銅器學報 3:100–27.

Kim Nakchung 김낙중
2009 *Yŏngsan'gang yuyŏk kobun yŏn'gu* 영산강유역 고분 연구 [A Study on Yŏngsan River Region Tombs]. Seoul: Hakyŏn Munhwasa 學研文化社.
2011 Pun'gu myo wa onggwan pun 분구묘와 옹관분 [Barrow Tombs and Jar Tombs]. In *Tongasia ŭi kobun munhwa* 동아시아의 고분문화, edited by Chungang Munhwaje Yŏn'guwŏn 중앙문화재연구원, pp. 201–38. Seoul: Sŏgyŏng Munhwasa.

Kim Sŭngok 金承玉
2011 Chungsŏbu chiyŏk Mahan kye punmyo ŭi insik kwa sikongganjŏk chŏn'gae kwajŏng 중서부 지역 마한계 분묘의 인식과 시공간적 전개과정 [Understanding and Spatio-temporal Extent of Mahan-Type Tombs in the Central Western Region]. *Han'guk sanggo sahakpo* 韓國上古史學報 71: 85–116.

Kim Wŏnyong 金元龍
1973 *Han'guk kogohak kaesŏl* 韓國考古學概說 [Remarks on Korean Archaeology]. Seoul: Ilchisa 일지사.

Kim Yongsŏng 金龍星
2009 *Silla wangdo ŭi koch'ong kwa kŭ chubyŏn* 신라왕도의 고총과 그 주변 [The High Tombs of the Silla Royal Capital and Their Surroundings]. Seoul: Hakyŏn Munhwasa 學研文化社.
2015 *Silla kobun kogohak ŭi t'amsaek* 신라 고분고학의 탐색 [Exploring Silla Tomb Archaeology]. Kwach'ŏn-si: Chininjin 진인진.

Kwŏn Oyŏng 권오영
2015 Mahan punmyo ŭi ch'ulhyŏn kwajŏng kwa choyŏng chipdan 마한 분구묘의 출현과정과 조영집단 [Emergence Process and Building Group of Mahan Barrow Tombs]. *Paekche hakpo* 百濟學報 14:37–58.

Lee, Dennis Hyun-Seung
2014 Keyhole-Shaped Tombs and Unspoken Frontiers: Exploring the Borderlands of Early Korean-Japanese Relations in the 5th–6th Centuries. PhD dissertation, Department of Asian Languages and Cultures, University of California–Los Angeles.
2018 Keyhole-Shaped Tombs in the Yŏngsan River Basin: A Reflection of Paekche-Yamato Relations in the Late Fifth–Early Sixth Century. *Acta Koreana* 21(1):113–35.

McBride, Richard D.
2020 Making and Remaking Silla Origins. *Journal of the American Oriental Society* 140(3):531–47.

Mizoguchi, Koji
2014 The Centre of Their Life-World: The Archaeology of Experience at the Middle Yayoi Cemetery of Tateiwa-Hotta, Japan. *Antiquity* 88:836–50.

2017   *The Archaeology of Japan: From the Earliest Rice Farming Villages to the Rise of the State.* Cambridge: Cambridge University Press.

MPCRI (Mahan-Paekche Culture Research Institute) 마한·백제문화연구소

2012   *Koch'ang Pongdŏng-ni 1 hobun* 고창 봉덕리 1호분 [Tomb 1 at Koch'ang Pongdŏng-ni]. Iksan: Mahan·Paekche Munhwa Yŏn'guso 마한·백제문화연구소.

No Chungguk 盧重國

1989   Han'guk kodae ŭi ŭmnak ŭi kujo wa sŏnggyŏk-kukka hyŏngsŏng kwajŏng kwa kwallyŏn hayŏ 韓國古代의 邑落의 構造와 性格-國家形成過程과 관련하여 [The Structure and Character of Ancient Korean Townships Relating to the State Formation Process]. *Taegu sahak* 大丘史學 38:1–49.

No Taedon 盧泰敦

1982   Samhan e taehan insik ŭi pyŏnch'ŏn 三韓에 대한 認識의 變遷 [Changing Conceptions of the Samhan]. *Han'guksa yŏn'gu* 韓國史研究 38:129–56.

Pai, Hyung Il

2000   *Constructing "Korean" Origins: A Critical Review of Archaeology, Historiography, and Racial Myth in Korean State-Formation Theories.* Cambridge, MA: Harvard University Press.

Pak Ch'anho 박찬호

2019   Wŏnsamguk~Samguk sidae sŏ haean kwŏnyŏk tajang pun'gu myo yŏn'gu 원삼국~삼국시대 서해안 권역 다장분구묘 연구 [A Study of Multiple-Burial Practices in the Western Coastal Region from the Proto-Three Kingdoms to Three Kingdoms Periods]. Master's thesis, Department of Archaeology and Art History, Chungbuk National University 충북대학교, Ch'ŏngju.

Pak Chiyŏng 박지영

2017   Wŏnsamguk~Samguk sidae Mahan-Paekche kwŏnyŏk ch'wirak punp'o ŭi sigonggan chŏk pyŏnhwa—pangsasŏng t'anso yŏndae wa GIS rŭl iyong han sihŏm chŏk kŏmt'o 원삼국~삼국시대 마한·백제 권역 취락 분포의 시공간적 변화—방사성탄소연대와 GIS를 이용한 시험적 검토 [Spatial and Temporal Changes in the Distribution of Villages in Mahan-Paekche Territory in the Proto-Three Kingdoms and Three Kingdoms Periods: A Pilot Study Using Radiocarbon Dating and GIS]. *Han'guk kogo hakpo* 韓國考古學報 104:40–77.

Pak Sunbal 박순발

2000   *Chugumyo ŭi kiwŏn kwa chiyŏksŏng kŏmt'o: Chungsŏbu chiyŏk ŭl chungsim ŭro* 주구묘의 기원과 지역성 검토: 중서부지역을 중심으로 [Origin and Regional Characteristics of Ditch Tombs Focusing on the Central Western Region]. *Ch'ungch'ŏnghak kwa Ch'ungch'ŏng munhwa* 충청학과 충청문화 2.

Pak Yŏngmin 박영민

2015   Chŏnbuk chiyŏk Mahan pun'gu myo sahoe ŭi yŏn'gu sŏnggwa wa kwaje 전북지역 마한 분구묘 사회의 연구 성과와 과제 [Outcomes and Tasks in Studies of Chŏnbuk Region Mahan Barrow Tomb Societies]. In *Mahan pun'gu myo pigyo kŏmt'o* 마한 분구묘 비교 검토, edited by Kwŏn Iji, pp. 237–84. Mahan yŏn'guwŏn ch'ongsŏ 마한연구원 총서 1. Seoul: Hagyŏn Munhwasa 學研文化社.

Paekche Institute of Cultural Properties (PICP) 백제 문화재 연구원

2012   *Sŏsan Yech'ŏn-dong yujŏk* 서산 예천동 유적 [The Site of Sŏsan Yech'ŏn-dong]. Puyŏ: PICP.

Schmid, Andre

1997   Rediscovering Manchuria: Sin Ch'aeho and the Politics of Territorial History in Korea. *Journal of Asian Studies* 56(1):26–46.

2002   *Korea between Empires 1895–1919.* New York: Columbia University Press.

Shen Yue 沈約

2018   *Songshu* 宋書. Beijing: Zhonghua shuju.

Shultz, Edward J.

2004   An Introduction to the "Samguk Sagi." *Korean Studies* 28:1–13.

Sin Ch'aeho 申采浩

1995   *Sin Ch'ae-ho yŏksa nonsŏlchip: Toksa sillon oe 35-p'yŏn* 申采浩歷史論說集: 讀史新論외 35편 [Collected Works of Sin Ch'aeho]. Edited by Chŏng Haeryŏm 丁海廉. Hyŏnsil ch'ongsŏ 3. Seoul: Hyŏndae Sirhaksa.

Sŏng Nakchun 성낙준

1983   *Yŏngsan'gang yuyŏk ŭi onggwan myo yŏn'gu* 영산강유역의 옹관묘 연구 [A Study on Yŏngsan River Region Jar Burials]. Paekche Munhwa 백제문화 15.

Wonkwang University Mahan Paekche Culture Institute (WUMPCI) 원광대학교 마한·백제문화연구소

2000   *Iksan Yŏngdŭng-dong yujŏk* 益山永登洞遺跡 [The Site of Iksan Yŏngdŭng-dong]. Iksan: Wŏn'gwang Taehakkyo Mahan·Paekche Munhwa Yŏn'guso 원광대학교 마한·백제문화연구소.

Xu, Stella
2016   *Reconstructing Ancient Korean History: The Formation of Korean-ness in the Shadow of History*. Lanham, MD: Lexington Books.

Yi Hŭijun 李熙濬
2011   Hanbando nambu ch'ŏngdonggi~Wŏnsamguk sidae sujang ŭi kwŏllyŏk kiban kwa kŭ pyŏnch'ŏn 한반도 남부 청동기~원삼국시대 수장의 권력 기반과 그 변천 [The Basis of Leadership on the Korean Peninsula from the Bronze Age to the Proto-Three Kingdoms Period and Its Evolution]. *Yŏngnam kogohak* 嶺南考古學 58:35–77.

Yi Hyŏnhye 李賢惠
1984   *Samhan sahoe hyŏngsŏng kwajŏng yŏn'gu* 三韓社會形成過程研究 [A Study on the Formation Process of Samhan Society]. Seoul: Ilchogak 一潮閣.

Yi Misŏn 이미선
2011   Kŭmgang yuyŏk chugu myo ŭi chiyŏk chŏk t'ŭkjing—Ch'ungch'ŏng chiyŏk ŭl chungsim ŭro 금강유역 주구토광묘의 지역적 특징 - 충청지역을 중심으로 [Regional Characteristics of Kŭm River Region Pit Tombs with Ditches—Focusing on the Ch'ungch'ŏng Region]. In *Che 23 hoe Kŭmgang yuyŏk Mahan munhwa ŭi chiyŏksŏng Hosŏ kogohak hoe haksul taehoe palp'yo yoji* 제23호 금강유역 마한문화의 지역성 호서고고학회 학술대회 발표요지. Sejong t'ŭkbyŏl si: Hosŏ Kogo Hakhoe 호서고고학회.

Yi Namsŏk 李南奭
2011   Kyŏnggi Ch'ungch'ŏng chiyŏk pun'gu myo ŭi kŏmt'o 경기충청지역 분구묘의 검토 [Examination of Kyŏnggi-Ch'ungch'ŏng Region Barrow Tombs]. In *Pun'gu myo ŭi sinjip'yŏng* 분구묘의 신지평. Ch'ŏnju: Chŏnbuk Taehakkyo Kogomunhwa Inryu Hakkwa.

Yi Sŏngju 李盛周
2000   Pun'gumyo ŭi insik 분구묘의 인식 [Conceptualizing Barrow Tombs]. *Han'guk sanggo sahakpo* 韓國上古史學報 32:75–109.

2009   Chokchangmyo wa kuk ŭi sŏngnip 族長墓와 '國의' 成立 [Chiefly Tombs and the Establishment of "Kuk"]. Edited by Choi Mong-lyong. *Han'guksa yŏn'gu hwibo* 한국사연구휘보 147.

2014   Chŏjang chesa wa sŏngch'an chesa: mokkwakmyo ŭi t'ogi pujang ŭl t'onghae pon ŭmsikmul ponghŏn kwa kŭ ŭimi 貯藏祭祀와 盛饌祭祀: 목곽묘의 토기부장을 통해 본 음식물 봉헌과 그 의미 [Storage and Feasting Rituals: Food Offerings Seen from the Storage of Pottery in Coffin Tombs and Their Meaning]. *Yŏngnam kogohak* 嶺南考古學 70.

Yi Sŏngjun 李晟準 and Kim Suhwan 金秀桓
2011   Hanbando kodae sahoe ŭi sunjang munhwa 韓半島 古代社會의 殉葬文化 [Human Sacrificial Culture in Ancient Societies of the Korean Peninsula]. *Han'guk kogo hakpo* 韓國考古學報 81:109–38.

Yi T'aekku 이택구
2008   Hanbando chungsŏbu chiyŏk Mahan pun'gu myo 한반도 중서부지역 馬韓 墳丘墓 [Mahan Barrow Tombs in the Central Western Region of the Korean Peninsula]. *Han'guk kogo hakpo* 韓國考古學報 66:48–89.

2015   Chŏnbuk chiyŏk Mahan pun'gu myo ŭi kujo wa ch'ult'o yumul 전북지역 마한 분구묘의 구조와 출토유물 [Structure and Excavated Artifacts of Chŏnbuk Region Mahan Barrow Tombs]. In *Mahan pun'gu myo pigyŏ kŏmt'o* 마한 분구묘 비교 검토, edited by Kwŏn Iji, pp. 201–36. Seoul: Hagyŏn Munhwasa 學研文化社.

Chapter 5

State Regulations or Human Sentiment
The Disappearance of Funerary Figurines in Ninth Century Chang'an and Luoyang

Ye Wa

After almost three decades, Lothar von Falkenhausen's influential article "On the Historiographical Orientation of Chinese Archaeology" (Falkenhausen 1993) is still relevant for his sincere criticism of the methodological problems of Chinese archaeology. His argument that the "planning and execution of archaeology" is "entirely along historiographical lines" (847) points to a major hurdle the discipline still needs to overcome. Nevertheless, it is impractical to research archaeological materials from historical periods without consulting written documents, so the problem becomes how to preserve the advantage of the evidence that only archaeology can provide and avoid framing issues only in terms of "history in the narrow sense." The question, as von Falkenhausen pointed out, is how to ask and answer questions that are based on archaeological evidence and not on the surviving documentary record. This essay asks a simple and direct question: how do we explain the decline and eventual disappearance of Tang funerary figurines, a historical fact revealed by the archaeological excavation of Tang tombs.

Tombs are a major focus of field archaeology of the Tang Dynasty (618–906 CE) in China. Most Tang tombs were discovered in the course of infrastructure development and thus were excavated in rescue fashion (Shaanxisheng 2008, 2018; Shaanxisheng and Jiang 2015; Zhongguo 1966, 1980, 2001). As a result, archaeological reports are often brief, and in most cases they record only the discovery of individual tombs. The lack of information on the layout of burial grounds, information crucial to understanding lineage relationships and social networks (especially through marriage) of the deceased, has impeded inquiry into social aspects of the Tang. Although von Falkenhausen (2006:401) saw archaeology as having a distinct strength in revealing "historical reality," the reports we have from the Tang significantly limit what we can say about funerary institutions. With rich data on individual tombs but poor information on "social patterns" revealed by tomb relationships, there is little information on the relative positions of tombs from which we can study the social relations of the deceased.[1] Nonetheless, archaeology reports reveal two important facets of Tang burial practices: changes in tomb structure and changes in the use of unperishable funerary objects, including ceramic figurines. Particular to medieval Chinese mortuary material culture is the tomb epitaph, a written eulogy carved in stone and buried with the dead. Information provided by epitaphs includes the lineage and official positions of the deceased, core social values of medieval oligarchies, and principles on which "aristocratic" Tang society was based (Tackett 2014; Twitchett 1973). Consequently, the three types of archaeological remains (tomb structures, ceramic figurines, and epitaphs) have become the focus of research in Tang mortuary archaeology in recent decades.

The results of such research have established a neatly ordered, rank-oriented mortuary system (Cheng and Zheng 2012; Qi 2006; Su 1995). It is indisputable that the official rank of the deceased played a role in Tang mortuary practice, and it is clearly shown in the archaeological data, yet funeral practices were not determined solely by the deceased's official rank. Focusing exclusively on rank obscures other historical realities and, as von Falkenhausen warned, plays into the hands of historical texts that attempted to make official rank the primary if not sole criterion in mortuary regulations. Therefore a major challenge in the historical archaeology of China is how to critically employ two distinct sets of data: archaeological remains and historic texts.

This paper addresses a key archaeological question that arises from the use of these two data sources. Specifically, it asks why sets of tomb figurines, long a staple of mortuary practice and found in tombs since the Western Jin Dynasty (281–317 CE; Li 2009; Shaanxisheng 2018), should change and eventually disappear from tombs in the Late Tang period (mid-ninth century CE). Based on archaeological reports, we know that the sets of four types of funerary figurines discussed in this paper were systematically placed in tombs only during the Western Jin Dynasty or fourth century CE. It is important to distinguish the different types of figurines found in earlier tombs from the set of figurines discussed here. Although figurines were common in Chinese mortuary practice, without understanding the historic context of how they were used, we cannot determine their social function. The aim of this research is not to fact check archaeological data against written documents that specified the number of funerary figurines depending on the official rank of the deceased; nor does it seek to show that the Tang legal statutes fully describe and explain Tang mortuary practices. Previous studies of Tang tomb structures and funerary figurines have already done precisely this (Cheng and Zheng 2012; Duan 1984; Qi 2006; Su 1995). In this study, the textual data are read as essential information for understanding funerary rituals, a key element for reconstructing mourning behavior in the period under consideration and, consequently, helping to explain changes in the use of funerary figurines seen in archaeological finds.

The archaeological data under consideration here come from non-imperial Tang tombs excavated in the two capital areas, Luoyang 洛陽 and Chang'an 長安 (Figure 5.1). All had epitaphs indicating the burial date, except for one, for which the excavator gave a reasonably accurate date based on archaeological evidence (Yu 1956:69). As the political, cultural, and economic centers of the dynasty, these two densely populated urban centers unsurprisingly have produced the largest amount of archaeological materials we have for this period. Furthermore, because the public display of funeral figurines was a key feature of funerary processions, their use is best manifested in urban settings, where onlookers naturally were drawn to observe them (*THY* 38:692). The texts analyzed in this study are government regulations on mortuary rites, including Tang-period legal codes, statutes, official memorials, decrees, and accounts. The documents in question, especially the legal texts, were designed to reinforce the aristocratic social order and to "promote socially desired behavior" (Johnson 1995:217).

Funerary Figurines in Archaeological Context

The four categories of figurines found in Tang tombs can be traced back to the fourth century CE (Li 2009; Xu 1989). They include tomb guardians of mythical animals and heavenly kings (*Tianwang* 天王); honor guards of a large number of horses, camels, and musicians; male and female attendants of the deceased; and household objects as well as domestic animals (Figure 5.2). These clay figurines come in various sizes, either painted or glazed. The use of funerary figurines from the late sixth to the early late ninth century is demonstrated in the graphs below (Figures 5.3 and 5.4). A total of 260 tombs in the graphs were discovered and excavated archaeologically; all had tomb epitaphs containing information on burial dates. Three tombs in Figure 5.2 were built prior to the establishment of the Tang Dynasty; they are included here to show that Tang mortuary practices were a continuation of past behaviors and that the change of dynasty had little impact on mortuary behavior. Of the 189 Sui and Tang tombs found in Xi'an and the 71 Tang tombs in Luoyang, the trend in the use of funerary figurines is clear.[2] It reached its peak in the middle of the eight century. During that period (711–754 CE), 94% of the tombs in Xi'an and close to 79% in Luoyang contained figurines. However, as compared to the Sui and Early Tang periods (592–710 CE), considerable change had already taken place. First, the overall number of tombs containing all four categories of figurines dropped significantly, from about 42% to 12% in Xi'an and from 71% to 16% in Luoyang. Second, the types of entombed figurines changed. Tomb guardians, the fierce-looking mythical creatures of category I—often elaborately manufactured and usually found at the entrance of burial chambers—decreased from appearing at 71% of tombs in the Xi'an area to 31%, and decreased from 76% to 26% in Luoyang (Figure 5.2). The same trend happened to the category II figurines, the classic examples of cosmopolitan life in Chang'an and Luoyang: the lavishly dressed riders, musicians, and performers, on horses and camels, sometimes attended by exotic-looking grooms (Figure 5.5). This type of figurine declined from appearing at 79% of tombs in Xi'an to about 57% and from

State Regulations or Human Sentiment 83

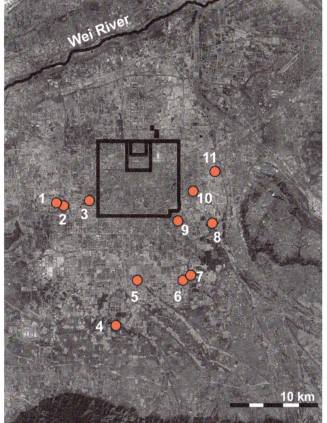

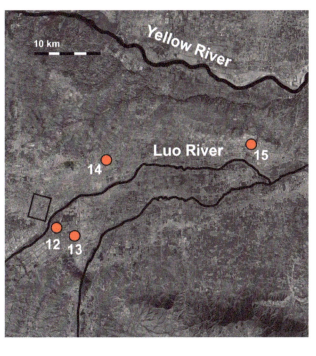

Figure 5.1. Map of site clusters mentioned in the text. A Group, Chang'an: 1. Xi'an West Power Station; 2. Jianjia; 3. Tumen; 4. Guodu; 5. Shangtapo; 6. Hanjiawan; 7. Dongzhaoyu; 8. Matengkong; 9. Qujiang; 10. Dengjiapo; 11. Guojiatan. B Group, Luoyang: 12. Luonan xinqu Tangmu; 13. Gualin; 14. Shilipu; 15. Yanshi Xingyuan.
Created by Bryan K. Miller.

84 Ye Wa

Figure 5.2. Category I tomb figurines: tomb guardians and heavenly kings (from Zhuge Fen's 諸葛芬 tomb, 687 CE).
Redrawn by the author after Xi'anshi 2015a.

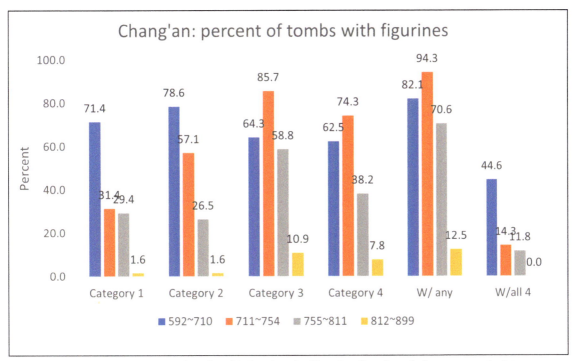

Figure 5.3. Percentage of tombs with figurines in Chang'an from late sixth century to the late ninth century. *Created by the author.*

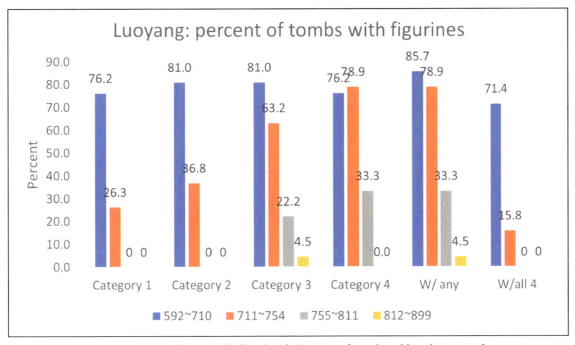

Figure 5.4. Percentage of tombs with figurines in Luoyang from the mid- to late seventh century to the late ninth century. *Created by the author.*

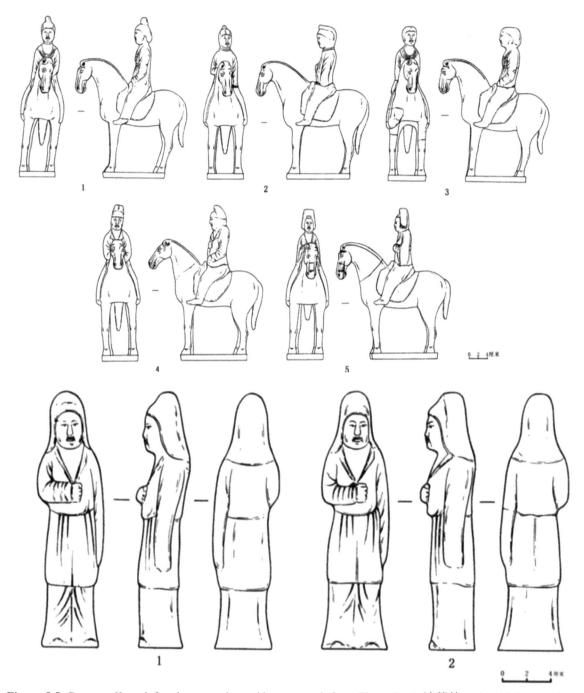

Figure 5.5. Category II tomb figurines: cavalry and honor guard (from Zhuge Fen's 諸葛芬 tomb, 687 CE). *Redrawn by the author after Xi'anshi 2015a.*

81% to 37% in Luoyang. At the same time, there was increased use of tomb attendant figurines (category III) in Xi'an and an increase in domestic animals (category IV) in both Xi'an and Luoyang; all figurines in these two categories were made with two-piece molds, requiring a relatively simple and straightforward technique compared to the figurines in categories I and II (Figures 5.5 and 5.6).

Figurine use decreased noticeably after 755, especially the second category of honor guards—only 27% of the Xi'an tombs had them, and none were in Luoyang.[3] The spectacular figurines in this category disappeared, replaced by a few unmounted horses or camels. Tomb guardians were further reduced: only a quarter of the tombs in the Xi'an area, and none in Luoyang, had guardians.

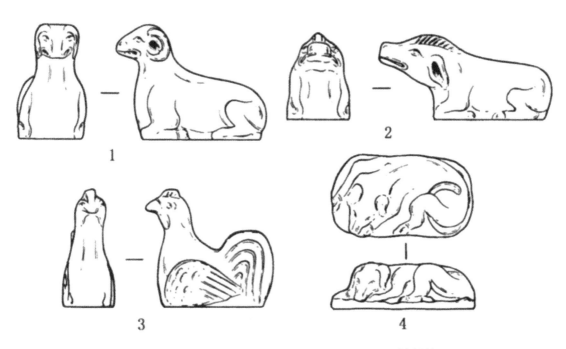

Figure 5.6. Category IV tomb figurines: animals (from Zhuge Fen's 諸葛芬 tomb, 687 CE).
Redrawn by the author after Xi'anshi 2015a.

The most popular figurines used in Xi'an and Luoyang, and also the longest lasting, were male and female attendants. They were always found in the burial chamber next to the coffin. After 755, a new type of small figurine bust started to appear in tombs; these had likely been dressed in perishable materials while in use. Household objects and domestic animals, always small in size and usually unpainted and unglazed, were found in all four periods in Xi'an but not in Luoyang.

The total number of figurines found in tombs also underwent changes. The database compiled for this study shows that prior to 711, about 18% of tombs in the Xi'an area contained more than 100 figurines. In the next period, the number of tombs containing more than 100 figurines increased to 21%, largely due to the use of category III and category IV figurines. The grave belonging to Feng Junheng 馮君衡 had 372 figurines.[4] Feng was the father of a powerful eunuch, Gao Lishi 高力士, under Emperor Xuanzong 玄宗 (r. 713–755; Shaanxisheng and Jiang 2015:686–90). In the next period (after 755 CE), only two tombs had more than 100 figurines—6% of the tombs in this period. Luoyang presents a similar result: prior to 711, 14% of tombs contained more than 100 figurines, with 17% in the following period. After 755, not a single tomb had more than 100 figurines.

It is indisputable that figurines in funerary processions during the Tang were a "medium for the competitive expression of status and status aspirations" (Cannon 1989:437), yet their disappearance from mortuary practice in the Late Tang was not entirely due to the fact that the practice lost its association with the higher classes when lower social classes increasingly adopted it (437). On the contrary, it is likely that the excessive display of figurines by high society triggered the government's suppression, since by Tang law the use of figurines was strictly regulated based on the deceased's official ranks (not inherited titles). The rich historic sources provide adequate information to address the question of the figures' disappearance.

Tang Mortuary Rites and the Historic Context of Funerary Figurines

Between 637 and 732, Tang emperors ordered scholars and officials to compile and revise the Tang rituals three times. The three ritual compendia, known as the *Zhenguan Rites* (貞觀禮, 637), the *Xianqing Rites* (顯慶禮, 658), and the *Kaiyuan Rites* (開元禮, 732), set the standards for rituals in various arenas of life in medieval China. No other rulers in Chinese history revised key dynastic rituals with such frequency. The surviving *Kaiyuan Rites* includes eight volumes on mortuary rites, detailing every step in the proper actions to take as the living dealt with death. The compilers explained the logic in the introduction of the *Kaiyuan Rites*:

記曰：「人生而靜，天之性也；感物而動，性之欲也。」欲無限極，禍亂生焉。聖人懼其邪放，於是作樂以和其性，制禮以檢其情，俾俯仰有容，周旋中矩 (*JTS* 21:815).

According to the *Books of Rites* [Record of Music]: "It belongs to the nature of man, as from Heaven, to be still at his birth. His activity shows itself as he is acted on by external things, and he develops the desires incident to his nature." Calamities and chaos will occur since desire has no limit. Because the sages feared the iniquitous release (of desire), they made music to harmonize man's nature, established rites to check man's emotions. As a result man's actions became correct, and their works followed the middle-way.[5]

Then the compilers gave their reasons for writing the funerary rites: "Filial piety and kindness will be manifest when mourning rites are established" (喪祭之禮立，則孝慈著; *JTS* 21:815).

Social order and filial piety, core Confucian values, were a key Tang concern in the newly specified rites. How were these intentions reflected in Tang mortuary practice? In other words, was the Tang government able to control some of the most important and widely practiced rituals in society? Did its subjects follow the regulations? How did Tang people manage the human emotions required by social morals while not overstepping the political boundaries that court regulations required? Does the disappearance of funerary figurines in the archaeological record have anything to do with the revision of the mortuary rites? Only by examining the function of the figurines in their historic context and their role in the court-issued regulations can we come up with a reasonable interpretation of the archaeological record.

Tang mortuary rites were compiled and approved by government authorities, based on existing ritual texts.[6] They contained complex rules for mourning. The *Kaiyuan Rites* (732 CE) describe the steps to be taken during a funeral. They start when death occurs (*chuzhong* 初終) and end with the ceremony for placing the deceased's spirit tablet in the family's memorial temple (*fumiao* 祔廟). There were 66 steps in all, and the whole procedure took "three years" (actually 25 months) to complete.

The Tang mortuary rites consisted of two major parts: procedures in private and in public settings.[7] Both parts left artifacts for archaeologists to study, although the remains are far from complete. My previous research on a Tang cemetery near Luoyang showed that artifacts associated with corpse preparation in private settings were subject to less change than those used in public settings—in this case the figurines (Ye 2005).

Above all, the purpose of the Tang mortuary rites was to exemplify the official ranking system in the public part of the funeral, to manifest the legitimacy of the Tang ruling class and political hierarchy in social settings. According to the Tang *Ordinance on Funerals and Burials* (*Sangzang ling* 喪葬令) and the rites, the deceased were grouped into four hierarchical classes based exclusively on official rank. If the deceased was female, the rituals were determined by her husband's rank. Although the use of official ranks as criteria in sumptuary regulations was not new to the Tang (*HHS* 6:3141–52), an instruction specifying the number of figurines based on the deceased's official rank was completely new in the Tang rites.

Except for personal belongings, all items used in funeral rituals in the public domain, including figurines, were based on the four status categories,[8] and the authorities certainly expected those performing the rituals to follow these rules. However, no matter how much the state wished that funeral rituals clearly express social distinctions, funerals were also an occasion for mourners to grieve publicly over their profound loss and especially to display their filial piety. Among the approved emotions were feelings of filial piety toward the older generation and benevolence toward one's siblings—both powerfully felt and socially approved sentiments. In fact, expressing one's remorse in a funeral was required by law. Not crying during the funeral contravened the sages' teachings and disregarded one's responsibility to correctly perform the rites (*THY* 38:699).

Patricia Ebrey (1991:32) has noted that "mourning austerities became the most widely used measure of filial piety." Officials were required to take two years of leave to mourn their parents. Cui Shanwei 崔善為, assistant director of the left in the Department of State Affairs (*Shangshusheng Zuocheng* 尚書省左丞), explained to the founding emperor Li Yuan 李淵 (r. 618–626) right after he took power in 619 that "mourning leave" for officials should be reestablished (*JTS* 1:1). He argued that "loyal officials can only be found among filial sons" (*THY* 38:688). To give positions to those who do not properly mourn their parents, he said, "will harm our customs" (*THY* 38:689).

The dual function of funeral rituals—to represent social and political distinctions and to display filial piety—were most apparent in public settings. In the *Kaiyuan Rites*, the ritual of corpse preparation treated the deceased as a corpse in its natural stage. Regardless of the political status of the deceased, everyone followed the same rituals of "soul calling" (*fu* 復), "washing" (*muyu* 沐浴), "dressing" (*xi* 襲),

"inserting grains and *han* in mouth" (*fanhan* 飯含),⁹ "the primary laying out" (*xiaolian* 小斂) "in which the corpse was prepared before being placed in the coffin," and "the final laying out" (*dalian* 大斂) or "placement in the coffin." Only during the funeral procession—in which a parade of carts, funeral paraphernalia, and mourners marched to the burial ground—did the deceased's social and political status became relevant in the funeral regulations. The funeral procession, which Gu Jiegang 顧頡剛 described as "the climax of the funeral" (Gu 1998 [1924]:429), was also an important moment for mourners to publicly display their devotion and filial piety to the deceased. Because of this dual function of the funeral rituals, it was extremely difficult for the state to enforce funeral regulations without violating human feelings. As we shall see, the Tang government specified both the quantity and quality of funerary goods, including figurines appropriate to the status of the deceased, and the mourners were supposed to adopt the same standards to express their grief and filial piety through those regulated objects. As a result of this conflict, funerary goods became both the center of mourners' attention in ritual ceremonies and a constant concern of the government edicts and regulations. More than anything else, the government wanted its people, especially the upper class, to obey the rules and follow the protocol in using such funerary items as figurines. In the end, the state appears to have prevailed. Under sustained pressure by the Tang government, funerary goods underwent rapid changes from the mid-eighth to the early ninth century (Cheng and Zheng 2012; Qi 2006; Xiao 2007), resulting in the disappearance of funerary figurines.

Excessive Funerals and Filial Piety

In the third month of the seventeenth year of the Zhenguan 貞觀 reign (643 CE), Emperor Taizong 太宗 (r. 627–649) issued an edict ordering his subjects to refrain from excessive funerals. It says:

雖送往之典，詳諸儀制，失禮之禁，著在刑書。而勳戚之家多流遁於習俗，閭閻之內或侈靡而傷風，以厚葬為奉終，以高墳為行孝，遂使衣衾棺槨，極雕刻之華，靈輴明器，窮金玉之飾。富者越法度以相尚，貧者破資產而不逮，徒傷教義，無益泉壤 (*ZGZY* 6:188).

Although the sending off rituals are specified in detail in [our] ritual regulations and the prohibition against violation of these rites is written in law, some honored and eminent families related by marriage have surrendered themselves to the common practice, and some commoners indulge in lavish spending and offended [good] customs. They send off their parents in excessive funerals and show their filial piety through grand tumuli. As a result, clothes and bedding, inner and outer coffins [for the deceased] are elaborately decorated; gold and jade are exhausted to make the decoration of hearses and *mingqi*. The rich exceed the regulations in competition for eminence, the poor bankrupt their families, and it is still not enough. This only harms our teachings and principles, and brings no benefit to the deceased.

This first recorded Tang edict on excessive funerals points out the reasons behind the practice: luxurious funerals and excessive spending were both a display of status and an expression of filial piety. The edict lists several funerary goods that the emperor considered to be the epitome of excessive spending. These included items commonly found in archaeological excavations: the funerary figurines and ceramic *mingqi*.

From the mourners' point of view, such funerary goods were a means of expressing feelings of filial piety for the deceased. When Yan Zhitui 顏之推 (531–597), a sixth century author, wrote his will, he told his sons not to use *mingqi* and other burial goods for his funeral (*YSJX* 20:601–2). Eighteenth century scholar Huang Shulin 黃叔琳 (1672–1756) explained that this was because Yan, in the chaotic political conditions of the time, "had been unable to give elaborate funerals to his parents and felt that his own funeral should not surpass those of his parents." Yan himself described his inability to offer proper funerals for his parents as "penetrating my heart and wounding my marrow" long after his parents' deaths. Huang sighed over the story, "How sorrowfully [this incident] touched the feelings of benevolent gentlemen and filial sons" (*YSJX* 20:597n1).

Dynastic histories also recorded many exemplary stories under the section "Biographies of Filial Persons and Loyal Friends" (*Xiaoyou* 孝友). Often, the stories described how filial sons overcame extreme difficulties to give their parents a proper burial. It is not unusual to read epitaphs that describe how people exhausted the family's possessions to have a splendid funeral (Kaiyuan 開元 083; Zhou and Zhao 1995:1211). This practice was often regarded as "being in accordance with the rites" and was praised by the community (Zhenyuan 貞元138; Zhou and Zhao 1995:1938–39).

In addition to the mourners' willingness to spend more on funerals to show their sincere feelings and moral obligations, society encouraged such behavior, and people formed organizations to help with one another's funerals. In 823 Li Deyu 李德裕, a surveillance commissioner of western Zhejiang (*Zhexi Guanchashi* 浙西觀察使), wrote a memorial describing the local custom of excessive funerals and the consequences:

閭里編甿，罕知報義。生無孝養可紀，歿以厚葬相矜。喪葬潛差，祭奠奢靡．．．或結社相資，或息利自辦。生業以之皆空，習以爲常，不敢自廢。人戶貧破，抑此之由 (*THY* 38:697).

Commoners and peasants rarely know how to repay [their parents'] kindness. Nothing they did left a record of filial piety when their parents were alive; but they boast of their excessive spending on their parents' funerals. These funerals and burials exceed the rank of the deceased, and they spend lavishly on the rituals. . . . Some form associations to support each other, some borrow money at interest so they can pay for the funerals themselves. Their means of subsistence are exhausted [but because] they are accustomed to it, they dare not abandon [the practice]. People and families are poor and bankrupt, all because of this.

In the eyes of the government, excessive funerals challenged the political hierarchy and corrupted the ranking system by overstepping protocol while exhausting people's resources. Even though we should be cautious in accepting written sources about the latter consequence, the cost of funerals was undeniably a burden for people (Ye 2005:appendix). As the result, suppressing extravagant funerals became a persistent concern of the Tang government.

The Funerary Goods Industry

Social pressure and customs are only part of the story of excessive funerals that broke the law. The funerary goods industry also contributed to the widespread practice. Bo Xingjian's 白行簡 (776–826) story of Li Wa 李娃 vividly recounts a competition between two rival funeral parlors (*xiongsi* 凶肆) in Chang'an, providing a firsthand look at the funeral goods industry and culture (*TPGJ* 484:3985–91). The story begins with two funeral shops competing to demonstrate which had the best funeral rentals. The competition took place along the Avenue of the Heavenly Gate (Tianmen jie 天門街), inside the capital's Imperial City. The two shops displayed their funeral equipment and goods (*xiongqi* 凶器) along each side of the grand central avenue. Chang'an residents, both gentlemen and ladies, came from every corner of the city, gathering by the tens of thousands on the day of the competition. Even the mayor was informed. From sunrise to midday, the crowd watched the spectacular and stunning funeral hearses and the majestic ritual paraphernalia from both shops, and they came to a decision that the eastern shop was superior. After learning the news, the western shop set up a stage for its singer. The singer had a long beard, carried a *duo* bell, and mounted the stage with a group of attendants. His powerful appearance and voice won a big roar from the crowd. Soon after this, the eastern shop set up its own stage facing the first. Its secret singer, a young scholar who had recently lost his lover, showed up with several funeral attendants holding *yi* (翣), the ritual placard. He started to sing the mourning song of Xielu 薤露. His voice was so clear and poignant that the nearby trees quivered. The crowd started to weep loudly even before he had finished. The western shop lost the competition, and the director of the western market disappeared so as to dodge the obligatory penalty of hosting a feast.

The story shows the highly competitive commercial nature of the Tang funeral business. Competitors had to come up with new products and ideas to appeal to the fickle tastes of the public. Indeed, funeral shops had existed in Chinese towns and cities long before the Tang Dynasty. Two Luoyang wards, named Cixiao 慈孝 (mercy and filial piety) and Fengzhong 奉終 (sending away), were engaged in the funeral business prior the mid-sixth century (*LYQLJ* 4:204).

The funeral business in medieval China included the sale of burial goods such as coffins and the rental of ritual paraphernalia. It was also a professional service, providing singers of funeral songs, coffin bearers, and paraphernalia bearers. Rentals included everything necessary for a funeral, including vehicles, signs, and carriers. People working in the commercial shops were paid for their services (*TPGJ* 484:3988).

Special kilns for making tomb figurines have been discovered near the Western Market (Xishi 西市) in Chang'an (Shaanxisheng 2008). Archaeologists have unearthed four pottery kilns and close to 10,000 fragments of figurine molds, tools, unglazed fragments, and tricolored figurines. Ceramic horses and human figures from the kilns are identical to those found in Tang tombs. The most important aspect of this excavation was the proximity of the kiln to the market and its exclusive focus on producing funerary goods.

The government had its own department to organize the supply of ceramic figurines for official funerals. Under the Directorate for Palace Buildings (*Jiangzuo jian* 匠作監), the Pottery Office (*Zhenguan shu* 甄官署) was in charge of manufacturing everything involving clay and stone, including funerary objects. The description of the Pottery Office's duties stated clearly that the office supplied *mingqi* to "those who are buried with special imperial orders, [but] the rest should prepare [these] on their own" (*DTLD* 23:18b). It also listed the number of *mingqi* each of the three official classes would have and the kinds of *mingqi* made by the court workshops:

三品以上九十事，五品以上七十事，九品以上四十事。當壙，當野，祖明，地軸，誕馬，偶人，其高各一尺。其餘音聲隊與僮僕之屬，威儀服玩，各視生之品秩所有，以瓦木為之，長率七寸 (*DTLD* 23:18b–19a).

Those of Ranks Three and above may have 90 pieces; those of Ranks Five and above [Ranks 4 and 5] may have 70 pieces; and those of Ranks Nine and above [Ranks 6 to 9] may have 40 pieces. [The *mingqi* they get are] *dangkuang* (Guardian of the pit), *dangye* (Guardian of the field), *zuming* (illuminator of the ancestor), *dizhou* (earth pivot), saddled horses, and human figures, each of them 1 *chi* tall.[10] The remaining [*mingqi*], representing musical bands, servants, paraphernalia, clothes, and adornments, depend on the deceased's rank while alive. They should be made of ceramic and wood, all 7 *cun* tall.

The court kilns not only produced *mingqi* following regulations; they also had to follow regulations in distributing products to members of the imperial family and officials according to rank. It is noteworthy that only those decedents with special funerary arrangements bestowed by the court could have *mingqi*, including figurines, from the imperial workshop; the rest had to prepare *mingqi* themselves. The commercial funerary shops were the sole suppliers for the rest of the population.

Tang Government Reactions and Policies Concerning *Houzang* (Excessive Funerals)

As mentioned above, from the beginning of the Tang, curtailing excessive funerals was on the mind of the government. In 643 Emperor Taizong issued an edict that declared excessive funerals as against "the teachings and principles" and that held offenders accountable to the law. The edict of said:

其公以下，爰及黎庶，送終之具有乖令式者，明加檢察，隨狀科罪。在京五品以上及勳戚之家，錄狀聞奏 (*ZGZY* 6:188).

[Officials] below the rank of minister and commoners who, [after] open inspection, [are found to have] used funerary items exceeding the regulations will have their case judged according to the law. Those above Rank 5 who work in the capital, and are members of honored and eminent families related to Us by marriage, will have their cases recorded and reported to the emperor.

In 681 Emperor Gaozong 高宗 (r. 649–683) issued an edict ordering Li Yixuan 李義玄—who at the time was chief executive of the Yongzhou prefecture (Yongzhou zhangshi 雍州長史), which included the capital Chang'an—to "arrest at whatever cost" those "merchants and rich people who exceed the rites by practicing excessive funerals" and "not to allow [excessive funerals] to happen anymore" (*JTS* 5:107). Punishment for those who violated the statue was 100 blows with a heavy stick (Johnson 1997:468; Liu 1996:118).

Rules and regulations for funerary equipment appeared in several documents issued by the Tang government, including the one mentioned above under the discussion of the Pottery Office. In addition to the number and size of the figurines and other *mingqi*, regulations on funerals also stipulated the size of grave plots, the height of tumuli, and aboveground features such as stelae and stone animals (*TD* 86:2351; *Kaiyuan Rites*, Volume 3, *TD* 108:2811–12). Although ritual texts put restrictions on certain articles used in corpse preparation (*TD* 138:3510–16), such regulations never appeared in imperial edicts, memorials, or supplementary regulations. Indeed, the state was almost entirely concerned with items used in public rituals—those that would have a visual impact and convey meaning in public. The *Tang Huiyao* (*THY* 38:691–98) and *Tang Da Zhaoling ji* (*TDZLJ* 80:418–19) preserve 23 records of similar regulations, dated from 623 to 841, showing the Tang government's persistent concern over the excessive use of funeral paraphernalia and objects for display in funeral processions. In 712, almost a century after the dynasty's founding, Tang Shao 唐紹, who had worked as chamberlain for ceremonials for years and was known as an expert on funeral rites, sent a memorial asking the emperor to reinforce the exiting mortuary regulations:

王公百官，竟為厚葬。偶人象馬，雕飾如生。徒以炫燿路人，本不因心致禮。更相扇動，破產傾資, 風俗流行, 下兼士庶。若無禁止, 奢侈日增。望請王公以下送葬明器, 皆依令式。 竝陳于墓, 不得衢路昇行 (*THY* 38:692).

Members of the imperial family and officials compete with each other in excessive funerals. [They make] figurines of humans and horse statues, carved and decorated as if they were alive. They do so only to dazzle onlookers, not because their minds are set on accomplishing the rites. They stir each other up, ruining their estates and losing their belongings. These fashions reach down to [ordinary] gentry and commoners. If we do not prohibit and stop it, the [longing] for extravagant and luxurious [funerals] will steadily increase. I hope that you will ask those [whose rank] is below the imperial family to follow the orders and codes on the use of *mingqi* for funerals. [They may] display [the *mingqi*] next to the tomb, but should not parade them on major streets.

The two crucial parts of Tang Shao's memorial are his condemnation of parading figurines during funeral processions and his asking officials of every position and rank (*baiguan* 百官) to follow regulations. To avoid public display of extravagance, his proposal was to stop the conspicuous figurine parade while permitting the use of figurines at the burial site in a more discreet way.

The Tang policy on mortuary practice remained basically unchanged until the mid-eighth century. After the early seventh century, the government had required families of the deceased to limit funerary spending. It concentrated its efforts on regulating the displayed items. In 716, four years after Tang Shao's famous memorial, the newly appointed palace attendant (*shizhong* 侍中), Song Jing 宋璟, and the vice minister of the secretariat (*zhongzhu shilang* 中書侍郎), Su Ting 蘇頲, presented a joint memorial urging the emperor to restrict official burials: "Frugality is the most revered virtue; extravagance is the greatest evil. In the past, virtuous men warned against tall tumuli and gentlemen opposed excessive burials." 儉, 德之恭; 侈, 惡之大。高墳乃昔賢所誡, 厚葬實君子所非 (*THY* 38:692–93).

These two powerful ministers strongly recommended that existing regulations be maintained and argued that it was improper to indulge human emotions:

情即無窮, 故為之制度. 不因人以動搖, 不變法以愛憎, 所謂金科玉條, 蓋以此也 (*THY* 38:693).

Human emotions are unlimited; that is why [we] make regulations to constrain them. [The regulations] should not waver because of the person, and the law should not be altered for love or hatred. This is what we call the gold standard and jade rule.

Nevertheless, despite repeated imperial injunctions, excessive spending on elaborate funerals never ceased. In 741, 25 years after the memorial of Song Jing and Su Ting, Emperor Xuanzong issued an edict instructing officials and commoners to follow ancient moral standards for frugal funerals. This edict ordered officials to reduce the number of *mingqi* used in funerals, the size of burial lots, and the height of tumuli (*THY* 38:693). Certain materials were banned from use in burial goods: "*Mingqi* . . . should be made from plain ceramics. They should not go so far as to use wood or [metals like] gold, silver, copper, and tin. [Figurine] clothing must not be so fancy like netted silk gauze, tabby weave silk, embroidery or painted fabrics" (*THY* 38:693).

The edict specifically mentioned an item not found on the earlier lists of regulations, the ritual platter, or *jipan* 祭盤. The ritual platter was allowed only if it was unornamented and was no larger than the size of a *yapan* 牙盤 (*THY* 38:693–94).[11] This item made of perishable materials gradually became the focus of the funeral procession, as described by Feng Yan 封演, an author who lived from mid-eighth to the early ninth century (*FSWJJJZ*:55–56).

One significant change in this edict is that for the first time the government allowed commoners—meaning those without official positions—to have figurines, as many as 15, in their graves (*THY* 38:693). It is difficult to judge whether this concession to commoners was sympathetic to their needs or merely legitimized current practice, for every account we have shows widespread violations of the ban on excessive funerals (*TDZLJ* 80:418–19; *THY* 38:691–98). To extend permission for the general population to use funerary figurines would certainly have relieved some of the cost of government enforcement. However, the cause for this change is less essential to our discussion than its influence on later government policies and the fate of funerary figurines. During the ninth century, edicts and memorials began to express more sympathy for the mourners.

Xuanzong's 741 edict can be considered a turning point in the fate of Tang funerary figurines, although it was not the final blow. By lifting the ban on commoners' use of figurines, the court deprived the elite and officials of their monopoly. Using the Xingyuan 杏园 Tang cemetery near Luoyang as an example, we find that the Middle Tang period (mid- to late eight century) had a slightly higher percentage (75%) of tombs containing figurines than the High Tang period (mid-seventh to mid-eighth century; 68%) but a much lower average number of figurines per tomb (12 vs. 20 in the High Tang). This trend indicates the wider accessibility and declining quality of figurines in the Middle Tang period, as they became common components of funerary assemblages (Zhongguo 2001).

In 808 the Chang'an mayor, Zheng Yuanxiu 鄭元修, who at the time was also imperial secretary of the Board of Punishment (*xingbu* 刑部), sent a memorial repeating old criticisms of excessive expenditures on funerals. He explicitly noted that "extravagant burials have long been common. Successive edicts and orders [to prohibit this practice] have been ineffective" (*THY* 38:695). Three years later, a new edict was issued on "regulations regarding funerals and burials of civil and military officials and commoners" (條流文武官及庶人喪葬). It repeated earlier regulations on funerals and burials but also made significant changes. These changes included restoring the numbers of permitted *mingqi* to numbers before the reduction ordered in 741 but adding restrictions on their size. Wood, previously banned as material for making grave figures, was now permitted, but the use of gold and silver, as well as feathers and fur, remained prohibited.

The most notable change in the 811 edict was that for the first time, instead of just requiring consumers to restrain their use of funeral goods, the government said that charges could be brought against those who made forbidden *mingqi*:

以前刑部尚書兼京兆尹鄭元修詳定品官葬給, 素有章程。歲月茲深, 名數差異, 使人知禁, 須重發明制, 庶可經久, 伏以喪葬條件, 明示所司。 如五作及工匠之徒, 捉搦之後, 自核准前後勅文科繩, 所司不得更之。喪孝之家, 妄有捉搦, 只坐工人。 亦不得句留, 令過時日 (*THY* 38: 696).

Previously, the imperial secretary of the Board of Punishments and the mayor of Chang'an, Zheng Yuanxiu, established detailed regulations for the offering of burial goods for ranked officials. There have always been articles and standards [for funerals and burials]. [But] over time, the names and numbers have changed. In order to let people know what is forbidden, we must again issue clear rules. Only in this way will they endure. The rules for funerals and burials should be set forth openly to those officials who are responsible. As for workers in the five government workshops (*wuzuo*) or craftsmen, after they are arrested, they must be charged based on the entire law, and no official may interfere in the matter. If any of the mourning and filial family [of the deceased] are seized by mistake, the workers alone must be held accountable. [The mourning and filial family members] may not be held, lest they miss the appointed time [for the funeral].

Never before had there been a threat of legal consequences for those who manufactured funerary goods. This decision was probably the result of many years of unsuccessful attempts to punish those who performed what the government considered extravagant funerals and burials. Punishing those who sold illegal numbers of funeral goods was perhaps the only effective measure the authorities could devise. The new regulations sympathized with mourners in allowing them to use more *mingqi* figures. This memorial was proclaimed by the powerful mayor of the capital, who was also the minister of punishment, whereas earlier memorials had originated in the Department of Ceremony, which had no power to charge offenders.

This policy change affected the archaeological record in a significant way. The database for this study shows that after 811, in the Chang'an area, only 14% of tombs contained figurines, with the largest number of figurines being eight. In Luoyang, only one out of 13 tombs (7%) had figurines. After 816, no Luoyang tombs contained figurines. After 850, there were none in Chang'an.

Making the regulations harsher, with criminal penalties on manufacturers, while easing the penalties on mourners, did not seem to stop extravagant funerals and burials. Thirty years later, in 841, the Censorate (*Yushitai* 御史臺) sent another memorial to the emperor complaining that "families of gentry and commoners rarely follow 'the funeral regulations.' Their excesses reach extremes, and their spending is great" (*THY* 38:698). The memorial testified to the difficulties in enforcing the law. To satisfy both the needs of families of the deceased and the policies of the government, the memorial made the following suggestion:

總以承前令式及制勅, 皆務從儉省, 減刻過多, 雖令人情易逾禁, 將求不犯, 實在稍寬。臣酌量舊儀, 創立新制, 所有高卑得體, 豐約合宜。 免令無知之人, 更懷不足之意 (*THY* 38:698).

In general, the previous rules, orders, and edicts all followed the principle of frugality. But the reductions ordered were excessive, so that human emotions naturally led people to exceed the limits. If we wish them not to transgress, we must be more lenient. We have deliberated on the old rituals and established new regulations so that superior and inferior obtain their proper places, and abundance and frugality are appropriately balanced. In this way, we will avoid causing the uneducated to feel unsatisfied.

To inform all people, the edict ordered that the new regulations be "announced and shown to all manufacturers and merchants," circulated in cities and markets, and posted on every city gate. It further ordered that "if there is a violation [of the new regulations], [authorities should] punish first the manufacturers and merchants for their crimes of selling [unlawful *mingqi*]" (*THY* 38:698).[12] The emperor approved the memorial.

This is the last surviving edict on mortuary practice issued before the fall of the Tang Dynasty in 907. It reveals that officials had recognized that the failure of government policy was caused by restrictions on human emotions (*renqing* 人情) that were too severe to be realistic. Such *renqing*, especially the devotion to filial piety, was directly related to a family's notion of a "proper" funeral. Throughout the Tang Dynasty, authorities struggled to control the mortuary practices of their subjects to maintain distinctions based on social status and the moral standard of frugality in funerals. They especially tried to stop extravagant funeral displays by restricting ritual goods used in processions. From Taizong's edict forbidding excessive funerals and burials in 641 to Tang Shao's suggestion to ban figurine parades in 712 to the later edict allowing commoners to use figurines and allowing officials more but smaller figures, from Song Jing's hard-hearted memorial to the Censorate's sympathy for the families of the deceased, the changes in policy were clear. Until the early ninth century, the government sought a middle ground between human emotions and stratified ritual propriety. The critical departure in Late Tang policy on mortuary practice was to punish the manufacturers and distributors. It is likely that such policies were one reason for the disappearance of large figurine assemblages that we see in the Middle/Late Tang tombs in both Chang'an and Luoyang.

Conclusion

Archaeological finds from Tang Dynasty tombs in Chang'an and Luoyang show that the peak period for the use of ceramic figurines was from the mid-seventh to the mid-eighth century, the High Tang (Qi 1990; Su 1995; Zhongguo 2001). Sometime in the mid-eighth century (730–740), the types of ceramic figurines in the capital region changed. Large tomb guardians and skillfully manufactured honor guards were replaced by small figures of attendants. In the early ninth century, traditional types of ceramic figurines disappeared almost completely, but zodiac animals and figurines with strong Daoist elements continued to appear in a few tombs.

Archaeologists have often explained the trajectory of ceramic figurine use as a reflection of the rise and decline of the Tang Dynasty, seeing the An Lushan rebellion (755–762) as a turning point and the beginning of the disappearance of *mingqi* figurines (Xie 1996; Zhongguo 2001). However, archaeological evidence does not fully support this statement. In fact, as discussed above, the archaeological record reveals that major changes occurred decades before the rebellion. The reduced use of the two most splendid Tang figurine types—the tomb guardians and the honor guards—surely lessened the impact of a funeral parade, which was the government's purpose in taming "extravagant funerals" and controlling activities in the public domain.

The changes in usage of figurines was likely the result of the Tang government's unrelenting effort to control mortuary practice and its intensified interference in funerary goods production. The government policies, written in the form of mortuary rites and regulations, had a fundamental flaw from the beginning. As Kutcher (1999) pointed out in his study of late imperial mourning practices, the conflict between filial piety to one's parents and obedience to the emperor—namely the state—was deeply imbedded in Confucian discourse, and this conflict was clearly exhibited in the dual functions of the funeral ritual. The strict policy of graded ritual ceremonies during the Early Tang was part of the government's overall design of mortuary rites. At the time, the newly established court needed to promote its own social status, since the founders of the Tang came from relatively humble family origins. They rewrote their own genealogy and promoted those who had followed them in the military conquest (Mao 1988:189–234; Twitchett 1973:47–86). The Early Tang funerary regulations, issued soon after the dynasty took power, were based strictly on official rank bestowed by the new government. The social differentiation to be conveyed by such rites was political in nature and origin. This policy denied access to grand funerals and burials to a significant portion of the elite (as well as commoners), which was the political objective, but it directly clashed with deep-rooted Confucian customs of filial piety. Once the beautiful figurines—symbols of privilege—became available on the market, it was difficult to control their use. A thriving industry and market provided the figurines found in all kinds of Tang tombs before the early eighth century, at least in the two capitals of the empire. Apparently, the government regulations were ineffective. However, the early disappearance of the most elaborate figurines—the tomb guardian figurines—was likely the result of the state's attention to those funeral procession figurines most closely associated with high official status.

When the Tang court and government finally came to acknowledge the human emotion of filial piety in funeral rituals, the first thing they did was to let commoners use figurines (the 741 edict). Following this were two more edicts, issued in the early and mid-ninth century, which allowed the use of more figurines. At the same time, the government placed increasing restrictions on the manufacturers, but it altered its basic conception of graduated rites based on social status. What we see among excavated figurines from the mid-eighth to early ninth century are basically small, simply decorated objects. It is hard to imagine that such figurines would "dazzle the onlookers" as in the funeral scene described by Tang Shao at the beginning of the eighth century. The previous glory and privilege associated with funerary figurines had already gone.

However, the disappearance of ceramic figurines, which is so dramatic in the archaeological record, does not mean that people abandoned all efforts at funeral display. Historical sources tell us that new types of funerary goods, made of paper and other perishable materials, began to appear in northern China sometime around the mid-eighth century, around the time the large tomb guardians disappeared. Feng Yan wrote that since the Xuanzong reign (712–755), people had been performing a road ritual (*daoji* 道祭) as a regular part of funerals. "Mourners set up ritual performance along the main road, erecting tent and curtains. The artificial flowers, fruit, figures, and animals made of dough . . . were thrown away as soon as the funeral hearse had passed," practices that "became more popular after the An Lushan rebellion" (*FSWJJJZ*:55–56). The use of new perishable materials had a major impact on the archaeological record: they did not survive. But these changes seen in the archaeological record may obscure important continuities in ritual practice.

Acknowledgments

I would like to thank Professor Lothar von Falkenhausen for his tireless support and guidance in my journey of searching through China's past, whether its medieval mortuary practice in densely populated urban areas or its Neolithic settlements dotting the banks of the Jing and Wei Rivers. Professor Elizabeth Carter pushed me to look at the archaeological evidence first in the initial research for this paper. Anke Hein's instructive suggestions were very helpful, and she and Bryan Miller provided useful input and criticism. Xiao Ye helped me with the data analysis. Michael Dalby proofread the paper and provided valuable comments.

Notes

1. Few archaeological reports on Tang tombs include maps of tomb layouts. One important exception is the report on the Tang tombs found in Yanshi of Henan (Zhongguo 2001). However, although the project excavated tombs from before and after the Tang period, the report discussed only the Tang tombs. This reflects the persistent practice of confining the attention of archaeological reports to a single dynastic period. This deprives readers of a wider perspective on the social significance of a cemetery—entombed members of a community whose lives were not limited to a single dynastic regime.

2. Tombs in these two charts represent only a small portion of the excavated tombs in Chang'an and Luoyang. A large number of tombs excavated in these areas contained no tomb epitaphs. Although archaeologists are able to establish the approximate date of the tombs, accurate dating is important to this study. Therefore I used only one tomb that had no epitaph, but the archaeologist was confident with the burial date he provided. References to the tombs are listed in the reference list.

3. The sample of Tang-period tombs from Luoyang is rather small, so we should treat the result with caution.

4. Feng died in 698 or 699, according to his epitaph. He was buried with his wife after she passed away in 729 (Zhang Boling 1995).

5. The translation of passages from the *Books of Rites* (Record of Music) are by Legge (1967). Other translations of quoted Chinese texts are done by the author, unless indicated otherwise.

6. The most comprehensive record of Tang rites is found in the *Tongdian* 通典 (Comprehensive Statutes of the Tang), compiled by Du You 杜佑 and completed in 801. The section entitled "Mortuary (or Inauspicious) Rites, History" (Xiongli凶禮, Yange沿革) comprises 27 volumes and includes 221 entries on mortuary practice from the Zhou through the Tang Dynasties (*TD* 79–105:2132–2760). It includes rules governing the wearing of mourning clothes, funerary procedures, the use of funerary objects, and rituals for mourning after the burial. It also includes the text of the *Da Tang Kaiyuan li* 大唐開元禮 (Rituals of the Kaiyuan Period of the Great Tang, or the *Kaiyuan Rites*), issued in

732, with eight volumes on mortuary rites (*TD* 134–40:3429–3586), which revised and combined the previous *Zhenguan Rites* and *Xianqing Rites.*

7 The special division is not only physically distinguished but also socially verified. Village funerals I have attended in both Henan and Shaanxi revealed this clearly (Ye 2005).

8 The four status categories were based on the nine official ranks. For example, the imperial order issued in 741 allowed Ranks 1 to 3 to have 70 figurines, Ranks 4 to 5 to have 40, and Ranks 6 to 9 to have 20. Those without official rank could have 15 figurines (*THY* 38:693).

9 A *han* might be either a bead made of precious stone or a coin.

10 One Tang *chi* equals 29.5 to 30 cm.

11 A *jipan*, according to Xuanzong's 741 edict, was a platter decorated with fake flowers and pavilions. It must have evolved into a more elaborated form. Feng Yan mentioned a *jipan* used in the funeral for Governor Xin Yunjing 辛雲京 (died 768) that was decorated with wooden figurines, depicting General Yuchi Jingde 尉遲敬德 fighting the Turks in battle, that looked like they were alive (*FSWJJJZ*:55–56).

12 "宣示一切供作行人，散榜城市及諸城門，令知所守。如有違犯，先罪供造行人賈售之罪."

References

DTLD see Li Longji
FSWJJJZ see Feng Yan
HHS see *Hou Han Shu*
JTS see *Jiu Tang Shu*
LYQLJ see Yang Xuanzhi
TD see *Tongdian*
TDZLJ see Song Minqiu
THY see *Tang Huiyao*
TPGJ see Li Fang
ZGZY see Wu Jing

310 Guodao Mengjin Kaogudui 310國道孟津考古隊
1993 Luoyang Mengjin Xishantou Tangmu fajue jianbao 洛陽孟津西山頭唐墓發掘報告 [A Brief Archaeological Report on the Excavation of a Tang Tomb in Xishantou, Mengjin, Luoyang]. *Huaxia kaogu* 華夏考古 1:52–68.

Cannon, Aubrey
1989 The Historical Dimension in Mortuary Expressions of Status and Sentiment. *Current Anthropology* 30(4):437–58.

Chen Anli 陳安利 and Ma Ji 馬驥
1988 Xi'an xijiao Tang Xichang xianling furen Shishi mu 西安西郊唐西昌縣令夫人史氏墓 [Tomb of Ms. Shi, Wife of Xichang County Magistrate, Tang Dynasty, in the Western Suburb of Xi'an]. *Kaogu yu wenwu* 考古與文物 3:37–40.

Cheng Yi 程義 and Zheng Hongli 鄭紅莉
2012 "Tang sangzangling" zhu mingqi tiao fuyuan de zai tantao "唐喪葬令" 諸明器條復原的再探討 [Further Discussion on the *Mingqi* Section Listed in the "Tang Mortuary Code"]. *Zhongyuan wenwu* 中原文物 5:79–86.

Cheng Zhaohui 程召輝
2020 Henan Luoyangshi Luolongqu Tang Wei? Fufu mu de fajue 河南洛陽市洛龙區唐卫?夫妇墓的發掘 [Excavation of Mr. and Mrs. Wei's Tomb in Luolong District, Luoyang, Henan]. *Kaogu* 考古 1:117–20.

Duan Pengqi 段鵬琦
1984 Tangdai muzang de fajue yu yanjiu 唐代墓葬的發現和研究 [The Excavation and Research of Tang Tombs]. In *Xin Zhongguo de kaogu faxian he yanjiu* 新中國的考古發現和研究 [Archaeological Excavations and Research in New China], edited by Zhongguo Shehui Kexueyuan Kaogu Yanjiusuo 中國社會科學院考古研究所, pp. 581–89. Beijing: Wenwu Chubanshe.

Ebrey, Patricia Buckley
1991 *Chu Hsi's "Family Rituals": A Twelfth-Century Chinese Manual for the Performance of Cappings, Weddings, Funerals, and Ancestral Rites*. Princeton, NJ: Princeton University Press.

Falkenhausen, Lothar von
1993 On the Historiographical Orientation of Chinese Archaeology. *Antiquity* 6(257):839–49.
2006 *Chinese Society in the Age of Confucius (1000–250 BC): The Archaeological Evidence*. Los Angeles: Cotsen Institute of Archaeology Press.

Feng Yan 封演
1958 [eighth–ninth century] *Fengshi wenjianji jiaozhu* 封氏聞見記校注 [Connotations on the Record of Hearing and Seeing of Mr. Feng]. Annotated by Zhao Zhenxin 趙真心. Shanghai: Shanghai Zhonghua Chubanshe.

Gu Jiegang 顧頡剛
1998 [1924] Liangge chubin de daozi zhang 兩個出殯的導子賬 [Two Lists of Funeral Processions].

In *Gu Jiegang Minsuxue lunji* 顧頡剛民俗學論集 [Collected Essays on Ethnographic Study by Gu Jiegang], pp. 428–38. Shanghai: Shanghai Wenyi Chubanshe.

Henansheng Gudaijianzhu Baohu Yanjiusuo 河南省古代建筑保護研究所 and Yanshishi Wenwu Guanliju 偃师市文物管理局
2009 Henan Yanshi sanzuo Tangmu fajue jianbao 河南偃師三座唐墓發掘簡報 [A Brief Archaeological Report on the Excavation of Three Tang Tombs in Yanshi, Henan]. *Zhongyuan wenwu* 中原文物 5:5–16.

Henansheng Wenhuajun Wenwu Gongzuodui Di'erdui 河南省文化局文物工作隊第二隊
1956 Luoyang 16 gongqu 76 hao Tangmu qingli jianbao 洛陽16工區76号唐墓清理简报 [A Brief Archaeological Report on the Excavation of No. 76 Tang Tomb in the Sixteenth Gongqu, Luoyang]. *Wenwu cankao ziliao* 文物參考資料 5:41–44.

Henansheng Wenwu Kaogu Yanjiusuo 河南省文物考古研究所 and Gongyishi Wenwu Baoguansuo 巩义市文物保管所
1996 Gongyishi Beiyaowan Han, Jin, Tang, Wudai muzang 巩义市北窑湾汉晋唐五代墓葬 [Tombs of the Han, Jin, Tang, and Five Dynasties in Beiyaowan of Gongyi City]. *Kaogu xuebao* 考古学报 3:361–97.

Hou Han Shu 后漢書 [History of the Eastern Han Dynasty]
1997 Beijing: Zhonghua shuju.

Hu Lingui 呼林貴, Hou Ningbin 侯寧彬, and Li Gong 李剛
1992 Xi'an Dongjiao Wei Meimei mu fajueji 西安東郊唐韦美美墓發掘记 [Excavation on a Tang-Period Tomb of Wei Meimei in the East Suburb of Xi'an]. *Kaogu yu wenwu* 考古與文物 5:58–63, 82.

Jiu Tang Shu 舊唐書 [Old History of the Tang Dynasty]
1997 Beijing: Zhonghua Shuju.

Johnson, Wallace
1995 Status and Liability for Punishment in the T'ang Code. *Chicago-Kent Law Review* 71(8):217–29.

Johnson, Wallace, trans.
1997 *The T'ang Code, Specific Articles*, Vol. 2. Princeton, NJ: Princeton University Press.

Kutcher, Norman
1999 *Mourning in Late Imperial China, Filial Piety and the State*. Cambridge: Cambridge University Press.

Legge, James, trans.
1967 *Li Chi: Book of Rites: An Encyclopedia of Ancient Ceremonial Usage, Religious Creed and Social Institutions*. New York: University Books.

Li Fang 李昉
1961 [925–996] *Taiping Guangji* 太平廣記 [Extensive Records of the Taiping Era]. Beijing: Zhonghua shuju.

Li Longji 李隆基
1991 [685–762] *Da Tang Liudian* 大唐六典 [The Six Statutes of the Tang]. Annotated by Li Linfu 李林甫 (683–753), Chikurō Hiroike 広池千九郎 (1866–1938), and Tomoo Uchida 内田智雄 (1905–1989). Xi'an: Sanqin Chubanshe.

Li Meitian 李梅田
2009 *Wei Jin Beichao muzang de kaoguxue yanjiu* 魏晉北朝墓葬的考古學研究 [Archaeological Studies on the Burials of the Wei, Jin, and Northern Dynasties]. Beijing: Shangwu Yinshuguan.

Li Yuzheng 李域铮
1985 Xi'an xijiao Tang Bishi Shinang mu qingli jianbao 西安西郊唐俾失十囊墓清理简报 [A Brief Archaeological Report on the Excavation of a Tang-Period Tomb of Bishi Shinang in the West Suburb of Xi'an]. *Wenbo* 文博 6:1–4.

Liu Junwen 劉俊文
1996 *Tang Lü shuyi qianjie* 唐律疏議箋解 [Annotations on the Tang Code]. Beijing: Zhonghua Shuju.

Luoyang Bowuguan 洛陽博物館
1980 Luoyang Guanlin Tangmu 洛陽关林唐墓 [Tang Tombs in Guanlin of Luoyang]. *Kaogu* 考古 4:379, 382–83.

Luoyang Di'er Wenwu Gongzuodui 洛陽第二文物工作隊 and Yanshixian Wenwu Guanli Weiyuanhui 偃師縣文物管理委員會
1991 Henan Yanshi Tang Liu Kai mu 河南偃师唐柳凯墓 [A Tang-Period Tomb of Liu Kai in Yanshi, Henan]. *Wenwu* 文物 1991:12:21–33.

Luoyang Xingshu Wenwuchu 洛陽行署文物处 and Yanshixian Wenguanhui 偃師縣文管會
1985 Yanshi Tang Li Yuanjing fufu mu fajue jianbao 偃师唐李元璥夫妇墓發掘簡報 [A Brief Archaeological Report on the Excavation of a Tang-Period Tomb of Mr. and Mrs. Li Yuanjing in Yanshi]. *Zhongyuan wenwu* 中原文物 1:19–22.

Luoyangshi Di'er Wenwu Gongzuodui 洛陽市第二文物工作隊

2005 Tang Cui Yuanlu fufu hezangmu 唐崔元略夫妇合葬墓 [Excavation of a Tang-Period Tomb of Mr. and Mrs. Cui Yuanlu]. *Wenwu* 2:52–61.

2007 Luoyang Tang Lu Zhaoji mu fajue jianbao 洛陽唐盧照已墓發掘簡報 [A Brief Archaeological Report on the Excavation of a Tang-Period Tomb of Mr. Lu Zhaoji]. *Wenwu* 文物 6:4–8.

Luoyangshi Wenwu Gongzuodui 洛陽市文物工作隊

1982 Luoyang Longmen Tang An Pu fufu mu 洛陽龙门唐安菩夫妇墓 [The Tomb of An Pu and His Wife in Luoyang Longmen, Tang Dynasty]. *Zhongyuan wenwu* 中原文物 3:14, 21–26.

2004 Luoyangshi Dongmingxiaoqu C5M1542 Tangmu 洛陽市東明小區C5M1542唐墓 [The Tang Tomb of C5M1542 in the Dongming Residential Compound of Luoyang City]. *Wenwu* 文物 7:55–66, 95.

2007 Henan Luoyangshi dongjiao shilipucun Tangmu 河南洛陽市東郊十里铺村唐墓 [A Tang Tomb in the Shilipu Village at the East Suburb of Luoyang, Henan Province]. *Kaogu* 考古 9:94–96.

2008a Luoyang Guanlinzhen Tangmu fajue baogao 洛陽关林镇唐墓發掘報告 [Excavation Report on the Tang Tombs in Guanlin Town, Luoyang]. *Kaogu xuebao* 考古學報 1:509–61.

2008b Luoyang Longmen Zhanggou Tangmu fajue jianbao 洛陽龙门张沟唐墓發掘簡報 [A Brief Archaeological Report on the Excavation of Tang Tombs in Zhanggou of Longmen, Luoyang]. *Wenwu* 文物 4:42–50.

Luoyangshi Wenwu Kaogu Yanjiuyuan 洛陽市文物考古研究院

2012 Luoyang Guanlin Tangdai Chen Hui mu faju jianbao 洛陽關林唐代陳暉墓發掘簡報 [A Brief Excavation Report on a Tang-Period Tomb of Chen Hui in Guanlin of Luoyang]. *Zhongyuan wenwu* 中原文物 6:4–8.

2013a Huangguan Zhang Chengsi mu fajue jianbao 宦官張承嗣墓發掘簡報 [A Brief Archaeological Report on the Excavation of the Tomb of Eunuch Zhang Chengsi]. *Luoyang kaogu* 洛陽考古 2:38–42.

2013b Tang Wu Youyi furen Lishi mu fajue jianbao 唐武攸宜夫人李氏墓發掘簡報 [A Brief Archaeological Report on the Excavation of a Tang-Period Tomb of Ms. Li, Wife of Wu Youyi]. *Luoyang kaogu* 洛陽考古 3:4–50.

2013c Tangdai Zhang Wenju mu fajue baogao 唐代張文俱墓發掘報告 [Report on the Excavation of a Tang-Period Tomb of Zhang Wenju]. *Zhongyuan wenwu* 中原文物 5:4–16.

2015 Luoyang Tangdai Daxi Xun fufu mu fajue jianbao 洛陽唐代達奚珣夫婦墓發掘簡報 [A Brief Archaeological Report on the Excavation of a Tang-Period Tomb of Mr. and Mrs. Daxi Xun in Luoyang]. *Luoyang kaogu* 洛陽考古 1:35–43.

2016 Luoyang Xinqu Tangmu C7M3138 fajue jianbao 洛陽新區唐墓C7M3138發掘簡報 [A Brief Archaeological Report on the Excavation of a Tang Tomb C7M3138 in the New District of Luoyang]. *Luoyang kaogu* 洛陽考古 4:28–34.

2018 Luoyang Tangdai Wang Xiongdan furen Weishi mu fajue jianbao 洛陽唐代王雄誕夫人魏氏墓發掘簡報 [A Brief Archaeological Report on the Excavation of a Tang-Period Tomb of Ms. Wei, Wife of Wang Xiongdan]. *Huaxia kaogu* 華夏考古 3:15–29.

Mao Hanguang 毛漢光

1988 *Zhongguo zhonggu shehuishi lun* 中國中古社會史論 [The Social History of Medieval China]. Taibei: Lianjing Chubanshi.

Qi Dongfang 齊東方

1990 Shilun Xi'an diqu Tangdai muzang de dengji zhidu 試論西安地區唐代墓葬的等級制度 [Discussion of Ranking System of Tang Tombs in Xi'an Area]. In *Jinian Beijing daxue kaogu zhuanye shanshi zhounian lunwenji* 紀念北京大學考古專業三十週年論文集 [Collected Papers in Commemoration of the Thirtieth Anniversary of the Department of Archaeology, Peking University], edited by Beijing Daxue Kaoguxi 北京大學考古系, pp. 286–308. Beijing: Wenwu Chubanshe.

2006 Tangdai de sangzang guannian xisu yu liyi zhidu 唐代的喪葬觀念習俗與禮儀制度 [A Study of the Tang Funeral Concept, Custom and Ritual Institution]. *Kaogu xuebao* 考古學報 1:59–82.

Sang Shaohua 桑紹華

1983 Xi'an nanjiao Sanyaocun faxian sizuo Tangmu 西安南郊三爻村发现四座唐墓 [Discovery of Four Tang-Period Tombs in Sanyao Village, Southern Suburb of Xi'an]. *Kaogu yu wenwu* 考古與文物 3:3–26.

1991 Xi'an Sanqiao cheliangchang gongdi faxian Tang Pei Liwu fufu mu 西安三橋車輛廠工地发现唐裴利物夫婦墓 [Discovery of the Tang-Period Tomb of Mr. and Mrs. Pei Liwu in the Construction Field of the Sanqiao Vehicle Factory, Xi'an]. *Kaogu yu wenwu* 考古與文物 6:25–31.

Shaanxi Kaoguzu Tangmu Gongzuozu 陝西考古組唐墓工作組
1960 Xi'an Dongjiao Tang Su Sixu mu qingli jianbao西安東郊唐蘇思勗墓清理簡報 [A Brief Archaeological Report on the Excavation a Tang-Period Tomb of Su Sixu in the Eastern Suburb of Xi'an]. *Kaogu* 考古 1:30–36, Plates 4–5.

Shaanxisheng Wenwu Baohu Yanjiuyuan 陝西省文物保護研究院 and Jiang Baolian 姜寶蓮
2015 *Ershishiji wushiniandai Shaanxi kaogu fajue ziliao zhengli yanjiu [shang, xia]* 二十世紀五十年代陝西考古發掘資料整理研究[上、下] [Compilation of the Archaeological Data Excavated in Shaanxi Province during the 1950s]. 2 vols. Xi'an: Shaanxi Xinhua Chuban Chuanmei Jituan, Sanqin Chubanshe.

Shaanxisheng Kaogu Yanjiusuo 陝西省考古研究所
1981 Xi'an Dongjiao sanzuo Tangmu qingliji西安東郊三座唐墓清理記 [Excavation Record of the Three Tang Tombs in the Eastern Suburb of Xi'an]. *Kaogu yu wenwu* 考古與文物 2:25–31.
2002 Tang Gao Lishi mu fajue jianbao唐高力士墓發掘簡報 [A Brief Archaeological Report on the Excavation of a Tang-Period Tomb of Gao Lishi]. *Kaogu yu wenwu* 考古與文物 6:21–32.

Shaanxisheng Kaogu Yanjiusuo peihe jijian kaogudui陝西省考古研究所配合基建考古隊
1990 Xi'an Jingshuicheng Tangmu qingli jianbao西安淨水廠唐墓清理簡報 [A Brief Archaeological Report on the Excavations of the Tang-Period Tombs at the Clean Water Factory in Xi'an]. *Kaogu yu wenwu* 考古與文物 6:59–65.

Shaanxisheng Kaogu Yanjiusuo 陝西省考古研究所 and Xi'anshi Wenwu Baohu Kaogusuo 西安市文物保護考古所
2003 Tang Chang'an nanjiao Wei Shenming mu qingli jianbao唐長安南郊韋慎名墓清理簡報 [A Brief Archaeological Report on the Tomb of Wei Shenming in the Southern Suburb of Tang Chang'an]. *Kaogu yu wenwu* 考古與文物 6:27–39, 43.
2005 Tang Sun Chengsi fufu mu fajue jianbao唐孫承嗣夫婦墓發掘簡報 [A Brief Archaeological Report on the Excavation of the Tang-Period Tomb of Mr. and Mrs. Sun Chengsi]. *Kaogu yu wenwu* 考古與文物 2:18–28.

Shaanxisheng Kaogu Yanjiuyuan 陝西省考古研究院
2006 Xi'anshi Nanjiao Matengkong Tangmu fajue jianbao 西安市南郊馬騰空唐墓發掘簡報 [A Brief Archaeological Report on the Excavation of the Tang-Period Tombs at Matengkong Village, in the Southern Suburb of Xi'an]. *Jianghan kaogu* 江漢考古 3:37–49.
2007 Tang Yin Zhongrong fufu mu fajue jianbao 唐殷仲容夫婦墓發掘簡報 [A Brief Archaeological Report on the Excavation of the Tang-Period Tomb of Mr. and Mrs. Yin Zongrong]. *Kaogu yu wenwu* 考古與文物 5:18–30.
2008 *Tang Chang'an Liquanfang Sancai Yaozhi* 唐長安醴泉坊三彩窯址 [The Tricolor Ceramic Kilns at the Liquan Ward in Chang'an of the Tang Dynasty]. Beijing: Wenwu Chubanshe.
2009 Tang Xue Yuanjia fufu mu fajue jianbao唐薛元嘏夫妇墓發掘簡報 [A Brief Archaeological Report on the Excavations of the Tang-Period Tombs of Mr. and Mrs. Xue Yuanjia]. *Kaogu yu wenwu* 考古與文物 6:3–10.
2011a Xi'an Chang'anqu wan Tang shiqi Linghu jiazu muzang fajue jianbao 西安市長安區晚唐时期令狐家族墓葬發掘簡報 [A Brief Archaeological Report on the Excavation of the Linghu Family Cemetery of the Late Tang in Chang'an District, Xi'an]. *Wenbo* 文博 5:15–22.
2011b Xi'anshi Chang'anqu Tang Qianfu sannian Tianshui Zhaoshi mu fajue jianbao西安市長安區唐乾符三年天水趙氏墓發掘簡報 [A Brief Archaeological Report on the Excavation of the Tang-Period Tomb of Ms. Zhao of Tianshui from the Third Year of the Qianfu Reign in Chang'an District, Xi'an]. *Sichuan wenwu* 四川文物 6:16–21.
2012 Xi'an Nanjiao Tang Zhenguan 17 nian Wang Lian fufu hezangmu fajue jianbao 西安南郊唐貞觀十七年王貞觀王憐夫婦合葬墓發掘簡報 [A Brief Archaeological Report on the Excavation of the Tang-Period Tomb of Mr. and Mrs. Wang Lian from the Seventeenth Year of the Zhenguan Reign, in the Southern Suburb of Xi'an]. *Wenbo* 文博 3:3–12.
2014 Tang Zhang Tai fufu mu fajue jianbao 唐張泰夫婦墓發掘簡報 [A Brief Archaeological Report on the Excavation of the Tang-Period Tomb of Mr. and Mrs. Zhang Tai]. *Wenbo* 文博 4:11–18.
2015 Tang Li Chui mu fajue jianbao唐李倕墓發掘簡報 [A Brief Archaeological Report on the

	Excavation of the Tang-Period Tomb of Li Chui]. *Kaogu yu wenwu* 考古與文物 6:3–22.
2016	Shaanxi Xi'an Tang Liu Zhi fufu mu fajue ianbao 陝西西安唐劉智夫婦墓發掘簡報 [A Brief Archaeological Report on the Excavation of the Tang-Period Tomb of Mr. and Mrs. Liu Zhi in Xi'an, Shaanxi]. *Kaogu yu wenwu* 考古與文物 3:18–31.
2017a	Shaanxi Xi'an Tang Liang Xingyi fufu mu fajue jianbao 陝西西安唐梁行儀夫婦墓發掘簡報 [A Brief Archaeological Report on the Excavation of the Tang-Period Tomb of Mr. and Mrs. Liang Xingyi in Xi'an, Shaanxi]. *Zhongyuan wenwu* 中原文物 2:9–23.
2017b	Shaanxi Xi'an Lifenghuizeyuan Tangmu fajue jianbao陝西西安立豐惠澤苑唐墓發掘簡報 [A Brief Archaeological Report on the Excavation of the Tang-Period Tombs at Lifenghuizeyuan in Xi'an, Shaanxi]. *Kaogu yu wenwu* 考古與文物 2:28–39.
2018	2008–2017 nian Shaanxi Sanguo, Sui, Tang, Song, Yuan, Ming, Qing kaogu zongshu 2008–2017年陝西三國隋唐宋元明清考古總述 [Review of the Archaeological Discoveries Dating from the Three Kingdoms to the Song-Yuan-Ming-Qing Periods in Shaanxi]. *Kaogu yu wenwu* 考古與文物 5:111–47.

Shaanxisheng Kaogu Yanjiuyuan 陝西省考古研究院, Shaanxisheng Lishi Bowuguan 陝西省歷史博物館, and Chang'anqu Lüyou Mizu Zongjiao Wenwuju 長安區旅游民族宗教文物局

2019	Shaanxi Xi'an Xiwei Tuyuhun gongzhu yu Ruru dajiangjun hezangmu fajue jianbao 陝西西安西魏吐谷渾公主與茹茹大將軍合葬墓發掘簡報 [A Preliminary Report on the Excavation of a Western Wei Period Joined Burial of a Tuyuhun Princess and a Ruru Grand General in Xi'an, Shaanxi]. *Kaogu yu wenwu* 考古與文物 4:36–60.

Shaanxisheng Kaogu Yanjiuyuan 陝西省考古研究院and Xibei Daxue Wenbo Xueyuan西北大學文博學院

2008	*Shaanxi Fengxiang Sui Tang mu* 陝西鳳翔隋唐墓1983–1990年田野考古發掘報告 [Tombs of the Sui and Tang Dynasties at Fengxiang of Shaanxi Province: The Excavation Report 1983–1990]. Beijing: Wenwu Chubanshe.

Shaanxisheng Kaogu Yanjiuyuan 陝西省考古研究院 and Xi'anshi Wenwu Baohu Kaogu Yanjiuyuan西安市文物保護考古研究院

2010	Xi'an Fengqiyuan Tang Guo Zhongwen mu fajue jianbao西安鳳栖原唐郭仲文墓發掘簡報 [A Brief Archaeological Report on the Excavation of a Tang-Period Tomb of Guo Zhongwen in Fengqiyuan, Xi'an]. *Wenwu* 文物 10:43–57.

Shaanxisheng Kaogu Yanjiuyuan Sui Tang Kaogu Yanjiubu 陝西省考古研究院隋唐考古研究部

2008	Shaanxi Sanguo Wei Jin Nanbeichao Sui Tang ji Song Yuan Ming Qing kaogu wushinian zongshu 陝西三國魏晉南北朝隋唐及宋元明清考古五十年綜述 [Summary of the Fifty Years of Archaeological Work of the Three Kingdoms, Wei, Jin, North and South Dynasties, Sui, Tang and Song, Yuan, Ming, Qing in Shaanxi]. *Kaogu yu wenwu* 考古與文物 6:161–97.

Shaanxisheng Wenwu Guanli Weiyuanhui 陝西省文物管理委員會

1958	Xi'an nanjiao Pangliucun de Tangmu 西安南郊龐留村的唐墓 [Tang Tombs Found in Pangliu Village, in the Southern Suburb of Xi'an]. *Wenwu cankao ziliao* 文物參考資料 10:40–43.

Song Minqiu 宋敏求

1992 [1070]	*Tang da zhaoling ji* 唐大詔令集 [The Edicts and Orders of the Tang]. Punctuated and proofread by Hong Pimo 洪丕謨, Zhang Boyuan 張伯元, and Shen Aoda 沈敖大. Shanghai: Xulin Chubanshe.

Su Bai 宿白

1995	Xi'an diqu de Tangmu xingzhi 西安的唐墓形制 [Types of Tang Tombs Discovered in Xi'an]. *Wenwu* 文物 12:41–50.

Tackett, Nicolas

2014	*The Destruction of the Medieval Chinese Aristocracy*. Cambridge, MA: Harvard University Asia Center.

Tang Huiyao 唐會要 [Social and Institutional Background of the Tang]

1998	Beijing: Zhonghua Shuju.

Tongdian 通典 [Comprehensive Regulations]

1988	Annotated by Wang Wenjin 王文錦et al. Beijing: Zhonghua Shuju.

Twitchett, Denis

1973	The Composition of the T'ang Ruling Class: New Evidence from Tunhuang. In *Perspectives on the T'ang*, edited by Arthur F. Wright and Denis Twitchett, pp. 47–86. New Haven, CT: Yale University Press.

Wu Jing 吳兢
[670–749] *Zhenguan zhengyao* 貞觀政要 [The Essentials of Governance from the Zhenguan Reign]. Shanghai: Shanghai Guji Chubanshe.

Xi'anshi Wenwu Baohu Kaogusuo 西安市文物保護考古所

2002a Tang Yao Wupi mu fajue jianbao 唐姚無陂墓發掘簡報 [A Brief Archaeological Report on the Excavation of the Tang-Period Tomb of Yao Wupi]. *Wenwu* 文物 12:72–81.

2002b Xi'an Dongjiao Tang Wen Chuo, Wen Sijian mu fajue jianbao 西安東郊唐溫綽、溫思暕墓發掘簡報 [A Brief Archaeological Report on the Excavation of the Tang-Period Tombs of Wen Chuo and Wen Sijian in the Eastern Suburb of Xi'an]. *Wenwu* 文物 12:37–49.

2004 Tang Kang Wentong mu fajue jianbao 唐康文通墓發掘簡報 [A Brief Archaeological Report on the Excavation of the Tang-Period Tomb of Kang Wentong]. *Wenwu* 文物 1:17–30, 61.

Xi'anshi Wenwu Baohu Kaogu Yanjiuyuan 西安市文物保護考古研究院

2012 Xi'an Tang Dianzhongshiyuyi Jiang Shaoqing ji furen Baoshou mu fajue jianbao 西安唐殿中侍御医蔣少卿及夫人寶手墓發掘簡報 [A Brief Archaeological Report on the Excavation of the Tang-Period Tombs of Jiang Shaoqing, the Imperial Physician-in-Attendance and His Wife, Ms. Baoshou, of the Tang Dynasty, in Xi'an]. *Wenwu* 文物 10:25–42.

2013a Xi'an Nanjiao Tangdai Zhang furen mu fajue jianbao 西安南郊唐代張夫人墓發掘簡報 [A Brief Archaeological Report on the Excavation of the Tang-Period Tomb of Ms. Zhang in the Southern Suburb of Xi'an]. Wenbo 文博 1:11–15, 17.

2013b Tangdai gu Jizhou sima Haojun furen Daxi Lingwan mu fajue baogao 唐代故濟州司馬郝君夫人達奚令婉墓發掘簡報 [A Brief Archaeological Report on the Excavation of the Tang-Period Tomb of Daxi Lingwan, Wife of Mr. Hao, Late Assistant Commander of Jizhou Region]. *Wenbo* 文博 4:11–17.

2013c Tang Guo Zhonggong ji furen Jintang zhanggongzhu mu fajue jianbao 唐郭仲恭及夫人金堂長公主墓發掘簡報 [A Brief Archaeological Report on the Excavation of the Tang Tomb of Mr. Guo Zhonggong and His Wife, the Elder Princess Jintang]. *Wenbo* 文博 2:13–18.

2014a Tang Taifu shaoqing Guo Qi fufu mu fajue jianbao 唐太府少卿郭鋊夫妇墓發掘簡報 [A Brief Archaeological Report on the Excavation of the Tomb of Mr. and Mrs. Guo Qi, Vice Minister of the Financial Department, Tang Dynasty]. *Wenbo* 文博 2014(2):10–15, 96.

2014b Xi'an Shangtapo Tang Wang fujun mu fajue jianbao 西安上塔坡唐王府君墓發掘簡報 [A Brief Archaeological Report on the Excavation of the Tang-Period Tomb of Mr. Wang, at Shangtapo Village in Xi'an]. *Wenbo* 文博 3:3–8.

2014c Xi'anshi Tang gu Xi zhizi Regui mu 西安市唐故奚質子熱瓌墓 [The Tang-Period Tomb of Prince Regui, a Hostage of the Xi Tribe, Found in Xi'an]. *Kaogu* 考古 10:29–42.

2014d Xi'an Majiagou Tang Taizhou sima Yan Shiwei fufu mu fajue jianbao 西安馬家沟唐太州司馬閻識微夫妇墓發掘簡報 [A Brief Archaeological Report on the Excavation of the Tang-Period Tomb of Mr. and Mrs. Yan Shiwei, Assistant Commander of Taizhou Region, at Majiagou Village of Xi'an]. *Wenwu* 文物 10:25–48.

2014e Tangdai gu Gaoyangjunjun Xushi furen mu fajue jianbao 唐代故高陽郡君許氏夫人墓發掘簡報 [A Brief Archaeological Report on the Excavation of the Tang-Period Tomb of Ms. Xu, Late Commandery Mistress of Gaoyang Prefecture]. *Wenbo* 文博 6:8–13.

2014f Zheng Qianyi fufu mu fajue jianbao 鄭乾意夫婦墓發掘簡報 [A Brief Archaeological Report on the Excavation of the Tomb of Mr. and Mrs. Zheng Qianyi]. *Wenbo* 文博 4:3–18.

2015a Xi'an Hangtiancheng liangzuo Tangdai bihuamu fajue jianbao 西安航天城兩座唐代壁画墓發掘簡報 [A Brief Archaeological Report on the Excavation of the Tang-Period Tomb Painted with Murals in Hangtiancheng, Xi'an]. *Wenbo* 文博 2:3–16.

2015b Tangdai Fujun furen Mishi mu qingli jianbao 唐代輔君夫人米氏墓清理簡報 [A Brief Archaeological Report on the Excavation of the Tang-Period Tomb of Ms. Mi, Wife of Mr. Fu]. *Wenbo* 文博 4:16–27.

2016a Tang Liangguo furen Wangshi mu fajue jianbao 唐涼國夫人王氏墓發掘簡報 [A Brief Archaeological Report on the Excavation of the Tang-Period Tomb of Ms. Wang, Mistress of the Liang Kingdom]. *Wenbo* 文博 6:3–10.

2016b Tangdai Du Jiang ji furen Zhaishi mu fajue jianbao 唐代杜江及夫人翟氏墓發掘簡報 [A Brief

Archaeological Report on the Excavation of the Tang-Period Tomb of Mr. Du and His Wife, Ms. Zhai]. *Wenbo* 文博 4:10–18.

2016c Xi'an Qujiang Moujiazhai Tangdai Yang Chou mu fajue jianbao 西安曲江繆家寨唐代杨籌墓發掘簡報 [A Brief Archaeological Report on the Excavation of the Tang-Period Tomb of Yang Chou, in Moujiazhai of Qujiang, Xi'an]. *Wenwu* 文物 7:15–22.

2018 Xi'an Tang gu Yanguo taifuren Lishi mu ji xiangguan wenti 西安唐故燕國太夫人李氏墓及相关问题 [The Tomb of Ms. Li, Late Grand Dowager of the Yan Kingdom of the Tang Dynasty in Xi'an and Related Issues]. *Zhongguo Guojia Bowuguan guankan* 中國國家博物館舘刊 2:6–18.

Xi'anshi Wenwu Guanlichu 西安市文物管理处

1991 Xi'an Xijiao Redianchang jijiangongdi Sui Tang mu qingli jianbao 西安西郊热电厂基建工地隋唐墓葬清理简报 [A Brief Archaeological Report on the Excavation of the Sui and Tang Tombs in the Construction Field of the Xi'an West Suburb Power Station]. *Kaogu yu wenwu* 考古與文物 4:50–95.

1991 Tang Dong Sengli mu qingli jianbao 唐董僧利墓清理簡報 [A Brief Archaeological Report on the Excavation of a Tang-Period Tomb of Dong Cengli]. *Kaogu yu wenwu* 考古與文物 4:96–105.

Xiao Xinqi 蕭新琦

2007 Shaanxi, Henan diqu chutu Tangsancai bijiao yanjiu 陕西，河南地区出土唐三彩比较研究 [A Comparative Study of Tang Sancai Earthen Wares in Shaanxi and Henan Provinces]. Master's thesis, Department of Archaeology and Museology, Jilin University, Changchun.

Xie Hujun 謝虎軍 and Liao Zizhong 廖子中

1996 Qianlun Luoyang chutu de Tangdai caihui taoyong 淺論洛陽出土的唐代彩繪陶俑 [A Preliminary Study of the Unearthed Painted Ceramic Figurines of the Tang Period from Luoyang]. In *Luoyang kaogu sishi nian—1992nian Luoyang kaogu xueshu yantaohui lunwenji* 洛陽考古四十年，1992年洛陽考古學術研討會論文集 [The Forty Years of Henan Archaeology: Collected Essays of the Conference on Luoyang Archaeology], edited by Ye Wansong 葉万松, pp. 343–51. Beijing: Kexue Chubanshe.

Xu Diankui 徐殿魁

1989 Luoyang diqu Sui Tang mu de fenqi 洛陽地區隋唐墓的分期 [The Periodization of the Sui and Tang Tombs in the Luoyang Area]. *Kaogu xuebao* 考古學報 3:275–304.

Yang Xuanzhi 楊衒之

1958 [?–555] *Luoyang Qielan ji* 洛陽伽藍記 [Records of the Luoyang Buddhist Temples]. Annotated by Fan Xiangyong 范祥雍. Shanghai: Shanghai Guji Chubanshe.

Yanshi Shangcheng Bowuguan 偃師商城博物館

1992 Henan Yanshixian sizuo Tangmu fajue jianbao 河南偃師縣四座唐墓發掘簡報 [A Brief Archaeological Report on the Excavation of the Four Tang-Period Tombs in Yanshi, Henan]. *Kaogu* 考古 11:1004–17.

1995 Henan Yanshi Tangmu fajue baogao 河南偃師唐墓發掘報告 [An Archaeological Report on the Excavation of the Tang Tombs in Yanshi, Henan]. *Huaxia kaogu* 華夏考古 1:14–31.

Yanshishi Wenwu Lüyouju 偃師市文物旅游局

2016 Luoyang Wei Xie fufu mu fajue jianbao 洛陽唐魏协夫妇墓發掘簡報 [A Brief Archaeological Report on the Excavation of a Tang-Period Tomb of Mr. and Mrs. Wei Xie]. *Luoyang kaogu* 洛陽考古 2:25–33.

Yanshixian Wenwu Guanli Weiyuanhui 偃师县文物管理委员會

1986 Henan Yanshixian Sui Tang mu fajue jianbao 河南偃師縣隋唐墓發掘簡報 [A Brief Archaeological Report on the Excavation of the Sui and Tang Tombs in Yanshi County]. *Kaogu* 考古 11:993–99.

Ye Wa

2005 Mortuary Practice in Medieval China: A Study of the Xingyuan Tang Cemetery. PhD dissertation, Department of Archaeology, University of California–Los Angeles.

Yu Weichao 俞偉超

1956 Xi'an Bailuyuan muzang fajuebaogao 西安白鹿原墓葬發掘報告 [An Archaeological Report of the Tomb Excavations in Bailuyuan, Xi'an]. *Kaogu xuebao* 考古學報 3:33–75, Plate 1–8.

Yun Anzhi 負安志 and Wang Yueli 王学理

1985 Tang Sima Rui mu qingli jianbao 唐司馬睿墓清理简报 [A Brief Archaeological Report on the Excavation of a Tang-Period Tomb of Sima Rui]. *Kaogu yu wenwu* 考古與文物 1:44–49.

Zhang Boling 張伯齡

1995 Tang Feng Junheng ji qi Maishi muzhi kaoshi 唐馮君衡暨妻麦氏墓誌考述 [Textural Study of the Epitaph of Feng Junheng and

His Wife Ms. Mai]. *Beilin jikan* 碑林集刊 1995:83–86.

Zhang Guozhu 張國柱 and Li Li 李力
1999   Xi'an faxian Tang sancai yaozhi 西安發現唐三彩窯址 [Kiln Remains of the Tang Tricolored Ceramics Found in Xi'an]. *Wenbo* 文博 3:49–57.

Zhang Quanmin 張全民 and Wang Zili 王自力
1992   Xi'an Dongjiao qingli de liangzuo Tangmu 西安東郊清理的兩座唐墓 [Excavation of the Two Tang Tombs in the Eastern Suburb of Xi'an]. *Kaogu yu wenwu* 考古與文物 5:51–57.

Zhang Xiaoli 張小丽 and Zhu Lianhua 朱连華
2015   Tang Taizong Minbu shangshu Dai Zhou fufu mu de xinfaxian 唐太宗民部尚书戴冑夫妇墓的新发现 [New Discovery of the Tomb of Mr. and Mrs. Dai Zhou, Minister of the Department of Civil Affairs Under Emperor Taizong]. *Wenwu tiandi* 文物天地 12:110–15.

Zhang Zhengling 張正嶺
1957   Xi'an Hansenzhai Tangmu qingliji 西安韓森寨唐墓清理記 [Excavation Record of a Tang Tomb at Hansenzhai in Xi'an]. *Kaogu tongxun* 考古通訊 5:57–62.

Zhengzhoushi Wenwu Kaogu Yanjiusuo 鄭州市文物考古研究所 and Gongyishi Wenwu Baohu Guanlisuo 鞏義市文物保護管理所
2005   Gongyi Changzhuang biandianzhan Dazhou shiqi muzang fajue jianbao 鞏義常莊變電站大周時期墓葬發掘簡報 [A Brief Archaeological Report on the Excavation of Tombs of the Wu Zetian Era at Changzhuang Substation in Gongyi]. *Zhongyuan wenwu* 中原文物 1:4–15.

Zhongguo Shehui Kexueyuan Kaogu Yanjiusuo 中國社會科學院考古研究所
1966   *Xi'an jiaoqu Sui Tang mu* 西安郊區隋唐墓 [Sui and Tang Tombs in the Xi'an Suburbs]. Beijing: Kexue Chubanshe.
1980   *Tang Chang'an chengjiao Sui Tang mu* 唐長安城郊隋唐墓 [Sui and Tang Tombs Adjacent to Tang Chang'an City]. Beijing: Wenwu Chubanshe.
2001   *Yanshi Xingyuan Tangmu* 偃師杏園唐墓 [The Tang Tombs in Yanshi Xingyuan]. Beijing: Wenwu Chubanshe.

Zhou Shaoliang 周紹良 and Zhao Chao 趙超
1992   *Tangdai muzhi huibian* 唐代墓志匯編 [A Collection of the Tang Epitaphs]. Shanghai: Shanghai Guji Chubanshe.

Part II

Ritual and Sacrifice

Chapter 6

No Sacrifice Too Great
A Measured Speculation on the Motive behind the Great Sanxingdui Hoards

Richard Ehrich

In 1986 two pits were discovered at Sanxingdui, Sichuan, filled with artifacts and artworks, many of them unlike any that had been seen before by archaeologists (Sichuansheng et al. 1987b, 1989). This discovery, possibly more than any other, fueled the flames of a major paradigmatic shift underway in Chinese archaeology at the time. Lothar von Falkenhausen (1996) famously described the new "regionalist paradigm," which included a focus on local developments in regions, such as Sichuan, that were traditionally not considered part of the cultural nexus where Chinese civilization had originated.

For the ancient proprietors of the Sanxingdui hoards (Figure 6.1), sending a shock through an academic discipline 3,200 years later was, with almost absolute certainty, unintended. This leaves us to determine why they left behind these wonderful things in the first place. The following is an attempt to come to grips with this question, which has been discussed many times by many scholars (e.g., Bagley 1988; Chen 1989; Falkenhausen 2002a, 2002b; Flad 2012; Li 1994; Sichuansheng 1999; Sun 1992, 2013; Xu 2001b; Xu Chaolong 1992; Zhao 1996, 2018). My goal is less to provide a definite answer than to improve the way we ask the question. Furthermore, I want to go beyond a general classification of the function of the hoards toward a search for the specific circumstance that incited this unusual course of action.

After I presented this paper at a workshop and symposium in Professor von Falkenhausen's honor in June 2019, he remarked that we should not rule out the possibility that apart from the two large hoards discovered in 1986 there could be more as yet undiscovered deposits out there. Six months later, in December 2019, came news that the Sanxingdui Team of the Sichuan Institute of Cultural Relics and Archaeology had indeed discovered a third large pit filled with artifacts (Tong and Cui 2019). Furthermore, in September 2020 the discovery of five more pits in the vicinity of the other three large pits was announced (Tong 2020). While I do not believe Professor von Falkenhausen would appreciate me praising the power of his premonition beyond that of any ancient court diviner, I would nevertheless use this example to illustrate his open-mindedness to possibilities unexplored and his ability to have exactly the right questions at hand when faced with any problem.

Missing Puzzle Pieces and Levels of Certainty

The discovery of the additional pits highlights one of the central concerns of this paper: how do we deal with information that we do not have? This situation mirrors that after the first two pits were revealed, when Robert Bagley remarked in the editor's preface to the catalog *Ancient Sichuan: Treasures from a Lost Civilization*, "Discoveries like Sanxingdui make us acutely aware that our statements about the past are always shaped by what has *not* been found (and by what our texts do *not* record). Do we now have all the pieces of a very peculiar puzzle? Or does

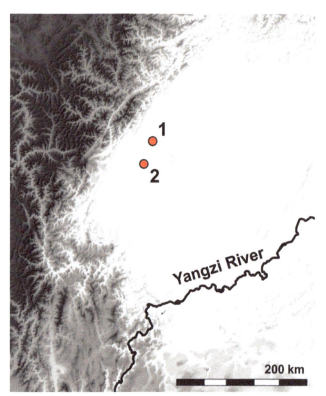

Figure 6.1. Map of sites mentioned in the text: 1. Sanxingdui; 2. Jinsha. *Created by Bryan K. Miller.*

the puzzle look peculiar because we are still missing large chunks?" (Bagley 2001:13; original emphasis). The discovery of the additional pits answers the first issue for us: we did not have all the pieces. Nor is it likely that we do now or that the puzzle will look any less peculiar once all the aspects of Pits 3–8 have been considered. Along with other empirical sciences, archaeology is in the challenging position that our datasets are always fragmentary. This effect is particularly severe with large-scale questions like "What motivated the deposition of the Great Sanxingdui Hoards?" Here there are so many missing puzzle pieces that we do not even know how large the puzzle is in the first place.

Given such an unclear foundation of evidence, the attempt to draw meaningful conclusions can be hazardous. Lars Fogelin (2007) observed that archaeologists, no matter what theoretical paradigm they subscribe to, generally tend to employ "inference to the best explanation" to form their hypotheses. Among the available explanations, the "best" is one that best accounts for a broad range of evidence while at the same time being as general, simple, modest, refutable, conservative, and able to address conflicting viewpoints as well as possible. However, as Fogelin (2007:606, 620) points out, even the best explanation might still not be very good. In his book *Thinking, Fast and Slow*, behavioral economist Daniel Kahneman (2011:85–88) describes the fallacy of "what you see is all there is"(WYSIATI), the tendency to jump to conclusions based on limited evidence. WYSIATI is an ever-present danger in archaeological reasoning and may blind us to the possibility that the best explanation might not have a lot of merit in many cases.

A possible way to address the pitfalls of WYSIATI lies in the concept of foils (Fogelin 2007:617). Foils are conflicting viewpoints that a good explanation should be able to address. In other words, they are doubts it is supposed to alleviate. However, the possibility of unseen evidence in archaeology constitutes a range of possible foils in and of itself, which explanations will find it harder and harder to address the broader they get. Thus any explanation, even if it is the best one possible given the known evidence, will lose in certainty the more encompassing it gets, since the chance it could be foiled by yet undetected evidence increases as well.

Different degrees of certainty exist on a spectrum, but for ease of reference, I propose three categories with fluid boundaries: *Initial observations*, such as "Pit 1 is 1.46 to 1.64m deep," carry the highest degree of certainty; there are very few foils that might be fielded against them. *Inferences*, such as "Pit 1 is a sacrificial hoard," are less certain, but if well supported they fill a vital role in the discussion. *Speculation*, such as "Pit 1 is the result of a sacrifice enacted by the theocratic rulers of Sanxingdui to reassert their power in the face of a crisis threatening their authority," contains very little certainty. For example, there are many possible ways in which the structure and contents of Pits 3 to 8, as soon as they are revealed, could contradict this explanation. Yet the answers to many questions that really matter to us fall in this realm. Hence I do not aim to invalidate speculation. Like the other parts of the spectrum, it is an essential part of the discourse. At the same time, its dangers need to be addressed.

Academic discourse ideally has a regulating function, which serves to weed out uncertainties without the need to qualify every statement. The regulating function is normally provided by other scholars pointing out issues of speculation or by a statement being revised after new evidence comes to light. However, while current academic discourse, which most of all encourages volume of publication, thrives on revisions, arguments, and counterarguments, one cannot help but notice that this is not the most efficient way to advance overall understanding. With the limited resources our field has, can we afford feuding at the expense of other causes much in need of attention?

All idealism aside, we have to be acutely aware of another danger—namely, the occasional tendency to put forth a statement that clearly has to be located in the speculative end of the spectrum and then use it as a foundation for a whole explanatory framework. Such shaky practice does not have to be confined to one scholar. Especially if the archaeologist putting forth the speculation has a certain authority in the field, the temptation for colleagues to take the statements for granted is undeniable.

As a proof of concept, an overview of the certainty levels of some main propositions made in this paper are provided at the end of it. In addition, there is a speculative narration of what might have happened at ancient Sanxingdui to warrant the deposition of the large hoards.

Terminology

I have been using the term *hoards* to denote Pits 1 and 2. I specifically write "Great Hoards" to distinguish them from other depositions at the site that are presented below. The exuberance of the term is intended to match the exuberance of the phenomenon. In Chinese they are commonly called *jìsìkēng* 祭祀坑. This term, which translates to "sacrificial pits," is used at the site museum and as the title of the main excavation report (Sichuansheng 1999). Of course, this term already interprets the intention and precludes alternative interpretations. A situation in which the term used to denote the subject matter of the discussion is by itself already on the inference side of the certainty spectrum should be avoided. The more neutral *qìwùkēng* 器物坑, which translates to "artifact pits," has been used in its stead, at times specifically to challenge the implication of sacrifice (Sun 2013). For the Chinese language side of the discussion, this may be a viable alternative as long as it is duly separated from settlement refuse pits, which after all tend to contain artifacts as well.

The term *hoard* denotes an archaeological feature category often employed in European archaeology (cf. Hein this volume). Its use here is not without problems. Hoards are commonly defined as deliberately laid depositions of artifacts or other remains of human activity, such as animal sacrifice (e.g., Eggert 2012:80). Hoards are also set apart from graves, which, although they would fit the above definition, constitute their own feature category due to their ubiquity in archaeology. The distinction exists only to make the typology more manageable, and it certainly has its gray areas, such as deposits outside the grave pit that formed part of the mortuary ritual or subsequent sacrifices to the deceased. Furthermore, even the distinction of hoards from settlement debris is sometimes blurry since the deliberate nature of the deposit has to be inferred. Is a forgotten stash of tools in an abandoned house a hoard? Another problem lies in the fact that the term *hoard* is often translated in Chinese as *jiàocáng* 窖藏, which implies the storage or secret stashing of artifacts but generally does not include sacrifice or other ritual as the main intention (Hein this volume).

Despite these reservations, using *hoard* here makes sense in that the features in question, Pit 1 and Pit 2, fit the broad definition provided above. Granted, this precludes the possibility that they could be graves, another premature assumption. Nevertheless, as shown below, the exclusion of the grave hypothesis is based on rather simple observations, such as the lack of human remains, and is hence not very contentious. Furthermore, with the use of terminology and definitions based in European archaeology, I hope to open up the discussion to concepts that have been applied to hoards in Europe. This usage is by no means prescriptive, of course. I find it useful in this particular text but will not insist on a Eurocentric renaming of the term in the larger discussion. I also use the terms *deposit* and *deposition* synonymously with *hoard*.

The Great Hoards in the Context of the Sanxingdui Site

In line with the epistemological framework just laid out, this discussion starts with the presentation of some basic observations concerning Pit 1 and Pit 2. As of the writing of this study, Pits 3–8 have not been excavated. Information revealed to the press indicates that at least the location, size, and orientation of Pit 3 are similar to those of Pits 1 and 2 (Wu 2020). But until the characteristics of the additional pits are fully revealed, they will have to remain "known unknowns."

A settlement at the Sanxingdui site was first established during the Late Neolithic period, in the early third millennium BCE (Sichuansheng et al. 1987a). After around 1600 BCE, the beginning of the Sanxingdui culture period, the settlement was surrounded by a large enclosure of rammed earth walls encircling an area of about 3km² (Figure 6.2). In addition, there was a structure identified as a palace in the northern part of the settlement, as well as a large platform consisting of rammed earth and, possibly rammed earth walls creating an internal division of the site.

After the end of the Sanxingdui culture period, around 1150 BCE, the site continues to show traces of occupation commonly assigned to the Shi'erqiao culture period. There is a debate as to whether these remains are so sparse as to indicate a decline of the settlement (e.g., Sun 1992, 2013) or whether they mark a continuation of the Sanxingdui culture occupation (Xu 2006).

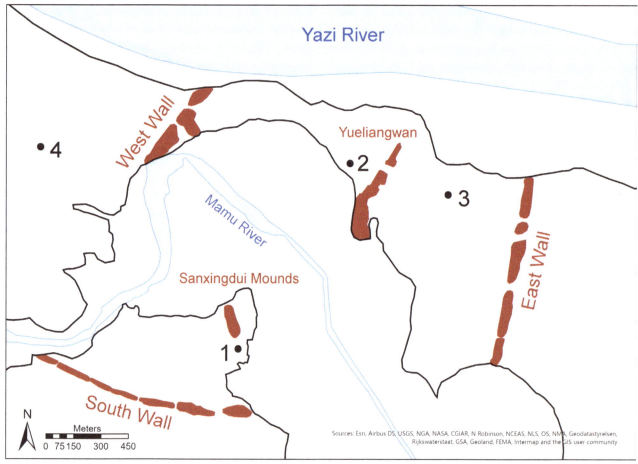

Figure 6.2. Map of the Sanxingdui site. 1. Pits 1–8; 2. Yueliangwan locus; 3. Cangbaobao pit; 4. Renshengcun cemetery. *Created by the author based on Flad 2012:308, Figure 15.2a; traced from satellite imagery in ArcGIS.*

Even in ancient times, the settlement area enclosed by the outer walls was bisected by a small river running through from west to east, the Mamu River, with a northward bend in the center of the site. South of the Mamu River, inside its bend and in a south-central location of the settlement, were three artificial mounds, of which one is preserved today. This is the Three Star Mound (Sānxīngduī 三星堆), after which the site is named. Pit 1 of the Great Hoards is located about 30m south of the Sanxingdui Mounds. Pit 2 is located another 30m southeast from Pit 1 (Sichuansheng 1999).

The creation of Pits 1 and 2 has been dated to around 1200 BCE (Sichuansheng 1999; Sun 2013). There are two ^{14}C dates from Pit 1 exhibiting a range between the twenty-first and the seventeenth centuries BCE, but these dates are deemed unreliable, since the sample material was charcoal and might be subject to the old wood effect (Sun 2013:15). Instead, the accepted absolute date is mainly derived from typological comparison of the bronze vessels in the hoards with bronze vessels from the Late Shang Dynasty of the Central Plains (Sun 2013:12–18). Important for the relative site chronology is the observation that ceramic sherds in the fill of Pit 1 date to the transition between the Sanxingdui culture period and the Shi'erqiao culture period (Sun 2013:16–17). The same goes for ceramics contained in occupation layers covering both pits. Altogether this means that in the common system of periodization at the Sanxingdui site, the deposition of the hoards appears to date to the very end of the Sanxingdui culture period.

The position of Sanxingdui among the cultures of Bronze Age China has been discussed in detail by Professor von Falkenhausen (2006). He demonstrated how both similarities with and divergences from other cultures are represented among the artifacts unearthed from Pits 1 and 2. The people of Sanxingdui, although having adopted or inherited many of the same styles, practices, and technologies as the people of the Shang culture in the Central Plains, appear to have taken their cultural expression on a different and unique trajectory (Falkenhausen 2006:232–33; Li 2018:304–7).

The Structure of the Pits and Their Relationship

In trying to determine the motive behind the depositions, a salient question is whether they were created at separate times or as part of the same action being conducted simultaneously at two different locations.

The main excavation report suggests that Pits 1 and 2 belong in the same general time frame but that Pit 1 dates earlier than Pit 2 (Sichuansheng 1999:427–31). The latter assertion is based on the ceramic content of the later occupation layers covering the pits. However, the applicability of this line of reasoning has been convincingly refuted both on typological and stratigraphical grounds by Sun Hua (2013:12). With the evidence at hand, it cannot be proven that one pit dates later than the other.

While the two depositions cannot currently be separated chronologically, the differences and commonalities among their structural aspects can be demonstrated in direct comparison (Table 6.1). In general terms, the two hoards are similar enough: large rectangular pits in a similar location and alignment filled with hundreds of artifacts in a certain sequence and then sealed with rammed earth, with many artifacts having been burned or broken. The overall idea behind the two depositions appears to be the same; they could be said to share a "hoard syntax" (Neumann 2012:14). Yet there are obvious differences in the particular ways the pits are laid out as well as in the makeup of their content. Pit 2 has a different shape than Pit 1 and lacks the tapering walls and the attached trench system that has been interpreted as access ramps (Sichuansheng 1999:19). Pit 2 also contained a lot more artifacts than Pit 1, but at the same time it did not feature the ash layers and animal bones found in Pit 1.

Thus, while the idea of depositing a hoard was the same in both cases, the execution was quite different. This can be taken as an argument for the hoards being buried at different times, unless we want to assume that we are dealing with different actors who competed in laying down the hoards at the same time but in different ways.

The fragmentation of the artifacts appears to be less a result of damage during their use and more a deliberate breaking. Similarly, the traces of burning appear to be from more than just an accidental fire; in a few instances, the heat was high enough to melt the bronze (Figure 6.3). It is not far-fetched to assume that the destruction of the artifacts was intentional and associated with their deposition.

Table 6.1. Structural comparison of Pit 1 and Pit 2

	Pit 1	Pit 2
Pit location	30 m S from Sanxingdui Mounds; S area inside enclosure	60 m SE from Sanxingdui Mounds; S area inside enclosure
Pit shape	rectangular	long rectangular
Pit alignment	NE–SW	NE–SW
Pit walls	slightly tapering	straight vertical
Access ramps	3	none
Area of pit bottom	4.01 x 2.80 m	5.00 x 2.00–2.10 m
Pit depth	1.46–1.64 m	1.40–1.68 m
Pit fill	rammed earth	rammed earth
Contents Layer 5	pottery vessels, larger jade artifacts	
Contents Layer 4	elephant tusks	
Contents Layer 3	ashes, bone residue	elephant tusks
Contents Layer 2	bronze heads, weapons	large bronzes
Contents Layer 1	small lithic artifacts	small bronzes, highly fragmented objects
Damage to objects	a lot of burned objects, some fragmentation	several burned objects, a lot of fragmentation
Suggested date	around 1200 BCE	around 1200 BCE

Note: Created by the author based on information from Sichuansheng 1999.

Figure 6.3. Bronze artifacts from Sanxingdui showing traces of burning and fragmentation. *Photos by the author.*

Other Hoards at Sanxingdui and Other Sites

The discovery of Pits 3–8 indicates that the burials of the two hoards in Pits 1 and 2 were not isolated cases. Even apart from Pits 1–8, there are several other features at Sanxingdui that could qualify as hoards, although their nature has been disputed. The first archaeological discovery at Sanxingdui, in 1929, was in fact a pit containing a large amount of stone and jade artifacts (Graham 1934). It was located at Yanjiayuanzi in the Yueliangwan area, in the center north of the settlement within the walled enclosure. The rectangular pit was about 2.3m long, 1m wide, and 1m deep. Its contents consisted of more than 400 jade artifacts, including dagger-axes, spearheads, *zhang* 章 scepters, *bi* 璧 disks, *cong* 琮 tubes, and large rings. Among these, 20 stone *bi* disks in groupings of different sizes were lined up alongside the walls of the pit.

Furthermore, in 2000 eight more pits were excavated at Yueliangwan (Zhao 2018:68). They included a rectangular pit with more than 100 complete small ceramic jars. In addition, there were shallow round pits containing fragments of jade artifacts, ceramic sherds, and pieces of burned clay. Other shallow pits contained ceramic vessels, whose mouths may have been sticking out of the ground. Apart from this, two pits containing what appears to be stone and jade raw material were discovered in the vicinity of Yueliangwan in 1964 and 1974, respectively (Sichuansheng 1999:15; Sun 2013:22).

In 1987 a pit was discovered at Cangbaobao, in the northeastern sector of the settlement, within the enclosure (Sichuansheng and Guanghan 1998). The pit was rectangular—2m long, 1m wide, and 0.4m deep. Apart from the large Sanxingdui hoards, it was the only pit at the site to contain bronze artifacts: three plaques. In addition, there were various jade implements and 21 stone *bi* disks, which were also arrayed according to size, similar to the situation in the Yanjiayuanzi pit. The pit also contained large amounts of ash and burned bones.

Sun Hua (2013:22–23) disputes the interpretation of any of the pits named above as "sacrificial pits." According to him, the pits at Yueliangwan containing stone and jade could have served as storage for raw material for the lithic industry. In addition, the Cangbaobao pit has the characteristics of a burial according to Sun (2013:23). He has to admit, however, that the ash and burned animal remains at Cangbaobao are reminiscent of Pit 1 (23). Furthermore, the similarities among the *bi* disk arrangements at Cangbaobao and Yanjiayuanzi are conspicuous. Combined with the absence of human remains and the unusual location of a burial outside any known cemetery, it seems appropriate to call the Cangbaobao feature a hoard. This interpretation can then be extended to the very similar Yanjiayuanzi pit and probably also to at least some of the other pits at Yueliangwan as well. The raw material storage hypothesis cannot be ruled out entirely for some of the pits, but it can hardly serve as an explanation for all of them.

Zhao Dianzeng (2018:68) goes one step further and includes among the possible "sacrificial pits" some pits at the Renshengcun cemetery that did not contain any discernible human remains as well as some pits within the settlement that contained large amounts of burned clay. The possibility that these features were the results of ritual activity certainly exists, but the evidence is insufficient to eliminate alternative explanations.

Outside of the Sanxingdui settlement, about 3km to the northwest, at Gaopian, another pit was discovered in 1976 (Ao 2006; Ao and Wang 1980; Zhao 2018:68). It was rectangular, about 1x 0.5m, and contained a bronze plaque similar to those in the Cangbaobao hoard, as well as jade knives, spearheads, and axes.

The hoards at Cangbaobao, Yanjiayuanzi, and Gaopian can be dated to within the Sanxingdui culture period but earlier than the large Sanxingdui hoards (Zhao 2018:69). Again we see some overlap in the preparation of the pits and the arrangement of artifacts, traces of a "hoard syntax." The custom to bury precious artifacts in a ritual context evidently existed already before the large hoards in Pit 1 and Pit 2 were deposited. However, the differences in scale are enormous. The creation of the large hoards does not follow naturally out of the already established depositional practice. Clearly, some exceptional circumstances must have led to the burying of the hoards in Pits 1 and 2. Nevertheless, on a conceptual level, certain elements in their creation recall practices already evident in the earlier hoards. It will be interesting to see how the hoards in Pits 3 to 8 fit into this picture.

The customs of hoard deposition did not stop after the large Sanxingdui hoards either. Most conspicuously, the Meiyuan Locus at the Jinsha site in Chengdu has yielded a large amount of buried bronzes, jades, gold artifacts, and elephant tusks similar to those in the Sanxingdui hoards (Chengdu 2004). Unlike Sanxingdui, to our current knowledge Jinsha does not feature extremely large hoards; instead there are several small deposits concentrated in a specific area of the site that has been termed a "sacrificial zone" (Flad 2012:315f.). It remains to be seen if Pits 1 and 2 at Sanxingdui, together with the six newly discovered hoards in close vicinity, constitute a "sacrificial zone" as well. The occupation of the Jinsha site begins at the end of the Sanxingdui culture period, around the time the Great Sanxingdui Hoards were deposited. It is not implausible that people moved from Sanxingdui to Jinsha around that time, bringing not only certain artifact styles with them but also traditions of hoard deposition.

The ritual deposition of artifacts in Bronze Age China was by no means limited to the Chengdu Plain. Other examples of this practice have been observed in southern Sichuan (Hein this volume), Hanzhong, the northeast, and the middle Yangzi River (Li 2018:300–303). The people of Sanxingdui were by no means alone in following this tradition, although the extreme to which they took it is outstanding.

The Argument for Sacrificial Pits

The proposition that Pits 1 and 2 are each the end product of a rite of sacrifice can be made with some certainty. This is the consensus among most scholars in the discussion (e.g., Bagley 1988; Chen 1989; Falkenhausen 2002a, 2002b; Li 1994; Sichuansheng 1999; Sichuansheng et al. 1987b, 1989; Wang 1996; Xu 2001a; Zhao 1996, 2018; but cf. Sun 2013). However, with the previously introduced certainty standards in mind, it is worth repeating how we get to this conclusion.

First of all, there is the principle of exclusion. All plausible foils to the sacrificial pit hypothesis can be rejected according to the evidence at hand, so that even the emergence of previously unknown evidence, say from Pits 3 to 8, is unlikely to undermine its probability. The deposition of both hoards is structured, deliberate, and made irreversible by sealing with rammed earth layers as well as the purposeful destruction of many artifacts in their inventory.

All these factors rule out an interpretation of either pit as a storage depot or a hastily created hiding spot of valuables in times of conflict. At the same time, the hoards do not make much sense as stashes of spoils created by a conquering party either. This hypothesis is contradicted by the irreversible nature of the deposition as well as the fact that even if, for instance, the ritual bronze artifacts were not much use for an outsider by themselves, they could have easily been melted down and recycled for instant material gain. This bounty depot hypothesis is not to be confused with the possibility brought up by Wang Yanfang (1996:106) of a conqueror celebrating victory by dedicating part of the spoils to divine sponsors. That would obviously qualify as a sacrifice. A further possibility could see invaders despoiling shrines or temples at Sanxingdui and, instead of stealing the contents, desecrating and burying them, due to a curse or taboo on the sanctified objects. This would still not explain the specific structure of the deposits (Xu 2001a:31n33) and is contradicted by some of the contents, such as the large amount of burned animal remains in Pit 1.

The possibility that Pits 1 and 2 are grave pits (Zhang 1989) is equally unlikely. First of all, there is the absence of any human remains. However, as demonstrated by the cemetery of the Sanxingdui site at Renshengcun (Sichuansheng 2004), the bone preservation is not good at all, so arguing from the absence of evidence here is dangerous and could be construed as an example of the WYSIATI fallacy. That being said, even allowing for the complete decay of human remains or the rare possibility of cremation burials (otherwise absent in the prehistory of Sichuan), the structure and layout of Pits 1 and 2 have no parallels among any other known burials. The lack of evidence in favor of the burial hypothesis justifies its elimination, but it does not rule out the pits being sacrificial pits related to the burial ceremony of some individual whose burial we have not found yet. As noted above, the line between mortuary features and sacrificial deposits can be blurry. However, burial or no burial, they would have to be sacrificial pits either way.

Unless there are other plausible alternatives yet to be proposed, the sacrificial pit hypothesis appears to be supported by the rejection of all foils. But what evidence positively speaks in its favor? In trying to argue against the sacrificial pit hypothesis, Sun Hua (2013:18f.) points out a major flaw that sometimes appears in arguments in favor of it (e.g., Sichuansheng 1999:440; Sichuansheng et al. 1989:19; Zhao 2018:70): just because a majority of the buried objects clearly had a ritual or religious function of some kind, that does not make the act of burying them a ritual or religious act. Sun is right. For the purpose of determining the intent behind their deposition, we have to look less at the nature of the objects themselves and more at the way they were treated in the context of the deposition.

First of all, there is the fact that the artifacts and animal remains were deposited in a specific order in both pits, forming distinct layers (Xu 2001a:31). There are no plausible practical reasons for this behavior. The most likely explanation would be the rules of a ritual performance. The logic behind these specific burial patterns might elude us forever, but their presence should suffice to indicate the presence of some sort of ritual enactment.

The excavators noted in the main report that while Pit 1 exhibited the layering of different artifact classes, the distribution of objects within each layer appeared haphazard (Sichuansheng 1999:19). They were not laid out in an orderly fashion as was the case, for example, in many of the hoards of bronze vessels throughout China. The fact that most objects were clustered at the southeastern end of the pit, the same end where the supposed access ramps are located, suggests that the objects were just tossed into the pit from there. This ostensibly "careless" treatment of the artifacts does not preclude a ritual performance, however. On the contrary, this could all be part of the ritual "killing" of the objects as part of the sacrifice (Xu 2001a:31).

Indeed, the intentional destruction of artifacts in Pits 1 and 2 can be understood as an additional measure to make the sacrificial exchange with the supernatural irreversible (Falkenhausen 2002a:21f). The practice of rendering artifacts unusable before their deposition has parallels among a very large amount of hoards in Europe (Brück 2016; Dietrich 2014). In the logic of sacrifice as described by Valerio Valeri (1994:106–7), this would represent the step of "renunciation"—essentially, sealing the deal of the exchange with the supernatural by ensuring that it cannot be reneged upon. The layers of rammed earth sealing the Great Hoards at Sanxingdui also support this being an act of renunciation. Another explanation for the destruction of the artifacts, possibly in addition to their renunciation, is that for the objects to become sacred, they have to be completely removed from human use (Valeri 1994:125n68).

Finally, the other deposits at Sanxingdui and other sites suggest that burying large amounts of artifacts was an established practice with certain recurring patterns. Again, ritual performance would be the most plausible explanation. It should be noted, however, that although the Yanjiadianzi and Cangbaobao hoards are considerable in size as well, their scale comes nowhere near the Great Hoards of Pits 1 to 3. There is a notable difference in content as well, as the wealth of metal artifacts in Pits 1 and 2 is not found in the smaller hoards. It appears that at the time of the deposition of the Great Hoards, a ritual practice of artifact sacrifice had already been in place. Yet the sheer size of the Great Hoards represented an entirely new approach to the tradition of sacrifice.

Reasons for the Sacrifice

The extraordinary scale of the Great Hoards in comparison with other depositions at Sanxingdui requires an explanation of motivating circumstances beyond a reference to established practices.

First, there is the question of whether the hoards are the result of one ritual performance enacted at different locations at the same time or multiple temporally distinct events. As mentioned above, the chronological relationship between Pits 1 and 2 cannot be clearly established at this point. However, from the absence of evidence that the hoards were deposited at different times does not follow, as (Sun Hua 2013:10–12) maintains, that they must have been deposited simultaneously. Again, we must take into account what we do not know. Even if we cannot see a difference in, say, the ceramic sequence, the resolution of that sequence is often low enough for decades or even generations to pass within the same step of the sequence. The only statement we can make is that the structural differences between Pit 1 and Pit 2 might point toward a chronological difference—a statement with an admittedly weak certainty.

The layering of the objects inside the hoards indicates that the deposition of each hoard was part of one act performed all at once as opposed to a piece-by-piece deposition over an extended period of time. This means that the artifacts to be deposited must have been collected over time so that they could all be buried together. Indeed, an idea brought up by Chen De'an in the main report on the Sanxingdui pits (Sichuansheng 1999:441f.) and taken up again by Sun Hua (2013:21)—that the artifacts deposited in the pits previously formed the inventory of a shrine or temple—does not seem unreasonable, especially given the presence of many elements among them that could be immobile or architectural. Furthermore, an idea brought forth by the same scholars—that the damage to the objects was sustained due to the said shrine or temple burning down—deserves consideration. Sun Hua (2013:21–22) observes that the traces of burning occur unevenly among the objects, which he takes to indicate that they were burned inside the temple as opposed to stacked on a pyre in an orderly fashion. It should be noted, however, that the burning on a pyre can certainly produce uneven burn marks and that the burning of only some of the objects could represent a *pars pro toto* gesture in a renunciation ritual.

As to the question of why the temple supposedly burned down, Sun (2013:46) puts forth the hypothesis that internal conflict created the conditions reflected in the hoards, presumably including the temple fire. As previously mentioned, even if the hoards were deposited in the context of conflict, they were still sacrificial—a votive of the spoils (Wang 1996:106). This is a possibility, but I do not believe it is very likely. Unless we assume that the two Great Hoards were deposited at the same time, we are looking at several events inciting their burial. This is likely supported by the newly discovered pits surrounding them. The close proximity of the great sacrificial pits suggests that they are referencing each other or a common signifier, making it implausible that they were buried by opposing factions or that only some of them were victory sacrifices. That would imply either that the inhabitants of Sanxingdui would gather a treasure trove of artifacts in their temple—only to have it raided and destroyed by outside forces time and again—or that the Sanxingdui people were very successful in raiding other communities, acquiring such immense amounts of wealth that they could afford sacrificing large parts of it—and then abandoning their settlement not long after. Both of these skepticisms apply if we follow Sun Hua's assumption of an internecine conflict in which one faction repeatedly raided the other.

Alternatively, there is the possibility that the ceremonies surrounding the deposition of the Great Hoards were intended to draw attention to a specific place. The study of Bronze Age hoards in Europe has revealed that their placement is almost always deliberate (Hansen et al. 2012; for a thorough discussion of the European research of hoards, see Hein this volume). Hoards were used in structuring space, be that in the creation of sacred landscapes in remote regions far from settled spaces or the elevation of built spaces within a settlement. It might seem counterintuitive that something that is usually hidden from view, as hoards usually are, might have the power to impact the conceptualization of space. Yet this fact enhances the concept, because as long as the performance that led to the creation of the hoard is in the memory of the audience, or canonized in the cultural memory through secondhand narration, it will achieve its effect (cf. Hansen 2016; Neumann 2012). When deposited in an irretrievable way, the objects cease to be physical and become idealized. Rowan Flad (2012) has pointed out how in the example of Sanxingdui and Jinsha, the deposition of valuable objects transforms their value. I think we can say concretely that in the terms of value theory (Papadopoulos and Urton 2012), one of the functions of hoards is to transform object value into place value.

As for Pits 1 and 2, statements about the meaning of their location are possible but fall largely in the speculative range of the certainty spectrum. The discovery of the six additional pits in the vicinity certainly indicates that the area had some significance for hoard deposition. The alignment of Pits 1 and 2 might reference the nearby Sanxingdui Mounds, which, as Sun Hua (2013:35ff.) and Zhao Dianzeng (2018:60ff.) have pointed out, have a prominent location in the center of the site, overlooking the Mamu River. While the hoards are not located on or among the mounds, it would have been enough for the mounds to be visible during the performance. Thus the individual location of the hoards may have been less important than the space around them that they are referencing. In fact, as the stratigraphy shows, Pits 1 and 2 were soon covered with settlement debris from roughly the same site phase as that of their creation, which could indicate that people continued to settle in the spot and there was no taboo against doing so. Instead, as long as the performance of the hoard creation would reference a place like the Sanxingdui Mounds, that place could be imbued with the value of the sacrificed objects. By extension, although this is speculative, the Sanxingdui Mounds, with their central location, can be taken to represent the settlement as a whole. A sacrifice as grand as that of Pit 1 and Pit 2 would be fitting to elevate the entire settlement in the eyes of not just its inhabitants but of outsiders as well.

Levels of Certainty

Figure 6.4 shows how the above statements about the ritual nature of the Great Sanxingdui Hoards can be sorted into the levels of certainty model introduced earlier. As previously noted, there are no strict boundaries between initial observations, inferences, and speculation. Any of the statements in the left column can be disputed, which is precisely why the diligent publication of excavation data is essential for this discussion. For example, the assertion that the depositions occurred toward the end of the settlement phase is contradicted by Jay Xu (2006), who advocates for a continuation of the Sanxingdui culture at Sanxingdui for about 200 more years after the depositions, during what is otherwise commonly referred to as the Shi'erqiao culture period. Further investigations into this period will have to show how much of a break with the preceding occupation phase it really represents. The inferences in this case are based on theories of ritual, space, and value, but they also follow from observations of the archaeological record. Speculation is in turn ideally based on the inferences, but at this level of uncertainty the questions remain open until new data and better models improve our understanding.

Note that the only reference to the religious context of the ritual—"What is the nature of the divine patron who receives the sacrifice?"—appears in the speculation column. As of yet, I have found no way to make any inferences about this question from the structure of the hoards. Furthermore, even using the artifacts contained in the hoards to tackle the ritual context of the deposition is problematic, since we do not know if the role some of the artifacts potentially played in their use life as ceremonial objects is the same as the role they played in the act of their sacrificial burial.

In lieu of a conclusion, this paper will end with a highly speculative attempt at answering the question posited in the beginning: "What was the intent behind the deposition of the large hoards?" While the narrative is rooted in inferences made above, the overall certainty still has to be rated as quite low.

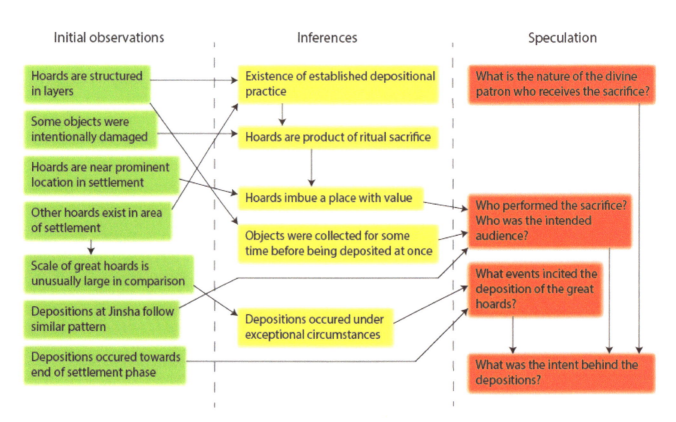

Figure 6.4. Levels of certainty in the case of the Sanxingdui hoards. The terms *hoards* and *depositions* refer to the Great Hoards of Pit 1 and Pit 2 unless otherwise noted. *Created by the author.*

A Speculation

The walled settlements of the Late Neolithic and Early Bronze Age Sichuan basin represented considerable endeavors of high risk and high reward for those involved. Their maintenance required a lot of people, but this concentration of people also led to a large accumulation of surplus wealth in these regional centers. The elites managing these centers could profit greatly from extracting this wealth, but they would have to keep the population together with the promise of protection from the natural elements and jealous neighbors. The sacrifice of material wealth to supernatural forces promising such protection would be a normal part of life in such a settlement. Some of it would take the form of large-scale events sponsored by the elites, but some of it might have been conducted on a private, individual level, represented by small depositions of food or minor objects that are very hard to trace archaeologically.

Toward the end of the Sanxingdui culture period, as we are nearing 1200 BCE, this arrangement was threatened in Sanxingdui. And it was not a singular threat, since there were at least three separate large-scale deposition events to deal with the threat. What events incited these drastic measures? Given the evident volatility of rivers in and around the Chengdu Plain in ancient times, severe environmental degradation involving flooding may have been the culprit (cf. Jia et al. 2017). Alternatively, the opening up of new trade routes with other parts of ancient China might have left Sanxingdui on the sidelines (Sun 2013:44ff.). For whatever reason, a large number of people left Sanxingdui to seek their fortune elsewhere. The Sanxingdui elites saw their power base wane. Their only chance to stem the tide of emigration would be to dial the ritual system meant to keep the people together up to the extreme and to stage such a conspicuous display of the destruction of disposable wealth that the whole region would talk of the grandeur of Sanxingdui. How the symbolism of destroying certain effigies—of elite figures? of priests? of gods?—fit into this is anybody's guess. Had the figures fallen out of favor for failing to provide the promised protection? Or was their sacrifice considered an honor to those depicted? The elites certainly did not sacrifice all their material wealth. The fact that we find hardly any metal objects outside these hoards is due to the fact that their owners carried the rest along as they moved on, and what they could not carry, they melted down and recycled.

Sanxingdui must have fallen on hard times indeed, since the lavish displays that the laying of the hoards entailed in an attempt to keep people interested in the settlement had to be conducted twice. Or perhaps it was a competition among an already factionalized elite. Either way, economic needs prevailed over ideological allegiance, and the population of Sanxingdui shrunk to a fraction of what it once was. Perhaps some of the people brought their customs with them down into the Chengdu Plain, to Jinsha, where the next phase of this social experiment would be staged.

In my opinion, one of Professor von Falkenhausen's feats has not been celebrated enough yet, and I would like to use my contribution to this Festschrift to draw more attention to it. It is the ability to choose names for things and for people (when translating them from or into Chinese). Of course, everybody is aware of his sublimely titled *Suspended Music: Chime-Bells in the Culture of Bronze Age China* (1994). But I will put it to debate that among all publications in archaeology, the best title is in fact one of Professor von Falkenhausen's contributions to the research of Sanxingdui (2002a). The name of the book, which he edited, is *Qiyi de tumu: Xifang xuezhe kan Sanxingdui* 奇異的凸目：西方學者看三星堆 (*Strange Protruding Eyes: Western Scholars' Perspectives on Sanxingdui*).

I think we should all take this as an inspiration to get better at naming things. Granted, this article may be a poor example. After all, I spend almost a full page deliberating whether or not to use the word *hoard*. All I will advocate for with this contribution is that we keep our eyes properly protruded to look out for the hidden foils that may affect the certainty of our explanations.

Acknowledgments

I thank Anke Hein for all her effort in putting this volume together as well as organizing the workshop and providing useful comments for the design of this paper. I greatly appreciate the feedback I received from Rowan Flad; a large part of this paper is inspired by his previous research on the subject. Helpful feedback was also provided by Ma Jian, Qian Yaopeng, Michael Müller, and Cori Hoover. I am grateful for the School of Cultural Heritage at Northwest University for providing a lot of the resources used in writing this paper. And of course I thank Lothar von Falkenhausen for inspiring this volume as well as this paper in the first place, as well as for many useful comments.

References

Ao Tianzhao 敖天照
2006   Guanghan Gaopian chutu Shangdai yuqi de buzheng 廣漢高駢出土商代玉器的補正 [Correction on the Shang Dynasty Jades Unearthed at Gaopian in Guanghan]. In *Sanxingdui yanjiu* 1 三星堆研究・第一輯 [Sanxingdui Research 1], edited by Sanxingdui Yanjiuyuan 三星堆研究院 and Sanxingdui Bowuguan 三星堆博物館, p. 127. Chengdu: Tiandi Chubanshe 天地出版社.

Ao Tianzhao 敖天照 and Wang Youpeng 王有鵬
1980   Sichuan Guanghan chutu Shangdai yuqi 四川廣漢出土商代玉器 [Shang Dynasty Jades Unearthed at Guanghan in Sichuan]. *Wenwu* 文物 9:76.

Bagley, Robert W
1988   Sacrificial Pits of the Shang Period at Sanxingdui in Guanghan County. *Arts Asiatiques* 43:78–86.
2001   Editor's Preface. In *Ancient Sichuan: Treasures from a Lost Civilization*, edited by Robert W. Bagley, pp. 12–13. Seattle: Seattle Art Museum.

Brück, Joanna
2016   Hoards, Fragmentation and Exchange in the European Bronze Age. In *Raum, Gabe und Erinnerung. Weihgaben und Heiligtümer in prähistorischen und antiken Gesellschaften* [Space, Gift, and Memory: Votive Goods and Sanctuaries in Prehistoric and Ancient Societies], edited by Svend Hansen, Daniel Neumann, and Tilmann Vachta, pp. 75–92. Berlin: Excellence Cluster 264 TOPOI.

Chen Xiandan 陳顯丹
1989   Guanghan Sanxingdui yi, erhao keng liangge wenti de tantao 廣漢三星堆一、二號坑兩個問題的探討 [Discussion of Two Questions Concerning Pits 1 and 2 at Sanxingdui in Guanghan]. *Wenwu* 文物 5:36–38.

Chengdu Shi Wenwu Kaogu Yanjiusuo 成都市文物考古研究所
2004   Chengdu Jinsha yizhi yiqu 'Meiyuan' didian fajue yiqi jianbao 成都金沙遺址一區'梅苑'地點發掘一期簡報 [Preliminary Report of Season One of the Excavations at the Meiyuan Locus of Area One of the Jinsha Site in Chengdu]. *Wenwu* 文物 4:4–65.

Dietrich, Oliver
2014   Learning from "Scrap" about Late Bronze Age Hoarding Practices: A Biographical Approach to Individual Acts of Dedication in Large Metal Hoards of the Carpathian Basin. *European Journal of Archaeology* 17(3):468–86.

Eggert, Manfred K. H.
2012   *Prähistorische Archäologie: Konzepte und Methoden* [Prehistoric Archaeology: Concepts and Methods]. 4th ed. Tübingen: UTB GmbH.

Falkenhausen, Lothar von
1994   *Suspended Music: Chime-Bells in the Culture of Bronze Age China*. Berkeley: University of California Press.
1996   The Regionalist Paradigm in Chinese Archaeology. In *Nationalism, Politics and the Practice of Archaeology*, edited by P. Kohl and C. Fawcett, pp. 198–217. Cambridge: Cambridge University Press.
2002a   Sanxingdui yizhi de xinrenshi 三星堆遺址的新認識 [New Insights from the Sanxingdui Site]. In *Qiyi de tumu: xifang xuezhe kan Sanxingdui* 奇異的凸目—西方學者看三星堆 [Strange Protruding Eyes: Western Scholars' Perspectives on Sanxingdui], edited by Lothar von Falkenhausen, pp. 3–78. Chengdu: Bashu Shushe.
2002b   Some Reflections on Sanxingdui. In *Papers from the Third International Conference on Sinology, History Section: Regional Culture, Religion, and Arts before the Seventh Century*, edited by I-Tien Hsing, pp. 59–97. Taipei: Institute of History and Philology, Academia Sinica.
2006   The External Connections of Sanxingdui. *Journal of East Asian Archaeology* 5(1):191–245.

Flad, Rowan
2012   Bronze, Jade, Gold, and Ivory: Valuable Objects in Ancient Sichuan. In *The Construction of Value in the Ancient World*, edited by John K. Papadopoulos and Gary Urton, pp. 306–35. Los Angeles: Cotsen Institute of Archaeology Press.

Fogelin, Lars
2007   Inference to the Best Explanation: A Common and Effective Form of Archaeological Reasoning. *American Antiquity* 72(4):603–25.

Graham, David Crockett
1934   A Preliminary Report of the Hanchou Excavation. *Journal of the West China Border Research Society* 6:114–31.

Hansen, Svend
2016   Gabe und Erinnerung—Heiligtum und Opfer [Gift and Memory—Sanctuary and Sacrifice]. In *Raum, Gabe und Erinnerung. Weihgaben und Heiligtümer in prähistorischen und antikenGe- sellschaften* [Space, Gift, and Memory: Votive Goods and Sanctuaries in Prehistoric and Ancient Societies], edited by Svend Hansen, Daniel Neumann, and Tilmann Vachta, pp. 211–36. Berlin: Excellence Cluster 264 TOPOI.

Hansen, Svend, Daniel Neumann, and Tilmann Vachta
2012   *Hortund Raum: Aktuelle Forschungen zu bronzezeitlichen Deponierungen in Mitteleuropa* [Hoard and Space: Current Research on Bronze Age Depositions in Central Europe]. Berlin: Walter de Gruyter.

Jia, Tianjiao, Chunmei Ma, Cheng Zhu, Tianhong Guo, JiajiaXu, Houchun Guan, Mengxiu Zeng, Ming Huang, and Qing Zhang
2017   Depositional Evidence of Palaeofloods during 4.0–3.6 Ka BP at the Jinsha Site, Chengdu Plain, China. *Quaternary International* 440:78–89.

Kahneman, Daniel
2011   *Thinking, Fast and Slow*. London: Penguin.

Li Anmin李安民
1994   Guanghan Sanxingdui yihao, erhao jisikeng suo fanying de jisi neirong, jisi xisu yanjiu廣漢三星堆一號、二號祭祀坑所反映的祭祀內容、祭祀習俗研究 [Research on the Content and Practices of Sacrifice Reflected in the Sacrificial Pits 1 and 2 at Sanxingdui in Guanghan]. *Sichuan wenwu*四川文物 4:11–15.

Li Min
2018   *Social Memory and State Formation in Early China*. Cambridge: Cambridge University Press.

Neumann, Daniel
2012   Hort Und Raum: Grundlagen und Perspektiven der Interpretation [Hoard and Space: Basics and Perspectives of Interpretation]. In *Hortund Raum: Aktuelle Forschungen zu bronzezeitlichen Deponierungen in Mitteleuropa* [Hoard and Space: Current Research on Bronze Age Depositions in Central Europe], edited by Svend Hansen, Daniel Neumann, and Tilmann Vachta, pp.5–21. Berlin: Walter de Gruyter.

Papadopoulos, John K., and Gary Urton
2012   *The Construction of Value in the Ancient World*. Los Angeles: Cotsen Institute of Archaeology Press.

Sichuansheng Wenwu Guanli Weiyuanhui四川省文物管理委員會, Sichuansheng Bowuguan四川省博物館, and Guanghanxian Wenhuaguan廣漢縣文化館
1987a   Guanghan Sanxingdui yizhi廣漢三星堆遺址 [The Sanxingdui Site in Guanghan]. *Kaoguxuebao*考古學報 2:227–54.

Sichuansheng Wenwu Guanli Weiyuanhui四川省文物管理委員會, Sichuansheng Wenwu Kaogu Yanjiusuo 四川省文物考古研究所, and Sichuansheng Guanghanxian Wenhuaju四川省廣漢縣文化局
1987b   Guanghan Sanxingdui yizhi yihao jisikeng fajue jianbao廣漢三星堆遺址一號祭祀坑發掘簡報 [Preliminary Report on the Excavation of Sacrificial Pit 1 at the Sanxingdui Site in Guanghan]. *Wenwu*文物 10:1–15.

Sichuansheng Wenwu Guanli Weiyuanhui四川省文物管理委員會, Sichuansheng Wenwu Kaogu Yanjiusuo四川省文物考古研究所, Guanghanshi Wenhuaju廣漢市文化局, and Guanghanshi Wenguansuo廣漢市文管所
1989   Guanghan Sanxingdui yizhi erhao jisikeng fajue jianbao廣漢三星堆遺址二號祭祀坑發掘簡報 [Preliminary Report on the Excavation of Sacrificial Pit 2 at the Sanxingdui Site in Guanghan]. *Wenwu*文物 5:1–20.

Sichuansheng Wenwu Kaogu Yanjiusuo四川省文物考古研究所
1999   *Sanxingdui jisikeng*三星堆祭祀坑 [The Sacrificial Pits at Sanxingdui]. Beijing: Wenwu Chubanshe文物出版社.

Sichuansheng Wenwu Kaogu Yanjiusuo Sanxingdui Yizhi Gongzuozhan四川省文物考古研究所三星堆遺址工作站
2004   Sichuan Guanghanshi Sanxingdui Yizhi Renshengcun tukengmu四川廣漢市三星堆遺址仁勝村土坑墓 [The Renshengcun Pit Graves at the Sanxingdui Site in Guanghan City, Sichuan]. *Kaogu*考古 10:14–22.

Sichuansheng Wenwu Kaogu Yanjiusuo Sanxingdui Gongzuozhan四川省文物考古研究所三星堆工作站 and Guanghanshi Wenwu Guanlisuo廣漢市文物管理所
1998   Sanxingdui yizhi Zhenwu Cangbaobao jisikeng diaocha jianbao三星堆遺址真武倉包包祭祀坑調查簡報 [Preliminary Report on the Survey of the Zhenwu Cangbaobao Sacrificial Pit at the Sanxingdui Site]. In *Sichuan kaogubaogaoji*四川考古報告集 [Sichuan Anthology of Archaeological Reports], edited by Sichuansheng Wenwu Kaogu Yanjiusuo四川省文物考古研究所, pp. 78–90. Beijing: Wenwu Chubanshe文物出版社.

Sun Hua 孫華
1992   Shilun Guanghan Sanxingdui yizhi de fenqi試論廣漢三星堆遺址的分期 [Discussion Attempt of the Chronology of the Sanxingdui Site]. *Nanfangminzukaogu*南方民族考古（第五辑）5:10–24.

2013   Sanxingdui qiwukeng de maicang wenti: Maicang niandai, xingzhi, zhuren he beijing三星堆器物坑的埋藏問題—埋藏年代、性質、主人和背景 [The Question of the Burying of the Sanxingdui Artifact Pits: Its Time, Structure, Actors, and Background]. *Nanfang Minzu Kaogu* 南方民族考古（第九輯）9:9–53.

Tong Fang 童芳
2020 Xin faxian 6 ge "jisikeng" Sanxingdui qidong dui jisiqu de shenru fajue yanjiu新發現6個'祭祀坑' 三星堆啓動對祭祀區的深入發掘研究 [New Discovery of 6 "Sacrificial Pits" at Sanxingdui Initiates Additional Excavations in the Ritual Area]. *Xinhuanet*, 2020, http://www.xinhuanet.com/2020-09/06/c_1126458726.htm.

Tong Fang 童芳 and Cui Kexin崔可欣
2019 Sanxingdui disanhao jisikeng zhanlu toujiao三星堆第三號祭祀坑嶄露頭角 [Third Sacrificial Pit Emerges at Sanxingdui]. *Xinhuanet*, 2019, http://www.xinhuanet.com/2019-12/20/c_1125370428.htm.

Valeri, Valerio
1994 Wild Victims: Hunting as Sacrifice and Sacrifice as Hunting in Huaulu. *History of Religions* 34(2):101–31.

Wang Yanfang王燕芳
1996. Sichuan xibu sanzhong wenhua leixing ji qi xiangguan wenti四川西部三種文化類型及其相關問題 [Three Culture Types in Western Sichuan and Related Questions]. In *Sichuan Kaogu Lunwenji* 四川考古論文集 [Anthology of Sichuan Archaeology], edited by Sichuan Sheng Wenwu Kaogu Yanjiusuo四川省文物考古研究所, pp. 104–17. Beijing: Wenwu Chubanshe文物出版社.

Wu Xiaoling吳曉鈴
2020 Zhongdafaxian: Sanxingdui faxian sanhao jisikeng! 重大發現：三星堆發現三号祭祀坑！ [Huge Discovery: Sacrificial Pit Number Three Discovered at Sanxingdui!]. *Guanchazhe* 觀察者, 2020, https://www.guancha.cn/politics/2020_02_10_535442.shtml.

Xu, Jay
2001a Sichuan before the Warring States Period. In *Ancient Sichuan: Treasures from a Lost Civilization*, edited by Robert W. Bagley, pp. 21–37. Seattle: Seattle Art Museum.
2001b Bronze at Sanxingdui. In *Ancient Sichuan: Treasures from a Lost Civilization*, edited by Robert W. Bagley, pp. 58–151. Seattle: Seattle Art Museum.
2006 Defining the Archaeological Cultures at the Sanxingdui Site. *Journal of East Asian Archaeology* 5(1):149–90.

Xu Chaolong徐朝龍
1992 Sanxingdui "jisishuo" changyi: Jiantan Yufu he Duyu zhi guanxi 三星堆'祭祀坑說'唱異—兼談魚鳧和杜宇之關係 [A Different Tone in the "Sacrificial Pits Hypothesis" at Sanxingdui: Additional Points on the Relationship between Yufu and Duyu]. *Sichuan wenwu*四川文物 5:32–38.

Zhang Minghua張明華
1989 Sanxingdui Jisikeng huifou shi muzang三星堆祭祀坑會否是墓葬 [Are the Sacrificial Pits at Sanxingdui Actually Burials?]. *Zhongguo wenwubao*中國文物報, June 2.

Zhao Dianzeng趙殿增
1996 The Sacrificial Pits at Sanxingdui. In *Mysteries of Ancient China: New Discoveries from the Early Dynasties*, edited by Jessica Rawson, pp. 232–39. New York: George Braziller.
2018 Sanxingdui jisi xingtai tantao三星堆祭祀形態探討 [Discussion of the Forms of Ritual at Sanxingdui]. *Sichuan wenwu*四川文物 2:59–73.

Chapter 7

Raw Material Hoards, Ritual Deposits, or Disturbed Burials?
Object Pits in the Mountains of Southwest China

Anke Hein

It may not be surprising that since I received my training in archaeology up to a master's degree in Germany, I often view archaeological material from China through a central European methodological lens. That I do so explicitly, and in a hopefully self-reflective manner, is the direct outcome of Lothar von Falkenhausen's research and teaching, both of which are international and broad in outlook and emphasize the strengths, weaknesses, and historical background of the disciplines at hand. In multiple papers, he has reflected on the history of archaeology, art history, and Sinology as well as the background of individual scholars and its influence on their work (e.g., Falkenhausen 1993, 1995, 2001a, 2009, 2017, 2018a). The most important example for me has been his work on antiquarianism, which compares Europe, East Asia in general, and China in particular (Falkenhausen 2010, 2015). Here I attempt to follow his example in applying insights gained from material in one region to material in another part of the world. By discussing non-mortuary, non-settlement deposits, which have most commonly been interpreted as ritual offerings, hidden treasures, or scrap metal collections, I furthermore hope to speak to both his long-held interest in ritual (e.g., Falkenhausen 2001b) and his current work on economy (Falkenhausen 2018b).

While graves and settlements are well-established find categories in archaeological research worldwide, objects appearing outside such contexts are more difficult to interpret. In the case of single finds made by non-archaeologists, even the exact find location may be unclear, and often no associated archaeological feature can be found. Such items are usually interpreted as random finds or lost items; but there is another group of non-mortuary, non-settlement finds consisting of one or more objects appearing in identifiable features such as pits. Often occurring in special locations such as streams and natural crevices, objects may be arranged in ways that strongly suggest deliberate deposition. Such discoveries—usually referred to as hoards, deposits, or caches—are a much-discussed find category in European archaeology, similar in importance to graves or settlements. Outside Europe, however, such finds receive considerably less attention.

In the Chinese context, many scholars discuss sacrifices in general, especially of humans or animals, mostly in burial contexts or for stately rituals (e.g., Campbell 2018; Flad 2012; Huang Zhangyue 1998; Kim 1994; Puett 2002; Shelach 1996; Sterckx 2011; Yuan and Flad 2005). As for items placed in non-mortuary pits, they have mostly been interpreted as sacrificial pits (*jisikeng* 祭祀坑). The most famous examples are probably the pits found at Sanxingdui in Sichuan, Southwest China (Ehrich this volume), but others have been reported from the middle reaches of the Yangzi River (Flad and Chen 2013:212–22). Nevertheless, these discoveries have not incited broader discussions of deposition practices, and finds less sensational than those at Sanxingdui have received little attention. Focusing on Southwest China, the present study shows that the relative frequency of non-mortuary deposits here and in other parts of China has been vastly underestimated. By way of introduction, I discuss the hoard/deposition phenomenon as defined in Europe, highlighting the difficulties of categorizing and interpreting such finds. Next I discuss the available evidence from Southwest China, paying particular attention to how local research practices may have caused hoards to go unrecognized. I show how the material from Southwest China differs from deposition practices in Europe, thus broadening the understanding of non-mortuary deposition practices within general frameworks of human behavior.

Framing and Terminology: Hoards and Deposits as Find Categories in European Archaeology

In Europe, research on prehistoric deposition practices in non-mortuary contexts commenced in the 1860s, with Jens Jacob Asmussen Worsaae working on finds from bogs and earth pits in Denmark. He argued that deposits constituted a meaningful find category in their own right (Worsaae 1866:326). In the discussions that followed, Conrad Engelhardt (1868:141) suggested that some such items or assemblages found in Scandinavia may have been meant for the use of the dead in the afterlife, as mentioned in the Søgur. Sophus Müller (1898) distinguished two main categories: "deposits" and "offerings," or votive finds. The former was meant to be retrievable; the latter was for the gods or the dead and was not to be retrieved by the living. The term *hoard* was suggested by Hans Seger (1935–1936) to cover both categories; he argued that the term *Hort* referred to a collection of treasures to be kept safe for religious or more mundane purposes, thus encompassing both of Müller's categories. In German, *Depot* and *Hort* are now used interchangeably, and in English the terms *hoard* and *deposit/deposition* are similar, sometimes modified by various *epiteta*, as in *wealth deposit* and *selective deposition*, as well as a range of qualifiers and other terms denoting specific contexts, contents, or assumed underlying motivation.

Issues of Terminology and Category Boundaries

As Helmut Geißlinger (1983:334) and many since (e.g., Eggert 2005 [2000]:78; Hansen 2002; Huth 2008) have pointed out, hoards/deposits are mostly defined by what they are *not*; they are finds not associated with graves or settlements. Cristoph Huth remarked that by calling them "gifts for the gods"—a term first used by Tullia Linders and Gullög Norquist (1987)—Hänsel and Hänsel (1997) made them a positively defined category, suggesting that all such finds were offerings, which is likewise problematic. Alternatively, these items may be seen as deliberately deposited rather than lost or forgotten (e.g., Stjernquist 1963:19). But what term should be used to refer to this type of finds? *Cache* and *treasure* (*Schatzfund*) are too narrow, as they suggest safekeeping of valuable items and do not include ritual deposits. The same applies to the term *hoard*. *Deposit* and *deposition* are largely synonymous, both describing something that has been laid down, by nature or humans, with *deposition* encompassing both the process and its outcome. One may argue that the word *deposit* is too neutral, as it can also refer to an archaeological or geological feature, such as a layer or a posthole. Hence some scholars prefer the established term *hoard*.

In German-language research, the words *Hort* and *Depot/Deponierung* (the equivalents of *hoard* and *deposit/deposition*) are applied interchangeably to Bronze Age metal finds and other items of perceived material value (such as amber beads; Ebbesen 1995). In contrast, ceramics are always referred to as Depot/Deponierung (e.g., Krenn-Leeb 2006), as are most finds from protohistoric periods (Hansen 2002:91). The reasons for this difference are unclear; it may be a convention following the first major publications on the respective phenomena and time periods. In the English-language literature, preference for the term *hoard* for metal items has historical reasons, going back to the twelfth century English treasure trove law, which was written to ensure that the crown received all newly discovered valuables without legal ownership. The law distinguished between collections meant to be recovered and those that were meant to remain in the ground, the latter including graves (Bradley 2013:124). Not surprisingly, the general tendency from the official side was to interpret any find of valuables not associated with graves as hoards or treasure that the crown could claim, thus shaping both terminology and general understanding of the finds.

Recent years have seen renewed debates on terminology, with scholars trying to find more neutral yet specific terms. Ester Oras (2012:61), for instance, suggested the term *wealth deposit*, defining it as one or more objects of value "hidden deliberately as an intended deposition of specifically chosen artefacts into a specifically chosen place in a specific manner." She argued that the term *wealth deposit* did not limit source material, number of objects, environment of concealment, or intent of deposition and was thus more suitable than the loaded terms *hoard* (meant for future use or safekeeping), *treasure* (usually referring to metal), *ritual/votive deposit*, or *sacrifice/offering* (the result of religious activity and not meant to be retrievable). *Wealth deposit* does, however, exclude anything of a value not immediately recognizable to the archaeologist or of no actual value whatsoever. Therefore *wealth deposit* does not provide a perfect solution to the terminology problem either.

Other scholars have been trying to establish more abstract and less interpretive terms, either keeping to the rather vague *deposit* (e.g., Joyce and Pollard 2010) or to slightly more narrow terms such as *structured deposit* (Richards and Thomas 1984), *selective deposit* (Fontijn 2008; Needham 1988), or *special deposit* (Cunliffe 1992). The latter term is rather vague, but some scholars working on Iron Age and medieval Britain are using it for intentionally hidden and/or specially treated objects (e.g., Hamerow 2006). Any intentionally deposited item was necessarily selected from a range of available materials, making the word *selective* unnecessary. The term *structured deposit* has been criticized as unhelpfully broad (Garrow 2012:85) and also criticized for excluding unique finds with no structural parallels to other discoveries (Oras 2012:67). The latter kind of finds are naturally difficult to interpret but may nevertheless be clearly identifiable as intentionally deposited. So the term *intentional deposit* seems most suitable.

Single artifact deposits are naturally difficult to distinguish from lost items or disturbed graves. Nevertheless, single items may be intentionally deposited for a variety of reasons. In the European context there are many single finds that have been intentionally broken, burned, and/or deposited in the same way as larger groups of items referred to as hoards or deposits (e.g., Jensen 1972). Horst (1977:168) distinguished between "classic single finds" of objects that were lost, "single finds of hoard character" (called "single-object hoards" by Bergmann 1970) that were deliberately deposited, and "hoards" that consist of at least two items. Mansen Eggert (2005 [2000]:79) adopted the term *single find of hoard character* (*Einzelfund mit Hortcharakter*) and furthermore suggested distinguishing between single finds of hoard character, a closed hoard (*geschlossener Hort*), and a non-closed hoard (*nichtgeschlossener Hort*). The former consists of items deposited at the same time. The latter is the product of several instances of deposition in the same place. Using slightly different terms, Gerald Görmer (2002, 2003, 2008) followed this three-part typology, speaking of "closed multi-piece deposits," "non-closed multi-piece deposits," and "single-object deposits." Svend Hansen (2002) criticized this plethora of long terms as unnecessarily complicated, arguing that "non-closed multi-piece deposits" was not only a mouthful but was also not clearly identifiable and thus unsuitable as a category. For single-object finds, he argued, it was impossible to distinguish lost items, objects from disturbed graves, and deliberately deposited objects. Hansen therefore distinguishes only two broad categories, *single find* and *hoard/deposit*, keeping the traditional terms for ease of communication and discussing composition and intent of deposition separately for each study.

While it is undeniably true that single finds are particularly difficult to interpret, even more so as they are often poorly documented and rarely scientifically excavated, the same applies to most multi-piece deposits. For Middle Bronze Age metal objects from the Netherlands, for instance, David Fontijn (2008:88) estimates that only about 4% came from excavations; 69% were reported by private individuals with some information on find location. For the others, context and location were entirely unknown. Both the Netherlands and Denmark have been thoroughly surveyed by both archaeologists and private detectorists; it is therefore assumed that the known metal hoards are representative in terms of distribution, size, and content (Fontijn 2001–2002:4; Levy 1982:4). The same may be said for metal hoards in the United Kingdom and other parts of Europe, but for ceramics and items of stone or other material, the coverage is much less certain. For regions where such finds—be they single- or multi-piece—are not seen as a category in their own right, the coverage is poor and the actual distribution of non-mortuary, selective, structured deposition practices is unclear. Additionally, non-archaeologists tend to retrieve only exceptional objects that they may stumble upon, leaving associated items such as stones, ceramics, animal bones, or distorted metal scraps in place and not investigating the surrounding area. A recent and rather prominent case in point is the Disk of Nebra, for which the deposition environment and overall hoard composition could later be reconstructed (Meller 2004). This bronze disk of about 30 cm in diameter—inlaid with a golden sun or full moon, lunar crescent, and stars, as well as two golden arcs that are later additions—has been dated to around 1600 BCE. It had been deposited together with two bronze swords, a chisel, two hatchets, and spiral bracelet fragments in a pit at Nebra, Saxony-Anhalt, Germany. There have been heated debates about its origin, date, and meaning, especially its alleged reflection of an early deep knowledge of the cosmos. Had the Disk of Nebra not been so exceptional, the case would probably never have been investigated with such care, and the context would have remained unknown.

Even with scientific excavation, less prominent components of metal hoards, such as slag, animal bones, or even non-metal containers, are generally not depicted in reports and often disregarded in further studies. Likewise, ceramic deposits—although common in both the Neolithic and the Bronze Age of Central Europe—are usually overlooked in studies on Bronze Age deposition practices. Given their very different composition, deposits containing ceramic vessels, stone tools, and/or animal bones are likely to have a somewhat different history or motivation from single-type weapon deposits, for instance, but such differences need to be systematically established and not assumed. The terminology used to refer to those finds thus needs to be considered carefully.

The Chinese-language literature has not seen similar discussions on suitable terminology for non-grave deposits; nevertheless, a number of different terms are being used. One is *sacrificial deposit* (*jisikeng*), mentioned above, a clearly interpretive term. Other terms used are *qiwukeng* 器物坑 (object pit), a choice that strives to stay neutral and not ascribe a specific function or meaning (Sun 2013), and *jiaocang* 窖藏, implying a secret storage without ritual character, the most common translation for the English word *hoard* (Ehrich this volume). In the Chinese context, the focus tends to be on deposits interpreted as sacrificial, in keeping with the broad interest in and long-lived discussion on sacrifice in Chinese archaeology mentioned above.

To avoid blanket interpretation in terms of function and underlying motivation, for the present paper I distinguish between two broad categories: chance finds (single- and multi-item) and deposits, the latter standing for intentional, selective, non-mortuary deposition. All chance finds are considered together with clearly intentional multi-item deposits, testing in each case if the find in question is indeed a deliberate, selective deposition or rather a random loss or disturbed grave. It is not always possible to decide this with absolute certainty, so unclear cases may have to be excluded from further analysis. The next step is to determine if these single finds or deposits can be interpreted as the results of sacrifice, concealment of valuables, accidental loss, or other kinds of human activities or natural processes. Here, too, a look at the European debate can help with developing a suitable approach.

Interpreting Intentional Deposits: The European Debate

The interpretation of non-mortuary intentional deposits varies widely over time and space, and the associated terminology, typology, and interpretations are very much the product of their time and place, but there are some general insights that will be helpful for analyzing the material from Southwest China.

The earliest discussion on the European material made it clear that there is too much diversity in assemblages to apply one explanation to all such finds, not even within the same region or period (e.g., Hundt 1955; Torbrügge 1985). Furthermore, the tendency to focus on extraordinary items, especially metal objects, has been shown to be rather unhelpful. Such a tendency is, however, prevalent all over the world; in both Europe and East Asia, it may be related to the perennial ties between antiques collecting, traditional antiquarianism, and modern archaeology (Falkenhausen 2010, 2015). Early in the history of research on deposition practices in Europe, it already became clear that there is a broad range of possible motivations for depositions, including trader deposits, workshop deposits, treasure hidden by private individuals or groups, various kinds of votive deposits, and items for the dead, to cite Schumacher's (1914) categories.

Since the 1970s, there has been an increasing interest in the social function of deposition practices. Several scholars suggested that the removal of such a large number of bronze items from circulation was meant to create artificial scarcity and ensure that the material retained its prestigious value (e.g., Kristiansen 1978; Levy 1982; Rowlands 1980) or that the deposition of such items took place in a potlatch-type act of conspicuous consumption that directly enhanced the prestige of the elites involved (Bradley 1984). As Fontijn (2001–2002:19) has pointed out, these interpretations all assume "that Bronze Age behavior was fundamentally structured by an economic rationality." Indeed, modern concepts of value can easily taint interpretations (pointed out by, e.g., Krenn-Leeb 2008, 2014; Stapel 1999). This danger may be mitigated by considering the entire assemblage and all deposition practices, including those involving ceramics, animal bones, and other items of no apparent value.

In the 1990s, the pendulum of interpretation started to swing back, with religious and far-reaching sociological interpretations becoming increasingly popular, finally leading to the automatic assumption that all deposits were "gifts to the gods," as the exhibition *Gaben an die Götter—Schätze der Bronzezeit Europas* (*Gifts to the Gods: Treasures of the European Bronze Age*) suggests (Hänsel and Hänsel 1997). Some scholars applied frameworks of gift exchange following Mauss (1990 [1925]) and Malinowski (1961 [1922]) or concepts of collective memory as developed by Halbwachs (1992 [1925]; Hansen 2002, 2005, 2012), but others were critical of potential over-interpretation of very patchy data (e.g., Huth 2008:151). Overall, there has thus been a constant back and forth between often rather narrow narratives of *Homo economicus* on one end of the spectrum and *Homo ritualis* on the other, interspersed with tales of caution emphasizing the complexity and variability of deposition phenomena throughout Europe.

Ethnographic evidence and religious studies perspectives have been helpful in interpreting the finds, showing that a clear dichotomy between sacred and profane, or ritual and economic, is clearly not appropriate for premodern cases. For instance, the profane versus ritual dichotomy has come to be criticized as being based on European post-Enlightenment concepts of rationality (e.g., Brück

1999). Based on ethnographic evidence and sociological studies, Joanna Brück argued that for non-Western, let alone prehistoric, groups, such antithetical thinking could not be assumed. Rather, she claims, in the past all spheres of life were permeated by ritual (Brück 1999:325). She suggests dropping the category of ritual altogether, but as Fontijn has pointed out, some human behaviors were set apart from everyday actions and could thus be termed ritual (2001–2002:21–22). This is where concepts of ritualization have proved useful—the idea of special activities meant to structure social reality through acts of performance that can leave material traces, such as deposits. Deposition practices, so Fontijn (2008:89) argued, are selective in both object and location choice, showing patterns that indicate a set of shared rules. This phenomenon has been called framing (Verhoeven 2002) or ritualization (Bell 1992). According to Catherine Bell (1992:74), "Ritualization is a way of acting that is designed and orchestrated to distinguish and privilege what is being done in comparison to other, usually more quotidian activities." These special activities, argued Bell (1992:91), are meant to structure social reality, especially in connection with community identity and solidarity, always through acts of performance involving sacred symbols (following Rappaport 1979).

Nevertheless, even where ethnographic and historical evidence is at hand, it remains nearly impossible to infer meanings of individual deposits or depositional practices. A problematic example can be found in Hänsel's (1998) work. He used historical accounts with no connection to the metal deposits he analyzed to interpret them either as gifts to "chthonic powers" or as connected with "the body of the king." Furthermore, referring to a single textual source is methodologically problematic and potentially misleading, not just for the European material but also in the Chinese context, where tendencies to rely uncritically on historical analogy are all too common (Falkenhausen 1993). Instead, various ethnographic and textual studies can be used to investigate structures of human behavior in a systematic fashion. Levy (1982) has consulted a broad range of ethnographic cases from all around the world to establish criteria by which offering rites leaving material remains could be identified and interpreted. According to her study, the main characteristics of offering rites that can be identified in the material record are choice of location, choice of objects, often an association with food, and a special arrangement of the deposited objects. She argues that it is "stereotyping of symbols which makes ritual communication clear to both the supernatural and natural world" and that ritual offerings or deposits were "made in a stereotyped way, of symbolically (and potentially materially) valuable objects, with the conscious purpose of communicating with the supernatural world" (Levy 1982:20).

I would argue that such references to texts and ethnographic studies must be accompanied by a systematic analysis of the archaeological material that identifies recurring patterns in deposition location, object types (including details of object production, raw material used, origin of items and materials, and object use life), assemblage composition, treatment, and arrangement. Some of these aspects have been used to analyze and classify deposits in the past, especially location choice and object treatment (e.g., Falkenstein 2011), but only rarely have all of them been viewed together. Instead, some scholars point out the importance of metal analysis with the aim of establishing source location and distribution (e.g., Bradley 2013; Huth 2008). Fontijn (2008) stressed the importance of object biographies, building on earlier research by Appadurai (1986) and others. Such ideas have been applied to Chinese material as well, both in art history and archaeology, albeit not in connection with deposition practices (e.g., Allard 2018; Clunas 1991). Based on European material, Fontijn convincingly argued that the link between the choice of specific objects and specific locations indicates socially agreed rules of deposition and/or taboos connected with certain items and locales (Fontijn 2008). These collective ideas and meanings, so he argued, are then combined with individual agency that may lead to slight variations in depositional patterns.

Indeed, patterns in assemblage composition and location choice are crucial to identifying and interpretting past behavioral patterns in relation to depositional practices, as are considerations of object production and usage prior to deposition. Furthermore, there is the issue of object treatment first emphasized by Frauke Stein (1976), who considered use wear, patina, and object breakage and other forms of treatment as crucial for interpreting hoard finds. There is, however, some disagreement as to how such patterns may be interpreted. While Stein argued that complete, unused objects denote a ritual function, others see unused objects as stock to be traded (Müller 1898). Some argued that breakage or fragmentation indicates a ritual context (Chapman 2000), with Louis Nebelsick (1997, 2000) even speaking of furious, ecstatic acts of violence and Brück (2006) of ritual killing. Others took a pragmatic approach, suggesting that fragmentation may have allowed for faster and more fuel-efficient remelting (Huth 2008:150). Many automatically assume that deposits in wet places, such as rivers and peat bogs, must have been intended to be non-retrievable and thus ritual in nature (e.g., Stein 1976), but others criticize this as a simplification, arguing that items placed in bogs might well be retrievable by the initiated but safe from people not familiar with the terrain (Geißlinger 1983:322).

I would argue that it is crucial to consider the context of assemblages from other types of sites to understand patterns of selectivity, particular treatment, or potentially special production for non-mortuary deposits. Indeed, in the European case, it has been shown that some deposits are similar in composition to grave assemblages (e.g., Brunn 1968, 1980; Ebbesen 1995; Hundt 1955). Therefore Richard Bradley (2013:136) argued that "hoards should not be investigated without paying equal attention to single finds and the artefacts deposited with the dead." I agree that it is crucial to investigate other contexts in which items similar to the ones observed in non-mortuary deposits have been found. Additionally, we have to consider which types of objects or object treatments may be exclusive to one find context or the other. I am not suggesting that each study on a specific segment of archaeological remains always needs to involve in-depth analysis of the entire range of contemporary finds, but I would argue that any study of non-mortuary, intentional, selective deposition practices has to be conducted with the entire range of contemporary material in mind, making comparisons where necessary and useful.

I also suggest that different types of deposits should first be considered together and may then be divided for further analysis based on structural differences. Given that single items may have been deposited following a logic similar to that for multi-piece assemblages, single finds should also be taken into consideration. But again, based on context and treatment of the item in question, part of the single finds will have to be labeled as coming from disturbed graves or having been lost or discarded, and some finds of unclear nature may have to be excluded from further discussions of non-mortuary deposition practices. The same applies to groups of objects, especially if found in a settlement context where both refuse pits and other kinds of deposits, such as storage pits, caches of hidden valuables, or lost items, may be found (e.g., Stapel 1999).

Below I distinguish between only two types: chance finds (single- and multi-item) and deposits, the latter standing for intentional, selective, non-mortuary deposition. Based on object type, treatment, and overall context, the single finds then must either be moved into the deposit category or be marked as disturbed graves, lost or discarded items, or single finds of unclear nature. Only at the next step of interpretation does it become useful to introduce further categories denoting motivation or intent of deposition, an issue that has been discussed heatedly in European archaeology.

Overall, I would argue that the key to identifying deposition as a practice rather than as a one-off individual act is the observation of repeated patterns, formal item combinations (including animal bones and other items that may not seem of any value to the modern observer), item treatment, and location choice. Here I follow Hundt (1955), Brunn (1968), and Fontijn (2001–2002) in arguing that deposition as a structured phenomenon reflects prehistoric rules of the proper way of doing things. An established practice does not necessarily imply that the underlying motivation was religious, as many scholars assume; otherwise, all repetitive acts (including cooking, object production, and refuse disposal) would have to have a religious motivation. Still, even everyday actions may have a ritual undertone, as the dichotomy between sacred and profane—or ritual and economic—is a modern one.

As far as location choice is concerned, it is not enough to consider only retrievability, as many early studies have done (e.g., Worssae 1866), or to distinguish simply between water/wetland and dryland deposits. Instead, placement in relation to graves, settlements, and other features, both human-made and natural, has to be taken into account. There are also some general assumptions that have to be avoided. For instance, as Alexandra Krenn-Leeb (2014) and others have pointed out, not all pits in settlements are refuse pits. Ceramic deposits made in connection with drinking/eating or offering rituals may appear in settlements as well. The treatment and composition of items helps to distinguish trash from deliberately chosen assemblages. Complete vessels in standardized sets likely indicate socially and culturally determined activities in connection with feasts and/or offering. In settlement contexts, ceramic deposits may be misidentified as refuse pits, while in other locales they may not be found at all. They will not trigger a metal detector or be reported if encountered when digging a well or building foundation, as the vessels will seem of little value to modern eyes.

All in all, it has become clear that focusing on behavioral practices is particularly useful for understanding deposits, including considering the process of object production (*chaîne opératoire*), the life history of objects, use wear, object treatment, deposition location, and potential connections between all these aspects. Furthermore, religion may be viewed as a kind of behavior rather than a precise set of ideas. Where nonlocal objects are found, it is furthermore worth considering the mechanisms by which foreign objects may be adapted and adopted into local practices, for instance via rituals.

In archaeological analysis, ideally, all these aspects of past behaviors should be considered together. The key to identifying deposition as practice rather than as one-off individual acts is the observation of repeated patterns and formalization of item combination, item treatment, and location choice. In such analyses, the focus needs to be on identifying recurring actions in space and time rather than on reconstructing long-lost motivations or meanings.

A Case Study from the Other Side of the World: Deposits in Southwest China

Based on insights gained from the European debate on intentional deposits, I discuss here all deposits and chance finds (both single- and multi-item) from the Liangshan region in Southwest China and consider their composition, treatment, and location compared with settlement and grave finds. I use the term *intentional deposits* for items placed in or on the ground or in a water source in a non-mortuary context. I use the term *chance finds* for single finds, which can consist of one or several items with unknown deposition context. These are evaluated based on a comparison with finds from graves, settlements, and clearly intentional object deposits to determine if they are indeed deposits, disturbed graves, or lost items. Ideally, the full life history of the objects would be reconstructed based on technological details, use wear traces, and signs of treatment, but as the reports on all these finds are sketchy at best, in most cases such detailed information is not available. Where available, such information is evaluated, but a systematic reconstruction of *chaîne opératoire*/use life for all items would require a separate study on the original material.

I focus on non-mortuary intentional deposits in Southwest China from the Liangshan region, in western Sichuan Province (Figure 7.1). Additionally, there are a number of chance finds, some of which may be object deposits as well (Table 7.1).

All these finds date between ca. 1600 BCE and 200 CE. They occur in the central Anning River valley and the adjacent river valleys of Puge County, where they are largely contemporary with megalithic graves, and also in the mountains of the southwest, southeast, and northeast, where they tend to be later in date and contemporary with stone-construction and earth-pit graves (Figure 7.2; Hein 2016, 2017a.)

Intentional Object Deposits

Two broad types of intentional deposits have been observed in two areas. Deposition pits in the Anning River valley and adjacent mountains contain ceramic vessels, sometimes associated with stone tools. Deposition practices in the southeast also involve bronze drums and bells. In all cases, the

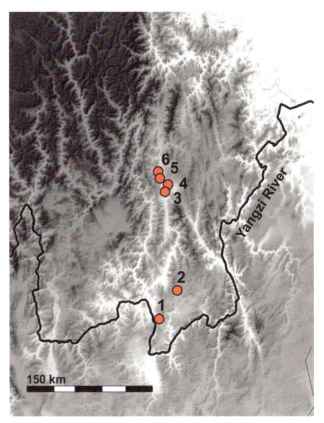

Figure 7.1. Location of object deposits in Southwest China: *Huili*: 1. Zhuanchangba; 2. Luoluochong; *Xichang*: 3. Dayangdui; 4. Beishan; 5. Yingpanshan; 6. Qimugou. *Created by Bryan K. Miller.*

objects are complete—though sometimes broken—and carefully arranged in recurring patterns, indicating socially and culturally agreed-upon practices. Given these differences, below these two phenomena are discussed separately.

Ceramic Deposits

Object pits containing carefully arranged complete ceramic objects have been reported from Xichang Dayangdui (Xichangshi et al. 2004), Maliucun (Sichuansheng et al. 2006a), Qimugou (Sichuansheng et al. 2006c), and Yingpanshan (Sichuansheng et al. 2006b), as well as from Puge Wadaluo (Liangshan 1983). Among them, we can distinguish between two different types of features:

1. Small round-oval or irregular pits containing one horizontally placed large jar or urn, sometimes combined with a few smaller ceramic vessels (Dayangdui Ka1-24, Qimugou W1, Yingpanshan W1-13)
2. Large, usually rectangular pits with a larger number of different kinds of medium-size and small vessels (Dayangdui H1-2, Maliucun H1, Puge Wadaluo H1).

Table 7.1. Deposits and chance finds from the Liangshan region

Site	Context	Objects
Huili 1994 (Huili "Gong'anju")	confiscated by police	8 bronze objects: 1 three-pronged sword, 1 short sword, 1 halberd, 1 bracelet, 2 knives, 1 spearhead, 1 staff head
Huili Guoyuan	chance find	1 Shizhaishan-type bronze drum buried upside down
Huili Hekoucun	chance find	1 bronze sword
Huili Luoluochong	1 pit	1 bronze drum buried upside down
Huili Yimen Xiacunxiang	chance find	1 bronze *yue* axe
Huili Zhuanchangba	1 pit	6 bronze bells
Jinyang Munagou	chance find	1 bronze sword, 1 bronze halberd
Ninglang Cunyi	chance finds	unclear number of bronze axes and other bronze objects, discovered over several years
Puge Wadaluo	1 pit	150+ ceramic vessels, 2 ceramic spindle whorls
Xichang Dayangdui (late phase)	2 pits	8 and 14 ceramic vessels, respectively; stacked neatly
Xichang Dayangdui (middle phase)	24 pits	1 to 8 ceramic vessels each; mostly two horizontally placed ceramic vessels, the larger one placed in the smaller one, with the bottom of the former intentionally broken, some with additional objects; filled with fine soil; no ash, charcoal, traces of fire, or bones
Xichang Maliucun	1 pit	20 ceramic vessels
Xichang Qimugou	1 pit	2 ceramic vessels
Xichang Yingpanshan	13 pits	1 to 5 ceramic vessels each; stone net weight in one
Yanyuan "Gong'anju"	confiscated by police	603 bronze objects (mostly weapons and tools; some ornaments, armor, horse gear, drums, bells, and items of unclear function), 2 iron objects, 24 composite weapons, 38 stone arrowheads, 9 stone grinding rods, 2 seashells, 1 god strip
Yongsheng Laoying	chance find	bundle of 20 much-corroded bronze swords, 0.6–0.8 m below surface; 1 bronze cauldron on surface; 1 bronze bracelet; 5 ceramic beakers
Yongsheng Longtan	chance finds	300+ bronze objects, mostly weapons
Yongsheng Yangjiaqing	chance find	1 ceramic beaker, 2 bronze drums, 2 bronze cups, several bronze ornaments
Zhaojue Sikaixiang	chance find	17 Han bronze coins 10 cm below surface

Type I Ceramic Deposits

The 24 pits at Dayangdui were found in Layer 5, which was devoid of other traces of cultural activity. The other layers at Dayangdui held earth-pit graves (Layer 6), megalithic graves, and two further pits (Layer 4). The pits in Layer 5 were arranged in two groups; those in the northern part of the site were east–west aligned, and those in the south were north–south aligned (Figure 7.3).

The ceramic vessels are of brown or red medium coarse ware, hand-thrown, rarely with a black slip, and of a quality similar to that of contemporary settlement and grave ceramics, all of them roughly made undecorated yellow-brown coarse ware. Most pits contained one urn or large jar, often with a row of upward-pointing lug-handles around the shoulder. The bottom of this vessel was nearly always intentionally broken and placed into a smaller jar. Only in a few cases

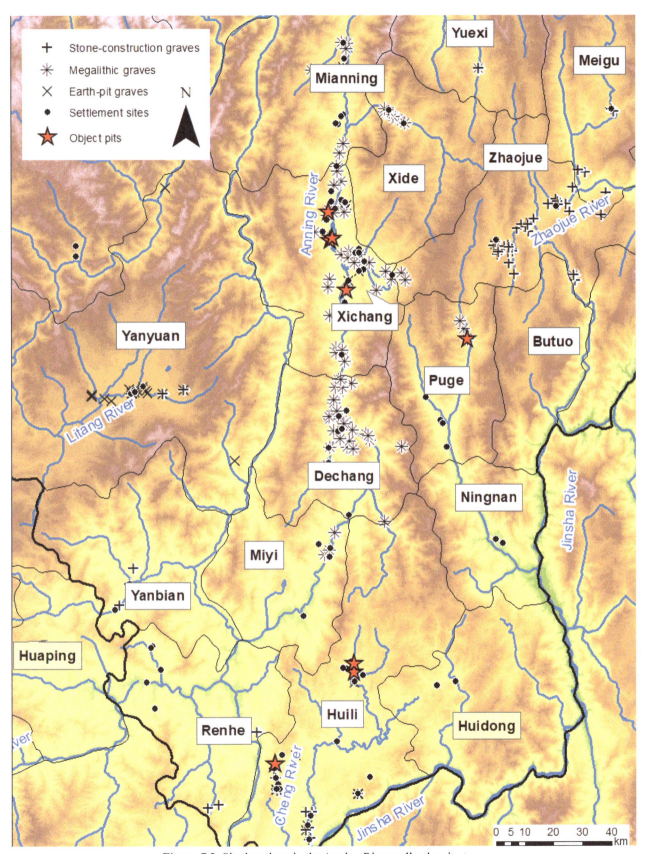

Figure 7.2. Site locations in the Anning River valley by site type.
Created by the author.

130 Anke Hein

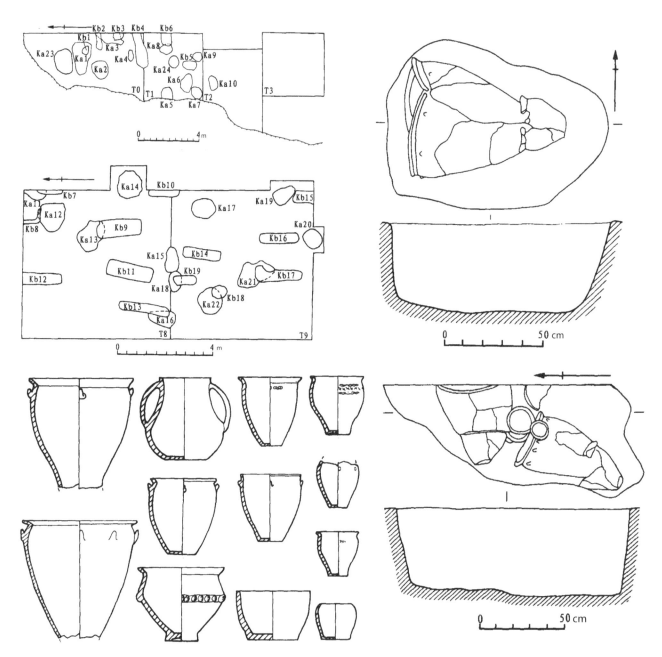

Figure 7.3. Top left: plan of object pits in the northern (top) and southern (bottom) part of Xichang Dayangdui; top right: plan of Ka21; bottom left: ceramic vessels from pits (1. Ka19:1; 2. Ka23:1; 3. Ka13:5; 4. Ka12:2; 5. Ka13:1; 6. Ka3:2; 7. Ka19:2; 8. Ka3:4; 9. Ka21:2; 10. Ka17:2; 11. Ka15:1; 12. Ka13:4); bottom right: plan of Ka3.
Drawn by the author after Xichangshi et al. 2004:Figures 9–17.

was the placement different: Ka3 contained two such vessel groups accompanied by three basins and one bowl; in Ka11 the vessels were placed mouth to mouth; in Ka2 they were positioned next to each other; Ka4-7 and Ka9 each held only one large jar with an intact bottom; Ka 13 had an assemblage composed of one jar, one double-handled jar, one cup, and one stemmed bowl; and in Ka14 two large jars of equal size and form were stacked on top of each other (Figure 7.3). In all cases, the vessels were horizontally placed in irregular pits just large enough to hold them. Furthermore, every object pit was paired with a larger, long rectangular pit with rounded corners containing fine yellow silt (Kb1-19). Such silt pits do not occur at Qimugou or Yingpanshan, but the vessel forms observed there are similar to those seen at Dayangdui.

The single-object Pit W1 at Qimugou was small and contained one urn and one jar, both made of gray-brown medium coarse ware without slip or decoration. The vessels were accompanied by charcoal indicating burning inside the pit. In this instance, the smaller vessel was placed inside the larger one, and the larger vessel seems to have been standing upright instead of lying on its side. The pits at Xichang Yingpanshan were mostly small and round (0.5–0.9 cm rim diameter; 0.1–0.3 m depth), with the exception of W2, which was considerably larger (1.3–1.62 rim diameter; 0.1–0.24 cm deep). In spite of its size, W2 contained only two large urns. The vessels from the pits at Yingpanshan were generally larger than those at Dayangdui (mostly 40–50 cm in height compared to 23–35 cm). Furthermore, they were slightly different in form, and none had lug-handles, but some did feature incised decoration, which is rare at Dayangdui. The ware quality and color, however, were similar between the two sites.

The vessel forms from Qimugou W1 were similar to those from the pits in Yingpanshan (very large urns with pointed-bottomed ovoid bodies, constructed necks, angular outward-flaring rims, wide openings, flat bottoms, and downward-sloping shoulders or high rounded shoulders, all without handles), and the sizes corresponded closely as well. The vessels at Yingpanshan were horizontally placed, but the bottoms had not been intentionally broken, and some contained red burned earth pellets and ash (W2, W5, W8, W11), which does not occur at Dayangdui. Some pits at Yingpanshan held only one large urn (W1, W3, W4, W9, W10, W12); others contained two vessels (W2, W5–W8), most of them urns as well; while W6 held one urn and one double-handled jar. W11 and W13 are exceptional, as their assemblages consist of five objects each. W11 held three urns or jars (they were too fragmented to allow reconstructing the exact form) and one vessel with a high ring-foot, possibly a beaker, all of them placed horizontally next to each other. W13 contained two urns layered on top of each other, with one bowl and one lid placed next to them. W12 is noteworthy as well, having yielded a large urn with a stone net-weight placed inside.

The vessels from all three sites are of red to brown coarse sand-tempered material and were hand-thrown or more rarely coil-built and fired at very low temperatures. The completeness of the vessels and the regularity of their placement and treatment make it clear that the deposits were not meant for mundane storage but were the outcome of ritualized actions. Because some of these vessels contained charcoal, they are often referred to as urn graves (*wenguanzang* 瓮棺葬); however, as none of them contained any bone remains or personal ornaments and many were even devoid of ash, this interpretation seems untenable. The pits could have been cenotaphs or ritual offerings, or they might contain objects used in ritual activities and then disposed of in a prescribed fashion. As no residue analyses were conducted at the time of excavation, it is difficult to tell whether they ever contained food or drink, but as the objects were placed horizontally, they were likely empty at the time of deposition.

The ceramics in Dayangdui on the one hand (we may call them Type Ia ceramic deposits) and in Qimugou and Yingpanshan on the other hand (Type Ib ceramic deposits) seem to have been used differently. Most of the large urns and jars at Dayangdui had a broken bottom and were placed in a smaller vessel. They might thus have been used for libation or some other kind of symbolic transition from one state or place to another. The fine yellow silt in the adjacent pits might have come from a special or sacred location, perhaps a place of origin of the group of people who dug them. At the other two sites, fire was involved in some way, but the vessels were intact, reflecting a different kind of ritual.

Both kinds of deposits are unique within the Liangshan region and do not seem to have any parallels in adjoining regions either. They have been compared to the urn graves at Yuanmou Dadunzi in Yunnan, but these contained charred bones of children placed in large urns covered either by another urn or jar or by a stone (Yunnansheng 1977). The urns had been horizontally placed as well but were of different form, roughly pill-shaped with a very small bottom and a narrow opening with a medium-high neck. Many urns contained additional objects, either ceramics (ewers or jars) or animal bones probably belonging to food offerings, or in one case 12 bone beads that might have belonged to a necklace. Similar urns containing the calcinated bones of infants accompanied by a few ornaments or small tools have furthermore been observed at the unpublished site of Yongsheng Duizi (Yunnansheng et al. 2010). The site of Mianning Xiaogoudi is likewise reported to have held 21 urn burials, but as the material remains unpublished, it is unclear if they were burials of infants or adults, what the urns looked like, and how they were positioned (Guojia 2009).

While the pits at Dayangdui clearly did not contain cremation burials, it is conceivable that the large vessels in the pits at Qimugou and Yingpanshan originally contained small bones that deteriorated in the unfavorable soil climate. As both sites, as well as Mianning Xiaogoudi, are very close to megalithic graves, which contained only bones of older men and women, it is possible that these three sites are cremation burials for children of the same group that buried their elderly in megalithic graves. If this was the case, then the object pits at Dayangdui would be either a completely unrelated phenomenon or a symbolic burial for infants whose bodies were deposed of elsewhere. As the pits at Dayangdui precede the megalithic graves at the same site, the latter explanation seems more plausible; the pits of Qimugou and Yingpanshan likely had a different behavioral context.

Type II Ceramic Deposits

Type II pits are large, roughly rectangular in form, and contain a larger number of smaller vessels neatly stacked in the center of the pit (Figure 7.4). The excavators interpret the feature at Wadaluo as a storage pit (*yaoxue* 窑穴) and the ones at Maliucun and Dayangdui as refuse pits (*huikeng* 灰坑)—that is, places for trash disposal. Given that the objects were complete and carefully stacked, these features are unlikely to have been refuse pits. However, their actual meaning is difficult to determine, and they may differ from site to site.

The three pits differ significantly in size and assemblage. Even though the Maliucun pit is much larger than the others (3.68 x 2.06 x 0.6 m as compared to 1–1.2 x 0.5 x 0.8 m), it held only 20 identifiable objects, while more than 150 vessels have been reported from Wadaluo. Dayangdui H1 contained 14, and H2 a mere eight vessels of slightly differing types (Figure 7.4). The ceramics from Dayangdui were all hand-thrown and made of red or brown sand-tempered clay, enhanced in some cases with an incised water ripple pattern, an impressed leaf vein pattern, or a black slip. Nearly all forms have wide outward-flaring rims, making them useful for drinking or pouring liquids.

The assemblages from Puge Wadaluo H1 and Xichang Maliucun H1 consist of fine gray-brown or black-brown high-fired clay ceramics, many of them highly polished or with black slip. In both pits, vessel forms associated with drinking, such as cups, beakers, ewers, and flasks, are most common, but there are stylistic differences between the two sites. The objects from Wadaluo are simple in form and undecorated, with flat bottoms; at Maliucun, complex vase and goblet forms with handles, spouts, ring-footed or pedestal-based bottoms, and line-decorated bodies are most common (Figure 7.5).

Megalithic graves have been observed at all three sites with this type of deposit, but so far only two of the graves at Dayangdui have been excavated. DM1 was devoid of objects, but DM2 contained five ceramic vessels of form and quality similar to vessels from the two object pits. The assemblage from Maliucun H1 closely resembles the ceramics from the megalithic graves of Xichang Bahe Baozi, which were located about 15 km from Maliucun (Xichang et al. 1978:Figure 7.4). Both sites are situated on the western bank of the Anning River. Liu Hong's (2009:91–92) interpretation of Maliucun as an offering pit used in connection with the multiple secondary burials of the megalithic graves is plausible and can be applied to Xichang Dayangdui H1 and H2 as well.

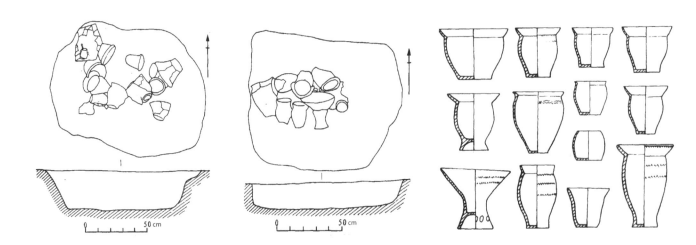

Figure 7.4. Plan of Dayangdui H1 (left) and H2 (middle); objects from Pits H1 and H2 and Grave DM2 (1. H1:1; 2. H2:6; 3. H2:1; 4. H2:3; 5. DM2:1; 6. H2:5; 7. H1:10; 8. DM2:4; 9. H1:13; 10. H1:6; 11. H2:2; 12. H1:5; 13. H2:4). *Drawn by the author after Xichangshi et al. 2004: Figures 13–15.*

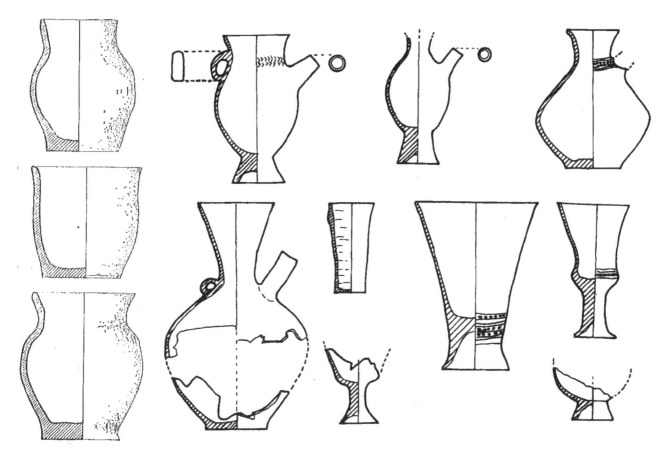

Figure 7.5. Objects from Puge Wadaluo H1 (after Liangshan 1983:Figures 9, 10, and 4); ceramics from Xichang Maliucun H1. *Drawn by the author after Sichuansheng et al. 2006a:Figures 1–2.*

For the object pit at Wadaluo, the situation is a little more difficult to assess. The megalithic graves excavated so far in Puge are very different in assemblage from what was found at Wadaluo (Liangshan et al. 1982). The graves contained mainly bronze, stone, bone, and tooth ornaments; bronze weapons and tools; and a very small number of pottery objects, the only overlap being a single centrally perforated spindle whorl in one of the graves resembling an object from the Wadaluo pit. The relationship between these two kinds of features therefore remains unclear. The ceramics at Wadaluo are reminiscent of objects from the stone grave M10 at Xichang Tianwangshan (Liangshan 1984:Figure 4), as well as vessels from earth-pit graves with or without stone installations in Puge, Zhaojue, and Huili (Liangshan 1981:Figure 7; Liangshan and Pugexian 1987:Figure 8.1; Liangshan et al. 1982:Figure 4; Tang 1999:Figure 2). Given this resemblance to artifacts from grave contexts, the object pit at Wadaluo might have been an offering connected with burial practices as well, be it in earth-pit, megalithic, or stone-construction graves.

Bronze Deposits

The only three known bronze deposits in the Liangshan region were discovered in Huili County at the border with Yunnan. They all contained large musical instruments made of bronze and dating probably to the last centuries BCE. At Huili Luoluochong (Huilixian 1977) and Guoyuan (Bao 1989), peasants found single bronze drums buried upside down. At Zhuanchangba (Tao 1982), locals encountered six bronze bells when digging a well. The bells were subsequently excavated by archaeologists, who noticed that they had been carefully stacked in three layers. The drum at Luoluochong was filled with gray-black earth, indicating that it had either contained organic material or been filled with a special kind of soil denoting ritual significance.

The drums from the two sites of Luoluochong and Guoyuan are very similar; they are both Shizhaishan-type drums, consisting of a flattened oval top and a trapezoidal outward-flaring lower part with a slightly stepped foot section (Figure 7.6). Four pairs of small braided double handles are distributed around the vessels, connecting the lower part of the top portion of a vessel to its middle. Both drums are of medium size, measuring 24.1 cm (Guoyuan) and 30.4 cm (Luoluochong) in height, with top diameters of 28.5 and 41 cm and bottom diameters of 34.5 and 50 cm. These drums are decorated in a similar fashion, carrying a star or sun motif inside several concentric circles on the top and several bands and panels of geometric and figural ornamentation around their bodies. The sides of the Luoluochong drum show the outlines of six boats with two or three rowers each, as well as four oxen with birds sitting on their backs and at their feet and additional birds shown in separate panels. The published picture of the Guoyuan drum is too small and unclear to show such details, but the excavation report describes the drum as carrying similar decorations of boats with two rowers each and standing oxen. Tang Xiang (1999), who had access to the original drums, furthermore remarks that the Guoyuan drum was most similar to Shizhaishan-type drums of the middle phase found both at Shizhaishan (for example, M3:3, M15:7, and M16:1) and at Lijiashan (for example, M24:36 and M24:42; Yunnansheng 1975:Figure 39; Zhongguo 1988:37–42). The Luoluochong drum strongly resembles a number of other drums from Shizhaishan (for example, M1:58 and M6:2; Li 1978:Figure 1.2), as well as drums from Yunnan, Guizhou, and Guangxi generally attributed to late Shizhaishan (Zhongguo 1988:43–47).

Shizhaishan-type drums, which are also referred to as Heger Style I drums, are very common throughout Southwest China and are either of similar size to those from Huili or larger. The alloys used in their production vary considerably, but it is unclear whether these differences were meant to influence the resulting sound or color or whether they had metallurgical reasons. It is generally assumed that the drums from Southwest China and Southeast Asia were cast in the lost-wax technique (Jiang 2008), although the occurrence of casting seams suggests that the piece-mold technique might have been used. The quality of these drums, as well as that of the Huili drums, is very high, contrasting with the lower quality of most other bronze objects from Huili. Tang Xiang (1999) therefore suggests that the drums were imported. The stylistic similarity with objects from Yunnan further supports this hypothesis.

What is most remarkable about the Huili drums is their mode of deposition. Most known bronze drums from China and Southeast Asia were retrieved from graves. Only the bronze drum from Cổ Loa Citadel near Hanoi was found in a pit (Higham 2002:122–23). This drum was exceptionally large (width: 73.6 cm; height: 57 cm), and it was filled with about 200 bronzes, including 20 kg of scrap pieces of various kinds of tools. It is unclear whether this was a storage hoard or a ritual offering. At the Phu Chanh site, about 40 km north of Ho-Chi-Minh City, a Shizhaishan/Heger I–type bronze drum was found positioned over a larger wooden jar of 50 cm diameter and 43.5 cm height (Bui 2008). Although the drum was interred in a large pit and

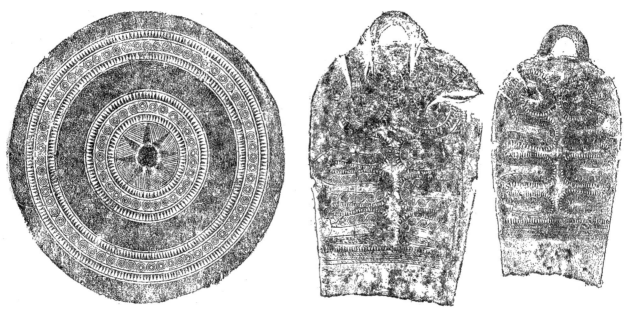

Figure 7.6. Rubbings of the drum from Huili Luoluochong and bells from Huili Zhuanchangba. For photographs of the drum from Huili Luoluochong, consult Huilixian 1977:Figure 1. For photographs of the drum from Huili Guoyuan, consult Bao 1989:Figure 1. *After Huilixian 1977:Figure 2 and Tao 1982:Figure 1.*

contained no bones, the site has been interpreted as a burial. At Prohear, Cambodia, some of the dead were buried with a bronze drum over the head (Reinecke et al. 2009), a phenomenon that resembles the common burial practices at Kele culture sites in Guizhou, where bronze kettles were employed for the same purpose (Guizhousheng 2008).

Combined with textual sources and ethnographic records, the archaeological material suggests a wide range of uses for bronze drums. Aside from the obvious function as musical instruments and signaling devices in rituals, celebrations, and war, they were employed in a burial context, most often as burial goods, presumably for the dead to use in the afterlife, or as objects that had been made ritually unusable as a consequence of their use in the burial ritual. Furthermore, drums could be used to cover the heads of the dead, and they could serve as containers for various kinds of offerings—for example, cowrie shells at Shizhaishan and other sites. Additionally, the drums probably served a wide range of purposes outside the grave, as suggested by some of the scenes depicted on cowrie containers (Tong 1983; Wang 1979).

What kind of inferences can be drawn from this material to help us understand the nature of the bronze drum deposits in Huili? It is fairly clear that at least the object form and possibly even the drums themselves were derived from the Dian cultural context. The use to which the drums were put in Huili, however, might have been very different from what was customary farther south. That the drums were placed upside down indicates that they may have served as containers rather than as musical instruments. Although their use as burial urns cannot be excluded—after all, bone does not preserve well in most of the Liangshan region—their upside-down placement into a pit without any accompanying objects suggests a ritual deposition possibly involving food or other organics.

The case of the six bells from Zhuanchangba is somewhat different. Although they were deposited in a pit just as the drums were, they hardly lend themselves to any other usage than as musical instruments, signaling devices, and/or objects with a symbolic meaning. These bells are clearly a set, given their nearly identical shape and decoration (Figure 7.6). They differ slightly in size, with heights of 43 cm to 49.5 cm and a maximum width of 22 cm to 30 cm, showing that they had been made from separate but very similar molds and would produce different tones. All six bells are decorated with line incisions of winding bands that remind us of snakes with patterns covering their bodies and four similar decorative bands below. These decorative bands closely resemble those on the drum from Luoluochong.

Bells of a similar form have been found in Yanyuan Laolongtou M4 and several sites west of Chuxiong in Yunnan (Li 1983:23; Liangshan and Chengdu 2009:Color Plate 7.1; Yunnansheng 1959:Figure 23; Yunnansheng 1964:Figure 9), nearly all of them in graves. The only exception are the bells from Fushilong, which were found 3 m below the surface without clear associated features, and the bells at Zhuanchangba, which came from a pit. The bells usually come in sets of six; the only exceptions are the single bell from Laolongtou and the three specimens from Xiangyun Jiancun in Yunnan. In all cases, the sizes and decorations are similar to those of the bells from Zhuanchangba—large animals with curved bodies or geometric motifs. Bells with a sheep's horn–shaped protrusion on top and straight or slightly outward-flaring sides have been found in great numbers all over Yunnan, Guangxi, Guangdong, and northern Vietnam. They were deposited in graves and are either undecorated or carry geometric motifs resembling those usually found on drums (Falkenhausen 1988:561–63). Both types of bells are thus restricted to Southwest China, but the second type is even more limited in its range of distribution.

According to the—admittedly very few—chemical analyses conducted on material from Southwest China, most bells and drums from Yunnan have a similar composition, consisting of 70–80% copper, 13–16% tin, and up to 13.7% lead (Falkenhausen 1993:105; Murowchick 1989:225–26). The bell from Laolongtou has an even higher tin percentage (30.46%) but a fairly low lead content (2.19%; Liu and Tang 2006:219), and the bells from Huili consist of nearly pure copper (92.49% copper and 7% tin; Falkenhausen 1993:105). Von Falkenhausen suggests that Dian bell manufacturers might have been aware of Chinese bronze casting rules calling for one part tin and six parts copper for musical instruments (Falkenhausen 1988:559). In later periods, so he argues, the southwestern bell casters seem to have moved away from these casting principles, as reflected in the very different composition of the Zhuanchangba bells.

This model of development, however, does not explain the composition of the similarly late bell from Laolongtou with its unusually high tin content. Such a high percentage of tin would have influenced the playing behavior unfavorably. It would have made the bell brittle and thus prone to breakage when struck. The tin might have been added to aid in the casting process and/or to enhance the color of the object, suggesting that the object's qualities as a musical instrument were not a primary concern. While the Dian had a specific casting tradition that may indeed have been informed by casting rules from the Central Plains, the casting techniques employed in the Liangshan area seem to represent a local practice that was much less refined.

Another factor to keep in mind is the availability of raw materials. As Murowchick has pointed out, lead levels in bronzes in northern China, northern Vietnam, and Cambodia are considerably higher than in artifacts from Southwest China, which could be due to the ready availability of tin in Southwest China, making it unnecessary to substitute lead (Murowchick 1989:226). Nevertheless, as high lead levels improve the flow of the material in casting (Falkenhausen 1988:225), technical considerations could have played a role as well. The casting techniques used for the bells in Huili and Shizhaishan have been compared to those common for small *ling* bells found as part of the personal attire in a number of graves throughout the Liangshan area and in Yunnan (Tao 1982). The *ling* bells, however, are usually much coarser in execution and only rarely carry any decoration. Those specimens recovered from Chuxiong Wanjiaba (Yunnansheng 1983) are of nearly pure copper with trace elements of other metals (Murowchick 1989:103), indicating no deliberate alloying, but two specimens retrieved from the antiquities market in Yanyuan have a relatively high tin content (7%–12%) combined with a low amount of lead (2%–4%).

The specific trace elements found in the bells from Zhuanchangba (Tao 1982), the deliberate alloying with lead, and the casting technique all speak for local production. The forms and decoration motifs, however, show an awareness of object traditions in the Dian culture realm. But the usage might have been different, making their sound and striking properties, and thus the actual alloy, immaterial to the metalworkers in Huili. The probable difference in usage and meaning would also explain the difference in interment.

Location Choice

As has become clear in the description above, the different types of object pits seem to have been preferentially located in different parts of the Liangshan region. All object pits containing bronzes have been found in Huili, Luoluochong, and Guoyuan. The two places with drum finds are located less than 3 km apart from each other. They are both less than 1 km south of the Cheng River and were built on level ground at an elevation of around 1800 m, low in relation with the overall terrain of Huili. The pit containing the bronze bells at Zhuanchangba similarly was located at an elevation of around 1800 m, on the eastern slope of a depression between the mountains, nearly 6 km from the nearest major river. All three sites are located within clusters of graves and settlement sites, all located at similar elevations and on similarly moderate slopes.

All three sites are located in places with easy access to Yunnan, particularly to Chuxiong, but are difficult to reach from the Anning River valley. The whole area is particularly rich in metal resources (especially copper and lead) and functions as the Liangshan region's gateway to Dian. It is therefore not surprising that the bronzes found in these pits show close similarity to finds from Chuxiong but differ markedly from the archaeological assemblages from the Anning River valley.

The pits with ceramic objects described above are located in a very different area. They mostly cluster around Xichang in the alluvial fan of the Anning River and thus at relatively low elevations (about 1,500 masl). Only Puge Wadaluo is located more than 44 km southeast, separated from the other sites by a high mountain chain and several rivers. Like the other sites, however, it is very close to a river, the Xiluo River, and—by local standards— it is at a moderate elevation of 1773 m and on a slope. The site is only 500 m from the megalithic graves of Puge Xiaoxingchang, indicating a direct relationship. Xichang Dayangdui and Maliucun are likewise extremely close to megalithic graves but on level ground on a wide alluvial plane and not on a mountain slope as observed in Puge. Furthermore, the ceramic assemblages from these two areas are very different from each other, indicating a difference both in ceramic tradition and in megalithic grave construction. However, the offering practices are similar.

It is difficult to tell whether special locations were chosen to conduct the rituals associated with the Xichang Dayangdui Layer 5, Qimugou, and Yingpanshan intentional deposits. Dayangdui is located on a human-made platform towering about 10 m above the surrounding landscape. The spot was used as an earth-pit grave cemetery before being used for ritual activities involving ceramic pits of the first type, and it was subsequently occupied by megalithic graves with associated ceramic pits of the second type. Qimugou first served as a settlement with associated graves, followed by a phase that saw the construction of a single grave accompanied by a ceramic pit. The site is very close to the river on level ground, a slightly elevated natural terrace with the mountains at its back and the river in front, making it similar to Dayangdui as well as to Yingpanshan but also to most other settlement and grave sites in the area.

Yingpanshan held several layers of settlement remains, object pits, and earth-pit graves, with object pits and graves occurring within the same layers. Given the close similarity between Qimugou and Yingpanshan and their spatial association with megalithic graves, it seems likely that the pits at these two sites were directly associated with burial rituals or might even have served as graves themselves. They are furthermore located less than 9 km from each other, while Dayangdui is more than 20 km farther south. Judging by their unique form and content, the pits at Dayangdui might thus belong to a separate tradition, commemorating the earlier burials at the same site, or they could have been the outcome of quite different kinds of ritualized actions, likely conducted by a group rather than individuals.

Chance Finds

Most single finds from the Liangshan region were made by private individuals with no subsequent excavation. Their original locations are thus unclear and their interpretations are problematic. As some of these are groups of objects rather than single items, it is more fitting to refer to them as chance finds rather than single finds. We can distinguish between two main categories with several subcategories:

1. Objects recovered from the antiquities market
2. Objects found and reported by local residents
    a. Discoveries followed up by excavation or surface survey
    b. Finds for which the original location has been reported but not further explored
    c. Objects kept in private households as heirlooms with a vague assignation as to find location

For the first category of objects, the deposition context is usually irretrievably lost. However, two large loots retrieved by the police in Huili and Yanyuan very likely come from one site or at least one river valley each. These finds have been analyzed elsewhere, and a comparison with grave finds in both locales has shown that they were probably assemblages from looted graves in Huili and the Yanyuan basin, respectively (Hein 2014). They will thus not be discussed here. Examples of 2a are, for instance, the bronze object pits from Huili, described above, as well as many graves that have been analyzed elsewhere together with other grave assemblages from the Liangshan region (Hein 2017b). Below I discuss only finds that could not be assigned to specific features.

Such finds with known location have been reported from Huili Hekoucun and Yimen Xiacunxiang; Ninglan Cunyi; Yongsheng Laoying, Longtan, and Yanjiaqing; and Zhaojue Sikaixiang (Guojia 2009). In most cases, no drawings or photographs have been published, making it difficult to assess the object types and potential significance of their occurrence. The bronze sword from Hekoucun was found at a slightly elevated spot on the eastern bank of the Jinshajiang, on level ground at 1771 m, close to the foot of the mountain. The weapon has been in the household of local peasants since 1971 and was recorded by archaeologists in March 1999 (Tang Xiang 1999). It has been described as a sword with a three-pronged hilt, measuring more than 32 cm in length. (It was broken at the tip.) The object was found 1.5 km from the grave site of Huili Yunshuancun and not far from Fenjiwan, Xiaotuanshan, and other sites that have both graves and settlement remains, none of which contain similar weapons. As many of the graves were severely disturbed and robbed, causing similar swords to appear on the antiquities market in Huili, the specimen from Hekoucun could have come from a grave, but it is unclear what kind of grave it was and what kind of objects it might have been associated with. At Huili Yimen Xiacunxiang, a single bronze *yue* axe was discovered on a second-level river terrace at 1,789 masl. Many of the earth-pit graves with or without stone installations in Huili contained bronze *yue* axes, for instance at Guojiabao, which is located 16 km away. The Xiacunxiang find may thus be from a disturbed grave or an actual object deposit.

The assemblages of surface finds in Yongsheng are very rich and all close to each other within the same valley, on level ground at around 1,600 masl; each collection site is close to a river. At Longtan, more than 300 bronze objects have been discovered, among them swords, halberds, spearheads, *yue* and *fu* axes, hoes, composite swords, bronze and iron spearheads, and ceramic jars. As no detailed descriptions or pictures of the objects have been published, it is difficult to compare them with provenience objects. However, composite swords are otherwise mainly known from Yanyuan Laolongtou and Han-period stone-cist graves from Yunnan and Sichuan, indicating that these finds might come from similar graves. Yongsheng Longtan and Yanjiaqing are very close as well and have yielded similar objects, indicating the presence of large cemeteries of several hundred graves. Ninglang Cunyi is located in a mountain valley as well but in a very narrow one at high altitude (2,195 masl), with no other known sites around. Nevertheless, as various kinds of bronze weapons have continuously come to light, excavations in this area would probably reveal a similar cemetery.

At Yongsheng Laoying, a bundle of 20 swords was found 0.6–0.8 m below surface, while a number of other items appeared on the surface (one bronze cauldron, one bronze bracelet, five ceramic beakers). The surface finds might have come from disturbed graves, but the bundling and burying of the swords suggests a deposit, maybe an offering to higher powers or items for several deceased in a group offering. The chance find of one bronze sword and one halberd in Jinyang Munagou, a place located on a first-level terrace at an elevation of 1,892 masl, may have been a disturbed grave as well, but as no images of the objects have been published, it is impossible to evaluate the material properly.

The situation in Zhaojue Sikaixiang is rather different. Here, a pile of 17 Han coins was discovered 10 m below the surface on the alluvial fan of a river at the considerable elevation of 2,444 masl but surrounded by even higher mountains. The location is close to a Han settlement site and a number of earlier and later graves and settlements, close to ancient roads and river courses. It is therefore highly likely that they were either offerings for safety on the road or money hidden for safekeeping in case of a bandit attack.

Discussion: The Nature of the Object Deposits in Southwest China

As is shown in this paper, the occurrence of an assemblage of intact objects in a pit can be the result of a wide variety of different behaviors. In the Liangshan region alone, three different kinds of practices were identified. These phenomena are deposits of precious metal objects (connected with the two separate traditions of interring either bells in their own right or single drums serving as containers for offerings), deposits of one large and one or several small ceramic vessels (connected with fire treatment and/or libation/transition rituals), and the interment of a larger number of ceramic vessels, probably in connection with burial rituals, as the spatial association with megalithic graves shows.

As has been shown elsewhere, the megalithic graves of the Anning River valley were the center of ritualized actions that took place at certain intervals and involved the building, reopening, and accessing of graves; eating/drinking and/or libation/food offerings in and around the graves; and potential processions or other forms of movement between graves located close to each other (Hein 2017b). One type of ceramic deposit was associated with these peri- or post-burial practices. The other type of ceramic deposits is the result of community-based ritualized actions of a different nature that did not involve graves and were earlier in date. Given that these earlier pits at Dayangdui are superimposed by megalithic graves that can be associated with ceramic deposits as well, the two customs may be linked. It was only in connection with megalithic graves, however, that the custom became widespread, especially during the late period, when similar deposits occurred all throughout the Anning River valley and even in the eastern mountains.

Ceramic deposits were generally located in the alluvial fans of rivers or on lower-level terraces and often close to settlements and/or burial sites rather than in special sacred locales, indicating that the ritualized acts conducted there were not secret but were closely linked to community life.

The pits at Xichang Dayangdui and Maliucun were clearly used in connection with the multiple secondary burials of the megalithic graves, either for offerings to the dead or for depositing objects used in ritual meals or other activities that precluded them from being employed in everyday consumption afterward; the same likely applies to Puge Wadaluo. The remaining ceramic deposits are very different in content, even though they are in the vicinity of megalithic graves. Xichang Qimugou and Yingpanshan might be either symbolic or actual urn burials originally holding the bones of infants and juveniles who for religious or social reasons could not be buried in the megalithic graves. Both sites are relatively close to each other. The ceramic pit of Xichang Dayangdui is located significantly farther south and reflects a very different practice. The pits at Dayangdui hold ceramics clearly used in libation rituals and are paired with pits containing fine yellow silt, which might have come from a special or sacred location, a custom that is unique within the Liangshan region and does not seem to have any parallels in adjoining regions either.

The bronze deposits are of a different nature. The drums are likely imports from the Dian culture sphere, deposited as ritual offerings of special objects, possibly in reference to the nearby river or other landmarks. The singular deposition of bronze bells was found 40 km farther southwest and separated by a high mountain ridge both from the other sites with bronze deposits and from the nearest river. The meaning of both groups of bronze deposits might nevertheless be similar, as they both contained ritual musical instruments used in graves in the Dian culture area but otherwise unknown from Huili. It is remarkable, however, that the bells were local products imitating foreign objects but not meant for actual use as musical instruments. All three deposits therefore show the high esteem in which Dian objects were held and reflect ways in which foreign items were received locally, in somewhat of a parallel to what Fontijn and others suggested for the case of imported bronzes in deposits in the Netherlands.

Bronze drums in particular have a wide distribution far beyond the Dian realm, extending throughout most of Yunnan and much of Southeast Asia. Apart from their usage in various rituals and as grave goods, historical sources show that the drums were symbols of authority as well as instruments for summoning the gods (Cooler 1995:9; Pirazzoli-t'Serstevens 1974:29–31). Pictographic evidence from Dian cowrie containers indicates that they might have had a similar function during earlier times as well. Alice Yao (2010) suggests that the drums might have symbolized formalized alliance networks, and it is conceivable that the specimens from the Liangshan region did indeed reach Huili as tokens of mutual political agreements between local groups and the Dian. This might apply to the drums found in Yanyuan as well, but there they were placed inside graves and not object pits, reflecting the high status, far-reaching connections, and political importance of the tomb owner. Yanyuan is furthermore characterized by the contrast between large and very richly furnished elite burials and small graves with only minimal equipment (Hein 2014), while the cemeteries in Huili speak of a society that—at least in death—seems to have been considerably more egalitarian (Hein 2014). The bronze drums therefore likely took on a slightly different meaning in these two places—in Huili as tokens of a bond between the Dian and the local community as a whole; in Yanyuan a symbol of elite exchange and high status of a few—which would explain the differences in deposition practice. The close connections with Yunnan visible in the assemblages from both regions and the lack of bronze drums and bells in other parts of the Liangshan region can be easily explained by geomorphological factors. Both areas are separated from the Anning River valley by high mountain ranges not easy to traverse, while in Huili the terrain gently slopes down toward Yunnan, making Huili the gateway to Dian. Yanyuan is farther from the region that the Dian inhabited in the past but has relatively easy access to northwestern Yunnan and thus indirectly to Dian.

The practice of depositing bronze objects in pits is unique within the Liangshan region, but the objects show clear signs of outside influence; so do many of the single finds. From a comparison of both the provenienced single finds and the objects retrieved from the antiquities market, it has become clear that most of them come from earth-pit graves with or without stone-construction parts in the southwest of the Liangshan region—that is, Yanyuan, Yongsheng, and Ninglang. Only a few may have been non-mortuary deposits of weapons, most prominently the bundle of swords at Yongsheng Laoying and maybe some of the single items as well. However, these occurrences are too rare to suggest the existence of a deposition custom as seen in Bronze Age Europe. Nevertheless, we have to keep in mind that the region is very under-researched and there no private detectorists systematically combing the landscape and reporting their findings. Looting is a major problem, but with artifacts retrieved from the antiquities market, it is virtually impossible to reconstruct the find context. The general assumption is that they come from looted graves, but this may not always be the case. The stash of Han coins from Zhaojue Sikaixiang is a singular occurrence of a different type and may be a one-off rather than a representative of a custom or behavioral pattern. Systematic field research is necessary to establish the nature of the actions underlying these finds.

Conclusion

The case study from the Liangshan region in Southwest China has shown how insights gained from the European debate on hoards/deposits can successfully be applied to other parts of the world. The study has confirmed that deposits need to be interpreted together with other kinds of archaeological finds for us to understand their significance—in the case of later ceramic deposits especially together with the megalithic graves. In the European context, it is generally agreed that single finds need to be considered together with multi-piece deposits, as single items can be offerings too. In Southwest China, however, all kinds of chance finds (meaning both single- and multi-piece finds) have to be evaluated together and compared with settlement and especially grave finds as well as deposits. In the European case, it is sometimes possible to evaluate items found by detectorists or other private individuals, as they often report where they found the items, which in turn makes further archaeological investigation possible. Unfortunately, in Southwest China, the majority of non-excavated finds were retrieved from the antiquities market, with no chance of reconstructing the original place of deposition. In all cases, stylistic and technological comparison can help situate the items to a degree. However, this can go only so far. Metal objects seem to have been traded and exchanged between the Dian area and surrounding regions, so it is impossible to determine where looted Dian items came out of the ground, in Yunnan or somewhere in Sichuan or Guizhou.

In the case of objects with clear provenience that come from non-mortuary deposits, for the European material, a multifaceted approach considering production, life history, treatment, and deposit location has been shown to be useful for determining the nature of deposits. In Southwest China, such research is hampered by the fact that many such finds have been published only in preliminary reports, with no information on traces of object production processes or use wear and only rarely information on object treatment or precise deposition location. Future research thus needs to revisit the original objects and excavation documentation where available to gain deeper insights into the details of past deposition practices.

Relying on only the published material, it has still been possible to gain some insights into local deposition practices. Some are different from the European material, while others show similarities in behavioral patterns. A particularly intriguing practice observable in both regions is the deposition of imported items that might reflect dealing with the foreign by integrating it into the local context via various ritual actions. A major difference can be seen in the type of items deposited. According to our current knowledge, in the Liangshan region, ceramic deposits seem to be more common than metal deposits. The present case study thus provides a further argument for refocusing the debate around hoards/intentional deposits to include also non-metal deposition practices instead of focusing only on issues of value and prestige. This will require taking a renewed look at items that may hold no apparent value for the modern observer, thus questioning our own perception of value, as done in a recent volume on that topic (Papadopulous and Urton 2012).

Like examples in Europe, the Liangshan region deposits result from a wide variety of different behaviors, making it clear that no single explanation will fit them all. Some deposits are related to graves (ritual refuse, items for the dead), others to non-mortuary-related ritualized actions (such as offerings). Others might be hidden treasure or offerings (coins). Of particular interest is the connection between ceramic deposits and megalithic graves, a phenomenon that may have been much more widely spread than the current number of reported cases indicates. In this case, only systematic survey and auguring around megalithic graves—something that has never been done before—can provide further insights.

Another lesson learned from the material at hand is the insight that seemingly similar deposits (that is, ceramic pits) may be the outcome of a variety of different behavioral patterns even if the assemblages superficially look alike. It is therefore crucial to consider object treatment, place of deposition, and association with other types of sites before suggesting an interpretation. This is an insight that may be applied to other parts of the world as well. Similarly, the phenomenon of "misunderstood" or redefined imported items that received new context and meaning via deposition practices may be applied to other regions too. Especially for bronze drums and the far-reaching exchange networks throughout Southwest China and Southeast Asia that they represent, it now seems advisable to reinvestigated how and where they were used and deposited to understand how they were understood and reinterpreted throughout this vast region.

At present, there are admittedly too few cases known from the Liangshan region to provide a conclusive interpretation, but there is enough to suggest that ceramic and bronze deposits are not one-off occurrences but were part of practices that so far have been underreported. Additionally, the material provides a useful case study outside Europe for testing general ideas on human behavior developed on the European material.

Acknowledgments

This paper is based on parts of my dissertation research conducted under the supervision of Lothar von Falkenhausen, to whom I owe great thanks for never-ceasing support and encouragement throughout my studies and to the present. This paper was originally presented at von Falkenhausen's sixtieth birthday celebration but has been much revised, with critical editorial help from von Falkenhausen as well as Rowan Flad and Bryan Miller. I would also like to express my thanks to Sun Hua, Jiang Zhanghua, Liu Hong, Tang Xiang, and everybody at the Chengdu City Institute of Archaeology, the Liangshan Yi Autonomous Prefecture Museum, and the Xichang City Museum who made this research possible.

References

Allard, Francis, Yan Sun, and Katheryn M. Linduff, eds.
2018   *Memory and Agency in Ancient China: Shaping the Life History of Objects*. Cambridge: Cambridge University Press.

Appadurai, Arjun
1986   *The Social Life of Things: Commodities in Cultural Perspectives*. Cambridge: Cambridge University Press.

Bao Yuehe 包月河
1989   Huili Guoyuanxiang chutu tonggu 會理果園鄉出土銅鼓 [A Bronze Drum Excavated at Huili Guoyuanxiang]. *Sichuan wenwu* 四川文物 5:66.

Bell, Catherine M.
1992   *Ritual Theory, Ritual Practice*. New York: Oxford University Press.

Bergmann, Joseph
1970   *Die ältere Bronzezeit Nordwestdeutschlands. Neue Methoden zur ethnischen und historischen Interpretation urgeschichtlicher Quellen* [The Older Bronze Age of Northwest Germany. New Methods of Ethnic and Historical Interpretation of Prehistoric Sources]. Vol. 2, *Kasseler Beiträge zur Vor- und Frühgeschichte*. Marburg: N. G. Elwert.

Bradley, Richard
1984   *The Social Foundations of Prehistoric Britain: Themes and Variations in the Archaeology of Power*. London: Longman.
2013   Hoards and the Deposition of Metalwork. In *The Oxford Handbook of the European Bronze Age*, edited by H. Fokkens and A. Harding, pp. 121–39. Oxford: Oxford University Press.

Brück, Joanna
1999   Ritual and Rationality: Some Problems of Interpretation in European Archaeology. *European Journal of Archaeology* 2(3):313–44.

2006 Fragmentation, Personhood and the Social Construction of Technology in Middle and Late Bronze Age Britain. *Cambridge Archaeological Journal* 16(3):297–315.

Brunn, Wilhelm Albert von
1968 *Mitteldeutsche Hortfunde der jüngeren Bronzezeit*. Berlin: De Gruyter.
1980 Eine Deutung spätbronzezeitlicher Hortfunde zwischen Elbe und Weichsel [An Interpretation of Late Bronze Age Hoards between Elbe and Weichsel]. *Bericht der Römisch-Germanischen Komission* 61:92–50.

Bui Chi Hoang
2008 The Phu Chanh Site: Cultural Evolution and Interaction in the Later Prehistory of Southern Vietnam. Proceedings of the 18th Congress of the Indo-Pacific Prehistory Association, Manila, Philippines, 20 to 26 March, 2006. *Bulletin of the Indo-Pacific Prehistory Association* 28:67–72.

Campbell, Roderick
2018 *Violence, Kinship and the Early Chinese State: The Shang and Their World*. Cambridge: Cambridge University Press.

Chapman, John
2000 *Fragmentation in Archaeology: People, Places, and Broken Objects in the Prehistory of South Eastern Europe*. London: Routledge.

Clunas, Craig
1991 *Superfluous Things: Material Culture and Social Status in Early Modern China*. Urbana: University of Illinois Press.

Cooler, Richard M.
1995 *The Karen Bronze Drums of Burma: Types, Iconography, Manufacture, and Use*. Leiden: E. J. Brill.

Cunliffe, Barry W.
1992 Pits, Preconceptions and Propitiation in the British Iron Age. *Oxford Journal of Archaeology* 11(1):69–83.

Ebbesen, Klaus
1995 Die nordischen Bernsteinhorte der Trichterbecherkultur [The Nordic Amber Hoards of the Funnel Beaker Culture]. *Prähistorische Zeitschrift* 70(1):32–89.

Eggert, Manfred K. H.
2005 [2000] *Prähistorische Archäologie: Konzepte und Methoden*. 2nd ed. Tübingen: A. Francke.

Engelhardt, Conrad
1868 Udsigt over Museet for de nordiske Oldsagers Tilvækst I Aarene 1863-67 [View of the Growth of the Nordic Antiquities Museum during 1863–67]. *Aarbøger for nordisk Oldkyndighed og Historie* 1868:81–166.

Falkenhausen, Lothar von
1988 Ritual Music in Bronze Age China: An Archaeological Perspective. PhD dissertation, Department of Anthropology, Harvard University, Cambridge, MA.
1993 On the Historiographic Orientation of Chinese Archaeology. *Antiquity* 67:839–49.
1995 The Regionalist Paradigm in Chinese Archaeology. In *Nationalism, Politics, and the Practice of Archaeology*, edited by P. L. Kohl and C. Fawcett, pp. 198–217. Cambridge: Cambridge University Press.
2001a Kwang-Chih Chang. *Artibus Asiae* 61:120–38.
2001b The Use and Significance of Ritual Bronzes in the Lingnan Region during the Eastern Zhou Period. *Journal of East Asian Archaeology* 3(1–2):193–236.
2009 Sidelights on the State of Sinology in Germany: Two Recent Festschriften with a Focus on Early and Early Imperial China. *China Review International* 16(1):33–65.
2010 Antiquarianism in East Asia: A Preliminary Overview. In *Reinventing the Past: Archaism and Antiquarianism in Chinese Art and Visual Culture*, edited by Wu Hung, pp. 35–66. Chicago: Center for the Art of East Asia.
2015 Antiquarianism in China and Europe: Reflections on Momigliano. In *Cross-Cultural Studies: China and the World. A Festschrift in Honor of Zhang Longxi*, edited by Qian Suoqiao, pp. 127–51. Leiden: Brill.
2017 East Asian Art History at UCLA. In *Global and World Art in the Practice of the University Museum*, edited by J. C. Davidson and S. Esslinger, pp. 96–114. New York: Routledge.
2018a Four German Art Historians in Republican China. In *Unmasking Ideology in Imperial and Colonial Archaeology: Vocabulary, Symbols, and Legacy*, edited by B. Effros and G. Lai, pp. 299–354. Los Angeles: Cotsen Institute of Archaeology Press.
2018b The Economic Role of Cities in Eastern Zhou China. *Archaeological Research in Asia* 14:161–69.

Falkenstein, Frank
2011 Zur Struktur und Deutung älterurnenfelderzeitlicher Hortfunde im nor-dalpinen Raum [About the Structure and

Interpretation of Late Urnfeld Hoards in the Northern Alps]. In *Bronzen im Spannungsfeld zwischen praktischer Nutzung und symbolischer Bedeutung. Beiträge zum internationalen Kolloquium* Münster 2008, edited by A. Jockenhövel and U. L. Dietz, pp. 71–105. Stuttgart: Franz Steiner Verlag.

Flad, Rowan K.
2012 Bronze, Jade, Gold and Ivory: Valuable Objects in Ancient Sichuan. In *The Construction of Value in the Ancient World*, edited by J. K. Papadoupoulos and G. Urton, pp. 258–87. Los Angeles: Cotsen Institute of Archaeology Press.

Flad, Rowan K., and Pochan Chen
2013 *Ancient Central China: Centers and Peripheries along the Yangzi River*. Cambridge: Cambridge University Press.

Fontijn, David R.
2001–2002 *Sacrificial Landscapes: Cultural Biographies of Persons, Objects and "Natural" Places in the Bronze Age of the Southern Netherlands, c. 2300–600 BC*. Analecta Praehistorica Leidensia. Leiden: University of Leiden.
2008 Everything in Its Right Place? On Selective Deposition, Landscape and the Construction of Identity in Later Prehistory. In *Prehistoric Europe: Theory and Practice*, edited by A. Jones, pp. 86–106. Chichester: Wiley-Blackwell.

Garrow, Duncan
2012 Odd Deposits and Average Practice: A Critical History of the Concept of Structured Deposition (with responses by Åsa Berggren, David Fontijn, Julian Thomas, Svend Hansen, and John Chapman and a reply by the author). *Archaeological Dialogues* 19(2):85–115.

Geißlinger, Helmut
1983 Depotfund, Hortfund [Deposits, Hoards]. In *Reallexikon der Germanischen Altertumskunde*, Vol. 5, edited by H. Beck, D. Geuenich, and H. Steuer, pp. 320–38. Berlin: De Gruyter.

Görmer, Gerald
2002 Zur Terminologie "Hortfunde" ("Depotfunde") und "Einzelfunde" [About the Terminology "Hoards" ("Deposits") and "Single Finds"]. *Archäologische Informationen* 25(1–2):89–90.
2003 Quellensystematik: Niederlegungen, Verlust und Wegwurffunde und unspezifische Funde [Source Systematics: Deposits, Lost Items, and Discarded Goods, and Unspecific Finds]. *Archäologische Informationen* 26(1):151–52.
2008 Einstückdepots, Flussdepots und Verluste [Single Piece Deposits, River Deposits, and Lost Items]. *Ethnographisch-Archäologische Zeitschrift* 49(2):227–34.

Guojia Wenwuju 國家文物侷
2009 *Zhongguo wenwu dituji: Sichuan fence* 中國文物地圖集:·四川分冊 [Atlas of Chinese Cultural Relics: Sichuan Volume]. Beijing: Wenwu Chubanshe 文物出版社.

Guizhousheng Wenwu Kaogu Yanjiusuo 貴州省文物考古研究所
2008 *Hezhang Kele erling lingling nian fajue baogao* 赫章可樂二〇〇〇年發掘報告 [Report on the Excavations at Hezhang Kele in the Year 2000]. Beijing: Wenwu Chubanshe 文物出版社.

Halbwachs, Maurice
1992 [1925] *On Collective Memory*. Translated by L. A. Coser. Chicago: University of Chicago Press.

Hamerow, Helena
2006 "Special Deposits" in Anglo-Saxon Settlements. *Medieval Archaeology* 50:1–30.

Hänsel, Alix
1998 Schatzfunde der alteuropäischen Bronzezeit—Gaben an die Götter? [Treasures from the Old European Bronze Age—Gifts to the Gods?] *Antike Welt* 29(5):423–30.

Hänsel, Alix, and Bernhard Hänsel, eds.
1997 *Gaben an die Götter: Schätze der Bronzezeit Europas. Ausstellung der Freien Universität Berlin in Verbindung mit dem Museum für Vor- und Frühgeschichte, Staatliche Museen zu Berlin, Preussischer Kulturbesitz* [Gifts for the Gods: Treasures from the European Bronze Age. Exhibition of the Free University of Berlin Together with the Museum of Prehistory, State Museums of Berlin, Prussian Cultural Heritage]. Berlin: Staatliche Museen Preussischer Kulturbesitz, Museum für Vor- u. Frühgeschichte.

Hansen, Svend
2002 Über bronzezeitliche Depots, Horte und Einzelfunde: Brauchen wir neue Begriffe? [About Bronze Age Deposits, Hoards, and Single Finds: Do We Need New Terms?] *Archäologische Informationen* 25(1–2):91–97.
2005 Über bronzezeitliche Horte in Ungarn—Horte als soziale Praxis [About Bronze Age Hoards in Hungary—Hoards as Social Practice]. In *Interpretationsraum Bronzezeit. Bernhard Hänsel von seinen Schülern gewidmet*, edited by

B. Horejs, R. Jung, E. Kaiser, and B. Terzan, pp. 211–30. Bonn: Habelt.
2012 Bronzezeitliche Horte: Zeitliche und räumliche Rekontextualisierungen [Bronze Age Hoards: Chronological and Spatial Recontextualizations]. In *Hort und Raum: Aktuelle Forschungen zu bronzezeitlichen Deponierungen in Mitteleuropa*, edited by S. Hansen, D. Neumann, and T. Vachta, pp. 23–48. Berlin: De Gruyter.

Hein, Anke
2014 Metal, Salt, and Horse Skulls: Elite-Level Exchange and Long-Distance Human Movement in Prehistoric Southwest China. In *Reconsidering the Crescent-Shaped Exchange Belt: Methodological, Theoretical and Material Concerns of Long-Distance Interactions in East Asia Thirty Years after Tong Enzheng*, edited by A. Hein, pp. 89–108. Oxford: Archaeopress.
2016 Local Developments on the Eastern Rim of the Tibetan Plateau: The Prehistoric Anning River Valley. *Archaeological Research in Asia* 5:72–87.
2017a Early Cultural Developments on the Eastern Rim of the Tibetan Plateau: Establishing a New Chronological Scheme for Southwest Sichuan. *Asian Perspectives* 56(1):2–54.
2017b *The Burial Record of Prehistoric Liangshan in Southwest China: Graves as Composite Objects*. Cham: Springer.

Higham, Charles
2002 *Early Cultures of Mainland Southeast Asia*. Chicago: Art Media Resources.

Horst, F.
1977 Jungbronzezeitliche Schwerter aus dem Elb-Havel-Gebiet [Early Bronze Age Swords from the Elbe-Havel-Region]. In *Archäologie als Geschichtswissenschaft: Studien und Untersuchungen. Karl-Heinz Otto zum 60. Geburtstag*, edited by J. Herrmann, pp. 165–75. Berlin: Akademie-Verlag.

Huang Zhanyue
1998 Human Sacrifice and Ancient Chinese Society. *Archaeological Review from Cambridge* 8:76–80.

Huilixian Wenhuaguan 會理縣文化館
1977 Sichuan Huili chutu de yimian tonggu 四川會理出土的一面銅鼓 [A Drum Excavated in Huili, Sichuan]. *Kaogu* 考古 (3):215–16.

Hundt, Hans-Jürgen
1955 Versuch zur Deutung der Depotfunde der nordischen jüngeren Bronzezeit unter besonderer Berücksichtigung Mecklenburgs [Attempt at Interpreting Northern Early Bronze Age Depositions from the Point of View of the Mecklenburg Finds]. *Jahrbuch des Römisch-Germanischen Zentralmuseums Mainz* 2:95–132.

Huth, Christoph
2008 Horte als Geschichtsquelle. In *Vorträge des 26. Niederbayerischen Archäologentages*, edited by K. Schmotz, pp.131–62. Rahden: VML Verlag.

Jensen, Jørgen
1972 Ein neues Hallstattschwert aus Dänemark: Beitrag zur Problematik der jungbronzezeitlichen Votivfunde [A New Hallstatt Period Sword from Denmark: Contribution on the Problem of Early Bronze Age Votive Finds]. *Acta Archaeologica* 43:159–84.

Jiang Yu 江瑜
2008 Zhongguo Nanfang he Dongnanya gudai tonggu zhuzao jishu tantao 中國南方和東南亞古代銅鼓鑄造技術探討 [A Discussion of Production Techniques of Ancient Drums from Southern China and Southeast Asia]. *Kaogu* 考古 6:85–90.

Joyce, Rosemary A., and Joshua Pollard
2010 Archaeological Assemblages and Practices of Deposition. In *The Oxford Handbook of Material Culture Studies*, edited by D. Hicks and M. C. Beaudry, 291–309. Oxford: Oxford University Press.

Kim Seung-og
1994 Burials, Pigs, and Political Prestige in Neolithic China. *Current Anthropology* 35(2):119–41.

Krenn-Leeb, Alexandra
2006 Gaben an die Götter? Depotfunde der Frühbronzezeit in Österreich [Gifts for the Gods? Early Bronze Age Depositions in Austria]. *Archäologie in Österreich* 17(1):4–17.
2008 Strategie und Stratagem: Überlegungen zu Tradition, Innovation und Legitimation anhand der frühbronzezeitlichen Depotfunde in Österreich [Strategy and Stratagem: Thoughts on Tradition, Innovation, and Legitimation Based on Early Bronze Age Deposits in Austria]. In *Vorträge des 26. Niederbayerischen Archäologentages*, edited by K. Schmotz, pp. 163–96. Rahden: VML.
2014 Tabuisierung—Inszenierung—Transformierung. Bemerkungen zum Phänomen deponierter Gefäßensembles im Ritualkontext [Taboo—Staging—Transformation. Comments on the Phenomenon of Depositing Vessel Assemblages in Ritual Contexts]. *Archäologie Österreichs* 25(1):26–31.

Kristiansen, Kristian
1978   The Consumption of Wealth in Bronze Age Denmark. A Study in the Dynamics of Economic Processes in Tribal Societies. In *New Directions in Scandinavian Archaeology*, edited by K. Kristiansen and C. Paludan-Müller, pp. 158–90. Copenhagen: National Museum of Denmark.

Levy, Janet E.
1982   *Social and Religious Organization in Bronze Age Denmark: An Analysis of Ritual Hoard Finds.* Oxford: BAR.

Li Chaozhen 李朝真
1983   Yunnan Xiangyun Jiancun shiguomu 雲南祥雲檢村石槨墓 [The Stone Cist Graves of Yunnan Xiangyun Jiancun]. *Wenwu* 文物 5:33-41, 99.

Li Weiqing 李偉卿
1978   *Zhongguo Nanfang tonggu de fenlei he duandai* 中國南方銅鼓的分類和斷代 [Typology and Dating of the Bronze Drums of Southern China]. *Kaogu* 考古 2:66–78.

Liangshan Yizu Diqu Kaogudui 涼山彝族地區考古隊
1981   Sichuan Liangshan Zhaojue shibanmu fajue jianbao 四川涼山昭覺石板墓發掘簡報 [Preliminary Report of Excavations Conducted on Stone Slab Graves in Zhaojue, Liangshan, Sichuan]. *Kaoguxue jikan* 考古學集刊 1:127–32.

Liangshan Yizu Zizhizhou Bowuguan 涼山彝族自治州博物館
1983   Sichuan Pugexian Wadaluo yizhi diaocha 四川普格縣瓦打洛遺址調查 [Survey of Wadaluo Site, Puge County, Sichuan]. *Kaogu* 考古 6:562–64.
1984   Sichuan Xichang Tianwangshan shihaomu qingli jianbao 四川西昌天王山十號墓清理簡報 [Preliminary Excavation Report of Tianwangshan Grave Number Ten, Xichang, Sichuan]. *Kaogu* 考古 12:1092–95.

Liangshan Yizu Zizhizhou Bowuguan 涼山彝族自治州博物館 and Chengdu Wenwu Kaogu Yanjiusuo 成都文物考古研究所, eds.
2009   *Laolongtou mudi yu Yanyuan qingtongqi* 老龍頭墓地與鹽源青銅器 [Laolongtou Cemetery and Yanyuan Bronzes]. Beijing: Wenwu Chubanshe 文物出版社.

Liangshan Yizu Zizhizhou Bowuguan 涼山彝族自治州博物館 and Pugexian Wenhuaguan 普格縣文化館
1987   Sichuan Puge Xiaoxingchang dashimu qun de diaocha yu qingli 四川普格小興場大石墓群的調查與清理 [Survey and Excavation of the Megalithic Grave Group of Sichuan Puge Xiaoxingchang]. *Wenwu ziliao congkan* 文物資料叢刊 10:155–58.

Liangshan Yizu Zizhizhou Bowuguan 涼山彝族自治州博物館, Pugexian Wenhuaguan 普格縣文化館, and Pugexian Kexue Jishu Qingbao Weiyuanhui 普格縣科學技術情報委員會
1982   Sichuan Pugexian Xiaoxingchang dashimu 四川普格縣小興場大石墓 [The Megalithic Graves of Xiaoxingchang, Puge County, Sichuan]. *Kaogu yu wenwu* 考古與文物 5:34–38.

Linders, Tullia, and Gullög Nordquist
1987   Gifts to the Gods: Proceedings of the Uppsala Symposium 1985. Uppsala: Acta Universitatis Upsaliensis.

Liu Hong 劉弘
2009   *Cong shan junling zhong de "lüzhou"—Anning hegu wenhua yicun diaocha yanjiu* 从山峻岭中的"绿洲"—安宁河谷文化遗存调查研究 [From an "Oasis" in the Mountains: Investigation of the Cultural Remains of Anning River Valley]. Chengdu: Bashu Shushe 巴蜀书社.

Liu Hong 劉弘 and Tang Liang 唐亮
2006   Laolongtou muzang he Yanyuan qingtongqi 老龍頭墓葬和鹽源青銅器 [Laolongtou Graves and Yanyuan Bronzes]. *Zhongguo lishi wenwu* 中國歷史文物 6:22–29.

Malinowski, Bronislaw
1961 [1922]   *Argonauts of the Western Pacific: An Account of Native Enterprise and Adventure in the Archipelagoes of Melanisian New Guinea.* New York: Dutton.

Mauss, Marcel
1990 [1925]   *The Gift: The Form and Reason for Exchange in Archaic Societies.* Translated by W. D. Halls. New York: Norton.

Meller, Harald, ed.
2004   *Der geschmiedete Himmel: Die weite Welt im Herzen Europas vor 3600 Jahren. Begleitband zur Sonderausstellung des Landesamtes für Denkmalpflege und Archäologie Sachsen-Anhalt* [The Welded Sky: The Wide World in the Heart of Europe 3,600 Years Ago. Publication Accompanying a Special Exhibition in the State Museum of Heritage Preservation and Archaeology, Saxony-Anhalt]. Stuttgart: Landesmuseum für Vorgeschichte Halle.

Müller, Sophus
1898   *Nordische Altertumskunde: Nach Funden und Denkmälern aus Dänemark und Schleswig gemeinfasslich dargestellt von Dr. Sophus Müller* [Northern Antiquarian Studies: Based on Finds and Ruins from Denmark and Shleswig,

Explained by Dr. Sophus Müller]. 2 vols. Strassburg: K. J. Trübner.

Murowchick, Robert Edwin
1989 The Ancient Bronze Metallurgy of Yunnan and Its Environs: Development and Implications. PhD dissertation, Department of Anthropology, Harvard University, Cambridge, MA.

Nebelsick, Louis D.
1997 Auf Biegen und Brechen: Ekstatische Elemente Bronzezeitlicher Materialopfer—Ein Deutungsversuch [Bending and Breaking: Ecstatic Elements in Bronze Age Material Offerings—An Attempt in Interpretation]. In *Gaben an die Götter: Schätze der Bronzezeit Europas. Ausstellung der Freien Universität Berlin in Verbindung mit dem Museum für Vor- und Frühgeschichte, Staatliche Museen zu Berlin—Preussischer Kulturbesitz*, edited by A. Hänsel and B. Hänsel, pp. 35–41. Berlin: Staatliche Museen Preussischer Kulturbesitz, Museum für Vor- u. Frühgeschichte.
2000 Rent Asunder: Ritual Violence in Late Bronze Age Hoards. In *Metals Make the World Go Round: the Supply and Circulation of Metals in Bronze Age Europe. Proceedings of a Conference Held at the University of Birmingham in June 1997*, edited by C. F. E. Pare, pp. 159–75. Oxford: Oxbow Books.

Needham, Stuart P.
1988 Selective Deposition in the British Early Bronze Age. *World Archaeology* 20(2):229–48.

Oras, Ester
2012 Importance of Terms: What Is a Wealth Deposit? *Papers from the Institute of Archaeology* 22:61–82.

Papadopoulos, John K., and Gary Urton, eds.
2012 *The Construction of Value in the Ancient World*. Los Angeles: Cotsen Institute of Archaeology Press.

Pirazzoli-t'Serstevens, Michèle
1974 *La civilisation du royaume de Dian à l'époque Han: d'après le matériel exhumé à Shizhai shan, Yunnan* [The Civilization of the Dian Kingdom during the Han Period: Based on Material Excavated from Shizhai Shan, Yunnan]. Publications de l'École française d'Extrême-Orient 94. Paris: École française d'Extrême-Orient.

Puett, Michael J.
2002 *To Become a God: Cosmology, Sacrifice, and Self-divinization in Early China*. Cambridge, MA: Harvard University Asia Center for the Harvard-Yenching Institute.

Rappaport, Roy A.
1979 *Ecology, Meaning, and Religion*. Richmond, CA: North Atlantic Books.

Reinecke, Andreas, Vin Laychour, and Seng Sonetra
2009 *The First Golden Age of Cambodia: Excavation at Prohear*. Bonn: DAI, KAAK.

Richards, Colin, and Julian Thomas
1984 Ritual Activity and Structured Deposition in Later Neolithic Wessex. In *Neolithic Studies: A Review of Some Current Research*, edited by R. S. Bradley and J. Gardiner, pp. 189–218. Oxford: BAR.

Rowlands, Michael
1980 Kinship, Alliance and Exchange in the European Bronze Age. In *Settlement and Society in the British Late Bronze Age*, edited by J. Barrett and R. Bradley, pp. 15–55. Oxford: British Archaeological Reports.

Schumacher, Karl
1914 Neolithische Depotfunde im westlichen Deutschland [Neolithic Deposits in Western Germany]. *Prähistorische Zeitschrift* 6:29–56.

Seger, Hans
1935–1936 Schlesische Hortfunde aus der Bronze- und frühen Eisenzeit [Bronze and Early Iron Age Hoards from Silesia]. *Alt-Schlesien* 6:85–182.

Shelach, Gideon
1996 The Qiang and the Question of Human Sacrifice in the Late Shang Period. *Asian Perspectives* 35(1):1–26.

Sichuansheng Wenwu Kaogu Yanjiusuo 四川省文物考古研究所, Liangshan Yizu Zizhizhou Bowuguan 凉山彝族自治州博物館, and Xichangshi Wenwu Guanlisuo 西昌市文物管理所
2006a Liangshanzhou Xichangshi Maliucun huikeng qingli jianbao 凉山州西昌市麻柳村灰坑清理简报 [Preliminary Excavation Report of the Refuse Pit of Maliucun, Xichang City, Liangshanzhou]. *Sichuan wenwu* 四川文物 1:11–12.
2006b *Anninghe liuyu dashimu* 安寧河流域大石墓 [The Megalithic Graves of the Anning River Valley]. Beijing: Wenwu Chubanshe 文物出版社.

Sichuansheng Wenwu Kaogu Yanjiusuo 四川省文物考古研究所, Liangshan Yizu Zizhizhou Bowuguan 凉山彝族自治州博物館, and Xichangshi Wenguansuo 西昌市文管
2006c Liangshanzhou Xichangshi Qimugou yizhi shijue jianbao 凉山州西昌市棲木溝遺址試掘簡報. *Sichuan wenwu* 四川文物 1:13–20.

Stapel, Andrea
1999 *Bronzezeitliche Deponierungen im Siedlungsbereich. Altdorf-Römerfeld und Altheim, Landkreis Landshut* [Bronze Age Depositions in Settlements. Altdorf-Römerfeld, Altheim, Landkreis Landshut]. Münster: Wasman.

Stein, Frauke
1976 *Bronzezeitliche Hortfunde in Süddeutschland: Beiträge zur Interpretation einer Quellengattung* [Bronze Age Hoards in Southern Germany: Contributions to the Interpretation of a Find Type]. Bonn: Habelt.

Sterckx, Roel
2011 *Food, Sacrifice and Sagehood in Early China*. Cambridge: Cambridge University Press.

Stjernquist, Berta
1963 Präliminarien zu einer Untersuchung von Opferfunden: Begriffsbestimmung und Theoriebildung [Preliminaries on an Analysis of Offerings: Defining Terms and Building Theories]. *Meddelanden från Lunds Universitets Historiska Museum* 1962–63:5–64.

Sun Hua 孙华
2013 Sanxingdui qiwukeng de maicang wenti: maicang niandai, xingzhi, zhuren he beijing 三星堆器物坑的埋藏問題—埋藏年代、性质、主人和背景 [The Issue of the Burial of the Sanxingdui Object Pits: The Issue of Time, Type, Actors, and Background of Burial]. *Nanfang minzu kaogu* 南方民族考古（第九辑）9:9–53.

Tang Xiang 唐翔
1999 Huili qingtong wenhua zongshu 會理青銅文化綜述 [Summary on the Huili Bronze Culture]. *Sichuan wenwu* 四川文物 4:51–57.

Tao Mingkuan 陶鳴寬
1982 Sichuan Huili chutu yizu bianzhong 四川會理出土一組編鐘 [A Bell Excavated in Huili, Sichuan]. *Kaogu* 考古 (2):216–17.

Tong Enzheng 童恩正
1983 Shilun zaoqi tonggu 試論早期銅鼓 [Discussing Early Drums]. *Kaogu xuebao* 考古學報 3:307–30.

Torbrügge, Walter
1985 Über Horte und Hortdeutung [About Hoards and Hoard Interpretations]. *Archäologisches Korrespondenzblatt* 15:15–23.

Verhoeven, Marc
2002 Ritual and Its Investigation in Prehistory. In *Magic Practices and Ritual in the Near Eastern Neolithic: Proceedings of a Workshop Held at the 2nd International Congress on the Archaeology of the Ancient Near East (ICAANE), Copenhagen University, May 2000*, edited by H.-G. Bebel, B. Dahl Hermansen, and C. Hoffmann-Jensen, pp. 5–42. Berlin: Ex Oriente.

Wang Ningsheng 王寧生
1979 Shilun Shizhaishan wenhua 試論石寨山文化 [A Discussion of Shizhaishan Culture]. In *Zhongguo Kaogu Xuehui diyici nianhui lunwenji* 中國考古學會第一次年會論文集 [Proceedings of the First Annual Meeting of the Chinese Archaeological Society], edited by Zhongguo Kaogu Xuehui 中國考古學會, pp. 23–45. Beijing: Wenwu Chubanshe 文物出版社.

Worsaae, Jens Jacob Asmussen
1866 Om nogle Mosefund fra Broncealderen [About Some Moor Finds from the Bronze Age]. *Aarbøger for nordisk oldkyndighed og historie* 1866:313–26.

Xichang Diqu Bowuguan 西昌地區博物館, Sichuansheng Bowuguan 四川省博物館, Sichuan Daxue Lishixi 四川大學歷史係, and Xichangxian Wenhuaguan 西昌縣文化館
1978 Xichang Bahe Baozi dashimu di'erci fajue jianbao 西昌壩河堡子大石墓第二次發掘簡報 [Preliminary Report of the Second Excavation Conducted at the Megalithic Graves of Xichang Bahe Baozi]. *Kaogu* 考古 2:86–90.

Xichangshi Wenwu Guanlisuo 西昌市文物管理所, Sichuansheng Wenwu Kaogu Yanjiusuo 四川省文物考古研究所, and Liangshan Yizu Zizhizhou Bowuguan 涼山彝族自治州博物館
2004 Sichuan Xichangshi Jingjiu Dayangdui yizhi fajue 四川西昌市經久大洋堆遺址發掘 [Excavations Conducted at Dayangdui Site, Jingjiu, Xichang City, Sichuan]. *Kaogu* 考古 10:23–35.

Yao, Alice
2010 Recent Developments in the Archaeology of Southwestern China. *Journal of Archaeological Research* 18:203–39.

Yuan Jing, and Rowan K. Flad
2005 New Zooarchaeological Evidence for Changes in Shang Dynasty Animal Sacrifice. *Journal of Anthropological Archaeology* 24(3):252–70

Yunnansheng Bowuguan 雲南省博物館
1975 Yunnan Jiangchuan Lijiashan gu muqun fajue baogao 雲南江川李家山古墓群發掘報告 [Report of Excavations Conducted at the Ancient Group of Graves of Lijiashan, Jiangchuan, Yunnan]. *Kaogu xuebao* 考古學報 2:97–156.

1977 Yuanmou Dadunzi xin shiqi shidai yizhi 元謀大墩子新石器時代遺址 [The Neolithic Site of Yuanmou Dadunzi]. *Kaogu xuebao* 考古學報 1:43–72.

Yunnansheng Bowuguan Kaogu Fajue Gongzuodui 雲南省博物館考古發掘工作對

1959 Yunnan Jinning Shizhaishan gu yizhi ji muzang 雲南晉寧石寨山古遺址及墓葬 [Ancient Site and Graves at Jining Shizhaishan, Yunnan]. *Kaogu xuebao* 考古學報 1:43–63, 146–55.

Yunnansheng Wenwu Gongzuodui 雲南省文物工作隊

1964 Yunnan Xiangyun Dabona muguo tongguan mu qingli baogao 雲南祥雲大波那木槨銅棺墓清理報告 [Report of Excavations of a Copper Coffin Tomb at Xiangyun Dabona, Yunnan]. *Kaogu* 考古 12:607–14.

1983 Chuxiong Wanjiaba gu muqun fajue baogao 楚雄万像垻古墓群發掘報告 [Excavation Report of the Ancient Grave Group of Chuxiong Wanjiaba]. *Kaogu xuebao* 考古學報 3:347–82.

Yunnansheng Wenwu Kaogu Yanjiusuo 雲南省文物考古研究所, Lijiangshi Bowuguan 麗江市博物館, and Lijiangshi Yongshengxian Wenwu Guanlisuo 麗江市永勝縣文物管理所

2010 *Yongsheng Duizi yizhi fajue* 永勝對子遺址發掘 [Excavations Conducted at Yongsheng Duizi Site]. Kunming: Kunming Chubanshe.

Zhongguo Gudai Tonggu Yanjiu Xuehui 中國古代銅鼓研究學會

1988 *Zhongguo gudai tonggu* 中國古代銅鼓 [The Ancient Bronze Drums of China]. Beijing: Wenwu Chubanshe 文物出版社.

Chapter 8

The Zooarchaeology of Oracle Bone Divination in Northwest China

Katherine Brunson, Li Zhipeng, Rowan Flad,
Qiao Hong, and Wang Qianqian

One of Lothar von Falkenhausen's most important contributions to Chinese archaeology is his ongoing work to make archaeological data from China more widely known and readily accessible to scholars both inside and outside of East Asia. Following in his footsteps, this paper presents a multilanguage, open-access database of oracle bone collections from China that can be used by researchers from around the world (https://opencontext.org/projects/27e90af3-6bf7-4da1-a1c3-7b2f744e8cf7). Using information from this online database, we conduct a preliminary analysis of trends in oracle bone divination in Northwest China. Our analysis draws inspiration from von Falkenhausen's approach, which emphasizes the importance of archaeological materials—not just historical sources—for gaining a complete and accurate understanding of changes in ancient Chinese ritual practices (Falkenhausen 2006). Most previous research on oracle bones has focused on inscribed texts written on Late Shang Dynasty oracle bones. In this paper, we examine uninscribed oracle bones from non-Shang cultural contexts. Our aim is to apply zooarchaeological approaches to the analysis of oracle bones and to examine the economic and social dimensions of oracle bone divination rituals in ancient Northwest China.

Worked bone artifacts provide an excellent medium for combining zooarchaeological perspectives on ritual and economy (Choyke 2006; Choyke and Bartosiewicz 2001; Choyke and O'Connor 2013; Russell 2012). The oracle bones found at many East Asian Neolithic and Bronze Age archaeological sites are a type of worked bone artifact that is especially useful in understanding how people selected animals for use in ritual practices. Oracle bones were usually made from flat bones, such as ungulate scapulae and turtle plastrons. Diviners would burn the bones and interpret the cracks that formed (Keightley 1978). The earliest oracle bones in China come from Neolithic sites in northern China that date to the late fourth millennium BCE (Flad 2008). Between the late third millennium and late second millennium BCE, oracle bone production became increasingly specialized and focused on a limited variety of animal taxa, as pyro-osteomancy came to be associated with individuals and institutions that held positions of power in early Chinese polities (Flad 2008; Keightley 1978, 2000). Hollows were systematically carved into these later oracle bones prior to burning, which helped produce more uniformly shaped cracks (Keightley 1978:18–27). Late Shang Dynasty (ca. 1250–1040 BCE) oracle bones excavated from the royal precinct at Anyang also contain the earliest written inscriptions in East Asia (Keightley 1999).

To date, most research on oracle bones has focused on inscriptions and epigraphy. Uninscribed oracle bones found outside of Shang Dynasty urban centers are rarely published in detail. Those that are usually do not include zooarchaeological data about the type of animal bone used or detailed information on how the bone was burned and carved. Metric data concerning divination marks are almost never reported (see Flad 2011:215–18 for a notable exception), and language differences among researchers and inconsistent data recording also pose challenges to research on broad interregional and temporal trends. As a result, the current literature on oracle bones may not accurately represent temporal and geographic trends in oracle bone divination across East Asia.

In the Oracle Bones in East Asia (OBEA) project, we are revisiting collections of oracle bones housed at institutes of archaeology and museums in China to collect representative data from uninscribed specimens. These data are compiled into a multilanguage online database published on Open Context (opencontext.org). In the following sections, we introduce the Open Context database and present data compiled from 99 oracle bones in the upper Yellow River valley (Gansu and Qinghai Provinces; Figure 8.1). These data make it possible to address four key aspects of oracle bone use in Bronze Age Northwest China:

1. When do oracle bones first appear in the archaeological record and when does oracle bone divination decline in popularity?
2. What factors influenced the selection of taxa used for oracle bone divination? Were animals selected due to local availability? Can other cultural factors explain the taxa used for making oracle bones?
3. Was the preparation and burning of oracle bones in Northwest China fundamentally different from the treatment of oracle bones in other regions?
4. What can the depositional contexts in which oracle bones are found reveal about the meaning of divination rituals and the social contexts in which divination was performed?

This paper takes Northwest China as a first case study for the project. The northwest has a comparatively large oracle bone dataset, and we have gathered additional contextual information during our fieldwork in the region. We find that most of the known oracle bones from Northwest China date to the Early Bronze Age Qijia culture period (ca. 2200–1600 BCE). Few oracle bones with earlier or later dates have been found in the region. During the Qijia culture period, pyro-osteomancy focused on caprine scapulae, and oracle bones were often used in rituals associated with the start of the use life of midden and storage pit features. These insights demonstrate how the online Oracle Bones in East Asia Project database can reveal regional and temporal trends in oracle bone production and use. They also provide a starting point for further research on the social and economic roles of sheep and goats in the Qijia culture.

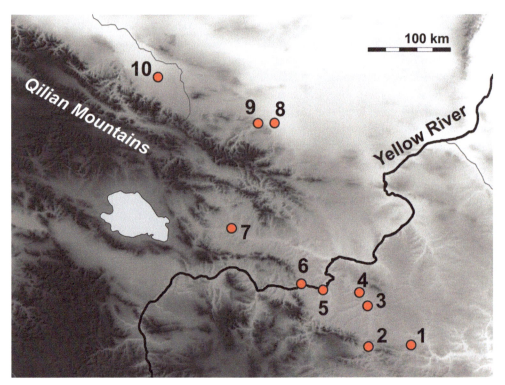

Figure 8.1. Map of sites mentioned in the text: 1. Fujiaman; 2. Mogou; 3. Qijiaping; 4. Huizuiwa; 5. Dahezhuang and Qinweijia; 6. Lajia; 7. Shenna; 8. Huangniangniangtai; 9. Shichengshan; 10. Donghuishan. *Created by Bryan K. Miller.*

Framing and Terminology: Methods Used by the OBEA Project on Open Context

The OBEA project is an ongoing endeavor to collect detailed and comparable information from oracle bones excavated from Neolithic and Bronze Age archaeological sites across East Asia. Data from oracle bones examined by OBEA project team members are collected at two levels of specificity. First, information is collected about the bone artifact as a whole. This includes information about archaeological excavation context (such as year excavated, excavation locus, and direct or associated dates), zooarchaeological data (such as taxon, side of the body, and standard size measurements), and production/manufacturing data (such as whether the bone was pretreated prior to burning, the number of carved hollows, and burn marks). Second, information is collected about each divination mark individually (such as location of the burn mark, shape and size of the hollow, and shape of cracks formed). Terminology and analytical categories used in the database were developed following Pak 2011. Detailed data collection protocols are available via the online project page (and see Figure 8.2 for an example).

The oracle bone database is published on Open Context in a multilanguage open-access format so that it can be used by researchers around the globe. It includes quantitative, georeferenced data that can be used to examine temporal and spatial trends in oracle bone manufacturing and use. Publishing the database on Open Context has several benefits:

1. Each oracle bone has its own record page with a stable, citable URI. All records undergo editorial review to ensure data quality.
2. Open Context's focus on application program interfaces (APIs) and linked open data (LOD) allows for greater data analysis and interoperability (Kansa and Kansa 2014). For example, all data are fully georeferenced and linked to detailed descriptions of the variables and data recording protocols. Taxonomic and anatomical terms are also cross-referenced to standard ontologies. The oracle bone data are searchable in ways that allow users to filter data according to criteria of interest or to download data into other formats.
3. All content on Open Context is freely available and archived with the University of California's California Digital Library for long-term preservation.

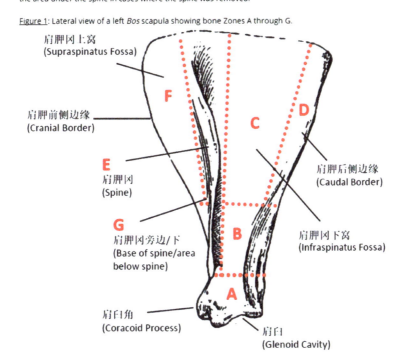

Figure 8.2. Example of data collection protocols linked to descriptive variables in the online oracle bone database. Clicking on "bone zones present" in the database reveals a diagram with code letters (A–G), used to describe parts of an ungulate scapula. *Created by the authors.*

Data sharing is an important part of cultural heritage management that ensures the long-term preservation of data from archaeological artifacts and dissemination of archaeological knowledge (Kansa 2015; Kansa and Kansa 2014; Kintigh et al. 2018; Lake 2012; Marwick et al. 2017; Richards and Winters 2015). Online data publication also facilitates large-scale synthetic research on archaeological collections (Kansa et al. 2018; Kintigh 2006; Kintigh et al. 2018). Recent analyses of zooarchaeological data published through other projects on Open Context reveal that despite differences in how data are collected and sorted, data sharing still allows for comparisons across large regions (Arbuckle et al. 2014; Lau and Kansa 2018). The oracle bone database provides systematically collected data that can be used in similar ways to examine trends in the development of oracle bone divination rituals across East Asia and the changing uses of animals in ritual practice. By making data openly available, we hope to facilitate collaborations and discussions among scholars interested in diverse topics, including zooarchaeology, oracle bone inscriptions, bone working, and ancient ritual technologies.

Data collection for the OBEA project is ongoing, but one region that is well represented in the current database is Northwest China. It provides us with a good starting point to examine what can be learned from specimens in the database.

Case Study: The Oracle Bones from Gansu and Qinghai Provinces
Domestic and Wild Taxa Available for Oracle Bone Divination in Northwest China

All the oracle bones reported here come from archaeological sites in the upper reaches of the Yellow River valley in what are now the eastern parts of Gansu and Qinghai Provinces. The earliest domestic taxa present in the region include pigs and dogs, which have been identified at sites dating back to ca. 6000–5000 BCE (Flad et al. 2007; Lü and Yuan 2018, 2019). Several West Asian domesticates were introduced to the region in the fourth and third millennia BCE at roughly the same time that oracle bone divination emerged. Domestic cattle and sheep first appear after about 2500 BCE (Flad et al. 2007; Lü et al. 2017; Lü and Yuan 2018, 2019). The timing for the arrival of domestic goats into the region is less clear; they do not appear to arrive in North China until after ca. 2300–1800 BCE (Yuan 2015:93–94). Although domestic yaks are important in the region today, the timing for yak domestication is not well understood. Yaks may not have been domesticated until after caprine pastoralism emerged in the region ca. 3000 BCE (Rhode et al. 2007). It is noteworthy that the adoption of pastoralism coincides with a climatic shift toward cooler and more arid conditions ca. 4300–2000 BCE (An et al. 2004). The arrival of cattle, sheep, and goats into the region was also part of Northwest China's increasing participation in trans-Eurasian exchange networks that involved the spread of plant and animal domesticates as well as new technologies such as metallurgy (Jaang 2015).

In addition to domestic taxa, the bones of many native wild ungulates in the region could have been used to make oracle bones. Gansu and Qinghai Provinces are home to wild bovids including gazelle, serow, argali, goral, Siberian ibex, Tibetan antelope, and blue sheep, also known as bharal (Smith and Xie 2013). Morphological criteria for distinguishing between the scapulae of these species are not well established (although see Wang 2017), and it is possible that people used wild bovid bones for divination in addition to bones from domesticated sheep and goats. The region is also home to many species of deer that could have been used in divination (Smith and Xie 2013). Oracle bones made from pig scapulae could represent either domestic pigs or wild boar.

Data Collected from Previously Published Oracle Bones

Data from 65 previously published mammalian scapula oracle bones are listed in Table 8.1. These data were compiled from information listed in published archaeological site reports. The oracle bones have not yet been reexamined in person by members of the OBEA project team, but they still provide basic information that contributes to our analysis.

Caprines (identified as *yang* 羊) are the most commonly identified taxa (50 out of 65 oracle bones; 77%), followed by cattle (identified as *niu* 牛) and pigs (identified as *zhu* 猪). Information about the appearance of divination marks is provided in some of the published reports (see Table 8.1), and occasionally it is possible to see the locations of the burn marks on oracle bones shown in photos or drawings. None of the oracle bones have carved hollows. All burn marks appear to be small and circular in shape. As far as can be determined, all bones were burned on the broad, flat portion of the blade of the scapula on the infraspinous fossa. The image of one caprine oracle bone from Huangniangniangtai (Figure 8.3) also shows one burn mark on the cranial side of the spine.

Data from Table 8.1 should be interpreted with caution. Taxonomic identifications of the oracle bones from reports published many decades ago may be incorrect.

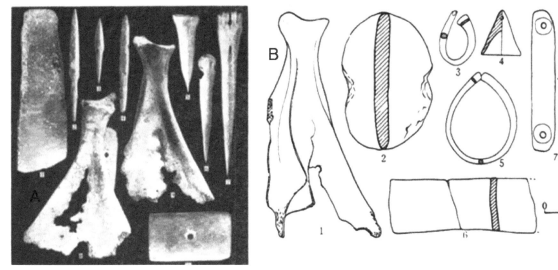

Figure 8.3. Oracle bones from Huangniangniangtai (left) and Donghuishan (right). Scapula T10:12 on the far left (A) was identified as a pig, but its morphology is similar to that of a bovid. Scapula 022 (B) was identified as a sheep/goat, but its morphology is similar to that of a pig. *Created by the authors after Gansusheng 1978:441 and Gansu and Jilin 1998:24.*

For example, in the report on Huangniangniangtai (Gansusheng 1978:441), the oracle bone T10:12 was identified in the main text as *zhu* 猪 (pig). From the image of this artifact, it is clear that the spine of the scapula is not shaped like that of a pig and the bone is more likely a caprine scapula. We have listed this specimen as a sheep/goat in Table 8.1. Similarly, an oracle bone from Donghuishan was identified as *yang* 羊 (sheep/goat), but the image shows that this bone is made from a pig scapula (Gansu and Jilin 1998:24–25). This specimen is listed as a pig in Table 8.1. Both of the misidentified specimens are shown in Figure 8.3.

Data Collected from Oracle Bones Examined by the OBEA Project Team

In addition to gathering information from published site reports, the OBEA project has collected primary data from 34 oracle bones housed at the Gansu Provincial Institute for Archaeology and Cultural Relics and the Qinghai Provincial Institute for Cultural Relics and Archaeology. A summary of these data is presented in Table 8.2. Measurements and other detailed information about these specimens are available online on Open Context.

As was the case for the oracle bones listed in Table 8.1, caprines (including specimens identified as sheep/goats and medium bovids) are the most commonly identified taxa (31 out of 34 specimens; 91%). Only two oracle bones were identified as large bovines, and one was identified as pig. None of the bones that we examined were carved prior to burning. All specimens had small circular burn marks located on the medial side of the blade. Sometimes the bone was burned on the spine of the scapula as well.

Summary of Trends in the Data

Below, we summarize general trends observed for the oracle bones listed in the previous sections in terms of chronology, taxa used, burn mark appearance and location, and excavation context.

Chronology

The earliest oracle bones from Fujiamen are reported as dating to the Shilingxia period of the Majiayao culture period (late third millennium BCE; Zhao 1995). The dates are based on stratigraphic association, but given the absence of other oracle bones from the Majiayao culture period, these dates should be taken with caution. We suspect that they may have a slightly later date. Almost all the other oracle bones date to the Qijia culture period (ca. 2200–1600 BCE). A few cases date to the Siba culture period (ca. 1950–1550 BCE) and Xindian culture period (ca. 1600–600 BCE). Three specimens may date to the Zhou Dynasty (1046–256 BCE) based on estimated dates for ceramics collected from the surface nearby, but these were from a private collection and were not excavated from secure contexts. The Zhou Dynasty dates should also be taken with caution. It is clear that the most intensive oracle bone use in the region took place at Qijia culture sites.

Table 8.1. Previously published oracle bones (OB) from sites in Gansu and Qinghai Provinces

Site	Location	Date	Total # OB	# Ovis/ Capra	# Large Bovine	# Pigs	# Unid.	Body Side
Fujiamen 傅家门	Wushan, Gansu	Majiayao culture, Shilingxia period (ca. 3900–2800 BCE)	6	2	1	1	2	Four shown in published images (two caprine, one cattle, and one pig) are from the left side.
Qinweijia 秦魏家	Yongjing, Gansu	Qijia culture (ca. 2200–1600 BCE)	3	3				ND
Huangniangniangtai 皇娘娘台	Wuwei, Gansu	Qijia culture (ca. 2200–1600 BCE)	26	21	1	4		Cattle scapula is a left. Images also show two left pig and two left caprine scapulae.
Huangniangniangtai 皇娘娘台	Wuwei, Gansu	Qijia culture (ca. 2200–1600 BCE)	13	9		4		ND
Dahezhuang 大何庄	Yongjing, Gansu	Qijia culture (ca. 2200–1600 BCE), in stratum dated to 1900 BCE	14	14				At least two lefts and two rights shown in published images.
Donghuishan 东灰山	Minle, Gansu	Siba culture (ca. 1950–1550 BCE)	1	1				right
Donghuishan 东灰山	Minle, Gansu	Siba culture (ca. 1950–1550 BCE)	2	1 (possible)		1		ND
		Total	65	50	2	10	2	

# Div. Marks	Div. Mark Description	Context Type	Context Description	Notes	Citation
Not specified. Images show one or two marks per bone.	Burned directly. No hollows.	pit (n = 1), building (n = 5)	One bone found in rectangular pit. Pile of five bones found in southeast corner of building F11.	Bones are reported to have inscribed symbols: S on the cattle scapula, = on the pig scapula, and / on one of the caprine scapulae.	(Zhao 1995)
Report states that burn marks range in number from two to four.	Burned directly. No hollows.	burial (n = 1)	One bone found in burial M23 inside two-handled *guan* vessel. Report does not provide detailed contextual information for the other two.		(Gansudui 1975)
Not specified. At least 10 marks visible on medial side of cattle scapula oracle bone shown in photo.	Burned directly. No hollows. Small circular marks.	pit (n = 1), burial (n = 1)	Cattle bone found at bottom of Pit H1. The cattle scapula appears to have been reused as a shovel and has a rectangular hole carved through the neck for hafting to a handle. One caprine bone found in Tomb M8 near the left leg of the human skeleton. Other bones appear to have been found in general fill layers and pits.		(Gansusheng 1960)
Report states that one pig bone had 13 marks (#T10:12, but the photo shows a sheep/goat scapula). Report states that one sheep bone had five marks (#H46:1).	Burned directly. No hollows.	ND	Unclear, but the bones appear to have been found in a mix of general fill layers and pits.		(Gansusheng 1978)
Report states that burn marks range in number from two to 24.	Burned directly. No hollows. Many small burn marks on medial side.	ND	Bones found next to circular stone features along with burials of cattle and caprine skeletons. Two bones found south of F3, one bone found south of F6, and three unburned bones found near F12.		(Zhongguo 1974)
At least one mark on all bones shown in image.	Circular burn mark on medial side.	ND	unclear		(Xu and Zhang 1995)
Pig has at least one mark on spine of scapula.	ND	ND	unclear; not found in burials	The text lists two caprine bones present. Only one is depicted in a drawing and photo. The image shows that this is a pig scapula with a characteristic curved spine.	(Gansu and Jilin 1998)

Table 8.2. Oracle bones from Gansu and Qinghai Provinces examined by the OBEA project

OB ID #	Site	Location	Year Ex.	Contents Type	Contents Description	Date	Ovis/ Capra	M. Bovid	M. Bovid or Cervid
QJP001	Qijiaping 齐家坪	Guanghe, Gansu	1975			Qijia (ca. 2200–1600 BCE)	x		
QJP002	Qijiaping 齐家坪	Guanghe, Gansu	1975			Qijia (ca. 2200–1600 BCE)	x		
QJP003	Qijiaping 齐家坪	Guanghe, Gansu	1975	Huikeng/ ash pit		Qijia (ca. 2200–1600 BCE)	x		
QJP004	Qijiaping 齐家坪	Guanghe, Gansu	1975	Huikeng/ ash pit		Qijia (ca. 2200–1600 BCE)	x		
QJP372	Qijiaping 齐家坪	Guanghe, Gansu	2016	Huikeng/ ash pit	Found at bottom of Pit H2 along with OB#373 and a complete corvid skeleton	Qijia (ca. 2200–1600 BCE)	x		
QJP373	Qijiaping 齐家坪	Guanghe, Gansu	2016	Huikeng/ ash pit	Found at bottom of Pit H2 along with OB#372 and a complete corvid skeleton	Qijia (ca. 2200–1600 BCE)			x
HZW374	Huizuiwa 灰嘴洼	Lintao, Gansu	2017	Huikeng/ ash pit	Found at bottom of Pit H3 with many stone cobbles	Xindian (ca. 1600–600 BCE)	x		
SCS375	Shichengshan 石城山	Wuwei, Gansu	2009		Not excavated. In private collection of Mr. Li Zongwen in Wuwei. Collected on surface in 2009.	Zhou Dynasty? (1046–256 BCE)	x		
SCS376	Shichengshan 石城山	Wuwei, Gansu	2009		Not excavated. In private collection of Mr. Li Zongwen in Wuwei. Collected on surface in 2009.	Zhou Dynasty? (1046–256 BCE)	x		
SCS377	Shichengshan 石城山	Wuwei, Gansu	2009		Not excavated. In private collection of Mr. Li Zongwen in Wuwei. Collected on surface in 2009.	Zhou Dynasty? (1046–256 BCE)	x		
MG461	Mogou 磨沟	Lintan, Gansu	?	burial	Oracle bone mixed with human bones from Mogou. From M1156R2.	Qijia (ca. 2200–1600 BCE)			x
LJ462	Lajia 喇家	Minhe, Qinghai	2003	pit		Qijia (ca. 2200–1600 BCE)	x (*Ovis*?)		
LJ463	Lajia 喇家	Minhe, Qinghai	2000	trench		Qijia (ca. 2200–1600 BCE)	x (*Ovis*?)		
LJ464	Lajia 喇家	Minhe, Qingahi	2005	Huikeng/ ash pit		Qijia (ca. 2200–1600 BCE)	x (*Ovis*?)		
LJ465	Lajia 喇家	Minhe, Qinghai	2002	trench?		Qijia (ca. 2200–1600 BCE)	x (*Ovis*?)		
LJ466	Lajia 喇家	Minhe, Qinghai	2003	Huikeng/ ash pit		Qijia (ca. 2200–1600 BCE)	x (*Ovis*?)		
SN467	Shenna 西宁沈那	Xining, Qinghai	1991	stratum		Qijia (ca. 2200–1600 BCE)	x (*Ovis*?)		

L. Bovid	Pig	Bone Zones	Body Side	# Div. Marks	Div. Mark Side	Notes
		A, B, E, F	R	> 1	medial	Carnivore chew marks on bone surface
		A, B, C, D, E, F	R	> 13	medial and lateral	
		A, B, C, D, E, F	L	7	medial	
		A, B, C, D, E, F	R	> 10	medial	
		A, B, C, D, E, F	L	5	medial	Cut marks on neck of scapula
		B, C, D, E, F	L	> 15	medial and lateral	Carnivore chew marks. Neck may have been burned. Six burn marks on the largest fragment and many more burn marks on smaller fragments from same specimen.
		A, B, C, D, E, F	R	0	medial	No clear burn mark, but bone is discolored and warped in one spot in the center of the blade where heat was applied.
		A, B, C, D, E, F	R	2	medial	Yang Yishi (from the Gansu Provincial Institute for Archaeology and Cultural Relics) has found materials dating to the Zhou period at the site and thinks the bones also date to the Zhou period.
		A, B, C, D, E, F	R	10	medial	Yang Yishi has found materials dating to the Zhou period at the site and thinks the bones also date to the Zhou period.
		A, B, C, D, E, F	L	6	medial	Yang Yishi has found materials dating to the Zhou period at the site and thinks the bones also date to the Zhou period.
		C, D, E, F	R	12	lateral	Many small burn marks on lateral side of the blade. One mark located farther toward the distal end.
		A, B, C, D, E, F	R	1	medial	One small burn mark on medial side near the proximal border. Root etching on the bone surface.
		A, B, C, D, E, F	L	3	medial	Bone looks like it comes from a juvenile individual (glenoid cavity is oval shaped). Small burn marks on the medial side of the blade near the proximal border.
		A, B, C, D, E, F	L	9	medial and lateral	Many small burn marks on the medial side and lateral side of the blade. Some are almost opposite one another. In these cases there are not clear cracks. There were probably even more burn marks in the broken part of the blade.
		A, B, C, D, E, F	R	1	medial	One small burn mark on the medial side of the blade. There were probably more burn marks on the broken part of the blade.
		A, B, C, D, E, F	R	7	medial	Many small burn marks on the medial side of the blade. There were probably more burn marks in the broken part of the blade.
		A, B, C, E, F	R	1	medial	The bone has an ID number from the storage facility (QK002094). Other contextual numbers are written on the bone, but the exact excavation context is unknown.

Table 8.2. Oracle bones from Gansu and Qinghai Provinces examined by the OBEA project *(continued)*

OB ID #	Site	Location	Year Ex.	Contents Type	Contents Description	Date	Ovis/ Capra	M. Bovid	M. Bovid or Cervid
SN468	Shenna 西宁沈那	Xining, Qinghai	1991	stratum		Qijia (ca. 2200–1600 BCE)		x	
SN469	Shenna 西宁沈那	Xining, Qinghai	1992	stratum		Qijia (ca. 2200–1600 BCE)			
SN470	Shenna 西宁沈那	Xining, Qinghai	1992	stratum		Qijia (ca. 2200–1600 BCE)			
SN471	Shenna 西宁沈那	Xining, Qinghai	1993	Huikeng/ ash pit		Qijia (ca. 2200–1600 BCE)	x (*Ovis?*)		
SN472	Shenna 西宁沈那	Xining, Qinghai	1992	Huikeng/ ash pit		Qijia (ca. 2200–1600 BCE)	x		
SN473	Shenna 西宁沈那	Xining, Qinghai	1993	Huikeng/ ash pit		Qijia (ca. 2200–1600 BCE)			
SN474	Shenna 西宁沈那	Xining, Qinghai	1992	stratum	The tag lists the following information: 92XS T34 (5) (硬土层) (7):3 (74).	Qijia (ca. 2200–1600 BCE)	x (*Ovis?*)		
SN475	Shenna 西宁沈那	Xining, Qinghai	1992	stratum	The tag lists the following information: 92XS T34 (5) (硬土层) (7):3 (74).	Qijia (ca. 2200–1600 BCE)		x (*Gazella?*)	
SN476	Shenna 西宁沈那	Xining, Qinghai	1992	Huikeng/ ash pit		Qijia (ca. 2200–1600 BCE)	x (*Ovis?*)		
SN477	Shenna 西宁沈那	Xining, Qinghai	1992	stratum		Qijia (ca. 2200–1600 BCE)	x (*Ovis?*)		
SN478	Shenna 西宁沈那	Xining, Qinghai	1992	stratum		Qijia (ca. 2200–1600 BCE)	x (*Ovis?*)		
SN479	Shenna 西宁沈那	Xining, Qinghai	1992	stratum		Qijia (ca. 2200–1600 BCE)	x (*Ovis?*)		
SN480	Shenna 西宁沈那	Xining, Qinghai	1992	stratum		Qijia (ca. 2200–1600 BCE)	x (*Ovis?*)		
SN481	Shenna 西宁沈那	Xining, Qinghai	1992	stratum		Qijia (ca. 2200–1600 BCE)		x (*Gazella?*)	
SN482	Shenna 西宁沈那	Xining, Qinghai	1992	stratum		Qijia (ca. 2200–1600 BCE)		x	
SN483	Shenna 西宁沈那	Xining, Qinghai	1992	stratum		Qijia (ca. 2200–1600 BCE)		x	
SN484	Shenna 西宁沈那	Xining, Qinghai	1992	?		Qijia (ca. 2200–1600 BCE)	x (*Ovis?*)		

L. Bovid	Pig	Bone Zones	Body Side	# Div. Marks	Div. Mark Side	Notes
		B, C, D, E, F	L	3	medial	The bone has only an ID number from the storage facility (QK002094). There is no other contextual information.
x		A, B, C, D, E, F	L	9	medial	This specimen appears to be from a young cow. It may be from the same individual as OB#470 based on size, appearance, and similar excavation context. However, the shape of the glenoid cavity is slightly more oval than OB#470.
x		A, B, C, D, E, F	R	5	medial	This specimen appears to be from a young cow. It may be from the same individual as OB#469 based on size, appearance, and similar excavation context. However, the shape of the glenoid cavity is slightly more circular than OB#469.
		A, B, C, D, E, F	R	7	medial	There are probably more divination marks at the edges of the broken parts of the blade, but these marks are not clear enough to record. There are fine cut marks on the medial neck.
		A, B, C, D, E, F	R	3	medial	Young individual. Unfortunately, the distal end is broken, so it is not possible to say for certain that this was an unfused scapula, but it appears to be from a young animal with an oval-shaped glenoid cavity.
	x	A, B, C, D, E, F	L	3	medial	Young individual (small size and glenoid cavity appears spongy). Three burn marks in a row in line with the caudal border.
		A, B, C, D, E, F	L	3	medial	The burn marks are not clear, but there is discoloration (probably from heating) around several of the breaks, suggesting that these were divination marks.
		A, B, C, D, E, F	R	0		No burn marks visible, but most of the blade is missing. Small size and circular glenoid cavity look more like goat than sheep. Maybe gazelle?
		A, B, C, D, E, F	L	1	medial	One discolored burned area is visible in the center of the blade. It is likely that there were more marks, but most of the blade is missing.
		A, B, C, D, E, F	L	9	medial	Many small circular burn marks on medial side of the blade.
		A, B, C, D, E, F	L	0		No burn marks visible, but most of the blade is missing. Circular breaks on the blade may have been the locations of burn marks.
		A, B, C, D, E, F	L	1	medial	One area of discoloration is probably a burn mark. Circular breaks on the blade may have been the locations of additional burn marks.
		A, B, C, D, E, F	R	3	medial	Three areas of discoloration are probably burn marks. Circular breaks on the blade may have been the locations of additional burn marks.
		A, B, C, D, E, F	R	0		No burn marks visible, but most of the blade is missing. Circular breaks on the blade may have been the locations of burn marks. Cut marks on medial side of neck.
		B, C, D, E, F	L	3	medial	Dog chew on distal end
		C, D, E, F	L	3	medial	Dog chew on distal end. Long scratch marks on medial side of blade.
		A, B, C, D, E, F	L	7	medial	No contextual information but probably from the 1992–1993 excavations at Shenna.

Taxa

Caprine scapulae make up the vast majority of oracle bones. Bovine and pig scapulae were also used occasionally. It is likely that most of the caprine oracle bones come from domesticated sheep or goats, but as mentioned earlier, it is possible that wild bovid bones are also present. For example, several of the oracle bones from Shenna were gracile in appearance and may have been made from gazelle scapulae. Taxonomic confirmation may only be possible for these and other specimens using biomolecular methods. To date, no turtle shell or other non-mammal oracle bones have been identified. Left and right scapulae are equally distributed. It does not appear that one side of the body was preferred over the other.

Burn Marks

We focus on the burn marks found on caprine bones, but similar burning patterns are apparent for the pig and bovine oracle bones as well. Burn marks are usually about 3 mm in diameter. Marks are primarily located on the medial side of the blade. Occasionally bones were also burned on the lateral side of the blade (LJ464) and on the spine of the scapula (QJP373 and QJP002). There are a few centimeters of separation between each burn mark. Figure 8.4 shows photographs of several oracle bones side by side. Burn marks are located on the thinnest part of the blade on the infraspinous fossa. Burn marks could have been made with a heated wooden stick. It is also possible that a heated metal tool was used because metal artifacts have been found at Qijia sites (An 1981).

While the number of burn marks varies from specimen to specimen, the broad proximal end of the scapula usually contains more marks than the narrower distal end. The largest number of burn marks recorded on a single bone was 15. (The bone was broken at the proximal end and may have contained even more marks.) Burn marks do not show consistent patterns in terms of their arrangements, but there is almost always one single mark at the V-shaped depression where the blade meets the neck of the scapula.

We did not observe consistent patterns in the shapes of cracks that formed (see supplemental data). Nonvisual aspects of bone burning—such as the sound of cracking—may have been more important than the shapes of cracks.

Depositional Contexts

Oracle bones were discarded in a variety of depositional contexts, most frequently in pits (*huikeng* 灰坑). There is a great deal of variability in how *huikeng* are defined and described in Chinse archaeological fieldwork. Here we assume that *huikeng* are storage pits or midden pit deposits filled with general refuse. Bones excavated from Qijia culture sites tend to occur singularly. Occasionally oracle bones were excavated in groups of two or three bones found together within a pit. The contextual information provided for most oracle bones includes only general information about the excavation locus. Specific information about where the bone was found within a pit is almost never reported. Only one previously published oracle bone was reported with sufficient detail to determine its location within a pit. Gansusheng (1960:Plate 1) included a photo of the cattle scapula during excavation of Huangniangniangtai Pit H1. The bone appears to have been found at the bottom of a circular pit, with the flat medial side of the blade facing up.

We were fortunate to excavate three oracle bones recently as part of the Tao River Archaeology Project (TRAP), which allowed us to note the location of these bones within pits. At the site of Qijiaping, oracle bones QJP372 and QJP373 were excavated from the bottom layer of Pit H2. Both of these scapulae are from the left side, indicating that they came from at least two different animals. A complete corvid skeleton was found at the bottom of the same pit. Corvids are used for augury in East Asia, and the placement of the crow together with the two oracle bones suggests that several divination rituals were performed when the pit was first opened.

At Huizuiwa, TRAP recovered an oracle bone (HZW374) made from a right scapula of a medium-size bovid, probably a domestic sheep. Figure 8.5. shows the oracle bone during excavation, when it was found lateral side up along with several large stones at the bottom of Pit H2. This scapula was one of only a few complete animal bones recovered from the pit. Most of the other faunal remains were small bone fragments that appeared to be food refuse and bone-working debris. The completeness of the scapula suggests that it was intentionally placed at the bottom of the pit rather than being thrown in as trash. The scapula has a circular discoloration in the center of the blade caused by heating. This burn mark is not as clear as the burn marks on most other oracle bones, and it may represent a failed attempt to burn the bone for divination.

Oracle bones have occasionally been recovered from tombs. At Huangniangniangtai, one caprine oracle bone was found near the left leg of a person buried in Tomb 8 (Gansusheng 1960:56). At Qinweijia, one sheep/goat oracle bone was found inside a *guan* 罐 ceramic vessel in a tomb (Gansudui 1975:68). At Mogou, a caprine oracle bone was found during the analysis of human remains excavated from Tomb M1156R2. The Mogou burials are still under study, and the exact location of the oracle bone within this tomb is unknown.

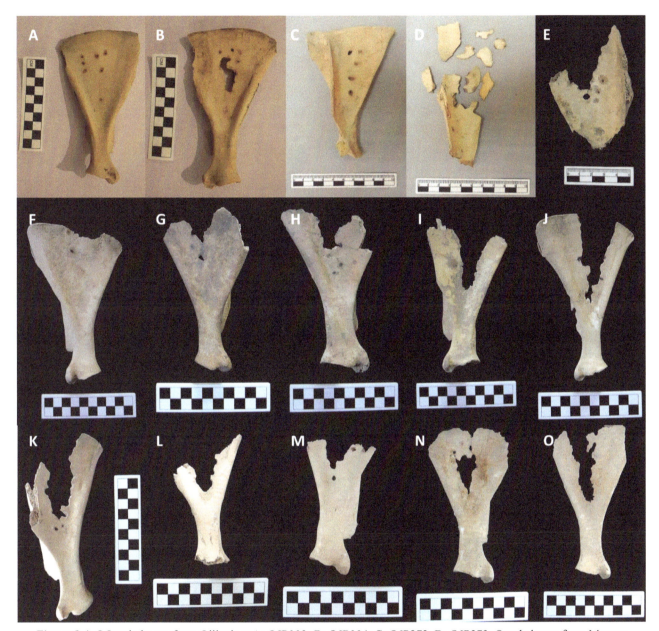

Figure 8.4. OOracle bones from Qijiaping: A: QJP003; B: QJP004; C: QJP372; D: QJP373. Oracle bones from Mogou: E: MG461. Oracle bones from Lajia: F: LJ462; G: LJ463; H: LJ464; I: LJ465; J: LJ466. Oracle bones from Shenna: K: SN471; L: SN472; M: SN474; N: SN477; O: SN479. *Photo by Katherine Brunson.*

Discussion

Our study reveals that oracle bones from Northwest China are unique in terms of their temporality, species used, and method of burning. The contexts where oracle bones were found provides clues about the meaning of divination rituals, but further zooarchaeological research is needed to understand the economic and social roles of sheep and goats in the Qijia culture.

Our data reveal that oracle bone divination in Northwest China experienced a sudden fluorescence during the Qijia culture period. As shown in Tables 8.2 and 8.3, only one site predating the Qijia culture has revealed oracle bones. The absence of oracle bones from Neolithic Majiayao culture sites besides Fujiamen is especially striking. While there are a small number of oracle bones from Neolithic and Chalcolithic sites in other regions of North China during

Figure 8.5. Bone HZW374 in situ at the bottom of Huizuiwa Pit H2. *Photo courtesy of TRAP.*

the late fourth millennium BCE (Flad 2008), we believe that oracle bone divination was not a common practice in Northwest China prior to the second millennium BCE.

In addition, oracle bones are only occasionally found at sites postdating the Qijia culture. Archaeological research in the region has traditionally focused on mortuary contexts, in which oracle bones are found only occasionally. It is possible that additional oracle bones will be recovered as more non-mortuary sites are excavated for the Xindian and Siba cultures, since they are more frequently found in residential areas. However, the current data suggest that oracle bone divination in Northwest China may have been a fairly short-lived practice that declined rapidly at the end of the Qijia culture, ca.1600 BCE. In the future, direct radiocarbon dates from oracle bones would help further refine the chronology of their use.

Qijia oracle bone divination appears to be unique in its focus on caprine scapulae. Caprines were used to make oracle bones in other regions of China as well (for example, in the middle Yellow River valley at sites such as Taosi and Zhoujiazhuang in Shanxi Province; Brunson et al. 2016), but at those sites, pig and cattle oracle bones are equally common or more common. Why were caprines so heavily favored in the northwest? And why, as our data suggest, might sheep have been favored over goats?

To address these questions, it is critical to integrate the oracle bone data with what is known in the broader zooarchaeological literature for the region. Zooarchaeological reports from Northwest China are limited, but the current evidence suggests that caprine bones, presumably from domesticated sheep and goats, become more common during the Qijia culture period compared to the preceding Majiayao culture period (Brunson et al. 2020; Flad et al. 2007; Lü and Yuan 2018, 2019). Caprine bones have been identified at Qijia culture sites including Dahezhuang (Zhongguo 1974), Qinweijia (Gansudui 1975), Shizhaocun (Zhou 1999), and Xishanping (Zhou 1999). The proportions of identified sheep and goat bones compared to other taxa are not provided in faunal reports from these sites. There is still much to learn about the relative distributions of caprines in zooarchaeological assemblages for this period, but it seems unlikely that their ubiquity alone can explain their preferred use in divination. For example, our analysis of faunal remains excavated from Qijiaping with TRAP suggests that pigs and sheep occur in similar frequencies (Brunson et al. 2020). If people selected taxa for divination purely based on availability, then we would expect to see more pig oracle bones in this region. Instead, there must have been cultural or ideological reasons why people chose to divine with caprine bones, especially sheep bones. Future zooarchaeological research at Qijia sites should carefully consider the different distributions of animals in quotidian deposits and in worked bone assemblages, including oracle bones.

The oracle bones from Northwest China are also unique in the ways they were burned. Unlike the more famous Shang Dynasty and Zhou Dynasty oracle bones, which were covered with intricately carved hollows, the bones in Northwest China were not treated prior to burning. Small burn marks were usually made on the medial side of the thinnest parts of the scapula blade. It remains to be seen why the number of burn marks and their specific placement on each scapula varied. Interregional patterns in burning practices may emerge in the future as the OBEA project continues to analyze oracle bones from other regions.

Given the unique nature of oracle bone divination in Northwest China, what might have been the possible social meanings of divination events? The depositional contexts of Qijia oracle bones provide some clues. Oracle bones were included in human burials at Huangniangniangtai, Qinweijia, and Mogou. It is possible that these personal items recorded an important divination event in the life of the deceased. The presence of oracle bones in tombs might also suggest that the deceased were diviners themselves. In either case, these oracle bones would have been a physical reminder of a ritual event in the life of that individual and may have had deep personal meaning. It is also possible that mourners used divination to decide when and where to bury the deceased person.

Oracle bone divination also appears to have been performed in shared public spaces. This is suggested by the fact that pits are the most common depositional context for oracle bones. In several cases, oracle bones were placed intentionally at the bottom of these pits, sometimes along with other divinatory objects, such as the crow found with oracle bones QJP372 and QJP373 in Qijiaping Pit H2. Divination rituals may have been performed to mark the start of the use life of these pits. Were these rituals similar to modern ribbon-cutting ceremonies—quick celebrations that are quickly forgotten—or were they more significant rituals that would have remained in the memory of community members during subsequent daily disposal of refuse into the pit? Unfortunately, the lack of detailed recording of most Qijia pit excavations limits our ability to draw further inferences. We second recent calls for more careful excavation and analysis of pit features in Chinese archaeology (Osing et al. 2017).

Many questions about the social roles of sheep, goats, and oracle bone divination in Qijia society remain to be explored. However, the new insights about oracle bones in Northwest China described above would not have been possible without systematically collected zooarchaeological and contextual data available through the OBEA project. Our results demonstrate the value of revisiting existing collections of oracle bones with new research methodologies and questions. As the database continues to grow and as more oracle bones from other regions are added, these artifacts will have even greater potential to contribute to our understanding of human–animal interactions in the societies of ancient East Asia.

Conclusions

Inspired by Lothar von Falkenhausen's contributions to international collaboration and his innovative uses of archaeological materials in research on ancient Chinese ritual practices, this article has shown how open-access zooarchaeological data collected by the OBEA project reveals patterns in oracle bone divination rituals. We have presented the first comprehensive regional analysis of oracle bones from Northwest China. Oracle bone divination in this region seems to have been largely restricted to the Qijia culture period. Caprine scapulae were a preferred raw material for making oracle bones, which suggests that sheep and goats had a special meaning in Qijia society. While the exact meaning of the small burn marks on the oracle bones remains a mystery, the depositional contexts of oracle bones in graves and at the bottom of pits indicate that these items had significance at both the personal and community levels. Divination events took place at the beginning of the use life of midden pits used by Qijia communities, suggesting that archaeologists should pay more attention to how materials were accumulated in pit features. Finally, our study demonstrates how the OBEA project's online database can be used to explore regional trends in oracle bone production. In the coming years, long-term preservation of archaeological data, development of open-access resources, and digital technologies will become increasingly important issues in Chinese archaeology. The OBEA project provides a model for future artifact databases—especially those that include faunal remains—and shows the value of revisiting and reanalyzing legacy collections in China.

Acknowledgments

We thank Anke Hein, Bryan Miller, and all the participants in the symposium in honor of Lothar von Falkenhausen. We also thank the Tao River Archaeology Project team, Zhou Jing and Yang Yishi at the Gansu Provincial Institute for Archaeology and Cultural Relics, the Shanna Field Station team, Wang Zhouwen, the Joukowsky Institute for Archaeology and the Ancient World at Brown University, the Center for Computational Molecular Biology at Brown University, the Esherick-Ye Foundation, Nina Hirai, and Audrey Lam. We thank Elizabeth Berger for drawing our attention to the oracle bone from a burial at the Mogou cemetery. Special thanks to Eric Kansa and the Open Context team.

References

An, Chengbang, Zhaodong Feng, and Lingyu Tang
2004 Environmental Change and Cultural Response between 8000 and 4000 cal. yr BP in the Western Loess Plateau, Northwest China. *Journal of Quaternary Science* 19(6):529–35.

An Zhimin 安志敏
1981 Zhongguo zaoqi tongqi de jige wenti 中国早期铜器的几个问题. *Kaogu xuebao* 考古学报 3:269–85.

Arbuckle, Benjamin S., Sarah Whitcher Kansa, Eric Kansa, David Orton, Canan Çakırlar, Lionel Gourichon, Levent Atici, Alfred Galik, Arkadiusz Marciniak, Jacqui Mulville, et al.
2014 Data Sharing Reveals Complexity in the Westward Spread of Domestic Animals across Neolithic Turkey. *PLOS ONE* 9(6):e99845.

Brunson, Katherine, Nu He, and Xiangming Dai
2016 Sheep, Cattle, and Specialization: New Zooarchaeological Perspectives on the Taosi Longshan. *International Journal of Osteoarchaeology* 26(3):460–75.

Brunson, Katherine, Lele Ren, Xin Zhao, Xiaoling Dong, Jing Zhou, Hui Wang, and Rowan K. Flad
2020 Zooarchaeology, Ancient mtDNA, and Radiocarbon Dating Provide New Evidence for the Emergence of Domestic Cattle and Caprines in the Tao River Valley of Gansu Province, Northwest China. *Journal of Archaeological Science: Reports* 31:102262.

Choyke, Alice M.
2006 Bone Tools for a Lifetime: Experience and Belonging. In *Normes techniques et pratiques sociales: de la simplicité des outillages pré-et protohistoriques*. Actes des XXIVe Rencontres Internationales d'archéologie et d'histoire d'Antibes, pp. 49–60. Antibes: APDCA.

Choyke, Alice M., and Laslo Bartosiewicz, eds.
2001 *Crafting Bone: Skeletal Technologies through Time and Space: Proceedings of the 2nd Meeting of the (ICAZ) Worked Bone Research Group, Budapest, 31 August–5 September 1999*. BAR International Series. Oxford: Archaeopress.

Choyke, Alice, and Sonia O'Connor, eds.
2013 *From These Bare Bones: Raw Materials and the Study of Worked Osseous Objects*. Oxford: Oxbow Books.

Falkenhausen, Lothar von
2006 *Chinese Society in the Age of Confucius (1000–250 BC): The Archaeological Evidence*. Los Angeles: Cotsen Institute of Archaeology Press.

Flad, Rowan K.
2008 Divination and Power: A Multiregional View of the Development of Oracle Bone Divination in Early China. *Current Anthropology* 49(3):403–37.
2011 *Salt Production and Social Hierarchy in Ancient China: An Archaeological Investigation of Specialization in China's Three Gorges*. Cambridge: Cambridge University Press.

Flad, Rowan K., Yuan Jing, and Shuicheng Li
2007 Zooarchaeological Evidence for Animal Domestication in Northwest China. In *Late Quaternary Climate Change and Human Adaptation in Arid China*, edited by David Madsen, Fa-hu Chen, and Xing Gao, pp. 167–204. Amsterdam: Elsevier.

Gansudui Zhongguo Kexue Yuan Kaogu Yanjiu Suo Gansu Gongzuo Dui 中国科学院考古研究所甘肃工作队
1975 Gansu Yongqing Qinweijia Qijia wenhua mudi 甘肃永靖秦魏家齐家文化墓地. *Kaogu xuebao* 考古学报 2:57–96.

Gansusheng Bowuguan 甘肃省博物馆
1960 Gansu Wuwei Huangniangniangtai yizhi fajue baogao 甘肃武威皇娘娘台遗址发掘报告. *Kaogu xuebao* 考古学报 2:53–71, 143–48.
1978 Gansu Wuwei Huangniangniangtai disici fajue baogao 武威皇娘娘台遗址第四次发掘报告. *Kaogu xuebao* 考古学报 4:421–48.

Gansusheng Wenwu Kaogu Yanjiusuo 甘肃省文物考古研究所 and Jilin Daxue Beifang Kaogu Yanjiushi 吉林大学北方考古研究室
1998 *Minle Donghuishan kaogu—Siba wenhua mudi de jieshi yu yanjiu* 民乐东灰山考古—四坝文化墓地的揭示与研究. Beijing: Kexue Chubanshe 科学出版社.

Jaang, Li
2015 The Landscape of China's Participation in the Bronze Age Eurasian Network. *Journal of World Prehistory* 28(3):179–213.

Kansa, Eric
2015 Contextualizing Digital Data as Scholarship in Eastern Mediterranean Archaeology. *CHS Research Bulletin* 3(2).

Kansa, Eric C., Sarah W. Kansa, Josh J. Wells, Stephen J. Yerka, Kelsey N. Myers, Robert C. DeMuth, Thaddeus G. Bissett, and David G. Anderson
2018 The Digital Index of North American Archaeology: Networking Government Data to Navigate an Uncertain Future for the Past. *Antiquity* 92(362):490–506.

Kansa, Sarah Whitcher, and Eric Kansa
2014 Data Publishing and Archaeology's Information Ecosystem. *Near Eastern Archaeology* 77(3):223–27.

Keightley, David N.
1978 *Sources of Shang History: The Oracle-Bone Inscriptions of Bronze Age China.* Berkeley: University of California Press.
1999 The Shang: China's First Historical Dynasty. In *The Cambridge History of Ancient China: From the Origins of Civilization to 221 BC*, edited by M. Loewe and E. L. Shaughnessy, pp. 232–91. Cambridge: Cambridge University Press.
2000 *The Ancestral Landscape: Time, Space, and Community in Late Shang China, ca. 1200–1045 BC.* China Research Monograph 53. Berkeley: University of California Press.

Kintigh, Keith
2006 The Promise and Challenge of Archaeological Data Integration. *American Antiquity* 71(3):567–78.

Kintigh, Keith W., Katherine A. Spielmann, Adam Brin, K. Selçuk Candan, Tiffany C. Clark, and Matthew Peeples
2018 Data Integration in the Service of Synthetic Research. *Advances in Archaeological Practice* 6(1):30–41.

Lake, Mark
2012 Open Archaeology. *World Archaeology* 44(4):471–78.

Lau, Hannah, and Sarah Whitcher Kansa
2018 Zooarchaeology in the Era of Big Data: Contending with Interanalyst Variation and Best Practices for Contextualizing Data for Informed Reuse. *Journal of Archaeological Science* 95:33–39.

Lü, Peng, Katherine Brunson, Yuan Jing, and Zhipeng Li
2017 Zooarchaeological and Genetic Evidence for the Origins of Domestic Cattle in Ancient China. *Asian Perspectives* 56(1):92–120.

Lü Peng 吕鹏 and Yuan Jing 袁靖
2018 Jiaoliu yu zhuanhua—Huanghe shangyou diqu xianqin shiqi shengye fangshi chutan (shang pian) 交流与转化—黄河上游地区先秦时期生业方式初探（上篇）[Exchange and Transformation—a Preliminary Study of Pre-Qin Agricultural Production Modes in the Upper Reaches of the Yellow River (Part 1)]. *Nanfang wenwu* 南方文物 2:170–79.
2019 Jiaoliu yu zhuanhua—Huanghe shangyou diqu xianqin shiqi shengye fangshi chutan (xia pian) 交流与转化—黄河上游地区先秦时期生业方式初探（下篇）[Exchange and Transformation—a Preliminary Study of Pre-Qin Agricultural Production Modes in the Upper Reaches of the Yellow River (Part 2)]. *Nanfang wenwu* 南方文物 2.

Marwick, Ben, J. d'Alpoim Guedes, C. M. Barton, L. A. Bates, M. Baxter, A. Bevan, E. A. Bollwerk, R. K. Bocinsky, T. Brughmans, A. K. Carter, et al.
2017 Open Science in Archaeology. *SAA Archaeological Record* 17(4):8–14.

Osing, N., M. Wu, and Y. He
2017 Preliminary Results from a Multi-methodological Approach on a Refuse Pit from the Middle Shang Period at Huanbei. Paper presented at the Eighty-Second Annual Meeting of the Society for American Archaeology, Vancouver, BC.

Pak, Chae-bok 朴載福
2011 *Xian Qin bufa yanjiu* 先秦卜法研究. Shanghai: Shanghai Guji Chubanshe 上海古籍出版社.

Rhode, David, David Madsen, P. Jeffrey Brantingham, and T Dargye
2007 Yaks, Yak Dung, and Prehistoric Habitation of the Tibetan Plateau. In *Late Quaternary Climate Change and Human Adaptation in Arid China*, edited by David Madsen, Fa-Hu Chen, and Xing Gao, pp. 205–24. Amsterdam: Elsevier.

Richards, Julian D., and Judith Winters
2015 Digging into Data: Open Access and Open Data. *European Journal of Post-Classical Archaeologies* 5:285–98.

Russell, Nerissa
2012 *Social Zooarchaeology: Humans and Animals in Prehistory.* Cambridge: Cambridge University Press.

Smith, Andrew T., and Yan Xie, eds.
2013 *Mammals of China.* Princeton, NJ: Princeton University Press.

Wang, Yiru
2017 Identifying the Beginnings of Sheep Husbandry in Western China. PhD dissertation, Department of Archaeology, University of Cambridge, Cambridge.

Xu Yongjie 许永杰 and Wei Zhang 张珑
1995 Gansu Minlexian Donghuishan yizhi fajue jiyao 甘肃民乐县东灰山遗址发掘纪要 [Report on Excavations Conducted at Donghuishan Site, Minle County, Gansu]. *Kaogu* 考古 12:1057–63.

Yuan Jing 袁靖
2015 *Zhongguo dongwu kaoguxue* 中国动物考古学 [Zooarchaeology of China]. Beijing: Wenwu Chubanshe 文物出版社.

Zhao Xin 赵信
1995   Gansu Wushan Fujiamen shiqian wenhua yizhi fajue jianbao 甘肃武山傅家门史前文化遗址发掘简报 [Preliminary Report on Excavations Conducted at the Prehistoric Site of Fujiamen, Wushan, Gansu]. *Kaogu* 考古 4:289–304.

Zhongguo Kexueyuan Kaogu Yanjiusuo Gansu Gongzuodui 中国科学院考古研究所甘肃工作队
1974   Gansu Yongjing Dahezhuang yizhi fajue baogao 甘肃永靖大何庄遗址发掘报告 [Excavation Report of Dahezhuang Site, Yongjing, Gansu]. *Kaogu xuebao* 考古学包 2:29–61.

Zhou, Benxiong 周本雄
1999   Shizhaocun yu Xishanping yizhi de dongwu yicun 师赵村与西山坪遗址的动物遗存 [Animal Bone Remains from Shizhaocun and Xishanping Sites]. In *Shizhaocun yu Xishanping* 师赵村与西山坪 [Shizhaocun and Xishanping], edited by Zhongguo Kexueyuan Kaogu Yanjiusuo 中国社会科学院考古研究所编著, pp. 335–39. Beijing: Zhongguo Dabaike Quanshu Chubanshe 中国大百科全书出版社.

Chapter 9

Emergence of Chime-Bells and *Li-yue* in the Zhou Dynasty

Kazuo Miyamoto

Chinese Society in the Age of Confucius (1000–250 BC): The Archaeological Evidence, published by Lothar von Falkenhausen in 2006, covers the period from the Western Zhou Dynasty to the Warring States and focuses on social changes based on ritual systems involving bronze vessels. In his research, von Falkenhausen uses a social archaeological approach to focus on kinship and social structures. His ideas about social change are related to reforms that took place in ritual systems during the Zhou Dynasty. According to his theory, two reforms in the ritual systems of the Zhou Dynasty took place from 1000 to 250 BC. One is the Late Western Zhou Ritual Reform, dating to about 850 BC. The other is the Middle Springs and Autumns Ritual Restructuring, which started about 600 BC.

Descriptions in the Chinese classic *Liji* 禮記 (*Book of Rites*) concerning a lineage split occurring over five generations, along with anthropological evidence, indicate that the lineage of elite classes of the Zhou Dynasty split during the Middle Western Zhou period. The split served to disturb the social order in the latter half of the Western Zhou period. Von Falkenhausen has demonstrated this process through research on Wei family bronze vessels based on analysis combined with research on inscriptions and the typology of bronze vessels.

The Late Western Zhou Ritual Reform restructured society in the wake of disturbances to order around 850 BC, five generations after the beginning of the Western Zhou period (Falkenhausen 2006). This reform consisted of a new ritual system involving bronze vessels used as food supply containers and excluded the use of drinking vessels for alcohol (Rawson 1989). I believe that the performance of ritual ceremonies involving the Zhou king and retainers from the elite class in the latter half of the Western Zhou period, as shown in inscriptions on bronze vessels, also signifies a reconstruction of the social order between the king and elite lineage. The subsequent Middle Springs and Autumns Ritual Restructuring is considered a reprise of the Late Western Zhou Ritual Reform and an attempt to update old standards in the face of changed social realities.

I believe that Lothar's book succeeds in providing an exhaustive elucidation of society during the Zhou period based on the archaeological analysis of various social divisions that together constituted society at different levels: gender, lineage, clan, ethnicity, and social classes. Lothar also succeeds in reconstructing the history of the Zhou period through scientific archaeological research without relying excessively on historical documents, the latter otherwise having been a feature of Chinese archaeological scholarship. This is one reason why his social archaeological theory, which was developed following the New Archaeology movement in the United States, has met with such appreciation, being adapted to the archaeology of the Zhou period in China.

In addition, I would like to mention influences in Lothar's research from Japanese archaeology, especially how he has combined analysis of typological chronologies with that of inscriptions on bronze vessels. I believe that his analytical results and theories concerning Chinese archaeology have made significant contributions to Chinese archaeological scholarship, just as the work of his teacher K. C. Chang did before him. Given his great contributions to Chinese archaeology, I aim to elaborate on his theory of ritual reform. There is a need to identify more concrete details about the content of the Late Western Zhou Ritual Reform and the Middle Springs and Autumns Ritual Restructuring.

Jessica Rawson has suggested that the ritual revolution in the Late Western Zhou consisted of new bronze ritual vessel types and bronze bells (Rawson 1999). She mentioned that "the bells added a completely new element to the rituals, that of resonant music," and that "their introduction, with many large pieces forming sets to produce music, would have made the rituals quite different from those held at earlier times" (Rawson 1999:436–38). In this paper, I focus on the chime-bells, which were one important ritual category added in the Late Western Zhou Ritual Reform.

History of Research and Remaining Issues

In his 2006 book (Falkenhausen 2006:48–49), Lothar mentions that "the decomposition of bronze vessel motifs during the Middle Western Zhou period and their near disappearance in Late Western Zhou bronzes, eventually led to a situation in which vessel decoration fulfilled just such a function." He goes on to mention that "people in Late Western Zhou did not suddenly cease to consume alcohol, but they do seem to have stopped sacrificing alcohol to their ancestors, and intimations of drunken trance— formerly perhaps a central component of ritual performances—vanish."

I would like to ask why people in the Late Western Zhou changed the ritual spirit and religion associated with their ancestor ceremonies. After the Late Western Zhou Ritual Reform, bronze vessel assemblages of the Zhou period were centered on sets of ding 鼎 (for meat) and gui 簋 (for grain) bronze vessels related to food consumption, and chime-bells related to music. Why did bronze vessel assemblages used as burial goods related to the Zhou sumptuary system change from those of the Shang Dynasty in the Western Zhou Dynasty?

In *Suspended Music: Chime-Bells in the Culture of Bronze Age China* (1993), von Falkenhausen mentioned that chime-bells were important items for the rules of propriety (*li*禮) in the Zhou Dynasty. It is important to note that new sets of bronze vessels, including chime-bells, emerged during the Middle Western Zhou period, accompanied by the decomposition of motifs popular during the Shang period.

Music in ancient China was very important for social order, as a means of harmonizing social classifications (Miyamoto 2020). But there are few examples of musical instruments in Shang ritual contexts. Musical bronze instruments first occur as grave goods in China in contexts chronologically corresponding with the Xia Dynasty, which some scholars associate with the Erlitou archaeological period. Later, instruments are found in connection with burials of the Zhou Dynasty. An exception is the category of bronze bells called *nao* 鐃in the Late Shang Dynasty. Textual sources such as the *Shuowen* 説文 in the Han period relate *nao* to warfare (Miyamoto 2020).

It is thought that the *nao* of northern China spread to the south of the Yangzi River from the Central Plains and that bigger bronze bells called *yongzhong* 甬鐘 originated from south of the Yangzi (Figure 9.1). Hayashi Minao, who was Lothar's supervisor when he studied at Kyoto University from 1984 to 1986, had previously posited such an idea (Hayashi 1981), and it was picked up by Lothar (1993). Later, Gao Zhixi became the first Chinese scholar to support this perspective, demonstrating that the decoration scheme of *yongzhong* originated from the enlarged *nao* bells of southern China. Gao showed that these enlarged *nao* bells originated from the Xianjiang River basin in Hunan Province (Gao 1997). Rawson (1999) argued that bells copied from the south appear in a set of three. Recently, Xiong Jianhua has argued that the enlarged *nao* bells and *bo* 鎛of southern China were the ancestors of the chime-bells of the Central Plains in China (Xiong 2013). Furthermore, it is thought that three-piece sets of *nao* dating to the Shang period could be related to sets of three *yongzhong* after the Middle Western Zhou period (Chang 2014).

In this paper, I begin by discussing the chronology of *nao* from the Late Shang period to the Early Western Zhou period. I will then move on to discuss the relationship between the *nao* of northern China and the enlarged *nao* bells of southern China. In doing so, we must also discuss the chronology of the enlarged *nao* bells of southern China. Based on archaeological evidence, *yongzhong* are thought to have originated from the *nao* bells of southern China. The designs of *mei* 枚 raised bosses and *xuan* 旋 decorative bands on *yongzhong* identified in historical texts (see Figure 9.2) were not seen in the *nao* of the Late Shang period in northern China (Gao 2009). I will shed light on how *yongzhong* emerged under the influence of the enlarged *nao* bells of southern China. In recent years, several new finds of *yongzhong* dating to the former half of the Western Zhou period in the Central Plains of China have been reported.

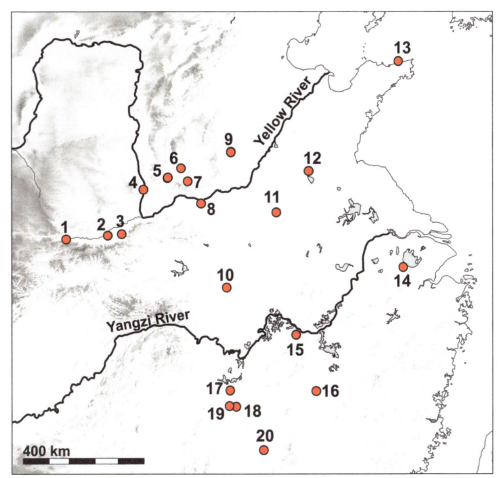

Figure 9.1. Map of sites mentioned in the text: 1. Zhuyuangou; 2. Puducun; 3. Zhangjiapo; 4. Liangdaicun; 5. Tianma-Qucun and Beizhao; 6. Dahekou; 7. Rujiazhuang; 8. Erlitou; 9. Yinxu (with Dasikong and Huayuanzhuang); 10. Yejiashan; 11. Taiqinggong; 12. Qianzhangda; 13. Huangcui (Tiancun); 14. Changxing (Xiaopu); 15. Liurongshan; 16. Dayangzhou (Xingan); 17. Qianjiazhou; 18. Huangmasai; 19. Beifangtan; 20. Xiajiashan.
Created by Bryan K. Miller.

I seek to resolve the issue described above with the help of these newly discovered materials and to provide new insights into the matter of the ritual reforms.

The Emergence of Nao Chimes

The *nao* chimes of northern China, which emerged during Yinxu 殷墟 Phase II of the Late Shang period, have been found in Grave 5 of Xiaotun 小屯 and other locations (Miyamoto 2020). The *nao* of northern China is a bronze bell with a round, hollow shank for gripping (Figure 9.3). Nao chimes are instruments meant to be handled, whereas *yongzhong* are suspended instruments. Bronze bells were also used in the Erlitou period for ritual ceremonies, but these disappeared with the appearance of Early and Middle Shang bronzes (Miyamoto 2020). The *nao* of northern China differ in form from the bronze bells of the Erlitou period, which abruptly emerged in the Late Shang period. It is curious to note that in Anyang, the capital of the Late Shang Dynasty, *nao* were not found in the tombs of kings, but several tombs belonging to members of the elite class contain these bronze bells. Nao bronze bells are usually found in sets of three among grave goods. The difference in size among *nao* from the Late Shang period indicates the existence of three size groups (Figure 9.4). It is believed that *nao* chimes made three separate musical sounds according to the three groups of scales of the *nao* of northern China (Miyamoto 2020). It is also believed that *nao* had a function as instruments different from that of the bronze bells of the Erlitou period, as they were used as single items among grave goods. At Anyang, large quantities of bronze

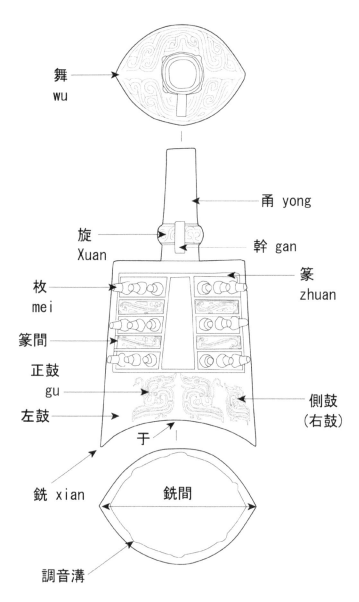

Figure 9.2. Nomenclature of *yongzhong* bells.
Created by the author.

weapons were found among the grave goods in some elite graves containing *nao*. Therefore the *nao* of northern China may be related to military affairs; the Chinese text *Shuowen* 說文, dating to the Han period, indicates that *nao* were used in army parades during warfare.

The second phase of Yinxu, which heralds the beginning of Late Shang bronzes, is the reign of Wuding 武丁, who restored the disturbed governability of the Shang Dynasty, as seen in the Chinese text *Shiji* 史記 (Mizoguchi and Uchida 2019). At this time, new bronze vessels like *hu* 壺, *guxing zun* 觚形尊, and *shuang'er gui* 双耳簋 were produced together with *nao* as part of ritual reforms enacted by Wuding (Miyamoto 2020). According to an analysis of a set of bronze vessels and their inscription style carried out by Mai Suzuki (2017), the *nao* of northern China were produced at Anyang in a workshop different from those that had produced the main bronzes.

Nao of the Late Shang period are classified according to the design of the bronze bell (Figure 9.3). In a new typology I am proposing here, Type 1 and Type 2 are classified as a mask design, like the *taotie* 饕餮 motif. Type 1 and Type 2 are differentiated on the basis of the cocoon form in the mask design. Type 1 is a type of round cocoon form, whereas Type 2 is a cocoon resembling a water buffalo horn with ears. Type 3 features double square grid lines, while Type 4 features a single square grid line that is similar in design to those seen in the Erlitou period.

A chronological scheme of *nao* in the Late Shang period (Figure 9.3) can be suggested based on the chronology of the grave pottery style of Yinxu. Type 1 underwent a typological change from Type 1a to Type 1b and eventually to Type 1c, which are classified by changes to the form of the nose and cheek according to the cultural phases of Yinxu. Type 2a emerged in the third phase of Yinxu and changed to Type 2b in the fourth phase of Yinxu. A typological change in mask design is seen in the nose and cheek of masks in Type 2.

Even in the early phase of the Western Zhou period, sets of three *nao* are still seen among grave goods (Figure 9.3). However, these graves are limited to members of elite Shang clans in the Early Western Zhou period. Type 1a is still the main type in the Western Zhou Dynasty. Type 1d emerged in the Early Western Zhou Dynasty, the result of a typological change in the nose form of the mask design. In the latter half of the Early Western Zhou period, Type 1d with *gan* 幹 (a suspension ring on the bell handle; see Figure 9.2) can be seen for the first time at Tomb 14 of Zhuyuangou 竹園溝, Baoji, Shangxi Province. At the same time, Type 4b with *gan* and *xuan* (a horizontal decorative band on the handle) was seen only in Tomb 1 of Dahekou 大河口, Shanxi Province. Type 4b with *gan* also has only *xuan* and was influenced by the *nao* bells of southern China. The function of *gan* is connected with strings for suspending bells. At this time, the *nao* of northern China started to be suspended when used (Miyamoto 2020).

In the middle phase of the Western Zhou period, in the Central Plains of China, the *nao* of northern China disappeared. *Nao* were replaced by *yongzhong*, though in the Middle Western Zhou Dynasty, *nao* are still seen in the peripheral area of the Central Plains, albeit only at Weihai, Shandong Province (Figure 9.3).

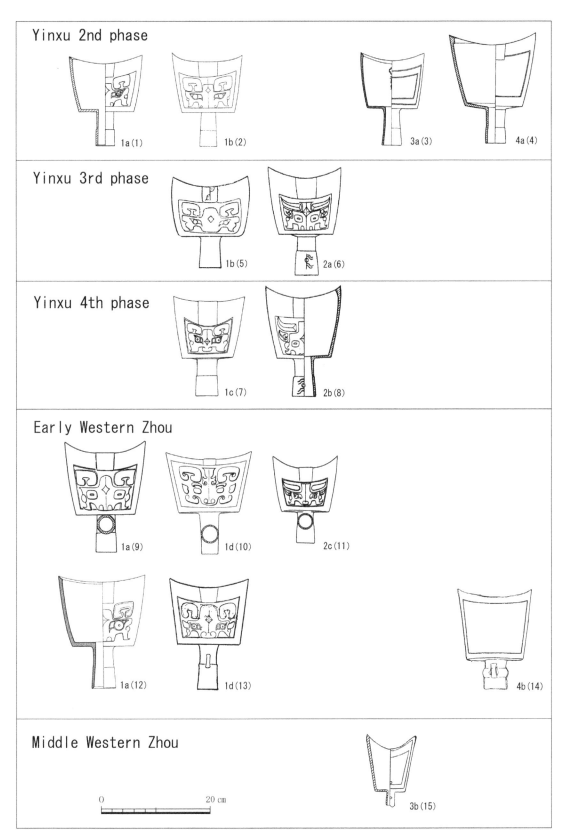

Figure 9.3. Chronology of *nao* of northern China in the Late Shang Dynasty and Early Western Zhou Dynasty: 1. Huayuanzhuang 54; 2. Dasikong 663; 3. Xiaotun 5; 4. Guojiazhuang 26; 5. Qijiazhuang East 269; 6. Guojiazhuang 160; 7. Dasikong 303; 8. Yinxu Xiqu 699; 9–11. Taiqinggong 1; 12. Qianzhangda 206; 13. Zhuyuangou 13; 14. Dahekou 1; 15. Huangcui 1. *Created by the author.*

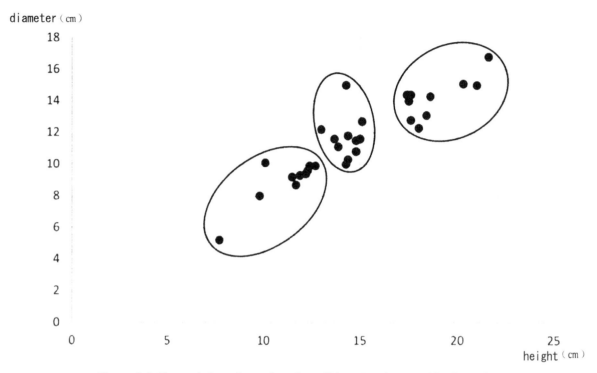

Figure 9.4. Size variation of *nao* of northern China. *Graph created by the author.*

The Emergence of Nao Bells in Southern China

The enlarged *nao* bells of southern China are classified according to their main design into four groups: Type A, a mask design; Type B, a modified mask design with a scroll design; Type C, a spiral design; and Type D, a *mei* raised-boss design (Gao 1984; Li 1996).

In this paper, I classify the designs on the enlarged *nao* bells of southern China into three groups, based on typological changes in design. Type 1 is a mask design, similar to the *taotie* motif (Hayashi 1981), which represents a modified form of a mask design. Type 2 indicates a typological change in the form of a spiral design. Type 3 is a raised line decoration with eyes in the grid lines comprised of faint raised lines and bands of circles.

Type 1 is classified into three subtypes (Figure 9.5). Type 1a is a *taotie* design and clear mask design. Type 1b modifies the mask design, in the process losing the meaning of the *taotie*. It keeps only the eye design, and other elements are changed to a scroll design. Type 1c has only a scroll design without an eye design.

Type 2 is classified into four subtypes (Figure 9.5). Type 2a is a kind of modified mask design consisting of a square grid with eye design. Type 2b consists of a modified eye design, like a spiral design inside a square grid. Type 2c is a modified eye design of Type 2b, which had been changed into a design of spirals and bosses in a square grid. With Type 2d, the bosses have been projected and changed to a *mei* design in a square grid.

Type 3 is classified into two subtypes (Figure 9.5), which feature the same eye design with a raised line decoration circled by faint raised lines and bands. Type 3a consists of a mask design similar to that of Type 2a. Type 3b modifies these stylistic motifs with a raised line decoration inside the grid lines, because of which the mask design loses the meaning of the *taotie* design.

The chronology of the enlarged *nao* bells of southern China indicates that the *xuan* design had been established, as in Types 1b, 1c, 2c, and 2d, in the latter half of this chronology. In fact, we do not know the function of the *xuan*. It could have served as a stopper for hanging the enlarged bell or been used with wire ropes to suspend the enlarged bell.

The taotie design of Type 1a found at Liurongshan 劉榮山, Hubei Province, is the same as that of that of Zhi-gui 执簋, which is synchronous with the second and third phases of Yinxu (Li 1996). Type 2a and Type 3a were found at Xingan, Jiangxi Province. Xiang Taochu believes that the Xingan 新干tomb dates to the third and fourth phases of Yinxu (Xiang 2010), although there are various theories as to the dating of this tomb, ranging from the Middle to the Late Shang period

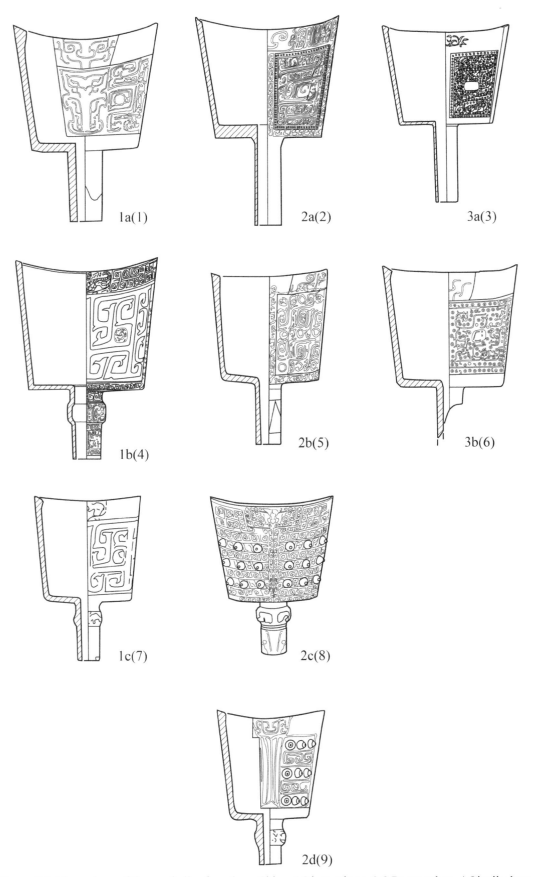

Figure 9.5. Chronology of the *nao* bells of southern China: 1 Liuronghsan, 2-3 Dayangzhou, 4 Qianjiazhou, 5 Huangmasai, 6 Liurongshan, 7 Beifengtan, 8 Changxing, 9 Xiajiashan. *Created by the author.*

(Falkenhausen 1993; Xiong 2013). Accordingly, Types 1a, 2a, and 3a are believed to date to the latter half of the late period of Shang bronzes. Type 1a, consisting of a *taotie* design, was produced in southern China and was influenced by the *nao* of northern China belonging to the Late Shang bronzes. At the beginning of the Late Shang, production techniques for bronze vessels spread to the Yangtze River basin, where people mined copper and tin ores. They produced enlarged bells, which developed from the *nao* of northern China, with modified mask ornamentation adapted from Late Shang bronzes (Hayashi 1981). The *nao* bells of southern China took on an almond-shaped cross section and musically used two tones (Falkenhausen 1993). But the fact that the *nao* bells of southern China are found as single bells suggests a different meaning behind their usage than that of the *nao* of northern China, which are found in sets of three. They became special ritual objects for people in southern China. It is believed that the dating of Types 1b, 1c, 2b, and 3b in southern China aligned with the early phase of the Western Zhou period, and the dating of Types 2c and 2d, featuring spirals and bosses (*mei*) in southern China, was contemporaneous with the Middle to Late Western Zhou period. This is according to Xiang Taochu's dating, which lacks clear archaeological evidence (Xiang 2010).

The Emergence of Yongzhong Bells

Yongzhong of the Western Zhou period are characterized by the presence of *xuan* and *mei*. The former has a stopper function for the bell, and the latter is a standard ornamentation scheme on *yongzhong*. Both are believed to have been influenced by the *nao* bells of southern China. *Yongzhong* emerged in the latter half of the Early Western Zhou period. The *xuan* appeared on the *nao* bells of southern China, as mentioned in the previous section. We must investigate connections between the standard ornamentation scheme of the *nao* bells of southern China and *yongzhong* of the Western Zhou period. First, we must set out a chronology for *yongzhong* to clarify these relationships.

Aya Nagasawa recently presented a chronology for the *yongzhong* of the Western Zhou period based on the combinations of design attributes (Nagasawa 2017), although Lothar had previously provided a rough outline for a chronology of chime-bells (Falkenhausen 1993). I would like to set out a new chronology for the *yongzhong* of the Western Zhou Dynasty based on the same design attributes as Nagasawa's, which I rework slightly. The design attributes of *yongzhong* consist of two categories: the *zhuan* 篆 grid line design and the main design, termed *gu* 鼓 (see Figure 9.2).

The most important attribute change the typology focuses on is a type of grid line (*zhuan* 篆). Nagasawa suggested a change in direction from an earlier *jia* 甲 type to a later *ding* 丁 type (Nagasawa 2017). In this paper, the naming and order of classification of the grid line *zhuan* will be changed from Nagasawa's (Figure 9.6). In the typology proposed here, the Type 1 grid line consists of a decoration in faint raised lines and bands of circles. The Type 2 grid line consists of a decoration in faint raised lines and bands of small studs. The Type 3 grid line consists of projected line contours. The Type 4 grid line consists of sunken line contours. I suggest that the Type 1 grid line is earliest because this type of grid line can be seen in the *nao* bells of southern China, such as Type 3 (Figures 9.5.3 and 9.5.6). Bands of circles eventually became bands of small studs—because I infer that whereas circles were first carved in the molds used for casting the bronze bells, the insides of the circles were later carved to form studs in the molds. This was a process of change in which a carved design was incorporated into the molds. In addition, Type 2 changed to Type 3, because when faint raised lines and bands of studs were carved, the whole section between the raised lines on the molds was carved to become protruding line contours. And sunken line contours should be protruding lines on the mold. The mold technique of producing the sunken line contour design is more complicated than that of the protruding line design. Therefore Type 3 developed into Type 4, as the technique used on molds for Type 4 was more complicated than that of Type 3.

Nagasawa classifies the main design of *gu* into two types (2017). In the present paper, the main design is classified into three types: scroll design, animal design, and bird-looking-back design (Figure 9.6). Nagasawa includes the latter two types as a single type. The three types here are called Type A, Type B, and Type C.

I suppose that the scroll design on *yongzhong* was introduced from the *nao* bells of southern China, as it is very similar to the main design in Type 1c (Figure 9.5.7). The scroll design (Type A) is also classified into three subtypes. Type A-a consists of a spiral design with multiple faint raised lines. Type A-b is a scroll design with double lines, and Type A-c is the same design with a single line (Figure 9.6). It is assumed that all subtypes underwent typological changes over time.

The animal design (Type B) and bird-looking-back design (Type C) are not seen in the *nao* bells of southern China, thus representing an original design of *yongzhong* in northern China (Figure 9.6). Type B is divided into two subtypes: Type B-a and Type B-b. Type B-a is a single animal with another small animal. Type B-b consists of a set of two identical symmetrical animals. Type B-a

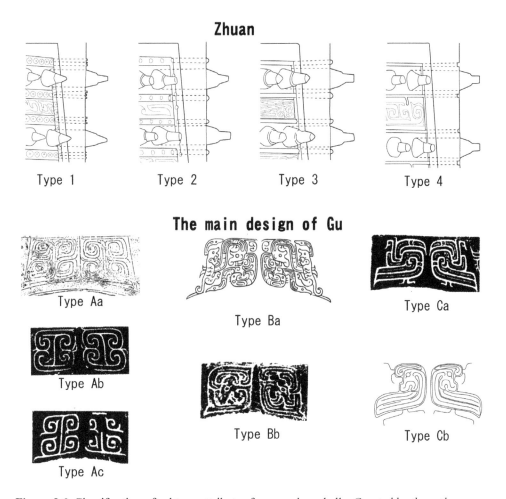

Figure 9.6. Classification of subtype attributes for *yongzhong* bells. *Created by the author.*

changed to Type B-b, as the representative design changed to become a symmetrical motif. Type C is also classified into two types, Type C-a and Type C-b. The bird design of Type C-a is a specific design and changes typologically into the degenerated design of Type C-b, for example with a modified leg design.

Such types of grid lines as *zhuan* and the main design (*gu*) change alongside each other, becoming defining aspects of types of *yongzhong* of the Western Zhou Dynasty. The matrix of grid line subtype and main design subtype is shown in Table 9.1. According to the table of subtypes, they can be grouped as A-a1 and A-a2, A-b2 and A-b3, and A-c3 and A-c4 types in the main A design; as B-a2 and B-b3 in the main B design; and as C-a3, C-a4, and C-b3 in the main C design. Table 9.2. shows the dating of types of *yongzhong* based on the bronze vessel chronology used for dating burials.

The earliest chime-bells, including four *yongzhong* and one *bo* 鎛, were discovered in Grave 111 of the Yejiashan 葉家山 cemetery in Suizhou, Hubei Province—a grave dating to the first half of the Western Zhou period (Hubeisheng Bowuguan et al. 2013). These *yongzhong* are Types A-a1 and A-a2 (Figure 9.7). Grave 111 is the grave of the Marquis of Zeng 曾 in the Early Western Zhou period. It is believed by some to be the grave of the fourth King Zhao昭王 in the latter half of the Early Western Zhou period (Zhang Changping 2013). Another theory is that it is the grave of the third King Kang 康王in the latter half of Early Western Zhou period (Zhang Tianweng 2016). Types A-b2 and A-b3 (Figure 9.7) are found at Tomb 7 of Zhuyuangou (Lu and Hu 1988), which is believed to date to the latter half of the Early Western Zhou period. It is believed that a group of Types A-a1 and A-a2 emerged, followed by the prompt appearance of a group of Types A-b2 and A-b3. Types A-c3 and Type A-c4 emerged continuously in the middle of the Western Zhou, and a group of Types B and Type C was established in the Late Western Zhou period based on evidence listed in Table 9.2.

Table 9.1. Combination of subtype attributes

	Type A-a	Type A-b	Type A-c	Type B-a	Type B-b	Type C-a	Type C-b
Type 1	○						
Type 2	○	○		○			
Type 3	○	○	○		○	○	○
Type 4		○	○			○	

Table 9.2. Collection of *yongzhong* found at graves of the Western Zhou Dynasty

Grave Name	Classification	Number	Dating
Yejiashan 111	A-a1	2	latter half of the Early Western Zhou
Yejiashan 111	A-a2	2	latter half of the Early Western Zhou
Dahekou 1017	A-a1	1	first half of the Middle Western Zhou
Dahekou 1017	A-a2	2	first half of the Middle Western Zhou
Zhuyangou 7	A-b2	2	latter half of the Early Western Zhou
Zhuyangou 7	A-b3	1	latter half of the Early Western Zhou
Puducun	A-a2	3	first half of the Middle Western Zhou
Rujiazhuang 1Yi	A-a2	2	latter half of the Middle Western Zhou
Rujiazhuang 1Yi	A-a3	1	latter half of the Middle Western Zhou
Zhangjiapo 163	A-c3	2	latter half of the Middle Western Zhou
Zhanjiapo 163	?	1	latter half of the Middle Western Zhou
Tianma, Qucun 7092	A-c4	1	latter half of the Middle Western Zhou
Beizhao 8	A-c4	2	first half of the Late Western Zhou
Beizhao 64	B-a3	1	latter half of the Late Western Zhou
Beizhao 93	C-a4	2	latter half of the Late Western Zhou
Liangdaicun 27		8	Early Springs and Autumns period
Liangdaicun 28	A-c4	8	first half of the Early Springs and Autumns period

Emergence of Chime-Bells and *Li-yue* in the Zhou Dynasty 177

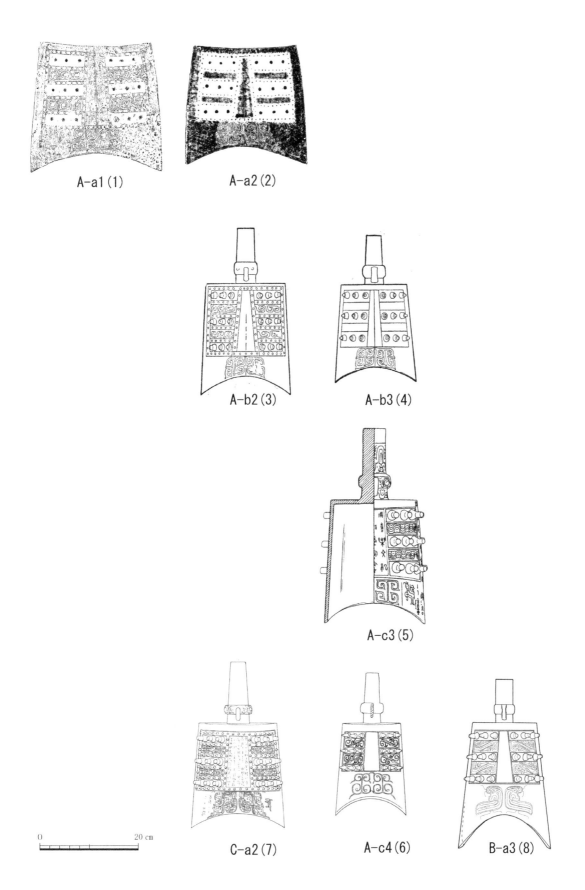

Figure 9.7. Chronology of *yongzhong* of the Western Zhou Dynasty: 1–2. Dahekou 1017; 3–4. Zhuyuangou 7; 5. Zhangjiapo 163; 6. Tianma-Qucun 7092; 7. Beizhao 64; 8. Beizhao 93. *Created by the author.*

The earliest *yongzhong* A-a1 type has Type 1 grid lines *zhuan* and a Type A-a main design. As already mentioned, these designs are related to the designs of *nao* bells of southern China. I believe that the standard ornamentation scheme and *xuan* of the *yongzhong* of northern China were introduced from those of the *nao* bells of southern China. Type 1 grid lines of *yongzhong* at Grave 111 at the Yejiashan cemetery are seen in Type 3 *nao* bells of southern China. Type 3b *nao* bells of southern China were found at the Liulongshan 劉榮山 site, Yangxin, Hubei Province, south of the territories of the Marquis of Zeng and the Marquis of Wo 噩 in the Western Zhou period.

It is known that in the latter half of the Early Western Zhou period, King Zhao 昭王 undertook large-scale military campaigns to the south, as seen in the Chinese text *Shiji* 史記 and inscriptions of bronze vessels in the Western Zhou period (Shaughnessy 1999). The purpose of southern military campaigns at the time was to obtain not only new territory but also metal raw materials. Recent compositional analysis indicates that raw materials used in producing bronzes from the Yu state found at the Zhuyangou and Rujiazhuang 如家庄 cemeteries in Shaanxi Province may come from the same source as those used in producing bronzes from the Zeng state found at the Yejiashan cemetery in Hubei Province (Li et al. 2020). This result suggests that ores of southern China were acquired by groups in the Central Plains of northern China in the Early Western Zhou period. I believe that the Western Zhou polity incorporated musical instruments from their original producers so as to rule the new territory. This situation resembled the emergence of the Shang Dynasty in that Shang people got bronze drinking vessels for alcohol, such as *jue* 爵 and *jia* 斝, from the Erlitou culture; bronze cooking vessels, such as *ding* 鼎 and *yan* 甗, from the Yueshi culture; and bronze serving vessels, such as *gui* 簋, from Shang itself, as ritual objects to symbolize, facilitate, and materialize rule over newly enlarged territory. People of three cultures—the Shang, Erlitou, and Yueshi—needed to join in the same ancestor ritual ceremony as the Shang royal family through the sharing the ritual goods of new lands (Miyamoto 2020).

The discussion above shows that *yongzhong* were developed under the influence of the *nao* bells of southern China in the latter half of the Early Western Zhou period. Therefore, Types 2c and 2d with the *xuan* and *mei* of the *nao* bells of southern China (Figure 9.5) should be dated to the Early Western Zhou period.

At the same time, other attributes of *yongzhong* could be related to the *nao* of northern China. Recently, a new discovery of chime-bells was made at the Dahekou 大河 □ cemetery in Yicheng, Shanxi Province. Grave 1 at the cemetery, which dates to the latter half of the Early Western Zhou Dynasty, contains three bronze bells of *nao* Type 4b (Figure 9.3.14), which are typologically related to those of the Late Shang period. These *nao* have *gan* that do not exist in the *nao* bells of southern China. Such gan also appear with an example of *nao* Type 1d (Figure 9.3.13) from Tomb 13 at Zhuyuangou, Baoji, Shangxi Province, which dates to the latter half of the Early Western Zhou period. Therefore, *gan* on *yongzhong* originated from *nao* in the Western Zhou period. The concept of a set of three *yongzhong* is another attribute originating from *nao*. *Yongzhong* occur in sets of three in grave goods, according to Table 9.2. *Gan* are used to suspend *nao*, and a set of three different sizes means a set of three tone sounds. These attributes pertain to *nao*'s function as instruments.

In this way, *yongzhong* emerged in the latter half of the Early Western Zhou Dynasty as a mixture of features of the *nao* of northern China and the *nao* bells of southern China. The form and design of *yongzhong* derived from *nao* bells of southern China, while the actual function of the instrument came from the *nao* of northern China. In the middle of the Western Zhou period, Types A-c3 and A-c4 were widespread. And the main designs of animals (Type B) and birds (Type C), which is a particular design of *yongzhong*, were widespread in the Late Western Zhou period. The set of three pieces of Types B and C of *yongzhong* produced three harmonious sounds proved by measurement of sound (Nakagawa 2017). The harmonious sounds produced by *yonzhong* chime-bells suggested the harmonization of ritual ceremonies in keeping with *li-yue* 禮樂 to maintain its social classified system of lineage. At the same time, the ritual reforms of the Late Western Zhou Dynasty were established in the new sets of bronze vessels with chime-bells of *yongzhong* and *bo*.

The Late Western Zhou Ritual Reform and the Establishment of *Li-yue*

In the transition of dynasties between the Xia and Shang, the set of bronze vessels changed. Bells and bronze drinking vessels for alcohol were limited to ritual ceremonies for ancestral worship during the Xia period. However, during the Early and Middle Shang period, bells were eliminated from use, and cooking and serving vessels were added to drinking vessels for alcohol in ritual ceremonies. Such changes in ritual objects related to changes in ritual ceremonies and religion in the sense that the Shang had a newly enlarged territory to rule over, with new lands mixed in with their different original ritual activities for worship of ancestors (Miyamoto 2020).

In the Late Shang period, new ritual bronze vessels such as *hu* 壺, *guxingzun* 觚形尊, and *shuang'ergui* 双耳簋 were introduced, with *nao* (bell instruments) in the original ritual bronze vessels, when Wuding 武丁 reformed the government by organizing new ritual activities for ancestors (Miyamoto 2020).

At the beginning of the Western Zhou period, the Zhou maintained the rules of the ritual system from the Late Shang Dynasty, given that the Zhou was a retainer under the Shang Dynasty. When the Zhou sought to enlarge its territory toward the south of the Yangzi in search of metal ores during the latter half of the Early Western Zhou period, it needed to incorporate different original ritual objects from south of the Yangzi River to facilitate its rule over new lands. In this process, *yongzhong* of northern China developed from the *nao* bells of southern China. At the same time, the bell instrument function was introduced from the *nao* of northern China in the Late Shang period and the Early Western Zhou period.

In the Middle Western Zhou period, Zhou society needed to sustain its social classification system of lineages with its own ritual ceremonies based on the supply of food for the ancestors (Falkenhausen 2006). I believe this is why the Zhou changed the set of bronze vessels during the Late Western Zhou Ritual Reform. The new set of bronze vessels consisted of chime-bells, including *yongzhong*. From this time onward, sets of three *yongzhong* sounded in harmony. This harmony of *yongzhong* means the beginning of *li-yue* 禮樂, which is harmonization in social order (Miyamoto 2020). The *yongzhong* changed to a set of typical chime-bells in the Middle Springs and Autumns period. This was the Middle Springs and Autumns Ritual Restructuring (Falkenhausen 2006).

Acknowledgments

Professor Lothar von Falkenhausen and I are around the same age. Our paths first crossed in 1984 during a series of research seminars organized by the late professor Hayashi Minao at the Institute of Research in the Humanities, Kyoto University, Japan. At that time, Lothar was a doctoral student at Harvard University and had gone abroad to study at Kyoto University under the supervision of Professor Hayashi Minao. Hayashi was also one of my teachers, specializing in Chinese archaeology. After Lothar's stay in Kyoto for two years, we met again unexpectedly at Beijing University, where I stayed for one year, from 1991 to 1992. Lothar was a visiting scholar at the Institute of Archaeology, Chinese Academy of Social Sciences, from 1990 to 1991 through a J. Paul Getty Fellowship after having obtained a PhD at Harvard University in 1988. We have since met occasionally in China, Japan, Korea, the United States, and Europe to exchange ideas on Chinese archaeology. In the Festschrift for von Falkenhausen, I had the honor of submitting an article about chime-bells, the theme of his doctoral dissertation, published by the University of California Press as *Suspended Music: Chime-Bells in the Culture of Bronze Age China*, in 1993. My research is supported by a JSPS KAKENHI grant-in-aid for scientific research: "Holistic Research on the Spread and Acculturation of Early Agriculture and the Processes behind the Establishment of Herding Societies in East Asia" (Kazuo Miyamoto 19H05593).

References

Chang Huaiying 常懷穎
2014　Lun Shang Zhou zhiji naozhong suizang 論商周之際鐃鐘随葬 [Nao as Grave Goods in the Transitional Time between Shang and Zhou]. *Jianghan kaogu* 江漢考古 2014(1):54–64.

Falkenhausen, Lothar von
1993　*Suspended Music: Chime-Bells in the Culture of Bronze Age China*. Berkeley: University of California Press.
2006　*Chinese Society in the Age of Confucius: (1000–250 BC): The Archaeological Evidence*. Los Angeles: Cotsen Institute of Archaeology Press.

Gao Zhixi 高至喜
1984　Zhongguo nanfang chutu Shang Zhou tongnao gailun 中国南方出土商周銅鐃概論 [Introduction of Bronze Nao Found in Southern China]. *Hunan kaogu jikan* 湖南考古集刊 2:128–35.
1997　Guanyu Jinhou Su bianzhong de laiyuan wenti 関于晋侯蘇編鐘的来源問題 [Issues Concerning the Origin of Chime-Bells of the Marquis of Jin]. *Wenwu* 文物 1997(3):62–63.
2009　Zailun Hunan chutu Shangdai shoumianwen tongnao de niandai ji xiangguan wenti 再論湖南出土商代獣面紋銅鐃的年代及相關問題 [Re-discussion on the Age and Related Issues of the Bronze Nao of Shang Dynasty Unearthed in Hunan]. *Hunansheng Bowuguangkan* 湖南省博物館刊 2009(5):44–54.

Hayashi Minao 林巳奈夫
1981　Yin, Seishu Jidai no Chihougata Seidouki 殷、西周時代の地方型青銅器 [Unusual Types of Ancient Chinese Bronzes during Yin and Western Chou Period]. In *Koukogaku memoire* 考古学メモワール 1980 [Memoirs of Archaeology, Kyoto University 1980], pp. 17–58. Tokyo: Gakuseisha 学生社.

Hubeisheng Bowugaun 湖北省博物館, Hubeisheng Wewu Kaogu Yanjiusuo湖北省文物考古研究所, and Suizhoushi Bowuguan隨州市博物館
2013 *Suizhou Yejiashan: Xizhou zaoqi Zengguo mudi* 隨州葉家山－西周早期曾国墓地 [Suizhou Yejiashan: Zeng State Cemetery in the Early Western Zhou Period]. Beijing: Wenwuchubanshe 文物出版.

Li, Chunyi李純一
1996 *Zhongguo Shanggu Chutu Yueqi Zonglun* 中国上古出土楽器総論 [General Remarks of Instruments Found at Prehistoric Times]. Beijing: Wenwu Chubanshe文物出版社.

Li Haichao 黎海超, Cui Jianfeng崔剣鋒, Wang Hong王 竑, and Ren Zhoufang 任周方
2020 Lun Yuguo bendi fengge tongqi de shengchan wenti 論強國本地風格銅器的生産問題 [A Discussion on the Production Issues of the Local Style Bronzes of the Yu State]. *Kaogu* 考古 2020(1):106–16.

Lu Liancheng and Hu Zhisheng廬連成·胡智生
1988 Baoji Yuguo Mudi 寶鶏強國墓地 [Yu State Graveyard in Baoji]. Beijing: Wenwu Chubanshe 文物出版社.

Miyamoto Kazuo
2020 *Higashi Ajia Seidouki Jidai no Kenkyu*東アジア青銅器時代の研究 [Research on the Bronze Age of East Asia]. Tokyo: Yuzankaku雄山閣.

Mizoguchi Koji and Uchida Junko
2018 The Anyang Xibeigang Shang Royal Tombs Revisited: A Social Archaeological Approach. *Antiquity* 92(363):709–23.

Nagasawa Aya
2017 Seishu Jidai no Henshou西周時代の「編鐘」 [Chime-Bells of the Western Zhou Dynasty]. *Komazawa shigaku* 駒澤史学, 70–97.

Rawson, Jessica
1989 Statesmen or Barbarians? The Western Zhou as Seen Through Their Bronzes. *Proceedings of the British Academy* 75:71–95.
1999 Western Zhou Archaeology. In *The Cambridge History of Ancient China from the Origins of Civilization to 221 BC*, edited by Michael Loewe and Edward L. Shaughnessy, pp. 352–449. Cambridge: Cambridge University Press.

Shaughnessy, L. Edward
1999 Western Zhou Archaeology. In *The Cambridge History of Ancient China from the Origins of Civilization to 221 BC*, edited by Michael Loewe and Edward L. Shaughnessy, pp. 292–351. Cambridge: Cambridge University Press.

Suzuki, Mai鈴木舞
2017 *Indai Seudouki no Seisantaisei* 殷代青銅器の生産体制 [Production System of Yin Bronzes]. Tokyo: Rokuichishobou六一書房.

Xiang Taochu 向桃初
2010 Cong Yinxu chutu tongnao kan nanfang tongnao de niandai從殷墟出土銅鐃看南方銅鐃的年代] [Dating of Southern Bronze Nao Viewed from Bronze Nao Found in Yinxu]. *Kaogu yu wenwu* 考古与文物 2:40–50.

Xiong Jianhua 熊建華
2013 *Hunan Shang Zhou qingtongqi yanjiu* 湖南商周青銅器研究 [Research on the Bronzes of Shang and Zhou Dynasties in Hunan District]. Changshe: Yuelu Shushe 岳麓書社.

Zhang Changping 張昌平
2013 Yejiashan mudi xiangguan wenti yanjiu 葉家山墓地相關問題研究 [Research on the Issues Related with Yejiaxhan Cemetery]. In *Suizhou Yejiashan: Xizhou zaoqi Zengguo mudi* 隨州葉家山－西周早期曾国墓地 [Suizhou Yejiashan: Zeng State Cemetery in the Early Western Zhou Period], edited by Hubeisheng Bowugaun 湖北省博物館, Hubeisheng Wewu Kaogu Yanjiusuo 湖北省文物考古研究所, and Suizhoushi Bowuguan隨州市博物館, pp. 270–84. Beijing: Wenwu Chubanshe文物出版.

Zhang, Tianwen 張天恩
2001 Shilun Suizhou Yejiashan mudi Zenghoumu de niandai he xulie 試論隨州葉家山墓地曾侯墓的年代和序列 [Essay of Dating and Order of Marquis Zeng Cemetery at Yejiashan Cemetery, Suizhou]. *Wenwu* 文物 10:44–54.

Chapter 10

Consuming the Herds
Animal Sacrifice and Offerings of the Xiongnu

Bryan K. Miller

From ceremonial bells to salt production, the collective works of Lothar von Falkenhausen span the realms of both ritual practice and economic systems. More importantly, much of his research demonstrates the ways in which dynamics of ritual and economy often intersect in specific material spheres. Just as the tradition of dual-evidence examination, as formulated by Wang Guowei in the early 1900s, shapes historical and archaeological research in East Asia, so has von Falkenhausen's research pushed the boundaries between domains of data, disciplines, and dynamics, fostering a multiperspective approach for individual inquiries (e.g., Falkenhausen 2006). This paper explicitly employs such a multivalent approach to archaeological remains to demonstrate how animal offerings in graves simultaneously embody economic and ritual institutions of steppe pastoral communities in the Xiongnu Empire in Inner Asia.

Animal offerings in mortuary arenas have been employed as key materials in assessments of cultural practice as well as social politics (Hayden 2009; Insoll 2010). They are often deemed sustenance for the deceased or other supernatural entities (Hesse et al. 2012; Schwartz 2017; Valeri 1994). However, more scrutiny of the contents and contexts of faunal remains deposited in graves reveals them to retain multiple functions and to be vestiges of manifold activities.

Livestock offerings in burials of Eurasian steppe societies are customarily discussed as both food for the dead and as reflections of pastoral economies (Hanks 2002). In the case of Inner Asia during the era of the Xiongnu Empire (ca. second century BCE to second century CE), burial sites containing offerings of horses, cattle, sheep, and/or goats are often categorized collectively as evidence of pastoralism, mostly in dichotomous contrast to realms of agricultural societies (e.g., Wu'en 2008; see Figure 10.1). Yet while livestock in graves may reflect the primacy of pastoral products in steppe societies, they are not mere reflections of herder lifeways; nor are they equivalents for herd compositions (Hanks 2002). The remains of livestock sacrifice and offering should be examined via multiple contexts to tease out their concurrent ritual, social, and economic significance in steppe communities.

The first step to expanding our understanding of faunal remains within mortuary arenas of the steppe is to expound the multidimensionality of animal sacrifice (Dietler and Hayden 2001; Hayden 2009; Hubert and Mauss 1964; Insoll 2010; Ucko 1969; Valeri 1994). Beyond the semantics of the term *sacrifice*—that is, to make sacred—the process of sacrifice is "situated in a network of practices . . . enacted prior to, coincident with, and subsequent to the killing . . . and can have multiple functions and meanings simultaneously" (Schwartz 2017:225). Yet if animal remains in the grave directly exhibit only one part of the process—the final deposition—how might we tease apart the multiple actions, or even multiple functions and meanings, that occurred in the course of animal sacrifice? Rowan Flad (2002) has shown how spatial distinctions in the placement of animal offerings of an otherwise seemingly similar

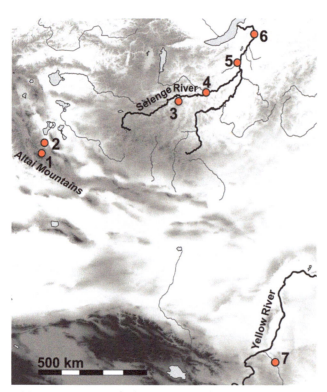

Figure 10.1. Map of Xiongnu cemeteries mentioned in the text. 1. Shombuuzyn-Belchir; 2. Takhiltyn-Khotgor; 3. Salkhityn Am; 4. Burkhan Tolgoi; 5. Derstui; 6. Ivolga; 7. Daodunzi. *Created by the author.*

nature within graves may indicate differences in the meanings of those offerings, the processes of sacrifice and deposition, or even separate ritual events. From this notion we may begin to consider numerous different treatments, not just the place where offerings are set, to further elucidate the multiple meanings of sacrificial offerings.

In the case of Xiongnu graves, we see not only a separation of spaces for animal offerings but also differences in the portions deposited and the artifacts with which offerings are set (Figure 10.2). While livestock were central to Xiongnu society and economy, whole animals were never deposited in graves. We are therefore forced to account for the remainder of the animal corpses. Why were certain parts placed in graves and others not, and what happened to those other portions? Why were different sets of portions of livestock often set apart from one another? Furthermore, since historical and archaeological evidence demonstrates Xiongnu communities to have augmented their pastoral subsistence economies with multiple resources, including hunting wild fauna and growing domestic crops, then why did animal offerings consist almost exclusively of the four categories of sheep, goats, cattle, and horses? This paper seeks to expand the spatial and temporal aspects of sacrificial offerings by considering the multitude of courses through which animals went before their final deposit in mortuary arenas. To accomplish this, I propose to examine the specific locations where animal deposits in graves are positioned as well as variations in the characteristics of those deposits. Through such multivariate analyses, we can begin to understand the multiple dimensions of animal sacrifice in the context of human burials by the Xiongnu.

Distinctions in Xiongnu Animal Offerings

In the era of the Xiongnu Empire, livestock offerings were prevalent throughout Inner Asia. Even if they did not occur within most graves, they did occur at the vast majority of sites. In a survey of more than 200 excavated cemeteries in northern China, Mongolia, and southern Siberia, out of well over 1,000 excavated graves, only about one-third contained livestock offerings (n = 346). Most of them contained the remains of only one or two animals. Thus the occurrence of livestock offerings was a primary means of distinction for those venerated via animal sacrifice. And while grave looting was widespread in the realms of the Xiongnu, with the vast majority of graves having been disturbed, looting targeted the body of the deceased and associated items. Hence, while many human bodies are absent, have only the lower portions intact, or remain articulated in half-dragged-out positions, the remains of animals, placed in adjacent or peripheral spaces of the main burial, often remain undisturbed, providing ample data for a structured study of animal sacrifice.

If we turn to the handful of fully excavated Xiongnu cemeteries to test this overall pattern, we see a range of investment in animal sacrifice in different communities. While some Early Xiongnu cemeteries, such as Daodunzi (27 burials; Ningxia et al. 1987) and Ivolga (216 burials; Davydova 1996), have only a small portion of graves with livestock offerings—18% and 10%, respectively—others, such as Derestui (130 burials; Minyaev 1998) and Salkhityn Am (31 burials; Ölziibayar et al. 2019), have 28% and 61%, respectively. This trend continues into the Late Xiongnu era, with cemeteries such as Burkhan Tolgoi (101 burials; Törbat et al. 2003) with livestock offerings in 78% of the graves. It was during this later era of the Xiongnu Empire that mortuary practices among the disparate communities of the empire became more standard and new types of monumental mortuary complexes, the square tombs, emerged for the uppermost echelons of the Xiongnu elite (Miller 2014). Although the structures and furnishings of mortuary spaces were greatly augmented in the later era, the patterns of differential placement and differential apportionment of animals for offering in mortuary arenas

Figure 10.2. Livestock offerings within the outer coffin versus those above the burial chamber, Grave 50, I'lmovaya pad', Russia. *Created by the author after Konovalov 1976.*

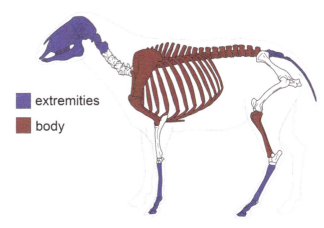

Figure 10.3. Common extremities and body portions of livestock in Xiongnu burials. *Created by the author.*

remained constant throughout the duration of the Xiongnu Empire. A structured examination of these two variables in treatment will allow for greater introspection into the range of activities associated with these animal offerings.

The first of these archaeologically visible distinctions is the physical partitioning of animal bodies (Figure 10.3). The exact set of portions taken from the original whole varies in each case, but sets of remains most often fall into two categories: (1) extremity and (2) body portions. Extremity portions consist primarily of the skull, often with axis and atlas portions of the cervical vertebrae, a practice of livestock offering in Inner Asia that has a deep history reaching back into the Bronze Age (see Taylor 2017; Zazzo et al. 2019). The head portions are often accompanied by distal components of appendages, including phalanges, carpals, and tarsals. Alongside these collective extremity portions are sometimes found caudal vertebrae and sacra. This recurrent combination of heads and hooves (and tails), so to speak, is not only the most frequent form of offering in Xiongnu burials; it also pervades all regions of Inner Asia with established Xiongnu communities (Figure 10.1). Such sets of animal portions in turn raise the question of what happened to the rest of the animal's body, which comprised, not accidentally, the portions with the most meat.

Body portions in Xiongnu burials consisted of most of the axial components related to the torso (thus excluding the head), as well as the more proximal components of appendages. The most frequently deposited of these body portions were ribs, thoracic vertebrae, lumbar vertebrae, and sacra (without the associated caudal vertebrae). And while limb bones of the front legs occur mostly in the context of other extremities, the meatier tibias, although rare, tended to occur with other torso body portions. The placement of body portions (Figure 10.4) within Xiongnu burials was not as frequent as the placement of sets of extremities (Figure 10.5), but it was still a relatively prevalent practice in Inner Asia. Some body portions, such as first ribs, occurred with sets of mostly extremity portions. However, for the most part, these two categories of animal portion sets were found in distinct spaces within burials, thus reinforcing the overall separate categories of extremity and body portions.

The partitioning of animal offerings into discrete spaces within the burials presents a second variable of distinction. Differences between animal portions appear to be reinforced by their grave spaces. While body portions are usually set in spaces closer to the deceased, whether within the actual coffin or within an adjacent antechamber, the more prevalent extremities were almost always placed outside the grave furnishings, sometimes on ledges or in niches of the grave pit and other times overtop the coffins (Figure

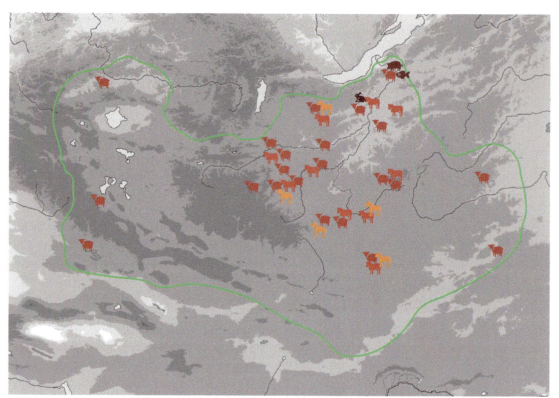

Figure 10.4. Locations of Xiongnu cemeteries with livestock body portion offerings from sheep/goat, cattle, and horse (and pig, fish, and rabbit). Line marks approximate extent of sites attributable to the Xiongnu.
Created by the author.

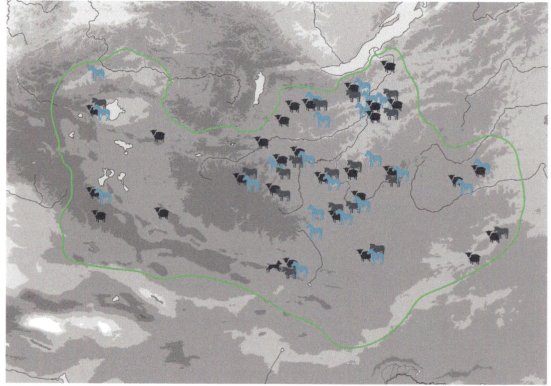

Figure 10.5. Locations of Xiongnu cemeteries with livestock extremity offerings from sheep/goat, cattle, and horse. Line marks approximate extent of sites attributable to the Xiongnu.
Created by the author.

10.2). If the nature of the animal remains—that is, which cuts—and their proximity to the deceased can provide hints as to their function, associated objects provide even clearer evidence. Among the well-documented graves examined for this study, approximately half of the body portions, and none of the extremities, were found within ceramic pots or other cooking vessels. When body portions were not within vessels, they were often placed alongside other feasting-related accoutrements, including iron knives, bone chopsticks, ladles, cups, bowls, cooking pots, and storage jars.

When jointly examined, these two variables of distinction provide valuable insights into the different, even if overlapping, meanings of animal offerings placed within Xiongnu graves. To explore these variables more fully, the patterns of physical and spatial apportionment are considered below for the two main categories of Xiongnu graves—standard ring graves of local elites and the larger square, mounded tombs of the regional elites—at the sites of Shombuuzyn-Belchir and Takhiltyn-Khotgor on the far western frontier, where ritual practices still adhered to standard mortuary rites within the core of the empire (Miller 2011).

Animal Offerings at Shombuuzyun-Belchir and Takhiltyn-Khotgor

Shombuuzyn-Belchir (SBR) is a small Xiongnu cemetery containing standard ring graves of local elites as well as several burials of persons of lesser status marked only by small piles of stones (Bayarsaikhan et al. 2011). To gain a sufficient test of the cemetery and its individuals, 15 of the 33 graves were excavated, sampling burials of all sizes and all areas of the cemetery. These included individuals of all ages—males, females, and subadults—and 12 of the 15 burials contained animal offerings. Even the tiny stone cist of a baby in SBR-36, marked by a pile of stones and placed abutting a ring grave of an older child, was accompanied by the head and cervical vertebrae of a sheep. In addition to these bones being articulated, skin, preserved by the dry conditions of the site, still covered the sheep portions, demonstrating that articulated offerings were likely deposited without any meat taken off. Along with a carnelian bead and a silk under-layer of swaddling wrapping the baby, the sacrifice of a sheep head gave further distinction to this grave occupant.

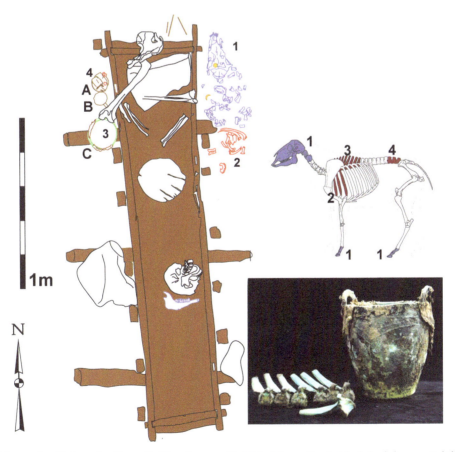

Figure 10.6. Livestock offerings for Grave 7, Shombuuzyn-Belchir, Mongolia. A: birch-bark box containing vertebrae; B: wooden ladle; C: bronze cauldron containing vertebrae and covered with animal skin. Numbers denote portions and placements of faunal remains. *Created by the author.*

One of the larger and richer ring graves, SBR-7, demonstrates the offering of both extremity and body parts of livestock remains as well as the spatial differentiation that further distinguished such sets (Figure 10.6). The skull, cervical vertebrae, and lower phalanges of a sheep (MNI =1) were placed to the left of the coffin (Figure 10.6.1), and in a separate pile beside these were set the first ribs of a sheep (Figure 10.6.2). On the other side of the coffin, among a collection of feasting wares, were other body portions of a sheep. A set of articulated thoracic vertebrae were placed within a bronze cauldron, with a covering of skin stretched overtop and a wooden ladle placed beside (Figure 10.6.3). Within an adjacent birch-bark box were placed three lumbar vertebrae of a sheep (Figure 10.6.4). Although the interior contents of the burial were heavily disturbed, with the remains of a body bent over and half ripped out of the coffin, the animal offerings and other materials around the coffin and at the edge of the grave pit remained relatively undisturbed.

Another large ring grave, SBR-16, which was similarly heavily looted of the contents of its coffin, also appears have retained its burial offering of livestock (Figure 10.7). The skulls, phalanges, and caudal vertebrae of at least four sheep/goats were set just to the north of the coffin, as they are in most Xiongnu grave pits, along with a bronze horse bell and iron fragments of a horse-riding bridle. But these were not the only remains of livestock offerings on behalf of the deceased. Outside the grave pit, several meters to the north, lay a line of stone pairs with highly fired and fragmented faunal remains amid some ash. This additional space for mortuary offerings, and the nature of the offerings deposited between sets of stones, further expands our understanding of Xiongnu practices of animal sacrifice (see fuller discussion in Miller et al. 2018). Whereas the offerings in the grave pit just outside the coffin consisted of only extremities, the pieces of animal bones set in the stone lines (n = 612 identifiable fragments) were almost all body portions (99%), mostly shaft fragments (n = 576), and were mostly from medium-size mammals,

Figure 10.7. Livestock offerings for Grave 16, Shombuuzyn-Blechir, Mongolia. A: bone and iron horse bridle pieces; B: bone composite bow plates. Numbers denote portions and placements of faunal remains. Animal icons denote proportions of burned faunal fragments. *Created by the author.*

likely sheep/goats (98%), in contrast to the very few findings of large mammals such as cattle or horses (Miller et al. 2018:1311–12).

These spatial divisions of animal offerings are even more pronounced in graves of larger sizes, which allow for more distinct compartmentalization of grave goods. The cemetery at Takhiltyn-Khotgor (THL), located in foothills within reach of the mountain site of Shombuuzyn-Belchir, contains numerous ring graves and square tombs (n = 129); the square tombs have both accompanying human graves and accompanying stone lines (Miller et al. 2009). One tomb complex, THL-64, was completely excavated and provides an ideal opportunity to examine the relationship between all three of the above-mentioned spaces for animal offerings and thereby different contexts for the different portions of animals offered (Figure 10.8).

The antechamber just north of the coffin contained body portions of a sheep or goat. In addition to three scattered

Figure 10.8. Livestock offerings for Tomb 64, Takhiltyn-Khotgor, Mongolia. A: iron ladle; B: bone chopsticks; C: painted wood tray. Numbers denote portions and placements of faunal remains. Animal icons denote proportions of burned faunal fragments. *Created by the author.*

ribs, the unfused shank bone and fully articulated set of thoracic vertebrae were placed together, with a pair of bone chopsticks above. Along with these portions of meat on the bone were placed a red-painted wooden tray, an iron ladle, and a large narrow-mouth storage jar (perhaps for holding grains)—the remnants of an assembly for feasting (Figure 10.8.1). Outside the wooden chamber, in a niche carved into the edge of the grave pit, the remains of three goats and one horse were found, each represented by skulls (with axis and atlas), lower front legs, and tails (sacra with caudal vertebrae; Figure 10.8.2).

In addition to these large offerings within the main tomb pit of THL-64 were small accumulations of burned fragmented animal bones within a stone line set to the north of the tomb mound, like the stone line of SBR-16 and its highly calcified animal offerings (Figure 10.8.3) (Miller et al. 2018:1307–9). While only some of the fragments are identifiable to species or portions (n = 347), the majority of them (85%) are from medium-size mammals. The collective bone fragments exhibit a far greater proportion of body than extremity components for both large (98% body) and small (97% body) livestock. In contrast to the preponderance for shaft fragments in the stone line at SBR-16, the stone line offerings for TH-64 were mostly ribs (n = 323). Although six distinct offering spaces of stone pairs were set, only three contained remains, and the last pair in the line contained the largest deposit by far (n = 337). The collective livestock offerings of the antechamber, grave niche, and stone line had highly varied treatments and contexts, intimate distinct meanings, and likely different sacrificial rites.

The Xiongnu Sacrificial Process

The collective evidence for multiple meanings and activities related to animal sacrifice forces us to think about the collective process of sacrifice. To elucidate processes of animal sacrifice further, scholars speak of an overall scheme of sacrifice (Hubert and Mauss 1964) consisting of a series of temporally distinct actions (Burket 1987) and even ritual codes like scripts for conduct (Hesse et al. 2012), all of which help structure the process of sacrifice (Schwartz 2012). In working with ethnographic data, Valeri (1994) divides the overall process into several stages of activity, highlighting the practice of separating the sacrificed body into portions that are "renounced" for presentation to the main benefactor of the ceremony—in the case of burials, the deceased—as well as portions that are consumed by the practitioners and participants in the ceremony. Thus, if we consider sacrifice as a process, then the offering materials found in ritual arenas such as graves constitute the material end of that process (Insoll 2010).

Building on these concepts of the multistage course of sacrificial offering, and reflecting upon the multiple variables of Xiongnu offerings discussed above, I propose here a scheme of the sacrificial process that gives weight to decisions and actions before the formal process of sacrificial killing begins and allows as well for multiple portions, places, and manners of consumption after the ceremonial induction and partitioning of the animal body. In the case of the Xiongnu, putative stages of sacrificial offerings may be summarized in five phases: (1) abnegation, (2) induction, (3) apportionment, (4) offering, and (5) consumption, each of which may entail ritualized actions or yield material remains (Figure 10.9).

Before the physical action of killing for sacrifice, an animal is chosen and subsequently taken from a herd (cf. Lepetz 2013a). The selection of the animal is done according to both the economics of the herd and ritual traditions, including religious beliefs or cultural prescriptions (Ottosson 1987). The selected animal then undergoes *abnegation* from the herd. Abnegation, or the relinquishing of a certain thing, in this case a portion of herd wealth, by a person or party is a renouncement of that portion of wealth or sustenance in order to accomplish another gain. It is an important part of the process of sacrifice, in so far as "giving up" and "giving away" an animal from one's herd should be considered a distinct action, indicative of particular ritual and economic issues before the action of "sacrificing"—that is, "making something sacred" (Schwartz 2017).

Abnegation of animals depended not only on what kinds of species were present in the herds of an offering household but also on the total number of available animals from which any could be culled for the purposes of offering. The economic capabilities of a person or household to provide animals had to be measured against the potential social or spiritual benefits of renouncing animals. Yet while the particular animal sacrificed clearly depended on the presence, and usually quantity, of potential animals in a local herd, the selection of animals would also have been highly dependent upon ritual prescriptions of Xiongnu culture as well as the social dynamics of each particular ritual event. The animals selected for renunciation thus reflect both economic and ritual decision-making. We must certainly refrain from quantitative reconstructions of herd compositions for local subsistence economies based on the animals found in graves (Hanks 2002), but we must also view the religious/cultural actions of offering animals as heavily affected by qualitative and quantitative constraints of local herds. In this way, ritual and economic variables intersect in the process of animal sacrifice.

A survey of animal remains at cemeteries shows offerings of sheep/goats, cattle, or horses to the deceased, and most often the extremities more than body portions, as a pattern consistent throughout the Xiongnu realms (Figure 10.4). Regional differences in herd compositions (cf. Bazargur 2005; Simukov 1934) surely affected the choices of animals that could be and were sacrificed, but these patterns are a reflection of ritual as well as economic practices (Figures 10.4 and 10.5). The introductory description of Xiongnu society in Chinese court histories lists horses, cattle, and sheep/goats as the society's primary herd animals, with camels and others as more unusual animals (*Shiji* 110:2879). But despite the presence of camels and yaks among the Xiongnu, attested by their depiction on prestigious belt ornaments (Brosseder 2011), neither of these animals has yet been found in Xiongnu graves. The process of selection for abnegation thus depended heavily on cultural as well as economic constraints related to herd animals.

The subsequent phase of *induction* for an animal mainly entailed the sacrificial killing of that animal. Induction theoretically includes other ritual actions, but, as in the case of the Xiongnu, we have neither material nor textual evidence for these—no vestiges of ritual codes, only remains of ritual actions. Chinese chronicles mention seasonal gatherings and ceremonies in Xiongnu society at which offerings are made to ancestors and deities, as well as daily offerings to the sun and moon by Xiongnu rulers (*Hanshu* 94A:3752; *Shiji* 110:2892). Yet we have no indication of what was offered or what transpired in those rituals, much less whether or not livestock sacrifice was part of those rituals. Chinese chronicles offer only a few examples showing how livestock were made sacred through killing in order to serve a variety of ceremonial acts involving the living and the supernatural.

There is one mention of the tendency of "shamans to bury sheep and cattle" in the ground in order for the Xiongnu to curse particular routes through hills and along riverbanks that could be taken by invading enemy forces, namely the Han Chinese (*Hanshu* 96B:3913). In this instance there is at least one mention that specific livestock (sheep or cattle) were slaughtered and subsequently buried as ritual offerings to appease deities and spirits. Another instance of ritual practice involving animal sacrifice demonstrates the use of a horse, although the blood oath ceremony for the Xiongnu–Han alliance for which it was employed was certainly of far greater significance than the curse of a river route. In this ceremony, a white horse was slaughtered at the top of a mountain, after which the participants drank from a ritual cup filled with alcohol stirred by a ritual spoon and imbued with gold bits shaved off using a ritual knife (*Hanshu* 94B:3801). Here we gain a brief view

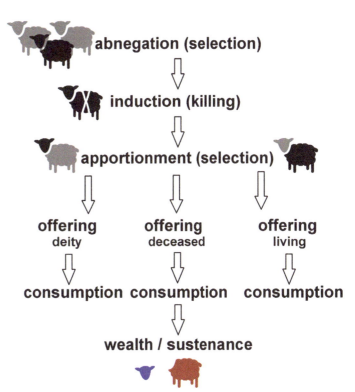

Figure 10.9. Schematic of the Xiongnu animal sacrificial process. *Created by the author.*

into paraphernalia used in rituals in which animal sacrifice played a part, though we do not know what happened to the sacrificed horse—whether it was buried, eaten, or both.

Archaeological remains of offerings in Xiongnu graves demonstrate that sacrificed animals most likely were subjected to a range of treatments after the slaughtering process of "making sacred." Once an animal's life had been formally taken and it was induced to sacred status, another phase of selection occurred: the animal was *apportioned* into elements, such as the extremities and body portions, which were then subjected to different treatments and/or placements. This second phase of selection, in which certain potions were set apart from others, ensued according to cultural and religious norms that dictated the meanings related to each part or set of parts (cf. Ottosson 1987).

From this point, different animal portions could serve different functions in different ceremonies of *offering*. Some could be deposited within mortuary settings, meant as direct offerings for the deceased. It is also at this juncture, however, that some portions of the animals could also serve in ceremonies for the benefit of others, be they spirits, deities, or living associates and ritual participants rather than the deceased (Burket 1987), leading them to be subjected to different treatments, deposited in separate spaces of the grave, or not at all deposited in mortuary spaces. The prime example is funeral feasts, in which the consumption of animals (or portions thereof) by the assembled living could account for the absence of many of the meaty body portions of animals deposited in graves (Hayden 2009). It is in this phase of offering, with specific placements and treatments, that we find the archaeological vestiges of animal sacrifice. From these remains we can postulate previous activities associated with abnegation, induction, and apportionment. And from the different treatments and contexts of the remains, we may also formulate multiple roles they served in mortuary rites and arenas.

The multiple categories of animal deposits—extremities, bodies, and burned pieces—intimate multiple ritual trajectories of animals that had been relinquished, slaughtered, and divided into distinct portions. If we review the case of SBR-7 (Figure 10.6), a single animal could, theoretically speaking, be divided such that (1) its head and hooves were set in one pile on the left side of the coffin (2), with its first ribs in an adjacent yet distinct pile, while on the other side of the coffin (3), its large and meaty thoracic vertebrae were placed in a cauldron for cooking and (4) several lumbar vertebrae (cooked?) were placed in a box for serving. Those portions not accounted for in the grave could have been delegated to a funerary ritual in which the living consumed the remaining ribs, vertebrae, and shaft bones. These latter categories of bones comprised the vast majority of identifiable fragments deposited in stone lines, suggesting that rituals such as those that produced stone line deposits could account for the consumption of many portions of the animals not present in Xiongnu graves (Miller et al. 2018).

While living ritual participants may have physically consumed animal portions, perhaps disposing of the bones through further ritualized renunciation that served yet another function, the deceased or other spiritual beings may have symbolically consumed the offerings. And while some animal portions could be seen as sustenance for the deceased, their presence in the graves might not preclude them from serving other purposes or embodying other meanings. Therefore, in regard to consumption, for the deceased or any others, I take on the broader interpretation of "consumption" beyond the meaning of bodily sustenance (*sensu* Miller 1995; Mullins 2011). To assert that offerings were merely food for the dead would be to greatly dilute their significance in mortuary and other ritual realms. The consumption of material goods—that is, their usage by a person or a community—is regularly discussed for non-sustenance yet feasting-related prestige items such as bronze cauldrons or painted lacquer cups in Xiongnu graves. Just as the possession of these accoutrements allowed an individual or household to host social gatherings of significant political potency, so did the possession of abundant animals, the prime source of wealth in the steppe, enable people to continually host gatherings. In this vein, livestock may have been offered to the deceased not only as direct sustenance but also as a representation of surplus, as materials representative of wealth as well as sustenance that were meant to accompany the deceased.

Heads and hooves may have stood as representations of whole domestic animals, which were the primary units of wealth in Xiongnu society. They were harvested for meat, milk, wool, leather, and bone—that is, for a broad range of consumables and craft goods. Livestock and their products were the main form of tax and tribute collected by the Xiongnu regime from the realms of Inner Asia (e.g., *Hanshu* 96B:3930), and they were the main materials taken by Xiongnu parties that raided the Han frontier (Hayashi 1990). Since the prime form of staple wealth in the steppe was livestock, this suggests that the presence of livestock in Xiongnu graves, especially when stripped of their greatest meat portions and placed separately from any feasting materials, may have been an offering not just of sustenance but of wealth.

These livestock were renunciations by the living conducted not only on behalf of the deceased but also for their own benefit (cf. Hubert and Mauss 1964). They could be sustenance for the living participants, just as they could be sustenance for the deceased in the afterlife. And by that argument, their renunciation (or abnegation) could be a demonstration of the wealth of the living, just as they could be representations of herd wealth accompanying the deceased into the afterlife—as portions that represented whole animals or perhaps even whole herds. In this vein, livestock in the graves were donations of material capital by living contributors for the deceased to accrue material capital as well as for the living to accrue social and symbolic capital.

Animal offerings in Xiongnu graves therefore represent a multitude of ritual activities and a multitude of ritual functions. The distinct apportionments and placements very likely relate to different functions in the mortuary spaces—for example, heads and hooves for wealth, ribs and vertebrae for feasting. Yet, as animal sacrifice was a process with several phases, animals may have served different functions at different phases of the overall process, not just the ones we infer from their final deposition in graves. An animal whose extremities were placed in a grave as a symbolic offering of wealth contributions from a herd of the living to a herd of the deceased may have its other body parts presented as sustenance consumed by funeral participants. I thus present the actions and meanings in this outline of animal sacrifice among the Xiongnu, as a working hypothesis of the multivariate process, in an effort to work toward a thicker description of livestock remains in burials and of livestock rituals in Xiongnu society.

Conclusion

For the Xiongnu, we find an emphasis in rituals of mortuary and non-mortuary realms on the sacrifice of herd animals. But sacrificed livestock in graves and elsewhere reflect more than just pastoralism, generally speaking. These remains represent a set of rituals that emphasized both the prevalence of pastoral subsistence and the primacy of herd animals in economics. Livestock offerings were wealth as well as sustenance, to be consumed and used in many ways by many recipients. The living, the dead, and even the deities all consumed the herds. But it is only through structured empirical examinations that we see how faunal remains embody the multiple manners, meanings, and milieu of animal sacrifice that reinforced ritual and economic systems of the steppe empire.

The varied forms, treatments, and placements of livestock remains in Xiongnu graves show that sacrificed animals were both physical items of economic capital and embodiments of larger social and cultural capital (*sensu* Bordieu 1986). The initial abnegation, or giving up/away, of the material capital was a means of investment for the accrual of social or symbolic capital, which ensured returns coming from the supernatural (deities or deceased) or from other living members of the community (Burket 1987: 43). We may therefore rightly assume that animal sacrifices dramatically performed and even altered social relations. They comprised a series of rituals intended for audiences not only of the supernatural but of the living funeral attendees as well (Swenson 2014) and were thereby imbued with potent costly signaling (Miller et al. 2018; Plourde 2009).

These broadened understandings of animal remains in Xiongnu graves rely heavily on a multitude of sources, material and textual, as well as a multitude of perspectives, economic and ritual. The interweaving of such a varied weft of data with warp threads of perspective for a single inquiry is a challenging endeavor, but one that von Falkenhausen, in his varied research, continues to execute with artful agility. The inquiry into animal sacrifice explored here is greatly inspired by von Falkenhausen's work and by von Falkenhauseun himself in motivating me to engage at an early stage in my academic career with multiple threads at once. This is certainly only a first step in moving toward a greater understanding of Xiongnu society, the first threads of a much larger tapestry.

Acknowledgments

Immeasurable thanks go of course to the many sponsors and organizers of the Festschrift celebration conference for Lothar von Falkenhausen at UCLA in June 2019, most of all to my coconspirators Anke Hein and Rowan Flad in working tirelessly for the event and for this subsequent volume to happen; and thanks to them both and to Maria Khayutina for their insightful comments on this paper. In addition to thanking Lothar himself profusely, I wish to give thanks as well to the cohort of creativity that he fostered and from which I benefited greatly during my years at UCLA. Many of the long-brewing ideas in this paper were inspired by those conversations and colleagues. Lastly, thanks are to be given to the Silk Road Foundation, the Henry Luce Foundation, and the National Museum of Mongolia, all of which provided support for the excavations in Khovd Province in western Mongolia that supplied the data for the case studies in this paper. Above all, I wish to thank Jamsranjav Bayarsaikhan, my collaborator and *n*ökhör in and out of the field.

References

Hanshu see Ban Gu
Shiji see Sima Qian

Allard, F., D. Erdenebaatar, N. Batbold, and B. K. Miller
2002   A Xiongnu Cemetery Found in Mongolia. *Antiquity* 76:637–38.

Balasse, M., A. Evin, C. Tornero, V. Radu, D. Fiorillo, D. Popovici, R. Andreescu, K. Dobney, T. Cucchi, and A. Bălăşescud
2016   Wild, Domestic and Feral? Investigating the Status of Suids in the Romanian Gumelniţa (5th Mil. Cal BC) with Biogeochemistry and Geometric Morphometrics. *Journal of Anthropological Archaeology* 42(June):27–36.

Ban Gu 班固
1962   *Hanshu* 漢書. Beijing: Zhonghua.

Bayarsaikhan, J., and B. K. Miller
2008   Khünnü bulshny takhilgiin baiguulamj bolon büttsiin zarim asuudal. *Nüüdelchdiin öv sudlal* 8:142–69.

Bayarsaikhan, J., Ts. Egiimaa, B. K. Miller, P. B. Konovalov, E. Johannesson, M. Machicek, J. Logan, and C. Neily
2011   Shombuuzyn Belchir dekh Khünnügiin dursgal. *Nüüdelchdiin öv sudlal* 11:156–83.

Bazargur, D.
2005   *Belcheeriin mal aj ahuin gazarzui*. Ulaanbaatar: Mongolian Academy of Sciences, Institute of Geography.

Benecke, N.
2003 Iron Age Economy of the Inner Asian Steppe. *Eurasia Antiqua* 9:63–83.

Bourdieu, P.
1986 The Forms of Capital. In *Handbook of Theory and Research for the Sociology of Education*, edited by J. Richardson, pp. 241–58. New York: Greenwood.

Brosseder, U.
2009 Xiongnu Terrace Tombs and Their Interpretation as Elite Burials. In *Current Archaeological Research in Mongolia: Papers from the First International Conference on "Archaeological Research in Mongolia,"* edited by J. Bemmann, H. Parzinger, E. Pohl, and D. Tseveendorzh, pp. 247–80. Bonn Contributions to Asian Archaeology 4. Bonn: VFG-Arch.

Brosseder, U., and B. K. Miller, eds.
2011 *Xiongnu Archaeology: Multidisciplinary Perspectives of the First Steppe Empire in Inner Asia*. Bonn Contributions to Asian Archaeology 5. Bonn: VFG-Arch.

Burket, W.
1987 Offerings in Perspective: Surrender, Distribution, Exchange. In *Gifts to the Gods: Proceedings of the Uppsala Symposium 1985*, edited by T. Linders and G. Nordquist, pp. 43–50. Uppsala: Acta Universitatis Upsaliensis.

Campbell, R.
2014 Introduction: Toward a Deep History of Violence and Civilization. In *Violence and Civilization: Studies of Social Violence in History and Prehistory*, edited by R. Campbell, pp. 1–22. Oxford: Oxbow.

Chang, C., and H. A. Koster
1986 Beyond Bones: Toward an Archaeology of Pastoralism. *Advances in Archaeological Method and Theory* 9:97–145.

Conolly, J.
2017 Costly Signalling in Archaeology: Origins, Relevance, Challenges and Prospects. *World Archaeology* 49:435–45.

Crubézy, E., J.-P. Verdier, B. Maureille, D. Erdenebaatar, Z. Batsaikhan, P.-H. Giscard, and H. Martin
1996 Pratiques funéraires et sacrifices d'animaux en Mongolie à la période proto-historique. Du perçu au signifié. A propos d'une sépulture Xiongnu de la vallée d'Egyin Gol (Région péri-Baïkal). *Paléorient* 22:89–107.

Cucchi, T., Dai Lingling, M. Balasse, Zhao Chunqing, Gao Jiangtao, Hu Yaowu, Yuan Jing, and J.-D. Vigne
2016 Social Complexification and Pig (Sus Scrofa) Husbandry in Ancient China: A Combined Geometric Morphometric and Isotopic Approach. *PLOS ONE* 11(7):1–20.

Davydova, A. V.
1995 *Ivolginskii arkheologicheskii kompleks I. Ivolginskoe gorodishche*, Arkheologicheskie pamyatniki Syunnu 1. St. Petersburg: AziatIKA.
1996 *Ivolginskii arkheologicheskii kompleks II. Ivolginskii mogil'nik*. Arkheologicheskie pamyatniki Syunnu 2. St. Petersburg: AziatIKA.

Dietler, M.
2010 Consumption. In *The Oxford Handbook of Material Culture Studies*, edited by D. Hicks and M. C. Beaudry, pp.209–28. Oxford: Oxford University Press.

Dietler, M., and B. Hayden, eds.
2001 *Feasts: Archaeological and Ethnographic Perspectives on Food, Politics, and Power*. Washington, DC: Smithsonian Institution Press.

Douglas, M., and B. Isherwood
1996 [1979] *The World of Goods: Towards an Anthropology of Consumption*. Routledge, New York.

Erdenebaatar, D., T. Iderkhangai, E. Mijiddorj, S. Orgilbayar, N. Batbold, B. Galbadrakh, and A. Maratkhaan
2015 *Balgasyn Tal dakh' Gol Mod 2-yn Khünnügiin Yazgurtny Bulshny Sudalgaa*. Ulaanbaatar: Mönkhiin Üseg.

Eregzen, G., S. Erdenesuvd, B. Batdalai, D. Mandakh, and S. Enkhbold
2017 Khentii aimgiin nutagt shineer bürtgesen Khünnügiin bulsh orshuulgyn dursgalt gaz-ruud. In *Mongolyn Arkheologi 2016*:136–48. Ulaanbaatar: Mongolian Academy of Sciences.

Falkenhausen, Lothar von
2006 *Chinese Society in the Age of Confucius (1000–250 BC): The Archaeological Evidence*. Los Angeles: Cotsen Institute of Archaeology Press.

Fan Ye 范曄
1965 *Hou Han shu* 後漢書. Beijing: Zhonghua.

Flad, R.
2002 Ritual or Structure? Analysis of Burial Elaboration at Dadianzi, Inner Mongolia. *Journal of East Asian Archaeology* 3(3–4):23–51.

Hanks, B.
2002 The Eurasian Steppe "Nomadic World" of the First Millennium BC: Inherent Problems within the Study of Iron Age Nomadic Groups. In *Ancient Interactions: East and West in Eurasia*, edited by K. Boyle, C. Renfrew, and M. Levine, pp. 183–97. Cambridge: McDonald Institute Monographs.

Hayashi T.
1990 The Development of a Nomadic Empire: The Case of the Ancient Turks (Tuque). *Bulletin of the Ancient Orient Museum* 11:135–84.

Hayden, B.
2009 Funerals as Feasts: Why Are They So Important? *Cambridge Archaeological Journal* 19:29–52.

Hesse, B., P. Wapnish, and J. Greer
2012 Scripts of Animal Sacrifice in Levantine Culture-History. In *Sacred Killing: The Archaeology of Sacrifice in the Ancient Near East*, edited by A. M. Porter and G. M. Schwartz, pp. 217–35. Winona Lake, IN: Eisenbrauns.

Honeychurch, W.
2015 *Inner Asia and the Spatial Politics of Empire*. New York: Springer.

Houle, J.-L., and L. Broderick
2011 Settlement Patterns and Domestic Economy of the Xiongnu in Khanui Valley, Mongolia. In *Xiongnu Archaeology: Multidisciplinary Perspectives of the First Steppe Empire in Inner Asia*, edited by U. Brosseder and B. K. Miller, pp. 137–52. Bonn Contributions to Asian Archaeology 5. Bonn: VFG-Arch.

Hubert, Henri, and Marcel Mauss
1964 *Sacrifice: Its Nature and Function*. Translated by W. D. Hall. Chicago: University of Chicago Press.

Insoll, T.
2010 Talensi Animal Sacrifice and Its Archaeological Implications. *World Archaeology* 42:231–44.

Jackson, H. E., and S. L. Scott
2003 Patterns of Elite Faunal Utilization at Moundville, Alabama. *American Antiquity* 68.3:552–72.

Johannesson, E. G.
2016 Echoes in Eternity: Social Memory and Mortuary Stone Monuments in Bronze–Iron Age Mongolia. In *Fitful Histories and Unruly Publics: Rethinking Temporality and Community in Eurasian Archaeology*, edited by K. O. Weber, E. Hite, L. Katchadourian, and A. T. Smith, pp. 79–107. Leiden: Brill.

Konovalov, P. B.
1976 *Khunnu v Zabaikal'ye*. Ulan-Ude: Buryatia.

Kradin, N. N.
2005 Social and Economic Structure of the Xiongnu of the Trans-Baikal Region. *Archaeology, Ethnology and Anthropology of Eurasia* 21:79–86.

Lepetz, S.
2013a Horse Sacrifice in a Pazyryk Culture Kurgan: The Princely Tomb of Berel' (Kazakhstan). Selection Criteria and Slaughter Procedures. *Anthropozoologica* 48(2):309–21.

2013b La Faune. In *L'Habitat Xiongnu de Boroo Gol*, edited by N. Pousaz, D. Ramseyer, Ts. Turbat, O. Akeret, D. Batsukh, Y. Dellea, M. Guélet, S. Lepetz, V. Serneels, and S. Thorimbert. Gollion: Infolio.

Lepetz, S., and F. Decanter
2013 Les restes d'animaux. In *Le Premier Empire des Steppes en Mongolie: Histoire du people Xiongnu et étude pluridisciplinaire de l'ensemble funéraire d'Egyin Gol*, edited by Mission Archéologique de L'Institut des Déserts et des Steppes, pp. 215–23. Dijon: Éditions Faton.

Ligneraux, Y.
2015 Tamiriin Ulan Khoshuu Rapport archéozoologique 2015. In *Peuplements humains et coévolution homme/milieu en Sibérie et dans la steppe euRASIatique au cours de l'Holocène*, edited by E. Crubézy, pp. 1–37. Toulouse: Université Paul Sabatier.

Linders, T., and G. Nordquist, eds.
1987 *Gifts to the Gods: Proceedings of the Uppsala Symposium 1985*. Uppsala: Acta Universitatis Upsaliensis.

Makarewicz, C.
2010 Animal Offerings and Winter Camp Use: Zooarchaeological and Isotopic Analyses of Faunas in Baga Gazaryn Chuluu. In *Dundgov' aimagt khisen arkheologiin sudalgaa: Baga Gazryn Chuluu*, edited by Ch. Amartuvshin and W. Honeychurch, pp. 436–49. Ulaanbaatar: BEMBI SAN.

2014 Winter Pasturing Practices and Variable Foddering Provisioning Detected in Nitrogen ($\delta^{15}N$) and Carbon ($\delta^{13}C$) Isotopes in Sheep Dentinal Collagen. *Journal of Archaeological Science* 41:502–10.

2017 Winter Is Coming: Seasonality of Ancient Pastoral Nomadic Practices Revealed in the Carbon ($\delta 13C$) and Nitrogen ($\delta 15N$) Isotopic Record of Xiongnu Caprines. *Archaeological and Anthropological Sciences* 9:405–19.

Martin, H.
2011 The Animal in the Xiongnu Funeral Universe: Companion of the Living, Escort of the Dead. In *Xiongnu Archaeology—Multidisciplinary Perspectives on the First Steppe Empire in Central Asia*, edited by U. Brosseder and B. K. Miller, pp. 229–42. Bonn Contributions to Asian Archaeology 5. Bonn: Rheinishe Friedrich-Wilhelms-Universität.

Miller, B. K.
2009 Power Politics in the Xiongnu Empire. Unpublished PhD dissertation, Department of East Asian Languages and Civilizations, University of Pennsylvania, Philadelphia.
2011 Permutations of Peripheries in the Xiongnu Empire. In *Xiongnu Archaeology—Multidisciplinary Perspectives on the First Steppe Empire in Central Asia*, edited by U. Brosseder and B. K. Miller, pp. 559–78. Bonn Contributions to Asian Archaeology 5. Bonn: Rheinishe Friedrich-Wilhelms-Universität.
2014 Xiongnu "Kings" and the Political Order of the Steppe Empire. *Journal of the Economic and Social History of the Orient* 57(1):1–43
2015 The Southern Xiongnu in Northern China: Navigating and Negotiating the Middle Ground. In *Complexity of Interaction along the Eurasian Steppe Zone in the First Millennium CE*, edited by J. Bemmann and M. Schmauder, pp. 127–98. Bonn Contributions to Asian Archaeology 6. Bonn: VFG-Arch Press.

Miller, B. K., F. Allard, D. Erdenebaatar, and C. Lee
2006 A Xiongnu Tomb Complex: Excavations at Gol Mod 2 Cemetery (2002–05). *Mongolian Journal of Anthropology, Archaeology and Ethnology* 2(2):1–21.

Miller, B. K., Zh. Baiarsaikhan, Ts. Egiimaa, P. B. Konovalov, and J. Logan
2009 Elite Xiongnu Burials at the Periphery: Tomb Complexes at Takhiltyn-khotgor, Mongolian Altai. In *Current Archaeological Research in Mongolia*, edited in J. Bemmann, H. Parzinger, E. Pohl, and D. Tseveendorj, pp. 301–14. Bonn Contributions to Asian Archaeology 4. Bonn: VFG-Arch.

Miller, Bryan K., Cheryl A. Makarewicz, Jamsranjav Bayarsaikhan, and Tömörbaatar Tüvshinjargal
2018 Stone Lines and Burnt Bones: Ritual Elaborations in Xiongnu Mortuary Arenas of Inner Asia. *Antiquity* 92(365):1310–28.

Miller, D.
1995 Consumption and Commodities. *Annual Review of Anthropology* 24:141–61.

Minyaev, Sergei S.
1998 *Dyrestuiskii mogil'nik: Archaeological Sites of the Xiongnu*, Vol. 3. St. Petersburg: AziatIKA.

Minyaev, Sergei S., and L. M. Sakharovskaya
2002 Soprovoditel'nie zahoroheniya "tsarskogo" kompleksa no. 7 v mogil'nike Tsaram. *Arheologicheskie Vesti* 9:86–118.
2007 Elitnii Kompleks zahoronenii Siunnu v padi Tsaram. *Rossiskaya Arheologiya* 1:194–201.

Mission archéologique française en Mongolie
2003 *Mongoli: le premier empire des steppes*. Arles: Actes sud.

Mullins, P. R.
2011 The Archaeology of Consumption. *Annual Review of Anthropology* 40:133–44.

National Museum of Korea, National Museum of Mongolian History, and Mongolian Institute of Archaeology
1999 *Mongolin Oglogchiin golin dursgal*. Seoul: National Museum of Korea.
2001 *Mongolin Morin tolgoin Hunnugiin uyeiin bulsh*. Seoul: National Museum of Korea.
2003 *Hudgiin tolgoin Hunnugiin uyeiin bulsh*. Seoul: National Museum of Korea.

Parker-Pearson, Michael
1993 The Powerful Dead: Archaeological Relationships between the Living and the Dead. *Cambridge Archaeological Journal* 3(2):203–29.

Navaan, D.
1999 *Khünnügiin öv soyol: arkheologiin sudalgaany material*. Ulaanbaatar.

Ningxia wenwu kaogu yanjiusuo寧夏文物考古研究所, Tongxinxian wenwu guanlisuo同心縣文物管理所, and Zhongguo shehui kexueyuan kaogusuo Ningxia kaoguzu中國社會科學院考古所寧夏考古組
1987 Ningxia Tongxinxian Daodunzi Handai Xiongnu mudi fajue jianbao 寧夏同心縣到墩子漢代匈奴墓地發覺簡報. *Kaogu* 考古 1987(1):33–37.

Ölzibayar, S., B. Ochir, and E. Urtnasan
2019 *Khünnügiin tüükh soyolyn sudalgaa (Salkhityn Amny dursgalt gazar)*. Ulaanbaatar: Mongolian Academy of Sciences.

Ottosson, M.
1987 Sacrifice and Sacred Meals in Ancient Israel. In *Gifts to the Gods: Proceedings of the Uppsala Symposium 1985*, edited by T. Linders and G. Nordquist, pp. 133–36. Uppsala: Acta Universitatis Upsaliensis.

Payne, S.
1973 Kill-off Patterns in Sheep and Goats: The Mandibles from Asvan Kale. *Anatolian Studies* 23:281–307.

Plourde, A. M.
2009 Prestige Goods and the Formation of Political Hierarchy. A Costly Signalling Model. In *Pattern and Process in Cultural Evolution: Origins of Human Behavior and Culture*, Vol. 2, edited by S. Shennan, pp. 265–76. Berkeley: University of California Press.

Porter, A. M., and G. M. Schwartz, eds.
2012 *Sacred Killing: The Archaeology of Sacrifice in the Ancient Near East*. Winona Lake, IN: Eisenbrauns.

Schwartz, G. M.
2012 Archaeology and Sacrifice. In *Sacred Killing: The Archaeology of Sacrifice in the Ancient Near East*, edited by A. M. Porter and G. M. Schwartz, pp. 1–32. Winona Lake, IN: Eisenbrauns.
2017 The Archaeological Study of Sacrifice. *Annual Review of Anthropology* 46:223–40.

Sh.U.A Arkhaeologiin khüreelen, Mongolyn Ündesnii muzei, and Solongosyn Ündesnii muzei
2011 *Duurlig narsny Khünnü bulsh I*. Seoul: National Museum of Korea.

Sima Qian 司馬遷
1959 *Shiji* 史記. Beijing: Zhonghua.

Simukov, A. D.
1934 Mongol'skie kochevki. *Sovremennaya Mongoliya* 4(7):40–47.

Swenson, E.
2014 Dramas of the Dialectic: Sacrifice and Power in Ancient Polities. In *Violence and Civilization: Studies of Social Violence in History and Prehistory*, edited by R. B. Campbell, pp. 28-60. Oxford: Oxbow.

Taylor, William
2017 Horse Demography and Use in Bronze Age Mongolia. *Quaternary International* 436(A):270–82.

Törbat, Ts.
2004 *Khünnügiin jiriin irgediin bulsh*. Ulaanbaatar: Mongolian State University of Education.

Törbat, Ts., Ch. Amartüvshin, and U. Erdenbat
2003 *Egiin Golyn sav nutag dakh' arkheologiin dursgaluud*. Ulaanbaatar: Mongolian State Pedagogical University.

Ucko, Peter J.
1969 Ethnography and the Archaeological Interpretation of Funerary Remains. *World Archaeology* 1:262–77.

Valeri, V.
1994 Wild Victims: Hunting as Sacrifice and Sacrifice as Hunting in Huaulu. *History of Religions* 34:101–31.

Wu'en Yuesitu 烏恩岳斯圖
2008 *Beifang caoyuan kaoguxue wenhua bijiao yanjiu—qingtong shidai zhi zaoqi Xiongnu shiqi* 北方草原考古學文化比較研究—青銅時代至早期匈奴時期. Beijing: Kexue.

Yerööl-Erdene, Ch.
2014 Gol Modny Khünnügiin yazguurtny orshuulgyn gazryn bairlal zuin sudalgaa. *Arkheologiin Sudlal* 34:236–44.

Yerööl-Erdene, Ch., J. Gantulga, J. Bemmann, U. Brosseder, G. McGlynn, and S. Reichert
2015 Orkhony Khöndii dekh Mongol-Germany Khamtarsan "Barkor" Tösliin Sudalgaany Ur'dchilsan ür dün. *Arkheologiin Sudlal* 35:198–227.

Zazzo, Antoine, Sébastian Lepetz, Jérôme Magail, and Jamyian-Ombo Gantulga
2019 High-Precision Dating of Ceremonial Activity around a Large Ritual Complex in Late Bronze Age Mongolia. *Antiquity* 93(367):80–98.

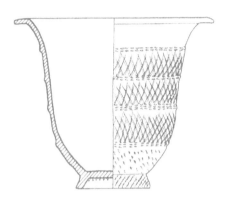

Part III

Technology, Community, Interaction

Chapter 11

Long-Distance Influences and Local Adoption
Technological Innovation in Ritual and Economy in Late Prehistoric Northwest China

Rowan Flad

Technology, Innovation, and the Significance of Margins

A central question in research on early complex societies concerns identifying stimuli for social change. Social change, and all its constituent components, is a core concern of the work that has been done by Lothar von Falkenhausen in his prolific career to date. Among his many contributions to the study of social change in early China are his publications that illustrate the complex relationships between different regions in early China. Instead of pursuing universal models of social change, von Falkenhausen attends to specific areas and times, and he brings rigorous consideration of local case studies into dialogue to illuminate larger pictures (Falkenhausen 2006a:19–20). In doing so, he shows that throughout the Bronze Age, East Asia was characterized not by coherent, bounded societies that easily fit into abstract categories or neatly follow at least partially anachronistic later textual accounts; rather they reflect a heterogeneous landscape of political, social, ritual, and economic topographies (an idea elaborated in Flad and Chen 2013). Such topographies include complex networks of interactions that involve a "multidirectional flow of goods among socio-political units of different degrees of complexity" (Falkenhausen 2006b:53). The article in which he makes that observation discusses the economic and social relationships between the Three Gorges region and other regions of the Yangzi River in China, particularly the core of the Chu state, where stratified polities had emerged by the first millennium BCE.

He observes that a view that considers these relationships through the lens of "cores" and "peripheries" overlooks the "mutually beneficial economic interactions" that characterized interregional interaction and "enduring relationships of economic interdependence" (Falkenhausen 2006b:53). How widespread and how ancient were such enduring relationships in early China? How do these relationships relate to the central question of identifying stimuli for social change?

In this essay I start with the premise that technology is a particularly important locus of social change. I discuss several definitions of technology and how they intersect. Their intersection focuses our attention on the process of making things in a social context. Furthermore, these definitions highlight how transformations in the associated practices that come from social margins (of various sorts) have the potential to be particularly impactful. I then turn my attention to two domains of technological innovation in the third and second millennia BCE in Northwest China—plant and animal domesticates for subsistence and stone and metal materials for craft production—and illustrate how changes in these two realms reflect the significance of social margins for change in social and technological practices at local and translocal scales.

Technology

Technology can be defined in many ways (Dobres 2000). The term is formulated as a "study of" (-ology) *techne* τέχνη, a Greek term for an art, craft, or skill. The history of technology as a term and concept has been considered many times (see Marx 2010 for an excellent overview). The concept has developed to simultaneously have both positive and negative connotations: technology can be seen as a facet of human behavior that allows us to make the world a better place and/or it can be that which may be the source of our destruction. This dual nature of technology emerges from the tension between the natural and unnatural—a tension highlighted in Cartesian ontologies but one that is mediated or transcended both in recent perspectives that highlight the agency of objects (Latour 2005a) and in some of the earliest theoretical work that interrogated the technology concept.

This dual nature can also be observed in related Chinese terms that are often used as the direct translation for *technology*. The most common colloquial translation is *jishu* 技術, which is composed of two characters. According to the *Ciyuan* 辭源, *ji* 技 refers to skill or talent, as well as ingenuity and ability, and *shu* likewise points to skill, as well as art, method, and technique. *Jishu* is found in early texts such as the *Shiji* 史記 and the *Hanshu* 漢書,[1] and therein it refers in particular to the arts of healing and divination. This association reflects the supernatural qualities associated with skill and ability inherent in the idea of technique. Other terms, such as *gongyi* 工藝 (arts and crafts), or just *gong* 工 (labor, work), have a more mundane focus on labor. Although it is also imbued with a sense of artistry, as a noun, *gong* refers to those who "engage in a broad range of activities . . . any craftsman (or woman) who made objects" (Barbieri-Low 2007:32), with *gongjiang* 工匠 an "all-inclusive term for craftspeople" (36) and with great artisans possessing *qiao* 巧, "an ambivalent term, packed with both positive and negative connotations" (45). Barbieri-Low uses the double meaning of the English term *crafty* to indicate the ambivalent nature of the term *qiao*, but we see this tension reflected in considerations of technology in Western philosophical discourse as well (see also Raphals 1992).

In 1877 Ernst Kapp published a treatise on the philosophy of technology titled *Grudnlinien einer Philosophie der Technik*, in which he proposed and discussed the idea of "organ projection" (Kapp 2018 [1877]; Kirkwood and Weatherby 2018). Organ projection involves the extension of the natural abilities of a human such that "every tool . . . presents the unique opportunity of moving beyond the immediate, superficial perception of things" (Kapp 2018 [1877]:24). Technology, for Kapp, includes all those things that are built off models of the natural world but extend the senses and abilities. In so doing, technology not only enables certain tasks to be carried out but also creates a sense of self-awareness that makes us human. That sense of awareness points to how "it is not only that the human is the measure of things, but also that the technological process allows us first to take the measure of the human" (Kirkwood and Weatherby 2018:xxxvi). As a follower of Kapp, George Canguilhem (1952:64) has influentially pointed out in his essay "Machine and Organism" that "technology allows man to live in continuity with life" rather than creating a situation in which we see "humankind as living in a state of rupture for which we ourselves are responsible because of science." Accordingly, there is no sharp divide distinguishing "technological" from other aspects of human activity. Instead, we should consider technologies and the technological as a framework for understanding the nature of the relationship between humans and the material world.

The framework building from Kapp has been succinctly outlined for us by the definition of technology provided by Marcel Mauss, who in a series of publications (1935, 1948, 1979 [1936]) reflected on the nature of technology. Technology, for Mauss, is the study of techniques, which in turn are defined as "traditional, effective acts."[2] This short definition is repeated throughout his publications, but he also expands on that definition of technique as "an assemblage of movements or actions, in general and for the most part manual, which are organized and traditional, and which work together towards the achievement of a goal known to be physical or chemical or organic" (translation from Schlanger 2006:149). There he intentionally (and I would argue unnecessarily) focuses his definition on the "purely material" in order to exclude "religious or artistic techniques," which are in my opinion effectively and usefully accommodated by the more elegant, simpler definition of techniques as "traditional, effective acts."

Each word in Mauss's definition does work. First, being *traditional*, techniques reflect cultural norms, particular ways of being in the world and the transmission of practices from one person to another. Techniques are social, and the study of techniques is therefore inherently a study of society. Second, being *effective*, techniques operate as organ projections that engage with natural phenomena to accomplish some goal. Third, techniques are *acts*—they involve bodily movement, gestures, and the physical manipulation of the material world.

The act of a technique is a particular concern not just of Mauss but of many of those whose work has been influenced by him. Perhaps foremost among these are André Leroi-Gourhan and Pierre Lemonnier. The impact of Leroi-Gourhan is most sustained through the ubiquitous reference in archaeological studies of technologies to the importance of understanding *chaînes opératoire*. These are sequences of stages, practices, and actions that together are responsible for the transformation of material into any object. This sequence of operations and actions reflects a "syntax" responsible for the creation of a product and "is born from the dialogue between the brain and the material realm" (Leroi-Gourhan 1993:114, 230–34; cited in Audouze 2002). This dialogue highlights the way in which actions on matter through gesture are the expression of group tendencies. Although Leroi-Gourhan emphasized the more general, evolutionary tendencies in technology as primary and "stylistic details" as expressions of cultural originality (see Lemonnier 1993:24), his inclusion of gesture as an important component of the *chaîne opératoire* approach has been taken up by Lemonnier (1986, 1992, 1993) and others (Dobres 2000, 2001, 2010; Lechtman 1977; Lechtman and Steinberg 1979). These authors emphasize the importance of choice and gesture in the unfolding of technology. As Lechtman and Steinberg (1979:141) point out, to understand technology, one must understand the technological process in its entirety, and that should include the technical aspects of the process as well as those associated with gesture and action.

The focus on gesture is central to Mauss's attention to "acts" and draws our attention to a variety of practices and elements that embody technology. Recently Wendrich (2013) has enumerated a number of these in her discussion of apprenticeship: dexterity, skill, endurance, memory, and properness. These various components of any act all are developed in the process of learning by doing and collectively constitute the active aspect of technique. Competence in them contributes to what Gell (1992:52) has called "technical virtuosity," which emerges from "practical mastery" (Bourdieu 1977 [1972]:15). The latter concept refers to "the informal, embedded, unexpressed (and inexpressible) ability to skillfully engage in any specific social activity" (Flad 2008:428). It is through these aspects of gesture and practice that *things* are imbued with the "enchantment" that is immanent in all forms of technical activity (Gell 1992).

The Thing

What is a "thing"? This loaded question has been the focus of philosophical ruminations for more than a century, starting perhaps with Husserl's (1997 [1907]) phenomenological musings more than 100 years ago on the thing and space, and subsequently developed most influentially by Heidegger (1971) in his essay "The Thing." Over the past decades, the ontological turn of New Materialist anthropology has taken up the significance of things, examining in a wide variety of contexts and, with quite a bit of theoretical reflection, how "things make us, just as much as we make things"—to quote the back of Daniel Miller's 2010 book *Stuff*.

In his discussion of things, Miller presents how the "stuff" that we make and that fills out the world within which we live provides the setting, or frame, for what is appropriate and inappropriate. He talks about how things can be invisible and taken for granted. Despite his positioning himself somewhat in opposition to a phenomenological position on things (Miller 2010:42), this point actually seems to me to correspond with Heidegger's (1971) notion of things being defined by "voids" and having an essence as "gatherings." Miller develops this even further in discussing "objectification" as "self-alienation" (explicitly following Hegel)—objects make us as we make them, and this "making" (Ingold 2013) creates society and culture.

Things have substance, and so they are composed of matter: "that which has mass and occupies space," to quote the *Oxford English Dictionary*. As with the chemical constitution of matter, it is the bonds in matter that are important. To push the metaphor further, chemical bonds, which are the lasting connections between atoms, ions, or molecules, can be strong or weak and are the result of a number of different types of behaviors. Latour's discussion of things similarly sees things as being defined by the stuff of which various types of bonds are composed (Latour 2005b:70). The Actor Network Theory, as elaborated by him and others (Latour 1993, 2005a; Van Oyen 2015), and the subsequent development of "symmetrical archaeology" (Olsen 2007; Whitmore 2007) emphasize connections between people, objects, and places in this thing-oriented literature. Voids, gathering, objectification, symmetry, and even entanglements (Hodder 2012), are all ideas that emphasize the notion of things in context—wrapped up in associations with people, place, and other objects.

To return to the broader question of defining technology, we can turn to Gell (1988:6), who clarifies that "technology, in the widest sense, is those forms of social relationships which make it socially necessary to produce, distribute and consume goods and services using 'technical' processes." For Gell, technical processes are those that exploit natural phenomena, and "social relations are the relations which are generated by the technical processes of which society at large can be said to consist, that is, broadly, the technical processes of the production of subsistence and other goods, and the production (reproduction) of human beings by domesticating them and breeding them" (Gell 1992:57). Here again, harking back to Kapp and Mauss, we see the interplay between human action and natural phenomena.

W. Brian Arthur has also highlighted this interplay in his discussion of the nature of technology (2009). As I elaborate more fully elsewhere (Flad 2017a), Arthur identifies three levels of abstraction in the concept of technology:

devices (or things), domains, and "the entire collection of devices and engineering practices available to a culture" (Arthur 2009:28–29). Arthur's primary intervention is to argue that technologies work similarly at each of these separate levels of abstraction. Whether one is focused on a device or other "means to fulfill a human purpose," a domain involving an "assemblage of practices or components," or the more totalizing "entire collection," Arthur claims that technologies always draw on natural phenomena and combine existing technologies, each of which is itself a technology. Arthur therefore is echoing Kapp, Mauss, Gell, and others in connecting human action to natural phenomena. He is also focusing our attention on the interconnections among technologies and between technologies and other aspects of social practice.

The interconnections highlighted here are central to what Brian Pfaffenberger (1992) develops in his discussion of "sociotechnical systems," which he presents as equivalent to technology. The sociotechnical systems concept emphasizes the interconnected nature of technologies and technological practice. For Pfaffenberger (1992:508), technology is not an "applied science" but instead is "an *activity system*, a domain of purposive, goal-oriented action in which knowledge and behavior are reciprocally constituted by social, individual and material phenomena." As an activity system, a technology, like society more broadly, is constantly in the process of becoming. This process of becoming, Pfaffenberger argues further, is not consistent with the "standard view of technology" (SVT), which is a teleological, unilinear, cumulative, evolutionist, fitness-oriented process through which humans have become separated from an authentic natural world and embedded in a fabricated, material world (1992:494). Instead, the traditional effective acts of technology are integrated in a situated context that depends on the existing technologies available to members of a social group and are contingent on all sorts of forces that effect choices and decision-making. This perspective is nicely incorporated into the definition of technology that has been proposed by Carrie Brezine and that I adopt. Technology is "a system of practices interrelating transformation of material resources, abstract and practical knowledge, social and political relationships, and cultural beliefs" (Brezine 2011:82). This definition incorporates (though not always explicitly) much of the emphasis up to this point on the systems of practices, the effective acts that comprise techniques, and the interconnected associations among groups of practices. Kapp, Mauss, Gell, Arthur, and Pfaffenberger may all have slightly different emphases, but they bring us to a nuanced, multifaceted, active, and networked understanding of technology and the things that make technology manifest.

Use and Innovation

If we accept that technology is a system, based on traditional effective acts, that ties together a variety of interrelated forces, affordances, practices, and beliefs, a central question emerges: where does change come from? As David Edgerton (1999) has pointed out, technology is not identical with innovation. In many studies of the history of technology, they are conflated, in part due to the aforementioned teleological assumptions of the SVT about the inevitable linear progress of technological advancement and assumptions that certain technologies will be adopted as a matter of course due to notions of technological superiority. Edgerton argues that attention needs to be paid to the histories of use because they are not the same as histories of innovation, and only by doing so can we attend to the geography, chronology, and sociology of the use of technology and how these may be distinct from those associated with various processes involving technology, such as invention, adoption, appropriation, diffusion, and disappearance, all of which contribute to the notion of innovation.

Although innovation as currently defined in the *Oxford English Dictionary* is the neutral "alteration of what is established by the introduction of new elements or forms," Godin (2016) and Leary (2019:114–19) have pointed out how *innovation* historically was a pejorative term, considered to be a vice associated with the questioning of authority, particularly the authority of the church. More recent positive connotations of innovation as being associated with creativity and progress emerge from the development of an association with technology (Godin 2016) and distancing from theological dogma—although this does not necessarily correspond with a secularization of the term, as *creativity, innovation*, and *craft* have taken on sacred connotations in their own right (see Kurlinkus 2014 for a discussion of *craft* as a "God term," for example). Within the framework of innovation as technological creativity, innovation is understood to involve a process through which new ideas are derived, acknowledged, accepted, and put into practice as a means to achieve a goal (Godin 2016). Nathaniel Erb-Satullo (2020) has recently distilled how this process of innovation is distinct from, but incorporates, the concept of invention.

Whereas innovation can be considered "the full process of initiating, systematizing, and transmitting technological change," invention is "the portion of the innovation process in which a new technical behavior is initiated, recognized, and developed to the point that it becomes systematic" (Erb-Satullo 2020:41). Invention, therefore, involves the generation of novelty and the new devices or practices that result. This is "a process of discovery and creation of ideas and things previously unknown" that involves the "renunciation of routine behaviors" (Lemonnier 1993:21). Innovation is the broader, more frequently recognizable process by which an adoption spreads and is sufficiently incorporated into social practice. For Lemonnier, building off Leroi-Gourhan, this involves transformation of tendencies (*tendances*), which are "the propensity that human groups have to perform the same technical actions *and* to develop very similar means of performing these actions" (Lemonnier 1993:29n29). Accordingly, tendencies tend to limit the range of possible techniques in a given context and themselves comprise traditional effective acts that are transformed in the process of innovation.

In addition to invention, innovation processes involve several related forms of technological transfer that involve some degree of building off of preexisting technologies. This process of borrowing from what already exists includes variations of adoption and appropriation. Differentiating these different forms involves understanding the degree to which technological practices and associated knowledge are shared. Entire sets are shared in varieties of adoption, including diffusion[3] and forms of biased transmission[4] (see Boyd and Richerson 1985, 1987; Eerkens and Lipo 2007; Henrich 2001). Appropriation involves the selection of individual components and varies among processes that may be characterized as acculturation, syncretism, bricolage, creolization, and hybridization (see Liebmann 2015). It should be clarified, however, that even in cases of novelty that we might characterize as invention, the derived technologies are constituted of components that are themselves technologies (following Arthur 2009). This implies that invention, like adoption and appropriation, involves some degree of borrowing.

As Wendrich points out (2013:4), even in cases where sharing seems most partial and indirect, the technological processes involved necessarily include the transfer of knowledge, which "encompasses the entirety of operational sequences, mental models, appropriate behavior, and involuntary gestures, within a social context" for whatever constituent parts are involved in the innovation process. Given the systemic definition of technology I have adopted, it seems important to recognize the significance of learning in any process of technology transfer and associated innovation, regardless of how complete or partial. Furthermore, in those contexts where the transfer of knowledge occurs between groups of people who learn collectively through sustained, shared sets of activities, it is useful to consider relevant "communities of practice" (Bowser 2008; Crown 2014; Minar 2001a, 2001b; Sassaman and Rudolphi 2001; Wendrich 2013; Wenger 1998). Whether at the level of the acting individual or a community of practice, however, "to be retained, a technological feature has to be *understood* as a potential means (or element of a means) of action on the material world. A new gesture, artefact, or complete sequence of technical operations has to be deciphered, appreciated and given a place in the light of a group's technical 'knowledge.' . . . [I]n a given society people or groups of people share sets of ideas regarding how a raw material or an artefact must be made, what it must look like, and how it should be used in order to fulfill a particular technical function" (Lemonnier 1993:14). A similar observation made by Bernbeck and Burmeister (2017:11) is that "most innovations, whether functional, symbolic, practical or other, had to be inserted carefully in to pre-existing social and cultural relations so as not to upset traditional lifeworlds."

Distance

Why must innovations "fit"? In large part it is because "what matters is not technology itself, but the social or economic system in which it is embedded" (Winner 1980:122). Technologies fit within the social context in which they are enacted. Technological changes or processes of innovation, consequentially, challenge existing social relations. "A successful innovation has as a prerequisite an integration into existing practical routines and structures of meaning," but "any innovation also leads at least in part to a disruption" (Bernbeck and Burmeister 2017:12).

Such challenges can be traumatic, but they can also present opportunities and new affordances. Technologies embody specific forms of power and authority and therefore new technologies, once introduced, create new "settings" in a particular community that transform social relations. Furthermore, they can "require, or be strongly compatible with particular kinds of political relationships" (Winner 1980:123). Some systems (such as railroads, as discussed by Winner) are inherently political, requiring institutions that call for, create and maintain a technology. But others, such as new agricultural practices or transformative production processes (including those discussed in this paper), are potentially political to the degree that related innovation processes transform social relationships in political ways.

Mary Helms (1993) has examined the cross-cultural evidence for an association between social power and distance, both spatial and temporal. Her extensive examples reflect an observation that has been documented in diffusion studies. In that literature it has been observed that "more radical novelties are more likely to stem from marginal[5] groups and especially from risk-taking individuals" (Schubert 2017:8). As Rogers has pointed out, innovators are venturesome: "He or she desires the hazardous, the rash, the daring and the risky" (Rogers 2003 [1962]:283). I argue that the significance of being on the outside is further emphasized in the sociological literature on social networks, which has highlighted the "strength of weak ties" (Granovetter 1973, 1983). The potential for real change comes from those whose ties are not so strong that they already belong to the same community of practice. Instead, weak ties provide a vector for innovation that can be adopted or appropriated. These apparently "weaker" ties within a network have outside impact on the connectivity and degrees of separation among nodes within a network and in their so-called "betweenness centrality" (see Collar et al. 2015 and citations therein). In the case study discussed below, the apparently marginal, or "outside," location of the Northwest China region relative to the Central Plains affords the possibility of creating weak ties within the broader set of connections and flows across Eurasia. Furthermore, at least metaphorically, the ideas of nodes and ties can be considered in relation to the networks of entanglements that connect people and things in technological practices, as discussed above (see also Knappet 2013).

Returning to Helms, her particular focus is "skilled crafting"—which she distinguishes from other types of manufacture as being political and ideological (rather than economic) and transformative (rather than rational and practical), thus reflecting the same emphases I have heretofore highlighted in the concept of technology. In her argument, skilled crafting is necessarily connected with persons of influence and power. I find her thoughts on the power of distance very insightful but would question some of her assumptions. Technologies and technological changes, rather than being subdivided into categories such as "skilled" and "economic" that are preordained by the identities of those involved, instead constitute Mauss's "traditional effective acts," all of which are transformative. Distance, the focus of Helms's discourse on power, is a factor that should be considered in the evaluation of how innovation occurs and how the changes in technologies that constitute innovation relate to broader social change.

What constitutes distance in the context of technological and social change can vary depending on the scale of analysis. Networks that extend outside a family can involve weak ties and marginal (that is, external) influences even within the scale of a larger community. Those that would seem to be more disruptive, however, are those that involve influence from beyond the community of practice that generates the traditions that constitute a technological act. The scale of meaningful technological change, therefore, would seem to be at the level of the community. Therefore it is at that level that we should focus our attention when trying to clarify technological *use* and technological *innovation*. We can try to do so by considering the traditions, effectiveness, and acts that constitute the use of technologies and then considering the role of margins and distance in innovation and chance. Although I argue our focus should be on the scale of community, to put the community in context we must first outline broader regional patterns. I argue that in eastern Eurasia, major transformations in technology occurred through technological transformations and innovation processes within communities and that some of the most significant ones are those that were apparently distant from the zone of core sociopolitical complexity in the Central Plains. Accordingly, I turn now to Northwest China and the region of the proto–Silk Road, where technological use and technological change in the second millennium BCE seemingly play a significant role in social change broadly across East Asia.

Northwest China and the Proto–Silk Road

The name proto–Silk Road refers to the connections, primarily of an indirect nature, that increasingly linked places across Eurasia in the third and second millennia BCE and that formed the historical foundation for routes of interaction that eventually coalesced, starting at the end of the first millennium BCE, into what geographer Ferdinand von Richthofen (building on several earlier uses of the term [Mertens 2019]) defined as the Seidenstrasse (Silk Road) in 1877 (Chin 2013; Flad 2017b). The region of particular interest for investigating the nature of technological change along the proto–Silk Road and how it impacted broader social changes encompasses the Hexi Corridor and adjacent regions of the upper Yellow River drainage in Gansu and Qinghai Provinces (Figure 11.1). Technological changes during the third and second millennia BCE in this region include the introduction of new domesticated plants and animals; the development of new craft technologies, including jade manufacture and bronze metallurgy; and transformations in existing ceramic technologies.

Synthesizing and building off a considerable corpus of previous scholarship, Jaang (2015) has thoroughly outlined the early evidence for many of the technological introductions into East Asia that have origins in western Eurasia. Her paper summarizes the earliest dates for certain key technologies, including wheat agriculture, caprine husbandry, and metallurgy, and the reader is pointed there for a more exhaustive treatment than is possible in this paper. Her emphasis is on the central role played by what she calls the Ejin River Transfer Zone (ERTZ)—a region that encompasses the Hexi Corridor and surrounding regions.

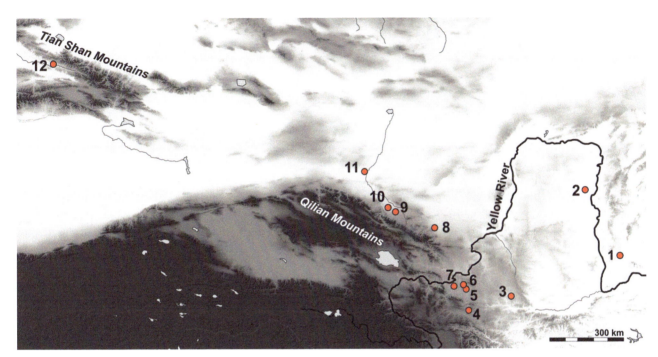

Figure 11.1. Map of sites mentioned in the text: 1. Taosi; 2. Shimao; 3. Dadiwan; 4. Mogou; 5. Qijiaping; 6. Huizuiwa; 7. Linjia; 8. Huangniangniangtai; 9. Donghuishan; 10. Xichengyi; 11. Huoshiliang/Ganggangwa; 12. Jartai Pass.
Created by Bryan K. Miller.

This neotoponym focuses attention on the central role that she proposes for the south–north drainage of the Ejin River—a now dry river that runs north to the basin of the also dry Lake Juyan north of Zhangye in the central Hexi Corridor. This river valley, Jaang has argued, was a critical thoroughfare in the early period of the historical Silk Roads (Jaang 2011), and its significance may extend quite a bit earlier as a principal route of technological transfer from steppe contexts to the north in Mongolia into the interaction networks south of the Gobi that are linked through the Hexi Corridor region. According to this model, the ERTZ acted as a location of technological percolation from which innovations spread east and west and served as a "major point of access to artifacts, innovations, and technologies from the steppe and the more distant reaches of Eurasia during the third and early second millennium BCE" (Jaang 2015:207). We might think of this as a degree of "betweenness centrality" in the larger Eurasian context.

The model she presents provides a plausible overview of the sequence of technological innovations. As she further points out, however, the process of innovation was quite contingent on local conditions and local receptiveness. Although the details of chronologies of innovation remain unfortunately unclear for many new technologies evident in the region, a brief further consideration of these historical processes points out that both subsistence and craft technologies in the region changed in nonuniform, complicated ways over the course of more than a millennium in order for new technologies to take hold. The community-level lived experience of those involved in innovation therefore seems to have been one that lacked marked change and involved adoption of artifacts and practices compatible with local lifeways in communities across Northwest China.

Subsistence Technology

As evidenced by the recent identification of a mandible attributed to Denisovans found in Xiahe, Gansu, Northwest China has been occupied by humans for at least 160,000 years (Chen et al. 2019). For most of the ensuing millennia of human activity in the region, sparsely distributed populations subsisted by hunting a variety of animals and gathering wild plant foods.

Domesticated Plants

Experiments in managing plant resources may have occurred in early Holocene contexts in the region. At the site of Dadiwan, for example, deeply stratified archaeological deposits indicate a transition from early hominin activity around 80,000 years ago, to microlithic technologies associated with hunter-gatherers near the end of the

Pleistocene, to a ceramic-using, sedentary agricultural subsistence technology (An et al. 2010; Bettinger et al. 2010a, 2010b; Zhang et al. 2010). Here, the transition to agriculture involved several cultural stages, over the course of which we see evidence for focused millet production and use starting as early as 6000 BCE. This evidence may reflect experimental intensification of millet stands and incipient agriculture (Bettinger et al. 2010a, 2010b), although some doubt the degree to which the earliest evidence at Dadiwan reflects millet agriculture per se (Leipe et al. 2019). This critique aside, there is consensus that millet agriculture had become established somewhere in North China by the sixth millennium BCE (Liu et al. 2016). The spread of millet agriculture resulted in population growth, but importantly this was not a uniform, inevitable, or ubiquitous process. Instead, there was a discontinuous spread of millet westward toward Central Asia, and more unevenly in adjacent regions (Leipe et al. 2019; Ventresca Miller and Makarewicz 2019). Around 1900 BCE, millet cultivation seems to have decreased in association with possible depopulation of some regions associated with a complex series of factors, including economic development, social stratification, and environmental changes.

Around this time we see increasing evidence for the introduction of domesticated plants from western Eurasia, particularly barley (*Hordeum vulgare*) and wheat (*Triticum* spp.). There has been an extensive recent discussion of the data that substantiate the chronology over which these Southwest Asian crops were increasingly used and incorporated into the agricultural practices of East Asia (Barton and An 2014; Chen et al. 2014; d'Alpoim Guedes and Bocinsky 2018; d'Alpoim Guedes et al. 2015; Dodson et al. 2013; Dong et. al 2017; Flad et al. 2010; Frachetti et al. 2010; Lister et al. 2019; Liu et al. 2014, 2017; Long et al. 2018; Ventresca Miller and Makarewicz 2019; Yang et al. 2019). Accordingly, it appears that both crops were introduced into parts of East Asia between 2600 and 1900 BCE. Somewhat surprisingly, some of the earliest accepted dates for wheat are found in eastern locales, specifically in Shandong and Liaoning, but these may have been the result of the introduction of exotic plants along north–south routes from the Eurasian steppe (Lee 2017; Long et al. 2018). In Northwest China, the Hexi Corridor seems to have been first populated by millet cultivators around 2800 BCE (Dong et al. 2018; Leipe et al. 2019). These populations were associated with the spread of painted pottery cultures from the upper Yellow River valley and surrounding areas toward the northwest along what has been described as a "painted pottery road" (Han 2012). By ca. 2000 BCE, wheat and barley had been introduced into this region, although the precise chronology is still under investigation. One anomalous wheat date of 4110 ± 250 BP (3368–1980 cal BCE) at Donghuishan (a site otherwise dated to the Siba culture; see Flad et al. 2010; Li and Mo 2004) is the earliest direct date in this region, with most other direct dates falling within the second millennium BCE. Other wheat and barley samples have been dated by association to the mid- to late third millennium BCE. They suggest that wheat and barley seem to be gradually and unevenly taken up as increasingly significant parts of the subsistence technology (Barton and An 2014; Dodson et al. 2013; Flad et al. 2010). Barley in particular seems to have become an important crop that facilitated the occupation of higher-elevation areas through the second millennium BCE (d'Alpoim Guedes et al. 2015). The degree to which wheat and barley became important components of the diet is an ongoing focus of archaeobotanical and isotopic analysis in Northwest China (Liu et al. 2014; Ma et al. 2014, 2016; Zhou and Garvie-Lok 2015). What seems to be the case is that the process of introduction was gradual and complex, and the introduced domesticates were treated as exotic goods that were slowly and unevenly fit into agricultural practices across North China (Long et al. 2018). I would argue that the metaphorical distance associated with introduced crops contributed to their value in the contexts where they became known.

As mentioned previously, millets are the dominant crop associated with agricultural practices in Northwest China until the introduction of wheat and barley (Barton et al. 2009). In order for wheat and barley cultivation to take hold, associated practices had to take hold in a social fabric that already engaged in millet farming. This would include new ways of scheduling agricultural activities and new forms of cuisine, all aspects of the technological innovations that would have been considered with shifting practices. Millets, which are C4 cultigens, are isotopically distinct from the C3 plants that dominate the natural vegetation in Northwest China and also include the introduced Southwest Asian domesticates (An et al. 2015a, 2015b; Atahan et al. 2014; Barton et al. 2009; Ma et al. 2014; Ma et al. 2015). Accordingly, isotopic ratios in the bones of humans and animals can be used as a proxy to determine the degree to which C4 plants (presumably millets) or C3 plants (including wheat and barley) were prevalent in diets. Isotopic methods show an increasing emphasis on millets through evidence of C4 plant uptake during the Neolithic in North China, followed by a shift toward increasingly C3 signatures after 1600 BCE (Ma et al. 2016; Zhou and Garvie-Lok 2015). The isotopic approach is somewhat ambiguous when we start to see this evidence for a shift from C4- to mixed C3/C4-focused diets. C3 plants are often thought to be wheat and barley in North China agricultural communities when these plants are attested or rice in other geographical contexts.[6] It is also possible, however, that C4 isotopic signatures reflect the direct or indirect intake of wild plants, particularly when humans are consuming grazing animals such as sheep and goats. Grazing animals intake C3 plants and pass on the isotopic signature to the humans who consume them, and animal husbandry is therefore a component of the subsistence technology that should be considered in this discussion.

Domesticated Animals

As was the case with introduced plant domesticates, the raising of newly introduced grazing animals must have involved incorporation into and "fit" with existing human–animal relationships as part of changing agricultural technologies. Sheep (*Ovis aries*) and goats (*Capra hircus*) appear in Northwest China starting in the third millennium BCE (Brunson et al. 2020; Flad et al. 2007; Wang 2017), following their initial domestication in areas around the Zagros Mountains in Southwest Asia. Among the earliest sheep in Northwest China are those at Shizhaocun, Hetaozhuang, and Lajia (Brunson et al. 2020; Cai et al. 2010; Jaang 2015). By the beginning of the second millennium, sheep and goats had been introduced to the middle Yellow River regions (Brunson et al. 2015; Yuan 2015). In Northwest China, some early evidence of sheep management comes from the sites of Huoshiliang and Ganggangwa, dating between 2300 and 1700 BCE, where isotopic values suggest that sheep were grazed beyond the agricultural zone, consuming both millet stubble and locally available grasses, a pattern that is consistent with long-distance transport (Atahan et al. 2011). These caprines may have been raised in small numbers as complements to the wild and other domesticated animals available. Initial caprine use therefore does not seem to have involved a transition to a more committed pastoral practice, nor to more transhumant mobility. Sheep and goats only gradually become increasingly important components of the subsistence package evident in zooarchaeological assemblages, however (Brunson et al. 2020). Accordingly, some groups that began to emphasize caprine raising may have adopted very new ways of interacting with the surrounding landscape compared to other communities.

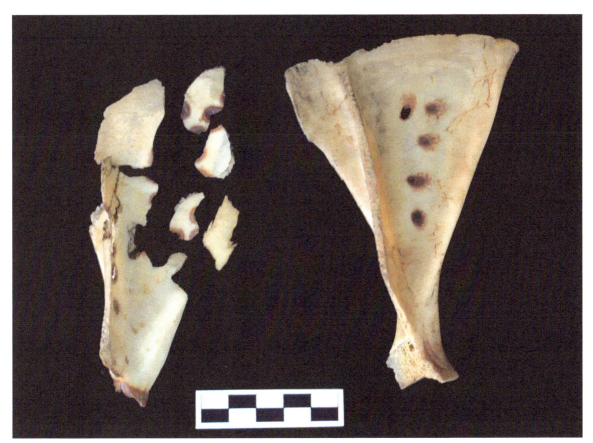

Figure 11.2. Qijia culture oracle bone (FCN4148) from 16GQ Trench 2 at Qijiaping. Excavated July 9, 2016. *Photo by the author.*

As this process occurred, caprines became an important medium for specialized ritual activity, as evidenced by the use of their bones in the practice of pyro-osteomancy—divination involving the burning of animal bones, which are sometimes called oracle bones (Flad 2008). Although the earliest evidence for oracle bone divination seems to involve the use of scapulae from wild animals (deer), sheep scapulae were used in Northwest China early in the development of this practice and continued to be considerably more ubiquitous than the bones of other taxa for this purpose through the second millennium BCE. Examples of this have been found in the recent Tao River Archaeological Project at the sites of Qijiaping, the type site of the Qijia culture (ca. 2300–1600 BCE), and Huizuiwa, a site of the Xindian culture (ca. 1600–600 BCE; Figure 11.2; Yiru 1959; also see Brunson et al. this volume, Figure 8.5). The apparent preference for caprines in divination practices in Northwest China illustrates their symbolic significance, and I argue that this value is related to their association with distant origins.

Domesticated cattle (*Bos taurus*), another Southwest Asian domesticate, has a similar process of introduction as well. Although wild cattle ranged across East Asia in earlier millennia, domesticated taurine cattle are introduced sometime in the early third millennium BCE and gradually emerge as one of the most significant animal domesticates in North China for various purposes, including traction, subsistence, and ritual (Lü 2010; Lü et al. 2014; Yu 2019). The way cattle were used and the degree to which they were important components of the local subsistence technologies in Northwest Chinese communities during the early phase of their introduction is not well understood and requires more sustained research, similar to that done in the middle and lower reaches of the Yellow River region (Brunson et al. 2015) and elsewhere (Wang 2018; Yu 2019). Were cattle in Northwest China raised in small numbers for occasional consumption or primarily for traction? Were other secondary products, such as milk, exploited (Wilkin et al. 2020)? To what extent do cattle in these communities reflect wealth, or were they used for ritual purposes? We currently do not have many data related to these questions, but we do know that cattle in the Central Plains of China became thoroughly embedded in ritual practices, such as divination and sacrifice, during the second millennium BCE (Campbell et al. 2011; Flad 2008). Their association with external origins likely contributed in an important way to the significance of cattle in ritual practices in the Central Plains. Like the aforementioned caprines, cattle are another example of introduced animals being incorporated into pre-existing ritual traditions.

Horses are a third category of animal technology reflecting changes associated with trans-Eurasian influences. As far as we can tell, they are not incorporated into subsistence practices in the same way as caprines, given that they are not a primary focus of consumption. The existing data provide sporadic and small-scale evidence of horse use in Northwest China around the beginning of the second millennium BCE (Flad 2008; Tie 2015). Somewhat later, in the last centuries of the second millennium, suddenly we have ample evidence of horse technology in the Central Plains, associated with the Late Shang state centered at Yinxu in Anyang (e.g. Linduff 2003; Mair 2003; Yuan and Flad 2006). The chronology of their incorporation at a relatively large scale into North China technological practices implies a rather slow and uneven process of change. Most of the data reflect a high value and ritualized set of functions associated with horses in this context, and these associations continued through the remained of the Bronze Age as horses continued to be used in the context of elite activities such as sacrifice and war (Dewall 1964; Lu 1993).

Summary

It will be through understanding a history of the use of wheat, barley, caprines, cattle, and horses—all "outside" innovations—that a fuller understanding of the adoption of these technologies will be had. Each of these elements of subsistence technologies reflects a nonuniform process of further innovation in the Northwest Chinese context. Unfamiliar plants and animals were adopted into local communities, and when they were, they had to fit local conditions and practices. There is some evidence of long-distance movement in association with these technologies, but there is yet little to no evidence of large-scale processes of demic diffusion of populations already familiar with these crops and domesticates. Instead, there may have been multiple waves of smaller-scale movements of people, intercommunity marriages, or other ways in which new ways of doing things and new materials and technologies were introduced into contexts where innovation might occur. Even in cases where people using technologies of distant invention migrated into Northwest China, an adjustment to new landscapes would have been required. Such adjustments would have required processes of technological innovation as these populations adapted to their new environment. The apparently slow process by which wheat, barley, caprines, cattle, and horses were taken up and became important within the overall subsistence technology systems reflects an uneven history of innovation that was complex and multidirectional. It is possible that at first these technologies were valued in part because of their association with distant places and unfamiliar practices. We see this reflected perhaps most clearly in the way that cattle and horses become central to ritual practices in the Central Plains of China, but it is also clearly evident in the exotic associations ascribed to wheat and barley and the preferential use of caprine bones for divination in Northwest China.

Craft Technology: Jade and Metals

Craft technologies are another set of practices that illustrate technological innovations in Northwest China during this period of social changes in the third and second millennia BCE. The cultural sequences of known Neolithic communities in this region from the Dadiwan culture (ca. sixth millennium BCE) onward are defined in large part based on elaborate painted pottery known primarily from burial sites. In particular, in North China painted ceramics—or their absence—are the primary means of identifying and distinguishing the phases of activity known as the Yangshao, Majiayao, Banshan, Keshengzhuang II, Machang, Xichengyi, Qijia, Siba, Xindian, Kayue, Zongri, Siwa, Yanbulak, Shanma, and Shajing cultures (among others). Although they are listed here in rough (overlapping) chronological order, I intentionally do not provide date ranges for each here, as every one of these chronological phases/regional cultures requires close, regionally specific consideration of the chronological range (see a recent example by Yang et al. 2019). These cultural traditions can be roughly mapped in space (Figure 11.3), and doing so illustrates that shared traditions of ceramic production do not indicate a wave of advance of some newly introduced population of innovators, wholly disconnected from local traditions during the transition from the third to the second millennia BCE (Jaffe and Flad 2018). Instead, while there were transformations in ceramic craft production, these seem to be based on longer-term familiarity with local resources and cultural connections that extend in multiple, different directions (Womack et al. 2019).

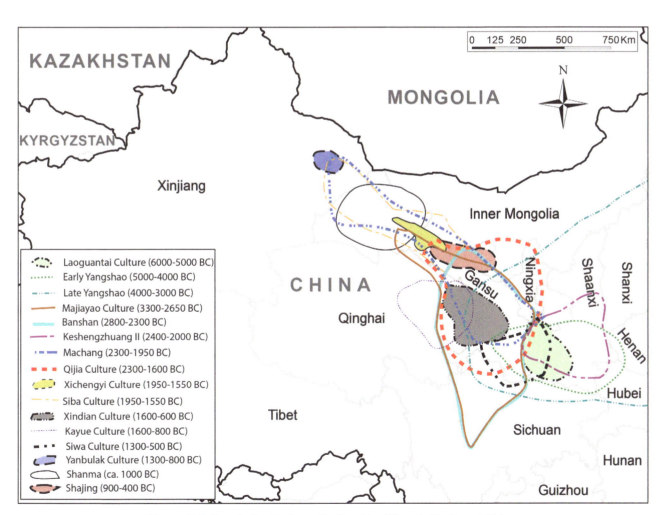

Figure 11.3. Rough distributions of cultural traditions in Northwest China.
Created by the author after Jaffe and Flad 2018.

Jade

One realm of craft production that shows this variety of directions of influence is jade,[7] whose importance in Northwest China increases during the second millennium BCE. The earliest jade objects in China were slit-ring ear ornaments created in Northeast China and adjacent regions (Ji and Deng 2018; Yang et al. 2006). Over time during the Neolithic, two regions of eastern China developed elaborate jade industries that reflect a widespread investment of hardstone minerals with high social value. These are associated with the cultural traditions termed Hongshan (ca. 4500–3000 BCE) in Northeast China and Liangzhu (ca. 3300–2100 BCE) in the lower Yangzi river region (Deng et al. 2015; Guo 1998; Hangzhou and Zhejiangsheng 2018; So 2019). Between these two regions there seems to have been some degree of interaction, and therefore these two trajectories of development should not be considered entirely distinct (Li Xinwei 2013). Instead, the significance of the development of jade manufacture in these two regions may reflect relatively innovative moments in a long-term, punctuated process by which jade obtained a collection of values and meanings that contributed to the important role this substance took on across East Asia in the Late Neolithic and Bronze Age. By the Late Neolithic, jade had become an unquestionable symbol of power in a variety of cultural contexts (Dematté 2006; Liu 2003), and Northwest Chinese traditions are no exception.

Qin Xiaoli summarized the development of hardstone use in Northwest China, particularly in relation to turquoise inlay, which became an elaborated part of the lapidary crafts in Northwest China in the Qijia culture (Qin 2010, 2016). As she outlines, the use of turquoise in Northwest China, starting in the third millennium BCE in association with Banshan and Machang burial traditions, was part of a broader set of practices of body ornamentation. Among these objects are turquoise-inlaid arm ornaments made of bone; these may be precursors to the more famous turquoise-inlaid bronze plaques associated with the Qijia culture. Associated with the changes in material culture that reflect the Qijia culture in the early second millennium BCE, the focus of craft production that resulted in the manufacture of elaborate objects for display and as markers of identity seems to have shifted from painted pottery manufacture to jade and bronze. Qijia culture jades are a significant component of the elite material culture associated with this tradition, and some Qijia jades may have been the produce of exploiting nephrite sources in the Maxianshan range, a source that would have been accessible through river cobbles, in particular in the Tao River valley (Figure 11.4). In the Northwest, particularly in association with the Qijia culture, the inclusion of jades in burials and the crafting of an increasing variety of jade objects reflect a development of jade as a substance that was important in social differentiation. The region where Qijia sites are distributed joined other places around the periphery of the Central Plains in magnifying the importance of this material, contributing to the processes by which jade became a ritually and culturally valuable symbolic medium.

Bronze

Another craft technology that plays a central role in social differentiation and integration in early China is bronze metallurgy. Bronze technology developed first in one or more places in Southwest Asia and nearby regions starting in the sixth millennium BCE (Hansen 2017; Roberts et al. 2009). The process by which bronze was manufactured incorporated existing pyrotechnologies associated with the production of ceramics and the awareness of various mineral ores and raw materials everywhere metallurgy became a local practice, so metallurgical innovations are in part a factor of material flows (Wilkinson 2014) as much as the adoption and appropriation of pyrotechnological techniques.

Across Eurasia, there is a general sense of chronological progression of metal technology from west to east, although that seems to have occurred in a "non-linear, non-uniform fashion" (Pigott 2018). Accordingly, the introduction of metallurgical practices into Northwest China is also seemingly nonlinear and nonuniform. The earliest evidence for local production of metal objects within China dates to around 2200 BCE (Dodson et al. 2009). This local production evidence comes from the sites of Huoshiliang and Ganggangwa on the Ejin drainage in the Hexi Corridor. There we see evidence for local communities adopting new technologies (namely metallurgy) while maintaining some connections in other aspects of material culture, particularly ceramics, to traditions with deep roots in the Gansu region. This situation reflects the persistence of some social distance among the groups that come into contact, even though some new technologies are adopted.

Even earlier is the evidence of bronze artifacts associated with Majiayao cultural materials, represented by a bronze knife found at the site of Linjia dated by association to 2900–2740 BCE (Bai 2002). To my knowledge, this solitary find is not connected with a secure provenience that can confirm its absolute chronology and remains rather anomalous. This is not to imply that the date should be doubted; as with the anomalous early Hexi wheat date mentioned above, the Linjia bronze artifact date is consistent with bronze objects of the same general type found in the Eurasian steppe. It is likely, however, that the object arrived in the Tao River valley, where Linjia is located, via

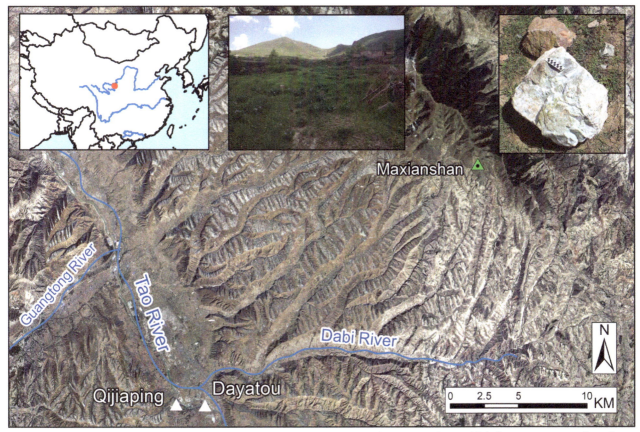

Figure 11.4. Maxianshan nephrite quarry location north of a tributary of the Dabi River, which flows east to west into the Tao River. Insets show the Maxianshan landscape and nephrite raw material at Maxianshan. *Created by the author.*

exchange networks, setting the stage (albeit in an ephemeral fashion) for the awareness of bronze objects among local third millennium BCE populations in the northwestern region. Members of some such populations, at places like those along the Ejin drainage, eventually started to engage in local bronze production using local resources.

Roughly contemporaneous with Huoshiliang and Gangangwa is a nearby site that contains debris associated with metallurgical production and local ceramic and burial traditions: Xichengyi, which is situated along the north–south–trending Heishui drainage in Zhangye County. Excavations there starting in 2010 have recovered remains from approximately 2100–1600 BCE associated with Late Machang through Siba cultural traditions. Dozens of copper and bronze artifacts have been discovered at Xichengyi (Dong et al. 2017; Jaang 2015), including awls, rings, knives, and buttons, as well as debris associated with local metal production. The metal production debris apparently comes from all three phases of activity at the site (Late Machang, Xichengyi II, and Siba) and thus can be dated to as early as ca. 2100 BCE (Chen et al. 2014). Other technological evidence, including the presence of mace heads found at the Huoshaogou cemetery (dating to the latest phase at Xichengyi), evidence of local casting of bronze mace heads using a stone mold at Xichengyi, and the presence of Southwest Asian cereal crops, all testify to connections to technologies introduced to the Hexi region from places farther west.

Elsewhere in Northwest China we have ample evidence of bronzes being made and used in the period between 2200 to 1600 BCE based on association with the Qijia culture tradition. Some sites, such as Huangniangniangtai in Wuwei, seem to be related to the earlier stages of that date range (Gansu Sheng Bowuguan 1960, 1978; Wang 2012; Wen 2021). Among the material culture excavated from Huangniangniangtai, dozens of small bronze implements were recovered. They included knives, awls, and other small tools and ornaments. Other Qijia culture sites, such as Mogou (Gansu and Xibei 2009a, 2009b; Mao et al 2009; Qian et al. 2009; Qian and Mao 2012) and Qijiaping (Chen 2013; Womack et al. 2017) in the Tao River valley, include bronze objects in graves, including similar bronze implements, bronze mirrors, and bronze plaques with turquoise inlay (Huang 2015; Jaang 2011; Qin 2014). These sites date to the later stages of the Qijia culture chronological range (Womack et al. 2017) and reflect clear connections with the developing bronze-using cultures of the Central Plains of North China (Fitzgerald-Huber 1995).

Elsewhere in North China we see a prolonged emergence of bronze production and use at roughly contemporaneous sites. One example is the site of Shimao, in Shenmu County, northern Shaanxi, where survey and preliminary analysis from 2012–2015 and excavations in 2016 have clarified the organization of this large walled site (Shaanxi et al. 2016; Sun et al. 2017, 2018). Among the finds within the area of the inner barbican that formed part of the defensive wall around the core of the site were fragments of stone molds used in the casting of bronze knives. The excavators assess the occupation of the site to be between 2300 and 1800 BCE and the casting evidence to date to at least as early as the end of this period (that is, before 1800 BCE). The earliest clear evidence of copper-based metal production in the Central Plains also dates to the end of the third millennium BCE based on association with Longshan material culture (Bai 2002; Mei et al. 2017). The locally produced metal objects include a small copper bell and both alloyed and unalloyed copper rings at the site of Taosi (Gao and He 2014).

In far Northwest China, in the western parts of Xinjiang, the earliest bronze production remains discovered so far are approximately the same age as the period of more extensive bronze use in the Tao River region—dating to approximately 1600 BCE based on recent excavations at the Jartai Pass site in Nilka County, Xinjiang (Ruan and Wang 2017). This site documents the earliest evidence of a settlement with local bronze production debris from the Ili River valley, for example. These remains show clear material similarities to sites from the broader central Asian region affiliated with the Andronovo culture (1800–1300 BCE). Other nearby studies of agropastoral communities also highlight these connections throughout the Ili region (Zhang and Festa 2020) and the Bortala Valley (Doumani Dupuy et al. 2019). Interestingly for the discussion of technological development, the Jartai Pass excavations have recovered the earliest pottery molds yet discovered in all of China (Ruan and Wang 2017), which might be counterintuitive given the assumption that the use of pottery molds in casting was a component of technology that has its roots in ceramic traditions farther to the east. The ceramic molds found at the Jartai Pass site were two-part molds used for casting awls and so are structurally and functionally similar to the stone molds known from earlier contexts, such as Shimao.

Ultimately, these technological developments in bronze production had a profound impact on the development of metal production and the rise of bronze-using civilizations within the Central Plains of North China. As was the case with the subsistence technologies discussed previously, and the development of jade technologies in the northeast, southeast, and northwest of China, the initially small-scale engagement with bronze as a medium for distinction became an important set of practices within the ritual and economic systems of the complex polities that emerged in the middle and lower Yellow River valleys during the second millennium BCE (Bagley 1999; Falkenhausen 2006a; Li 2021; Rawson 1993).

The introduction of metal into East Asia was a process that involved the adoption of ideas about smelting ores to create metal objects. However, recent research has highlighted how the ways of making and using metals in the Central Plains of China were radically different from those of Central Asia, such that the transmission of metal production technology cannot be considered a straightforward process of adoption. As Edgerton (1999:122) points out, there is a "general tendency to attribute important effects to technologies which have what might be called high cultural visibility." But highly visible technologies are not necessarily pervasive throughout society, and social value is sometimes even framed such that ubiquity and cultural value are negatively correlated (see Papadopoulos and Urton 2012).

In craft technologies, we see processes that must be thought about simultaneously at different spatial scales and over an extended period of time. At the local scale, a sufficient degree of ubiquity and familiarity was necessary for certain crafts to be engaged in by local artisans and incorporated into the broad repertoire of a community. However, individual exotic objects had some allure due to scarcity at the local level, providing they were sufficiently available at the regional scale for their association with distant places to be salient. On the regional scale, consequently, such processes might eventually result in an increasing ubiquity that could foster a degree of familiarity with the technology in question sufficient for adoption and further innovation. Through this iterative innovation process, the power associated with objects that reference marginal regions would have become increasingly incorporated into growing communities and super-community polities during the Bronze Age in China. In addition to being a region in which we see evidence at the community level of social and technological development, the Northwest China region incorporating parts of Gansu, Qinghai, and Xinjiang seems to have played an important role in the process of technological and social change in the Central Plains of the lower Yellow River valley in ways that were fundamental to the development of what is often framed as the origins of Chinese civilization. Innovations fit into or developed within communities within Northwest China in an apparently heterogeneous and patchwork process. In that process, associations related to distance cause certain technologies to be highly valued, and these high values were enhanced in ways that further built up the power of distance over the course of the second millennium BCE.

Conclusion

In studies of the history of technology, we have a tendency to emphasize novelty rather than use and to fixate on invention rather than innovation. We study "innovations which succeed later" (Edgerton 1999:124) rather than those that are characteristic, pervasive, or meaningful in the ways of living and ways of knowing that characterize a particular period in time. In archaeology this tendency is exacerbated by a focus on trying to understand those stimuli to which the cause of social change can be attributed. In some cases, this has led to the aforementioned evolutionist SVT-based disposition in the grand narrative of technological and social change (Pfaffenberger 1992). This SVT perspective sees technology essentially as progress itself (Marx 2010). Consequently SVT carries an assumption that progress is not itself in need of explanation and understanding. Instead, emphasis is placed on catalysts for change—thus emphasizing the notion of innovation while at the same time not really explaining the process of innovation.

Here I have contextualized the significance of novelty associated with social and spatial margins in order to place it securely within a framework of use, as one source of variation that plays a significant role in East Asia in the process of innovation through the related practices of adoption and appropriation. I have focused on several subsistence and craft technologies that play critical roles in the emergence of economic and ritual practices that were crucial in the social contexts of emerging complex societies in the Central Plains. In these concluding comments, I want to focus attention on the active nature of appropriation and adoption, and in doing so I want us to reconsider assumptions about the nature of "progress." Instead of seeing technology as progress itself, we should return to the perspective that considers technology as a means of progress (Marx 2010), a perspective linked to the idea of sociotechnical systems (Pfaffenberger 1992), particularly in those cases, as Marx (2010:567) discusses, where technological processes are intimately linked with institutions and practices that involve collective practices institutionalized on a broad social level,[8] but also in the technological practices of everyday life.

I think a new take on technological progress is required—one that considers innovation through the lens of social progressivism as a process that requires work and occurs only under certain conditions. Progressivism need not assume progress. Although traditional progressivism rooted in the reason and humanism of the Enlightenment emerged in a time in which this philosophy was inextricably tied to notions of moral development, cultural evolution, and the roots of social Darwinism, a reframing of social progressivism focuses on how progress requires active effort and striving for a better political reality actively built and based on learning from the past (Pinker 2018). Contexts where we see the historical significance of processes of innovation laying the foundation for integrated systems of ritually and economically significant technologies are examples of technological progressivism at play in processes of social change.

In the innovations in subsistence and craft technologies focused on in this essay, the newly introduced technologies did not quickly replace other existing technologies. Instead we seem to see processes of experimentation and incorporation—innovation through adoption that reflects a recognition of the value of certain technologies and associated practices without a whole-scale social transformation. There are many other examples where similar cases of innovations have been observed in the contexts of even more radical and sudden social transformations, such as the contexts of violent and transformative encounters between indigenous New World populations and Europeans (e.g., Van Valkenburgh et al. 2017). We must envision the patchwork of cultures and communities across ancient China to be one in which the tensions of the "familiar" and the "strange"[9] were constantly being negotiated in the process of technological transformation in prehistory. These processes of innovation likely involved various members of a given community—young and old, men and women, those of higher status and those who were not, and both insiders and outsiders. It seems that a familiarity with the unfamiliar, however, had a consequential impact on the technological changes that we observe. Weak ties to those who did things differently not only brought people into contact with new plants, animals, materials, and ways of doing but also gave them an ability to make changes based on those contacts. This must have involved an evaluation of the costs and benefits of doing things differently.

Such seemingly economic calculations were inherently tied to ritual practices and the construction of value. Exotic things could become valuable and imbued with some degree of usefulness when they could also be accepted as something that was not too costly to create or use. Consequently, the concern with economy and ritual at the heart of this volume and infused throughout the work of Lothar von Falkenhausen is central to an investigation of technology.

Acknowledgments

This paper is a heavily revised version of a presentation given at the celebration of the sixtieth birthday of Lothar von Falkenhausen. The written manuscript benefited greatly from the constructive critiques of a number of colleagues, including the coeditors of this volume, Anke Hein and Bryan Miller, as well as Paula Doumani-Dupuy, Nathaniel Erb-Satullo, Christian Tryon, and Liye Xie. I also wish to recognize my colleagues on the Tao River Archaeology Project, especially Zhou Jing, Wang Hui, Andrew Womack, and Yitzchak Jaffe, for conversations that contributed to the ideas in this paper and to recognize the participants in a graduate seminar on the archaeology of technology in the spring semester of 2018.

Notes

1. See examples in the biography of Huozhi in the *Shiji* 史記·貨殖列傳: "醫方諸食技術之人，焦神極能，為重繆也" and in the Yiwen chapter of *Hanshu*, Vol. 30: 漢書．卷三〇．藝文志："漢興有倉公，今其技術晻昧，故論其書，以序方技為四種."
2. "Acte traditionnel efficace" (Mauss 2012:375).
3. Diffusion concerns the spread of a practice or technology, communication about it, the time it takes to occur, and the social system involved (Rogers 2003 [1962]).
4. Biased transmission is discussed extensively in the cited literature and references therein as a concern with those factors that affect the way humans acquire behaviors directly, through attention to or concern with prestige and through practices of conforming (Henrich 2002).
5. Which I take to mean "distant," not "disenfranchised" or "subaltern."
6. Rice (*Oryza sativa*) is an important domesticate in southern latitudes in China and even in the lower Yellow River region of North China but is not common in Northwest China contexts. (See Fuller 2012 for a broad summary of rice agriculture.)
7. The term *jade* is used in Chinese archaeology, art history, and material culture studies to refer to a range of hardstone minerals, including hemijades (nephrite and jadeite; Wen and Jing 1992) and pseudojades (distinct minerals such as turquoise, marble, quartz, chalcedony, and others; Middleton and Freestone 1995).
8. Marx discusses, for example, the railway system and telegraph, which are sociotechnical systems that require a certain degree of institutional and social integration to be set up and to work.
9. To reference one of the main foci of the discipline of anthropology: the process of making the strange familiar and the familiar strange (see Myers 2011)

References

An, Cheng-Bang, Weimiao Dong, Yufeng Chen, Hu Li, Chao Shi, Wei Wang, Pingyu Zhang, and Xueye Zhao
2015a Stable Isotopic Investigations of Modern and Charred Foxtail Millet and the Implications for Environmental Archaeological Reconstruction in the Western Chinese Loess Plateau. *Quaternary Research* 84(1):144–49.

An, Cheng-Bang, Weimiao Dong, Hu Li, Pingyu Zhang, Yongtao Zhao, Xueye Zhao, and Shi-Yong Yu
2015b Variability of the Stable Carbon Isotope Ratio in Modern and Archaeological Millets: Evidence from Northern China. *Journal of Archaeological Science* 53:316–22.

An Chengbang, Ji Duxue, Chen Fahu, Dong Guanghui, Wang Hui, Dong Weimiao, and Zhao Xueye
2010 Evolution of Prehistoric Agriculture in Central Gansu Province, China: A Case Study in Qin'an and Li County. *Chinese Science Bulletin* 55(18):1925–30.

Arthur, W. Brian
2009 *The Nature of Technology*. New York: Free Press.

Atahan, Pia, John Dodson, Xiaoqiang Li, Xinying Zhou, Liang Chen, Linda Barry, and Fiona Bertuch
2014 Temporal Trends in Millet Consumption in Northern China. *Journal of Archaeological Science* 50:171–77.

Atahan, Pia, John Dodson, Xiaoqiang Li, Xinying Zhou, Songmei Hu, Fiona Bertuch, and Nan Sun
2011 Subsistence and the Isotopic Signature of Herding in the Bronze Age Hexi Corridor, NW Gansu, China. *Journal of Archaeological Science* 38:1747–53.

Audouze, Francoise
2002 Leroi-Gourhan, a Philosopher of Technique and Evolution. *Journal of Archaeological Research* 10(4):277–306.

Bagley, Robert W.
1999 Shang Archaeology. In *The Cambridge History of Ancient China: From the Origins of Civilization to 221 BC*, edited by Michael Loewe and E. L. Shaughnessy, pp. 124–231. Cambridge: Cambridge University Press.

Bai Yunxiang 白雲翔
2002 Zhongguo de zaoqi tongqi yu qingtongqi de qiyuan 中國的早期同期與青銅器的起源 [The Emergence of Early Copper and Bronze Objects in China]. *Dongnan wenhua* 東南文化 2002(7):25–37.

Barbieri-Low, Anthony J.
2007   *Artisans in Early Imperial China*. Seattle: University of Washington Press.

Barton, Loukas, and Cheng-Bang An
2014   An Evaluation of Competing Hypotheses for the Early Adoption of Wheat in East Asia. *World Archaeology* 46(5):775–98.

Barton, Loukas, Seth D. Newsome, Fa-Hu Chen, Hui Wang, Thomas P. Guilderson, and Robert L. Bettinger
2009   Agricultural Origins and the Isotopic Identity of Domestication in Northern China. *Proceedings of the National Academy of Sciences* 106(14):5523–28.

Bernbeck, Reinhard, and Stefan Burmeister
2017   Archaeology and Innovation: Remarks on Approaches and Concepts. In *The Interplay of People and Technologies: Archaeological Case Studies on Innovation*, edited by S. Burmeister and R. Bernbeck. pp. 7–20. Berlin: Universität Berlin.

Bettinger, Robert L., Loukas Barton, and Christopher Morgan
2010a   The Origins of Food Production in North China: A Different Kind of Agricultural Revolution. *Evolutionary Anthropology* 19:9–21.

Bettinger, Robert L., Loukas Barton, Christopher Morgan, Fahu Chen, Hui Wang, Thomas P. Guilderson, Duxue Ji, and Dongju Zhang
2010b   The Transition to Agriculture at Dadiwan, People's Republic of China. *Current Anthropology* 51(5):703–14.

Bourdieu, Pierre
1977 [1972]   *Outline of a Theory of Practice*. Cambridge: Cambridge University Press.

Bowser, Brenda J.
2008   Leaning and Transmission of Pottery Style: Women's Life Histories and Communities of Practice in the Ecuadorian Amazon. In *Cultural Transmission and Material Culture: Breaking Down Boundaries*, edited by M. T. Stark, B. J. Bowser, and L. Horne, pp. 105–29. Tucson: University of Arizona Press.

Boyd, Robert, and Peter J. Richerson
1985   *Culture and the Evolutionary Process*. Chicago: University of Chicago Press.
1987   The Evolution of Ethnic Markers. *Cultural Anthropology* 2(1):65–79.

Brezine, Carrie J.
2011   Dress, Technology and Identity in Colonial Peru. PhD thesis, Department of Anthropology, Harvard University, Cambridge, MA.

Brunson, Katherine, He Nu, and Dai Xiangming
2015   Sheep, Cattle, and Specialization: New Zooarchaeological Perspectives on the Taosi Longshan. *International Journal of Osteoarchaeology* 26:460–75.

Brunson, Katherine, Ren Lele, Zhao Xin, Wang Hui, Zhou Jing, and Rowan Flad
2020   Zooarchaeology, Ancient mtDNA, and Radiocarbon Dating Provide New Evidence for the Emergence of Domestic Cattle and Caprines in the Tao River Valley of Gansu Province, Northwest China. *Journal of Archaeological Science: Reports* 31:102262.

Cai Dawei 蔡大偉, Tang Zhuowei 湯卓煒, Chen Quanjia 陳全家, Han Lu 韓璐, and Zhou Hui 周慧
2010   Zhongguo mianyang qiyuan de fenzi kaoguxue yanjiu 中國綿羊起源的分子考古學研究 [Archaeological Systematics of the Origins of Sheep in China]. *Bianjiang kaogu yanjiu* 邊疆考古研究 [Archaeological Research on the Borderlands] 9:291–300.

Campbell, Roderick B., Zhipeng Li, Yuling He, and Jing Yuan
2011   Consumption, Exchange and Production at the Great Settlement Shang: Bone-Working at Tiesanlu, Anyang. *Antiquity* 85:1279–97.

Canguilhem, George
1952   Machine and Organism. In *Incorporations*, edited by J. Crary and S. Kwinter, pp. 44–9. New York: Zone.

Chen, Fahu, Frido Welker, Chuan-Chou Shen, Shara E. Bailey, Inga Bergmann, Simon Davis, Huan Xia, Hui Wang, Roman Fischer, Sarah E. Freidline, Tsai-Luen Yu, et al.
2019   A Late Middle Pleistocene Denisovan Mandible from the Tibetan Plateau. *Nature* 569:409–12

Chen, F. H., G. H. Dong, D. J. Zhang, X. Y. Liu, X. Jia, C. B. An, M. M. Ma, Y. W. Xie, L. Barton, X. Y. Ren, et al.
2014   Agriculture Facilitated Permanent Human Occupation of the Tibetan Plateau after 3600 BP. *Science* 347(6219):248–50.

Chen Pin 陈玭
2013   Qijia wenhua de fenqi yu yuanliu—yi Qijiaping yizhi wei zhongxin 齊家文化的分期與源流—以齊家坪遺址為中心 [The Periodization and Origin of the Qijia Culture— Focusing on the Qijiaping Site]. PhD thesis, Department of Archaeology, Peking University, Beijing.

Chin, Tamara
2013 The Invention of the Silk Road, 1877. *Critical Inquiry* 40(1):194–219.

Collar, Anna, Fiona Coward, Tom Brughmans, and Barbara J. Mills
2015 Networks in Archaeology: Phenomena, Abstraction, Representation. *Journal of Archaeological Method and Theory* 22(1):1–32.

Crown, Patricia L.
2014 The Archaeology of Crafts Learning: Becoming a Potter in the Puebloan Southwest. *Annual Review of Anthropology* 43(1):71–88.

d'Alpoim Guedes, J., and R. K. Bocinsky
2018 Climate Change Stimulated Agricultural Innovation and Exchange across Asia. *Science Advances* 4(10):4491–4503.

d'Alpoim Guedes, Jade, Hongliang Lu, Anke M. Hein, and Amanda H. Schmidt
2015 Early Evidence for the Use of Wheat and Barley as Staple Crops on the Margins of the Tibetan Plateau. *Proceedings of the National Academy of Sciences* 112(18):1–6.

Demattè, Paola
2006 The Chinese Jade Age: Between Antiquarianism and Archaeology. *Journal of Social Archaeology* 6(2):202–26.

Deng Cong 鄧聰, Cao Jinyan 曹錦炎, Zhejiangsheng Wenwu Kaogu Yanjiusuo 浙江省文物考古研究所, and Xianggang Zhongwen Daxue Zhongguo Kaogu Yishu Yanjiu Zhongxin 香港中文大學中國考古藝術研究中心, eds.
2015 *Liangzhu yugong: Liangzhu yuqi gongyi yanliu lunji* 良渚玉工: 良渚玉器工藝源流論集 [Liangzhu Jades: Essays on Prehistoric Jade Technologies in China]. Hong Kong: Zhongguo Kaogu Yishu Yanjiu Zongxin.

Dewall, Magdalene von
1964 *Pferd und Wagen im frühen China*. Bonn: Habelt.

Dobres, Marcia-Anne
2000 *Technology and Social Agency: Outlining a Practice Framework for Archaeology*. Oxford: Blackwell Publishers.
2001 Meaning in the Making: Agency and the Social Embodiment of Technology and Art. In *Archaeological Perspectives on Technology*, edited by M. B. Schiffer, pp. 47–76. Albuquerque: University of New Mexico Press.
2010 Archaeologies of Technology. *Cambridge Journal of Economics* 34(1):103–14.

Dodson, John R., Xiaoqiang Li, Ming Ji, Keliang Zhao, Xinying Zhou, and Vladimir Levchenko
2009 Early Bronze in Two Holocene Archaeological Sites in Gansu, NW China. *Quaternary Research* 72:309–14.

Dodson, J. R., X. Li, X. Zhou, K. Zhao, N. Sun, and P. Atahan
2013 Origin and Spread of Wheat in China. *Quaternary Science Review* 72:108–11.

Dong, Guanghui, Yishi Yang, Xinyi Liu, Haiming Li, Yifu Cui, Hui Wang, Guoke Chen, John Dodson, and Fahu Chen
2018 Prehistoric Trans-continental Cultural Exchange in the Hexi Corridor, Northwest China. *Holocene* 28(4):621–28.

Doumani Dupuy, Paula N., Peter Weiming Jia, Alison Betts, and Dexin Cong
2019 Pots and Potters of the Bronze Age of North-West Xinjiang. *Antiquity* 93(371):1231–48.

Edgerton, David
1999 From Innovation to Use: Ten Eclectic Theses on the Historiography of Technology. *History and Technology* 16(2):111–36.

Eerkens, Jelmer W., and C. P. Lipo
2007 Cultural Transmission Theory and the Archaeological Record: Providing Context to Understanding Variation and Temporal Changes in Material Culture. *Journal of Archaeological Research* 15:239–74.

Erb-Satullo, Nathaniel L.
2020 Archaeomaterials, Innovation and Technological Change. *Advances in Archaeomaterials* 1:36–50.

Falkenhausen, Lothar von
2006a *Chinese Society in the Age of Confucius (1000–250 BC): The Archaeological Evidence*. Los Angeles: Cotsen Institute of Archaeology Press.
2006b The Salt of Ba: Reflection on the Role of the "Peripheries" in the Production Systems of Bronze Age China. *Arts Asiatiques* 61:45–56.

Fitzgerald-Huber, Louisa G.
1995 Qijia and Erlitou: The Question of Contact with Distant Cultures. *Early China* 20:19–67.

Flad, Rowan K.
2008 Divination and Power: A Multi-regional View of the Development of Oracle Bone Divination in Early China. *Current Anthropology* 49(3):403–37.
2017a Urbanism as Technology in China. *Archaeological Research in Asia* 14:121–34.

2017b   Where Did the Silk Road Come From? In *The China Questions*, edited by M. Szonyi and J. Rudolph, pp. 237–43. Cambridge, MA: Harvard University Press.

Flad, Rowan, and Pochan Chen
2013   *Ancient Central China: An Archaeological Study of Centers and Peripheries along the Yangzi River*. Cambridge: Cambridge University Press.

Flad, Rowan K., Yuan Jing, and Li Shuicheng
2007   Zooarchaeological Evidence for Animal Domestication in Northwest China. In *Late Quaternary Climate Change and Human Adaptation in Arid China*, edited by D. B. Madsen, Chen FaHu, and Gao Xing, pp. 163–99. Amsterdam: Elsevier Press.

Flad, Rowan Kimon, Shuicheng Li, Xiaohong Wu, and Zhijun Zhao
2010   Early Wheat in China: Results from New Studies at Donghuishan in the Hexi Corridor. *Holocene* 20(6):955–65.

Frachetti, Michael D., Robert N. Spengler, Gayle J. Fritz, and Alexei N. Mar'yashev
2010   Earliest Direct Evidence for Broomcorn Millet and Wheat in the Central Eurasian Steppe Region. *Antiquity* 84:1–18.

Fuller, Dorian Q.
2012   Pathways to Asian Civilizations: Tracing the Origins and Spread of Rice and Rice Cultures. *Rice* 4:78–92.

Gansu Sheng Bowuguan 甘肃省博物馆
1960   Gansu Wuwei Huangniangniangtai yizhi fajue baogao 甘肃武威皇娘娘台遗址发掘报告 [Report on the Excavations at the Site of Huangniangniangtai in Wuwei, Gansu]. *Kaogu xuebao* 考古学报 [Acta Archaeologica Sinica] 1960(2):53–71.
1978   Wuwei Huangniangniangtai yizhi disici fajue 武威皇娘娘台遗址第四次发掘 [The Fourth Excavations at Huangniangniangtai in Wuwei, Gansu]. *Kaogu xuebao* 考古学报 [Acta Archaeologica Sinica] 1978(4):421–48.

Gansu Sheng Wenwu Kaogu Yanjiusuo 甘肃省文物考古研究所 and Xibei Daxue Wenhua Yichan yu Kaoguxue Yanjiu Zhongxin 西北大學文化遺產與考古學研究中心
2009a   Gansu Lintan Mogou Qijia wenhua mudi fajue jianbao 甘肅臨潭磨溝齊家文化墓地發掘簡報 [Preliminary Report on the Excavations of the Qijia Culture Cemetery at Mogou in Lintan, Gansu]. *Wenwu* 文物 2009(10):4–24.
2009b   Gansu Lintan xian Mogou Qijia wenhua mudi 甘肅臨潭縣磨溝齊家文化墓地 [The Qijia Culture Cemetery at Mogou in Lintan County, Gansu]. *Kaogu* 考古 2009(7):10–17, 100–103.

Gao Jiangtao 高江涛 and He Nu 何駑
2014   Taosi yizhi chutu tongqi chutan 陶寺遺址出土銅器初探 [A Preliminary Investigation of Copper Objects Excavated from the Taosi Site]. *Nanfang wenwu* 南方文物 [Cultural Relics in Southern China] 1:91–95.

Gell, Alfred
1988   Technology and Magic. *Anthropology Today* 4(2):6–9.
1992   The Technology of Enchantment and the Enchantment of Technology. In *Anthropology, Art, and Aesthetics*, edited by J. Coote and A. Shelton, pp. 40–63. Oxford: Clarendon Press.

Godin, Benoît
2016   Technological Innovation: On the Origins and Development of an Inclusive Concept. *Technology and Culture* 57(3):527–56.

Granovetter, M.
1973   The Strength of Weak Ties. *American Journal of Sociology* 78:1360–80.
1983   The Strength of Weak Ties: A Network Theory Revisited. *Sociological Theory* 1:201–33.

Guo Dashun 郭大順
1998   Hongshan wenhua yuqi tezheng ji qi shehui wenhua yiyi zai renshi 紅山文化玉器特徵及其社會文化意義再認識 [A New Understanding of the Characteristics of the Hongshan Jades and Their Social and Cultural Significance]. In *Dongya yuqi* 東亞玉器 [East Asian Jade: Symbol of Excellence], Vol. 1, edited by Tang Chung (Deng Cong 鄧聰), pp. 140–47. Hong Kong: Centre for Chinese Archaeology and Art, Chinese University of Hong Kong.

Han Jianye 韓建業
2012   "The Painted Pottery Road" and Early Sino-Western Cultural Exchanges. *Anabasis* 3:25–42.

Hangzhou Liangzhu Yizhi Guanliqu Guanli Weiyuanhui 杭州良渚遺址管理區管理委員會 and Zhejiangsheng Wenwu Kaogu Yanjiusuo 浙江省文物考古研究所, eds.
2018   *Liangzhu yuqi* 良渚玉器 [Liangzhu Jades]. Beijing: Kexue Chubanshe.

Hansen, Svend
2017   Key Techniques in the Production of Metals in the 6th and 5th Millennia BCE: Prerequisites, Preconditions and Consequences.

In *Appropriating Innovations: Entangled Knowledge in Eurasia, 5000–1500 BCE*, edited by J. Maran and P. W. Stockhammer, pp. 136–48. Oxford: Oxbow.

Heidegger, Martin
1971   The Thing. In *Poetry, Language, Thought*, pp. 163–84. New York: Perennial Classics.

Helms, Mary W.
1993   *Craft and the Kingly Ideal: Art, Trade and Power*. Austin: University of Texas Press.

Henrich, Joseph
2001   Cultural Transmission and the Diffusion of Innovations: Adoption Dynamics Indicate That Biased Cultural Transmission Is the Predominate Force of Cultural Change. *American Anthropologist* 103(4):992–1013.
2002   Decision Making, Cultural Transmission, and Adaptation in Economic Anthropology. In *Economic Anthropology: Theory at the Turn of the Century*, edited by J. Ensminger, pp. 251–95. New York: Rowman and Littlefield.

Hodder, Ian
2012   *Entangled: An Archaeology of the Relationships between Human and Things*. Malden, MA: Wiley-Blackwell.

Huang Tsui-mei 黃翠梅
2015   Gongneng yu yuanliu: Erlitou wenhua lusongshi tongpaishi yanjiu 功能與源流：二里頭文化鑲綠松石銅牌飾研究 [Function and Origin: Research on the Turquoise-Inlay Bronze Plaques of the Erlitou Culture]. *Gugong xueshu jikan* 故宮學術季刊 [Palace Museum Journal] 33(1):97–122.

Hursserl, Edmund
1997 [1907] *Thing and Space*. Dordrecht: Springer.

Ingold, Tim
2013   *Making: Anthropology, Archaeology, Art and Architecture*. New York: Routledge.

Jaang, Li
2011   Long-Distance Interactions as Reflected in the Earliest Chinese Bronze Mirrors. In *The Lloyd Cotsen Study Collection of Chinese Bronze Mirrors*, Vol. 2, *Studies*, edited by L. von Falkenhausen, pp. 34–49. Los Angeles: Cotsen Institute of Archaeology Press.
2015   The Landscape of China's Participation in the Bronze Age Eurasian Network. *Journal of World Prehistory* 28:179–213.

Jaffe, Yitzchak, and Rowan Flad
2018   Prehistoric Globalizing Processes in the Tao River Valley, Gansu, China? In *Globalization in Prehistory: Contact, Exchange, and the "People without History*," edited by N. Boivin and M. D. Frachetti, pp. 131–61. Cambridge: Cambridge University Press.

Ji Ping 吉平 and Deng Cong 鄧聰
2018   *Hamin yuqi yanjiu* 哈民玉器研究· [Research on the Jades of Hamin]. Beijing: Zhonghua Shuju.

Kapp, Ernst
2018 [1877] *Elements of a Philosophy of Technology*. Minneapolis: University of Minnesota Press.

Kirkwood, Jeffrey West, and Leif Weatherby
2018   Introduction: The Culture of Operations: Ernst Kapp's Philosophy of Technology. In *Elements of a Philosophy of Technology: On the Evolutionary History of Culture*, edited by J. W. Kirkwood and L. Weatherby, ix–xliii. Minneapolis: University of Minnesota Press.

Knappett, Carl
2013   *Network Analysis in Archaeology: New Approaches to Regional Interaction*. Oxford: Oxford University Press.

Kurlinkus, William Campbell
2014   Crafting Designs: An Archaeology of "Craft" as God Term. *Computers and Composition* 33:50–67.

Latour, Bruno
1993   *We Have Never Been Modern*. Translated by Catherine Porter. Cambridge, MA: Harvard University Press
2005a   *Reassembling the Social: An Introduction to Actor Network Theory*. Oxford: Oxford University Press.
2005b   Third Source of Uncertainty: Objects Too Have Agency. In *Reassembling the Social: An Introduction to Actor Network Theory*, edited by B. Latour, pp. 63–86. Oxford: Oxford University Press.

Leary, John Patrick
2019   *Keywords: The New Language of Capitalism*. Chicago: Haymarket Books.

Lechtman, Heather
1977   Style in Technology—Some Early Thoughts. In *Material Culture: Styles, Organization and Dynamics of Technology*, edited by H. Lechtman and R. S. Merrill, pp. 3–20. St. Paul, MN: West Publishing.

Lechtman, Heather, and Arthur Steinberg
1979   The History of Technology: An Anthropological Point of View. In *The History and Philosophy of Technology*, edited by G. Bugliarello and D. B. Doner, pp. 135–60. Urbana: University of Illinois Press.

Lee, Gyoung-Ah
2017 The Chulmun Period of Korea: Current Findings and Discourse on Korean Neolithic Culture. In *Handbook of East and Southeast Asian Archaeology*, edited by J. Habu, P. V. Lape, and J. W. Olsen, pp. 451–81. New York: Springer-Verlag.

Leipe, Christian, T. Long, Elena A. Sergusheva, Mayke Wagner, and Pavel Tarasov
2019 Discontinuous Spread of Millet Agriculture in Eastern Asia and Prehistoric Population Dynamics. *Science Advances* 5(9):1–9.

Lemonnier, Pierre
1986 The Study of Material Culture Today: Toward an Anthropology of Technical Systems. *Journal of Anthropological Archaeology* 5(2):147–86.
1992 *Elements for an Anthropology of Technology*. Ann Arbor: Museum of Anthropology, University of Michigan.
1993 Introduction. In *Technological Choices: Transformation in Material Cultures since the Neolithic*, edited by P. Lemonnier, pp. 1–35. London: Routledge.

Leroi-Gourhan, Andre
1993 *Gesture and Speech*. Translated by Anna Bostock Berger. Cambridge, MA: MIT Press.

Li Shuicheng 李水城 and Mo Duowen 莫多闻
2004 Donghuishan yizhi tanhua xiaomai niandaikao 東灰山遺址碳化小麥年代考 [Considering the Dating of Wheat at the Site of Donghuishan]. *Kaogu yu wenwu* 考古與文物 [Archaeology and Cultural Relics] 2004(6):51–60.

Li Xinwei
2013 The Later Neolithic Period in the Central Yellow River Valley Area, c. 4000–3000 BC. In *A Companion to Chinese Archaeology*, edited by A. P. Underhill, pp. 213–35. Malden, MA: Blackwell Publishing.

Li, Yung-ti
2021 *Kingly Crafts: The Archaeology of Craft Production in Late Shang China*. New York: Columbia University Press.

Liebmann, Matthew
2015 The Mickey Mouse Kachina and Other "Double Objects": Hybridity in the Material Culture of Colonial Encounters. *Journal of Social Archaeology* 15(3):319–41.

Lin Meicun
2016 Seima-Turbino Culture and the Proto–Silk Road. *Chinese Cultural Relics* 3(1–2):241–62.

Linduff, Kathryn M.
2003 A Walk on the Wild Side: Late Shang Appropriation of Horses in China. In *Prehistoric Steppe Adaptation and the Horse*, edited by Marsha Levine, C. Renfrew, and K. Boyle, pp. 139–62. Cambridge: McDonald Institute for Archaeological Research.

Lister, Diane L., Huw Jones, Hugo R. Oliveira, Cameron A. Petrie, Xinyi Liu, James Cockram, Catherine J. Kneale, Olga Kovaleva, and Martin K. Jones
2019 Barley Heads East: Genetic Analyses Reveal Routes of Spread through Diverse Eurasian Landscapes. *PLOS ONE* 13(7):e0196652.

Liu Li
2003 "The Products of Minds as Well as of Hands": Production of Prestige Goods in the Neolithic and Early State Periods of China. *Asian Perspectives* 42(1):1–40.

Liu, Xinyi, Dorian Q. Fuller, and Martin Jones
2016 Early Agriculture in China. In *The Cambridge World History*, edited by G. Barker and C. Goucher, pp. 310–34. Cambridge: Cambridge University Press.

Liu, Xinyi, Emma Lightfoot, Tasmin C. O'Connell, Hui Wang, Shuicheng Li, Liping Zhou, Yaowu Hu, Giedrė Motuzaitė Matuzevičiūtė, and Martin K. Jones
2014 From Necessity to Choice: Dietary Revolutions in West China in the Second Millennium BC. *World Archaeology* 46(5):661–80.

Liu, Xinyi, Diane L. Lister, Zhijun Zhao, Cameron A. Petrie, Xiongsheng Zeng, Penelope J. Jones, Richard A. Staff, Anil K. Pokharia, Jennifer Bates, Ravindra N. Singh, et al.
2017 Journey to the East: Diverse Routes and Variable Flowering Times for Wheat and Barley En Route to Prehistoric China. *PLOS ONE* 12(11):e0187405.

Long, Tengwen, Christian Leipe, Guiyun Jin, Mayke Wagner, Rongzhen Guo, Oskar Schröder, and Pavel Tarasov
2018 The Early History of Wheat in China from C14 Dating and Bayesian Chronological Modelling. *Nature Plants* 4:272–79.

Lu Liancheng
1993 Chariot and Horse Burials in Ancient China. *Antiquity* 67(257):824–38.

Lü Peng 吕鹏
2010 Zhongguo jiayang huangniu de qiyuan jiqi zai zongjiao yishi zhong de yingyong 中國家養黃牛

的起源在宗教儀式中的應用 [The Significance of the Origins of Cattle Raising in China to Ritual and Religious Practices]. *Zhongguo shehui kexueyuan gudai wenming yanjiu zhongxin tongxun* 中國社會科學院古代文明研究中心通訊 [Reports of the Research Center on Ancient Civilizations of the Chinese Academy of Social Sciences] 20:10–16.

Lü Peng 呂鵬, Yuan Jing 袁靖, and Li Zhipeng 李志鵬
2014 Zailun Zhongguo jiayang huangniu de qiyuan: Shangque "Zhongguo dongbei diqu quanshixinzaoqi huangniu de xingtaixue he jiyinxue zhengju" yiwen 再論中國家養黃牛的起源：商榷'中國東北地區全是新早期黃牛的形態學和基因學證據'疑問 [Another Discussion of the Origins of Domesticated Cattle in China: Considering the "Evidence from Morphology and Genes of Early Holocene Cattle in Northeast China"]. *Nanfang wenwu* 南方文物 [Relics from the South] 2014(3):48–59.

Ma, Minmin, Guanghui Dong, Emma Lightfoot, Hui Wang, Xinyi Liu, X. Jia, K. R. Zhang, and Fahu Chen
2014 Stable Isotope Analysis of Human and Faunal Remains in the Western Loess Plateau, Approximately 2000 Cal BC. *Archaeometry* 56:237–55.

Ma, Minmin, Guanghui Dong, Xinyi Liu, Emma Lightfoot, Fahu Chen, Hui Wang, Hu Li, and Martin K. Jones
2015 Stable Isotope Analysis of Human and Animal Remains at the Qijiaping Site in Middle Gansu, China. *International Journal of Osteoarchaeology* 25(6):923–34.

Ma Minmin, Dong Guanghui, X. Jia, Wang Hui, Y. Cui, and Chen Fahu
2016 Dietary Shift after 3600 Cal Yr BP and Its Influencing Factors in Northwestern China: Evidence from Stable Isotopes. *Quaternary Science Reviews* 145:57–70.

Mair, Victor H.
2003 The Horse in Late Prehistoric China: Wresting Culture and Control from the "Barbarians." In *Prehistoric Steppe Adaptation and the Horse*, edited by Marsha Levine, C. Renfrew, and K. Boyle, pp. 163–87. Cambridge: McDonald Institute for Archaeological Research.

Mao Ruilin 毛瑞林, Qian Yaopeng 錢耀鵬, Xie Yan 谢焱, Zhu Yunyun 朱芸芸, and Zhou Jing 周靜
2009 Gansu Lintan Mogou Qijia wenhua mudi fajue jianbao 甘肅臨潭磨溝齊家文化墓地發掘簡報 [Preliminary Report on the Excavations of the Qijia Culture Cemetery at Mogou in Lintan, Gansu]. *Wenwu* 文物 [Cultural Relics] 2009(10):4–24.

Marx, Leo
2010 Technology: The Emergence of a Hazardous Concept. *Technology and Culture* 51(3):561–77.

Mauss, Marcel
1935 Les techniques du corps. *Journal de Psychologie* 32(3–4):271–93.
1948 Les techniques et la technologie. *Journal de Psychologie* 41:71–78.
1979 [1936] Body Techniques. In *Sociology and Psychology Essays*, edited and translated by Ben Brewster, pp. 97–123. London: Routledge & Kegan Paul.
2012 *Techniques, Technologie et Civilisation*. Paris: Presses Universitaires de France.

Mei, Jianjun, Yongbin Yu, Kunlong Chen, and Lu Wang
2017 The Appropriation of Early Bronze Technology in China. In *Appropriating Innovations: Entangled Knowledge in Eurasia, 5000–1500 BCE*, edited by J. Maran and P. W. Stockhammer, pp. 231–40. Oxford: Oxbow.

Mertens, Matthias
2019 Did Richthofen Really Coin "The Silk Road"? *Silk Road* 17:1–9.

Middleton, Andrew, and Ian Freestone
1995 The Mineralogy and Occurrence of Jade. In *Chinese Jade: From the Neolithic to the Qing*, edited by Jessica Rawson, pp. 413–23. London: British Museum Press.

Miller, Daniel
2010 *Stuff*. Cambridge: Polity Press.

Minar, C. Jill
2001a Learning and Craft Production: An Introduction. *Journal of Anthropological Research* 57(4):369–80.
2001b Motor Skills and the Learning Process: The Conservation of Cordage Final Twist Direction in Communities of Practice. *Journal of Anthropological Research* 57(4):381–405.

Myers, Robert
2011 The Familiar Strange and the Strange Familiar in Anthropology and Beyond. *General Anthropology* 18(2):1, 7–9.

Olsen, Bjørnar Julius 2007. Keeping Things at Arm's Length: A Genealogy of Symmetry. *World Archaeology* 39(4):579–88.

Papadopoulos, John K., and Gary Urton, eds.
2012   *The Construction of Value in the Ancient World*. Los Angeles: Cotsen Institute of Archaeology Press.

Pfaffenberger, Bryan
1992   Social Anthropology of Technology. *Annual Review of Anthropology* 21:491–516.

Pigott, Vincent C.
2018   The Bactria-Margiana Archaeological Complex (BMAC), the Seima-Turbino Horizon and a Possible Eastward Transmission of Tin-Bronze Technology through Later Third Millennium BCE Central Asia to the Altai Mountains/Eastern Steppe. In *How Objects Tell Stories: Essays in Honor of Emma C. Bunker*, edited by Katheryn M. Linduff and Karen S. Rubinson, pp. 191–221. Turnhout: Brepols.

Pinker, Steven
2018   *Enlightenment Now: The Case for Reason, Science, Humanism, and Progress*. New York: Viking.

Qian Yaopeng 錢耀鵬 and Mao Ruilin 毛瑞林
2012   Gansu Lintan Mogou Qijia wenhua mudi fajue ji zhuyao shouhou 甘肅臨潭磨溝齊家文化墓地發掘及主要收穫 [Main Results of the Qijia Culture Cemetery Excavation at Mogou in Lintan, Gansu]. In *Kaoguxue yanjiu (jiu)—Qingzhu Yan Wenming xiansheng bashi shouchen lunwenji* 考古學研究（九）—慶祝嚴文明先生八十壽辰論文集 [Archaeological Research 9: A Collection of Essays in Celebration of Yan Wenming's 80th Birthday], edited by Beijing Daxue Kaogu Wenbo Xueyuan 北京大學考古文博學院 and Beijing Daxue Zhongguo Kaoguxue Yanjiu Zhongxin 北京大學中國考古學研究中心, pp. 638–56. Beijing: Wenwu Chubanshe 文物出版社.

Qian Yaopeng 钱耀鹏, Zhou Jing 周静, Mao Ruilin 毛瑞林, and Xie Yan 谢焱
2009   Gansu Lintan Mogou Qijia wenhua mudi fajue de shouhuo yu yiyi—2008 niandu quanguo shida kaogu xinfaxian zhi yi 甘肅臨潭磨溝齊家文化墓地發掘的收穫與意義— 2008年度全國十大考古新發現"之一 [The Results and Significance of the Excavations of the Qijia Cemetery at Mogou in Lintan, Gansu—One of the Top Ten Archaeological Discoveries of 2008]. *Xibei daxue xuebao (zhesheban)* 西北大學學報（哲社版）[Journal of Northwest University (Philosophy and Social Science)] 39(5):5–10.

Qin Xiaoli 秦小麗
2010   *Zhongguo gudai zhuangshipin yanjiu: xinshiqi shidai—zaoqi qingtong shidai* 中國古代裝飾品研究: 新石器時代—早期青銅時代 [Research on Early Neolithic Bronze Decoratives in China]. Shanxi: Shanxi Shifan Daxue Chubanshe.

2014   Zhongguo gudai xiangqian gongyi yu lvsongshi zhuangshipin 中國古代鑲嵌工藝與綠松石裝飾品 [Ancient Chinese Inlay and Turquoise Ornaments]. In *Xia Shang duyi yu wenhua* (er) 夏商都邑與文化（二）[Cities and Culture of the Xia and Shang Dynasties (2)], edited by Zhongguo Shehui Kexueyuan Kaogu Yanjiusuo 中國社會科學院考古研究所, pp. 296–326. Beijing: Zhongguo Shehui Kexue Chubanshe.

2016   Turquoise Ornaments and Inlay Technology in Ancient China. *Asian Perspectives* 55(2):208–39.

Raphals, Lisa
1992   *Knowing Words: Wisdom and Cunning in the Classical Traditions of China and Greece*. Ithaca: Cornell University Press.

Rawson, Jessica
1993   The Ancestry of Chinese Bronze Vessels. In *A History from Things: Essays on Material Culture*, edited by S. Lubar and W. D. Kingery, pp. 51–73. Washington, DC: Smithsonian Institution Press.

Roberts, B. W., C. P. Thornton, and Vincent C. Pigott
2009   Development of Metallurgy in Eurasia. *Antiquity* 83:1012–22.

Rogers, E. M.
2003 [1962] *Diffusion of Innovations*. New York: Free Press.

Ruan Qiurong 阮秋榮 and Wang Yongqiang 王永强
2017   Xinjiang Nilekexian Jirentai Goukou yizhi 新疆尼勒克縣吉仁台溝口遺址 [The Jartai Pass Site in Nilka County, Xinjiang]. *Kaogu* 考古 [Archaeology] 2017(7):57–70.

Sassaman, Kenneth E., and Wictoria Rudolphi
2001   Communities of Practice in the Early Pottery Traditions of the American Southeast. *Journal of Anthropological Research* 57(4):407–25.

Schlanger, Nathan, ed.
2006   *Marcel Mauss: Techniques, Technology and Civilisation*. New York: Durkheim.

Schubert, Cornelius
2017   Innovation Minus Modernity? Revisiting Some Relations of Technical and Social Change. In *Appropriating Innovations: Entangled Knowledge in Eurasia, 5000–1500 BCE*, edited by J. Maran and P. W. Stockhammer, pp. 4–11. Oxford: Oxbow.

Shaanxi Sheng Kaogu Yanjiuyuan 陝西省考古研究院, Yulin Shi Wenwu Kaogu Kantan Gongzuodui 榆林市文物考古勘探工作隊, Shenmu Xian Wenti Guangdianju 神木縣文體廣電局, and Shenmu Xian Shimao Yizhi Guanlichu 神木縣石峁遺址管理處
2016 *Faxian Shimao gucheng* 發現石峁古城 [The Discovery of the Shimao Site]. Beijing: Wenwu Chubanshe.

So, Jenny F.
2019 Meeting Nature's Challenge: Jade in Prehistoric China (c. 4000–2000 BCE). In *Early Chinese Jades in the Harvard Art Museums*, edited by J. F. So, pp. 49–73. Cambridge, MA: Harvard Art Museums.

Sun Zhouyong 孫周勇, Shao Jing 邵晶, Di Nan 邸楠, Kang Ningwu 康宁武, Zhao Yi 趙益, Shao Anding 邵安定, and Xia Nan 夏楠
2017 Shaanxi Shenmuxian Shimao chengzhi Huangchengtai didian 陝西神木縣石峁城址皇城台地點 [The Huangcheng Locus at the City Site of Shimao, Shaanxi]. *Kaogu* 考古 [Archaeology] 2017(7):46–56.

Sun, Zhouyong, Jing Shao, Li Liu, Jianxin Cui, Michael F. Bonomo, Qinghua Guo, Xiaohong Wu, and Jiajing Wang
2018 The First Neolithic Urban Center on China's North Loess Plateau: The Rise and Fall of Shimao. *Archaeological Research in Asia* 14:33–45.

Tie Yuanshen 鐵元神
2015 Zhongguo beifang jiama qiyuan wenti chutan: yi Ganqing diqu wei tantao zhongxin 中國北方傢馬起源問題初探—以甘青地區為探討中心 [Preliminary Discussion of the Origin of Domesticated Horses in North China—Making the Gansu-Qinghai Region the Center of Investigation]. *Nongye kaogu* 農業考古 [Agricultural Archaeology] 2015(1):241–48.

Van Oyen, Astrid
2015 Actor-Network Theory's Take on Archaeological Types: Becoming, Material Agency and Historical Explanation. *Cambridge Archaeological Journal* 25(1):63–78.

Van Valkenburgh, Parker, S. J. Kelloway, K. L. Privat, B. Sillar, and J. Quilter
2017 Rethinking Cultural Hybridity and Technology Transfer: SEM Microstructural Analysis of Lead Glazed Ceramics from Early Colonial Peru. *Journal of Archaeological Science* 82:17–30.

Ventresca Miller, Alicia R., and Cheryl A. Makarewicz
2019 Intensification in Pastoralist Cereal Use Coincides with the Expansion of Trans-regional Networks in the Eurasian Steppe. *Scientific Reports* 9(1):8363.

Wang Hui 王輝
2012 Gan Qing diqu xinshiqi qingtong shidai kaoguxue wenhua de puxi yu geju 甘青地區新石器青銅時代考古學文化的譜係與格局 [Variants and Patterns in the Neolithic and Bronze Age Cultures of the Gansu-Qinghai Region]. *Kaoguxue yanjiu* 考古學研究 [Archaeological Research] 9:210–43.

Wang, Juan
2018 *A Zooarchaeological Study of the Haimenkou Site, Yunnan Province, China*. Oxford: BAR.

Wang, Yiru
2017 Identifying the Beginnings of Sheep Husbandry in Western China. PhD thesis. Department of Archaeology, University of Cambridge, Cambridge.

Wen, Chenghao
2021 Huangniangniangtai: A Qijia Gateway Community in the Hexi Corridor. *Bulletin of the Museum of Far Eastern Antiquities* 82:181–208.

Wen Guang and Jing Zhichun
1992 Chinese Neolithic Jade: A Preliminary Geoarchaeological Study. *Geoarchaeology* 7(3):251–75.

Wendrich, Willeke, ed.
2013 *Archaeology and Apprenticeship: Body Knowledge, Identity, and Communities of Practice*. Tucson: University of Arizona Press.

Wenger, E.
1998 *Communities of Practice: Learning, Meaning and Identity*. Cambridge: Cambridge University Press.

Whitmore, Christopher
2007 Symmetrical Archaeology: Excerpts of Manifesto. *World Archaeology* 39(4):546–62.

Wilkin, Shevan, Alicia Ventresca Miller, William T. T. Taylor, Bryan K. Miller, Richard W. Hagan, Madeleine Bleasdale, Ashley Scott, Sumiya Gankhuyg, Abigail Ramsøe, S. Uliziibayar, et al.
2020 Dairy Pastoralism Sustained Eastern Eurasian Steppe Populations for 5,000 Years. *Nature Ecology and Evolution* 4(3):346–55.

Wilkinson, Toby C.
2014 *Tying the Threads of Eurasia: Trans-regional Routes and Material Flows in Transcaucasia, Eastern Anatolia and Western Central Asia, c. 2000–1500 BC*. Leiden: Sidestone Press.

Winner, Langdon
1980 Do Artifacts Have Politics? *Daedalus* 109(1):121–36.

Womack, Andrew, Yitzchak Jaffe, Lingyu Hung, Zhou Jing, Wang Hui, Li Shuicheng, Pochan Chen, and Rowan Flad
2017 Mapping Qijiaping: New Work on the Type Site of the Qijia Culture. *Journal of Field Archaeology* 42(6):488–502.

Womack, Andrew, Hui Wang, Jing Zhou, and Rowan Flad
2019 Continuity and Change: A Petrographic Analysis of Clay Recipes in Late Neolithic Northwestern China. *Antiquity* 93(371):1161–77.

Yang Hu 楊虎, Liu Guoxiang 劉國祥, and Deng Cong 鄧聰, eds.
2006 *Yuqi qiyuan tansuo—Xinglongwa yuqi yanjiu yu tulu* 玉器起源探索—興隆洼玉器研究與圖錄 [The Origins of Chinese Jade Culture—Xinglongwa Jades Research and Catalog]. Hong Kong: Chinese University of Hong Kong Press.

Yang, Yishi, Lele Ren, Guanghui Dong, Yifu Cui, Ruiliang Liu, Guoke Chen, Hui Wang, Sheven Wilkin, and Fahu Chen
2019 Economic Change in the Prehistoric Hexi Corridor (4800–2200BP), Northwest China. *Archaeometry* 61(4):957–76.

Yang, Yishi, Shanjia Zhang, Chris Oldknow, Menghan Qiu, Tingting Chen, Haiming Li, Yifu Cui, Lele Ren, Guoke Chen, Hui Wang, and Guanghui Dong
2019 Refined Chronology of Prehistoric Cultures and Its Implication for Re-evaluating Human–Environment Relations in the Hexi Corridor, Northwest China. *Science China Earth Sciences* 62(1674–7313):1578.

Yiru 怡如 [pseud.]
1959 Wenwu gongzuo baodao: Gansusheng Wuwei Qijia wenhua yizhi zhong faxian bugu 文物工作報導: 甘肅省武威齊家文化遺址中發現卜骨 [Report on Cultural Relics Research: Oracle Bones Found in Qijia Culture Contexts in Wuwei, Gansu]. *Wenwu* 文物 [Cultural Relics] 1959(9):71–73.

Yu, Chong
2019 *The Origin of Cattle in China from the Neolithic to the Early Bronze Age*. Oxford: BAR.

Yuan Jing 袁靖
2015 *Zhonguo dongwu kaoguxue* 中國動物考古學 [Chinese Zooarchaeology]. Beijing: Wenwu Chubanshe.

Yuan Jing and Rowan K. Flad
2006 Research on Early Horse Domestication in China. In *Equids in Time and Space*, edited by M. Mashkour, pp. 124–31. Oxford: Oxbow.

Zhang Chi and Marcella Festa
2020 Archaeological Research in the Ili Region: A Review. *Asian Perspectives* 59(2):338–84.

Zhang Dongju, Chen Fahu, Robert L. Bettinger, Loukas Barton, Ji Duxue, Christopher Morgan, Wang Hui, Cheng Xiaozhong, Dong Guanghui, T. P. Guilderson, and Zhao Hui
2010 Archaeological Records of Dadiwan in the Past 60 ka and the Origin of Millet Agriculture. *Chinese Science Bulletin* 55(16):1636–42.

Zhang, Menghan, Shi Yan, Wuyun Pan, and Li Jin
2019 Phylogenetic Evidence for Sino-Tibetan Origin in Northern China in the Late Neolithic. *Nature* 569:112–15.

Zhou, Ligang, and Sandra J. Garvie-Lok
2015 Isotopic Evidence for the Expansion of Wheat Consumption in Northern China. *Archaeological Research in Asia* 4:25–35.

Chapter 12

Organization of Copper Mining and Smelting along the Middle Yangzi River

Shi Tao

The introduction of bronze metallurgy brought not only new technology but also a new knowledge system and worldview to the heartland of China (Chang 1983, 1990). In bronze metallurgy, the first step is mining of the necessary raw materials, such as copper, lead, and tin, so exploration and extraction of these resources are critical for archaeologists to comprehensively understand bronze metallurgy and its social impacts. Archaeologists need to first understand how copper resources were extracted in mines and how they were smelted. In his book *Chinese Society in the Age of Confucius*, Professor Lothar von Falkenhausen (2006) listed several open issues of importance for understanding the Late Bronze Age of China, such as demographic growth and population movements, territorial control and expansion, and such social groups as the military, merchants, entrepreneurs, artisans, and professionals. He asserted that apart from settlements and cemeteries, other types of Late Bronze Age sites, particularly "resource-exploitation and manufacturing sites would provide crucial information on the technical and economic background of the artifacts on which our archaeological chronologies are based" (Falkenhausen 2006:420).

Professor von Falkenhausen's assertion is a reminder that we should pay more attention to resource-rich regions, which are normally distributed in remote, mountainous regions. As several scholars point out, a constant flow of important natural resources was critical to state formation in early China (e.g., Chang 1983; Hubei 2001:502–3; Liu and Chen 2003; Tong 1998). Hence studying the extraction of key natural resources is significant for reconstructing the political-economic landscape of early China. How were key natural resources extracted in early China? What roles did local inhabitants play in resource procurement? How can we look at the relationship between resource extraction and political economy in early centers, such as Erlitou and Zhengzhou? To answer these questions, this article chooses the Tonglüshan mining region in the middle Yangzi River valley as an example and analyzes archaeological remains excavated from metallurgical sites.

Archaeological investigations of copper mines have long been carried out in China. Archaeologists have excavated several important mining and smelting sites in the Zhongtiao Mountains (e.g., Li 1993), the middle Yangzi River valley (e.g., Anhui and Nanling 2002; Huangshi 1999; Liu and Lu 1998), the Liaoxi region (Jilin and Neimenggu 2014), and so on. Moreover, related accompanying studies have been carried out in many aspects, such as the origin of copper metallurgy in China, copper technology, and the ancient copper trade, laying a good foundation for exploring the organization of mining and smelting in this article. In recent decades, archaeologists and archaeometallurgists have started to focus on the organization of metal mining and smelting based on archaeological remains in mining areas in other parts of the world. For example, Pigott (1998), Raber (1987), and Shennan (1998) discussed the organization of copper production, respectively, in the Phu Lon region of Northeast

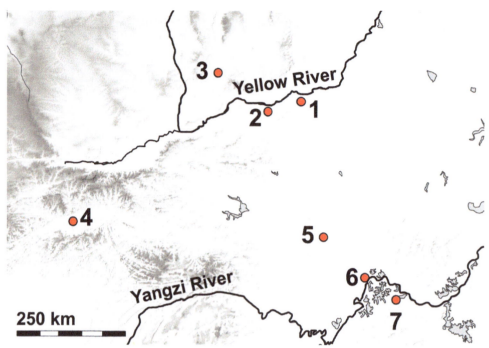

Figure 12.1. Major sites (1–6) and study area (7) mentioned in the text: 1. Zhengzhou; 2. Erlitou; 3. cemetery of the Marquises of Jin; 4. Hanzhong; 5. Yejiashan; 6. Panlongcheng; 7. Tonglüshan region. *Created by Bryan K. Miller.*

Thailand during the last two millennia BCE, in the Polis region in western Cyprus from the eighth century BCE to the fifteenth century CE, and in the Mitterberg region of the eastern Alps during the second millennium BCE. They pointed out that metal production in these regions was carried out on a small scale and was not directly controlled by any single political entity. In contrast, Cantarutti (2013) and Salazar et al. (2013) analyzed archaeological materials from, respectively, the mining complex of Los Infieles in north-central Chile and the Atacamenian territory of northern Chile under Inca rule and suggested that metal mining and metallurgy in the two regions was directly controlled by the Inca state. These and other cases from other parts of the world provide a comparative perspective and lay the foundation for my investigation.

Copper mining and smelting, which are usually interrelated activities, are the focus in this paper. The middle Yangzi River valley region possesses the largest deposit of copper resources in China and is home to many ancient metallurgical sites. While the region extends over more than 500 km from west to east, its mining and smelting sites are primarily concentrated in three regions: Daye-Yangxin, Jiujiang-Ruichang, and Tongling-Nanling (Figure 12.2; Wei 2007:26). Early mining and smelting sites have been found in all three areas, especially in the Daye-Yangxin region, where the Tonglüshan mine currently yields best-preserved assemblages. Through analysis of the mining and smelting sites in and around the Tonglüshan mine, this paper seeks to disentangle the changes in production modes over a long run and to discuss the resource strategies of early states in China.

Tonglüshan

In the Daye-Yangxin district, copper mining and smelting activities likely date to the Longshan period (ca. 2300–1800 BCE), also known as the post-Shijiahe period in the middle Yangzi River region, based on archaeologists having uncovered metallurgical remains at the Dalupu and Xiezidi sites, which are located close to the Tonglüshan mine (Hubei and Huangshi 2010; Hubei et al. 2013:63). A survey in the district of Daye City discovered more than 10 Erlitou-period sites (ca. 1800–1520 BCE), which were hypothesized to be related to copper mining and smelting (Huangshi 1984). Direct evidence of early mining activities comes from Tonglüshan, which has long been the most important copper mine in Daye City (Huangshi 1999). The mining region is located to the southeast of the Yangzi River in Hubei Province (Figure 12.4) and covers an area of 7.8 km², rising gradually from the north to the south. The spatial distribution of ore bodies is separated into two belts, one 2,100 m long by 300–350 m wide and the other 1,850 m long by 100 m wide. Due to the area's long formation process, the Tonglüshan mine contains

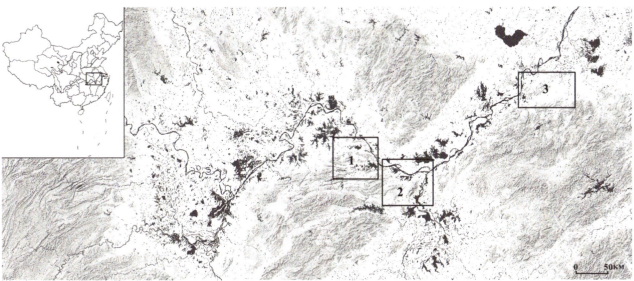

Figure 12.2. Distribution of ancient mining and smelting sites in the middle Yangzi River valleys: 1. Daye-Yangxin district; 2. Jiujiang-Ruichang district; 3. Tongling-Nanling district. *Drawn by the author based on Wei 2007:26, Figure 2.2.*

Figure 12.3. Mining galleries at Location 2, Orebody VII, at the Tonglüshan mine. *Photo by the author.*

a diverse range of ores. Based on the symbiotic relations of minerals, these ores could be categorized to three types, including copper-iron ores, copper ores, and copper-sulfur ores, the first two of which (including malachite, native copper, chalcocite, and cuprite) were probably the main focuses of early miners.

Continuous archaeological excavations have been carried out in the Tonglüshan region, with archaeologists uncovering a large quantity of mining and smelting assemblages in the mining area. Based on current archaeological information, two types of mining methods were probably adopted—surface and underground extraction.

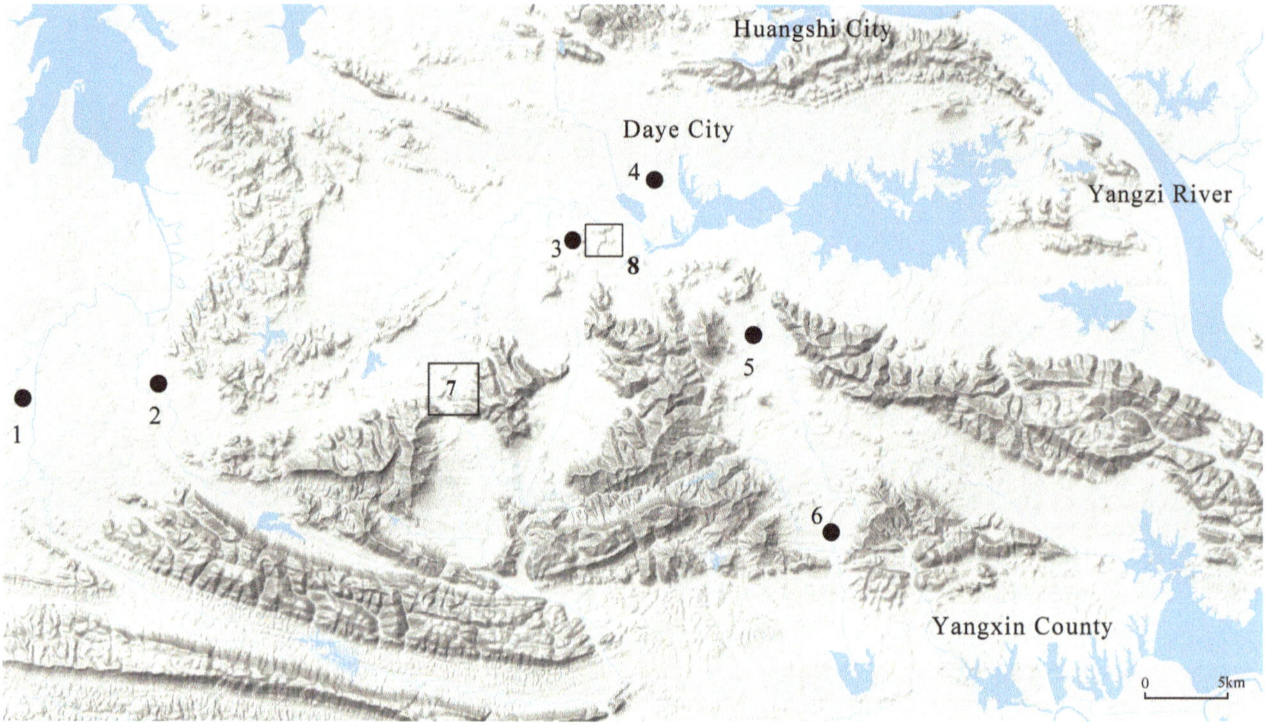

Figure 12.4. Major sites in and around the Tonglüshan region mentioned in this text: 1. Ewangcheng; 2. Xianglushan; 3. Caowangcheng; 4. Xiezidi; 5. Wulijie; 6. Dalupu; 7. Tongshankou copper mine; 8. Tonglüshan mine and preservation zone. *Created by the author.*

Archaeologists have discovered surface activities in seven locations, but the dates of operation are very hard to determine. Underground workings were widely used by ancient miners at Tonglüshan, with a series of excavations uncovering nearly 500 galleries and shafts during the 1970s and 1980s. In these workings, archaeologists collected a large quantity of mining tools made of wood, bamboo, iron, and bronze. These included not only tools for breaking hard rocks, such as axes, adzes, spades, and hammers, but also tools probably used for transporting ores, such as baskets, wood wheels, and so on. The styles of ceramic sherds and radiocarbon dating of wood from galleries suggest that these underground workings were opened as early as 3260 ± 80 BP, roughly contemporaneous with the Late Shang period (ca. 1300–1046 BCE) in China's archaeological context (Figure 12.3). Archaeologists also discovered three smelting sites during the 1970s and 1980s, while a recent survey further found 12 ancient smelting sites in the Tonglüshan mine (Hubei and Daye 2012). The operating time scale of these smelting sites ranges from the Eastern Zhou period (771–221 BCE) to the Qing Dynasty (1636–1912). Although most of these sites were not well preserved because of modern activities, materials from the sites could still provide much information about the organization of early mining in the Tonglüshan region. The following discussion analyzes these mining and smelting sites in detail.

Identifying Organization of Mining and Smelting

This section primarily discusses the model adopted to measure the organization of mining and smelting in the middle Yangzi River valley. Due to the absence of textual evidence about early mining and smelting activities in the distant mountains, anthropological and archaeological reconstructions of production modes are significant to this investigation. Anthropologists and archaeologists have devised a series of concepts to characterize the organization of ancient production. Four parameters are usually adopted to assess organization of production: context, concentration, scale, and intensity (Costin 1991). Acquisition of raw materials was normally considered the first step of the metallurgical production process (Miller 2007:145–46), so mining and smelting could also be measured within the four parameters. Archaeologists can examine these variable parameters through direct and indirect lines of evidence. Direct evidence includes production loci and debris, while indirect evidence includes standardization, efficiency, skills, and other factors. Since indirect evidence mostly takes final products as its focus and usually cannot directly reflect production processes, its effectiveness for evaluating organization has been questioned by many anthropologists and archaeologists (e.g., Arnold 2000; Costin 1991). Moreover, as the remains of mining and smelting activities—such as workings, smelting slag, and mining and smelting implements—are mostly direct evidence for evaluating their organization, this article does not take indirect evidence as the focus, although I touch on it when necessary.

Context delineates the relationship between specialists and demands. Specialists were initially conceptualized as two extreme types—independent specialists and attached specialists—along a continuum (e.g., Costin 1991; Lewis 1996). Independent specialists normally produce utilitarian goods based on general consumers' demands, while attached specialists normally produce prestige or high-value goods based on sponsorship from elites or governments. However, this conceptualization was critiqued by several archaeologists, who proposed that context of production should be defined as a parameter based on "the relationship between producers and those who control the distribution of products" instead of the relationship between manufacturers and types of products (Clark 1995; Flad 2011:24). Moreover, context was not conceptualized as two dichotomies along a continuum. Rather, independent specialists are defined as those who own the rights of completely controlling their products; otherwise contexts should be defined as attached (Flad 2011:25). Moreover, attached production does not mean that all procedures of production have to be directly controlled by those who made decisions about distribution, but it varies in many forms (Flad 2011:25). As Costin (2001) points out, for example, raw materials were usually not directly regulated or highly restricted, even if other procedures of production were strictly controlled. To understand the nature of context, therefore, archaeologists have to carefully explore the relationship between steps of production and distribution. Generally, the archaeological indicators of attachment include a close relationship with governmental facilities, bounded workshop or production units, artifacts relating to administration, and so on, while those of independent production probably yield no or few links with these features.

My discussion in this paper is an attempt to understand the context of mining and smelting of copper resources, which are the first steps in the operational sequence of bronze metallurgy. According to the above standards, attached mining and smelting would probably yield a close link with governmental features. Since mining normally occurs deep in mountainous areas, miners are anticipated be at a distance from large-scale governmental departments. However, it is expected that some artifacts relating to administration would be discovered in or near workings. Smelting is a little more complicated. If smelting occurs near mining workings in mountains, it is also anticipated that some artifacts or features relating to administration would be discovered near the location of smelting activities. If smelting occurs in settlements outside of mines, apart from artifacts relating to administration, it is also possible that large-scale governmental facilities or departments would be discovered at a close distance. In the context of independent mining and smelting, artifacts relating to administration would probably not be discovered, and metallurgical workshops would not be bounded and placed close to governmental departments or elite residences. Rather, they would possibly be close to ordinary domestic structures.

Concentration mainly describes the spatial distribution of production and the relationship between production and landscape, with two extremes—dispersed production, in which production is evenly distributed throughout the region, and nucleated production, in which production is concentrated in a limited number of production centers. For dispersed metallurgical activities, it is anticipated that metallurgical remains would be found in most communities in and around the Tonglüshan mine. In contrast, for nucleated production, it is possible that several kinds of metallurgical remains could be clustered in specific production centers, forming what archaeometallurigists call a mining district (e.g., O'Brien 2015; Stöllner 2014).

The third parameter, as Costin (1991) discussed, is scale of production, which describes the constitution of production units. According to her usage, scale includes two variables: group size and how specialists are involved in production activities. One extreme of scale is individual or kin-based production; the other is large-scale or industrial production. Identifying scale through direct evidence is normally based on the size of production facilities and the output per production unit. Large-scale production generally results in large quantities of refuse and larger facilities (Flad 2011:22). When identifying the scale of mining and smelting activities, it is anticipated that large-scale production would leave a tremendous amount of smelting slag and products, large furnaces or crucibles, permanent mining or smelting communities, and so on (O'Brien 2015:269; Raber 1987; Stöllner 2014). However, small-scale mining and smelting activities are more likely to leave few traces, and those could be easily obliterated by subsequent occupations or mining operations (Stöllner 2014). Also, the facilities, furnaces, and crucibles likely to be used in small-scale mining and smelting activities are not only smaller; they are also usually impermanent.

The last parameter, intensity, refers to the time specialists devote to production activities. One extreme of intensity is part-time production; the other is full-time. Accordingly, scheduling is an important factor in identifying the intensity of specialists (Hagstrum 2001). The most effective way to identify intensity is to examine the range of economic activities based on their remains (Costin 1991). Household- or village-based mining and smelting activities would normally leave not only deposits of metallurgical refuse but also remains related to other types of economic activities. Conversely, full-time operations usually leave only remains closely related to mining and smelting.

Measuring Organization of Mining and Smelting at Tonglüshan

Tonglüshan is the best-investigated mine in the sphere of Chinese archaeology. Surveys in and around this region have discovered metallurgical sites dating from the Longshan period to the Qing Dynasty. By adopting the parameters mentioned above, and based on currently available materials, this paper argues that the organization of mining and smelting in the Tonglüshan region differed before and after the Springs and Autumns period (771–ca. 450 BCE), as detailed below (Figure 12.4).

Concentration

By adopting a regional approach, it is easy to observe the differences in spatial distribution before and after the Springs and Autumns period. Before this era, settlements related to mining and smelting were all distributed around the Tonglüshan and other mines, at least several kilometers away from the mountains where the copper resources were deposited. Three metallurgical communities that existed before the Springs and Autumns period have been discovered near the Tonglüshan and other mines: Dalupu, Xiezidi, and Xianglushan.

The Dalupu and Xiezidi sites have been excavated, and based on ceramic typology, archaeologists have uncovered assemblages from two periods: the Longshan period and the Late Shang–Western Zhou period (ca. 1046–771 BCE). The Xianglushan site has not been excavated, but a survey of the site has collected assemblages from the Longshan and Western Zhou periods (Hubei et al. 2015). The three metallurgical communities were all located on the plains or in basins near the Tonglüshan mine, at least several kilometers from the copper resource heartlands. For example, the Dalupu site is located about 15 km southeast of the Tonglüshan mine and several kilometers to the west of the nearest mountain with copper mines. The tableland where the Dalupu site is located is in a small intermountain basin, with a small stream flowing in front of it. The Dalupu site is only 8 ha in size. The Xiezidi site is located on a plain, approximately 5 km north of the Tonglüshan copper mine, at the intersection of the Jianghan Plain and Tonglüshan Mountain. The Xianglushan site is a little farther away, located at the intersection of a small mountain and a plain about 30 km to the southwest of the Tonglüshan copper mine and 20 km from another important copper deposit, the Tongshankou copper mine (Hubei et al. 2015). Archaeologists have discovered metallurgical remains at these three sites, attesting that the inhabitants of the three communities carried out metallurgical activities from the Longshan to the Western Zhou period. However, as mentioned above, their distance from the copper mines suggests that their metallurgical activities were dispersed rather than nucleated.

During the Springs and Autumns period, the spatial distribution of mining and metallurgical activities changed, with some smelting sites being set up closer to mining sites in copper mines. Although archaeologists have discovered large quantities of mining remains in the workings of Tonglüshan and have asserted that mining there began as early as the Late Shang period, smelting sites are not evidenced until the Springs and Autumns period (Huangshi 1999). According to a recent survey, at least 15 smelting sites existed in the Tonglüshan mine, all at a distance of about 100–500 m from the copper mines (Figure 12.5; Huangshi 1999; Hubei and Daye 2012).[1] Modern exploitations have damaged most of these sites, with only one, Lujianao, remaining relatively well preserved (Hubei and Daye 2013a). Based on the ceramic sherds that have been collected, the earliest sites can be dated to the Eastern Zhou period and the latest to the Qing Dynasty (Hubei and Daye 2013a). Archaeologists have excavated at four of these sites: Yanyinshanjiao, a smelting site at Orebody XI, Lujianao, and Kexitai (Huangshi 1999; Hubei and Daye 2013a, 2013b). The earliest assemblage from the four sites came from the smelting site on Orebody XI, which yielded ceramic sherds dating to the Late Western Zhou period. However, the smelting furnaces at Orebody XI dated to the Springs and Autumns period. Once integrated, the assemblages from the survey suggest that large-scale mining and smelting activities may have started in the Springs and Autumns period.

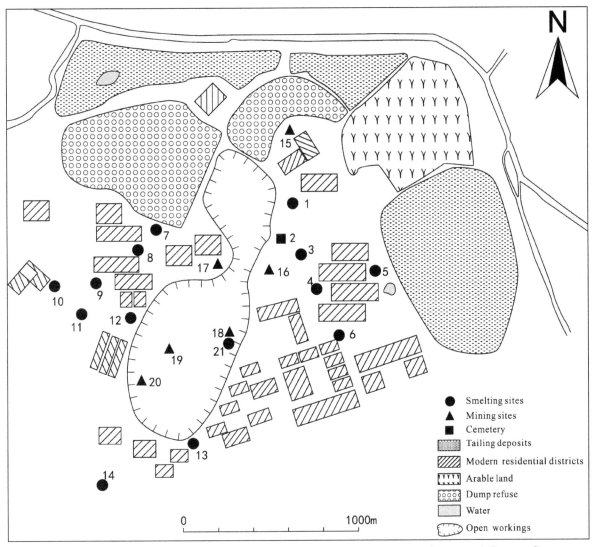

Figure 12.5. Distribution of mining and smelting sites at the Tonglüshan preservation zone: 1. Daquan Caowan; 2. Sifangtang cemetery; 3. Yanyin Shanjiao; 4. Xiongjialong; 5. Zhongzui; 6. Tuzangshan; 7. Qingshan Xiaoqu; 8. Kexitai; 9. Chenru Houbeishan; 10. Lujianao; 11. Wangjiatang; 12. Maocaoshan Dongpo; 13. Maoshan; 14. Nan Dongqiao Caojiawan; 15. Wuya Bulintang; 16. Tonglüshan Museum (a mining site at Orebody VII); 17–21. Possible locations of mining sites at Orebodies IV, XI, II, and I and a smelting site at Orebody XI. *After Shi 2021:Figure 4.*

Scale

It is difficult to determine scale of production absolutely based on archaeological materials. In most circumstances, one can distinguish only the scale of production activities based on comparison. Hence this paper does not directly estimate the scale of mining and smelting activities under the two different organizational forms. The incompleteness of the archaeological evidence does not really allow archaeologists to know the scale of ancient mining and smelting accurately. Thus this paper assesses the scale of mining and smelting before and after the Springs and Autumns period through comparison.

Until now, no mining and smelting communities before the Springs and Autumns period have been discovered by archaeologists inside the Tonglüshan mine; neither have they found any large deposits of smelting refuse nor large-scale metallurgical facilities. According to the above standards, all lines of evidence indicate that mining and smelting at Tonglüshan were probably carried out on a relatively small scale before the Springs and Autumns period. It is possible that ancient miners preliminarily processed and smelted copper ores in situ and brought copper ingots back to their communities. It is also possible that ancient miners directly brought copper ores back to their communities for smelting. The metallurgical remains excavated at the Dalupu and Xiezidi sites attest to this possibility (Hubei et al. 2013).

The metallurgical remains from the Dalupu and Xiezidi sites show that mining and smelting activities in the two communities occurred on a relatively small scale (Hubei and Huangshi 2010; Hubei et al. 2013). Small-scale mining and smelting activities are indicated by a small amount of mining- and smelting-related assemblages, including copper ores, furnace debris, and smelting slag, as well as finished metal objects as an indirect reflection. Few mining and smelting remains at the two sites date from the Longshan period. At the Dalupu site, the Longshan-period mining and smelting remains include only four pieces of ore, one piece of furnace debris, and four pieces of smelting slag. Significantly more mining and smelting remains from the Late Shang–Western Zhou period have been found. Apart from tiny pieces that archaeologists did not bother to collect, these remains include 14 pieces of ore, 31 pieces of smelting slag, and two pieces of furnace debris. The excavators published information on all the associated features, and it is on the basis of these data that we can infer the scale and frequency of smelting activities during this period. The attached charts of the excavation report record a total of 196 ash pits, 46 of which (23%) yielded pieces of smelting slag. However, the amount of smelting slag in each was very small, and the individual pieces of smelting slag were normally only several centimeters in length. Thus, while the currently available materials show that the frequency of metallurgical activities during the Late Shang–Western Zhou period was much greater than during the Longshan period, the limited amount of metal objects and smelting refuse indicated above suggests that the metallurgical activities at the Dalupu community were small on scale. Additionally, seven possible furnace bases dating from the Late Shang–Western Zhou period have also been excavated. Each is 1–1.5 m long and less than 1 m wide. The small furnaces reflect the small-scale smelting activities at Dalupu during this period.

The metallurgical remains from the Xiezidi site are considerably fewer in number than those from Dalupu. The Longshan-period metallurgical remains include only a single piece of malachite and a stone anvil, which was likely used for crushing copper ores. Similar to Dalupu, metallurgical remains from the Western Zhou period increased significantly in number at Xiezidi. They include two bronze arrowheads, one hematite whetstone, one copper ingot, one string of lead-tin alloy, two ceramic molds, one piece of furnace debris, and three undetermined bronze objects. Archaeologists have discovered neither large facilities related to metallurgy nor large deposits of smelting slag, suggesting that only small-scale production was done at Xiezidi before the Springs and Autumns period.

In contrast, the scale of mining and smelting became much larger in the Springs and Autumns period. It has been calculated that the smelting refuse at Tonglüshan amounted to 400,000 metric tons, accumulated to a thickness of 3 m. Surveys in the Tonglüshan mine have not found any smelting sites before the Springs and Autumns period, so it is hypothesized that most of the smelting refuse in the Tonglüshan region was produced during or after this era. A recent survey attests that smelting sites were established close to the Tonglüshan mine and were active from the Springs and Autumns period to the Qing Dynasty (Hubei and Daye 2012). If smelting activities were continuously carried out at the Tonglüshan mine, the average production rate of slag was 148 metric tons per year (400,000 metric tons divided by 2,700 years). Based on data from the Polis region in western Cyprus, Raber (1987) obtained a slag:metal ratio of 9.26:1, if we calculate copper production from the quantities of slag left by early smelting. Adopting this ratio, the mean annual production of metal at Tonglüshan was approximately 15 metric tons per year. This rate assumes a continuous operation over the entire dynastic period. However, smelting activities were not likely to be carried out at an average rate. For instance, the absence of remains from the Yuan Dynasty (1271–1368) suggests that the Tonglushan mine was idle during this time. Therefore, when it was active, the production rate was probably considerably larger than suggested by the average rate. But the average rate would be sufficient to show that the scale of exploitation greatly increased vis-à-vis that reflected by metallurgical remains at Dalupu and Xiezidi, even though some factors unavoidably cannot be incorporated in the calculation.

Starting from the Springs and Autumns period, many smelting locales were set up in the Tonglüshan mine. Archaeologists have uncovered several of them. At the Yanyinshanjiao locus, excavations uncovered assemblages from four periods: the Springs and Autumns period, the Warring States period (ca. 450–221 BCE), the Han Dynasty (202 BCE–220 CE), and the Qing Dynasty. The Springs and Autumns assemblage is the most important of these (Hubei and Daye 2013b). The features of this period include a layer of a beneficiation field (a field used to select useful ores and remove useless minerals), tailings (the wastes of beneficiation), a clay pool, and a furnace. Together these constitute an intact operational sequence of metal production from beneficiation, washing, and smelting to ingot making. At the Lujianao locus, archaeologists uncovered furnaces and working shelters dating to the Han Dynasty and collected ceramic sherds and other objects dating to the Tang (618–907) to Song (960–1279) Dynasties and the Ming (1368–1644) to Qing Dynasties (Hubei and Daye 2013a). These features suggest that permanent mining and smelting communities had been constructed by the Springs and Autumns period. Moreover, the survey discovered layers of smelting slag at almost all loci distributed in the Tonglüshan mine. The tremendous deposits of smelting slag, permanent infrastructures, the intact operational sequence, and the closeness to mines show that the scale of copper mining and smelting in the Tonglüshan region was much larger than that before the Springs and Autumns period.

Intensity

To interpret intensity of production, it is most important to look at the range of economic activities in which households (or other production units) were involved. Scheduling is an important factor in estimating intensity of production. Costin (1991) pointed out that efficiency is also an important factor. It is obvious that the sites close to the copper mines at Tonglüshan were more efficient in terms of their mining, transportation, and smelting activities than were those communities outside the mine. Hence this paper mainly focuses on the economic activities in which these communities participated.

The archaeological information from the Dalupu, Xiezidi, and Xianglushan sites attests that their inhabitants participated in multiple types of economic activities before the Springs and Autumns period (Hubei and Huangshi 2010; Hubei et al 2013, 2015). At the Dalupu site, for example, the metallurgical remains comprise only a tiny amount of the Longshan and Late Shang–Western Zhou assemblages. A large amount of agricultural and textile production tools was uncovered in the Longshan assemblage, indicating that agriculture and household craft production probably dominated the economy of the Dalupu community during the Longshan period. Although the quantity of metallurgical remains increased significantly during the Late Shang–Western Zhou period, metallurgy probably still occupied a small proportion of the economy in the Dalupu community. A total 106 stone tools have been excavated; most were agricultural production tools. They include knives, axes, spades, and adzes. Textile production was also important in the economy, as evidenced by 87 ceramic spindle whorls. Moreover, 43 ceramic paddles and anvils—tools for making ceramics—have been excavated, showing that ceramic production was another important component of the economy at Dalupu. These materials clearly show that Dalupu inhabitants participated in diverse economic activities during the Late Shang–Western Zhou period. Based on the number of these tools found, it appears that metallurgy was only a small portion of all production activities.

Similar ranges of economic activities have been discovered at Xiezidi and Xianglushan. As shown in Figure 12.6., the economy of the Xiezidi community was agriculture-based, including such other economic activities as textile production and ceramic production, with metallurgy probably being only a minor economic activity. The Xianglushan site has not been excavated, but a survey of the site has identified assemblages from the Longshan and Western Zhou periods. A total of 25 metallurgical remains have been collected in the Western Zhou assemblage, including 11 pieces of furnace debris and 19 pieces of smelting slag. Additionally, one stone axe, one stone adze, and two ceramic spindle whorls were collected. Since the site has not been excavated, it is not possible to estimate the mode of metallurgical production. However, current materials indicate that agriculture and metallurgy were both carried out in the Xianglushan community during the Western Zhou period, with metallurgy being only one of the tasks in which inhabitants engaged.

Based on the materials from the three sites, it can be readily concluded that mining and smelting around the Tonglüshan mine before the Springs and Autumns period was probably a part-time activity. Although the materials are still few, the two ceramic molds retrieved from Xiezidi suggest that these communities could not only smelt copper ores before the Springs and Autumns period, they could produce some final metal products, even though we still do not know how sophisticated their metallurgical technologies were.

During the Springs and Autumns period, the intensity of mining and smelting started to change at Tonglüshan in two aspects. First, unlike the communities that predate the Springs and Autumns period, the economic activities of the communities in the Tonglüshan mine were all mining- and smelting-related. Among the sites that have been excavated, none has yielded remains relevant to other types of economic activities. For example, objects excavated at the Yanyinshanjiao site include iron ores, copper ores, native copper, smelting slag, furnace debris, splints, bamboo objects, and a small amount of ceramic sherds (Hubei and Daye 2013b). Except for the ceramic sherds, which were probably related to ancient miners' meals, the other objects are all related to metallurgical activities. No agriculture-related production tools, such as stone axes, adzes, or ceramic spindle whorls, have been excavated. Similarly, at Lujianao, archaeologists have yet to excavate any agriculture-related production tools (Hubei and Daye 2013a).

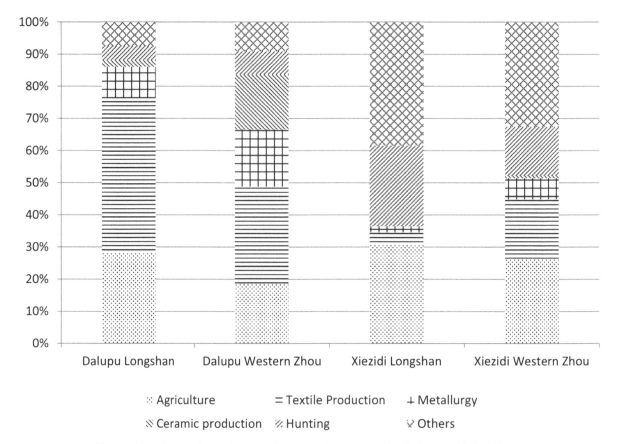

Figure 12.6. Comparison of production-related remains at the Dalupu and Xiezidi sites. *Redrawn from Hubei and Huangshi 2010; Hubei et al. 2013.*

The large number of objects related to metallurgy and the absence of agricultural and other production tools suggest that the communities present in the Tonglüshan mine region after the Springs and Autumns period were probably specifically established for metallurgy. Second, it should be emphasized that the production content in these communities was different from that in Dalupu and Xiezidi. No casting remains, such as molds, have been excavated at these sites, showing that these communities probably specialized in production of copper ingots instead of final products (Hubei and Daye 2013b).

Context

Generally, as mentioned above, attached production is usually archaeologically indicated by the existence of artifacts relating to administration and close relationships with governmental facilities. This type of evidence should not be found if mining or smelting were independently carried out. The recent excavation of the Sifangtang cemetery has shed much light on the context of mining and smelting in the Tonglüshan mine. The Sifangtang cemetery is located to the north of the Tonglüshan Museum and covers an area of 1.5 ha (Hubei and Daye 2015). Until now, a total of 258 tombs have been excavated. Of these, 246 are dated to the Western and Eastern Zhou periods. Although a detailed excavation report has not been published yet, it can be concluded that most of these tombs were built during the Springs and Autumns period, since of the 123 currently published tombs, three have been dated to the Western Zhou period while the other 120 have been dated to the Springs and Autumns period (Chen et al. 2017). Contemporaneous with the Sifangtang cemetery, Orebody VII was exploited during the Springs and Autumns period. Hence it can be concluded that the cemetery was closely related to copper mining in Tonglüshan. The tomb occupants of the Sifangtang cemetery were likely workers and staff who undertook the tasks of exploiting and monitoring mining and smelting at Tonglüshan (Hubei and Daye 2015).

The existence of the Sifangtang cemetery shows that a regulatory system for copper mining and smelting had been built up at Tonglüshan during the Springs and Autumns period. Although three tombs dated to the Western Zhou period, it is hard to determine whether an administrative system had been established at that time. However, the 120 tombs and the large amount of materials excavated at Tonglüshan attest to the existence of such an administration during the Springs and Autumns period. In the Sifangtang cemetery, according to Chen and Chen (2015), the scales of tombs suggest status differentiation. Two types of tombs have been identified. One type includes only two tombs: M1 and M34, whose areas are much larger than those of the other tombs. The occupant of M1 was interred in a double coffin, whereas others were interred in only a single coffin or none at all. Moreover, the other tombs range in size from 2–3 m^3, much smaller than both M1 and M34. This status differentiation suggests that a regulatory system related to copper mining and smelting was probably set up at Tonglüshan. However, the occupants of these tombs were probably low-status staff rather than high-status elites (Chen and Chen 2015; Chen et al. 2017). This argument is supported by the fact that the grave goods interred in all tombs were very few in number, and those retrieved from M1 do not largely outnumber those found in other tombs. Additionally, jade objects similar to those found in M1 were also retrieved from smaller tombs. These lines of evidence show that there was probably not marked status differentiation between the two types of tombs (Chen and Chen 2015).

It can also be seen that military forces were present at Tonglüshan during the Springs and Autumns period. Archaeologists have excavated bronze weapons from 13 tombs at Sifangtang, such as *ge* daggers and a *pi* sword, suggesting that the tomb occupants were probably soldiers responsible for controlling and protecting copper mining at Tonglüshan (Chen and Chen 2015; Chen et al. 2017; Hubei and Daye 2015). These lines of evidence show that copper mining and smelting in the Tonglüshan mine were probably directly controlled by state powers during the Springs and Autumns period. While there is, of course, no clear evidence of a state's direct control after the Springs and Autumns period, from the existence of many smelting sites dating from this era, it is anticipated that remains related to state control will be discovered in future fieldwork.

Discussion

By considering four parameters of the organization of production, this paper summarizes the diachronic change in mining and smelting in the middle Yangzi River valley and concludes that copper mining and smelting activities in the Tonglüshan region were organized differently before and after the Springs and Autumns period. Before the Springs and Autumns period, the organization of copper mining and smelting can be characterized as follows:

1. Settlements that conducted copper mining and smelting activities were distributed far from copper mines.
2. The scale of mining and smelting was relatively small.
3. Miners and smelters were part-time, and metallurgy occupied only a small proportion of their economies, which were dominated by agriculture and other kinds of craft production.
4. Copper mining and smelting were probably household- or village-based.

In contrast, the organization of copper mining and smelting from the Springs and Autumns period onward and can be summarized as follows:

1. Smelting sites were normally distributed close to workings, normally within several hundred meters. The concentration of smelting sites around copper mines formed what archaeometallurgists call a mining district (e.g., O'Brien 2015; Stöllner 2014).
2. The scale of mining and smelting was much larger than in previous periods.
3. Mining and smelting were the primary tasks of the workers in the Tonglüshan mine. No evidence of agricultural work has been discovered, suggesting that workers were highly specialized. These workers were responsible only for making copper ingots, which were probably transported to larger metallurgical centers and cast into final products there.
4. An administrative and protective system was established.

The differences in organization of mining and smelting are important for the discussion of resource strategies in ancient China diachronically. As mentioned above, copper mining and smelting before the Springs and Autumns period was small-scale, part-time, and household- or village-based. Under this mode, metallurgy was probably a supplemental part of a mainly agrarian economy; miners and smelters were primarily agriculturalists, whose principal work was plant cultivation and other types of craft production rather than metallurgy. Moreover, the existence of many types of metallurgical remains shows that metallurgical communities needed to accommodate a variety of metal production procedures, such as mining, smelting, and casting. Taken together, these factors would likely hinder the efficiency of mining and smelting, leading to low rates of metal production. Thus it is very unlikely these activities fell under direct state control, since the high economic, political, and military costs thereof would have lessened their efficiency and made them unattractive. It is hard to imagine that early states would spend much energy directly controlling copper resource extractions and smelting given the few benefits they would receive from the resultant small supply of copper resources. The sporadic mining and smelting activities, as a supplemental part of economy, were more likely to be a risk avoidance or profit maximization strategy of local communities.

The absence of state control in the Tonglüshan region suggests that copper resources could possibly flow physically "freely." As a supplemental part of local economy, local communities indeed determined the directions of resource flow. Therefore the directions of copper resource flow would be random to some extent. Recently published articles pertinent to movement of metals, with methods of scientific testing, support this argument. For example, Liu et al. (2019) integrated data from published chemical analyses of bronze objects from the Erligang-period sites (ca. 1550–1400 BCE) Panlongcheng and Zhengzhou, as well as bronze objects from the Hanzhong basin, and argued that Panlongcheng and Zhengzhou, even though they shared a large amount of metal, differed partially in their access to sources of raw metal. As for copper, copper-containing nickel was present but rarely found at Zhengzhou. It is possible that metals from Hanzhong were transported to Panlongcheng and remelted there. Lead isotope analysis of bronze objects from the Early Western Zhou–period site Yejiashan shows that copper sources were diverse (Yu et al. 2016). Copper was not only from the Tonglüshan region but also probably from the eastern Qinling Mountains. Moreover, Li and Cui (2018) integrated information from bronze inscriptions, ceramic assemblages, and scientific testing of trace elements of bronze objects from the cemetery of the Marquises of Jin (at Beizhao, Quwo [Shanxi]) and found that, during the Western Zhou and Early Springs and Autumns period, bronze objects in the Jin state in southern Shanxi Province also imported copper resource from the middle Yangzi River regions. These studies resemble my conclusion in this article: copper mining and smelting before the Springs and Autumns period were not directly controlled or monopolized by states.

The absence of control over copper mining and smelting does not mean early states did not take actions to secure their resource supply. Take the Erligang period as an example. It is widely accepted that Panlongcheng was set up as an outpost of the Erligang state, as demonstrated by the existence of a wall-enclosed settlement measuring 7.5 ha at Panlongcheng and by the similarities of ceramics, bronze vessels, and tombs between Panlongcheng and Zhengzhou (Hubei 2001). The metallurgical remains suggest that Panlongcheng also conducted bronze metallurgy, and some of the copper resources probably came from Tonglüshan region. However, the close sociopolitical link between Panlongcheng and Zhengzhou does not mean the same degree of link between Panlongcheng and Tonglüshan. Based on my above analysis, copper mining and smelting in Tonglüshan before the Springs and Autumns period were not controlled by states. Rather I propose that they were local activities that supplemented local economies. Therefore the relationship between Panlongcheng and Tonglüshan was more possibly based on trade instead of control. The close sociopolitical link between Panlongcheng and Zhengzhou, and the local mode of copper mining and smelting, suggests that the Erligang state's copper resource strategy more possibly focused on distribution rather than resource extraction. That is to say, the state set up the Panlongcheng outpost and undertook the absorption and transportation of copper resources instead of directly controlling resource mining and smelting due to the aforementioned high cost-efficiency rate. This model of resource strategy resembles my analysis of copper mining and smelting in the Tonglüshan mine, the archaeological materials from Panlongcheng and Zhengzhou, and the data of scientific testing on bronze objects in early China.

Although current archaeological information shows that metallurgical production was attached to elites from the beginning of the Chinese Bronze Age (Chang 1983; Liu and Chen 2003), copper mining and smelting in the Tonglüshan area had been directly controlled by ancient states only since the Springs and Autumns period. Multiple lines of evidence show that mining and smelting became a specialized activity starting in the Springs and Autumns period. Smelting sites in the Tonglüshan mine undertook the tasks of producing copper ingots, which were supposed to be transported to larger metallurgical centers outside the region, such as the wall-enclosed settlements Wulijie, Ewangcheng, and Caowangzui (Chen and Lian 2018:48; Daye 1983; Hubei 2006).[2] Smelting remains dating to the Springs and Autumns period have also been discovered at Wulijie and nearby sites, suggesting that smelting activities were still carried out in communities outside the Tonglüshan mine during this period.

We can suggest why ancient states started to control copper mining and smelting in the Springs and Autumns period. As mentioned by von Falkenhausen (2006), Chinese society underwent an abrupt transformation during the Eastern Zhou period, featuring the innovation of a centrally administered bounded territory, the emergence of bronze coinage, rapid increase of population, prosperity of mercantile activities, and so on. The change in the organization of copper mining and smelting was synchronic with and likely related to these transformations. For example, "the development of the former nucleated polities to territorial states" required a tightening strategy of territorial control during the Eastern Zhou period (Stumpfeldt 1970, from Falkenhausen 2006:406). Hence the exact bordering of territory was one of the most important affairs for states. As copper was a key resource in ancient China, direct control of copper mining and smelting probably became an effective strategy to declare states' ownership. Moreover, with the emergence of bronze coinage and the fast-developing economy, states needed a high degree of central control over copper mining and smelting to sustain their economic stability (Glahn 2016:72). In general, the change of the copper mining and smelting mode coincides with the grand Chinese history.

Acknowledgments

This study was financially sponsored by the Chiang Ching-kuo Foundation for International Scholarly Exchange (Grant DD048-A-15), National Social Science Fund of China (Grant 21CKG005), and Sichuan University (Grant 2022CX15). I would like to thank Professor Lothar von Falkenhausen, Li Min, Anke Hein, Rowan Flad, and Bryan Miller for their kind suggestions. Chen Shuxiang, Xi Qifeng, and Hu Changchun from Hubei Provincial Institute of Archaeology gave me a chance to visit the Tonglüshan site and introduced their knowledge of copper mining. I would like to thank Maria Khayutina and other reviewers for their suggestions and comments.

Notes

1 During the 1970s and 1980s, archaeologists excavated six mining sites at Orebodies I, II, IV, VII, and XI and two smelting sites at Orebody XI and Kexitai Village. Except for the mining site at Orebody VII and the smelting site at Kexitai, the sites are not marked on maps published in 2012 and 2018. I speculate their locations based on the map and descriptions of their locations in the excavation report published in 1999.

2 According to current materials, Wulijie was constructed in the transitional period from the Western Zhou to the Eastern Zhou and was abandoed in the Middle Springs and Autumns period, Ewangcheng was constructed in the Warring States period and was continuously occupied to the Qing Dynasty, and Caowangzui was constructed in the Springs and Autumns period and was abandoned in the Western Han Dynasty (202 BCE–8 CE) (Chen and Lian 2018:47–48).

References

Anhui Sheng Wenwu Kaogu Yanjiusuo 安徽省文物考古研究所 and Nanling Xian Wenwu Guanlisuo 南陵縣文物管理所
2002 Anhui Nanling xian gu tongkuang caiye yizhi diaocha yu shijue 安徽南陵縣古銅礦采冶遺址調查與試掘 [Survey and Test Excavation of Ancient Copper Mining and Smelting Sites in Nanling County, Anhui]. *Kaogu* 考古 2002(2):45–54.

Arnold, Dean E.
2000 Does the Standardization of Ceramic Pastes Really Mean Specialization? *Journal of Archaeological Method and Theory* 7(4):333–73.

Cantarutti, Gabriel E.
2013 Mining Under Inca Rule in North-Central Chile: The Los Infieles Mining Complex. In *Mining and Quarrying in the Ancient Andes: Sociopolitical, Economic and Symbolic Dimensions*, edited by Nicholas Tripcevich and Kevin J. Vaughn, pp. 185–211. New York: Springer.

Chang Kwang-chih 張光直
1983 *Art, Myth and Ritual: The Path to Political Authority in Ancient China*. Cambridge, MA: Harvard University Press.
1990 Cong Shang Zhou qingtongqi tan wenming yu guojia de qiyuan 從商周青銅器談文明與國家的起源 [Origins of Civilization and States Based on Bronze Vessels of Shang and Zhou]. In *Zhongguo Qingtong Shidai* II 中國青銅時代（二集）[Chinese Bronze Age, Vol. 2], by Chang Kwang-chih, pp. 115–30. Beijing: Sanlian Shudian.

Chen Lixin 陳立新 and Chen Shuxiang 陳樹祥
2015 Shilun Daye Tonglüshan Sifangtang mudi de xingzhi 試論大冶銅綠山四方塘墓地的性質 [A Discussion on the Nature of the Sifangtang Cemetery at Tonglüshan, Daye City]. *Jianghan kaogu* 江漢考古 2015(5):95–102.

Chen Shuxiang 陳樹祥 and Lian Hong 連紅, eds.
2018 *Tonglüshan Kaogu Yinxiang* 銅綠山考古印象. Beijing: Wenwu Chubanshe.

Chen Shuxiang 陳樹祥, Luo Jingjing 羅晶晶, and Zhao Yibo 趙藝博
2017 Chuguo jinglüe E dongnan tongkuang ziyuan de kaoguxue guancha 楚國經略鄂東南銅礦資源的考古學觀察 [An Archaeological Observation of Chu's Regulation on Copper Resources in Southeastern Hubei]. *Hubei Ligong Xueyuan xuebao* 湖北理工學院學報 34(2):1–7.

Clark, John E.
1995 Craft Specialization as an Archaeological Category. *Research in Economic Anthropology* 16:267–94.

Costin, Cathy Lynne
1991 Craft Specialization: Issues in Defining, Documenting, and Explaining the Organization of Production. *Archaeological Method and Theory* 3:1–56.
2001 Craft Production Systems. In *Archaeology at the Millennium: A Sourcebook*, edited by Gary M. Feinman and T. Douglas Price, pp. 273–327. New York: Springer.

Daye Xian Bowuguan 大冶縣博物館
1983 Ewangcheng yizhi diaocha jianbao 鄂王城遺址調查簡報. *Jianghan kaogu* 江漢考古 1983(3):23–28.

Falkenhausen, Lothar von
2006 *Chinese Society in the Age of Confucius (1000–250 BC): The Archaeological Evidence*. Los Angeles: Cotsen Institute of Archaeology Press.

Flad, Rowan
2011 *Salt Production and Social Hierarchy in Ancient China*. Cambridge: Cambridge University Press.

Glahn, Richard von
2016 *The Economic History of China*. Cambridge: Cambridge University Press.

Hagstrum, Melissa
2001 Household Production in Chaco Canyon Society. *American Antiquity* 66(1):47–55.

Huangshi Shi Bowuguan 黃石市博物館
1984 Daye gu wenhua yizhi kaogu diaocha 大冶古文化遺址考古調查 [Archaeological Survey of Ancient Sites in Daye City]. *Jianghan kaogu* 江漢考古 1984(4):8–16.
1999 *Tonglüshan gu kuangye yizhi* 銅綠山古礦冶遺址 [Ancient Mining and Smelting Sites in Tonglüshan]. Beijing: Wenwu Chubanshe.

Hubei Sheng Wenwu Kaogu Yanjiusuo 湖北省文物考古研究所
2001 *Panlongcheng: 1963–1964 nian kaogu fajue baogao* 盤龍城—1963–1964年考古發掘報告 [Palongcheng—Report of 1963–1964 Excavations]. Beijing: Wenwu Chubanshe.
2006 *Daye Wulijie—chunqiu chengzhi yu zhouwei yizhi kaogu baogao* 大冶五裡界—春秋城址與周圍遺址考古報告 [Wulijie in Daye—Archaeological Report of the Springs and Autumns Wall-Enclosed Settlement and Nearby Sites]. Beijing: Kexue Chubanshe.

Hubei Sheng Wenwu Kaogu Yanjiusuo 湖北省文物考古研究所 and Daye Shi Tonglüshan Gu Tongkuang Yizhi Baohu Guanli Weiyuanhui 大冶市銅綠山古銅礦遺址保護管理委員
2012 Hubei sheng Daye shi Tonglüshan gu tongkuangye yizhi baohuqu diaocha jianba 湖北省大冶市銅綠山古銅礦冶遺址保護區調查簡報 [Preliminary Survey Report of the Conservation Area of Mining and Smelting Sites at Tonglüshan, Daye City, Hubei Province]. *Jianghan kaogu* 江漢考古 2012(4):18–34.
2013a Daye shi Tonglüshan Lujianao yelian fajue jianbao 大冶市銅綠山盧家塰冶煉遺址發掘簡報 [Preliminary Excavation Report of the Smelting Site at Lujianao in Tonglüshan, Daye City]. *Jianghan kaogu* 江漢考古 2013(2):3–21.
2013b Hubei Daye Tonglüshan Yanyinshanjiao yizhi fajue jianbao 湖北大冶銅綠山岩陰山腳遺址發掘簡報 [Preliminary Excavation Report of the Yanyinshanjiao Site in Daye City, Hubei]. *Jianghan kaogu* 江漢考古 2013(3):7–26.
2015 Daye Tonglüshan Sifangtang mudi di yi ci kaogu zhuyao shouhuo 大冶銅綠山四方塘墓地第一次考古主要收穫 [Result of the First Excavation at the Sifangtang Cemetery at Tonglüshan, Daye City]. *Jianghan kaogu* 江漢考古 2015(5):35–44.

Hubei Sheng Wenwu Kaogu Yanjiusuo 湖北省文物考古研究所 and Huangshi Shi Bowuguan 黃石市博物館
2010 Daye Xiezidi yizhi 2009 nian fajue jianbao 大冶蟹子地遺址2009年發掘簡報 [Preliminary Report of 2009 Excavation at the Xiezidi Site in Daye City]. *Jianghan kaogu* 江漢考古 2010(4):18–62.

Hubei Sheng Wenwu Kaogu Yanjiusuo 湖北省文物考古研究所, Beijing Keji Daxue Yejin Yu Cailiaoshi Yanjiusuo 北京科技大學冶金與材料史研究所, Daye Shi Bowuguan 大冶市博物館, and Daye Ewangcheng Baohuzhan 大冶鄂王城保護站
2015 Hubei Daye shi Xianglushan yizhi diaocha jianbao 湖北大冶市香爐山遺址調查簡報 [Preliminary Survey Report at the Xianglushan Site in Daye City, Hubei]. *Jianghan kaogu* 江漢考古 2015(2):29–39.

Hubei Sheng Wenwu Kaogu Yanjiusuo 湖北省文物考古研究所, Hubei Sheng Huangshi Shi Bowuguan 湖北省黃石市博物館, and Hubei Sheng Yangxin Xian Bowuguan 湖北省陽新縣博物館
2013 *Yangxin Dalupu* 陽新大路鋪 [The Dalupu Site in Yangxin]. Beijing: Wenwu Chubanshe.

Jilin Daxue Bianjiang Kaogu Yanjiu Zhongxin 吉林大學邊疆考古研究中心 and Neimenggu Zizhiqu Wenwu Kaogu Yanjiusuo 內蒙古自治區文物考古研究所
2014 Neimenggu Keshiketeng qi Xiquegou yizhi fajue jianbao 內蒙古克什克騰旗喜鵲溝遺址發掘

簡報 [Preliminary Report of the Excavation at Hexigten Banner in Inner Mongolia]. *Kaogu* 考古 2014(9):3–15.

Lewis, Brandon S.
1996 The Role of Attached and Independent Specialization in the Development of Sociocultural Complexity. *Research in Economic Anthropology* 17:357–88.

Li Haichao 黎海超 and Cui Jianfeng 崔劍鋒
2018 Shi lun Jin, Chu jian de tongliao liutong 試論晉、楚間的銅料流通. *Kaogu yu wenwu* 考古與文物 2018(2):96–101.

Li Yanxiang 李延祥
1993 Zhongtiaoshan gu tong kuangye yizhi chubu kaocha 中條山古銅礦冶遺址初步考察 [Preliminary Survey of Ancient Copper Mining and Smelting Sites in the Zhongtiao Mountains]. *Wenwu jikan* 文物季刊 2:64–78.

Liu Li and Chen Xingcan
2003 *State Formation in Early China*. London: Duckworth.

Liu, Ruiliang, A. Mark Pollard, Jessica Rawson, Xiaojia Tang, Peter Bray, and Changping Zhang
2019 Panlongcheng, Zhengzhou and the Movement of Metal in Early Bronze Age of China. *Journal of World Prehistory* 32:393–428.

Liu Shizhong 劉詩中 and Lu Benshan 盧本珊
1998 Jiangxi Tongling tongkuang yizhi de fajue yu yanjiu 江西銅嶺銅礦遺址的發掘與研究 [Excavation and Study of Copper Mine Sites in Tongling, Jiangxi Province]. *Kaogu xuebao* 考古學報 1998(4):465–96.

Miller, Heather M.
2007 *Archaeological Approaches to Technology*. London: Elsevier.

O'Brien, William
2015 *Prehistoric Copper Mining in Europe*. Oxford: Oxford University Press.

Pigott, Vincent C.
1998 Prehistoric Copper Mining in the Context of Emerging Community Craft Specialization in Northeast Thailand. In *Social Approaches to an Industrial Past: The Archaeology and Anthropology of Mining,* edited by A. Bernard Knapp, Vincent Pigott, and Eugenia W. Herbert, pp. 205–25. London: Routledge.

Raber, Paul
1987 Early Copper Production in the Polis Region, Western Cyprus. *Journal of Field Archaeology* 14(3):297–312.

Salazar, Diego, César Borie, and Camila Oñate
2013 Mining, Commensal Politics, and Ritual Under Inca Rule in Atacama, Northern Chile. In *Mining and Quarrying in the Ancient Andes: Sociopolitical, Economic, and Symbolic Dimensions*, edited by Nicholas Tripcevich and Kevin J. Vaughn, pp. 253–74. New York: Springer.

Shennan, Stephen
1998 Producing Copper in the Eastern Alps during the Second Millennium BC. In *Social Approaches to an Industrial Past: The Archaeology and Anthropology of Mining*, edited by A. Bernard Knapp, Vincent C. Pigott, and Eugenia W. Herbert, pp. 191–204. London: Routledge.

Shi, Tao
2021 Copper Mining and Metallurgy in the Zhongtiao Mountains and Yangzi River Valleys in Early China. *Asian Perspectives* 60(2):382–416.

Stöllner, Thomas R.
2014 Methods of Mining Archaeology. In *Archaeometallurgy in Global Perspective: Methods and Syntheses*, edited by Benjamin W. Roberts and Christopher P. Thornton, pp. 133–60. New York: Springer.

Stumpfeldt, Hans
1970 *Staatsverfassung und Territorium im antiken China: Über die Ausbildung einer territorialen Staatsverfassung*. Düsseldorf: Bertelsmann Universitätsverlag.

Tong Weihua 佟偉華
1998 Shangdai qianqi Yuanqu pendi de tongzhi zhongxin—Yuanqu Shangcheng 商代前期垣曲盆地的統治中心—垣曲商城. *Zhongguo lishi bowuguan guankan* 中國歷史博物館館刊 1:89–100.

Wei Guofeng 魏國鋒
2007 Gudai qingtongqi kuangliao laiyuan yu chandi yanjiu de xin jinzhan 古代青銅器礦料來源與產地研究的新進展 [New Developments of Study on Raw Materials and Provenances of Ancient Bronzes]. PhD dissertation, Department for the History of Science and Scientific Archaeology, University of Science and Technology of China, Hefei.

Yu Yongbing 郁永彬, Chen Jianli 陳建立, Mei Jianjun 梅建軍, Chen Kunlong 陳坤龍, Chang Huaiying 常懷穎, and Huang Fengchun 黃鳳春
2016 Guanyu Yejiashan qingtongqi qian tongweisu bizhi yanjiu de jige wenti 關於葉家山青銅器鉛同位素比值研究的幾個問題. *Nanfang wenwu* 南方文物 2016(1):94–102.

Chapter 13

Erlitou and Nanwa
Contextualizing White Ceramics in Early Bronze Age China

Lee Hsiu-ping

"Whatever the answer, we are dealing with a highly complex situation of interaction [in different regions of Bronze Age China] in which living habits, aesthetic tastes, technical abilities, and economic structures are intertwined."
—Lothar von Falkenhausen,
Chinese Society in the Age of Confucius

Working from the premise that Erlitou was the political center of Early Bronze Age China, scholars have traditionally characterized the interregional interactions between Erlitou and its adjoining regions in center–periphery terms: it is assumed that the political center strongly influenced and even dominated its neighbors (e.g., Zhongguo Shehui 2003:97). Based on new archaeological evidence, however, I conducted a comparative analysis of archaeological contexts, which permitted me to explore various models of possible patterns of interregional interaction within the central Yellow River region (Lee 2018). This previous research covered three geographic areas: the Henan region, in which Erlitou was located, and the important nearby Hedong and Henei regions. The research results suggested a highly complex interaction network among these three regions, including military conflicts, competition for metal resources, and peaceful coexistence. Though that work mainly focused on analyzing the relationship among the Henan, Hedong, and Henei regions, it also revealed that interactions among sites within a specific region, or even within an archaeological unit, were likewise highly complex. One of the best examples is the relationship between Erlitou and Nanwa, which I explore further in the following pages.

Lothar von Falkenhausen's advice and scholarship strongly influenced the aforementioned work. His research on Bronze Age China (e.g., Falkenhausen 2006) demonstrates how scholars, using sound archaeological data, might rethink fundamental yet crucial questions in Chinese archaeology by moving beyond traditional interpretations. One such set of concerns relates to interregional interaction in early China, which has traditionally been dominated by political interpretations of center–periphery relations emphasized in Chinese academia. Interactions at this scale can alternatively be explored from a variety of viewpoints, including economics. The exchange of metal resources and bronze objects, for instance, might have played a crucial role in the interaction network between the Erlitou culture in the Henan region and the Dongxiafeng culture in the Hedong region (Lee 2018:459–66), although this hypothesis requires further archaeological evidence and is subject to further tests and modifications. The present article focuses on white ceramics, which functioned as a category of ritual vessels in the Erlitou culture. Examples have been discovered at both Erlitou and Nanwa. Although the materials were similar, the meaning of white ceramics was very different at these two sites: Erlitou was a consumption metropolis whereas Nanwa was a production center. The present paper investigates the interaction patterns between these two sites by focusing on the production–consumption relationship involving white ceramics.

"Interaction" and Erlitou

The term *interaction* refers to the various ways in which different human groups or societies in different regions come into contact with one another. Interaction is both a universal phenomenon in world history and a significant research topic in archaeology. Basic forms of interaction include exchange, emulation, colonization, and conquest, some of which occasionally overlap (Stein 2002:903). Archaeological research in this area is usually classified as the study of interregional interaction, intersocietal contact, culture change, or culture contact (e.g., Cusick 1998; Schortman and Urban 1992; Stein 2002).

Generally speaking, there are at least three scales of interaction. The large scale, such as the interaction between Han China in East Asia and the Roman Empire in Europe, connects vast and distant areas. The medium scale involves contact between neighboring regions, such as the Erlitou culture in western Henan and the Dongxiafeng culture in southwestern Shanxi. The small scale covers the relationship between sites within a specific region or archaeological unit, such as Erlitou and Nanwa, both of which were located in western Henan and which archaeologists associate with the Erlitou culture. These three different scales of interaction can shape complex interactive networks among regions, societies, and human groups. Archaeological research often places greater emphasis on the large and medium scales of interaction, because they are typically regarded as the major causes of crucial historical events, such as the fall of the Western Zhou Dynasty: some scholars believed it was defeated by its northwestern neighbor, the Quanrong (犬戎, the "dog barbarians"; e.g., Li Feng 2006). Nonetheless, the small scale of interaction can provide insights into the emergence, development, maintenance, and even collapse of a society, polity, or civilization, quite simply because the small scale of interaction can be the internal basis for external relations, such as intersocietal contact and cultural change.

This article focuses on the small scale of interaction—that between two sites, Erlitou and Nanwa (Figure 13.1)—in the middle Yellow River valley in early China during the second quarter of the second millennium BCE. Erlitou, located in western Henan, was not only the type site of the Erlitou culture but more significantly was also one of the most important political centers in early Chinese history, sometimes thought to represent the capital of the Xia Dynasty or the "Erlitou state" (e.g., Liu and Chen 2003; Zhongguo Shehui 2003). By contrast, Nanwa, situated around 33 km southeast of Erlitou, was a small settlement within the Erlitou culture sphere.

As Liu Li has observed, during the Erlitou period (ca. 1750–1530 BCE), white ceramics were important prestige goods (Liu 2003; Liu et al. 2004, 2007), material symbols to show a higher social, political, and economic status of their owners. It is worth noting that, despite the different

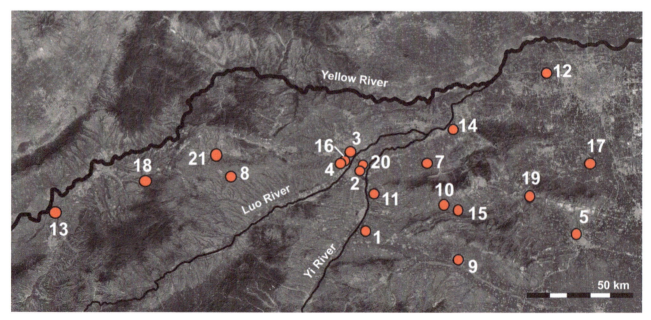

Figure 13.1. Map of site clusters mentioned in the text: 1. Baiyuan; 2. Cuoli; 3. Dongganggou; 4. Sunqitun; 5. Dongzhuang; 6. Erlitou; 7. Huizui; 8. Lusi; 9. Meishan; 10. Nanwa; 11. Nanzhai; 12. Niangniangzhai; 13. Qilipu; 14. Shaochai; 15. Shidao; 16. Dongmagou; 17. Xinzhai; 18. Xiyacun; 19. Yucun; 20. Zaojiashu; 21. Zhengyao. *Created by Bryan K. Miller.*

dimensions and functions of Erlitou and Nanwa, considerable amounts of white ceramics, particularly ritual vessels such as *jue* 爵, *gui* 鬶, and *he* 盉 (Figure 13.2), were widely distributed across both sites. White ceramics unearthed from Erlitou and Nanwa thus offer key archaeological evidence to help us explore the interaction between these places.

Luan Fengshi (2010) has suggested that white ceramics made with kaolinite were already regarded as a type of prestige good prior to the Erlitou period, during the Neolithic era. According to analysis of residues, white ceramic *gui* pitchers found at the Liangchengzhen site in Rizhao City, Shandong Province, and dated to the Longshan period (ca. 2600–2000 BCE) were used to store alcohol, implying that white ceramics might be employed in feasting or ritual activities (Mai et al. 2005). Moreover, within elite graves and at higher-ranking settlements, white ceramics were usually discovered. During the Neolithic period, kaolinite-based white ceramics might have independently originated in two regions: the central Yangzi River valley to the south and the Haidai region to the north. In the Haidai region, kaolinite was used to manufacture utilitarian wares and, more frequently, ritual vessels such as *gui* pitchers from around 3000 to 2000 BCE. In the Central Plains, some white ceramics that might have been introduced from the Haidai region first appeared during this time. In the following Erlitou period, white ceramics spread extensively across the Erlitou culture sphere in the Central Plains. The majority of the white ceramics known to date were found at the Erlitou type site (Zhongguo Erlitou 1985, 1992, 2015; Zhongguo Shehui 1995, 1999, 2014). Additionally, white ceramics were discovered at other sites that belonged to the Erlitou culture (Figure 13.1; Table 13.1).

One of the most crucial questions related to white ceramics during the Erlitou period is *where* these prestige goods were made. Based on neutron activation analysis (NAA), researchers have suggested that Nanwa might have been one of the production centers of white ceramics at this time (Han et al. 2007). Moreover, based on the results of ICP-MS trace elements and TIMS Sr isotopic analysis, researchers have suggested that some of the white ceramics found at Erlitou might have been made and imported from Nanwa, though other pieces might have come from other unknown sites (Li et al. 2009, 2010; Liu et al. 2007). The general consensus is that white ceramics found at Erlitou were not locally made but imported from other sites, and Nanwa is one of the candidates. As a result, it is possible to discuss the interaction patterns between Erlitou and Nanwa from the perspective of a production–consumption relationship involving white ceramics.

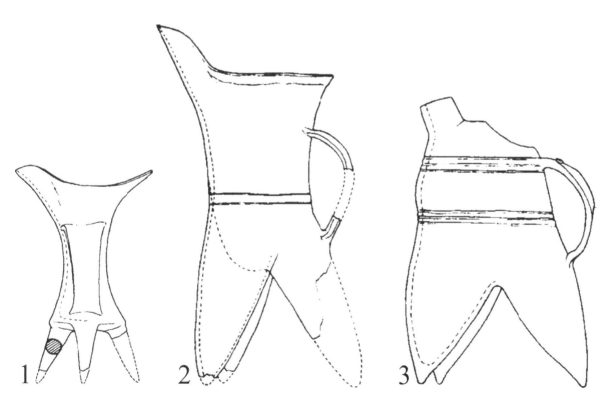

Figure 13.2. White ceramic ritual vessels from Erlitou (1. *jue*; 2. *gui*; 3. *he*).
Redrawn by the author after Zhongguo Shehui 1999:Figures 81.4, 80.1, 81.2.

Table 13.1 Sites with white ceramics in the Erlitou culture sphere

No.	Site Name	Site Name in Chinese	Reference
1	Baiyuan, Yichuan	白元, 伊川	Luoyang Diqu Wenwuchu 1982
2	Cuoli, Luoyang	矬李, 洛陽	Luoyang Bowuguan 1978a
3	Donggangou, Luoyang	東乾溝, 洛陽	Zhongguo Shehui 1989
4	Dongmagou, Luoyang	東馬溝, 洛陽	Luoyang Bowuguan 1978b
5	Dongzhuang, Yuzhou	董莊, 禹州	Henan Sheng and Yu Xian 1991
6	Erlitou, Yanshi	二里頭, 偃師	Zhongguo Shehui 1999, 2014
7	Huizui, Yanshi	灰嘴, 偃師	Zhongguo Shehui Henan Diyi 2010
8	Lusi, Mianchi	鹿寺, 澠池	Henan Sheng Wenhuaju 1964
9	Meishan, Ruzhou	煤山, 汝州	Zhongguo Shehui Henan Er Dui 1982
10	Nanwa, Dengfeng	南窪, 登封	Zhengzhou Daxue 2014
11	Nanzhai, Yichuan	南寨, 伊川	Henan Sheng 1996, 2012
12	Niangniangzhai, Xingyang	娘娘寨, 滎陽	Zhengzhou Shi and Henan Sheng Wenwu Guanliju 2014
13	Qilipu, Sanmenxia	七里鋪, 三門峽	Huanghe Shuiku 1960
14	Shaochai, Gongyi	稍柴, 鞏義	Henan Sheng 1993
15	Shidao, Dengfeng	石道, 登封	Beijing Daxue and Henan Sheng 2007
16	Sunqitun, Luoyang	孫旗屯, 洛陽	Henan Wenwu 1955
17	Xinzhai, Xinmi	新砦, 新密	Beijing Daxue and Zhengzhou Shi 2008
18	Xiyacun, Sammenxia	西崖村, 三門峽	Henan Sheng 1989
19	Yucun, Dengfeng	玉村, 登封	Han Weizhou et al. 1954
20	Zaojiaoshu, Luoyang	皂角樹, 洛陽	Luoyang Shi 2002
21	Zhengyao, Mianchi	鄭窯, 澠池	Henan Sheng and Mianchi Xian 1987

Unlike earlier research, which studied the production–consumption relationship between Erlitou and Nanwa in general (Han et al. 2007; Li et al. 2008, 2009, 2010; Liu 2003; Liu et al. 2004, 2007), mainly by observing that Erlitou was a consumption center and that Nanwa was a production settlement for white ceramics, this article examines how and why the consumption of white ceramics at Erlitou strongly affected the rise and fall of Nanwa. I consider archaeological contexts that contained white ceramics and compare the similarities and differences between the functions, values, and meanings of objects as they were transferred from production sites to consumption sites. This comparison elucidates interaction patterns between production and consumption settlements. Fortunately, the published archaeological data from both Erlitou and Nanwa provide extensive contextual information about white ceramics unearthed from these two sites. The developmental trajectories of settlement plans at both Erlitou and Nanwa are relatively clear, setting solid spatial foundations for our analysis. Furthermore, the excavation reports of these two sites provide sound numerical data for white ceramic sherds, revealing useful information, such as classification, quantity, finding location, and relative chronology (Zhengzhou Daxue 2014:819–901; Zhongguo Shehui 2014:5:Appendices 9-5A, 9-5B).

The following discussion investigates interaction between these production and consumption locales for white ceramics through a detailed examination of the two sites. For each location I provide (1) a summary of the developmental trajectory of the settlement plan and (2) an analysis of the patterns of numerical data and the archaeological contexts for white ceramics. I conclude that the demand for white ceramics in a consumption settlement, such as Erlitou, might have impacted the rise and fall of a production center, such as Nanwa, and finally point out some topics for future study.

Nanwa and Erlitou
Nanwa
Settlement Plan

Nanwa, located in the valley between the Song and Ji Mountains (Figure 13.1), about 20 km southwest of Dengfeng City, Henan Province, is a small Erlitou culture settlement. The Kuangshui River flows through its northern and western parts. For the Erlitou period, the occupation of Nanwa can be subdivided into five successive phases (Table 13.2). The excavation area covers three main parts: Northern Area I (NA I), Central Area I (CA I), and Southern Area II (SA II) (Figure 13.3; Zhengzhou Daxue 2014:1–2, 7–10, 630–31).

Nanwa was already occupied in Phase I (Erlitou Phase IB), but only a few features were discovered in the three excavation areas dated to this period, including 15 ash pits and a well. G1, a moated enclosure with an irregular shape, was probably constructed during this period. The western and northern parts of G1 remain poorly defined (Figure

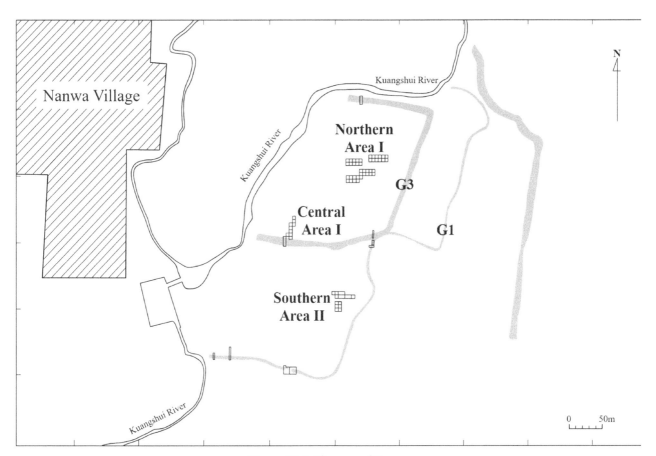

Figure 13.3. Site map of Nanwa.
Redrawn by the author from Zhengzhou Daxue 2014:Figure 1-3.

13.3). The area surrounded by G1 and the Kuangshui River is around 11.3 ha in size, demarcating the size of Nanwa during the Erlitou period (Zhengzhou Daxue 2014:20–4, 36, 624, 781, 817–18, 839, 884–85, 887, 901).

Nanwa reached its maximum occupation during Phases II and III (Erlitou Phase II). At least 279 ash pits dated to these two periods were distributed across the site. The other moated enclosure, G3, was probably built in Phase II. The western part of G3 is also poorly defined, though it also connects to the Kuangshui River. It is noteworthy that the settlement plan in Phases II and III may indicate the existence of a specialized ceramics workshop area fortified by G3. In Phase II, a house was surrounded by three kilns and a well at NA I; in Phase III, a kiln and three wells were situated in the same area. In addition, at SA II, a kiln and a well dated to Phase II were also discovered, suggesting another area for ceramics production (Zhengzhou Daxue 2014:25–40, 819–95).

Nanwa started to decline in Phase IV (Erlitou Phase III). Only 89 ash pits and one grave dated to this period were found, revealing a decrease in human activity at Nanwa. Despite this decline, the moated enclosure G3 was still in use (Zhengzhou Daxue 2014:62–63, 628, 819–95). No kilns dated to Phase III have been found, but white ceramic sherds dated to this period were discovered, suggesting that white ceramics probably continued being produced at Nanwa during this period.

In Phase V (Erlitou Phase IVA), evidence for human activity at Nanwa is quite sparse. Only 10 ash pits and one grave dated to this period have been unearthed. Additionally, the moated enclosure G3, though it had not yet been filled up, was abandoned. Importantly, according to the excavation report, there is no evidence for natural disaster or military conflict at Nanwa during this period (Zhengzhou Daxue 2014:64, 629, 781). However, the authors of the report offer no alternative reason to explain the abandonment of Nanwa.

Clearly, Nanwa was a fortified settlement associated with ceramics manufacture during the Erlitou period. The two moated enclosures, G1 and G3, were probably constructed during Phases I and II, respectively. G1 marks the spatial dimensions of Nanwa, and G3 indicates its core region. In the area surrounded by G3 (NA I), kilns and wells were densely distributed during Phases II and III, implying the existence of a workshop area for making ceramics. In addition, the area between G1 and G3 (SA II) might have been another area for ceramics production during Phase II. Thus one of the main activities at Nanwa was probably the production of ceramics, including white ceramics (Han et al. 2007; Li et al. 2008, 2009, 2010; Liu et al. 2007). Accordingly, the functions of G1 and G3 were to fortify this industrial locality (Zhengzhou Daxue 2014:781). The developmental trajectory of Nanwa's settlement plan, which reached its peak in Phases II and III and started to decline in Phase IV, corresponds with the distribution trends of white ceramic sherds (discussed below). More significantly, these distribution trends are another indicator for explaining the rise and the fall of this industrial settlement.

White Ceramics and Their Archaeological Contexts

The excavation report for Nanwa provides useful numerical data for analyzing the distribution trends and the archaeological contexts of white ceramics over time at Nanwa (Zhengzhou Daxue 2014:819–901). Because white ceramics at Nanwa were found exclusively in non-grave contexts, no complete white ceramic vessels were discovered. Among 207 white ceramic fragments collected from Nanwa, eight whose relative dating are uncertain will be excluded in the following discussion. Despite these limitations, the data still offer useful clues to help us investigate the distribution trends of white ceramics at Nanwa.

Table 13.2 Absolute and relative chronology of Erlitou and Nanwa

Absolute Chronology[1]	Relative Chronology	
	Erlitou	Nanwa
ca. 1750–1680 BCE	Phase IA	
	Phase IB	Phase I
ca. 1680–1630 BCE	Phase IIA	Phase II
	Phase IIB	Phase III
ca. 1630–1580 BCE	Phase IIIA	Phase IV
	Phase IIIB	
ca. 1580–1530 BCE	Phase IVA	Phase V
	Phase IVB	

Phase I (Erlitou Phase IB)

At least eight white ceramic fragments dated to Phase I were discovered (Table 13.3): six in NA I, one in CA I, and one in SA II. One was collected from a well; the others were collected from ash pits. All white ceramic sherds found were fragments of ritual vessels, including *jue* and *gui* (or *he*). Although kilns from this phase have not been discovered at Nanwa, white ceramics might have been made at Nanwa. Such speculation, however, must be tested through ceramic provenance analysis. If confirmed, this would suggest that white ceramic ritual vessels were being made at Nanwa during Phase I, but the scale of production was quite small. Since the sherds were found in ash pits and a well, they might be production waste or the remains of local ceramics consumption. It is worth noting that the percentage of white ceramics (9.41%) among all ceramics in the assemblage (Table 13.3) may be overestimated due to a small sample size.

Phase II (Erlitou Phase IIA)

Compared to the previous period, the quantity of white ceramic sherds found in Phase II contexts is much higher, but the percentage of white ceramics was slightly lower than in Phase I. At least 105 white ceramic fragments (9.16%) were found at Nanwa (Table 13.3): 81 in NA I, 21 in SA II, and three in the moat G1. Most of them were collected from ash pits. As mentioned above, three kilns dated to this period were located in NA I and another was in SA II. Thus the quantity of kilns and white ceramic sherds have a positive correlation. NA I, fortified by G1 and G3, might have been a primary area for white ceramics production. Additionally, SA II, located between G1 and G3, might have been a secondary area. Most of these white ceramic products were ritual vessels, including 64 *gui* (or *he*), 16 *jue*, and one *gu* 觚. In addition, some utilitarian white ceramic vessels, including one tripod *ding* 鼎 cauldron, one tripod *yan* 甗 steamer, and three *guan* 罐 pots, were found. In addition to vessels, nine net sinkers made with white ceramics were also discovered. It is possible that—since Nanwa was the production center for white ceramics—potters also used this valuable raw material to make not only prestige goods but also utilitarian objects. Thus only white ceramic ritual vessels (and maybe a few utilitarian ones) made at Nanwa were exported to other settlements and neighboring regions. However, various sorts of white ceramics, including ritual and utilitarian vessels and net sinkers, were not only made but also used locally at this production center. The production and use of utilitarian objects made with kaolinite might also indicate that Nanwa was a production center for white ceramics during the Erlitou period.

Phase III (Erlitou Phase IIB)

In comparison with the preceding stage, the quantity and percentage of white ceramic sherds at Nanwa decreased considerably during Phase III; only 57 white ceramic fragments (5.02%) were found (Table 13.3). Most were collected from ash pits, but four came from wells. All the sherds were discovered in NA I, except for one, which was found in SA II. This distribution pattern corresponds with the layout of Nanwa during this period, when there was only one kiln in NA I. The archaeological evidence suggests that NA I was still a production area for white ceramics during Phase III, though comparing to Phase II, its scale of production was much smaller during this stage. It is possible, however, that SA II simply stopped making white ceramics. Ritual vessels, including *jue*, *gui*, and *he*, were still the most common white ceramics found at Nanwa. Other white ceramic objects were also unearthed: four net sinkers and one bell, which might have reflected the high status of its

Table 13.3. Numerical data of white ceramics at NanwaNumerical data of white ceramics at Nanwa

Chronology	Quantity of White Ceramics	Quantity of Entire Ceramic Assemblage	Percentage of White Ceramics
Phase I	8	85	9.41%[2]
Phase II	105	1146	9.16%
Phase III	57	1135	5.02%
Phase IV	25	842	2.97%
Phase V	4	172	2.33%
Total	199	3380	

owner in Erlitou society, since bells were also found in six higher-raking graves at Erlitou, but made from bronze (Zhongguo Erlitou 1984:37–38; 1985:1093; 1986:320, 1992:295; Zhongguo Shehui 1999:137; 2014:1003–4). In short, during Phase III, Nanwa was still a production center for white ceramics and probably continued to export products, such as ritual vessels, to other settlements, but its scale of production was reduced. This situation also mirrors the decline of Nanwa itself.

Phase IV (Erlitou Phase III)
Twenty-five white ceramic fragments (2.97%) were found in Phase IV contexts at Nanwa (Table 13.3): 23 in NA I and two in CA I. All the white ceramics were found in ash pits. Although no kilns dated to this period were discovered at Nanwa, these sherds might still have been locally made or might simply belong to remains dated to earlier stages. Most of these white ceramic remains are fragments of ritual vessels, but some are from utilitarian objects, including two pots and two net sinkers. The scale of production during this period had been radically reduced, if white ceramics were still made at Nanwa during Phase IV at all. At the same time, the settlement itself continuously declined.

Phase V (Erlitou Phase IVA)
During Phase V, the settlement was almost entirely abandoned, and only four white ceramic fragments (2.33%) dated to this period were uncovered at Nanwa (Table 13.3). All of them were fragments of ritual vessels. Although ritual vessels made from white ceramics were quite rare at Nanwa during this period, this does not mean that ritual vessels had lost their significance in the Erlitou culture. In fact, many ritual vessels made from clay, kaolinite, and even bronze still played an important role in ceremonies and feasts and were buried in graves, particularly at Erlitou (see discussion below). However, from the perspective of Nanwa, Erlitou seemingly no longer required white ceramic ritual vessels made at Nanwa.

Based on the analysis of white ceramic finds and their archaeological contexts at Nanwa, during its early stages, particularly in Phase II—the most prosperous period for Nanwa—the production scale of white ceramics reached a peak. Starting from Phase III, the scale of production of white ceramics gradually declined until Phase V (Table 13.3). As a production settlement, Nanwa strongly relied on the manufacture and export of white ceramic products, especially ritual vessels. In addition to production, how white ceramics were distributed to consumption settlements, such as Erlitou, is another intriguing question.

Erlitou

Settlement Plan

Erlitou, situated in the Luoyang basin of western Henan, was one of the largest settlements in East Asia during the early half of the second millennium BCE. The relative chronology of Erlitou includes four successive phases, each of which can be subdivided into early and late stages (Table 13.2; Zhongguo Shehui 2014:25). According to the latest ^{14}C dating, the absolute chronology of Erlitou from Erlitou Phase I to Phase IV spanned the period from around 1750 to 1530 BCE (Zhongguo Shehui 2014:1236). Since its discovery in 1959, Erlitou has been excavated for more than 60 years. However, because many significant excavation results have not been published, the developmental trajectory of Erlitou's settlement plan remains in parts unclear, except for the palatial area and the fortified workshop area.

Erlitou was occupied from Erlitou Phase I. Archaeological remains were widely distributed in its southeastern and central parts, covering about 100 ha (Figure 13.4). Because the cultural layers belonging to Erlitou Phase I were severely damaged, it is difficult to assess whether Erlitou was an individual settlement or several smaller settlements (Zhongguo Shehui 2014:1657).

Archaeological remains dated to Erlitou Phase II are widely distributed throughout the entire site, covering an area of around 300 ha (Figure 13.4). It is crucial to point out that the core area of Erlitou, namely the highest location of the entire site, had been occupied during Erlitou Phase I. The core area of Erlitou consisted of the palatial area in the center, the fortified workshop area in the south, a "sacrificial area" in the north, and elite residential areas surrounding the palatial area. Outside the core area, residential areas for commoners were situated to the west and north of this site. In addition, more than 400 graves, distributed across various residential areas and even inside the palace complexes, have been found. Furthermore, kilns and remains associated with bone production were discovered in different parts of Erlitou (Chen and Li 2016; Zhongguo Shehui 1999:129, 2014:17, 1657–63).

On the one hand, in a hierarchical society such as Erlitou, various prestige goods, including jade, bronze, and such distinctive ceramics as white ceramics, were consumed by local elites to display their status and wealth (Li 2008:27–29). On the other hand, the preferences of local elites at Erlitou also defined the value of these elite goods in their local setting. We might nonetheless ask whether the value system within this hierarchical society stayed the same throughout all periods or whether it changed over time. The following on the distribution of white ceramics at Erlitou will investigate this intriguing issue.

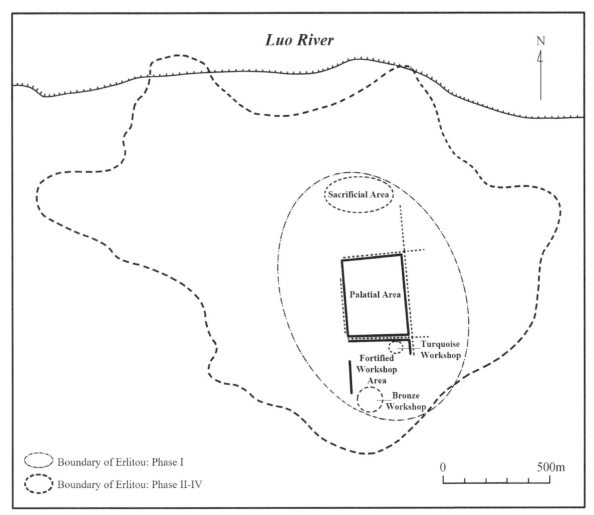

Figure 13.4. Site map of Erlitou. *Redrawn by the author from Zhongguo Shehui 2014:Figures 11-2-1-1 and 11-2-2-1*

White Ceramics and Their Archaeological Contexts

Since the discovery of Erlitou in 1959, large amounts of white ceramics have been collected from this huge settlement through long-term excavation. However, most of the relevant data have not published, and even *Yanshi Erlitou* (Zhongguo Shehui 1999), the first official report, documented only the excavation results from 1959 to 1978. Fortunately, the most recent excavation report *Erlitou: 1999–2006* (Zhongguo Shehui 2014), a five-volume monograph, provides a complete account of white ceramics from the excavations carried out between 1999 and 2006. These newly released data permit the investigation of distribution patterns and the archaeological contexts for white ceramics at Erlitou. The following discussions therefore mainly focus on data contained in the new excavation report.

Before conducting any analyses, three issues concerning the data need to be mentioned. First, because the excavations from 1999 to 2006 were mainly carried out in the palatial area, particularly in its northeastern portion, most of the white ceramic sherds are concentrated in this specific area, rather than in the fortified workshop area and the eastern boundary area, which were also excavated between 1999 and 2006. Despite this biased dataset, the distribution of white ceramics in the palatial area over time still reveals general trends in usage and frequency for these prestige goods. Second, since most of the data from other relevant sources may belong to Erlitou Phase II, the following analysis of white ceramics dated to this period also covers data from both the new excavation report and the first excavation report, *Yanshi Erlitou* (Zhongguo Shehui 1999), preliminary reports (Zhongguo Erlitou 1985, 1992, 2015), and *Erlitou Taoqi Jicui* (*Cream of the Pottery from Erlitou*; Zhongguo Shehui 1995). Finally, because the relative dating of some white ceramic remains found at Erlitou is uncertain, the following discussion excludes these data.

Erlitou Phase IB

White ceramics appeared at Erlitou no later than Erlitou Phase IB. In layers dated to this period, only nine white ceramic fragments were found (Table 13.4). It is important to notice, however, that the percentage of white ceramics among the whole ceramic assemblage dated to this period (15%) was the highest among all phases. This result may be overestimated because of the relatively small sample size. All white ceramic fragments were located in the northeastern part of the palatial area, in which Foundation 3 was built during Erlitou Phase IIA. Six were collected from a ditch, G10, and the others from an ash pit, H119. Most of the white ceramics were ritual vessels, including *gui*, *he*, and *jue*. Although the quantity of white ceramics in Erlitou Phase IB was small, it is worth noting that all the white ceramics were distributed in the northeastern part of the palatial area. Because white ceramics—prestige goods showing the higher status of their owners in Erlitou society—were found concentrated in this specific area, the northeastern part of the palatial area might play a significate role in the entire site during Erlitou Phase I.

Erlitou Phase IIA

At least 51 white ceramic fragments were found in Erlitou Phase IIA contexts at Erlitou, but only 8.15% of them were white ceramics (Table 13.4). Among these white ceramic fragments, 43 came from the palatial area and eight came from the northern fortified workshop area; 41 of the 43 fragments found in the palatial area were concentrated in the northeastern part of Foundation 3. Most of these were found in a ditch, G38. Some were found in ash pits, roads, and cultural layers, and three were found in a grave, 2001 V M1, which is located in the central courtyard of Foundation 3. Besides three white ceramic fragments, including two *he* and one *jue*, 2001 V M1 contained other prestige goods, such as one jade handle-shaped object and one lacquerware. Moreover, a layer of cinnabar was set in the bottom of this grave (Zhongguo Shehui 2014:991–97). Based on the archaeological evidence, the occupant of 2001 V M1 was likely a high-ranking elite in Erlitou society. In addition, two white ceramic fragments were uncovered in the southwestern part of the palatial area. Finally, all white ceramic fragments found in the fortified workshop area were unearthed from ash pits, seven of these fragments in the turquoise workshop. As in the previous period, most of the white ceramics uncovered from layers dated to this period were ritual vessels; only three were *zun* 尊 storage jars.

The fact that most white ceramic fragments were discovered in the palatial area suggests that local elites might have been the major consumers of white ceramics at Erlitou in Erlitou Phase IIA. White ceramics were probably used not only in daily practices but also for special events, such as ceremonies and feasts. Moreover, as analyzed above, white ceramic vessels were buried in at least one elite grave. In addition, few white ceramic sherds were uncovered in the turquoise workshop. This situation suggests that due to specialized crafts for producing turquoise objects, some craftsmen might have had a high social status and the means to use white ceramic vessels. Of course, another possibility is that some craftsmen might have been members of local elites, who therefore could use and even own white ceramics.

Table 13.4. Numerical data of white ceramics at Erlitou

Chronology	Quantity of White Ceramics	Quantity of Entire Ceramic Assemblage	Percentage of White Ceramics
IB	9	60	15.00%[3]
IIA	51	626	8.15%
IIB	146	1049	13.92%
IIIA	29 (44)	286 (301)	10.14% (14.62%)
IIIB	23 (43)	362 (382)	6.35% (11.26%)
IVA	4	166	2.41%
IVB	195 (235)	1836 (1876)	10.62% (12.53%)
Total	532	4460	

Note: Data in parentheses might be overestimated.

Erlitou Phase IIB

At least 146 white ceramic fragments dated to Erlitou Phase IIB were found at Erlitou. More importantly, the percentage of white ceramics among the whole ceramic assemblage increased to 13.92%, which was higher than in Erlitou Phase IIA contexts (Table 13.4). Most of the white ceramics dated to Erlitou Phase IIB were discovered within the palatial area, particularly concentrated in Foundation 3, in which 108 white ceramic fragments were collected from ash pits, ditches, roads, and cultural layers. White ceramic objects were also buried in two graves, 2002 V M3 and M4, both of which were situated in the southern courtyard of Foundation 3. In 2002 V M3, three white ceramic bamboo-hat-shaped objects (*doulixingqi* 斗笠形器; Figure 13.5) were unearthed on or near the head of the occupant. A small hole can be found at the center of these peculiar white ceramic objects, suggesting they might be a kind of ornament. In addition, many other prestige goods, such as a famous turquoise dragon-shaped object (*longxingqi* 龍形器; Figure 13.6), one jade handle-shaped object, a set of seashell ornaments, a bronze bell, lacquerwares, turquoise beads, and many ceramic ritual vessels, were also buried in 2002 V M3 (Zhongguo Shehui 2014:998–1006). In 2002 V M4, another higher-ranking grave, one white ceramic *he* was discovered next to other prestige goods (Zhongguo Shehui 2014:1007–11). In addition to appearing in Foundation 3, white ceramics were also uncovered from the northeastern and southwestern parts of the palatial area. White ceramics also appeared in various other parts of this huge settlement: 16 fragments in the northern fortified workshop area, including in the turquoise workshop; 13 in the eastern boundary of site; four between the palatial area and the fortified workshop area; and two outside the northern wall of the palatial area. All white ceramic remains found outside the palatial area were collected from ash pits, ditches, roads, and cultural layers. During Erlitou Phase IIB, most of the white ceramics recovered were ritual vessels. In addition, two *zun* jars and one *guan* pot were also found.

In comparison with the previous period, during Erlitou Phase IIB, more white ceramic remains were used and also distributed widely to various parts of Erlitou. In other words, white ceramics were more common and more widespread in Erlitou society during this period than before. Of course, most of these white ceramic objects were still concentrated in Foundation 3. This situation suggests that the major consumers of white ceramics might still have been local elites, who used these prestige goods for daily consumption or for special occasions. In addition, white ceramics might also have been used by non-elites, who might

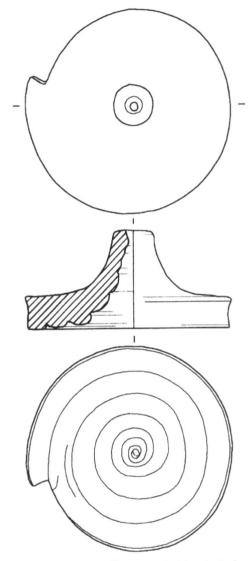

Figure 13.5. *Doulixingqi* (diameter 5.9–6.1 cm). *Redrawn by the author from Zhongguo Shehui 2014:Figure 6-4-3-4-2B 2.*

have lived in the fortified workshop area and even on the eastern boundary of this large settlement. Given the popularity of white ceramics, a greater number of non-elites not only had the ability to imitate local elites in their consumption of prestige goods but also attempted to do so.

In addition to the numerical data from *Erlitou: 1999–2006*, at least 17 white ceramic remains dated to Erlitou Phase II have been documented in other sources, such as *Yanshi Erlitou* (Zhongguo Shehui 1999), preliminary reports (Zhongguo Erlitou 1985, 1992, 2015), and *Erlitou Taoqi Jicui* (Zhongguo Shehui 1995). All these objects were ritual vessels. It is worth noting that eight white ceramic fragments were found in the bronze workshop in the southern fortified workshop area; six were unearthed from

Figure 13.6. *Longxingqi* (length 64.5 cm). *Photo by the author.*

four white ceramic fragments were recovered from graves (Zhongguo Shehui 1995:46, 97, 104, 351, 355; Zhongguo Erlitou 1985:1090, 1992:296). As I have discussed (Lee 2018:166–67), particular features, such as circular features, rectangular pits, and many graves, including some buried with prestige goods, were found in this area. However, since the occupants of these graves were not human sacrifices, it is more appropriate to connect these features and graves with religious practices rather than with specific sacrificial events documented in historical texts. Limited archaeological evidence suggests that the occupants of graves buried with white ceramics in the "sacrificial area" might have had high status. For example, in Grave M49, 10 burial goods were found: a white ceramic *gui*, other ritual and utilitarian ceramic vessels, and one lacquerware, which is also a material symbol reflecting the high status of its owner (Li 2008:27; Zhongguo Erlitou 1992). Moreover, at least three white ceramic fragments were uncovered in the palatial area. Two of them were found in two graves, M22 and M23, located in the southwestern part, specifically to the southeast of Foundation 1, which was constructed in Erlitou Phase IIIA (Zhongguo Shehui 1999:132, 134). Therefore the occupants of M22 and M23 might also have been members of the local elite in Erlitou society. The other white ceramic was unearthed to the south of Foundation 3 (Zhongguo Shehui 1999:116). Finally, to the northwest of the site, which might have been a residential area for commoners (Zhongguo Shehui 2014:1663), one white ceramic fragment was discovered in Grave M2. According to the limited information, at least 10 ceramic vessels were buried in this grave (Zhongguo Shehui 1995:159, 359–60).

In short, during Erlitou Phase II, and particularly its later stage, white ceramics were widely distributed across various parts of Erlitou. More importantly, some non-elite inhabitants of the settlement, such as specialized bronze and turquoise craftsmen, might have used and owned these prestige goods, indicating the popularity of white ceramics at Erlitou during this period.

graves and two from cultural layers (Zhongguo Shehui 1995:43, 46, 86, 94, 114, 131, 351, 354–57, 1999:134–35). This situation indicates that specialized bronze craftsmen might have had access to white ceramics for daily use and even for taking to their graves. Thus some bronze makers, like some turquoise craftsmen mentioned above, possibly a had high status within Erlitou society during Erlitou Phase II. Beyond the bronze workshop, one white ceramic fragment was collected from an ash pit outside the western wall of the fortified workshop area (Zhongguo Erlitou 2015:48). In the "sacrificial area" to the north of the palatial area,

Erlitou Phase IIIA

According to numerical data published in *Erlitou: 1999–2006*, only 44 white ceramic fragments dated to Erlitou Phase IIIA were discovered. But compared to Erlitou Phase IIB, the percentage of white ceramics among the whole ceramic assemblage slightly increased, to 14.62% (Table 13.4), seemingly implying that this sort of prestige good perhaps still played an important role in Erlitou society during this period. All white ceramic fragments were found in ash pits and cultural layers, and most were concentrated in the northeastern part of the palatial area. During

Erlitou Phase IIIA, Foundation 3 was abandoned, while Foundation 4 was built in the southern part of Foundation 3. Most of the white ceramic fragments found in the northeastern part of the palatial area were discovered in the north of Foundation 4, which was vacant land with some ash pits during Erlitou Phase IIIA, before the construction of Foundation 2 in Erlitou Phase IIIB (Zhongguo Shehui 2014:1659–60). Additionally, two white ceramic fragments were unearthed from the southwestern part of the palatial area, with another one in the eastern boundary of the site. As to the types of white ceramics, in addition to ritual vessels, the numerical data reveal 16 *zun* jars collected from Layer ④B of Locus 2003 V T32 in the northeastern part of the palatial area. Based on the numerical data above, the likelihood that 16 *zun* jars were collected from one specific excavation unit is low, since this kind of vessel made from white ceramics was not so popular at Erlitou, according to the data analyzed in this article. It is highly likely that the quantity of white ceramic *zun* jars has been overestimated. If we treat these 16 *zun* jars as one, only 29 white ceramic vessels can be dated to Erlitou Phase IIIA, and the percentage of white ceramics decreases to 10.14%. In other words, with conservative consideration, the quantity of white ceramics might range between 29 and 44 (10.14% and 14.62%, respectively). Therefore it is highly possible that in Erlitou Phase IIIA, not only the quantity but also the percentage of white ceramics might be smaller than those found in Erlitou Phase IIB (Table 13.4).

After experiencing a peak for white ceramics consumption in Erlitou Phase IIB, the quantity and percentage of these prestige goods began to decrease in Erlitou Phase IIIB. This applies to white ceramics found not only in the palatial area but also throughout the settlement. However, a decline in the quantity and percentage of white ceramics at Erlitou did not mean the decline of the metropolis itself.

Erlitou Phase IIIB
Compared to the previous period, a similar quantity of white ceramics can be dated to Erlitou Phase IIIB; 43 fragments were found at Erlitou (Table 13.4). Among them, 29 fragments were uncovered within the palatial area. However, 20 of them came from Pond D2HC. This pond was located in the northern courtyard of Foundation 3 and was constructed during Erlitou Phase IIA. It was then filled and leveled up for the construction of Foundation 2 during Erlitou Phase IIIB (Zhongguo Shehui 2014:1308–9). Thus the white ceramics collected from Pond D2HC might belong to Erlitou Phase II. If this assumption is correct, then only 23 white ceramic vessels can be dated to this period and the percentage of white ceramics among the whole ceramic assemblage was 6.35% (Table 13.4). The other white ceramic fragments from the palatial area were found in ash pits and cultural layers in its northeastern and southern parts. In addition, six white ceramic fragments were found in cultural layers in the turquoise workshop, six fragments were found cultural layers in the eastern boundary of the site, and two fragments were found in an ash pit between the palatial area and the fortified workshop area. Most of the white ceramics were fragments of ritual vessels. However, three of them were utilitarian vessels, including one tripod *ding* cauldron, one tripod *yan* steamer, and one *guan* pot, which might have been used for cooking. The tripod *yan* steamer was not a typical vessel in local Erlitou culture, though it was common in neighboring archaeological units, such as the Xiaqiyuan culture, which was situated between the Taihang Mountains to the west and the Yellow River to the east (e.g., Liu Xu 1990). Due to the lack of compositional analysis, it is still uncertain whether this tripod steamer (Zhongguo Shehui 2014:1031) was made locally or imported from a neighboring area. All in all, the quantity and percentage of white ceramics in Erlitou Phase IIIB were smaller than in Erlitou Phase IIIA, but white ceramics had wider distribution than in the previous period.

Erlitou Phase IVA
Erlitou Phase IVA is the period during which the smallest amount of white ceramics was found at Erlitou. Only four white ceramic *he*, whose percentage among the whole ceramic assemblage was merely 2.41% (Table 13.4), were unearthed. All were collected from ash pits and cultural layers in the eastern boundary of the site rather than in the palatial area. Of course, that no white ceramics were found in the palatial area might simply be a coincidence. However, it is certain that white ceramics did not play a crucial role throughout Erlitou during Erlitou Phase IVA. This decline in white ceramics at Erlitou might have already begun, as noted above, during Erlitou Phase IIIA.

Erlitou Phase IVB
Surprisingly, the quantity and percentage of white ceramics dramatically increased at Erlitou during Erlitou Phase IVB. At least 235 white ceramic fragments, whose percentage within the whole ceramic assemblage from the period was 12.53%, were found (Table 13.4). Accordingly, the quantity and percentage of white ceramics dated to Erlitou Phase IVB were much larger than those found during Erlitou Phase IIB. During Erlitou Phase IVB, the palatial area is still the area in which most of the white ceramics were found. At least 94 white ceramic fragments were collected

in the palatial area. Sixty-four of them were concentrated in Foundation 6, which was also located in the northeastern part of the palatial area, built during Erlitou Phase IVB. It is noteworthy that 40 of them were collected from the rammed earth of Foundation 6. Since this foundation was constructed with earth dug up from older cultural layers elsewhere at Erlitou, the white ceramic sherds found from the rammed earth of Foundation 6 might be dated to earlier periods. Based on this assumption, the quantity of white ceramics dated to Erlitou Phase IVB should be reduced to 195 and the percentage of white ceramics among the whole ceramic assemblage should be adjusted to 10.62%. The other 24 white ceramic fragments found in Foundation 6 were mainly collected from roads and cultural layers, except for four from ash pits. The other white ceramic remains in the palatial area were almost all discovered in its northeastern part, which was extensively excavated between 2002 and 2006; two more remains were recovered from its southwestern part. Beyond the palatial area, at least 58 white ceramic fragments were found in cultural layers and ash pits in the eastern boundary of the site; 38 fragments were found in the turquoise workshop, located in the western part of the rammed-earth wall, Q3, and in the northern and northeastern parts of the fortified workshop area; and 41 fragments were found in cultural layers and ash pits between the palatial area and the fortified workshop area. Finally, four fragments were found in ash pits and a ditch outside the eastern wall of the palatial area. It is important to note that no white ceramics dated to Erlitou Phase IVB were collected from graves. Most of the recovered white ceramics were ritual vessels such as *jue*, *gui*, and *he*, though a few storage vessels such as *zun* and *gang* 缸 were also found.

A large amount of white ceramics dated to Erlitou Phase IVB was found at Erlitou. On the one hand, according to the archaeological evidence mentioned above, due to the construction of Foundation 6 in this period, some white ceramic sherds that originally belonged to earlier periods might have been churned up from the lower cultural layers. On the other hand, it seems that white ceramics were once again popular during Erlitou Phase IVB, probably throughout the entire site—not only in the palatial area but also in the fortified workshop area and in the eastern boundary of Erlitou. In consideration of the developmental trend of white ceramics in this metropolis between Erlitou Phase IB and Erlitou Phase IVA, the fact that a large amount of white ceramics suddenly appeared at Erlitou during Erlitou Phase IVB is extremely surprising. The main cause of this unusual phenomenon demands further investigation.

Discussion

Based on the analysis of numerical data, especially the percentage of white ceramics among the entire ceramic assemblage and the archaeological contexts for white ceramics from the production settlement of Nanwa and the consumption metropolis of Erlitou discussed above, it is possible to explore interaction patterns between these two sites in detail.

Numerical Data

With an exception for data dated to Erlitou Phase IB at both sites that may be overestimated, the relative quantities of white ceramics at Nanwa and Erlitou from Erlitou Phase IIA to Erlitou Phase IVA reveal a similar long-term trend (Tables 13.3 and 13.4).

The peaks of the presence of white ceramics at both sites occurred during Erlitou Phase II, indicating that white ceramics were frequently used across both Nanwa and Erlitou during this period. Given that Nanwa was a production center, as discussed above, the potters there made more white ceramics to satisfy the demand of consumption settlements such as Erlitou. As Erlitou was a consumption settlement, the local people, especially the local elites, imported plenty of white ceramics and probably used these prestige goods in both their daily lives and for special events, such as ceremonies, feasts, and funeral rites.

Nevertheless, after flourishing during Erlitou Phase II, the relative quantities of white ceramics gradually diminished between Erlitou Phase IIIA and Erlitou Phase IVA. As a production center, Nanwa experienced a serious decline not only in the production of white ceramics but also, more significantly, in the development of the settlement itself. Eventually, after Erlitou Phase IVA, Nanwa was abandoned entirely. At the same time, Erlitou merely experienced a decline in the demand for white ceramics, and this huge settlement continuously developed until the end of Erlitou Phase IVB. Thus, starting in Erlitou Phase IIIA, the people of Erlitou, including local elites—inhabitants of the most important consumption settlement—were not eager to use or even own white ceramics (in contrast to those in Erlitou Phase II). In other words, starting in Erlitou Phase IIIA, the taste or fashion that regarded white ceramics as a sort of prestige good within Erlitou culture changed. One of the most likely reasons for the change of taste or fashion was the appearance of bronze ritual vessels, especially *jue*, which displaced the significance of white ceramic ritual vessels in Erlitou Phase III. It is nonetheless highly likely that the decline of Nanwa, one of the production centers of white ceramics, might have had a positive correlation with the decreasing demand for white ceramics in Erlitou society.

Archaeological Context

An analysis of the archaeological context for white ceramics also provides insight into the production–consumption relationship between Nanwa and Erlitou. During the thriving period of white ceramics production, namely Erlitou Phase II, kilns appeared at Nanwa, particularly in NA I, which was enclosed by Moat G3. More specifically, during Erlitou Phase IIA, in which the quantity and percentage of white ceramics reached their peak at Nanwa, at least three kilns were found in NA I and one in SA II. Although the quantity and percentage of white ceramics started to diminish in Erlitou Phase IIB, one kiln was discovered in NA I at Nanwa. In other words, the production scale of Nanwa, as a center for the production of white ceramics, might be reflected in the numerical data of kilns and white ceramic remains. From Erlitou Phase IIIA, few white ceramics were produced. Although no kiln was found at Nanwa, white ceramics were probably still being made at this site, though the scale of production was much smaller. In addition, although white ceramics might also have been used in the daily life of the production settlement, this sort of prestige good was seemingly not buried in graves as a burial good at Nanwa. One possible reason is that white ceramics were mainly exports and exchange goods, which were used at Erlitou. Another possible reason is that, due to lower social statuses, the potters at Nanwa were prevented from burying white ceramics in their graves. There is of course a third possible explanation: white ceramics were indeed buried within the graves at Nanwa, but excavators have not yet found them.

The analysis of the archaeological context shows that white ceramics played an important role in Erlitou society as a means to display the status of owners. In the consumption metropolis of Erlitou, during Erlitou Phase II, white ceramics were mainly distributed in the palatial area, in which local elites held special events and even dwelled. Furthermore, white ceramic objects, including not only ritual vessels but also objects such as ornaments, were also buried in high-ranking elite graves with other prestige goods, such as jade, turquoise, and lacquerware. In addition, the taste or fashion for white ceramics as prestige goods was not restricted to local elites but also influenced other locals, particularly turquoise and bronze craftsmen. However, from Erlitou Phase IIIA, the taste or fashion of Erlitou, whose inhabitants had viewed white ceramics as prestige goods, changed. During this period, white ceramics decreased dramatically and were seemingly no longer buried within elite graves. At the same time, ritual vessels, particularly *jue*, started to be made with bronze during Erlitou Phase III, and these bronze vessels were also buried in elite graves at that time. In other words, it is highly likely that bronze replaced white ceramics and became the most significant raw material for making ritual vessels for consumption by local elites.

In sum, based on the analyses of numerical data and the archaeological context of white ceramics conducted above, the interaction patterns between Nanwa and Erlitou can be defined within a production–consumption relationship. On the one hand, the producers at Nanwa provided white ceramics to the consumers at Erlitou; on the other hand, the demand for white ceramics at Erlitou directly impacted the rise and fall of Nanwa.

Suggestions for Future Research

In closing, two important issues about white ceramics at Erlitou and Nanwa need to be addressed. First, as shown above, during Erlitou Phase IVB, the quantity and percentage of white ceramics at Erlitou increased dramatically. This increase did not correspond with the developmental trend of the usage of white ceramics in this metropolis, particularly from Erlitou Phase IIB to Erlitou Phase IVA, which reflects a long-term decrease related to the percentage of white ceramics among the entire ceramic assemblage (Table 13.4). According to recent research, two relevant issues related to Erlitou Phase IVB could be take into consideration in exploring this phenomenon. In the first place, the abandonment of Erlitou, or more specifically the end period of the occupation of the palatial area by local elites, is still debatable. Some scholars suggest that the palatial area was occupied by local elites until the end of Erlitou Phase IV (e.g., Xu 2006; Xu and Liu 2008; Xu et al. 2004; Zhongguo Shehui 2014:1658, 1661–62; Zou 1980). Others argue that from Erlitou Phase IVB, Erlitou might have been occupied by nonlocals (e.g., Du 2003; Gao et al. 1998; Zhao 2016; Zhongguo Shehui 2003). In the second place, the period covered by Erlitou Phase IVB in this metropolis is also debatable. The latest excavation report, *Erlitou: 1999–2006*, suggests that Erlitou Phase IVB was equal to Lower Erligang Phase I (Zhongguo Shehui 2014:25, 1654). However, recent research suggests that some remains previously dated to Erlitou Phase IVB at Erlitou should in fact be dated to Lower Erligang Phase II (Li 2018:87). In other words, Erlitou Phase IVB at Erlitou might span the entire Lower Erligang period, during which Zhengzhou Shang City and Yanshi Shang City flourished. In my view, a clarification of these two issues related to the nature of Erlitou Phase IVB would help us investigate the unusual development of the usage of white ceramics at Erlitou during this period.

Second, after the decline of Nanwa during Erlitou Phase IVA, this production center for white ceramics thrived again during the Yinxu period, namely the Late Shang period. It is worth noting that during the Yinxu period, many fine white ceramics also appeared in graves at Anyang, the final capital of the Shang Dynasty (Guo 1951; Liang and Kao 1962, 1965, 1967, 1968, 1970, 1974, 1976; Zhongguo Anyang 1982, 1987, 2017). Although some scholars suggest that the raw material for these fine white ceramics, namely kaolinite, probably came from the east of the Taihang Mountains near Anyang (Yue et al. 2017), we still have to ask: Did the revival of Nanwa have a definitive relationship with the consumption of white ceramics in the Late Shang capital? This is an intriguing topic to be explored in future research.

In sum, the research on white ceramics at Erlitou and Nanwa provides a crucial case study for investigating interaction patterns within the Erlitou culture from an economic perspective. This case study also should prompt us to inquire into various possible interaction patterns in early China more generally through the comparative analysis of archaeological contexts.

Let me close this article with an insightful statement from Lothar von Falkenhausen, which motivates me to explore various possible patterns of interaction in early China. In chapter 5, "Ethnic Contrasts within the Zhou Culture Sphere (ca. 1050–350 BCE)," in *Chinese Society in the Age of Confucius (1000–250 BC)*, von Falkenhausen analyzes how so-called aliens interacted with high-ranking Zhou aristocratic lineages and the Qin core population. As he has mentioned, the interaction between different human groups that lived in different social, political, economic, and cultural settings is highly complex. I believe one possible approach to investigating this interaction in early China is the comparative analysis of archaeological contexts, which is inspired by von Falkenhausen: "To feel somewhat confident about inferring an ethnic association . . . one needs both a clear archaeological context for the 'alien' evidence, and a well-documented non-'alien' background to contrast it with" (Falkenhausen 2006:233).

Acknowledgments

This article serves as a supplement to my dissertation, "Erlitou and Its Neighbors: Contextualizing Interregional Interaction in the Central Yellow River Region in Ancient China" (Lee 2018). First of all, I would like to thank Anke Hein, the organizer of the workshop, for celebrating Lothar von Falkenhausen's sixtieth birthday and for giving me this opportunity to pursue the particular argument made above. Also, I would like to thank Hein and Rowan K. Flad for reviewing the draft of this article and for providing thoughtful and considerable comments for the revision. When I was still working on my dissertation, von Falkenhausen also offered me many valuable suggestions. In closing, I would like to dedicate this article to Lothar von Falkenhausen, for both his kind encouragement and his thoughtful advice between 2011 and 2018. *Herzlichen Glückwunsch zum Geburtstag!*

Notes

1   In fact, the official report, based on the latest results of 14C dating from Erlitou, merely mentions that Erlitou Phase I dates from 1750 to 1680 BC and that Erlitou Phases II, III, and IV date from 1680 to 1530 BC (Zhongguo Shehui 2014:1236).

2   The percentage may be overestimated due to a small sample size.

3   The percentage may be overestimated due to a small sample size.

References

Beijing Daxue Kaogu Wenbo Xueyuan 北京大學考古文博學院 and Henan Sheng Wenwu Kaogu Yanjiusuo 河南省文物考古研究所
2007   *Dengfeng Wangchenggang kaogu faxian yu yanjiu* 登封王城崗考古發現與研究. Zhengzhou: Daxiang Chubanshe.

Beijing Daxue Zhendan Gudai Wenming Yanjiu Zhongxin 北京大學震旦文明研究中心 and Zhengzhou Shi Wenwu Kaogu Yanjiuyuan 鄭州市文物考古研究院
2008   *Xinmi Xinzhai: 1999–2000 nian tianye kaogu fajue baogao* 新密新砦: 1999–2000年田野考古發掘報告. Beijing: Wenwu Chubanshe.

Chen Guoliang 陳國梁
2014   Luelun Erlitou yizhi de weiyuan zuofang qu 略論二里頭遺址的圍垣作坊區. In *Xia Shang duyi yu wenhua (er)* 夏商都邑與文化 (二), edited by Zhongguo Shehui Kexueyuan Kaogu Yanjiusuo 中國社會科學院考古研究所, pp. 92–108. Beijing: Zhongguo Shehui Kexue Chubanshe.

Chen Guoliang 陳國梁 and Li Zhipeng 李志鵬
2016   Erlitou yizhi zhigu yicun de kaocha 二里頭遺址製骨遺存的考察. *Kaogu* 考古 2016(5):59–70.

Cusick, James G.
1998   *Studies in Culture Contact: Interaction, Culture Change, and Archaeology*. Carbondale: Southern Illinois University Press.

Du Jinpeng 杜金鵬
2003 "Yanshi Shang cheng jiebiaoshuo" jiexi "偃師商城界標說" 解析. In *Huaxia wenming de xingcheng yu fazhao* 華夏文明的形成與發展, edited by Henan Sheng Wenwu Kaogu Yanjiusuo 河南省文物考古研究所, pp. 252–64. Zhengzhuo: Daxiang Chubanshe.

Falkenhausen, Lothar von
2006 *Chinese Society in the Age of Confucius (1000–250 BC): The Archaeological Evidence*. Los Angeles: Cotsen Institute of Archaeology Press.

Gao Wei 高煒, Yang Xizhang 楊錫璋, Wang Wei 王巍, and Du Jinpeng 杜金鵬
1998 Yanshi Shang cheng yu Xia Shang fenjie 偃師商城與夏商分界. *Kaogu* 考古1988(10):66–70.

Guo Baojun 郭寶鈞
1951 Yi jiu wu lin nian chun Yinxu fajue baogao 一九五〇年春殷墟發掘報告. *Zhongguo kaogu xuebao* 中國考古學報 5:1–61.

Han Guohe 韓國河, Zhao Weijuan 趙維娟, Zhang Jihua 張繼華, and Zhu Junxiao 朱君孝
2007 Yong zhongzi huohua fenxi yanjiu Nanwa baitao de yuanliao chandi 用中子活化分析研究南窪白陶的原料產地. *Zhongyuan wenwu* 中原文物 2007(6):83–86.

Han Weizhou 韓維周, Ding Boquan 丁伯泉, Zhang Yongjie 張永傑, and Sun Baode 孫寶德
1954 Henan Dengfeng xian Yucun gu wenhua yizhi gaikuang 河南登封縣玉村古文化遺址概況. *Wenwu cankao ziliao* 文物參考資料6:18–24.

Henan Sheng Wenhuaju Wenwu Gongzuodui 河南省文化局文物工作隊
1964 Henan Mianchi Lusi Shang dai yizhi shijue jianbao 河南澠池鹿寺商代遺址試掘簡報. *Kaogu* 考古1964(9):435–40.

Henan Sheng Wenwu Kaogu Yanjiusuo 河南省文物考古研究所
1996 Henan Yichuan xian Nanzhai Erlitou wenhua muzang fajue jianbao 河南伊川縣南寨二里頭文化墓葬發掘簡報. *Kaogu*考古 1996(12):36–43.
2012 *Yichuan kaogu baogao* 伊川考古報告. Zhengzhou: Daxiang Chubanshe.

Henan Sheng Wenwu Yanjiusuo 河南省文物研究所
1989 Shaan xian Xiyacun yizhi de fajue 陝縣西崖村遺址的發掘. *Huaxia kaogu* 華夏考古 1989(1):15–47.
1993 Henan Gongxian Shaochai yizhi fajue baogao 河南鞏縣稍柴遺址發掘報告. *Huaxia kaogu* 華夏考古1993(2):1–45.

Henan Sheng Wenwu Yanjiusuo 河南省文物研究所 and Mianchi Xian Wenhuaguan 澠池縣文化館
1987 Mianchi xian Zhengyao yizhi fajue baogao 澠池縣鄭窯遺址發掘報告. *Huaxia kaogu* 華夏考古1987(2):47–95.

Henan Sheng Wenwu Yanjiusuo 河南省文物研究所 and Yu Xian Wenguanhui 禹縣文管會
1991 Henan Yu xian Ying he liang'an kaogu diaocha yu shijue 河南省禹縣潁河兩岸考古調查與試掘. *Kaogu* 考古1991(2):97–108, 146.

Henan Wenwu Gongzuodui Di'erdui Sunqitun Qingli Xiaozu 河南文物工作隊第二隊孫旗屯清理小組
1955 Luoyang Jianxi Sunqitun gu yizhi 洛陽澗西孫旗屯古遺址. *Wenwu cankao ziliao* 文物參考資料9:58–64.

Huanghe Shuiku Kaogu Gongzuodui Henan Fendui 黃河水庫考古工作隊河南分隊
1960 Henan Shaan xian Qilipu Shang dai yizhi de fajue 河南陝縣七里鋪商代遺址的發掘. *Kaogu xuebao* 考古學報1960(1):25–49.

Lee Hsiu-ping 李修平
2018 *Erlitou and Its Neighbors: Contextualizing Interregional Interaction in the Central Yellow River Region in Ancient China*. PhD dissertation, Cotsen Institute of Archaeology, University of California–Los Angeles.

Li Baoping 李寶平, Liu Li 劉莉, Zhao Jianxin 趙建新, Chen Xingcan 陳星燦, Feng Yuexing 俸月星, Han Guohe 韓國河, and Zhu Junxiao 朱君孝
2008 Chemical Fingerprinting of Whitewares from Nanwa Site of the Chinese Erlitou State: Comparison with Gongxian and Ding Kilns. *Nuclear Instruments and Methods in Physics Research, Section B, Beam Interactions with Materials and Atoms* 266:2614–22.

Li Baoping 李寶平, Liu Li 劉莉, Chen Xingcan 陳星燦, Zhao Jianxin 趙建新, Feng Yuexing 俸月星, Xu Hong 許宏, Han Guohe 韓國河, and Zhu Junxiao 朱君孝
2009 Yanshi Erlitou yizhi chutu baitao chandi de chubu tantao ji si tongweisu fenxi de zhongyao yiyi 偃師二里頭遺址出土白陶產地的初步探討及鍶同位素分析的重要意義. In *'09 gu taoci kexue jishu 7 guoji taolunhui lunwenji* '09古陶瓷科學技術7國際討論會論文集, edited by Luo Hongjie 羅宏傑 and Zheng Xinmiao 鄭欣淼, pp. 65–70. Shanghai: Shanghai Kexue Jishu Wenxian Chubanshe.

Li Bao-Ping 李寶平, Liu Li 劉莉, Chen Xing-Can 陳星燦, Zhao Jian-Xin 趙建新, J. Drennan, A. Greig, Feng Yue-Xing 俸月星, M. Lawrence, Xu Hong 許宏, Han Guo-He 韓國河, Zhu Jun-Xiao 朱君孝, and Zhang Song-Lin 張松林
2010 Chemical Comparison of Rare Chinese White Pottery from Four Sites of the Erlitou State: Results and Archaeological Implications. *Archaeometry* 52.5:760–76.

Li Feng 李峰
2006 *Landscape and Power in Early China: The Crisis and Fall of the Western Zhou, 1045–771 BC.* Cambridge: Cambridge University Press.

Li Hongfei 李宏飛
2018 Erlitou wenhua di si qi wanduan yicun niandai xiaxian de tantao 二里頭文化第四期晚段遺存年代下限的探討. *Kaogu* 考古 2018(11):82–91.

Li Zhipeng 李志鵬
2008 Erlitou wenhua muzang yanjiu 二里頭文化墓葬研究. In *Zhongguo zaoqi qingtong wenhua: Erlitou wenhua zhuanti yanjiu* 中國早期青銅文化：二里頭文化專題研究, edited by Zhongguo Shehui Kexueyuan Kaogu Yanjiusuo 中國社會科學院考古研究所, pp. 1–123. Beijing: Kexue Chubanshe.

Liang Ssu-yung 梁思永 and Kao Ch'ü-hsün 高去尋
1962 *Hou Chia Chuang*, Vol. 2, *HPKM 1001* 侯家莊第二本 1001號大墓. Taipei: Institute of History and Philology, Academia Sinica.
1965 *Hou Chia Chuang*, Vol. 3, *HPKM 1002* 侯家莊第三本 1002號大墓. Taipei: Institute of History and Philology, Academia Sinica.
1967 *Hou Chia Chuang*, Vol. 4, *HPKM 1003* 侯家莊第四本 1003號大墓. Taipei: Institute of History and Philology, Academia Sinica.
1968 *Hou Chia Chuang*, Vol. 6, *HPKM 1217* 侯家莊第六本 1217號大墓. Taipei: Institute of History and Philology, Academia Sinica.
1970 *Hou Chia Chuang*, Vol. 5, *HPKM 1004* 侯家莊第五本 1004號大墓. Taipei: Institute of History and Philology, Academia Sinica.
1974 *Hou Chia Chuang*, Vol. 7, *HPKM 1500* 侯家莊第七本 1500號大墓. Taipei: Institute of History and Philology, Academia Sinica.
1976 *Hou Chia Chuang*, Vol. 8, *HPKM 1550* 侯家莊第八本 1550號大墓. Taipei: Institute of History and Philology, Academia Sinica.

Liu Li 劉莉
2003 The Products of Minds as Well as of Hands: Production of Prestige Goods in the Neolithic and Early State Periods of China. *Asian Perspectives* 42:1–40.

Liu Li 劉莉 and Chen Xingcan 陳星燦
2003 *State Formation in Early China.* London: Duckworth.

Liu Li 劉莉, Chen Xingcan 陳星燦, Lee Yun Kuen 李潤權, Henry Wright, and Arlene Rosen
2004 Settlement Patterns and Development of Social Complexity in the Yiluo Region, North China. *Journal of Field Archaeology* 29:75–100.

Liu Li 劉莉, Chen Xingcan 陳星燦, and Li Baoping 李寶平
2007 Non-State Crafts in the Early Chinese State: An Archaeological View from the Erlitou Hinterland. *Bulletin of the Indo-Pacific Prehistory Association* 27:93–102.

Liu Xu 劉緒
1990 Lun Wei Huai diqu de Xia Shang wenhua 論衛懷地區的夏商文化. In *Jinian Beijing daxue kaogu zhuanye san shi zhounian lunwenji* 紀念北京大學考古專業三十週年論文集, edited by Beijing Daxue Kaoguxi 北京大學考古系, pp. 171–210. Beijing: Wenwu Chubanshe.

Luan Fengshi 欒豐實
2010 Haidai diqu shiqian baitao chulun 海岱地區史前白陶初論. *Kaogu* 考古 2010(4):58–70.

Luoyang Bowuguan 洛陽博物館
1978a Luoyang Cuoli yizhi shijue jianbao 洛陽矬李遺址試掘簡報. *Kaogu* 考古 1978(1):5–17.
1978b Luoyang Dongmagou Erlitou leixing muzang. 洛陽東馬溝二里頭類型墓葬. *Kaogu* 考古 1978(1):18–22.

Luoyang Diqu Wenwuchu 洛陽地區文管會
1982 Yichuan Baiyuan yizhi fajue jianbao 伊川白元遺址發掘簡報. *Zhongyuan wenwu* 中原文物 1982(3):7–14.

Luoyang Shi Wenwu Gongzuodui 洛陽市文物工作隊
2002 *Luoyang Zaojiaoshu: 1992–1993 nian Luoyang Zaojiaoshu Erlitou wenhua juluo yizhi fajue baogao* 洛陽皂角樹：1992–1993年洛陽皂角樹二里頭文化聚落遺址發掘報告. Beijing: Kexue Chubanshe.

Mai Gewen 麥戈文, Fang Hui 方輝, Luan Fengshi 欒豐實, Yu Haiguang 于海廣, Wen De'an 文德安, Wang Chenshan 王辰珊, Cai Fengshu 蔡鳳書, Gelixin Huo'er 格里辛霍爾, Jiali Feiman 加里費曼, and Zhao Zhijun 趙志軍
2005 Shandong Rizhao shi Liangchengzhen yizhi Longshan wenhua jiu yicun de huaxue fenxi: jiantan jiu zai shiqian shiqi de wenhua yiyi 山東

日照市兩城鎮遺址龍山文化酒遺存的化學分析: 兼談酒在史前時期的文化意義. *Kaogu* 考古 2005(3):73–85.

Schortman, Edward M., and Patricia A. Urban
1992　*Resources, Power, and Interregional Interaction.* New York: Plenum Press.

Stein, Gil J.
2002　From Passive Periphery to Active Agents: Emerging Perspectives in the Archaeology of Interregional Interaction. *American Anthropologist* 104.3:903–16.

Xu Hong 許宏
2006　Erlitou 1 hao gongdian jizhi shiyong niandai chuyi 二里頭1號宮殿基址使用年代芻議. In *Erlitou yizhi yu Erlitou wenhua yanjiu* 二里頭遺址與二里頭文化研究, edited by Du Jinpeng 杜金鵬 and Xu Hong 許宏, pp. 64–77. Beijing: Kexue Chubanshe.

Xu Hong 許宏, Chen Guoliang 陳國梁, and Zhao Haitao 趙海濤
2004　Erlitou yizhi juluo xingtai de chubu kaocha 二里頭遺址聚落型態的初步考察. *Kaogu* 考古 2004(11):23–31.

Xu Hong 許宏 and Liu Li 劉莉
2008　Guanyu Erlitou yizhi de xingsi 關於二里頭遺址的省思. *Wenwu* 文物2008(1):42–52.

Yue Zhanwei 岳占偉, Jing Zhichun 荊志淳, Yue Hongbin 岳洪彬, Niu Shishan 牛世山, Tang Jigen 唐際根, He Yuling 何毓靈, and Guo Meng 郭夢
2017　Yinxu baitao de chubu yanjiu 殷墟白陶的初步研究. *Nanfang wenwu* 南方文物2017(4):64–74.

Zhao Haitao 趙海濤
2016　Erlitou yizhi Erlitou wenhua si qi wanduan yicun tanxi 二里頭遺址二里頭文化四期晚段遺存探析. *Nanfang wenwu* 南方文物2016(4):115–23.

Zheng Guang 鄭光
1985　Yanshi xian Erlitou yizhi 偃師縣二里頭遺址. In *Zhongguo kaoguxue nianjian (1985)* 中國考古學年鑑 (1985), pp. 162–63. Beijing: Wenwu Chubanshe.

Zheng Guang 鄭光, Yang Guozhong 楊國忠, Zhang Guozhu 張國柱, and Du Jinpeng 杜金鵬
1984　Yanshi xian Erlitou yizhi 偃師縣二里頭遺址. In *Zhongguo kaoguxue nianjian (1984)* 中國考古學年鑑 (1984), pp. 128–29. Beijing: Wenwu Chubanshe.

Zhengzhou Daxue Lishi Wenhua Yichan Baohu Yanjiu Zhongxin 鄭州大學歷史文化遺產保護研究中心
2014　*Dengfeng Nanwa: 2004–2006 nian tianye kaogu baogao* 登封南窪: 2004–2006年田野考古報告. Beijing: Kexue Chubanshe.

Zhengzhou Shi Wenwu Kaogu Yanjiuyuan 鄭州市文物考古研究院 and Henan Sheng Wenwu Guanliju Nan Shui Bei Diao Wenwu Baohu Bangongshi 河南省文物管理局南水北調文物保護辦公室
2014　Xingyang Niangniangzhai yizhi Erlitou wenhua yicun fajue jianbao 滎陽娘娘寨遺址二里頭文化遺存發掘簡報. *Zhongyuan wenwu* 中原文物2014(1):4–12.

Zhongguo Shehui Kexueyuan Kaogu Yanjiusuo 中國社會科學院考古研究所
1989　*Luoyang fajue baogao: 1955–1960 nian Luoyang Jianbin kaogu fajue ziliao* 洛陽發掘報告: 1955–1960年洛陽澗濱考古發掘資料. Beijing: Beijing Yanshan Chubanshe.
1995　*Erlitou taoqi jicui* 二里頭陶器集粹. Beijing: Zhongguo Shehui Kexue Chubanshe.
1999　*Yanshi Erlitou: 1959 nian–1978 nian kaogu fajue baogao* 偃師二里頭: 1959年–1978年考古發掘報告. Beijing: Zhongguo Dabaikequanshu Chubanshe.
2003　*Zhongguo kaoguxue: Xia Shang juan* 中國考古學: 夏商卷. Beijing: Zhongguo Shehui Kexue Chubanshe.
2014　*Erlitou: 1999–2006* 二里頭: 1999–2006. Beijing: Wenwu Chubanshe.

Zhongguo Shehui Kexueyuan Kaogu Yanjiusuo Anyang Dui 中國社會科學院考古研究所安陽隊
1987　Yinxu 259, 260 hao mu fajue baogao 殷墟259, 260號墓發掘報告. *Kaogu xuebao* 考古學報1987(1):99–117.

Zhongguo Shehui Kexueyuan Kaogu Yanjiusuo Anyang Gongzuodui 中國社會科學院考古研究所安陽工作隊.
1982　Anyang Houjiazhuang Beidi yi hao mu fajue jianbao 安陽侯家莊北地一號墓發掘簡報. *Kaoguxue jikan* 考古學季刊2:35–40.
2017　1978 nian Anyang Yinxu wanglingqu Houjiazhuang Beidi yi hao mu fajue baogao 1978年安陽殷墟王陵區侯家莊北地一號墓發掘報告. *Jianghan kaogu* 江漢考古 2017(3):20–56.

Zhongguo Shehui Kexueyuan Kaogu Yanjiusuo Erlitou Dui 中國社會科學院考古研究所二里頭隊
1983　1980 nian qiu Henan Yanshi Erlitou yizhi fajue jianbao 1980年秋河南偃師二里頭遺址發掘簡報. *Kaogu* 考古1983(3):199–205, 219.
1985　1982 nian qiu Yanshi Erlitou yizhi jiu qu fajue jianbao 1982年秋偃師二里頭遺址九區發掘簡報. *Kaogu* 考古1985(12):1085–93, 1108.

Zhongguo Shehui Kexueyuan Kaogu Yanjiusuo Erlitou Gongzuodui 中國社會科學院考古研究所二里頭工作隊

1984　1981 nian Henan Yanshi Erlitou muzang fajue jianbao 1981年河南偃師二里頭墓葬發掘簡報. *Kaogu* 考古1984(1):37–40.

1986　1984 nian qiu Henan Yanshi Erlitou yizhi faxian de jizuo muzang 1984年秋河南偃師二里頭遺址發現的幾座墓葬. *Kaogu* 考古1986(4):318–23.

1992　1987 nian Yanshi Erlitou yizhi muzhang fajue jianbao 1987年偃師二里頭遺址墓葬發掘簡報. *Kaogu* 考古1992(4):294–303.

2015　Henan Yanshi shi Erlitou yizhi qiangyuan he daolu 2012–2013 nian fajue jianbao 河南偃師市二里頭遺址牆垣和道路2012–2013年發掘簡報. *Kaogu* 考古2015(1):40–58.

Zhongguo Shehui Kexueyuan Kaogu Yanjiusuo Henan Diyi Gongzuodui 中國社會科學院考古研究所河南第一工作隊

2010　Henan Yanshi shi Huizui yizhi xizhi 2004 nian fajue jianbao 河南偃師市灰嘴遺址西址2004年發掘簡報. *Kaogu* 考古2010(2):36–46.

Zhongguo Shehui Kexueyuan Kaogu Yanjiusuo Henan Er Dui 中國社會科學院考古研究所河南二隊

1982　Henan Linru Meishan yizhi fajue baogao 河南臨汝煤山遺址發掘報告. *Kaogu xuebao* 考古學報1982(4):427–76.

Zou Heng 鄒衡

1980　Shilun Xia wenhua 試論夏文化. In *Xia Shang Zhou kaoguxue lunwenji* 夏商周考古學論文集, pp. 95–182. Beijing: Wenwu Chubanshe.

Chapter 14

Archaeology of Community
Changing Settlement Patterns from the Yingpanshan to the Shi'erqiao Period in Ancient Sichuan, China

Lin Kuei-chen

In recent decades, researchers have gradually pieced together the cultural history of the prehistoric Chengdu Plain (see Table 14.1) and have begun to study its origins through numerous excavations and regional surveys conducted or published in recent years (e.g., Chengdu and Chengdu 2017; Chengdu and Dayi 2015a, 2015b, 2016; Chengdu and Xinjin 2016; Lei Yu 2014; Liu et al. 2017; Sichuan et al. 2013, 2016). Many speculations and models have been devised to account for the sociopolitical forms at each stage of cultural development. Such studies typically treat societies from this region through an evolutionary lens, with each inexorably marching toward a complex state. To consider the entire region as a coherent, progressive entity has the advantage of providing an outline for an overall trend, though this is not without its own problems, as constituent societies are hardly homogeneous. In a series of articles, Lothar von Falkenhausen demonstrated—by discussing the Sanxingdui 三星堆 site (Falkenhausen 2003; Falkenhausen, ed. 2003) and the Zhuwajie 竹瓦街 site (Falkenhausen 2001) on the Chengdu Plain, the Moutuo 牟托 site (Falkenhausen 1996) on the upper Min River, and various Bronze Age sites in the upper Han River basin (Falkenhausen 2011)—that these societies can have multidirectional connections with other regions and have had many forms of exchange. He broadly compared related settlements, their production and economic modes, and how these might relate to their social and ritual systems, with special attention to the coexistence of different sources of material cultures and their implications. He observed that the uses and symbolic meanings of things are permutable when transported to other societies (Falkenhausen 2003). With many possibilities for exchange relationships, Falkenhausen (2006b) also convincingly argued, societies that used to be thought of as peripheries or subordinated can be understood to be independent of other, seemingly stronger polities, sometimes even taking more active roles in the management of desirable resources. Such insights into diverse and changeable economic modes, social relationships, and external connections have influenced this paper.

We often lack clear or recognizable boundaries when thinking about the nature of a society, whether it was an urban center or a rural region. The bonds that maintained such a society were also diverse. Some were even subtle, shaped by brief and ritual systems and extended kin networks that were biologically or socially constructed (Falkenhausen 2006a). In a similar manner, the organization, or lack of thereof, of households, as well as supra-household activities for each community, also diverged. By comparing the different periods of western Sichuan, this paper attempts to investigate the most important communal activities, production, and rituals that helped to maintain a community and might help to delineate its scope.

The value of using "community" as an analytical unit between household and region or state is that it provides a context for supra-household interactions and communal activities that is able to reflect both the ecosystem and human relationships. To form a community and a community identity is to have a group of interrelated people who share the

Table 14.1. Archaeological cultures prevailing on the Chengdu Plain and the Hengduan Mountains mentioned in the text

Culture or Phase	Period	Note
Yingpanshan 營盤山	3300–2600 BC	
Baodun 寶墩	2700–1700 BC	includes Sanxingdui I
Sanxingdui 三星堆	1700–1150 BC	Sanxingdui II–III
Shi'erqiao 十二橋	1200–600 BC	includes Jinsha, Xinyicun, and Sanxingdui IV

same interests and attend to communal activities (Goldstein 2000). Such a space is not neutral but is an important context for social interactions (Yaeger and Canuto 2000:1). It is also a moderately sized unit, allowing archaeologists to assess changes in accumulated daily practices and how such changes might be related to long-term and large-scale cultural transformations (see Birch 2013). To define an analytical unit like this can also provide a viable way to study settlement patterns, which often include a wide range of scales, from the inner layout of a settlement to intersite relations in a region. A community specifically describes the space and layout inside a settlement and, more importantly, the communal activities, daily life, and relationships within such a space (see Birch 2013:6). These activities and interactions, based on consanguinity, affinity, or neighborhood, thus produce patterned behaviors, habitus, or idiosyncrasies that render such spaces and material culture recognizable in archaeology. A community, which provides a scope for social interactions and sets the social background for material remains, is therefore an archaeologically meaningful unit (Chang 1968).

Despite the distinction in the level of abstraction and different emphases, "settlement" and "community" remain interrelated concepts. To compare different settlement patterns over time is to discover how a community or communities can be distinctively produced. Not only do we have to acknowledge the manner in which the landscape shaped a community; we also expect to discover how ancient people identified themselves and used communal activities, including rites, (ceremonial) feasts, collaborative production, infrastructure projects, and trade, to consolidate their identities while eliminating social tensions (Flad 2012; Lin 2019), thereby distinguishing themselves from others. It is also noted that human relationships in communal life might be multiple, contextual, and changeable. However, despite its seemingly small scale and delimitation in a domestic space composed of house lots (Sutro and Downing 1988:33), a community is susceptible to larger social and cultural changes and should not be considered in isolation.

To consider particular social groups as "natural" or "real" communities, though (re)constructed by archaeologists, unlike the "imagined communities" posited by Benedict Anderson (1991) in 1983, emphasizes people's everyday lives and interactions in daily practice. Natural communities, however, were constituted not solely through blood ties but also through certain cultural and social means, such as co-residence, religion, and fictive consanguinity (Falkenhausen 2006a:166; Wang 1997), processes of which people may not have been fully conscious. These exercises of social construction have often been materialized and can be identified through archaeological features or material remains, such as ritual paraphernalia. In forming a sense of a community, in which participants share common interests and have the same experiences, we can thus observe the processes through which humans and things mutually define one another. The methods devised to study communities in the following cases therefore focus on the spatial distributions of physical (e.g., walls and ditches) and invisible (e.g., artifact styles or ways to form an assemblage) boundaries that delimit a community. I also pay special attention to how people sharing similar interests might interact in spaces during communal activities, such as ritual gatherings or labor-intensive constructions that promoted community cohesion and identity.

Beginning: Whose Ancestors from the Highlands?

Bounded by high mountains, the Mao Xian 茂縣 basin on the upper Min 岷 River once hosted Yingpanshan 營盤山 (3300–2600 BC; Chengdu et al. 2018), the largest known settlement of this region during the Neolithic period. The prominent landscape and traffic routes, mostly through river valleys, must have influenced the manner of communication between Yingpanshan people and external, far-flung regions. Such a landscape might have also shaped their community identity (see Herrera 2007 about landscapes and identities). Although the reason remains unclear, it is apparent that painted pottery and vessels with double-layered rims with small openings (*shuangchun shi xiaokou ping* 雙唇式小口瓶), found in Yingpanshan and nearby sites, were transmitted from Majiayao 馬家窯 culture and possibly also Yangshao 仰韶 culture locations to the north, in modern Gansu and Qinghai Provinces (Chengdu et al. 2018; Hung et al. 2011). These sites have yielded painted pottery scattered across not only the upper Min River and upper Dadu 大渡 River in northwestern Sichuan but also the lower Dadu River in southwestern Sichuan (Figure 14.1). Some scholars have suggested that waves of migrants coming from the north via these river valleys and their tributaries owe to climate deterioration, especially a cooling event in about 5500 BC (e.g., Chen and Wang 2004), and possibly also population pressure (Li 2011). Such movements might have been further encouraged by the similar landscape and living conditions in western Sichuan and the upper Yellow River and the mobility of the migrants' livestock, which was their major subsistence (Yuan and Luo 2014).

When painted pottery was introduced to the upper Min drainages from the north, the inhabitants of the region seemingly also began to adopt subsistence economies that prevailed in the north, such as millet cultivation (both broomcorn and foxtail; Zhao and Chen 2011) and high-intensive domestication of pigs, in which pigs were fed with household foods or leftovers (Barton et al. 2009; Lee et al. 2018). Some scholars thus suggest that Neolithic sites on the upper Min River should be thought of as a regional phase of the Yangshao culture (Chen and Wang 2004) or the Majiayao culture (He 2011, 2015), implying a lifestyle aligned with that in the north. However, although such a lifestyle on the upper Min River was seemingly shaped by external cultures, it was inevitably transformed by the inner structure of local societies (see Yaeger and Canuto 2000:2) through a process of indigenization. Local potters, for instance, made ceramic vessel types that were similar to imports from the north, but they lacked painted decorations

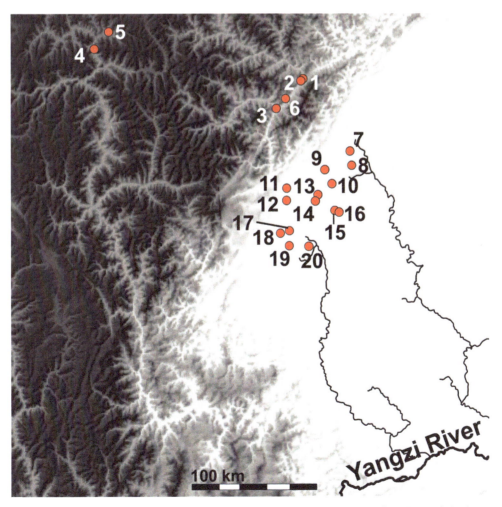

Figure 14.1. Neolithic sites on the upper Min River mentioned in the text: 1. Yingpanshan; 2. Boxi; 3. Jiangweicheng; 4. Konglongcun; 5. Haxiu; 6. Shawudu. *Created by Bryan K. Miller.*

(Hung et al. 2011). Moreover, they also made ceramics found exclusively in this region. This juxtaposition of three production modes—exotic pots, imitations of mixed styles, and local types—shows how the inhabitants of the upper Min River responded to external impetuses derived from human migrations, itinerant potters, or trade.

Excavations at Yingpanshan have uncovered a hard-stamped floor extended to several hundred square meters, beneath which there are four human sacrifices (Chengdu et al. 2018:6). The excavators speculate that the area with hard-stamped earth was a plaza where ritual and some public activities were held (Jiang and Chen 2003). During such activities, social interactions were intensified and a certain level of decision-making or consensus-finding could have been reached. In addition, the Yingpanshan inhabitants were able to exploit a wide range of environmental resources, such as bovids, deer, bears, dogs, boars, monkeys, shells, fish, birds, millet, peaches, walnuts, plums, and apricots, as seen in the many faunal and floral remains unearthed from the site (Chengdu et al. 2018:540, 575; He 2009; Zhao and Chen 2011). In all senses, the society was not simply an attachment or outpost of the Majiayao, even though its people exhibit some similarities in their material culture.

In this region, traffic was funneled through corridors (Huo 2005). As a result, the settlement pattern in the upper Min River was shaped by the landscape. This landscape created passable valleys that connected people to external regions as well as to local natural resources. Settlements scattered along the river drainages formed a dendritic structure (Figure 14.2). Settlements also tended to cluster around the convergence of small drainages and developed into nexuses, such as the Yingpanshan site, when the landform permitted. Such nexuses might have been critical for the circulation of materials, technologies, and ideas. Distribution modes and communications with the north must have also influenced the distribution of later settlements, including those with stone-slate burials.

The stone-slate funeral customs popular in the western Sichuan highlands were perhaps influenced by the culture of the Zongri 宗日 site in Qinghai, again via corridors on the eastern edge of the Qinghai-Tibet Plateau or the Hengduan 橫斷 Mountains, and extended farther south to the Lancang 瀾滄 River drainage in Northwest Yunnan. Such customs had been popular for a long time, from the end of the second millennium BC to the Han Dynasty (202 BC–AD 220). They possess, however, some regional diversity, especially during the Bronze Age, and cannot be lumped into a single group (Luo 2012; Yuan and Luo 2014:115). At some sites, stone coffins or related features were deposited directly above the Neolithic depositions with nothing between them, although there is a chronological gap between the two periods of deposition. Jars discovered in many of these stone-slate funerals as burial goods (e.g., Chen 2012; Luo 2012:281–87; Xie 2005), which are similar to those of the Qijia 齊家 culture (ca. 2500–1500 BC) in the north, suggest that connections between western Sichuan and its north were seemingly not interrupted.

However, cultural centers gradually shifted to the lowlands in what is today modern Chengdu City, starting around 3000 BC, when the Guiyuanqiao 桂圓橋 site, located in the foothills, was occupied (Sichuan et al. 2013; Wan and Lei 2013). While the population of the Chengdu Plain increased, it is believed that the pottery production of Yingpanshan influenced Baodun 寶墩 potters living in the foothills of the western Sichuan mountains (which I discuss further in the following section). This influence is exemplified by some Baodun ceramic prototypes that can be traced back to Yingpanshan ceramics, especially jars with impressed decorations on their rims and vats with deep bellies (Figure 14.3). Some archaeologists (e.g., He 2016; Huang and Zhao 2004; Jiang 2004, 2015) therefore consider the upper Min River valleys to be the origin of the Baodun culture and its succeeding cultures on the Chengdu Plain, perhaps through some transitional phase, such as the yet little studied Guiyuanqiao culture (3100–2100 BC).

Organizing the Public: The Emergence of Walled Settlements on the Chengdu Plain

The Baodun period (ca. 2500–1700 BC) was a turning point, during which large settlements emerged and developed into regional centers on the Chengdu Plain. A number of walled settlements successively appeared,[1] first in the foothills of the mountains and then farther toward the center of the Chengdu Plain (Flad and Chen 2013:106; Jiang 2015; Zhou 2010). This shift from the highlands to the lowlands might indicate that flooding conditions and the environment, which tormented the lowlands, had come under greater control after the late Neolithic period. In addition, rice was introduced probably from the middle Yangzi River at this time or slightly earlier (Chengdu and Xinjin 2011b; Sichuan 2015a) and replaced millet as the most important crop, although millet might still have served as a complement (d'Alpoim Guedes 2011; Huo 2009; Jiang 2015). It is likely that the adoption of rice as the major staple crop and the growing of two or more kinds of crops complementarily would have reduced food crises during climate fluctuations and further induced food surpluses (d'Alpoim Guedes 2011). With an increase in the number of sites and

Figure 14.2. Neolithic sites on the eastern edge of Qinghai-Tibet Plateau. *Redrawn by the author from Hung et al. 2011.*

site sizes, the cultivation of rice seemingly also caused population growth, as was the case in the domestication core on the lower Yangzi (Fuller and Qin 2009). The Baodun settlement, for instance, expanded from 60 to 276 ha due to population growth and was enclosed by double walls and ditches, making the settlement the largest known on the Chengdu Plain and the fourth largest on the East Asian continent at the time (Chengdu and Xinjin 2011a; He 2015).

The new subsistence practice might also have changed their lifestyle and manner of storing and consuming surplus food. At least eight large buildings, a few possible storage houses, and a number of house foundations have been unearthed at Baodun, accompanied by burials, pottery kilns, and considerable quantities of ash pits (He 2015; He and Tang 2020; Jiang 2015). Among the large buildings, F1 and F3, with sizes of 210 m² and 300 m², respectively, are located at the Gudunzi 鼓墩子 locus near the center of the inner enclosure (Chengdu and Xinjin 2012; He and Tang 2020; Jiang 2015). The settlement can be further divided into several parts, with naturally or artificially raised lands. Archaeologists suggest that the enclosure might have been a collective settlement that included a number of smaller residential areas, each of which possessed a few graves and ash pits, which might be thought of themselves as small settlements (Jiang 2015). In some sections, artificial ditches were directed to connect with ancient rivers, likely forming simple drainage and irrigation systems (Chengdu and Xinjin 2016). The potters produced ceramic vessels of high quality, which were carefully made, from the selection of clay to firing controls (Chengdu et al. 2000). Pots were mostly made in fine wares and fired under high temperatures. They tend to be large and most suitable for storage. The burials were very simple and contained no grave goods. They were, however, consistently oriented to either NW–SE or SW–NE, indicating some communal planning and ordering that might reflect a shared belief system. Interestingly, such orientations were followed not only by other peer settlements enclosed by walls but also by later people on the Chengdu Plain. For instance, the cemeteries unearthed from the Gaoshan 高山 site, which is roughly contemporaneous to the Baodun site, contain at least 100 burials arranged following these orientations (Chengdu and Dayi 2015a; Liu et al. 2017; Zhou et al. 2015). The Yangguang Didai 陽光地帶 II locus, which had been used for cemeteries for about 500 years (ca. 1400–900 BC) at the Jinsha 金沙 site, yielded 290 burials oriented in the same directions (Chengdu and Chengdu 2017).

Despite this shared ideology, people did not nucleate at a single settlement center during the Baodun period. On the contrary, the population was distributed across other walled settlements that contained important features besides their artificial walls. For instance, the foundation of a large house, which was about 550 m² based on the cobbles, was found in the center of Pi Xian Gucheng 郫縣古城. It might have been a locus for public gatherings or communal ceremonies like those recently unearthed at the Baodun type site mentioned above (Chengdu and Pi Xian 2001). Such public spaces, while providing opportunities for gatherings and interactions, would have promoted community integration (see Birch 2013).

The construction of the walls themselves would have required the cooperation and organization of considerable labor. An estimation suggests that 4,000 people would have been required to work concertedly for a month to construct simply the inner walls of the Baodun type site, which is 60 ha (Flad and Chen 2013:84). This effort to organize labor to accomplish a task or activities (in this case, the construction of walls) helps us delineate the

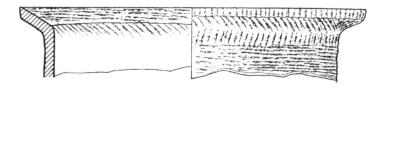 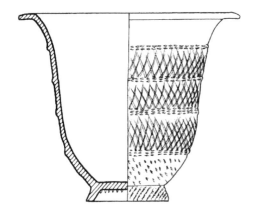

Figure 14.3. Ceramics of the first phase discovered at the Baodun site. Left: jar rim with impressed cord marks (IIIT2130:129). Right: vat with everted rim and deep belly (IIIT2130:128). *Redrawn by the author after Chengdu et al. 2000:108.*

presence of a community. The organization of community mobilization does not automatically demonstrate the existence of hierarchical leadership or social stratification, and there is no clear sign of differentiation in burial treatments or residential forms. Instead, cooperative and collective decision-making is possible (see also Birch 2013:14; Kowalewski 2006). In addition, the several walled settlements provide no evidence of intersite domination and subordination relationships, despite their unequal sizes. The walled settlements formed communities that were able to sustain themselves, whereas different communities also shared ceramic types, residential architectural styles, burial forms, and probably an ideological system. Some political forms, including chiefdoms or peer polities, have been proposed to account for the social structure of the walled settlements on the Chengdu Plain (Duan 1999:46; Peng 2003). They seem to have been decentralized and not united into a larger polity, perhaps because each settlement was a self-contained system that had maintained some degree of equilibrium without the need for a higher decision-making system.

Population was also distributed in the small sites outside the walled enclosures, especially during the third and fourth phases of the Baodun period (Jiang 2015). According to Jiang Zhanghua's observations (2015) on recent surveys and excavations, these small sites are very likely to be hamlets, composed of a few houses, burials, ash pits, and sometimes kilns in a simple structure. The overall population was seemingly sustainable in this broad land and may not have necessarily led to population pressure. Ian Kuijt (2000) has cautiously argued for a distinction between the two, echoing Robert Drennan's (1988) suggestion that we need to distinguish residential density within a settlement from regional population density. Unlike the simultaneous population explosion in northern China, the residential density inside the walled enclosure was not very high, and small villages, which enjoyed some degree of autonomy, can be found dispersed outside the walls in many parts of the Chengdu Plain, which also suggests that the carrying capacity of the environment was large. It should be noted that the costs of aggregation in a densely populated region or area can be high, often coming at the expense of privacy and control over natural surroundings and resources, which is not always an intended consequence (see Kowalewski 2013). Therefore, while some villages were attached to the walled settlements, others might have elected for greater autonomy. Undoubtedly, however, these small villages, together with the walled settlements, shared the same cultural atmosphere, according to their material cultures, subsistence technologies, and burial customs.

During this period, there were residential concentrations in the several settlement centers, which formed communities not only defined by the walls but also shaped by the construction tasks of public architectures. Nevertheless, there were still many autonomous village communities outside the walled enclosures. These villages were dispersed either between walled settlements (CPAS 2010) or farther away. The relationship between outside villages and walled communities is unclear. The walls might have served as shelters during flooding events, for instance (Sun 2000:392; Xu 2001; see also Flad and Chen 2013:84), or been the foci of communal activities, especially larger buildings near the centers of the Baodun type site and Pi Xian Gucheng. However, such gatherings were temporary or periodic and occurred during special events. Land and food resources had remained sustainable, until people were inundated by flooding events during the late Baodun period. Possible environmental degradation is reflected in some locations, wherein river sand depositions interrupted the stratigraphy of the late Baodun (Jiang 2015).

The Space of Nucleation: Sacred and Mundane Power in One House?

It is not until the Sanxingdui period (ca. 1700–1150 BC) that a production tradition that combined foreign and local characteristics took shape (again) more clearly, after Yingpanshan had been abandoned. At the end of the Neolithic period, much of the regional population gathered into Sanxingdui, a settlement initially developed during the first phase of the Baodun period but that flourished only after the decline of other walled settlements. This also marks the second phase of the Sanxingdui culture and the beginning of the Bronze Age on the Chengdu Plain. The further concentration of the population also caused the expansion and fortification of the settlement, for which walls were built to encompass an area of 500 ha. Inside this area, sections of walls surrounded spaces possibly used for special events or activities, including the Cangbaobao 倉包包 district, where jade and stone artifacts have been discovered, and the Yueliangwan 月亮灣 district, where a large building, Qingguanshan 青關山 (900 m^2), was built on an artificially raised platform with burned floors (Sichuan 2015b). The platform was also the highest locus in the settlement. With uncertainty, some archaeologists have proposed that the platform mound was the residence of high-class rulers (see Sun 2013). The construction of these outer and interior walls would have required more substantial labor than that of most Baodun culture walls (Flad and Chen 2013:92).

Some scholars have argued that the society was stratified and ruled by ritualized political authority (e.g., Duan

1999:108), while others have suggested secular and deified powers in separate domains. For example, Sun Hua (2013) argues that Sanxingdui society once hosted two ethnic groups corresponding to the hairstyles and costumes of human statues found in the sacrificial pits. They managed secular and sacred matters, respectively. The political structure of the society is unclear, however. In addition, social groups seem to have grown even more diverse during the later Shi'erqiao 十二橋 culture period, especially in Jinsha 金沙 society (Lin 2019). In either case, religious activities were occasions during which great wealth was spent and were the most important impetus for the manufacturing and importation of precious goods for ritual paraphernalia, which can be seen in the depositions in ritual-related contexts. The concentration of such social wealth was unmistakably displayed in the sacrificial pits, where both locally made and exotic precious goods were deposited (Sichuan 1999).

This coexistence of multiple production traditions at Sanxingdui might be described as a coalescent society (Lehmer 1954; see Kowalewski 2006), in which two material styles or archaeological traditions blended, usually because of immigration or invasion. In some cases, large-scale warfare caused communities to become nucleated (Kowalewski 2006). Whereas warfare cannot be confirmed in the case of Sanxingdui (see Jiang 2015), the blending of different material cultures is suggested by artifacts found in the sacrificial pits, which combine both local and nonlocal working traditions. Nonlocal traditions include Erlitou 二里頭 (ca. 1900–1500 BC), Erligang 二里岡 (ca. 1500–1300 BC), and Yinxu 殷墟 (ca. 1300–1046 BC) in the Central Plains; Shijiahe 石家河 (ca. 2600–2000 BC) in the middle Yangzi River; and the Longshan 龍山 cultures (ca. 3000–1900 BC) of Shandong, Shaanxi, and Shanxi (Falkenhausen 2003:205). From the existence of unfinished remains, it is also clear that imitations of imports were occasionally manufactured locally at the Sanxingdui site. The contexts of use for these items in local ritual occasions and their social values apparently differed from prototypes in their original societies (Flad 2012). The newly constructed cultural values would have gradually been acknowledged and shared by members of the Sanxingdui community through their repeated participation in public activities, such as ritual ceremonies. Outside the walls, material cultures similar to that at Sanxingdui can also be found in the neighboring area of about 1200 ha, but perhaps not as widely distributed as the Baodun or Shi'erqiao cultures.

Both external influences and religious activities were intensified during this period, and many exotic artifacts, technologies, and ideas were adopted and instituted during ritual occasions. People nucleated in the settlement center, with only a few villages dispersed beyond the river drainage. Meanwhile, large pottery vessels, such as closed-spouted *he* 盉 pitchers, were found in the site and were possibly used for warming and/or serving liquids (Du 1992), as can be seen in the sometimes smoky traces at their bases. They are said to have a northern origin and look particularly close to samples from Erlitou and the middle Yangzi River. Similar items as well as other large pottery vessels were found in the Shi'eriqiao type site (for example, IT16:50; Sichuan and Chengdu 2009:104) and in the Jinsha sacrificial zone (for example, IT7309:19) outside Sanxingdui. They might have been part of ritual paraphernalia, beyond their practical uses, and might have been related to ceremonial feasts for their large volume (see Blitz 1993). As Katherine Spielmann (2002) has pointed out, socially valued goods, which have effects on social transactions, and ceremonial feasts are both critical parts of rituals (see also Chang 1976:117; Dietler 2001; Hayden 1995), along with the production or acquisition of related items. Brain Hayden (2003) notes that in Southeast Asian tribal societies, important domesticated animals and plants were not only forms of wealth but were also primarily or even exclusively used during feasting occasions.

Such seemingly extravagant religious activities could not always maintain community cohesion. As a result, the society shrank and a portion of the people were displaced to Shi'erqiao and Jinsha, where they encountered other social groups and developed new settlement centers. The reason why is unknown, though scholars have speculated about the depletion of natural and social resources, the existence of external forces (from the east or north), or both, judging from the concentrated deposition of so many precious goods in the sacrificial pits (e.g., Jiang 2015; Zhou 2010).

Distributed Centers: Ritual or Production Centers?

In contrast with the Sanxingdui culture, small village communities and perhaps multiple settlement centers were distributed across the Chengdu Plain during the Shi'erqiao culture period (1200–600 BC; Sichuan and Chengdu 2009). The Shi'erqiao type site grew to be a regional settlement center before the Sanxingdui center was fully dispersed. Another center developed 5 km away, at Jinsha, around 1000 BC, while the Shi'erqiao settlement at Xinyicun 新一村 (Chengdu 2004; Zhou et al. 2012) remained important in some social dimensions (Figure 14.4).

For example, Shi'erqiao (Xinyicun) yielded remains of large houses, divinatory oracle bones, a jade *ge* 戈 dagger, and a semi-finished stone *cong* 琮 tube (Sichuan and

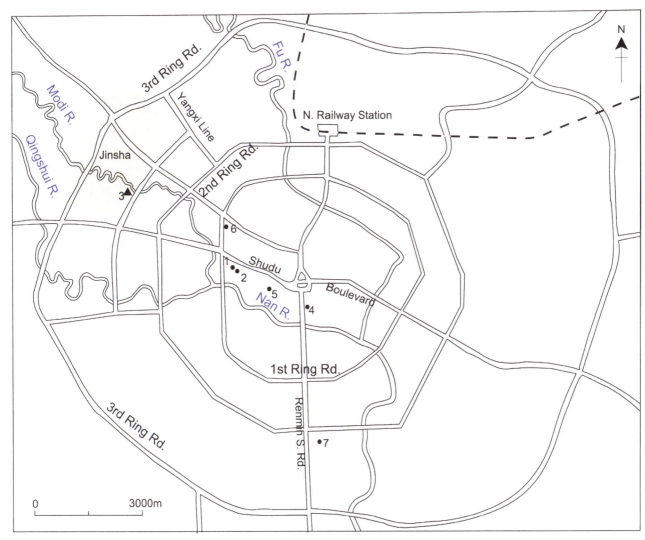

Figure 14.4. Shi'erqiao site cluster in modern Chengdu City: 1. Shi'erqiao; 2. Xinyicun; 3. Jinsha-Meiyuan; 4. Zhihuijie; 5. Fangchijie; 6. Fuqintai Xiaoqu; 7. Minjiang Xiaoqu. *Redrawn by the author from Chengdu 2006.*

Chengdu 2009; Zhou 2016). These items and loci were probably related to ritual occasions. A nearby site, Zhihuijie 指揮街 (Sichuan and Chengdu 1987), yielded similar oracle bones. Another site in the neighborhood, Fangchijie 方池街 (Chengdu and Chengdu 2003), yielded a kneeling human figure in stone, which has otherwise been found only in the sacrificial zone of the Jinsha site (the Meiyuan 梅苑 locus) and in sacrificial Pit 1 and Yueliangwan at the Sanxingdui site (Figure 14.5). Both the Fangchijie and Zhihuijie sites are associated with the Shi'erqiao culture and are part of the Shi'erqiao site cluster. The association of these items with rituals is clear, and such scattered finds further mystify the nature of these Shi'erqiao culture sites. Some scholars contrast the Shi'erqiao site (including Xinyicun) and the Jinsha site, suggesting that the former was possibly a production center responsible for the manufacturing of at least part of the ritual paraphernalia buried in the Jinsha sacrificial zone whereas the latter was a center for worship (e.g., Zhou 2016). While at present it's impossible to confirm, the uses of oracle bones for divination and the presence of large houses in the Shi'erqiao site intimate a connection to decision-making and public gatherings, as I suggest elsewhere (Lin 2019). The space, as a place where divination ceremonies were held, would have been very special, even if was not a production center. Importantly, the site also maintained some level of practical production, according to the ceramic and small-tool remains. The space was not specialized for particular activities.

Despite the still unclear nature of these communities and the possible differences in their division of functions,

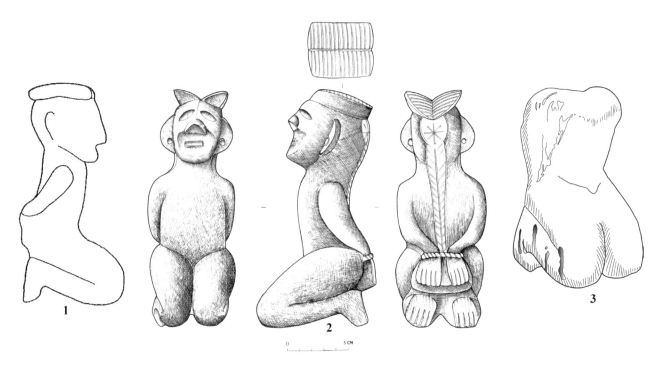

Figure 14.5. Stone kneeling human figures discovered in 1. Fangchijie (84CFT12, height 50 cm; Chengdu and Chengdu 2003:307, Figure 9); 2. Meiyuan (L19:17); 3. Sanxingdui (86T13138, head missing, height 11.5 cm).
Redrawn by the author from Chengdu and Chengdu 2018:287, Figures 85, and Sichuan and Chengdu 2009:751, Fig. 46.

they shared the same cultural code. I have proposed elsewhere (Lin 2013, 2019) that ceramic pointed-bottomed saucers (*jiandizhan* 尖底盞) represent the cultural idiosyncrasy of Shi'erqiao culture. Such items can be found in the core area of the Jinsha settlement (composed of the Meiyuan, Lanyuan 蘭苑, and Sanhe Huayuan 三和花園 loci; Chengdu and Chengdu 2018), with a very high level of standardization. They were less standardized in the other parts of the Jinsha settlement. They were least carefully made in remote villages in mountainous areas, such as Shaxi 沙溪 at Ya'an 雅安 (Sichuan et al. 1990). Although these diverse areas all produced the same items, the remote villages lacked daily interactions with the settlement centers and might not have shared community identities with the core.

The Jinsha settlement center itself probably constituted multiple lineages, each producing their own pottery and each possessing their own cemetery, judging from the spatial separation between household groups. Jiang (2015:74), based on pottery types, has suggested that there was a wave of migration from the Three Gorges area to the Chengdu Plain during the transition from Sanxingdui to Jinsha (ca. 1200 BC). This incorporation of the new social groups would have further enhanced the diversity of both the population and its material culture in Jinsha. This might also explain why millet, the major crop cultivated in the Three Gorges area, regained attention on the Chengdu Plain after a decline during the Baodun period. According to a recent floral flotation result from the Yangguang Didai 陽光地帶 II locus at Jinsha, the amount of millet remains is slightly higher than that of rice grains (Yan et al. 2017:477), whereas cultivated rice was 45% of all floral remains (including non-grains) and millet was only 1.6% in the Baodun type site (Chengdu and Xinjin 2011b).

Several batches of sacrificial depositions at Jinsha (Meiyuan) show the possible presence of multiple social groups in the greater Jinsha community, which used rites and ceremonies to compete and negotiate with one another (Flad 2012). As in the Sanxingdui settlement, ritual activities and production activities related to them also integrated the different social pieces of Shi'erqiao into a community that shared cultural values through frequent interactions. The considerable quantities of precious goods deposited in the Meiyuan sacrificial zone, together with a cluster of large buildings and pottery kilns found at the Sanhe Huayuan locus, in the center of the Jinsha settlement, suggest the importance, frequency, and scale of ritual events and public gatherings. This core area also features Lanyuan, where a residential area and a cemetery with more than 100 burials, all in the simplest form, were found. The compound was also surrounded by many ash pits and pottery kilns. In fact, across the Jinsha settlement, individual cemeteries, though associated with respective residential groups, were mostly oriented in the same direction, as seen in Baodun culture and Sanxingdui culture sites. This does not necessarily indicate a plan instituted by a definite ruling authority, though it reflects some shared ideological system. In addition, despite the distinct ritual paraphernalia, social stratification is seemingly absent in other dimensions. Different lineages or social groups, occupying different sections inside the Jinsha community, were seemingly only loosely connected. These sections were also (supra-) household-level production loci that were able to work collectively when required.

Further, unlike Sanxingdui, whose related settlements were nearly all concentrated on the Tuo 沱 River drainage, settlements were more widely distributed across multiple places on the Chengdu Plain during the era in which Jinsha became the regional center. Some were active and developed into larger communities that owned or produced ritual items and large buildings. For instance, the Shi'erqiao-Xinyicun site containing the aforementioned large arc structure, which features large logs and ground beams, was possibly another center, besides the Jinsha settlement, that produced both ritual and practical items. The remains of raw materials and semi-finished products, as well as metalworking tools, are found in situ. The semi-finished stone *cong* tube is particularly intriguing because it is a far less delicate imitation of the Liangzhu 良渚 tradition (ca. 3300–1900 BC; Zhou 2016). Meanwhile, a 10-tiered jade *cong*, likely made in a site of the Late Liangzhu culture, was deposited in the northeast corner of the Meiyuan locus, together with bronzes and ivory. They are all clearly part of the ritual paraphernalia.

The Liangzhu tradition was not the only source of inspiration for Shi'erqiao crafters. Some crafters residing in Jinsha also produced stone *cong* following the traditions of the Qijia culture or other Longshanoid phases in northern China. *Cong* produced in these northern traditions often have simpler designs, without human-beast figures or eyes. Their overall shapes and heights are also divergent. These northern cultures had influenced the production traditions of the Chengdu Plain, including the manufacturing of *cong* items, since the Sanxingdui period (Falkenhausen 2003). The production of stone *cong* then declined. Crafters in the Jinsha core turned to jade, in addition to stone, to produce *cong* (Zhou and Wang 2019), while still following the Longshan tradition.

It is clear that stone *cong* found in Jinsha or Xinyicun, though made from less valuable materials, were special and important goods used in ritual occasions, which made them socially valued. The production of items like these is unrelated to survival problems or practical technology (see Hayden 1998). When moving to Jinsha, where multiple social groups aggregated, people not only continued to use ceramic assemblages from earlier phases but also produced ritual paraphernalia similar to that used by their predecessors, such as the Sanxingdui people, by which they sought a sense of belonging with the past or their ancestors. However, material cultures also evolved according to the resources available to residents. During this transformation, they also realigned themselves as part of a newly developing community and reconstructed their identities. In doing so, although the people of the Shi'erqiao period continued to adopt diverse production traditions, as the Sanxingdui people created their connections, the adoption of foreign items or technologies again were subject to local social circumstances. Their users may have added or completely replaced the social meanings of the objects. The incorporation of imports into local societies is, in my opinion, like domestication in some dimensions that involves not only morphological modifications but also cultural processes, in which species or items are gradually integrated into local communities and social structures through a certain extent of adaptations (Clutton-Brock 1992). In the case of the Shi'erqiao, the (re)incorporation of imports into its society permitted its newly aggregated members and their material things to define each other mutually.

In a loosely organized society like the Shi'erqiao, members are able to adjust and accommodate different production traditions using the natural resources available to them. A willingness to follow (and not simply receive) different traditions to make similar items, such as *cong*, signals the diversity of the Jinsha community and suggests that this society had entered a stage of experimentation using new materials. According to Zhou and Wang (2019), although the Sanxingdui had exploited bronze resources and had many bronze items in their ritual paraphernalia, bronze, jade, and gold items were hardly present in the initial deposition in the Meiyuan sacrificial zone. These materials became common only later, during the second phase of the Jinsha site. The shift from stone to jade *cong*, along with other developed valued goods, perhaps reveals the new adoption or reacquisition of resources. The presence of so many valued objects further confirms the central importance of the Jinsha settlement. However, in comparison with Sanxingdui, the reduction in bronze materials and the replacement of some bronze types with jade might be ascribed to a shortage of bronze resources and/or people's changing tastes (Flad 2012; Lin 2019). Because multiple communities were able to access precious imports and produce special items, this also suggests that ritual and prestige technologies were not monopolized. For instance, oracle bone divinations were rituals newly arrived in the Chengdu Plain from the middle Yangzi River, which in turn had been introduced from the Central Plains. The divinations were not restricted to or monopolized in Shi'erqiao, although related knowledge and practices might have been mastered by a limited number of ritual specialists. They followed certain complex procedures, though not completely consistent everywhere, to prepare and generate divination hollows and marks on the surfaces of oracle bones (Flad 2008; Luo 1988) before the burn marks could be interpreted. In such a society without clear social stratification, ritual craft specialists who possessed the ability to materialize ideological icons might also have been the primary practitioners of rites and naturally played an important role on such occasions (see Spielmann 1998).

Beyond the two likely settlement centers, Shi'erqiao and Jinsha, a number of small villages, such as Zhihuijie, Fangchijie (mentioned above), Minshan Fandian, and Fuqintai Xiaoqu (Figure 14.4), have been found nearby. To the northwest of Jinsha, a few sites have also been found. They were mostly house clusters associated with farmlands, sometimes accompanied by a few kilns, some of which had been used since the Baodun period. These smaller and somewhat dispersed sites, as situated in the vicinity of the Jinsha settlement, can be considered the suburb of the Jinsha center, and they might have occasionally interacted with residents living in the urban area. However, the boundaries between them and the center might have been vague. In the even farther-reaching outer layers (currently Xindu 新都, Pi, and Wenjiang 溫江 Counties), there are also archaeological sites displaying the characteristics of the Shi'erqiao culture (Jiang 2015). The total number of Shi'erqiao sites exceeds those of Baodun and certainly of Sanxingdui, though their scale might not necessarily be larger. The external connections of Shi'erqiao also reached beyond the Chengdu Plain.

The western highlands, which seemingly became the margin after settlement centers gradually shifted to the center of the Chengdu Plain, no longer possessed larger settlements and continued to be marginalized as the Chengdu Plain and its eastern neighbors intensified their interactions. There are, however, many stone-slate burials that were deposited in the area during the Shi'erqiao period, judging from grave goods. Pointed-bottomed vessels and jars with ring feet (Figure 14.6) discovered from the stone-slate burials at Yingpanshan (Chengdu et al. 2013), for instance, bear characteristic features of the Shi'erqiao culture. There were also pits for human sacrifices, with individuals whose diets seem closer to the inhabitants and domestic animals of the Chengdu Plain instead of those of mountainous areas (Lee et al. 2018). Across the Hengduan Mountains, there were still caches, hoards, and ritual deposits, other than grave goods, that displayed connections to many regions (Falkenhausen 1996; Hein this volume). These deposits are diverse in origin, featuring items not only from the upper Yellow River, as seen in pottery styles, but also from the Chengdu Plain, the middle Yangzi River, the steppe, and the south, indicating that the area was still active in a network of exchange with the outside world. These locations, featuring stone coffins and related deposits, are hubs that should not be neglected. Such findings should force us to reconsider the relationship between the highlands and the lowlands. In any case, the variable distances between these settlements or outposts and the urban centers in the lowlands would have influenced the density of the interactions between them and created graduated levels of affinity.

Discussion

From the material evidence and the presence of various exotic goods in important collective activities, notably ritual occasions, it is clear that diverse external cultures influenced the societies of western Sichuan from the Yingpanshan to the Shi'erqiao period. Yinpangshan potters used local raw clays to make pottery both in their own style and in imitation of Majiayao imports. Their affinity to the north and their transformation of exotic elements into their local culture is clearly reflected in their pottery making, showing one way in which innovations or technologies were introduced to and adopted by local societies (Flad this volume). Local styles and community identities were also shaped during the accommodation of these newly constructed or transformed cultural values shared by residents. The primary sources for these exotic stimuli and their interactions changed over time, from the northern to the eastern bounds. By the time of the Baodun period, the middle Yangzi River had come fundamentally to influence people's ways of life on the Chengdu Plain, including rice cultivation (d'Alpoim Guedes 2011) and wall construction techniques (Yu 2004).

Both the Baodun and Shi'erqiao periods featured multiple settlement centers with many dispersed small villages scattered around, though the reason for this settlement pattern might not have been the same. Population diversity might also have differed. While the Baodun culture did not face the same population pressure or powerful external pressure to form a nucleated society, like the Sanxingdui

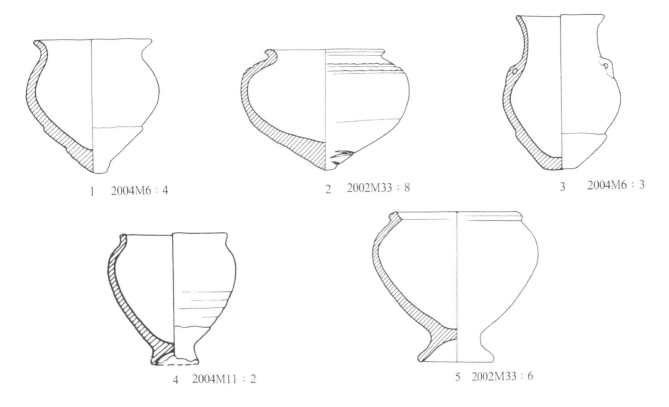

Figure 14.6. Pointed-bottomed vessels (1–3) and jars with a ring foot (4–5) discovered in the stone-slate burials at Yingpanshan. *Redrawn by the author after Chengdu et al. 2013:37.*

settlement, the Shi'erqiao culture lacked the requisite hinterlands, which were otherwise separated by river courses. Flooding on the Chengdu Plain, though better controlled from the Baodun period or slightly earlier, still created threats that possibly forced the people of the Baodun culture to build walls to prevent such disasters. The walled enclosures, regardless of their locations on the Chengdu Plain, were all constructed in the same manner, though they differed from their counterparts in northern China. To mobilize labor to accomplish such a large-scale task might further convey a sense of participation and union inside of these respective communities.

Some archaeologists (e.g., He 2016; Jiang 2004, 2015) have proposed to trace parts of the ceramic types of the Baodun culture back to Yingpanshan prototypes. This "inheritance" of ceramics and shared material cultures might lead to a sense of a common origin and might have influenced how Baodun people formed their ideological system, including their funeral orientations. With such a system, these walled enclosures, along with other dispersed villages, were parts of a larger regional culture—the Baodun culture—and were to some extent interrelated. Although such

relationships among Baodun settlements have been little investigated (except for the Chengdu Plain Archaeological Survey; see CPAS 2010), they would have influenced the way different groups of people aggregated the Sanxingdui.

As to Shi'erqiao, I have previously argued that pointed-bottomed saucers might have been a proxy for the Shi'erqiao culture, delineating not a territory under the direct control of ruling elites but a sphere of cultural idiosyncrasy (Lin 2019). Items like stone and jade *cong* made in different styles and following different traditions coexisted in one society, perhaps suggesting divergent group interests and circumstantial identities inside a society, just as the spatial distribution of different styles of artifacts can be employed to outline the scope of a social group (Dietler and Herbich 1998; Sackett 1977, 1990). These boundaries between social groups inside a community are subtler and easier to cross than those constructed by pottery types, such as pointed-bottomed saucers. However, such circumstantial identities, if continuously repeated, may become profound ones.

The Shi'erqiao culture was more like a loosely coalescent society that took over part of the people from Sanxingdui, along with the traditions of the ritual paraphernalia and ceramic vessel assemblage, while people indigenous to the locale and coming from other parts of the Sichuan basin also added to the diversity of the population. Different scales of rituals and related production, whose remains were deposited several times in a successive manner, were needed more frequently than during the Sanxingdui period, perhaps because of competition among social groups (Flad 2012) and/or attempts to reduce tensions and enhance concordance. Together with Shi'erqiao ceramics that had been distributed as far away as the mountainous area in western Sichuan and southern-middle Shaanxi, ritual ceremonies and some key items delineated graduated levels of a sense of community. This shared ideological system and the social values of artifacts, strengthened by communal activities, provided opportunities for divergent social groups to negotiate and coordinate, which also helped in the construction of community identity and cultural idiosyncrasy.

Both Sanxingdui and Jinsha featured ceremonies of a grand manner. To bring them about, people would have been required to organize in some manner to exploit scarce natural resources and to practice prestige technologies (Hayden 1998). However, the two settlements were divergent in their production modes: while Sanxingdui was more concentrated, Shi'erqiao, including Jinsha, was more distributed at the household and supra-household level. Among such distributed production loci, the urban center, the Meiyuan locus at Jinsha, maintained the most diverse ritual production. It inherited items from Sanxingdui and at the same time adopted new imports that had not been incorporated into the Chengdu Plain before, such as a new style of *cong*. This coexistence of new and transformed imports reveals a process like domestication and re-domestication (Larson and Fuller 2014), in which special objects, like living creatures, were gradually recognized and integrated into the community, a process that produced their meanings within the social structure. In such a process, the objects' natures or traits may be selectively reproduced or replaced according to people's interests. To reproduce, local producers might adopt materials available to them to imitate imports, adding exclusive details, such as special motifs or other manufacturing signatures. The functions of the objects or ways to use them in coordination with other items were also modified to fit local situations, as suggested by the ritual paraphernalia in Sanxingdui, Jinsha, and later Moutuo (Falkenhausen 1996, 2003).

In comparison with the settlement center, the surrounding village communities of Jinsha would have been less involved in the generation of social meanings for ritual items, even if they were not prohibited from producing ritual items. With various levels of proximity to the centers, they appear to have exercised different rural economies, which produced only a small portion or nothing at all in terms of items related to ritual activities. The production and manipulation of ritual items, such as stone/jade *cong*, *ge*, kneeling human figures, and, most surprisingly, oracle bones, was not completely monopolized and can be found in the neighboring communities, such as Xinyicun and Zhihuijie. However, settlement centers, especially the Jinsha core, display the most diverse types of ritual production. The ability to generate and even control the meanings of the ritual items, including their uses and deposition, reveals the central role of the community. These gradational variations in production modes in different communities, whether they were part of an urban city or smaller villages in the suburbs, are where we might sketch the invisible boundaries of a community when real walls are absent, as in the case of Shi'erqiao culture. Such an investigation into the spatial distribution of communities along with their production modes might also hint at the mutable and nearly untraceable scopes of divergent social groups.

In comparing the settlement patterns and production modes of different periods, it becomes clear that the driving forces behind communities in this region and their reactions to the same stimuli were disparate. Those societies influenced by external forces and those possessing well-developed connections with other regions, if seemingly passive, transformed those pressures into local elements by selection and generated new social meanings, a process that was contextual and depended on environmental resources, social structures, ideological and ritual systems, and demographic compositions and diversity. Local preferences and choices since the period of Yingpanshan have allowed societies of the region to "creatively absorb, recombine, and transform" elements of various origins (Falkenhausen 2003:218) and thus develop their own production traditions. In such continuous selection processes, both the preceding societies and current social groups played a role in setting and shaping their social conditions, including economic modes. Chronological comparison of archaeological cultures permits us a clearer view of their transitions and transformation, allowing us to inspect the elements influencing a newly developed community in the process of constructing its cultural values. These case studies also suggest the different manners in which people adopted new ways of life, including transitions in subsistence strategies and production modes for both ritual and daily needs.

It is also by dissecting the production traditions and working groups inside a community that we can study intraregional relationships. Although the settlement patterns along with political forms seem dispersed and only loosely organized during some periods, ritual and ideological systems remained the important sources for maintaining social cohesion while also providing symbolic capital for different lineages and social groups in competitive ceremonies and performances. Such religious activities and the ensuing interactions allowed members to negotiate their social capital (Bourdieu 1986). During the Bronze Age, the mountainous areas and the rural villages might maintain certain autonomy with their own self-contained economies and exchange with the ritual/production centers in a somewhat mutually beneficial manner (Falkenhausen 2006b). They were not simply exploited, passive peripheries as one might assume. Through their gradational participation in ritual systems, community identities were also formed at multiple levels and were sometimes mutable.

Acknowledgments

I would like to thank my lifelong adviser, Lothar von Falkenhausen, for his guidance, advice, and comments on this manuscript and my other work. This article celebrates his sixtieth birthday. I also thank the editors, Anke Hein and Rowan Flad, who helped me clarify my viewpoints toward a clearer argument, and Bryan Miller, who helped me deal with the figures and revision issues. Maria Khayutina also helped me clarify my argument. I thank her.

Before the manuscript was presented at the conference, my colleagues gave me valued comments on the earliest version. In particular, Chen Kwang-tzuu 陳光祖 carefully read my article and shared insights with me. Wang Ming-ke 王明珂 kindly suggested ethnographic data. Li Shang-ren 李尚仁 gave me suggestions about the structure of the article. Liang Yuen-gen 梁元禎 also carefully read my English words. Lee Hsiu-ping 李修平 provided me comparable cases from his working area. During the conference, Katherine Brunson gave me feedback and kindly shared her oracle bone database. I thank all of them.

Notes

1 So far, eight walled enclosures have been discovered. They are the Baodun type site (Chengdu et al. 2000; Chengdu and Xinjin 2011a, 2012, 2016; He 2015), the Gaoshan site (Chengdu and Dayi 2015a; Liu et al. 2017), the Yandian 鹽店 site (Chengdu and Dayi 2015b, 2016), the Zizhu 紫竹 site (Chengdu and Chongzhou 2016), the Mangcheng 芒城 site (Chengdu and Dujiangyan 1999), the Shuanghe 雙河 site (Chengdu 2002), the Pi Xian Gucheng 郫縣古城 site (Chengdu and Pi Xian 2001), and the Yufu 魚鳧 site (Chengdu 2001). Among them, the Zizhu, Mangcheng, Shuanghe, and Baodun sites have double walls.

References

Anderson, Benedict R. O'G.
1991 *Imagined Communities: Reflections on the Origin and Spread of Nationalism*. London: Verso.

Barton, Loukas, Seth D. Newsome, Fahu Chen, Hui Wang, Thomas P. Guilderson, and Robert L. Bettinger
2009 Agricultural Origins and the Isotopic Identity of Domestication in Northern China. *Proceedings of the National Academy of Sciences* 106(14):5523–28.

Birch, Jennifer
2013 Between Villages and Cities: Settlement Aggregation in Cross-Cultural Perspective. In *From Prehistoric Villages to Cities: Settlement Aggregation and Community*, edited by Jennifer Birch, pp. 1–22. New York: Routledge, Taylor & Francis.

Blitz, John H.
1993 Big Pots for Big Shots: Feasting and Storage in a Mississippian Community. *American Antiquity* 58:80–96.

Bourdieu, Pierre
1986 The Forms of Capital. In *Handbook of Theory and Research for the Sociology of Education*, edited by J. G. Richardson, pp. 241–58. London: Greenwood Press.

Chang, Kwang-chih
1968 Toward a Science of Prehistoric Society. In *Settlement Archaeology*, edited by Kwang-chih Chang, pp. 1–9. Palo Alto, CA: National Press Books.
1976 *Early Chinese Civilization: Anthropological Perspectives*. Cambridge, MA: Harvard University Press.

Chen Wei 陳葦
2012 Xian Qin shiqi de Qingzang Gaoyuan donglu 先秦時期的青藏高原東麓 [The Eastern Edge of Qinghai-Tibet Plateau in the Pre-Qin Period]. Beijing: Kexue Chubanshe.

Chen Weidong 陳衛東 and Wang Tianyou 王天佑
2004 Qianyi Minjiang shangyou Xinshiqi shidai wenhua 淺議岷江上游新石器時代文化 [Discussion on the Neolithic Cultures in the Upper Min River]. *Sichuan wenwu* 四川文物 2004(3):15–21.

Chengdu Institute of Cultural History and Archeology, ed.
2006 *Jinsha Site: A 21st Century Discovery of Chinese Archaeology*. Beijing: China Intercontinental Press.

Chengdu Pingyuan Guoji Kaogu Diaochadui (CPAS) 成都平原國際考古調查隊

2010 Chengdu Pingyuan quyu kaogu diaocha 成都平原區域考古調查 (2005–2007) [Archaeological Survey in the Chengdu Plain, 2005–2007]. *Nanfang minzu kaogu* 南方民族考古 2010(6):255–78.

Chengdu Shi Wenwu Kaogu Gongzuodui 成都市文物考古工作隊

2002 Sichuan Chongzhou Shi Shuanghe shiqian chengzhi shijue jianbao 四川崇州市雙河史前城址試掘簡報 [Brief Report on the Test Excavation at the Shuanghe Site in Chongzhou City, Sichuan]. *Kaogu* 考古 2002(11):963–79.

Chengdu Shi Wenwu Kaogu Yanjiusuo 成都市文物考古研究所

2001 Wenjiang Xian Yufucun yizhi 1999 niandu fajue 溫江縣魚鳧村遺址1999年度發掘 [The 1999 Excavation Season at Yufucun Site, Wenjiang County]. *Chengdu kaogu faxian* 成都考古發現 1999:40–53.

2004 Chengdu Shi'erqiao yizhi Xinyicun fajue jianbao 成都十二橋遺址新一村發掘簡報 [Excavation Report on the Xinyicun Locus of the Shi'erqiao Site in Chengdu City]. *Chengdu kaogu faxian* 成都考古發現 2002:172–208.

Chengdu Shi Wenwu Kaogu Yanjiusuo 成都文物考古研究所, Aba Zangzu Qiangzu Zizhizhou Wenwu Guanlisuo 阿壩藏族羌族自治州文物管理所, and Mao Xian Qiangzu Bowuguan 茂縣羌族博物館

2013 *Mao Xian Yingpanshan shiguanzang mudi* 茂縣營盤山石棺葬墓地 [Cemetery of Stone-Coffin Tombs at Yingpanshan in Mao County]. Beijing: Wenwu Chubanshe.

2018 *Mao Xian Yingpanshan Xinshiqi shidai yizhi* 茂縣營盤山新石器時代遺址 [The Yingpanshan Neolithic Site in Mao County I-III]. Beijing: Wenwu Chubanshe.

Chengdu Shi Bowuguan Kaogudui 成都市博物館考古隊 and Chengdu Shi Wenwu Kaogu Yanjiusuo 成都市文物考古研究所

2003 Chengdu Fangchijie gu yizhi fajue baogao 成都方池街古遺址發掘報告 [Report on the Excavation of the Fangchijie Site in Chengdu City]. *Kaogu xuebao* 考古學報 2003(2):297–316.

Chengdu Shi Wenwu Kaogu Gongzuodui 成都市文物考古工作隊 and Dujiangyan Shi Wenwuju 都江堰市文物局

1999 Sichuan Dujiangyan Shi Mangcheng yizhi diaocha yu shijue 四川都江堰市芒城遺址調查與試掘 [On the Survey and Test Excavation at the Mangcheng Site in Dujiangyan City, Sichuan]. *Kaogu* 考古 1999(7):14–27.

Chengdu Shi Wenwu Kaogu Gongzuodui 成都市文物考古工作隊 and Pi Xian Bowuguan 郫縣博物館

2001 Sichuan Sheng Pi Xian Gucheng yizhi 1998-1999 niandu fajue shouhuo 四川省郫縣古城遺址1998–1999年度發掘收穫 [The Yield of the 1998–1999 Excavation in the Gucheng Site, Pi County, Sichuan]. *Chengdu kaogu faxian* 成都考古發現 1999:29–39.

Chengdu Shi Wenwu Kaogu Yanjiusuo 成都市文物考古研究所, Sichuan Daxue Lishixi Kaogu Jiaoyanshi 四川大學歷史系考古教研室, and Waseda Daigaku Chōkō Ryūiki Bunka Kenkyūsho 早稻田大學長江流域文化研究所

2000 *Baodun yizhi: Xinjin Baodun yizhi fajue he yanjiu* 寶墩遺址--新津寶墩遺址發掘和研究 [The Baodun Site: The Excavation and Study of the Baodun Site in Xinjin County]. Tokyo: Apu (APR).

Chengdu Wenwu Kaogu Yanjiuyuan 成都文物考古研究院 and Chengdu Jinsha Yizhi Bowuguan 成都金沙遺址博物館

2017 *Jinsha yizhi—Yangguang didai erqi didian fajue baogao* 金沙遺址——陽光地帶二期地點發掘報告 [Excavation Report on the Yangguang Didai II Locus at Jinsha Site]. Beijing: Wenwu Chubanshe.

2018 *Jinsha yizhi jisiqu chutu wenwu jingcui* 金沙遺址祭祀區出土文物精粹 [The Essence of Unearthed Cultural Relics in the Sacrificial Area of the Jinsha Site]. Beijing: Wenwu Chubanshe.

Chengdu Wenwu Kaogu Yanjiusuo 成都文物考古研究所 and Chongzhou Shi Wenwu Guanlisuo 崇州市文物管理所

2016 Chongzhou Shi Zizhu Gucheng diaocha, shijue jianbao 崇州市紫竹古城調查、試掘簡報 [Brief Report on the Test Excavation and Survey in the Zizhu Walled Site in Chongzhou City]. *Chengdu kaogu faxian* 成都考古發現 2014:40–57.

Chengdu Wenwu Kaogu Yanjiusuo 成都文物考古研究所 and Dayi Xian Wenwu Guanlisuo 大邑縣文物管理所

2015a 2012–2013 niandu Dayi Xian Gaoshan Gucheng yizhi diaocha shijue jianbao 2012–2013年度大邑縣高山古城遺址調查試掘簡報 [Brief Report on the Survey and Test Excavation of the Gaoshan Walled Site in Dayi County, 2012–2013]. *Chengdu kaogu faxian* 成都考古發現 2013:1–44.

2015b Dayi Xian Yandian Gucheng yizhi 2013 nian fajue jianbao 大邑縣鹽店古城遺址2013年發掘簡報 [Brief Report on the Excavation of the Yandian Walled Site in Dayi County, 2013]. *Chengdu kaogu faxian* 成都考古發現 2013:45–65.

2016 Dayi Xian Yandian Gucheng yizhi 2002–2003 nian fajue jianbao 大邑縣鹽店古城遺址2002–2003年發掘簡報 [Brief Report on the Excavation of the Yandian Walled Site in Dayi County, 2002–2003]. *Chengdu kaogu faxian* 成都考古發現 2014:58–88.

Chengdu Wenwu Kaogu Yanjiusuo 成都文物考古研究所 and Xinjin Xian Wenguansuo 新津縣文管所

2011a Xinjin Baodun yizhi diaocha yu shijue jianbao 新津寶墩遺址調查與試掘簡報 (2009–2010年) [Brief Report on the Survey and Test Excavation at the Baodun Site, Xinjin County (2009–2010)]. *Chengdu kaogu faxian* 成都考古發現 2009:1–67.

2011b Xinjin Baodun yizhi 2009 niandu kaogu shijue fuxuan jieguo fenxi jianbao 新津寶墩遺址2009年度考古試崛浮選結果分析簡報 [Brief Report on the Archaeobotanical Flotation Results of the 2009 Test Excavation at the Baodun Site of the Xinjin County]. *Chengdu kaogu faxian* 成都考古發現 2009:68–82.

2012 Xinjin Xian Baodun yizhi Gudunzi 2010 nian fajue baogao 新津縣寶墩遺址鼓墩子2010年發掘報告 [Report on 2010 Season of Excavation at the Gudunzi Locus at the Baodun Site in Xinjin County]. *Chengdu kaogu faxian* 成都考古發現 2012:1–63.

2016 Xinjin Xian Baodun yizhi 2012–2013 niandu kaogu fajue jianbao 新津縣寶墩遺址2012–2013年度考古發掘簡報 [Brief Report on the 2012–2013 Season of the Excavation at the Baodun Site in Xinjin County]. *Chengdu kaogu faxian* 成都考古發現2014:14–39.

Clutton-Brock, Juliet
1992 The Process of Domestication. *Mammal Review* 22(2):79–85.

d'Alpoim Guedes, Jade
2011 Millets, Rice, Social Complexity, and the Spread of Agriculture to the Chengdu Plain and Southwest China. *Rice* 4(3):104–13.

Dietler, Michael
2001 Theorizing the Feast: Rituals of Consumption, Commensal Politics, and Power in African Contexts. In *Feasts: Archaeological and Ethnographic Perspectives on Food, Politics, and Power*, edited by Michael Dietler and Brian Hayden, pp. 65–114. Washington, DC: Smithsonian Institution Press.

Dietler, Michael, and Ingrid Herbich
1998 *Habitus*, Techniques, Style: An Integrated Approach to the Social Understanding of Material Culture and Boundaries. In *The Archaeology of Social Boundaries*, edited by Miriam T. Stark, pp. 232–63. Washington, DC: Smithsonian Institution Press.

Drennan, Robert D.
1988 Household Location and Compact versus Dispersed Settlement in Prehispanic Mesoamerica. In *Household and Community in the Mesoamerican Past*, edited by Richard R. Wilk and Wendy Ashmore, pp. 273–93. Albuquerque: University of New Mexico Press.

Du Jinpeng 杜金鵬
1992 Fengding he yanjiu 封頂盉研究 [Study on Closed-Spouted He Vessels]. *Kaogu xuebao* 考古學報 1992(1):1–34.

Duan Yu 段渝
1999 *Zhengzhi jiegou yu wenhua moshi: Ba Shu gudai wenming yanjiu* 政治結構與文化模式: 巴蜀古代文明研究 [Political Structure and Cultural Models: Research on the Ancient Civilization of Ba and Shu]. Shanghai: Xuelin Chubanshe.

Falkenhausen, Lothar von
1996 The Moutuo Bronzes: New Perspectives on the Late Bronze Age in Sichuan. *Arts Asiatiques* 1996(51):29–59.

2001 The Chengdu Plain in the Early First Millennium BC: Zhuwajie. In *Ancient Sichuan: Treasures from a Lost Civilization*, edited by Robert W. Bagley, pp. 177–201. Seattle: Seattle Art Museum and Princeton University Press.

2003 The External Connections of Sanxingdui. *Journal of East Asian Archaeology* 5(1–4):191–245.

2006a *Chinese Society in the Age of Confucius (1000–250 BC): The Archaeological Evidence*. Los Angeles: Cotsen Institute of Archaeology Press.

2006b The Salt of Ba: Reflection on the Role of the "Peripheries" in the Production Systems of Bronze Age China. *Arts Asiatiques* 2006(61):45–56.

2008 Stages in the Development of "Cities" in Pre-Imperial China. In *The Ancient City: New Perspectives on Urbanism in the Old and New World*, edited by Joyce Marcus and Jeremy A. Sabloff, pp. 209–28. Santa Fe: School for Advanced Research Press.

2011 Hanjiang shangyou pendi de qingtongshidai de ruogan guancha 漢江上游盆地的青銅時代的若干觀察 [Preliminary Remarks on the Bronze Age of the Upper Han River Basin]. In *Hanzhong chutu Shang dai qingtongqi* 漢中出土商代青銅器 IV [Shang Bronzes from Hanzhong IV], edited by Cao Wei 曹瑋, pp. 517–69. Chengdu: Ba Shu Shushe.

Falkenhausen, Lothar von, ed.
2003 *Qiyi de tumu: Xifang xuezhe kan Sanxingdui wenhua* 奇異的凸目--西方學者看三星堆文化 [Strange Protruding Eyes: Western Scholars Look at the Sanxingdui Culture]. Chengdu: Ba Shu Shushe.

Flad, Rowan
2008 Divination and Power: A Multiregional View of the Development of Oracle Bone Divination in Early China. *Current Anthropology* 49(3):403–37.
2012 Bronze, Jade, Gold, and Ivory: Valuable Objects in Ancient Sichuan. In *The Construction of Value in the Ancient World*, edited by John K. Papadopoulos and Gary Urton, pp. 306–35. Los Angeles: Cotsen Institute of Archaeology Press.
2013 The Oracle Bones of Zhongba: Divination at an Early Salt Production Site. In *Salt Archaeology in China,* Vol. 3, *Ancient Salt Production and Landscape Archaeology in the Upper Yangzi Basin: The Site of Zhongba in Perspective*, edited by Li Shuicheng and Lothar von Falkenhausen, pp. 294–337. Beijing: Kexue Cubanshe.

Flad, Rowan K., and Pochan Chen
2013 *Ancient Central China: Centers and Peripheries along the Yangzi River*. Cambridge: Cambridge University Press.

Fuller, Dorian Q., and Ling Qin
2009 Water Management and Labour in the Origins and Dispersal of Asian Rice. *World Archaeology* 41(1):88–111.

Goldstein, Paul S.
2000 Communities without Borders: The Vertical Archipelago and Diaspora Communities in the Southern Andes. In *The Archaeology of Communities: A New World Perspective*, edited by Marcello A. Canuto and Jason Yaeger, pp. 182–209. London: Routledge.

Hayden, Brian
1995 Pathways to Power: Principles for Creating Socioeconomic Inequalities. In *Foundations of Social Inequality*, edited by T. Douglas Price and Gary M. Feinman, pp. 15–86. New York: Plenum Press.
1998 Practical and Prestige Technologies: The Evolution of Material Systems. *Journal of Archaeological Method and Theory* 5(1):1–55.
2003 Were Luxury Foods the First Domesticates? Ethnoarchaeological Perspectives from Southeast Asia. *World Archaeology* 34(3):458–69.

He Kunyu 何錕宇
2009 Qianlun dongwu kaoguxue zhong liangzhong rouliang gusuan fangfa—yi Yingpanshan yizhi chutu de dongwu guge weili 淺論動物考古學中兩種肉量估算方法—以營盤山遺址出土的動物骨骼為例 [A Brief Discussion on Two Methods of Estimating Meat Quantity in Zooarchaeology—Taking the Faunal Remains Unearthed from Yingpanshan Site as an Example]. *Kaogu yu wenwu* 考古與文物 2009(5):95–99.
2011 Gansu Dongxiang Linjia yizhi fenqi de zai renshi—jianlun Yingpanshan yizhi de fenqi, niandai yu wenhua shuxing 甘肅東鄉林家遺址分期的再認識—兼論營盤山遺址的分期、年代與文化屬性 [Recognition of the Periodization of Linjia Site in Dongxiang, Gansu: Also on the Periodization, Date, and Cultural Affiliation of the Yingpanshan Site]. *Sichuan wenwu* 四川文物 2011(4):29–39, 42.
2015 Baodun yizhi: Chengdu Pingyuan shiqian daxing juluo kaogu xinjinzhan 寶墩遺址：成都平原史前大型聚落考古新進展 [The Baodun Site: New Discoveries of the Largest Prehistoric Settlement on the Chengdu Plain]. *Zhonghua wenhua yichan* 中華文化遺產 2015(6):26–31.
2016 Shilun Baodun wenhua de yuantou 試論寶墩文化的源頭 [On the Origin of Baodun Culture]. *Nanfang minzu kaogu* 南方民族考古 12:11–26.

He Kunyu 何錕宇 and Tang Miao 唐淼
2020 Baodun wenhua juluo xingtai yanjiu 寶墩文化聚落形態研究 [On the Settlement Patterns of the Baodun Culture]. *Zhonghua wenhua luntan* 中華文化論壇 2020(3):71–82.

Herrera, Alexander
2007 Social Landscapes and Community Identity: The Social Organisation of Space in the North-Central Andes. In *Socialising Complexity: Structure, Interaction and Power in Archaeological Discourse*, edited by Sheila Kohring and Stephanie Wynne-Jones, pp. 161–85. Oxford: Oxbow Books.

Huang Haode 黃昊德 and Zhao Binde 趙賓德
2004 Baodun wenhua de faxian ji qi laiyuan kaocha 寶墩文化的發現及其來源考察 [On the Discovery and Origin of the Baodun Culture]. *Zhonghua wenhua luntan* 中華文化論壇 2004(2):14–18.

Huo Wei 霍巍
2005 Lun Hengduan shanmai didai xian Qin liang Han shiqi kaoguxue wenhua de jiaoliu yu hudong 論橫斷山脈地帶先秦兩漢時期考古學文化的交流與互動 [On the Exchange and Interaction of the Archaeological Cultures in the Pre-Qin Period and Han Dynasties in the Hengduan Mountains]. In *Zangyi zoulang: lishi yu wenhua* 藏彝走廊：歷史與文化 [Tibetan-Yi Corridor: Its History and Culture], edited by Shi Shuo 石碩, pp. 272–99. Chengdu: Sichuan Renmin Chubanshe.

2009 Chengdu Pingyuan shiqian nongye kaogu xinfaxian ji qi qishi 成都平原史前農業考古新發現及其啟示 [New Archaeological Discoveries of Prehistoric Agriculture in the Chengdu Plain and Its Implications]. *Zhonghua wenhua luntan* 中華文化論壇 2009(11):155–58.

Hung Ling-yu 洪玲玉, Cui Jianfeng 崔劍鋒, Wang Hui 王輝, and Chen Jian 陳劍
2011 Chuanxi Majiayao leixing caitao chanyuan fenxi yu tantao 川西馬家窯類型彩陶產源分析與探討 [Analysis and Discussion of Majiayao-Style Painted Pottery Discovered in Western Sichuan]. *Nanfang minzu kaogu* 南方民族考古 7:1–58.

Inomata, Takeshi
2007 Classic Maya Elite Competition, Collaboration, and Performance in Multicraft Production. In *Craft Production in Complex Societies: Multicraft and Producer Perspectives*, edited by Izumi Shimada, pp. 120–33. Salt Lake City: University of Utah Press.

Jiang Cheng 蔣成 and Chen Jian 陳劍
2003 2002 nian Minjiang shangyou kaogu de shouhuo yu tansuo 2002年岷江上游考古的收穫與探索 [The Harvest and Exploration of the Archaeology Work in the Upper Min River in 2002]. *Zhonghua wenhua luntan* 中華文化論壇 2003(4):8–12.

Jiang Zhanghua 江章華
2004 Minjiang shangyou Xinshiqi shidai yicun xinfaxian de jidian sikao 岷江上游新石器時代遺存新發現的幾點思考 [Some Thoughts on the New Discoveries of the Neolithic Remains along the Upper Min River]. *Sichuan wenwu* 四川文物 2004(3):10–14.

2015 Chengdu Pingyuan xian Qin juluo bianqian fenxi 成都平原先秦聚落變遷分析 [Analysis on the Pre-Qin Settlements of the Chengdu Pain]. *Kaogu* 考古 2015(4):67–78.

Kowalewski, Stephen A.
2006 Coalescent Societies. In *Light on the Path: The Anthropology and History of the Southeastern Indians*, edited by Thomas J. Pluckhahn and Robbie Franklyn Ethridge, pp. 94–122. Tuscaloosa: University of Alabama Press.

2013 The Work of Making Community. In *From Prehistoric Villages to Cities: Settlement Aggregation and Community*, edited by Jennifer Birch, pp. 201–18. New York: Routledge, Taylor & Francis.

Kuijt, Ian
2000 People and Space in Early Agricultural Villages: Exploring Daily Lives, Community Size, and Architecture in the Late Pre-Pottery Neolithic. *Journal of Anthropological Archaeology* 19(1):75–102.

Larson, Greger, and Dorian Q. Fuller
2014 The Evolution of Animal Domestication. *Annual Review of Ecology, Evolution, and Systematics* 2014(45):115–36.

Lee Chengyi 李政益, Lin Kuei-chen 林圭偵, Chen Jian 陳劍, Andrea Czermak, and Yuan Haibing 原海兵
2018 Mao Xian Yingpanshan yizhi liangge renlei geti zhi shipu jiegou: yabenzhi jiaogyuan xulie yangben ji gujiaoyuan zhi tan, dan tongweisu fenxi 茂縣營盤山遺址兩個人類個體之食譜結構：牙本質膠原序列樣本及骨膠原之碳、氮同位素分析 [Diets of Two Human Individuals at the Yingpanshan Site of the Mao County: Carbon and Nitrogen Isotope Analyses on the Sequence Samples from Their Dentin Collagen and from Their Bone Collagen]. In *Mao Xian Yingpanshan Xinshiqi shidai yizhi (zhong)* 茂縣營盤山新石器時代遺址（中）[The Yingpanshan Neolithic Site in Mao County II], edited by Chengdu Shi Wenwu Kaogu Yanjiusuo 成都文物考古研究所, Aba Zangzu Qiangzu Zizhizhou Wenwu Guanlisuo 阿壩藏族羌族自治州文物管理所, and Mao Xian Qiangzu Bowuguan 茂縣羌族博物館, pp. 525–39. Beijing: Wenwu Chubanshe.

Lehmer, Donald J.
1954 *Archeological Investigations in the Oahe Dam Area, South Dakota, 1950–51*. Washington, DC: U.S. Government Printing Office.

Lei Yu 雷雨
2014 Sichuan Guanghan Sanxingdui yizhi 2012–2013 nian kaogu xinshouhuo 四川廣漢三星堆遺址2012–2013年考古新收穫 [New Archaeological

Discoveries at Sanxingdui Site in Guanghan, Sichuan from 2012 to 2013]. In *2013 Zhongguo zhongyao kaogu faxian* 2013 中國重要考古發現 [Major Archaeological Discoveries in China in 2013], edited by Guojia Wenwuju 國家文物局, pp. 46–51. Beijing: Wenwu Chubanshe.

Li Shuicheng 李水城
2011　Shiguanzang de qiyuan yu kuosang—yi Zhongguo weili 石棺葬的起源與擴散——以中國為例 [The Origin and Spread of Stone-Cist Burials—A Case Study of China]. *Sichuan wenwu* 四川文物 2011(6):64–69.

Lin Kuei-chen 林圭偵
2013　Pottery Production and Social Complexity of the Bronze Age Cultures on the Chengdu Plain, Sichuan, China. PhD dissertation, Cotsen Institute of Archaeology, University of California–Los Angeles.
2019　On Craft Production and the Settlement Pattern of the Jinsha Site Cluster on the Chengdu Plain. *Asian Perspectives* 58(2):366–400.

Liu Xiangyu 劉祥宇, Zhou Zhiqing 周志清, and Chen Jian 陳劍
2017　Chengdu Shi Dayi Xian Gaoshan gucheng 2014 nian fajue jianbao 成都市大邑縣高山古城2014年發掘簡報 [Preliminary Report on the 2014 Excavation at Gaoshan Site in Dayi County, Chengdu]. *Kaogu* 考古 2017(4):3–13.

Luo Erhu 羅二虎
1988　Chengdu diqu bujia de chubu yanjiu 成都地區卜甲的初步研究 [Preliminary Research on Oracle Bones in the Chengdu Area]. *Kaogu* 考古 1988(12):1122–29.
2012　*Wenhua yu shengtai, shehui, zuqun: Chuan Dian Qingzang minzu zoulang shiguanzang yanjiu* 文化與生態、社會、族群：川滇青藏民族走廊石棺葬研究 [Culture and Ecology, Society, and Ethnic Groups: Study on the Stone-Coffin Funerals in the Qinghai-Tibet Ethnic Corridor in Sichuan and Yunnan]. Beijing: Kexue Chubanshe.

Peng Bangben 彭邦本
2003　Gucheng, qiubang yu gu Shu gongzhu zhengzhi de qiyuan—yi Chuanxi pingyuan guchengqun weili 古城、酋邦與古蜀共主政治的起源——以川西平原古城群為例 [Ancient Cities, Chiefdoms, and Common Leader Politics in Ancient Shu: Exemplified by the Ancient Walled Site Cluster on the Western Sichuan Plain]. *Sichuan wenwu* 四川文物 2003(2):18–22.

Sackett, James R.
1977　The Meaning of Style in Archaeology: A General Model. *American Antiquity* 42(3):369–80.
1990　Style and Ethnicity in Archaeology: The Case for Isochrestism. In *The Uses of Style in Archaeology*, edited by Margaret Wright Conkey and Christine Ann Hastorf, pp. 32–43. Cambridge: Cambridge University Press.

Sichuan Daxue Bowuguan 四川大學博物館 and Chengdu Shi Bowuguan 成都市博物館
1987　Chengdu Zhihuijie Zhou dai yizhi fajue baogao 成都指揮街周代遺址發掘報告 [Report on the Excavation of the Zhou Site at Zhihuijie, Chengdu City]. *Nanfang minzu kaogu* 南方民族考古 1:171–210.

Sichuan Sheng Wensu Kaogu Yanjiusuo 四川省文物考古研究院
1999　*Sanxingdui jisikeng* 三星堆祭祀坑 [The Sacrificial Pits at Sanxingdui]. Beijing: Wenwu Chubanshe.
2015a　Sichuan Shifang Shi Guiyuanqiao yizhi fuxuan jieguo yu fenxi 四川什邡市桂圓橋遺址浮選結果與分析 [Results and Analysis of the Flora Flotation of Guiyuanqiao Site in Shifang, Sichuan]. *Sichuan wenwu* 四川文物 2015(5):81–87, 94.
2015b　Sichuan Guanghan Shi Sanxingdui yizhi Qingguanshan Zhanguomu fajue jianbao 四川廣漢市三星堆遺址青關山戰國墓發掘簡報 [Excavation Report on Qingguanshan Warring States Tombs at the Sanxingdui Site, Guanghan City, Sichuan Province]. *Sichuan wenwu* 四川文物 2015(4):5–9.

Sichuan Sheng Wenwu Kaogu Yanjiuyuan 四川省文物考古研究院 and Chengdu Wenwu Kaogu Yanjiusuo 成都文物考古研究所
2009　*Chengdu Shi'erqiao* 成都十二橋 [The Shi'erqiao Site of the Chengdu City]. Beijing: Wenwu Chubanshe.

Sichuan Sheng Wenwu Kaogu Yanjiuyuan 四川省文物考古研究院, Deyang Shi Bowuguan 德陽市博物館, and Shifang Shi Bowuguan 什邡市博物館
2013　Sichuan Shifang Guiyuanqiao Xinshiqi shidai yizhi fajue jianbao 四川什邡桂圓橋新石器時代遺址發掘簡報 [Preliminary Report on the Excavation at the Neolithic Guiyuanqiao Site in Shifang City, Sichuan]. *Wenwu* 文物 2013(9):4–12.

Sichuan Sheng Wenwu Kaogu Yanjiusuo 四川省文物考古研究所, Deyang Shi Wenwu Kaogu Yanjiusuo 德

陽市文物考古研究所, and Shifang Shi Wenwu Baohu Guanlisuo 什邡市文物保護管理所
2016 Sichuan Shifang Shi Jiantaicun yizhi IV, V, VI qu fajue jianbao 四川什邡市箭台村遺址IV、V、VI區發掘簡報 [Preliminary Report on the Excavation at the IV, V, VI Districts at Jiantaicun Site, in Shifang City, Sichuan]. *Sichuan wenwu* 四川文物 2016(2):51–20.

Sichuan Sheng Wenwu Guanli Weiyuanhui 四川省文物管理委員會, Sichuan Sheng Wenwu Kaogu Yanjiusuo 四川省文物考古研究所, and Sichuan Sheng Ya'an Diqu Wenwu Guanlisuo 四川省雅安地區文物管理所
1990 Ya'an Shaxi yizhi fajue ji diaocha baogao 雅安沙溪遺址發掘及調查報告 [Excavation and Survey Report on the Shaxi Site in Ya'an]. *Nanfang minzu kaogu* 南方民族考古 3:293–339.

Spielmann, Katherine A.
1998 Ritual Craft Specialists in Middle Range Societies. In *Craft and Social Identity*, edited by Cathy Lynne Costin and Rita P. Wright, pp. 153–60. Arlington, VA: American Anthropological Association.
2002 Feasting, Craft Specialization, and the Ritual Mode of Production in Small-Scale Societies. *American Anthropologist* 104(1):195–207.

Sun Hua 孫華
2000 *Sichuan pendi de qingtong shidai* 四川盆地的青銅時代 [The Bronze Age of the Sichuan Basin]. Beijing: Kexue Chubanshe.
2013 The Sanxingdui Culture of the Sichuan Basin. In *A Companion to Chinese Archaeology*, edited by Anne P. Underhill, pp. 147–68. Chichester: John Wiley & Sons.

Sutro, Livingston D., and Theodore E. Downing
1988 A Step toward a Grammar of Space: Domestic Space Use in Zapotec Villages. In *Household and Community in the Mesoamerican Past*, edited by Richard R. Wilk and Wendy Ashmore, pp. 29–50. Albuquerque: University of New Mexico Press.

Wan Jiao 萬嬌 and Lei Yu 雷雨
2013 Guiyuanqiao yizhi yu Chegndu Pingyuan Xinshiqi wenhua fazhan mailuo 桂圓橋遺址與成都平原新石器文化發展脈絡 [The Guiyuanqiao Site and the Development of the Neolithic Culture in the Chengdu Plain]. *Wenwu* 文物 9(2013):59–63.

Wang Ming-ke 王明珂
1997 *Huaxia bianyuan: lishi jiyi yu zuqun rentong* 華夏邊緣——歷史記憶與族群認同 [On Chinese Borderlands: Historical Memory and Ethnic Identity]. Taipei: Yuncheng.

Xie Chong'an 謝崇安
2005 Lüelun Xinan diqu zaoqi pingdi shuang'er guan de yuanliu ji qi zushu wenti 略論西南地區早期平底雙耳罐的源流及其族屬問題 [A Brief Discussion on the Origin and the Ethnic Group of the Users of Flat-Bottomed Amphorae in Southwest China in Ancient Times]. *Kaogu xuebao* 考古學報 2005(2):127–60.

Xu, Jay
2001 Sichuan before the Warring States Period. In *Ancient Sichuan: Treasures from a Lost Civilization*, edited by Robert W. Bagley, pp. 21–37. Seattle: Seattle Art Museum and Princeton University Press.

Yaeger, Jason, and Marcello A. Canuto
2000 Introducing an Archaeology of Communities. In *The Archaeology of Communities: A New World Perspective*, edited by Marcello A. Canuto and Jason Yaeger, pp. 1–15. London: Routledge.

Yan Xue 閆雪, Jiang Ming 姜銘, and Zhou Zhiqing 周志清
2017 Yangguang didai erqi didian fuxuan jieguo fenxi baogao 陽光地帶二期地點浮選結果分析報告 [Analytical Report on the Flotation Results at the Yangguang Didai II Locus]. In *Jinsha yizhi—Yangguang didai erqi didian fajue baogao* 金沙遺址——陽光地帶二期地點發掘報告 [Excavation Report on the Yangguang Didai II Locus at Jinsha Site], edited by Chengdu Wenwu Kaogu Yanjiuyuan 成都文物考古研究院 and Chengdu Jinsha Yizhi Bowuguan 成都金沙遺址博物館, pp. 476–92. Beijing: Wenwu Chubanshe.

Yu Weichao 俞偉超
2004 Sichuan diqu kaogu wenhua wenti sikao 四川地區考古文化問題思考 [Reflections on the Archaeological Cultures in Sichuan]. *Sichuan wenwu* 四川文物 2004(2):3–5.

Yuan Guangkuo 袁廣闊 and Luo Yi 羅伊
2014 *Cong kaogu faxian kan Zhongyuan yu Xinan diqu zaoqi wenhua de guanxi* 從考古發現看中原與西南地區早期文化的關係 [Investigating the Relationship between Central Plains and the Early Culture in Southwest China from Archaeological Discoveries]. Beijing: Shehui Kexue Wenxian Chubanshe.

Zhao Zhijun 趙志軍 and Chen Jian 陳劍
2011 Shichuan Mao Xian Yingpanshan yizhi fuxuan jieguo ji fenxi 四川茂縣營盤山遺址浮選結果及分析 [Results and Analyses of Floating Carried Out at the Yingpanshan Site, in Mao County, Sichuan]. *Nanfang wenwu* 南方文物 2011(3):60–67.

Zhou Zhiqing 周志清

2010 Jinsha yizhi juluo xingtai de chubu renshi 金沙遺址聚落型態的初步認識 [Preliminary Understanding of the Settlement Pattern of the Jinsha Site]. In *Zhongguo juluo kaogu de lilun yu shijian: jinian Xinzhai yizhi fajue 30 zhounian xueshu yantaohui lunwenji (diyiji)* 中國聚落考古的理論與實踐：紀念新砦遺址發掘30週年學術研討會論文集（第一輯）[Theory and Practice of Chinese Settlement Archeology: To Commemorate the 30th Anniversary of the Excavation in Xinzhai, Conference Proceedings (No. 1)], edited by Zhongguo Shehui Kexue Yuan Kaogu Yanjiusuo 中國社會科學院考古研究所 and Zhengzhou Shi Wenwu Kaogu Yanjiuyuan 鄭州市文物考古研究院, pp. 165–75. Beijing: Kexue Chubanshe.

2016 Xinyicun yizhi xin chutu shicong he yuge guancha 新一村遺址新出土石琮和玉戈觀察 [On a Stone Cong and a Jade Ge Recently Unearthed from the Xinyicun Site]. *Chengdu wenwu* 成都文物 2016(2):64–68.

Zhou Zhiqing 周志清, Chen Jian 陳劍, Liu Xiangyu 劉翔宇, and Bai Tieyong 白鐵勇

2015 Quyu xitong diaocha fangfa zai Chengdu Pingyuan dayizhi juluo zhong de shijian yu shouhuo—yi Gaoshan Gucheng yizhi weili 區域系統調查方法在成都平原大遺址聚落考古中的實踐與收穫--以高山古城遺址為例 [Systematic Regional Survey on the Large Settlements of the Chengdu Plain: Exemplified by the Gaoshan Gucheng Site]. *Zhonghua wenhua yichan* 中華文化遺產 2015(6):32–37.

Zhou Zhiqing, 周志清, Qiu Yan 邱豔, Zuo Zhiqiang 左志強, and Yi Li 易立

2012 四川成都市Shi'erqiao Xinyicun didian Shang Zhou zhi Sui Tang shiqi yizhi fajue qingkung 十二橋遺址新一村地點商周至隋唐時期遺址發掘情況 [On the Excavation of the Shang/Zhou-Sui/Tang Site at Xinyicun, Shi'erqiao in Chengdu, Sichuan]. *CCR News* 中國文物報 2012(5):11.

Zhou Zhiqing 周志清 and Wang Zhankui 王占魁

2019 Jinsha yizhi "jisiqu" chutu shicong guancha 金沙遺址"祭祀區"出土石琮觀察 [On the Stone Cong Unearthed from the Sacrificial Zone at Jinsha Site]. *Chengdu wenwu* 成都文物 2019(2):1–7.

Chapter 15

China for Asia
Bencharong and Peranakan Porcelains in the Eighteenth and Nineteenth Centuries

Ellen Hsieh

Chinese porcelain exported in the eighteenth and nineteenth centuries is best known for products customized for western Europe and North America (Mudge 1981; Pitts 2017; Sargent 2012). While these porcelains were produced for particular groups, in the final decades of the eighteenth century, total exports to Western countries decreased due to increasing competition from European wares. Indeed, even China's traditional overseas markets in Asia were gradually taken over by European products (Finlay 2010; Skowronek 1998). From Japan and the Philippines to Java, English creamwares with transfer-printed motifs[1] became common in the cultural layers of the contemporaneous era across archaeological sites of Asian port cities (Cuevas et al. 2000; Oka 2008; Sakai 2007). The new fashion of foreign wares graced the dining tables of the well-off. European factories, recognizing this overseas market, produced plates with designs particularly for Southeast Asia (Floor and Otte 2013). Meanwhile, a large amount of Chinese low-quality blue-and-white porcelain products were still shipped to this region. However, they were most likely associated with a wave of poor Chinese migrant workers called "new guests" (*sinkhek* 新客), who met the increasing need for labor against the backdrop of the European imperial agenda in Southeast Asia.[2]

Compared with the above-mentioned trend of increasing European ceramic consumption, the presence of overglazed polychrome Bencharong and Peranakan porcelains in Southeast Asia is exceptional. Both porcelains were produced in Jingdezhen in Jiangxi Province, a town that enjoyed fame for its centuries-old Chinese porcelain manufacturing, before shipment to distinct destinations. The Bencharong was made for the Siamese royal court, and the Peranakan was strongly associated with the Peranakan Chinese at the Straits Settlements, namely Penang, Malacca, and Singapore. Peranakan Chinese were those whose Chinese ancestors had settled in Southeast Asia before the new wave of Chinese immigration during the nineteenth century, and this term is used widely across today's Malaysia and Indonesia to differentiate them from China-born merchant and migrant communities.[3] Considering the partial Chinese ancestry of the Siamese nobles, some scholars have categorized Bencharong and Peranakan porcelains together as ceramics produced for overseas Chinese (Harris 1990; Miksic 2009). Both Bencharong and Peranakan porcelains were critical mediums in rituals used to build relationships and social identities. However, this paper challenges such an exclusive view of the consumption patterns of both Chinese exports. A sherd of Bencharong porcelain found in an archaeological site in Spanish Manila and a set of Peranakan porcelain dishes identified at the wall of a mosque at Cirebon reveal alternative destinations for these wares.

In the middle of the eighteenth century, Southeast Asia was gradually taken over by Europeans politically and economically. Nevertheless, Chinese and creolized Chinese[4] were the most active among the groups conducting actual trade in European colonies and indigenous autonomous states. Tracing the social lives of Bencharong and Peranakan porcelains from a symbolic perspective in their original contexts and from an economic perspective in their abnormal contexts not only enhances our understanding of the complex multicultural worlds the various creolized Chinese communities of Southeast Asia inhabited but also sheds light on the connections among them (Appadurai 1986; Malkin 2011). The original cultural value and usages of Bencharong and Peranakan porcelains were indeed altered in the unusual cases found in the Philippines and Indonesia, but their unanticipated journeys enrich our understanding of the connectivity of the region (Figure 15.1).

This paper is dedicated to Lothar von Falkenhausen, who always encouraged me to explore objects that raised my curiosity and to never let current national boundaries limit the scope of my research (Falkenhausen 1995). Questions like "What does it mean to be Chinese?" and "What is Chinese culture?" are never easy to answer. The prevailing image of Chinese communities in Southeast Asia is an isolated and exclusive one, yet the culture-crossing groups discussed in this paper developed local identities to various degrees while maintaining connections not only with the motherland in southern China but also with each other.

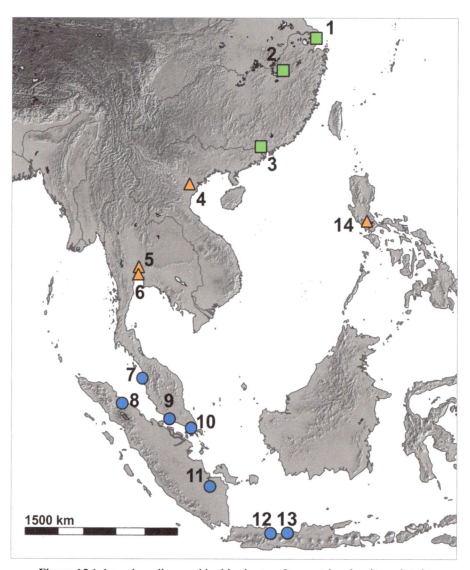

Figure 15.1. Locations discussed in this chapter. Orange triangle: sites related to Bencharong. Blue circle: sites related to Peranakan. Green square: related sites in China. 1.Shanghai; 2.Jingdezhen; 3.Canton; 4.Bat Trang; 5.Ayutthaya; 6.Bangkok; 7.Penang; 8.Medan; 9.Malacca; 10.Singapore; 11.Palembang; 12.Cirebon; 13.Pekalongan; 14.Manila.
Created by Bryan K. Miller.

Figure 15.2. Examples of Bencharong porcelain at the Chao Sam Phraya Museum, Thailand.
Photo taken by the author.

Bencharong and Peranakan Porcelains

Historically speaking, Bencharong (meaning "five colors" in Sanskrit)[5] porcelain was Chinese polychrome porcelain ordered by the Siamese court. The origin of Bencharong can be traced back to the late period of Ayutthaya (1350–1767 CE), and demand for this product continued through the late nineteenth century (Chantrapakajee 2019; Robinson 1979, 1982). Bencharong porcelain can be easily distinguished from other contemporary Chinese porcelain by its typical forms, such as bowls with pagoda-shaped lids, as well as motifs using Siamese Buddhist symbols and figures (Figure 15.2). Some of the forms and motifs of Bencharong were shared with Siamese metal wares, whereas other motifs resembled patterns from silk and cotton textiles ordered from India. Also characteristic are bright colors, including red, black, white, green, blue, and purple. In most cases, only the exterior of the wares was colored, but there are also examples of both exterior and interior decoration. A ware named Lainumthong (also written Lai Nam Thong) is usually considered the "sister" of Bencharong (Robinson 1979; Rooney 2017). Sharing similar shapes and patterns with the latter, Lainumthong is characterized by its opulent gilded decorations. Produced after the late eighteenth century or early nineteenth century, Lainumthong is of higher quality than Bencharong in both form and decoration and was made exclusively for imperial use. A few pieces can also be found in the royal collections of Cambodia and Laos, formerly tributary states to Siam (Groussin 2003).

In addition to daily use in the regal household, Bencharong porcelain was mostly used for relationship-building activities, such as royal dining, tea service for monks and visiting dignitaries, and betel chewing (Rooney 2017). During the reign of Chulalongkorn (Rama V; r. 1868–1910 CE), these traditional functions for Bencharong declined, accompanied by westernization trends promoted by the king, although it remained a status symbol. It also became more accessible for the well-off. In this later period, European-inspired products, such as candleholders and western-style teapots, became part of the Bencharong assemblage; some of them even turned into decorative materials on religious buildings such as Wat Arun in Bangkok (Figure 15.3).

Bencharong porcelain was originally thought to have been fired in Jingdezhen and painted in Canton (Guangzhou), similar to other exported wares for the West (Groussin 2003; Robinson 1979). However, several sherds with motifs identical to those of Bencharong discovered in Jingdezhen in recent years have revealed that the products were directly finished in the porcelain city (Rooney 2017).

Figure 15.3. A Bencharong ware (bottom center) inlaid at the wall as part of the decoration (Wat Arun, Thailand).
Photo taken by the author.

Robinson (1991) argues that aside from the regular supply from China, during the transition period between the rule of Ayutthaya and the rule of Rama I (r. 1782–1809 CE), there might have been difficulty in acquiring Bencharong from China; some high-fired stoneware copies might have been ordered from Bat Trang, Vietnam. These stoneware products feature common Bencharong motifs, but their shapes disclose their origin. Today, some Thai villages imitate the old Bencharong products, and the name Bencharong in the modern Thai context refers to colored porcelain with classical Siamese shapes and motifs, regardless of the object's place of manufacture (Rooney 2017). Bencharong continues to be a symbol of Siam, and its patterns have become a source for modern Thai designers (Sadsunk 2013).

Peranakan porcelain is a kind of polychrome enameled porcelain made for the wealthy Peranakan Chinese in the Malay world, especially those who were based in the Straits Settlements. Peranakan means "locally born" in Malay, and Peranakan Chinese refers to locally born people who can trace their origins to China. Alternative names of Peranakan porcelain include Nonya or Nyonya ware, because it is believed that the designs of the wares were selected by *nonya*, the female members of the community (Kee 2004, 2009; Lim 1981; Rudolph 1998; Tan 1988, 1993).[6] And since Peranakan porcelain was manufactured in Jingdezhen and exported through Shanghai, it was historically called Kiangsi (Jiangxi) ware or Shanghai ware. Apart from the Straits Settlements, some Peranakan Chinese communities inhabiting today's southern Thailand and Indonesia also possessed pieces of Peranakan porcelain (Wibisono et al. 2012).

Although some examples can be dated back to the mid-nineteenth century, Peranakan porcelain objects were mainly imported during the Peranakan golden age (between the 1870s and 1920s), when this creole community enjoyed ascendancy in political, economic, and material domains in European colonial societies (Knapp 2012; Rooney 2017). Pieces dated after the 1920s are rare and of relatively inferior quality, which is mainly due to the decline of Jingdezhen and the shift to European wares (Rudolph 1998).

Peranakan Chinese communities are known for unique cultural practices that blend Chinese, Malay, and European elements. In their ceramic consumption, based on ethnographic records and memories sustained within the community, rich Peranakan Chinese families picked English transferwares for daily usage, Chinese blue-and-white porcelain for funerals and the mourning period, and colorful Peranakan wares for weddings, birthdays, anniversaries, and the Lunar New Year (Lee and Chen 2006; Rudolph 1998). In the case of weddings, important rituals that ensured the sustainability of the Peranakan Chinese community and its family businesses, Peranakan porcelain can be further split into two categories: serving wares for the ceremony and feast, such as tea sets, dishes, bowls, and spoons, and gifts for the bride, such as boxes for hair oil or spittoons associated with the popular betel nut chewing habit. Regarding the pieces used for dining, Lim (1981) notes that quantity mattered: being able to display a certain amount of Peranakan wares was essential for the reputation of the family. Chia (1994) specifically noted that a set of Peranakan wares contained 144 pieces. It is also interesting to note that in his classic ethnography, Tan (1988) observed that although the Peranakan Chinese preferred to eat with fingers in daily life, they used forks, spoons, or chopsticks during weddings when they sat next to non-Peranakan Chinese.

Peranakan porcelain is characterized by its vibrant colors and feminine motifs. Rose pink, powder blue, and mustard green are the dominant colors among these fully enameled pieces, which leads to a discussion of the possible relationship between Peranakan wares and Chinese *famille rose* and *famille verte* porcelains from the eighteenth century (Feller 1982; Lim 1981). The motif combining the phoenix and peony flowers was the most popular pattern, leaving a feminine impression (Figure 15.4). Luck symbols, such as butterflies and double-happiness characters, and Chinese-style Buddhist motifs were not uncommon. Human figures were rarely present. In fact, they may have been avoided on purpose to respect the Malays, among whom the Peranakan lived closely (Lim 1981:24).[7] The form of the wares was mostly Chinese, but a few European-influenced products, such as soap dishes and teacups with handles, can also be seen. Today, together with beadwork, dresses, accessories, and furniture, Peranakan porcelain is one of the most recognized material cultures of Peranakan Chinese heritage in Southeast Asia.

Although Bencharong and Peranakan porcelains are distinctive from each other in appearance, some similarities can be observed since they were produced at the same

Figure 15.4. Examples of Peranakan porcelain at the Pinang Peranakan Mansion, Malaysia. *Photo courtesy of NG Xin Yi.*

Figure 15.5. A sherd of Bencharong porcelain from the Mehan Garden site, the Philippines. *Photo taken by the author.*

kiln complex and their manufacturing periods overlapped during the second half of the nineteenth century. First, the enamel technique produced a thick and opaque glaze on the surface of both porcelains, in contrast to other Jingdezhen overglaze polychrome products, such as those for the court and armorial wares decorated with coats of arms for the West. Second, several forms, such as cylindrical teapots with low, dish-like lids and round-bodied covered jars with lids with lion designs, were shared between the Bencharong and the Peranakan.[8] Despite shared forms, the Bencharong and Peranakan porcelains can still be easily distinguished based on colors and motifs. In other words, it was only at the final coloring stage of the porcelain production process that Peranakan wares and late Bencharong wares clearly diverged. Rooney (2017) considered these particular shapes as a "Chinese influence" on Behcharong porcelain. However, from Jingdezhen potters' viewpoint, this trend might simply reflect the standardization of the industry as it reached its new height responding to an influx of orders. In addition, the presence of European-influenced shapes among Bencharong and Peranakan porcelains reminds us how the development of an early modern European *civilité*, alongside the importation and use of china (Finlay 2010; Pitts 2017), circulated back to Asia.

As summarized above, Bencharong and Peranakan are mainly treated as ritual wares or heirlooms and are attributed to particular groups. However, two cases—a Bencharong porcelain sherd in the archaeological collection from a site in Manila and a set of Peranakan plates identified among wall decorations at a mosque in Java—jointly provide alternative narratives for these colorful products.

Wares in Abnormal Contexts

A sherd newly identified as Bencharong porcelain is part of the collection from the Mehan Garden archaeological site in Manila. It is the mouth rim of a lotus-paneled bowl with the so-called Himaphan-forest-flowers motif,[9] one of the most common patterns of Bencharong porcelain (Figure 15.5). From the remaining sherd, we can see that the ware was fully glazed, but only the exterior is decorated. Although the colored glazes were mostly oxidized and are partially gone, making the original colors hard to determine, it is still evident that each panel was enameled with different colors and that the flower designs within each division varied. Similar ware can be found in the collection of the Chao Sam Phraya Museum at Ayutthaya (Figure 15.2; center piece in the upper row). Robinson (1982) places this type of design in the Rama I period category, while Sng and Bisalputra (2011) suggest that the style was quite common during the eighteenth century.

Located next to the Spanish Walled City, the Mehan Garden site was part of the former settlement for nonconverted Chinese until the late seventeenth century. Later on, before the site became a botanical garden in 1858, it was an open area next to the city moat. A large amount of archaeological materials dating from the eighteenth to the early twentieth century suggests that part of this area may have been residential or used as a dump for people who lived in the Walled City before and while the garden was being built (Cuevas et al. 2000; Jago-on et al. 2003).

Just as this sherd of Bencharong found its way far afield from the Siamese upper class to Spanish Manila, an unusual sample of Peranakan porcelain has been identified at an Islamic monument in Java. Masjid Sunan Gunung Jati and its associated cemetery are at the outskirts of Cirebon. The cemetery not only serves as a popular place for Javanese Muslim pilgrimages but also embraces various groups of people, regardless of their religious and ethnic backgrounds, coming to ask for blessings (Sanusi 2010). Like other notable sites along the north coast of Java, the mosque and the adjoining cemetery are characterized by porcelain adornments (Agustina and Ekasari 2018). In addition to square wall tiles from the Netherlands and England, full pieces of dishware from the Netherlands, England, and China, complete pieces of the seventeenth century to modern times, were combined and inlaid in the walls.

In this site, four pieces of Peranakan porcelain were identified at the tomb of Sunan Gunung Jati (1448–1568 CE), founder of the Cirebon Sultanate and a revered Islamic saint, (Figure 15.6). The dishes feature the same design on the visible interior: a peach is placed at the center, surrounded by two red roundels containing Chinese double-happiness characters and two pink peonies with extra curly vines. The double-happiness characters were written in a rough and compact way. Kee (2009) has dated a similar plate (one of few not fully enameled products) to the reign of Tongzhi (r. 1861–1875 CE). The four dishes were placed together as a set surrounding a blue-and-white transferware, probably from England, further distinguished from other decorations by lines of brown-and-white square tiles with European port scenery.

Discussion: The Social Lives of Polychrome Porcelains and the Networks of Creolized Chinese in Southeast Asia

Although potters from China and Japan had produced specific types of ceramics for Southeast Asian markets for centuries, those wares were not made for specific customers. In contrast, Bencharong and Peranakan porcelains were requested by particular groups in this region. What was the nature of these primary connections with China? And what was the potential for these wares to circulate beyond these major connections?

Orders for Bencharong and Peranakan porcelains were facilitated by prosperous trading activities between Siam and China and between the Straits Settlements and China. After the Dutch massacred the Chinese in Batavia in 1740 and the Spanish excluded non-Catholic Chinese from the Philippines in 1755, the Chinese junk trade in Southeast Asia switched considerably to non-European port cities in the following century. Siam, the most substantial local power in the region, became the new business center

Figure 15.6. Peranakan porcelain at the wall of Masjid Sunan Gunungjati, Indonesia.
Photo taken by the author.

to meet the growing demand from China (Reid 2001 [1996]). This has been called the "Chinese century" in Southeast Asia, as Chinese traders and migrants became vital resources for local rulers between the mid-eighteenth century and the mid-nineteenth century (Reid 2015). In the case of Siam, an open ethnic policy and similar religions facilitated Chinese integration into local society. Unlike in European colonies, a rigid system of stratification based on ethnicity was not applied in Siam until the reign of Rama VI (r. 1910–1925 CE). People of full or partial Chinese ancestry achieved high positions in the court and dominated both internal and external commerce, including royal tributary trade with China (Kuhn 2009). By the 1820s, the trade activity of Siam had been taken over by the Straits Settlements, especially Singapore, where Peranakan Chinese actively served as middlemen between the British and the traditional Chinese and indigenous business groups in the region (Reid 2001 [1996]).

The preferential demand from royal Siamese and the Peranakan Chinese for Bencharong and Peranakan porcelain, in contrast to concurrent global trends of ceramic consumption, could be interpreted as a form of cultural persistence, despite the expansion of European imperialism during the eighteenth and nineteenth centuries. Importantly, the persisting culture I refer to here is not "Chinese culture," although some consumers of these wares were of Chinese descent, but rather particular Southeast Asian cultures. In this region, using materials from China in rituals essential to sustaining local identity, or as gifts to facilitate social relationships, has been a common strategy. This point is particularly evident when we consider the fact that Peranakan porcelain made the elite Peranakan Chinese distinct not only from the Malays but also from non-Peranakan Chinese elites who did not consume the same wares. The presence of European-influenced products among Bencharong and Peranakan porcelains further implies that the Chineseness of these products was not critical to a certain degree for their owners.

Because orders for Bencharong and Peranakan porcelains were quite limited compared to those for other mass-produced products from Jingdezhen, the wares found in the "abnormal contexts" of Manila and Cirebon were most likely related to the trade connections between Siam and the Philippines and between the Straits Settlements and Java, respectively. The city of Manila heavily relied on junks managed by the Chinese and Chinese mestizos before it became a free port in 1834. Considering that the neighborhood of nonconverted Chinese was moved to another location during the eighteenth century, the Bencharong bowl found next to the Walled City could have belonged to either Spanish or Chinese mestizos.[10] Notably, the latter had a much higher population than the former and had a better connection with the junk trade. However, perhaps because of Christianization, Chinese mestizos in the Philippines did not develop a strong preference for Chinese-made, ritual-use materials like their counterparts along the Malacca Strait. Converting to Catholicism was a business strategy for some Chinese traders in the early Spanish Philippines (Chan 1978). After continuous missionary work and intermarriage with indigenous communities, the Chinese mestizo communities, officially labeled a separate ethnic group by the Spanish in the middle of the eighteenth century, were characterized as being "more Spanish than the Spanish, more Catholic than the Catholics" (Skinner 2001 [1996]; Wickberg 1964:99) in their cultural practices. Nevertheless, Chu (2002) emphasized the persistence of the Chineseness of the Chinese mestizos as part of their fluid identity. The presence of a Bencharong bowl in Manila, of course, cannot stand in for this entire argument, but it may denote the complex relationship between ethnicity and material culture in the social lives of these porcelain wares. The linkage between overseas Chinese communities in Manila and Siam is known but rarely addressed, and the fact that the Bencharong porcelain found in Manila was not decorated with an overtly Siamese Buddhist figure might have made it a proper gift from Siam to Chinese mestizos.

Placing the Peranakan porcelains as tributes at the mosque in Cirebon, one of the critical centers for Javanese Islam, tells a parallel story. As one of the old trade ports along the coast of northern Java, Cirebon is known for its rich cultural heritage, such as architectures hybridizing Hindu, Javanese, Chinese, and European elements and the local batik design characterized by a Chinese-style cloud. During the mid-nineteenth century, the city flourished due to colonial cash crops from the Dutch cultivation system as well as maritime trade. Despite living in very different colonial environments, Peranakan Chinese in Indonesia and the Straits Settlements shared material culture to some extent. For example, it is well-known that batik sarongs made in Pekalongan in northern Java—another outstanding material culture of the Peranakan Chinese—were the most fashionable and precious among the Peranakan Chinese communities. With regard to the use of Peranakan porcelain in the Indonesian archipelago, Wibisono et al. (2012) note that it played a more critical role in the Peranakan communities close to the Straits Settlements, such as Medan and Palembang, whereas in other places it served as a complement. The diverse consumption of Peranakan porcelain by Peranakan Chinese of the Malay world provides a hint as to why and how double-happiness plates that were normally used in Chinese wedding contexts ended up at an Islamic tomb.

The heterogeneous nature of the Peranakan Chinese was reflected in religious practices. As noted by Wibisono et al. (2012), the majority of Peranakan Chinese in Indonesia practiced Buddhism or Taoism. However, Hoadley (1988) and Taylor (2005) indicate that historically, the ethnic Chinese Muslim and Peranakan Chinese communities contributed to the spread of Islam at the port cities of Indonesia and that the Peranakan Chinese were close to the Javanese elites at Cirebon. Since the Peranakan Chinese in Java did not have as strong an attachment with Peranakan porcelain as their counterparts living along the strait, it seems that the pieces decorating the masjid might have been offered by a person of local Javanese culture, whether Peranakan Chinese or Muslim. This last owner might not even have understood the meaning of the Chinese characters on the plates (see Falkenhausen 1999). Instead, offering the wares as tiles for wall decoration in a tradition that can be traced back to the time of the Majapahit Kingdom (Sakai and Ohashi 2017) might have been more meaningful.

Concluding Remarks

Studying Bencharong and Peranakan porcelains, the china made for Asia, we see the entanglement of Chinese and non-Chinese elements among the objects as well as people; we see how regional economic networks and smaller-scale ritual networks integrated with each other. Discussions of overseas Chinese communities during the eighteenth and nineteenth centuries are usually based on current-day national boundaries in Southeast Asia and focus on the *sinkheks*, while the Peranakan and mestizo Chinese are largely ignored due to their ambiguous positions in national narratives (Hun 2017; Lee 2013). Moreover, among scholarship of these creolized communities, the majority focuses on their development in each colony, while their cross-border connectivity is rarely explored (Salmon 2000). More research in this direction is needed to reveal the diverse identities of these peoples and the complexity of their networks in the region before their further incorporation into global trends.

Acknowledgments

I would like to thank the National Museum of the Philippines for access to its archaeology collection and Takashi Sakai for identifying the Bencharong porcelain sherd. I would also like to thank Attha Atthasit for directing me to search for Bencharong porcelain in Bangkok, and Huang Wei for offering more information about discovery of the Bencharong sherds at Jingdezhen as well as the current scholarship on Bencharong porcelain in China. Finally, I thank Regalado Trota José for providing information about the Mehan Garden site.

Notes

1. The ware decorated with transfer-printing technique was developed in the 1750s. The motifs were first engraved on copper plates. Then pigments were applied to the plates, and images were printed on a specific paper. The paper was quickly applied (transfer printed) to a biscuit-fired ceramic object.
2. Other than the overseas Chinese markets, some of these products were redistributed to the Arabic world. See Sakai and Hsieh (2023).
3. Peranakan Chinese communities were fully developed during the British colonial period in the Straits Settlements, and most ethnographic research focuses on people in these cities (Clammer 1979, 1980; Tan 1988). However, there are Peranakan Chinese in other cities and rural areas in mainland and island Southeast Asia, with vast diversities (Tan et al. 2015). The Peranakan Chinese are also known as Baba-Nonya (*baba* refers to the males and *nonya* refers to the females of the community). The latter term is more commonly used in the Straits Settlements while the former is widely embraced by overseas Chinese with a similar background in Malaysia and Indonesia.
4. The term *creolized Chinese* in this paper is adapted from Skinner's "Creolized Chinese Societies in Southeast Asia" (1996), where he highlights how the Chinese in various parts of Southeast Asia culturally integrated with local societies.
5. The Sanskrit roots of the name Bencharong are from *panch* (five) and *rang* (color). It is possible that this word was translated from the Chinese *wucai*五彩.
6. A *nonya* could be Chinese, Malay, or a descendant of Chinese–Malay intermarriage. Some Peranakan Chinese were creole in terms of language (they developed a language mainly based on Malay but containing a lot of Hokkien words) and other cultural practices.
7. As Lim (1981) notes, there is a general prohibition against idols in Islam, and most Malay were already Muslims at the time. Lim does not mention how the prohibition was practiced in the Malay world, however, and animal figures (for example, birds) were not prohibited, since Garuda remained a popular figure.
8. Examples of the teapots can be found in Kee 2009:125–31, vs. Rooney 2017:168–72; covered jars can be found in Kee 2009:168–86, vs. Rooney 2017:111.
9. In Buddhist belief, Himaphan is a legendary forest where mythological creatures live.
10. In the context of the Spanish colonial Philippines, Spanish mestizos are descendants of Spanish–indigenous intermarriage, whereas Chinese mestizos are descendants of Chinese–indigenous intermarriage. The population of Chinese mestizos increased over time relative to the Spanish mestizos and was active in overseas Chinese networks. It is more likely that the owner of the ware discussed here was a Chinese mestizo, although the author does not exclude the possibility of association with Spanish mestizos, who were a significant minority in the colony and also participated in trade.

References

Agustina, Ina Helena, and Astri Mutia Ekasari
2018   Study of Cultural Heritage in Astana Village Cirebon District. In *The 8th Rural Research and Planning Group International Conference*, edited by Suratman, M. Baiquni, and Surani Hasanati, pp. 264–72. Yogyakarta: Gadjah Mada University Press.

Appadurai, Arjun, ed.
1986   *The Social Life of Things: Commodities in Cultural Perspective*. New York: Press Syndicate of the University of Cambridge.

Chan, Albert
1978   Chinese–Philippine Relations in the Late Sixteenth Century and to 1603. *Philippine Studies* 26(1–2):51–85.

Chantrapakajee, Suthipob
2019   The Stream of Merchandise at Ayutthaya, an International Maritime Market. In *Ancient Maritime Cross-Cultural Exchanges: Archaeological Research in Thailand*, edited by Amara Srisuchat and Wilfried Giessler, pp. 136–65. Bangkok: Fine Arts Department, Ministry of Culture.

Chia, Felix
1994   *The Babas Revisited*. Singapore: Heinemann Asia.

Chu, Richard T.
2002 The "Chinese" and the "Mestizos" of the Philippines: Towards a New Interpretation. *Philippine Studies* 50(3):327–70.

Clammer, John R.
1979 *The Ambiguity of Identity Ethnicity Maintenance and Change among the Straits Chinese Community of Malaysia and Singapore.* Singapore: Institute of Southeast Asian Studies.
1980 *Straits Chinese Society.* Singapore: Singapore University Press.

Cuevas, N. T., S. C. B. Jago-on, and J. G. Belmonte
2000 The Mehan Garden Archaeology Project: A Preliminary Report. *National Museum Papers* 10(2):69–90.

Dangkong, Palawat
2019 Phrabāth s̄mdĕc phracêāxyů̄h̄ạw (rạchkāl thī̀ 10) พระบาทสมเด็จพระเจ้าอยู่หัว (รัชกาลที่ ๑๐) [His Majesty the King (Rama 10)], https://www.facebook.com/photo.php?fbid=2334111086651794&set=a.2334168536646049&type=3&theater, accessed May 10, 2019.

Falkenhausen, Lothar von
1995 The Regionalist Paradigm in Chinese Archaeology. In *Nationalism, Politics, and the Practice of Archaeology*, edited by Philip Kohl and Clare Fawcett, pp. 198–217. Cambridge: Cambridge University Press.
1999 Inconsequential Incomprehensions: Some Instances of Chinese Writing in Alien Contexts. *Res* 35:42–69.

Feller, John Quentin
1982 *Chinese Export Porcelain in the 19th Century: The Canton Famille Rose Porcelains.* Salem, MA: Peabody Museum of Salem.

Finlay, Robert
2010 *The Pilgrim Art: Culture of Porcelain in World History.* Berkeley: University of California Press.

Floor, Willem, and Jaap Otte
2013 European Ceramics for the East. *Aramco World* 64(3):34–40.

Groussin, Gérard
2003 *La Porcelaine Sino-thaïe: Bencharong et Lai Nam Thong.* Paris: Kailash.

Harris, Mark
1990 *Muzium Negara Kuala Lumpur: Sejarah dan Kebudayaan Malaysia.* Kuala Lumpur: Pepin Press.

Hoadley, Mason C.
1988 Javanese, Peranakan, and Chinese Elites in Cirebon: Changing Ethnic Boundaries. *Journal of Asian Studies* 47(3):503–17.

Hun, Pue Giok
2017 "Our Chinese": The Mixedness of Peranakan Chinese Identities in Kelantan, Malaysia. In *Mixed Race in Asia: Past, Present and Future*, edited by Zarine L. Rocha and Farida Fozdar, pp. 147–61. London: Routledge.

Jago-on, Sheldon Clyde B., Nida T. Cuevas, and Joy G. Belmonte
2003 Mehan Garden Archaeology. *Proceedings of the Society of Philippine Archaeologists* 1:110–14.

Kee, Ming-Yuet
2004 *Straits Chinese Porcelain.* Kuala Lumper: Kee Ming-Yuet Sdn Bhd/Cross Time Matrix Sdn Bhd.
2009 *Peranakan Chinese Porcelain: Vibrant Festive Ware of the Straits Chinese.* Tokyo: Tuttle.

Knapp, Ronald G.
2012 *The Peranakan Chinese Home: Art and Culture in Daily Life.* Tokyo: Tuttle.

Kuhn, Philip A.
2009 *Chinese among Others: Emigration in Modern Times.* Lanham, MD: Rowman & Littlefield.

Lee, Khoon Choy
2013 *Golden Dragon and Purple Phoenix: The Chinese and Their Multi-Ethnic Descendants in Southeast Asia.* Hackensack, NJ: World Scientific.

Lee, Peter, and Jennifer Chen
2006 *The Straits Chinese House: Domestic Life and Traditions.* Singapore: National Museum of Singapore.

Lim, Suan Poh
1981 Nonya Ware. In *Nonya Ware and Kitchen Ch'ing: Ceremonial and Domestic Pottery of the 19th–20th Centuries Commonly Found in Malaysia*, edited by William Willetts and Suan Poh Lim, pp. 17–30. Selangor: Southeast Asian Ceramic Society.

Malkin, Irad
2011 *A Small Greek World: Networks in the Ancient Mediterranean.* New York: Oxford University Press.

Miksic, John N.
2009 Research on Ceramic Trade, within Southeast Asia and between Southeast Asia and China. In *Southeast Asian Ceramics: New Light on Old Pottery*, edited by John N. Miksic, pp. 70–99. Singapore: Southeast Asian Ceramic Society.

Mudge, Jean McClure
1981 *Chinese Export Porcelain for the American Trade: 1785–1835*. 2nd ed. Plainsboro, NJ: Associated University Presses.

Oka, Yasumasa
2008 Dejima shutsudo no Yōroppa tōki wo megutte 出島出土のヨーロッパ陶器をめぐって [Concerning the European Ceramics Excavated at Dejima]. In *Kuni shitei Dejima Oranda shōkan ato: Kapitan heya ato hoka nishigawa kenzōbutsu-gun hakkutsu chōsa hōkoku-sho* 国指定 出島阿蘭陀商館跡:カピタン部屋跡ほか西側建造物群発掘調査報告書 [Dejima Dutch Archaeological Site: Excavation Report on Chief Factor's Residence and Other Western Buildings], edited by Nagasaki City Board of Education, pp. 1–25. Nagasaki: Nagasaki City Board of Education.

Pitts, Martin
2017 Globalization and *China*: Materiality and Civilité in Post-Medieval Europe. In *The Routledge Handbook of Archaeology and Globalization*, edited by Tamar Hodos, pp. 566–79. London: Routledge.

Reid, Anthony
2001 [1996] Flows and Seepages in the Long-term Chinese Interaction with Southeast Asia. In *Sojourners and Settlers: Histories of Southeast Asia and the Chinese*, edited by Anthony Reid, pp. 15-50. Honolulu: University of Hawai'i Press.
2015 *A History of Southeast Asia: Critical Crossroads*. Malden, MA: Wiley Blackwell.

Robinson, Natalie V.
1979 Bencharong and Lai Nam Thong Ceramics. In *The Artistic Heritage of Thailand: A Collection of Essays*, pp. 139–49. Bangkok: Sawaddi Magazine, National Museum Volunteers.
1982 *Sino-Thai Ceramics: In the National Museum, Bangkok, Thailand, and in Private Collections*. Bangkok: Department of Fine Arts.
1991 Comparison of Transitional Bencharong and Probable Bat-Trang Enameled Wares. *Journal of the Siam Society* 79(2):48–60.

Rooney, Dawn F.
2017 *Bencharong: Chinese Porcelain for Siam*. Bangkok: River Books.

Rudolph, Jürgen
1998 *Reconstructing Identities: A Social History of the Babas in Singapore*. Aldershot: Ashgate.

Sadsunk, Suwit
2013 Fabric Printing Design, Inspired from the Five-Color Porcelain (Benjarong). *International Journal of Humanities and Social Sciences* 7(5):1292–96.

Sakai, Takashi
2007 Banten Tirutayasa iseki Buton Worio jōseki hakkutsu chōsa hōkoku-sho バンテン・ティルタヤサ遺跡 ブトン・ウォリオ城跡発掘調査報告書 [Excavation Research Report of Tirtayasa Site, Banten and Wolio Castle Ruins, Buton]. Jakarta: NPO Association of Asian Culture Properties Cooperation and Pusat Penelitian dan Pengembangan Arkeologi Nasional.

Sakai, Takashi, and Ellen Hsieh
2023 A Thousand Years of Connections between the Indian Ocean region and Southeast Asia. In *Historical Archaeology in the Indian Ocean*. Edited by Mark William Hauser and Julia Haines. Gainesville: University Press of Florida. (in press).

Sakai, Takashi, and Koji Ohashi
2017 *Hizen Wares Excavated from Royal Capital Sites in Indonesia: Trowulan and Other Sites*. Tokyo: Yuzankaku.

Salmon, Claudine
2000 Chinese Merchants in Southeast Asia. In *Asian Merchants and Businessmen in the Indian Ocean and the China Sea*, edited by Denys Lombard and Jean Aubin, pp. 329–51. Oxford: Oxford University Press.

Sanusi, Burhanudin
2010 Jum'ata in the Graveyard: An Anthropological Study of Pilgrims in the Grave of Sunan Gunung Jati Cirebon, West Java. *Journal of Indonesian Islam* 4(2):317–40.

Sargent, William R.
2012 *Treasures of Chinese Export Ceramics: From the Peabody Essex Museum*. New Haven, CT: Yale University Press.

Skinner, G. William
2001 [1996] Creolized Chinese Societies in Southeast Asia. In *Sojourners and Settlers: Histories of Southeast Asia and the Chinese*, edited by Anthony Reid, pp. 15–93. Honolulu: University of Hawai'i Press.

Skowronek, Russell K.
1998 The Spanish Philippines: Archaeological Perspectives on Colonial Economics and Society. *International Journal of Historical Archaeology* 2(1):45–1.

Sng, Jeffery, and Pim Praphai Bisalputra
2011   *Bencharong and Chinaware in the Court of Siam.* Bangkok: Chawpipope Osathanugrah.

Tan, Chee Beng
1988   *The Baba of Melaka: Culture and Identity of a Chinese Peranakan Community in Malaysia.* Selangor Darul Ehsan: Pelanduk Publications.
1993   *Chinese Peranakan Heritage in Malaysia and Singapore.* Shah Alam: Fajar Bakti.

Tan, Yao Sua, Kamarudin Ngah, and Mohd Shahrul Imran Lim Abdullah
2015   Negotiation of Identity and Internal Contradictions: The Terengganu and Kelantan Peranakan Chinese Foodways Compared. *Asian Ethnicity* 16(4):411–27.

Taylor, Jean Gelman
2005   The Chinese and the Early Centuries of Conversion to Islam in Indonesia. In *Chinese Indonesians: Remembering, Distorting, Forgetting*, edited by Tim Lindsey and Helen Pausacker, pp. 148–64. Singapore: Institute of Southeast Asian Studies.

Wibisono, Lily, Mary Northmore, Rusdi Tjahyadi, and Musa Jonatan, eds.
2012   *Indonesian Chinese Peranakan: A Cultural Journey.* Jakarta: Indonesian Cross-Cultural Society.

Wickberg, Edgar
1964   The Chinese Mestizo in Philippine History. *Journal of Southeast Asian History* 5(1):62–100.

Part IV

Objects and Meaning

Chapter 16

The Xi'an Kharoṣṭhī Inscription
A New Translation

Minku Kim

Prologue

My guru Lothar von Falkenhausen is a formidable polyglot. His erudition is inimitable and his intellectual spectrum vast, reaching beyond the conventional disciplinary bounds of sinology and across the "silk routes," his preferred plural emphasizing the erratic and ephemeral nature of the ancient trans-Eurasiatic trade network (Falkenhausen 2010). He has even written rigorously about silk itself (Falkenhausen 1999, 2000).

While I was at UCLA, he encouraged me to study any rarefied languages that could be useful to my own study of Buddhist art and archaeology. Even though my regional focus lies in China, I was blessed to learn Sanskrit, Tocharian, and Tibetan as liberally I saw fit. This important seed of training enabled me to venture into Gāndhārī, the language at stake below, during my postdoctoral study—indeed, the same Andrew W. Mellon postdoctoral fellowship that he had held nearly two decades earlier at Stanford. (I cannot easily imagine a more delightful opportunity than what was also given to me at Stanford by Al Dien and Fred R. Porta, who ran a small weekly lunchtime seminar, where Brāhmī and Kharoṣṭhī were often on our table.) The current paper, whatever its value, owes its raison d'être to all the support, inspirations, and revelations Professor von Falkenhausen has offered me since 2004 when I had such great luck to be introduced to him in South Korea.

Two Kharoṣṭhī Inscriptions from China Proper

Kharoṣṭhī is one of the two earliest known Indic scripts (Salomon 1998:42–56, 2007). Primarily used in the northwestern part of the Indian subcontinent, namely Gandhāra, it generally records a local language spoken in the region (Figure 16.1). Modern scholars coined the term Gāndhārī to designate this distinctive Middle Indo-Aryan vernacular language, named after its toponym, Gandhāra (Bailey 1946; Salomon 2018). In the past few decades, Gāndhārī has been getting more attention for the role it played in the early transmission of Buddhism, especially Mahāyāna, to China (Bernhard 1970; Karashima 2013; Nattier 1990) through the Tarim basin (Figure 16.1), a region where oasis polities once flourished around the vast desert of Taklamakan.

Outside Greater Gandhāra, the largest corpus of Gāndhārī and of Kharoṣṭhī as well is found in a region called Chinese Turkestan or Xinjiang (Rapson et al. 1929). These materials, often along with their parallel findings written in Chinese, provide the earliest evidence of literacy practiced in the region (Hansen 2004). Most Kharoṣṭhī materials were found along the southeastern fringes, corresponding to the former domain of Kroraina or Loulan 樓蘭/Shanshan 鄯善 (Figure 16.1; Brough 1965, 1970; Enoki 1963). To further pinpoint, the foremost epicenter within Kroraina is Caḍota (Jingjue 精絕) or Niya 尼雅/Nīña (Nirang 泥壤; Figure 16.1). The local vernacular, or Krorainic proper, was an Iranian language, but these Iranian speakers distinctively adopted Gāndhārī in writing their documents.[1] This literary form of Gāndhārī recorded in these documents differs considerably from that of mainstream Gāndhārī in morphology, phonology, and orthography (Burrow 1937, 1940; Fussman 1989). We may therefore call this Krorainic Gāndhārī. Despite differences in nomenclature, this "dialect" is identical to Sten Konow's (1867–1948) Central Asian Prakrit or Thomas Burrow's (1909–1986) Niya Prakrit (Burrow 1936; Konow 1936). Following the aforesaid coinage of the name Gāndhārī by Harold Walter Bailey (1899–1996) in 1946 and the brilliant contributions made in recent decades by Richard G. Salomon and his protégés around the world, Gāndhārī is perfectly apposite to describe the given literary dialect of Kroraina too. In any case, Krorainic Gāndhārī is witnessed in these excavated documents mainly as an administrative language whose geographic range reaches from the vicinities of Caḍota proper, including Sāca (or Endere) in the west (Figure 16,1), to the Lop Nur basin in the east, the very political center of Kroraina (Meng 2017).

It is rare to come across Kharoṣṭhī writing, thus Gāndhārī, anywhere east of Kroraina. The current count stands at a meager three samples (Lin 1996:200–201). Dunhuang (Gansu) is the provenance of the first specimen. Written on a badly dilapidated piece of silk (T.XII.a.ii.20), the sample was discovered by Aurel Stein (1862–1943) in 1907 during his second expedition to the Tarim basin (Stein 1921:2:777; 1921:4:Plate 39). Its findspot is a refuse pit attached to a ruined watchtower, only a short distance from the famous Jade Gate (Yumenguan 玉門關; Figure 16.1) along the so-called Dunhuang Limes (meaning "path" in Latin). This pit also yielded the famous "lost postbag" of Sogdian letters, the crucial trove of materials for the study of the Eastern Middle Iranian language and Sino–Sogdian relations (Grenet and Sims-Williams 1987; Grenet et al. 1998; Henning 1948; Reichelt 1931; Sims-Williams 2001, 2005). Notwithstanding this tantalizing and intriguing indication of a close sociocultural nexus across Kharoṣṭhī and Sogdian literacy, this fragile specimen has long been unaccounted for after the first edition was published by Rapson et al. (1929:266). Even the International Dunhuang Project, the multinational collaborative led by the British Library, omits from its catalog this singular Kharoṣṭhī entry.[2] I hope that its omission in the online database does not indicate the loss of the physical specimen itself. The group of scrap textiles found in the same refuse pit was pouched together and is now on loan to the Victoria and Albert Museum (Stein.48) from the National Museum, New Delhi. Today I cannot pursue any further whether the pouch in question—a conservatory work, possibly, by Stein's "recording angel" Florence Mary Glen Lorimer (1883–1967) herself (Wang 1998)—still contains the specimen or whether it remains somewhere in India, as Stefan Baums suspects.[3] The specimen is listed (CKD 708) in the indispensable online platform that Baums and Andrew Stuart Glass have

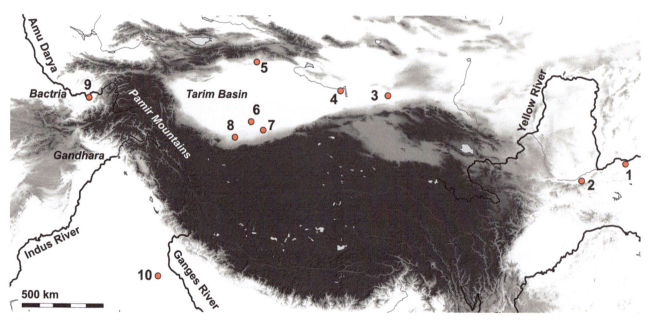

Figure 16.1. Map of sites mentioned in the text: 1. Luoyang; 2. Xi'an; 3. Dunhuang; 4. Loulan; 5. Kucha; 6. Niya; 7. Endere; 8. Karadong; 9. Ai Khanoum; 10. Mathurā. *Created by Bryan K. Miller.*

Figure 16.2. Luoyang Kharoṣṭhī inscription (CKI 193), Stone A. Length 45.7 cm. From a suburb of Luoyang; discovered by an archaeological expedition conducted by Peking University in 1924. Arthur M. Sackler Museum of Art and Archaeology at Peking University. *Photo taken by the author.*

been maintaining, in which the corpus is divided into four subcategories: inscriptions, documents, manuscripts, and coins—thus the abbreviations CKI (Corpus of Kharoṣṭhī Inscriptions), CKD (Corpus of Kharoṣṭhī Documents), and so forth.[4]

East of Dunhuang lies China proper. Here we have two Kharoṣṭhī inscriptions (CKI 170 and 193) noted thus far, one of which is the current focus of this paper. Regrettably, neither was retrieved from a controlled scientific excavation. We hear only in retrospect that they were collected from somewhere near or within Luoyang (Henan) and Xi'an (Shaanxi), respectively (Figure 16.1). Both cities were former imperial capitals, or at least important urban centers, in North China, but our inquiries about the exact findspots and the archaeological contexts thereof have been fruitless.

The Luoyang inscription (CKI 193) is written on a contiguous curvature of a now fragmented stone monument, only a fraction of which—possibly no more than one-third of the original writing—was collected in 1924 from an unspecified location in what was then a suburb of Luoyang, after having been severely weathered already (Figures 16.2 and 16.3). Now those pieces are being stored in two separate venues in Beijing: the Arthur M. Sackler Museum of Art and Archaeology at Peking University (Stone A) and the National Museum of China (Stones B and C). Since the grand reopening of the latter in 2011, Stones B and C have been on public display in a permanent gallery the basement, but their order is reversed (Stone B would more correctly be put to the right of Stone C). It was not until the early 1960s that the script—once misunderstood to be Palmyrene and used to stir up a wild fancy about the presence of Jews in early medieval Luoyang (Prévost 1924)—was correctly recognized as Kharoṣṭhī (Brough 1961). The decipherment by John Brough (1917–1984) was a breakthrough. Unfortunately, with no in situ information available to us, doubt remains about the original monument's form and function. A dominant view is that these stones originally were part of a well coping (Lin Meicun 1989). One may rule out other possibilities, however. For instance, the fragments may, albeit in some inscrutable way, amount to an appendage belonging to a Buddhist image (Institut de sinologie 1925:Plate 7; Kim 2014).

Before moving on to the other Kharoṣṭhī example from the Chinese heartland, which is the main topic of this paper, let me briefly call attention to the controversial date of the Luoyang inscription, because the issue will matter later in this discussion. Most scholars today favor an early chronology, reinforced by the influential reanalysis done by Lin Meicun 林梅村 (1989). In particular, a late Eastern Han (25–220) date is treated as a fait accompli (Rhie 1999:340–41). More deliberately, the National Museum's plaque narrows the date to the reign of Eastern Han emperor Ling Di

Figure 16.3. Luoyang Kharoṣṭhī inscription (CKI 193), Stones B (left) and C (right). Length 27.9 cm (B) and 20.3 cm (C). National Museum of China (Beijing). *Photo taken by the author.*

靈帝 (168–189), which I suspect to be a secondary confirmation bias originally brought by circumstantial inferences presented in Lin's paper. But before Lin's authoritative work, Brough (1961:525–27), who initially read the inscription, was far more circumspect in dating. Brough alluded to only a slim possibility of an Eastern Han date precisely because he was striking a balance with what he knew from historical texts indicating that there was *some* contemporary presence of Buddhism in Luoyang (Maspero 1934; Zürcher 1984:197). In other words, this may constitute a circular argument that the inscription evinces activities of Buddhism in the Eastern Han capital. One can now assign a post-Han date, whether by a margin of some decades or even centuries (Kim 2014, 2022). Based on its paleographic parameters alone, Brough (1961:527) previously speculated that the inscription could be as late as 400. More importantly, we cannot ignore the parallel corpus of Kharoṣṭhī uncovered in Kroraina, the largest and closest body of evidence comparable with the inscription (Enoki 1963; Konow 1923). The testimony is unequivocal. Those Krorainic materials are post-Han, which Brough (1965, 1970) too ascribed to between the mid-third and the early fourth centuries. This chronology—now more precisely recalibrated to span between ca. 239 and ca. 328 CE (Atwood 1991:165)—must be, I argue, the baseline for the Luoyang inscription. I see no reason why the Luoyang inscription has to deviate from this timeline so as to fall before 220. The Luoyang inscription might not be any significantly earlier than the materials from Kroraina (Kim 2014, 2022). The hard temporal median of the Krorainic corpus lies toward the last quarter of the third century, namely around the heyday of the Western Jin 晉 (266–316). It is not surprising to imagine a flourishing Gāndhārī-literate (if not Gāndhārī-speaking) community in Luoyang at that time. Indeed, we do not have any unarguably Buddhist object from Luoyang that clearly dates earlier (Kim 2011:chapter 3; Kim 2022).

The Xi'an inscription (CKI 170) is written on a gilt bronze image of the Buddha (Figure 16.4). For the sake of convenience, let me call this image the Kharoṣṭhī Buddha. It must be noted that this inscription, as a Buddhist dedicatory written in Kharoṣṭhī on a metal image, is unique not only within China but also across the pan-Gāndhārī Buddhist world. Whether within or outside Gandhāra proper, very few images bear dedicatory inscriptions, and those that do are either stone or stucco, not metal. Notwithstanding such singularity, the Kharoṣṭhī Buddha was discovered by sheer luck. It was rescued in 1979 from what was then Chang'an County's retail outlet (*menshibu* 門市部) for recycling "waste goods" (*feiguwuzi* 廢舊物資; Han 1998). Were it not for the item's exchangeable value as scrap metal, this serendipity would have missed the attention of the Xi'an Municipal Office of Cultural Heritage, and the irreplaceable inscription would have vanished for good. Lothar von Falkenhausen has reasoned that this utterly plebeian origin story makes a good argument for its authenticity (Kim 2011:7n6, 2015:299n3). It is only disappointing that nothing much is known about how this "recyclable" item ended up the neighborhood shop. According to hearsay, it was assembled with other "junk" from Shifosi 石佛寺 Village in the township of Huangliang 黃良, under the same jurisdiction as the present-day Chang'an district. Fortunately, this rural locality in the southern suburb of Xi'an, skirting

Figure 16.4. Kharoṣṭhī Buddha. Gilt bronze. Height 13.4 cm. Reputedly found in Shifosi Village, Huangliang, Chang'an, Xi'an (Shaanxi) in 1979. Xi'an Museum (Ding 丁 3gtc47).
Photo taken by the author.

the northern foot of the Zhongnan 終南 Mountains, remains underdeveloped, and we may await an archaeological breakthrough in the near future.

Throughout the following decade, few people in Xi'an paid attention to the Kharoṣṭhī Buddha. That long silence was broken by Han Baoquan 韓保全, then director of the Xi'an Museum, where the Kharoṣṭhī Buddha had been deposited. He made a rubbing of the hitherto unread inscription and passed it on to Lin Meicun (1991) via the late Su Bai 宿白 (1922–2018), the most preeminent Buddhist archaeologist in China of the past century. Lin realized that this first rubbing was not sufficient, so a new pair was prepared for him. Lin did not see the real inscription and proceeded to study it like a traditional antiquarian. Unfortunately, the newer rubbings were not perfectly serviceable either, as we judge from what Lin published (1991:131). For instance, the upper and far left sides look fuzzy. Perhaps to help clarify such inadequacies, Lin supplemented his own handwritten copy (131), but that kind of chirographic facsimile demonstrates only what the scribe is up to, without adding precision.

To overcome any shortcomings of the existing rubbings, my current study makes primary use of a naked-eye observation. Since June 2014, I have observed the Kharoṣṭhī Buddha in and out of Xi'an. Actually, it was again Lothar von Falkenhausen, when I happened to catch up with him on the quaint campus of Northwest University, who advised me where I should go the next day to see the image. I subsequently reread the inscription from the photographs I had been taking, although photography is never free of problems. In 2004 the image was brought overseas to the Metropolitan Museum of Art in New York for a major exhibition curated by James Watt Chi-yan (Qu Zhiren 屈志仁; Howard 2004:91), but since my first physical encounter with it in the Xi'an Museum, the Kharoṣṭhī Buddha has become a frequent traveler. It even came to my native city of Seoul in the fall of 2015 (Kungnip Chungang Pangmulgwan 2015:88–89). Also, with the increasing force of the so-called Belt and Road Initiative by the Chinese government, the Kharoṣṭhī Buddha has taken a consummate spot symbolizing an ancient analogue of how modern Chinese society conceives of the silk routes. A representative event was the joint exhibition presented by the Palace Museum and the Indian National Museum, possibly the largest in scale and magnitude ever dedicated to Buddhist art in China (Fang and Li 2016:1:314; 2016:2:75). Between September 2016 and December 2017, the touring show took the Kharoṣṭhī Buddha on the road from Beijing to Fuzhou (Fujian), Hangzhou (Zhejiang), and Chengdu (Sichuan). The Kharoṣṭhī Buddha returned to Hangzhou for another ambitious Buddhist-themed exhibition between November 2018 and February 2019 (Zhejiang Sheng Bowuguan 2018:38). Most recently, it revisited Beijing at the Tsinghua University Art Museum in late 2019 (Qinghua and Shaanxi 2019:419).

Despite this recent spike in interest, the Xi'an inscription has not yet received the attention it deserves. For instance, all these publications uncritically repeat Lin Meicun's preliminary report of 1991. Now, greatly benefited by new insight offered by the internet project directed by Baums (2020), let me try a new reading.

Xi'an Inscription: New Translation

The inscription in question lies on the bottom rear of the tiny (13.5 cm high) Buddha image running along its narrow base. As Kharoṣṭhī is written from the right to left (like its better-known relatives Hebrew and Arabic), the inscription begins underneath the Buddha's right knee and terminates around his upper left thigh (Figure 16.5). This inscribed surface has not avoided the elements entirely, but most letters are clearly legible. These would amount to 27 *akṣara*s (or alphasyllabaries) in total, although Lin Meicun (1991) figured an extra. For easy reference, I sequence each *akṣara* by an Arabic numeral:

lýi	va	ka	sa	pa	na	ha	ta	su	ca	ma	re	ga	pu
1	2	3	4	5	6	7	8	9	10	11	12	13	14

tre	ka	sta	ka	pa	ḍi	ma	pu	ja	ya	bha	va	tu
15	16	17	18	19	20	21	22	23	24	25	26	27

From here on in, I will show this number in brackets when an *akṣara* is mentioned. Above all, paleography is basic. For those who have any familiarity with Kharoṣṭhī, one very prominent, albeit odd, trait to notice here concerns *ga* [13], *ja* [23], and *ḍi* [20] (Glass 2000:56–60, 64–67, 78–80). Those letters carry an elongated cauda (tail) or differentiating line.[5] As a diacritic expediency—like what the *cédille* does in French—these tails denote intervocalic fricativization or Iranian-like spirants (Konow 1931; Rapson et al. 1929:295 passim). In compliance with the practice of Edward James Rapson (1861–1937) and his colleagues, who employed an acute accent (´) when deciphering Stein's corpus, Lin Meicun (1991:120) adopted such superscription as *ǵa* [13], *j́a* [23], and *ḍ́a* [20] (Rapson et al. 1929:Plate 14, nos. 27, 48, 67). For *j́*, however, Lin (1991:130n17) made a typo (*j̇*), which has been cited unchecked in all secondary scholarship (Howard 2004:91; Rhie 2002:326–27). However, these superscribed accents have become obsolete, since Baums and Glass are making use of the underscore (_) instead (https://gandhari.org/dictionary); graphically, the underlining is more intuitive. I am following suit in this new standard.

The next important feature to be mentioned is the dedicatory formula. Again, those who are familiar with Gandhāra will easily see how vividly the closing of the Xi'an inscription echoes what we have seen from this Urheimat of Gāndhārī writing. Regarding the vast distance blocked by the Pamirs (Figure 16.1) in between, the concordance is a beautiful one. Also, this normative command of the language further dispels any remaining worries about the authenticity of the inscription, inasmuch as it is practically impossible to imagine such an unusually knowledgeable forger dwelling obscurely in pre-Reform China, whose trade could be sold for this ridiculously cheap return. In 2010 Richard Salomon personally shared his opinion that the inscription does not seem fake (Kim 2011:7n6). The early medieval scribe who wrote the inscription was someone familiar with this genre of writing, as demonstrated widely across the domain of the Kuṣāṇa Empire and beyond. The boilerplate formula is the final phrase of blessing, *pujaya bhavatu* [22 through 27]. Here *bhavatu* is the third-person-singular imperative of the verb √*bhū* (be), exactly as the Sanskrit parallel conjugates. In English, this can be translated as "May it be!" The preceding *pujaya* is obviously an analogue of *pūjā* (homage) in Sanskrit. The *-aya* termination is the singular dative declension of *puja* (Burrow 1937:§52).

This Sanskritic *-aya* ending is worth elaborating, because it is the *-e* termination (also dative) that is far more common in the mainland Gāndhārī corpus.[6] The elision from *-aya* to *-e* is regularly expected (Burrow 1937:§6; Lin 1991:123). Thus the idiosyncrasy of *pujaya* can now be quickly demonstrable thanks to the efficient internet database provided by Baums and Glass. Within Greater Gandhāra, at least 39 exemplars of *puyae* can be gleaned from various receptacles, including images (CKI 117, 161, 192, 222, 835), architectural members (53, 69, 93, 453, 1113), well or tank copings (56, 57, 158, 830), reliquaries (33, 46, 50, 60, 65, 153, 159, 172, 177, 178, 242, 251, 326, 331, 403, 442, 455, 466, 564), and other vessels (367, 391, 404, and 1161). Nor is their geographic range limited to Gandhāra proper; they can be found beyond the Hindu Kush in Bactria (CKI 755; Figure 16.1) and as far as along the Gangetic basin in Mathurā (CKI

Figure 16.5. Detail of Figure 16.4 (opening of CKI 170 below the right knee). *Photo taken by the author.*

48; Figure 16.1). Intriguingly, the only unelided -*aya* ending I can find—indeed, also in the same imperative formation of *puyaya bhavatu*—is found in the famous stone pentad image, formerly in the collection of Claude de Marteau in Brussels (CKI 232; Fussman 1974:54–58; Rhi 2018:43–44) and recently (September 2020) auctioned off at Christie's in New York (18241, Lot 609). That this rare combination of -*aya* dative with the imperative dedication is noted in these two peculiar devotional images may well be a coincidence, about whose significance I am unable to investigate any further. I can only say that the artistic styles are quite disparate from each other. But the testimony of this stone image from Gandhāra proves that this Sanskritized -*aya* ending of the Xi'an inscription is not an implausible anomaly (Salomon 2001). Intriguing as it may be, the Luoyang inscription exhibits the more prevailing *puyae*. Again, I cannot investigate the reason for this contrast between these two exemplars from China proper today.

With regard to *pujaya*, there is another phonology that I call Sanskritizing. In Gāndhārī, the voiced stop *j* is a rarity, while the intervocalic *j* is routinely softened into *y* (Burrow 1937:§17). Baums, too, has kindly instructed me in a personal communication that *j* is equivalent to *y*. But our Xi'an inscription retains the fricative medial *ja* instead of *puyaya, though this is not unexpected. For instance, the schist lid of a reliquary now stored in the Ashmolean Museum (EA1995.72) bears two episodes of dedication dated to Years 156 and 172, presumably of the Indo-Scythian Azes era (CKI 328; Baums 2012:238–39). Here both *pujae* and *pujae* are co-present, even in the same line of the dedication dated to 156, and *puyae* is in that of 172. These three—*j*, *y*, and *j*—were interchangeable. Therefore *puja*- may well be warranted in our inscription too.

The rest of the inscription is not as easy to read. Admittedly, my grip of Gāndhārī is less proficient than Lin Meicun's (1991). Therefore, when any emendation is necessary below, I consult the authority of Baums via his up-to-date online edition.

The first major problem in Lin's reading (1991) is *videḍame, which is replaced as *paḍima* [19 through 21] above. Initially, an emendation of *paḍime had been offered by Salomon, as credited in Baums's web platform with the date of April 8, 2011. The final -*ma* [21] is Baums's own, dated to April 16, 2011, presumably as a response to that of his teacher. Setting aside this final *akṣara* for now, let me first unpack how self-contradictory was Lin's guess of *vi-. Evidently, the same letter *pa* had been correctly read as such by him in *sapana* [4 through 6], although this very *pa* [5] is a bit smaller than the given *akṣara* in question. Additionally, as in *puja* [22 and 23] and *putre* [14 and 15],

Lin was correct about the *akṣara*, which is modified into *pu* only by the attached vowel sign. That Lin was wrong about *vi*- is out of the question. The *-*deḍa*- that follows can be a more complicated problem. But as Salomon's emendation suggests, what Lin had parsed as dual *akṣaras* cannot be so. When compared with other *akṣaras*, before and after which even cadence of space is maintained, the clutter of writing is too narrow internally to make two *akṣaras*. This also speaks to why Lin's chirographic edition (1991:131) ought to be used with caution. Here Lin ostensibly widened the distance between what he deems as *de and *ḍa. But the single *akṣara* is the retroflex *ḍi* [20] carrying a fricative cauda running to the lower right. Presumably, Lin was not ready to envision that cauda here and thus made the error.

Finally, the terminal -*ma* [21] is given by Baums. This is easily reaffirmed, as the same nasal labial recurs in nearly identical size on the eleventh *akṣara* (-*ma*). It is also clear that the given *ma* lacks the diacritic for the -*e* vowel. Thus here stands *paḍima*, the feminine word meaning "image," corresponding to *pratimā* in Sanskrit (Kim 2019:207–8). In the case of this word, of particular interest to art historians, I call it directive (dir.), again following the practice of Baums's online dictionary. In Krorainic Gāndhārī, there is no morphological distinction between nominative and accusative, both ending in -*a* (Burrow 1937:§51), although here we can distinguish a nominative sense.[7]

Next is the opening of the inscription, *citaka [1 through 3] according to Lin Meicun (1991:120). Even for Lin himself, this conclusion would have been hard to believe; he had to hyper-correct it to *Cittaka, which he understood as a personal name. This conjecture has been cited unconditionally again and again in all subsequent literature. Part of the reason this is difficult to follow is physical. That portion of the inscription starts tightly in the narrow area below the right knee of the Buddha, where it has been more susceptible to the test of time (Figure 16.5). Baums has offered a critical rereading, *lýiva ka* (dated to July 17, 2018), which I hear was made possible thanks to high-resolution photographs taken by Lukas Nickel in Xi'an, who offered them via Jason Neelis to Baums in 2018. I can only say that it was such ingenious work by Baums to figure out the softened *l* conjunct of *lýi* here. The phoneme *lýi* is not unknown, especially in the Krorainic onomasticon. For instance, Lýipeya is a well-attested name (Padwa 2007:325–26). Lýiva itself, as inflected into Lýivana and Lýivaṃma, is also seen in the Krorainic corpus (CKD 104, 118, 263, 596, and 601). And Livarazma (CKD 12 and 43) may well be interpreted as Lýivrasma with the same root, Lýiva (Padwa 2007:325). That a personal name opens the inscription is a reasonable assumption. The remaining question is whether the name is

Lýiva or any succeeding syllables are part of the name. At the UCLA conference in June 2019, I treated the ensuing *ka* as a suffix, possibly, for a diminutive or affectionate effect (Burrow 1937:§74). I assumed the conceived form *Lýivaka would be approximate to such names as Lýipatga (or Lpatga) observed in Kroraina (Padwa 2007:325). After consulting Baums, I realized that he leans more toward Lýiva. I have no gut to go against any of his premonitions. Lýiva is likely the name of the one who donated this devotional image.

Before coming back to *ka-* [3], let me briefly comment on the phonology of this donor's name, especially because this directly addresses the ethno-linguistic identity of that individual. This lateral approximant of the palatal with the diacritic cauda—that is, *lý*—is not of mainland Gāndhārī at large. The postconsonantal ý, once misrepresented as *p* by Burrow (1937:§31), is another idiosyncrasy of Krorainic dialect, presumably reserved to local, non-Indic (but possibly Iranian) vocabularies. Since this sound is not witnessed in Gandhāra proper, some used to wonder, along with other presumptions based on similar observations and relatable historical information, whether the local vernacular was Tocharian (Burrow 1935; Meng Fanren 2017; Schmidt 2018). Such dualism or dichotomy between the vernacular (Iranian) spoken by the majority of people and the completely disparate literary language (Gāndhārī) adopted among a few scribes is too unlikely and cannot be dealt with in this paper. Relevant, however, is what this characteristically Krorainic onomastics of Lýiva tells about the Buddha image from Xi'an: that the donor was from Kroraina. I revisit this significance in the following section.

In connection to this distinctive token of Kroraina implied in the donor's name, the inscription bears another lexical element that points to the same region of origin. This is what Baums identified as *tasuca* [8 through 10] in June 2018. Along with the preceding *ha* [7], this was another judicious emendation by Baums to Lin's (1991) greatly perplexing *eda buca* ("this Buddha"?). But how tempting this unaspirated palatal -*ca* was apropos the bewildering etymology of *puch'ŏ* 부처 in Korean—and the possibly corresponding parallel *hotoke* ほとけ in Japanese—for the Indic word of origin, *buddha* (Pellard 2014)! Frequently witnessed across the Krorainic corpus, *tasuca* is widely accepted to be a local official title (Burrow 1937:94, s.v.). Its exact function remains vague, even though Frederick William Thomas (1867–1956) once conjectured about an "interpreter-in-chief" (Thomas 1934:78). His reasoning stemmed from Alexander Wylie's (1815–1887) translation of the term *yizhang* 譯長, which is rather randomly quoted in the *Hou Han shu* 後漢書 (*juan* 96, 3875) upon the introduction of Shanshan and its governance (Wylie 1881:24).

But we cannot yet verify whether this Chinese record had anything to do with *tasuca*. Whatever this job was for, *tasuca* here, ending in -*a*, also attributes to the nominative subject. Lýiva was *tasuca*, the prestigious title from his faraway homeland in Kroraina, with which he identified when having the Buddha image cast in China.

The next word is *maregaputre* [11 through 15], the initial decipherment of which by Lin Meicun (1991) remains uncontested. Lin (1991:122, 126) views Maregaputra as a *tatpuruṣa* (or a dependent determinative compound); I concur. The genitive component *putra* (son), too common an Indic onomasticon, needs no further explanation. Lin was also right in that Marega is well recognized in Middle Indo-Aryan, especially Iranian. As a case in point from Greater Gandhāra, he particularly points to Konow's edition (1929:165–70, 184) of the famous Mahāsāṃghika inscription (CKI 159), written on a metal reliquary discovered by Charles Masson (1800–1853) from Wardak Stupa 1 at Khavada (present-day Khowat or Khawat, in Maidan Wardak, Afghanistan) and now in the British Museum (1880.93). Here the form makes a suffix, as in Vaga-marega and Hasthunaḥ-marega (Baums 2012:243–44). And these two *marega*-suffixed names are exactly repeated in a similar reliquary vase (CKI 509)—also found at Khowat around 2002 and containing birch-bark texts and other precious deposits (Baums 2012:245–46; Falk 2008). In any case, these intense cultural and linguistic junctures noted between Iranian and Gāndhārī are not new, having also been carried away to Kroraina—and eventually even farther east to our Buddha image, most plausibly cast in China proper. Finally, Lin (1991:122) successfully notes three exemplars of Marega (Padwa 2007:165) found in Niya (CKD 431 and 432) and Loulan (CKD 756), all of which have been listed in the "Index Verborum" (Rapson et al. 1929:362) prepared by Rapson and Peter Scott Noble (1899–1987). In addition to the name Lýiva [1 and 2] and the official title *tasuca* [8 through 10], Marega may well also be understood as almost exclusively indicative of Kroraina.

In this case, however, I must differ from Lin's view (1991:122) of the -*e* ending as locative singular. Lin's position was not without merit, because such a locative is often declined in Krorainic Gāndhārī, although -*aṃni* would be a more normative form (Burrow 1937:§58). Also, the place in the sentence, at least as it was assumed by Lin (1991:123), would easily expect a locative to stand as the benefactor of the dedicative speech given. But now, with the thoroughly revised edition presented by Baums, it seems more in line with this long string of address—from the very opening of the inscription to the word in question here—that this is a nominative subject as a whole. In Krorainic morphology, -*e* can modestly be a nominative as well (Burrow 1937:§53). In his online dictionary, Baums too glossed the form as directive. Our Lýiva has also to be a Marega-putra.

This departure from Lin's grammar leads us to the baffling five letters (*ka sa pa na ha*) sitting between Lýiva and *tasuca*. Because the former is a name and the latter a title, I assumed the string concerned a title too—germane to the person. But, having been unsure of its meaning, I could not help but force a wild interpretation at the conference. The bold hypothesis was about some phonetic analogy between *sapana* [4 through 6] and the notorious Middle Chinese hybrid word *sabo* 薩薄 (EMC *sat bak*)—or any of its presumable equivalents, such as *safu* 薩甫 (EMC *sat puəˀ*) and *sabao* 薩保/°-寶 (EMC *sat pawˀ*)—observed as early as the Eastern Wei (534–550) to mean "caravan leader," "merchant chief," or even "Persian priest" (Hucker 1985:395, s.v. 4828; Zhao Chao 2016). Eventually, I ventured that *sapana* was a secondary loan from the Chinese word, conjecturing that the Sinicized word of Indo-Iranian origin, perhaps from *s'rtp'w* (Dien 2019), translated back to Krorainic Gāndhārī. Now I revoke that fanciful thinking.

Instead I now draw attention to the kind of Indian currency referred to as *kasapana* in Greek inscriptions found in Ai Khanoum (Figure 16.1; Bernard 1978:Figures 17–18; Mairs 2014:49–50; Rapin 1983:326–30). The Greek wording may be closely linked to the Pāṇinian coin weight measure *kārṣāpaṇa* (De Romanis 2020:330). According to Rapson (1908:clxxix), however, its Prakrit is *kāhāpana*, and it is hard to neglect the significant gap in time between when these coins circulated in Gandhāra, by 150 BCE, and the centuries-later date of the Xi'an Buddha. But honestly, because of the lack of a better alternative, I provisionally settle that *kasapanaha* here is a Krorainic derivative of *kārṣāpaṇa*, with the final *-ha* an indeclinable emphatic particle making such stressing effect as *-gha* or *-ha* would do in Sanskrit (Monier-Williams 1899:375, 1286, s.vv.). Inasmuch as the ensuing *tasuca* concerns political authority, it sits well if the preceding phrase discusses financial power (or an office thereof?). Its meaning would lie in shades of "with *kārṣāpaṇa*," "moneyed," "wealthy," or something of that kind.

At the outset, however, Lin (1991:121) matched *sapana* with *sattva* (being) in Sanskrit. But for the singular nominative *sattva*, Gāndhārī is *satva*. In the actual corpus, what we observe is that *sapaṇa* replaces the genitive plural *sattvānām* (Burrow 1936:424; 1937:§43; Lüders 1909). For instance, such *sapaṇa* as in the *sarva-sapaṇa* (*sarva-sattvānām*) formation is witnessed on CKI 57 (a stone tank, bearing the date Year 113, discovered in Kāldarra Nadī in Swāt) and CKI 158 (a well coping, bearing the date Year 41, discovered in Ārā in Punjab), both now in Lahore Museum (Konow 1929:cviii, 65–66, 162–65). Here, unlike our *sapana*, the retroflex *ṇ* is present. But its distinction from the dental (*n*) was already not vital in Kroraina (Burrow 1937:§34). They are the same sound.[8] Additionally, the *-ana* termination is for the plural genitive in Krorainic Gāndhārī as well (Burrow 1937:§52). No wonder that Lin too was aware that his take on *sapana* as singular instrumental seemed a bit of a stretch, and thus he had to hyper-correct it as **sapena*. To me, a more fundamental problem was already that *satva* itself is rarely demonstrated in existing onomastics either as a part of a binomen (say, Lýivaka Satva) or a long compound (say, Lýivakasatva). For instance, Mariner Padwa's onomasticon (2007) lists no individual's name involving the putative component *satva*. Nevertheless, I remain sympathetic to Lin's challenge in deciphering this difficult inscription for the first time. I submit my *kasapanaha* only as a working proposition.

The last untouched word is now *kastaka* [16 through 18]. Lin (1991:122) originally read the initial as *pa*, but it was emended by Ingo Strauch in April 2011, as documented in the internet edition by Baums, and one can easily see why. The *akṣara* looks almost identical to the final *-ka* [18], although sometimes the head hooks that distinguish *ka* from *pa* are not always clear in actual Kharoṣṭhī manuscripts. The real problem, however, is that I cannot unpack its meaning. For the conference paper, I inferred that this was a main predicate, for we have yet to encounter one. Then I suspected something inflected with the verb √*kṛ* (make), because, along with *prati-*√*sthā* (set up), this frequently makes a past participle causative in Kuṣāṇa Buddhist dedicative speeches (Schopen 1988–1989). If so, the matching Gāndhārī conjugations would rather be *karavida*, *karavedi*, or even *karavite* (Salomon 1985–1986:284). I must ditch the obsolete idea. It does not look like a verb.

The next logical step would be to check if *kastaka* belongs to the subsequent, disparate imperative clause along with the aforesaid nominative *paḍima* [19 through 21].[9] Would this *-aka* suffix be what makes the passive voice (Burrow 1937:§§110–11)? For the mere sake of offering an answer here instead of nothing, I speculate this to be a Krorainic passive participle (of √*sthā*)—meaning something like "established"—although the prefixed *ka-* remains inscrutable in this scenario too. I would not want to posit a scribal error when my command of Gāndhārī is undeniably limited; I leave any necessary corrections to Baums and other experts of the language. But here, at least, I can conclude with a tentative translation: "Lýiva, moneyed *tasuca*, son of Marega [causes to establish this image]. Let the established image be for the homage [of him]!"

The Socioeconomics of Buddhist Image Making in Fourth Century China

The difficulties I encounter in this translation owe to my philological ineptitude, but I also want to point out inexplicit ellipses lurking in this terse dedicatory speech, like the seeming omission of the main verb in the first clause. For our scribe, however, any ellipsis would have been inevitable; there is simply no space left to be more verbose.

To imagine this scribe at least conceptually helps us to touch upon more fundamental issues beyond philology—the socioeconomic context in which the image was produced in post-Han China. This brings us to the question of the identification of Kroraina as the donor's origin. His title (*tasuca*) and name (Lýiva) both serve as unflinching indicators of Kroraina. Lin Meicun (1991:120 passim) too took heavy references to the corpus of Kroraina—or Krorayina as he spells and which equated with Loulan but was not inclusive of Caḍota (120)—and its language, what he calls Krorayinese (127–28; Bailey 1938:21). But he was not eager to build any special relationship between the inscription and Kroraina. In retrospect, I surmise that he was hardly ready to do so precisely because he did not catch either of the lexical items as being a signature of Kroraina. Instead, he was far more anxious to connect the image's historical milieu with Gandhāra proper, or what he calls Greater Yuezhi, particularly by way of the suffix *marega* attested in, for example, the Wardak reliquary (Lin Meicun 1991:122 passim). Notwithstanding the problem that he had, perhaps too simplistically, identified the people (or peoples) of Greater Yuezhi 月氏 with the ethnonym Yuezhi °-支, which is associated with such crucial early Sinicized Buddhist figures as Zhi Qian 支謙 (Lin 1991:124–29) and Zhu Fahu 竺法護 (Dharmarakṣa), it seems far-fetched to say that our donor was akin to anybody whose name carries the same subcomponent *marega*, especially at some historically significant level. There could be many Jacks and Jills across Gandhāra, Kroraina, and China who are barely related. Yes, all Kharoṣṭhī writings of Kroraina would eventually revert to the Urheimat Gandhāra in origin. But ample Kroraina-specific evidence in this inscription allows us to consider that this Buddha image came into being through an agent essentially situated at a much relatively shorter distance from China proper than where Lin Meicun pointed to in the west of the Pamirs.

The linchpin in any consideration linking our Kharoṣṭhī Buddha to certain "Chinese" manufacture is an art historical assumption, mainly, stylistic (see below). Nevertheless, one can still say that the Buddha's drapery, the thickened robe covering both shoulders, is indicative of inspiration *ultimately* deriving from Gandhāra. But this is almost an invariable aspect of early Chinese Buddha art. The real problem is that the image carries a conspicuously unusual motif: lozenge diapers of various sizes and designs engraved on the pedestal, which are, as far as I am aware, missing in any similar gilt bronze Buddhas made in China proper (Kim 2015). Even so, we cannot confidently ascribe its place of production to Kroraina, where we know of no clear trace of metal image making (Rhie 1999:357–426). Nor is this scarcity in metal tradition unique to Kroraina among its neighbors within the Taklamakan. With few remarkable exceptions, the absence of metallic images is widely noted through all these ruined oases. Despite such idiosyncratic application of the lozenge diapers, the Chinese production of the image seems most likely.

I have elsewhere ruminated about the significance of these lozenge patterns (Kim 2015). They are reminiscent of those distinctive "diamond" decorations routinely accompanying thrones depicted specifically in murals painted on the rock-cut Buddhist caves in Kucha (Figure 16.1; Xinjiang Weiwu'er et al. 1997:Figure 29). Thus I argued that they may well be cognate. Given our lack of identical specimens from Kroraina itself, however, I am unable to make a full historical assessment of what these lozenge diapers tell us. For instance, the design on our Kharoṣṭhī Buddha is also different from those regular-shaped diamonds of Kucha. The Kuchean patterning is so orderly that one wonders if they were meant to symbolize the exalted *vajrāsana* on which the historical Buddha-to-be was seated for his final meditation (Cunningham 1892:Plates X.11, XIII), whereas the Kharoṣṭhī Buddha's throne seems rather to have been covered by a layer of rug carrying a bold geometric design simply for the sake of decoration. In any case, this rug-like draping over the throne is so uncommon in China proper that its appearance on the Kharoṣṭhī Buddha suggests that it could also have been a feature valid in Kroraina, where such rugs must have been a daily commodity. But since we have no salient evidence of these diapers outside Kucha applied to the Buddha's throne, today let me attempt an explanation in two directions. For one, within the Tarim basin itself, Kroraina and Kucha might well have maintained substantial exchange with each other, so that sometimes one region could have affected artistic idioms of Buddha images made in the other. For another, the nexus, a rather haphazard and hybrid outcome, was made within China proper through interactions between exclaves from these different local communities of the Tarim basin already settled within some Chinese metropolises. Alternatively, the rug diapers could have been within Lýiva's special bespoke instruction. Whatever the process, the Kharoṣṭhī Buddha must have been commissioned and produced in China proper and reaffirms the very complex and wide-ranging linguistic, ethnic, social, cultural, and political conditions that the expatriate from Kroraina had been facing in his life, relocated probably in Chang'an, including diverse Indian, Iranian, Tokharian, and Chinese elements, among others.

Out of these various multicultural undercurrents, our primary concern lies with the Gāndhārī-literate enclave to which our Lýiva belonged. That his dedicatory speech is written in Krorainic Gāndhārī for the given Chinese-made product may indicate that he could have expected a similar readership within the part of China where he was positioned. Potentially, he had prioritized his fellow émigré Krorainans, say, over Chinese neighbors by the choice of this exclusive language. It is also intriguing to ask if the scribe and/or engraver was a different person from Lýiva. I am inclined to believe they are one and the same, regarding the mastery of given calligraphy. With the data available today, though, we cannot determine the size of Lýiva's presumed compatriot community in China proper, if there was any. But it would not have been big enough to be equipped with, for instance, its own industrial, especially metalworking infrastructure. Upon commissioning the image, Lýiva would have approached any workshop in town that suited to him, presumably a long-established local business rather than one specifically Krorainan-heritaged, as it were. Such artistic features as attenuated but pointed physiognomy, sharply ribbed and parallelized drapery, and schematically cascading apron-like folds suggest this local "Chinese" workshop scenario. The appointed artisan at work probably was not too conversant with what this peculiar Krorainan Buddhist patron was envisioning. Thereby the image became an amalgam of Krorainan and Sinicized characteristics, the single extant combination thus far known.

Last but not least, it is an art historian's obligation to date the Kharoṣṭhī Buddha with the current exercise of epigraphic reassessment. The special trade of art history is now much anticipated here, especially inasmuch as the terse inscription is undated. This absence of an absolute date is indeed unfortunate, as in the case of the tantalizing Luoyang inscription, which lost most of its dated part also. We cannot pinpoint the exact year when either of these two rare examples of Kharoṣṭhī was written in China proper. Even so, we can work with some ballpark figures. As mentioned above, the corpus of Krorainic materials ranges between ca. 239 and ca. 328 CE (Atwood 1991:165). Our Buddha image should not deviate much from that. The earliest margin is not of much concern, because by the 230s, Buddhist image-making activities had barely started in China. Of course, a few scholars prefer to assign a late Eastern Han date to some undated specimens (Whitfield 2005), but that view is not prevalent. Alternatively, the latest margin has been identified by Lin Meicun (1990) as being as late as 359 (or even 383), based on poignant divorce deeds (CKD 788) discovered in 1981. While Lin's (1990:290) calculus was a rough process, we know that Loulan was abandoned in 376 after a dynastic collapse (Hansen 2017:76), which I assume was catastrophic in the history of Gāndhārī literacy in Kroraina and eventually anywhere in the east. But Kharoṣṭhī writing should not have instantly and completely withered away upon this watershed moment. Scribes could have lived on for a generation or two at least, especially those who emigrated out of Kroraina. Could this political calamity of Kroraina have been the underlying sociopolitical context of our Kharoṣṭhī Buddha? In any case, I propose that the Buddha's date is not far removed from 376.

Judging from art historical criteria, this mid- to late fourth century dating can also be supported. Our major benchmark must be the monumental former Avery Brundage (1887–1975) Buddha bearing the 338 date, now stored in the Asian Art Museum of San Francisco (B60B1034). As the earliest extant absolute Chinese date-bearing freestanding Buddhist devotional image, this gilt bronze Buddha in many ways features simpler elements than the Kharoṣṭhī Buddha, and so is it comparatively viable to sequence our Kharoṣṭhī Buddha after 338. Marylin M. Rhie (1937–2020), a most rigorous practitioner of such formalist methodology, once speculated a date between the 360s and the 380s (Rhie 2002:334). I too find this is a sensible chronology. On the other hand, Angela F. Howard (2004:91) suggested ca. 300 instead, primarily by comparison with Karadong (Figure 16.1; Debaine-Francfort et al. 2001). But insofar as the Kharoṣṭhī Buddha was produced in China proper, I am not convinced how relative chronology informed by a site located in Khotan (Xinjiang) would serve as a basis for our case. I am in favor of the late fourth century, with a terminus ante quem around 400, indeed.

Howard (2004:91) made the important observation that the Kharoṣṭhī Buddha "was cast in one piece." I hope this is reliable and accurate information, although our eyes cannot really see the deep inner side of the hollow image, and sometimes assumptions are dramatically shattered by modern imaging devices. Meanwhile, the most impactful breakthrough has been the radiographic analyses, albeit done on other images, by Donna Strahan (2010a, 2010b), which revealed that some early Chinese bronze images were cast by the piece-mold method, a long-forgotten indigenous Chinese technique in use since the Bronze Age (Strahan 2010a:Figure 9). Based solely on stylistic considerations, I have presumed that the Kharoṣṭhī Buddha was a product of a workshop in China proper, and even if this contradicts Howard's brief reporting, I still believe there is a chance that our Buddha is cast out of multiple sectional molds. If so, its Chinese manufacture and earlier date are incontrovertibly proven. By the fifth century, the more "international" lost-wax process was gradually gaining its currency in China too.

Afterword

As a final note I wish to bring up another precious thing that I learned from my teacher Lothar von Falkenhausen—to respect, befriend, and collaborate with our wonderful colleagues in mainland China. In 2017 I approached Su Rongyu 蘇榮譽 (Chinese Academy of Sciences) to find a way to conduct lab testing, and in 2018 I applied for joint research funding with Yang Junchang 楊軍昌 (Northwestern Polytechnical University), but this pet project of mine went into hibernation. Now it is time that I get back to work and have our Kharoṣṭhī Buddha X-rayed—at last.

Acknowledgments

Funding for this study was provided by the Faculty of Arts, CUHK, through the Direct Grant for Research (4051129). I am most thankful to Stefan Baums, who kindly read the earlier manuscript and offered invaluable corrections and suggestions. Any lingering or newly introduced errors and infelicities must remain mine. I also thank Lukas Nickel for sharing his unpublished close-up photographs, which facilitated some otherwise unclear readings. R. Lanier Anderson, J. P. Daughton, Sonya S. Lee, and Klaas Ruitenbeek all helped the project through the various stages.

Notes

1. I thank Stefan Baums for alerting me that it is now almost universally considered wrong to view the vernacular language of Krorainia itself as Tocharian (or, even more distinctively, as Tocharian C).
2. International Dunhuang Project, British Library, http://idp.bl.uk, accessed February 10, 2022.
3. Once again I thank Baums for sharing his wisdom through email.
4. Stefan Baums and Andrew Glass, *Catalog of Gāndhārī Texts*, https://gandhari.org/catalog, accessed February 10, 2022.
5. I thank Baums for alerting me that these caudae are not unique to Kroraina but also exist in Gandhāra proper.
6. I thank Baums for correcting me, who once misunderstood the case to be the locative.
7. I thank Baums for enlightening me that *paḍima* here is a subject.
8. I thank Baums for reaffirming my position.
9. Without Baums, I would never be capable of considering this possibility. I also thank him for enlightening me that *kastaka* might well be a noun.

References

Atwood, Christopher
1991 Life in Third-Fourth Century Cadh'ota: A Survey of Information Gathered from the Prakrit Documents Found North of Minfeng (Niyä). *Central Asiatic Journal* 35(3–4):161–99.

Bailey, H. W.
1938 *The Content of Indian and Iranian Studies: An Inaugural Lecture Delivered on 2 May 1938*. Cambridge: Cambridge University Press.
1946 Gāndhārī. *Bulletin of the School of Oriental and African Studies* 11(4):764–97.

Baums, Stefan
2012 Catalog and Revised Texts and Translations of Gandharan Reliquary Inscriptions. In *Gandharan Buddhist Reliquaries*, edited by David Jongeward, Elizabeth Errington, Richard Salomon, and Stefan Baums, pp. 200–51. Seattle: Early Buddhist Manuscripts Project.

Baums, Stefan, ed.
2020 CKI 170—Cháng'ān Buddha Statue, *Catalogue of Gāndhārī Texts*, https://gandhari.org/a_inscription.php?catid=CKI0170, accessed September 1, 2020.

Bernard, Paul
1978 Campagne de fouilles 1976–1977 à Aï Khanoum (Afghanistan). *Comptes rendus des séances de l'Académie des Inscriptions et Belles-Lettres* 122(2):421–63.

Bernhard, Franz
1970 Gāndhārī and the Buddhist Mission in Central Asia. In *Añjali: Papers on Indology and Buddhism*, edited by Jayadeva Tilakasiri, pp. 55–62. Peradeniya: University of Ceylon.

Brough, John
1961 A Kharoṣṭhī Inscription from China. *Bulletin of the School of Oriental and African Studies* 24(3):517–30.
1965 Comments on Third-Century Shan-Shan and the History of Buddhism. *Bulletin of the School of Oriental and African Studies* 28(3):582–612.

1970 Supplementary Notes on Third-Century Shan-Shan. *Bulletin of the School of Oriental and African Studies* 33(1):39–45.

Burrow, Thomas
1935 Tokharian Elements in the Kharoṣṭhī Documents from Chinese Turkestan. *Journal of the Royal Asiatic Society* 67(4):667–75.
1936 The Dialectical Position of the Niya Prakrit. *Bulletin of the School of Oriental Studies* 8(2–3):419–35.
1937 *The Language of the Kharoṣṭhī Documents from Chinese Turkestan*. Cambridge: Cambridge University Press.
1940 *A Translation of the Kharoṣṭhī Documents from Chinese Turkestan*. London: Royal Asiatic Society.

Cunningham, Alexander
1892 *Mahābodhi or the Great Buddhist Temple under the Bodhi Tree at Buddha-Gaya*. London: W. H. Allen.

Debaine-Francfort, Corinne, Thibaud Fournet, Joël Suire, and Augustin Cornet
2001 Les plus anciens sanctuaires bouddhiques du Xinjiang: Essai de reconstitution d'une architecture et de son décor. In *Keriya, Mémoires d'un fleuve: Archéologie et civilisation des oasis du Taklamakan*, edited by Corinne Debaine-Francfort and Abduressul Idriss, pp. 82–91. Suilly-la-Tour: Findakly.

De Romanis, Federico
2020 *The Indo-Roman Pepper Trade and the Muziris Papyrus*. Oxford: Oxford University Press.

Dien, Albert E.
2019 Consideration of Some Aspects of the Sogdian Experience in China: From *sabo* to *s'rtp'w*. In *Early Medieval North China: Archaeological and Textual Evidence*, edited by Shing Müller, Thomas O. Höllmann, and Sonja Filip, pp. 301–40. Wiesbaden: Harrassowitz.

Enoki, Kazuo 榎一雄
1963 The Location of the Capital of Lou-lan and the Date of Kharoṣṭhī Inscriptions. *Memoirs of the Research Department of the Toyo Bunko* 22:125–71.

Falk, Harry
2008 Another Reliquary Vase from Wardak and Consecrating Fire Rites in Gandhāra. In *Religion and Art: New Issues in Indian Iconography and Iconology*, edited by Claudine Bautze-Picron, pp. 63–80. London: British Association for South Asian Studies.

Falkenhausen, Lothar von
1999 Inconsequential Incomprehensions: Some Instances of Chinese Writing in Alien Contexts. *Res* 35:42–69.
2000 Die Seiden mit chinesischen Inschriften. In *Die Textilien aus Palmyra: Neue und alte Funde*, edited by Andreas Schmidt-Colinet, Anne-Marie Stauffer, and Khaled Al As'ad, pp. 58–81. Mainz: Philipp von Zabern.
2010 Notes on the History of the "Silk Routes": From the Rise of the Xiongnu to the Mongol Conquest (250 BC–AD 1283). In *Secrets of the Silk Road*, edited by Victor H. Mair, pp. 58–68. Anaheim: Bowers Museum of Cultural Art.

Fang Yan 方妍 and Li Yuanming 李園明, eds.
2016 *Fantian dongtu bingdi lianhua: Gongyuan sibai dao qibai nian Yindu yu Zhongguo diaosu yishu* 梵天東土並蒂蓮華: 公元400–700年印度與中國雕塑藝術. Beijing: Gugong.

Fussman, Gérard
1974 Documents épigraphiques kouchans. *Bulletin de l'École française d'Extrême-Orient* 61:1–66.
1989 Gandhari écrite, gandhari parlée. In *Dialectes dans les litteratures indo-aryennes*, edited by Colette Caillat, pp. 433–501. Paris: College de France.

Glass, Andrew
2000 A Preliminary Study of Kharoṣṭhī Manuscript Paleography. Master's thesis, Department of Asian Languages and Literature, University of Washington, Seattle.

Grenet, Frantz, and Nicholas Sims-Williams
1987 The Historical Context of the Sogdian Ancient Letters. In *Transition Periods in Iranian History*, edited by l'Association pour l'avancement des Études Iraniennes, Deutsche Forschungsgemeinschaft, and Istituto Italiano per il Medio ed Estremo Oriente. pp. 101–22. Leuven: Peeters.

Grenet, Frantz, Nicholas Sims-Williams, and Étienne de la Vaissière
1998 The Sogdian Ancient Letter V. *Bulletin of the Asia Institute* 12:91–104.

Han Baoquan 韓保全
1998 Chang'an chutu de quluwenming liujintong zaoxiang 長安出土的佉盧文銘鎏金銅造像. *Shoucangjia* 收藏家 29(3):21.

Hansen, Valerie
2004 Religious Life in a Silk Road Community: Niya during the Third and Fourth Centuries. In *Religion and Chinese Society*, edited by John Lagerwey, pp. 279–315. Hong Kong: Chinese University Press.

2017 *The Silk Road: A New History with Documents.* Oxford: Oxford University Press.

Henning, W. B.
1948 The Date of the Sogdian Ancient Letters. *Bulletin of the School of Oriental and African Studies* 12(3–4):601–15.

Howard, Angela F.
2004 Seated Buddha in Meditation. In *China: Dawn of a Golden Age, 200–750 AD*, edited by James C. Y. Watt, p. 134. New York: Metropolitan Museum of Art.

Hucker, Charles
1985 *A Dictionary of Officials Titles in Imperial China.* Stanford, CA: Stanford University Press.

Institut de sinology
1925 *Institut de sinologie de l'Université nationale de Pékin.* Mâcon: Protat Frères.

Karashima Seishi 辛嶋静止
2013 Was the Aṣṭasāhasrikā Prajñāpāramitā Compiled in Gandhāra in Gāndhārī? *Annual Report of the International Research Institute for Advanced Buddhology* 16:171–88.

Kim, Minku
2011 The Genesis of Image Worship: Epigraphic Evidence for Early Buddhist Art in China. PhD dissertation, Department of Art History, University of California–Los Angeles.
2014 Two Kharoṣṭhī Inscriptions from China Proper: Gāndhārī-Speaking Communities and the Agent of Early Buddhist Art in China. Unpublished paper read at the annual meeting of the Association for Asian Studies (AAS), Philadelphia.
2015 The Kuchean Connection: The Kharoṣṭhī-Inscribed Buddha from Xi'an and Its Stylistic Problems. In *Qiuci Shiku baohu yu yanjiu guoji xueshu yantaohui lunwenji* 龜茲石窟保護與研究國際學術研討會論文集, edited by Xinjiang Qiuci Yanjiuyuan 新疆龜茲研究院, pp. 296–302. Beijing: Kexue chubanshe.
2019 Where the Blessed One Paced Mindfully: The Issue of *Caṅkrama* on Mathurā's Earliest Freestanding Images of the Buddha. *Archives of Asian Art* 69(2):181–216.
2022 The Archaeology of Early Chinese Buddhism: Rethinking "Han Buddhism and the Western Region." In *Chinese Buddhism and the Scholarship of Erik Zürcher*, edited by Jonathan A. Silk and Stefano Zacchetti, pp. 23–93. Leiden: Brill.

Konow, Sten
1923 The Royal Dates in the Niya Inscriptions. *Acta Orientalia* 2(2):113–41.
1929 *Kharoṣṭhī Inscriptions with the Exception of Those of Aśoka.* Calcutta: Government of India Central Publication Branch.
1931 Note on a Kharoṣṭhī Akṣara. *Bulletin of the School of Oriental Studies* 6(2):405–9.
1936 Note on Khotanī Saka and the Central Asian Prakrit. *Acta Orientalia* 14:231–40.

Kungnip Chungang Pangmulgwan 國立中央博物館
2015 *Kodae pulgyo chogak taejŏn* 古代佛像彫刻大展. Seoul: T'ongch'ŏn Munhwasa 通川文化社.

Lin Meicun 林梅村
1989 Luoyang suochu quluwen jinglan tiji: Jianlun Dong Han Luoyang de sengtuan yu fosi 洛陽所出佉盧文井欄題記: 兼論東漢洛陽的僧團與佛寺. *Zhongguo Lishi Bowuguan guankan* 中國歷史博物館館刊 13–14:240–49.
1990 A New Kharoṣṭhī Wooden Tablet from China. *Bulletin of the School of Oriental and African Studies* 53(2):283–91.
1991 A Kharoṣṭhī Inscription from Chang'an. In *Ji Xianlin jiaoshou bashi huadan jinian lunwenji* 季羨林教授八十華誕紀念論文集 1, edited by Li Zheng 李錚 and Jiang Zhongxin 蔣忠新, pp. 119–31. Nanchang: Jiangxi Renmin.
1996 Kharoṣṭhī Bibliography: The Collections from China (1897–1993). *Central Asiatic Journal* 40(2):188–220.

Lüders, Heinrich
1909 The Māṇikiāla Inscription. *Journal of the Royal Asiatic Society of Great Britain and Ireland* 41(3):645–66.

Mairs, Rachel
2014 *The Hellenistic Far East: Archaeology, Language, and Identity in Greek Central Asia.* Berkeley: University of California Press.

Maspero, Henri
1934 Les origines de la communauté bouddhiste de Lo-yang. *Journal asiatique* 225:87–107.

Meng Fanren 孟凡人
2017 *Niya yizhi yu Yutian shi yanjiu* 尼雅遺址與于闐史研究. Beijing: Shangwu.

Monier-Williams, Monier
1899 *A Sanskrit–English Dictionary: Etymologically and Philologically Arranged with Special Reference to Cognate Indo-European Languages.* Oxford: Clarendon Press.

Nattier, Jan
1990 Church Language and Vernacular Language in Central Asian Buddhism. *Numen* 37(2):195–219.

Padwa, Mariner
2007 An Archaic Fabric: Culture and Landscape in an Early Inner Asian Oasis (3rd–4th Century CE Niya). PhD dissertation, Department of Inner Asian and Altaic Studies, Harvard University, Cambridge, MA.

Pellard, Thomas
2014 The Awakened Lord: The Name of the Buddha in East Asia. *Journal of the American Oriental Society* 134(4):689–98.

Prévost, Georges
1924 Les inscriptions hébraïques du Musée de l'Université du Gouvernement chinois à Pékin. *Bulletin Catholique de Pékin* 11(134):407–10.

Qinghua Daxue Yishu Bowuguan 清華大學藝術博物館 and Shaanxi Lishi Bowuguan 陝西歷史博物館, eds.
2019 *Yu tian jiuchang: Zhou Qin Han Tang wenhua yu yishu* 與天久長: 周秦漢唐文化與藝術. Shanghai: Shanghai Shuhua.

Rapin, Claude
1983 Inscriptions économiques de la trésorerie hellénistique d'Aï Khanoum. *Bulletin de correspondance hellénique* 107(1):315–72.

Rapson, Edward James
1908 *Catalogue of the Coins of the Andhra Dynasty, the Western Kṣatrapas, the Trsikūṭaka Dynasty, and the "Bodhi" Dynasty*. London: British Museum.

Rapson, Edward J., Auguste M. Boyer, Émile Senart, and Peter S. Noble
1929 *Kharoṣṭhī Inscriptions Discovered by Sir Aurel Stein in Chinese Turkestān*. Oxford: Clarendon Press.

Reichelt, Hans
1931 Die alten Briefe. In *Die soghdischen Handschriftenreste des Britischen Museums*, Vol. 2, *Die nicht-buddhistischen Texte*, pp. 1–56. Heidelberg: Carl Winters Universitätsbuchhandlung.

Rhi, Juhyung
2018 Positioning Gandhāran Buddhas in Chronology: Significant Coordinates and Anomalies. In *Problems of Chronology in Gandhāran Art*, edited by Wannaporn Rienjang and Peter Stewart, pp. 35–51. Oxford: Archaeopress.

Rhie, Marylin M.
1999 *Early Buddhist Art of China and Central Asia*, Vol. 1, *Later Han, Three Kingdoms and Western Chin in China and Bactria to Shan-shan in Central Asia*. Leiden: Brill.
2002 *Early Buddhist Art of China and Central Asia*, Vol. 2, *The Eastern Chin and Sixteen Kingdoms Period in China and Tumshuk, Kucha and Karashahr in Central Asia*. Leiden: Brill.

Salomon, Richard
1985–1986 A New Kharoṣṭhī Inscription. *Indologica Taurinensia* 13:283–87.
1998 *Indian Epigraphy: A Guide to the Study of Inscriptions in Sanskrit, Prakrit, and the Other Indo-Aryan Languages*. New York: Oxford University Press.
2001 Gāndhārī Hybrid Sanskrit: New Sources for the Study of the Sanskritization of Buddhist Literature. *Indo-Iranian Journal* 44:241–52.
2007 Gāndhārī in the Worlds of India, Iran, and Central Asia. *Bulletin of the Asia Institute* 21:179–92.
2018 *The Buddhist Literature of Ancient Gandhāra: An Introduction with Selected Translations*. Somerville, MA: Wisdom.

Schmidt, Klaus T.
2018 Eine dritte tocharische Sprache: Lolanisch. In *Nachgelassene Schriften*, edited by Stefan Zimmer, pp. 161–274. Bremen: Hempen.

Schopen, Gregory
1988–1989 On Monks, Nuns, and "Vulgar" Practices: The Introduction of the Image Cult into Indian Buddhism. *Artibus Asiae* 49(1–2):153–68.

Sims-Williams, Nicholas
2001 The Sogdian Ancient Letter II. In *Philologica et Linguistica: Historia, Pluralitas, Universitas (Festschrift für Helmut Humbach)*, edited by Maria Gabriela Schmidt and Walter Bisang, pp. 267–80. Trier: Wissenschaftlicher Verlag.
2005 Towards a New Edition of the Sogdian Ancient Letters: Ancient Letter 1. In *Les Sogdiens en Chine*, edited by Étienne de La Vaissière and Éric Trombert, pp. 181–93. Paris: École française d'Extrême-Orient.

Stein, Aurel
1921 *Serindia: Detailed Report of Exploration in Central Asia and Westernmost China Carried Out and Described Under the Orders of H. M. Indian Government*. 5 vols. Oxford: Clarendon Press.

Strahan, Donna
2010a   Piece-Mold Casting: A Chinese Tradition for Fourth- and Fifth-Century Bronze Buddha Images. *Metropolitan Museum Studies in Art, Science, and Technology* 1:133–53.
2010b   Creating Sacred Images of the Buddha: A Technical Perspective. In *Wisdom Embodied: Chinese Buddhist and Daoist Sculpture in the Metropolitan Museum of Art*, edited by Denise Patry Leidy and Donna Strahan, pp. 26–45. New Haven, CT: Yale University Press.

Thomas, F. W.
1934   Some Notes on the Kharoṣṭhī Documents from Chinese Turkestan. *Acta Orientalia* 13:44–80.

Wang, Helen.
1998   Stein's Recording Angel: Miss F. M. G. Lorimer. *Journal of the Royal Asiatic Society*, 3rd series, 8(2):207–28.

Whitfield, Roderick
2005   Early Buddha Images from Hebei. *Artibus Asiae* 65(1):87–98.

Wylie, Alexander
1881   Notes on the Western Regions: Translated from the *Tsëën Han Shoo*, Book 96, Part 1. *Journal of the Anthropological Institute of Great Britain and Ireland* 10:20–73.

Xinjiang Weiwu'er Zizhiqu Wenwu Guanli Weiyuanhui 新疆維吾爾自治區文物管理委員會, Baicheng Xian Kezi'er Qianfodong Wenwu Baoguansuo 拜城縣克孜爾千佛洞文物保管所, and Beijing Daxue Kaoguxi 北京大學考古系
1997   *Kezi'er shiku* 克孜爾石窟. Beijing: Wenwu 文物.

Zhao Chao 趙超
2016   Jieshao huke Zhai Mensheng mumen zhiming ji shipingfeng 介紹胡客翟門生墓門志銘及石屏風. In *Suteren zai Zhongguo: Kaogu faxian yu chutu wenxian de xinyinzheng* 粟特人在中國：考古發現與出土文獻的新印證, Vol. 2, edited by Rong Xinjiang 榮新江 and Luo Feng 羅豐, pp. 67–84. Beijing: Kexue.

Zhejiang Sheng Bowuguan 浙江省博物館
2018   *Foying lingqi: Shiliuguo zhi Wudai fojiao jintong zaoxiang* 佛影靈奇：十六國至五代佛教金銅造像. Beijing: Wenwu.

Zürcher, Erik
1984   Beyond the Jade Gate: Buddhism in China, Vietnam and Korea. In *The World of Buddhism: Buddhist Monks and Nuns in Society and Culture*, edited by Heinz Bechert and Richard Gombrich, pp. 193–211. London: Thames and Hudson.

Chapter 17

Solidified *Qi* Clouds
Reconsideration of the Form and Name of *Boshan* Incense Burners

Zhang Hanmo

Exploring the ritual and religious meaning of an art motif based on taxonomic information proves a fruitful method in Professor Lothar von Falkenhausen's research (Falkenhausen 2004, 2006a, 2017). Just as the number of a set of certain buried ritual objects may indicate the social status of a tomb occupant, the form and decoration of an object often reflects people's religious thinking and practice of a time. Inspired by von Falkenhausen's teaching and research, this chapter is a reexamination of the artistic design of *boshan* 博山 incense burners, specifically focusing on the form of the covers, which have long been considered representations of mountains where mythical and legendary figures in premodern Chinese literature, often called immortals, allegedly dwell. I argue that a reconsideration of the religious connotation is needed, since the previous identification of the form of a *boshan* incense burner's cover is unreliable in light of observations of the rendering of mountain motifs in Han pictorial art. This also suggests the necessity of rethinking the naming of this kind of object following a reidentification of its form.

To be more specific, this study addresses the issue of how to identify the mountain-like art motifs, which are the most noticeable feature defining *boshan* incense burners. Do these mountain-like motifs indeed represent layers of steep peaks designed to rise and fall on the outside of the cover and the upper body of the incense burner container, as has long been thought? The answer to this question not only directly relates to the naming of this type of incense burner from an iconographical perspective but is also related to the interpretation of the mountain-like art motifs in terms of their religious connotations. As a matter of fact, the term *boshan lu* 博山爐, or *boshan* incense burner, first appeared and gradually gained popularity in literary works after the Han (202 BCE–220 CE), while inscriptions on an object discovered at Maoling 茂陵 indicate that in the Early Western Han (202 BCE–8 CE), standard *boshan* incense burners were called *xunlu* 熏爐. These burners produced smoke by burning a specific kind of fragrant grass. Calling these objects incense burners (in modern Chinese, *xianglu* 香爐) may be anachronistic, as incense in the conventional sense—joss sticks made of fragrant resins—had not yet come into wide use during the Early Han period; resinous incense was introduced to China from Southeast Asia and Central Asia during the Han period at the earliest. Until then, only herbs, such as *xuncao* 薰草 (*Ocimum basilicum* L.), were used in incense burners (Sun 2008:13–15). Nevertheless, this anachronism has long been considered an acceptable rendering inspired by the mountain-like motifs characterizing *boshan* incense burners.

More interesting is the uncertainty of the meaning of the term *boshan*. Whether or not this refers to the seemingly mountainous design has not been fully evaluated. This is to say, we have not examined the designs on the covers of *boshan* incense burners to see whether they really represent mountains; nor have we discovered the true connection between the mountain-like designs on the covers of *boshan* incense burners and the term *boshan*. This article offers my suggestions on these two questions.

Boshan and Sacred Mountains

Archaeological finds suggest that incense burners appeared in the Late Neolithic Hongshan 紅山 culture in northeastern China, though they confidently have been identified as such only in Western Zhou contexts (Figure 17.1). By the Warring States period, they are archaeologically ubiquitous throughout the domain nowadays recognized as China, indicating that incense burners might have been widely used in people's daily life at the time (Wang L. 2013:10). The *boshan lu* is a special type of incense burner.[1] A *boshan* incense burner, viewed typologically, looks like a *dou* stemmed bowl, including a container with a body and cover at the top, a circular base or plate at the bottom, and a thin stem in the middle connecting the top and the bottom parts (Erickson 1992:6). What is typically used to distinguish a *boshan lu* from other types of incense burners is its mountain-shaped cover, represented in particular by a few Early Western Han bronze incense burners discovered in Shaanxi and Hebei Provinces. Famous examples are a gilt incense burner with a long bamboo-shaped stem found in a pit near a Western Han tomb at Maoling, Shaanxi Province (Xianyang and Maoling 1982) and two bronze incense burners from the tombs of Liu Sheng 劉勝 (165–113 BCE) and his wife Dou Wan 竇綰 excavated at Mancheng 滿城, Hebei Province (Zhongguo and Hebei 1980a, 1980b).

It is worth noting that not all the covers on top of incense burners are mountain-shaped. In addition to mountains, one often sees covers in the shape of tree leaves or geometrical designs (see, e.g., Erickson 1992:7–13; Wang L. 2013:18). And not all objects with mountain-shaped covers are incense burners. Mountain-shaped designs, often labeled *boshan* designs, also appear on the covers of excavated objects identified as miniatured cylindrical *zun* 樽 vessels, *ding* 鼎 tripods, *hu* 壺 kettles, inkstones, or knobs (*se rui* 瑟枘) to tighten zither strings (Wang L. 2013:16, 18–19). Interestingly, objects with mountain-shaped covers are sometimes called vessels with *boshan* covers even when they are not incense burners (Wang L. 2013:19–20), while incense burners with covers with leafy, floral, or geometrical designs are sometimes still labeled *boshan* incense burners (Lian 2014:31–66). Such inconsistencies complicate the study of *boshan* incense burners by creating unnecessary confusion in definition. For convenience of discussion, this study adopts Susan Erickson's definition of a *boshan* incense burner by emphasizing the mountain-shaped cover of the container on the top as its main feature. Thus only when an incense burner includes a container on the top with a mountain-shaped cover can the incense burner be explicitly identified as a *boshan* incense burner (Erickson 1992:7–8). To Erickson, the mountain-shaped

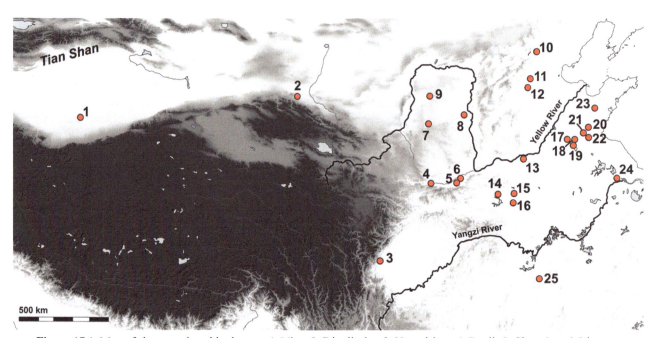

Figure 17.1. Map of sites mentioned in the text: 1. Niya; 2. Dingjiazha; 3. Yangzishan; 4. Baoji; 5. Chang'an; 6. Lintong; 7. Dingbian; 8. Mizhi; 9. Etuoke; 10. Maoling; 11. Mancheng; 12. Dingxian; 13. Zhengzhou; 14. Xichuan; 15. Nanyang; 16. Xinye; 17. Zoucheng; 18. Tengzhou; 19. Weishan; 20. Yinan; 21. Feixian; 22. Linyi; 23. Anqiu; 24. Xihu xiang; 25. Mawangdui.
Created by Bryan K. Miller.

design constitutes the most important characteristic of a *boshan* incense burner and distinguishes it from other types of incense burners. The object she employs as the standard form of a *boshan* incense burner is that excavated from Liu Sheng's tomb (Figure 17.2).

Liu Sheng's gilt bronze incense burner has a round base, a stem, and a container with a body and cover. The excavation report accurately points out that the base and stem of this incense burner are made into a single part riveted to the body of the container. The description of the decoration, however, seems to be more than a recounting of the details of the design. There is a lack of necessary discussion on iconology in identifying the dragons and the mountain-shaped art motifs mentioned in the report. For example, the report confidently says that the designs of the stem and base resemble "three dragons jumping out of the rolling waves to hold up the body of the container at the top" (Zhongguo and Hebei 1980a:63), yet it is difficult to identify the surface of the sea and its rolling waves. Moreover, with no discussion of their iconographic connotations, the report takes for granted that the multiple layers of mountain-like designs on the cover are representations of mountains. Following such an understanding without further consideration, the animal and human figures as well as "layers of steep peaks designed to rise and fall on the outside of the cover and the upper body of the incense burner container" (Zhongguo and Hebei 1980a:63) are arguably interpreted as parts of a grand hunting scene. The validity of this sort of unverified assumptions is questionable. In this case, to understand the decoration as a whole, the issue of identifying the mountain-like motifs on the cover of the incense burner container must first be addressed.

Those who consider the artistic design on the cover of a *boshan* incense burner to be a representation of mythic and legendary mountains rely on an antiquarian tradition going back to Song antiquarianism (Lin 2008:65; Ruan 2012:49), as shown in the *Kaogu tu* 考古圖 (*Illustrated Catalog of Examined Antiquity*) by the Song antiquarian Lü Dalin 呂大臨 (1040–1092). This catalog incorporates a woodcut illustration of a *boshan* incense burner as well an explanation of its origin, form, and function. According to Lü Dalin's description, the origin of *boshan* incense burners may have been connected with the consumption of luxury goods by the Han and Jin 晉 (265–420) imperial families. As for the form of a *boshan* incense burner and the function of its base plate, Lü explains that "the burner resembles *boshan* in the sea, with a plate at the base containing hot water emitting fragrant vapor, mimicking the movement of the sea" (Lü 2016:153).

Interestingly, the illustration of the *boshan* incense burner incorporated in the *Kaogu tu* does not accurately represent the form of the cataloged object; nor can the reader locate in the corpus of premodern Chinese literature any reference leading to the decipherment of the expression "*boshan* in the sea." Yet Lü's interpretation of the form of *boshan* incense burners has heavily influenced further studies of this specific type of burner. Following Lü's description, when exploring the connection between the form of *boshan* incense burners and people's religious mentality from an iconographic perspective, most scholars consider the mountain-like design on the cover of a *boshan* incense burner to be a representation of the imaginary mountains floating in the Eastern Sea. These mountains, namely Mount Penglai 蓬萊, Mount Fangzhang 方丈, and Mount Yingzhou 瀛洲, allegedly are homes to immortals, even though Boshan has never been listed as one of these mountains (Lian 2014:41–43).

Figure 17.2. *Boshan* incense burner excavated from the tomb of Liu Sheng, king of Zhongshan (r. 154–113 BCE), Mancheng, Hebei Province. *From Zhongguo 2006a:172.*

The *Xiqing Gujian* 西清古鑒 (*Appreciating Antiques at the Xiqing Study*), a later catalog sponsored by the Qing emperor Qianlong 乾隆 (r. 1736–1795), lists a greater number of *boshan* incense burners than the *Kaogu tu*. The creators' noticeable effort to be as accurate as possible in drawing and describing the featured *boshan* incense burners is impressive. Based on the information recorded in transmitted texts, this catalog clearly states that the manufacture and use of *boshan* incense burners started during the Han Dynasty. More importantly, it points out that, instead of functioning as a container for hot water as Lü Dalin thought, the base of a *boshan* incense burner was actually a receptacle for the ashes of the fragrant grass burned in the container above. The reason for this challenge to Lü's observation lies in the discovery of holes in the base plates, a discovery that dismisses the possibility of a plate functioning as a water container and, to a certain extent, challenges Lü's observation that the form of a *boshan* incense burner recalls mountains the immortals dwelled on in the Eastern Sea (Shanghai Shudian 2012:825–27).

The study of *boshan* incense burners in the West began with Berthold Laufer (1874–1934) in the early twentieth century (Laufer 1909:174–98) and has continued to the present day. Consulting the "Feng shan shu" 封禪書 ("Writings on *Feng* and *Shan* Rituals") chapter of the *Shiji* 史記 and relevant information in the *Jigu lu* 集古錄 (*Records on Collecting Antiques*) by Ouyang Xiu 歐陽修 (1007–1072), Laufer inferred that *boshan* incense burners began to be created during the reign of Emperor Wu 武 of Han (r. 141–87 BCE). He argues that they resulted directly from Emperor Wu's performance of *feng* 封 and *shan* 禪 rituals to worship Mount Tai and other nearby hills or mountains. Thus he linked the form and the making of *boshan* incense burners to the religious practice of worshipping sacred mountains during the Han. Archibald G. Wenley challenged Laufer's inference by questioning the late date of the textual materials that Laufer employed in comparison with the period when *boshan* incense burners began to be made (Wenley 1948–1949). The earliest textual evidence in Laufer's argument is dated to the fourth century CE, more than 500 years after Emperor Wu's time. According to Wenley, this is too late to provide a valid picture of the events happening several hundred years earlier. Based on the technology of gold, silver, and precious stones inlaid in a *boshan* incense burner he acquired for the Freer Gallery of Art in 1947, Wenley traced the making of *boshan* incense burners to the Warring States period, around the time when the batch of bronzes found at Jincun 金村 of Luoyang 洛陽 were made.

Nearly half a century after Wenley's article was published, Susan Erickson attempted to answer Wenley's question on the date of the invention of *boshan* incense burners on the basis of new archaeological discoveries unavailable to either Laufer or Wenley. Erickson argued that the technology of gold or silver inlay frequently was used not only to make *boshan* incense burners but also to make other bronzes during the Han. This means that the technology of gold or silver inlay used in the decoration of *boshan* incense burners was not necessarily a technique exclusively limited to the Warring States period; nor is Wenley's conclusion that the burners date to this period unassailable. Erickson argues that the *boshan* incense burner acquired by Wenley was probably also made in the Western Han, just like the incense burners found near Maoling, Xi'an, and at Mancheng, Hebei, to satisfy the needs of Han imperial and noble families (Erickson 1996–1997).

Influenced by Laufer, Erickson furthered the study of *boshan* incense burners' typological and iconographic aspects. For example, she observes that *boshan* incense burners are connected with incense burners and *dou* vessels from a typological perspective, but following Laufer, she singles out the mountain-shaped design on the cover of *boshan* incense burners as the most noticeable defining factor of this type of vessel. She also agrees with Laufer that the invention and function of *boshan* incense burners were associated with Western Han imperial and noble families fulfilling their luxury and religious needs. For instance, the mountain-shaped design reflects, from an iconographic perspective, Wudi's worship of sacred mountains to obtain longevity. To be more specific, she agrees that *boshan* incense burners may have been first invented on the occasion of Wudi's dispatching magicians overseas to search for elixirs or to present sacrifices to Mount Tai in a ritual, religious context closely related to immortality (Erickson 1992).

When Erickson makes a typological connection between *boshan* incense burners and high-pedestaled *dou* vessels dated to as early as the Warring States period, she traces the form of the *boshan* objects, especially the mountain-like design of the covers, to the *dou*. In doing so, she considers *boshan* incense burners to be a local invention. Jessica Rawson, however, suggests a foreign origin of the form of *boshan* incense burners based on her observation that the overall shape of *boshan* incense burners resembles that of incense burners widely used in Achaemenid Persia. According to her observations, the Western Han *boshan* incense burners may have adopted some of the elements of Achaemenid incense burners—for instance, the perforated cone-shaped cover and, in some cases, the motif of a bird standing on the top of the cover (De Luca 2019). Knowing that covers of this shape were not meant to denote mountains in their Achaemenid and other West Asian contexts, Rawson does not take into account a possible West Asian origin of a mountain-related semantic dimension in the design of Early Western Han *boshan* incense burners or any possible adoption of external cultural meanings by incense burner makers of the Han. Instead she emphasizes people's ability in Early Han to thoroughly transform foreign elements to serve their own purposes, and she interprets the mountain-like motif as a representation of sacred mountains in the Eastern Sea completely in the context of Han religious mentality (see Rawson 2006, 2013).

Lian Chunhai 練春海 strongly disagrees with Rawson on her proposal of a possible foreign origin of the overall design of *boshan* incense burners (Lian 2014:43–44). The similarities between the design of *boshan* incense burners and that of incense burners used in ancient Persia and on the Siberian steppes, according to Lian, is oversimplified by Rawson. Lian dismisses the three elements discussed in Rawson's article—the conical form of the container and cover design, the chain linking the container with the cover, and the bird motif on top of the cover—as evidence demonstrating the similarities and possible connection between *boshan* and Persian incense burners. As Lian argues, these are not defining features of *boshan* incense burner designs. Lian considers the overall shape of *boshan* incense burners to be a direct successor to Chinese incense burners developed locally (Lian 2014:56–57).

A more provocative point Lian Chunhai makes is his rejection of the idea that the design of *boshan* incense burners reflects the religious thinking in worshipping sacred mountains during the Han, an idea that has been widely accepted by many (see, e.g., Lin 2008; Sun 2008:413–19; Wang L. 2013; Wu 1984; Yang 1991, 2004). As mentioned earlier, Lü Dalin was one of the earliest scholars who connected the design of the *boshan* cover with sacred mountains floating in the sea. Despite the lack of textual support, Lü's idea greatly influenced later studies on *boshan* incense burners and has rarely been challenged. Lian Chunhai, however, considers the interpretation of *boshan* as a kind of mountain to be a misconception (Lian 2014:41–43). This term, he argues, has nothing to do with Mount Hua or with the three mountains where immortals allegedly dwell; rather, the interpretation of the designs should focus on the botanic and dragon motifs as well as the religious connotations these motifs may convey. He considers the term *boshan* to be a synonym of *fusang* 扶桑, a spiritual tree that is symbolized by a dragon in some transmitted texts. Inspired by Chao Fulin's 晁福林 analysis of the form of the Chinese character for dragon (*long* 龍), Lian identifies the shape of the *boshan* incense burner as a representation of the head of a dragon. He therefore argues that Han imperial artisans deliberately created *boshan* incense burners to cater to Emperor Wu's taste for activities that promised longevity and immortality (Lian 2014:44–52; a similar argument is found in Lian 2013).

By questioning the widely held equation of the design of a *boshan lu* cover with the symbol of a sacred mountain or a mountain where immortals dwell, Lian touches upon the critical issue raised at the beginning of this article: the meaning of *boshan* censer covers. The alternative interpretation of the mountain-like designs on *boshan* incense burners offered by Lian, however, puts too much weight on the botanic features and dragon elements seen in some *boshan lu* designs. Like the features emphasized in Rawson's study, these are not the defining factors characterizing a *boshan* incense burner. As Erickson points out, the reason *boshan* is used as the name for this special type of incense burner is its mountain-like design on the cover. Most of the examples given in Lian's discussion to illustrate his argument are not typical *boshan* incense burners. Even when examining the unique design of the incense burner discovered at Maoling, Lian mainly focuses on the bamboo and dragon designs on the stem and base of the incense burner, while leaving the features of its cover out of the discussion. It is worth mentioning that Lian's identification of the overall shape of the container and the cover as flower buds (Lian 2014:44–46) is not beyond question. Similarly, although the dragon figure as part of the decoration appears in the designs of the *boshan* incense burners discovered in both the Maoling pit and Liu Sheng's tomb, it is not an indispensable artistic element seen in all *boshan* incense burners.

In short, Lian's article raises very important questions regarding previous studies on *boshan* incense burners and challenges the equation of the design of *boshan* incense burners with the symbol of a sacred mountain in which immortals live. In reinterpreting the design of *boshan* incense burners as religious symbols, however, Lian's argument falls short of necessary iconographic support. In fact, neither Lian nor anyone else has ever offered an examination of mountain motifs in Han pictorial art to back up their arguments. In the sections that follow, I first explore how mountains are presented in Han pictorial art. Then I compare the mountain motifs with the mountain-like designs on the covers of *boshan* incense burners to see whether they are related. If the mountain-like designs do not represent mountains, we further need to explore why *boshan* incense burners were given this name.

Mountain Motifs in Han Pictorial Art

Mountain motifs in Han pictorial art generally represent two different types of mountains: sacred mountains where immortals allegedly dwell and natural, realistic mountains seen in ordinary people's lives. Based on mythological records preserved in transmitted texts and our understanding of people's religious mentality during the Han, sacred mountains are generally associated with two different religious centers: Mount Kunlun 昆侖 in the west and the three legendary islands or mountains—Penglai, Fangzhang, and Yingzhou—to the east. Mount Kunlun is usually presented as the headquarters of the Queen Mother of the West and her entourage, which includes winged immortals (*yuren* 羽人), strange animals, and a rabbit that makes elixirs for her, while the three legendary islands or mountains to the east are most closely connected with the symbolism of the *boshan* incense burners.[2] The idea that the *boshan* designs represent the three legendary mountains floating in the Eastern Sea probably originates from what is said in Lü Dalin's *Kaogu tu*. Such a connection lacks support or evidence, whether textual or material. In fact, whether or not the *boshan* decoration symbolizes mountains, let alone the three legendary mountains, is examined later in this article. For this reason, for the time being, our discussion on the representation of sacred mountains focuses on images of Mount Kunlun.

The images of Mount Kunlun appear differently on different materials in Han pictorial art. On the surface of lacquered coffins, silk paintings, and carved stones and bricks of different periods, for instance, Mount Kunlun is depicted as three connected peaks, as mushroom-shaped or tree-shaped peaks, or as hourglass-shaped terraces (Figure 17.3).[3] Among the various forms, the mushroom- and tree-shaped designs remain consistent over time, whereas the three-peaked and hourglass-shaped designs differ depending on where and when they were produced (Figure 17.4; see Wang Y. 2011:30–31; Wu 1989:118–22). It is worth noting that the identification of all the different types of symbols as representations of Mount Kunlun relies on the Queen Mother of the West (and later the King Father of the East) and her entourage being represented together with the mountain symbols. This inference is apparently backed up by transmitted mythological records stating that the Queen Mother of the West resides on Mount Kunlun.[4]

For this reason, as long as the symbol of a mountain is juxtaposed with the Queen Mother, it usually follows that the symbol represents Mount Kunlun, even if the shape of the symbol completely differs from all the iconological representations of Mount Kunlun mentioned above. Take, for example, the pictorial design on a carved brick discovered in Zhengzhou 鄭州, Henan Province, dated to the Han Dynasty (Li 2000:51, Figure 12; Wang

Figure 17.3. Queen Mother of the West and mushroom-shaped Mount Kunlun. Ink-squeeze rubbing of a pictorial stone relief from a tomb discovered at Songshan 宋山 near the town of Mandong 滿硐 in Jiaxiang 嘉祥, Shandong Province. Eastern Han Dynasty. *Courtesy Xu Chengrui* 徐呈瑞, *Peking University Han Art Institute*.

Solidified *Qi* Clouds 319

There are several ways to present ordinary mountains in Han pictorial art. One method is to use triangles, shaded or not, to symbolize hills or mountains. They are usually upright triangles, in many cases connected to one another and sometimes of the same size. To make these triangles more recognizable as hills or mountains, tree motifs may also be added to the scene, either on or around the triangular designs. A good example of this sort of representation is a picture carved on a stone excavated from Weishan Dao 微山島 in Weishan County in Shandong Province, which is dated to the reign of Emperor Xuan 宣帝 (r. 74–49 BCE) or that of Emperor Yuan 元帝 (r. 49–33 BCE) of the Western Han Dynasty (Figure 17.5). A rectangular grave occupies the center of the picture. A group of people are standing or seated in front of the grave, and a pair is working near its right side. Behind the grave stand three triangles symbolizing mountains. The three triangles stand side by side, dotted with tree motifs between and behind them to indicate the location and surroundings of the tomb.

Another example of this kind, found in the Wolonggang 臥龍崗 district of Nanyang 南陽 City, Henan Province, illustrates a hunting scene in a mountainous setting (Jin and Xin 2009a:81). In the foreground, a hunter, half-squatting or probably running, is leading three hounds to capture a running fawn. A row of triangles of different sizes, partly overlapping each other, symbolizes mountains and makes up the background of the hunting scene. Tree motifs are not used in this case, but the triangles of different sizes convey the idea of a mountainous setting.

Figure 17.4. Queen Mother of the West, King Father of the East, and hourglass-shaped, three-peaked Mount Kunlun. From Shipan 石盘 in the Lishi 离石 district of Lüliang 吕梁, Shanxi Province 山西. Eastern Han Dynasty. *From Jin and Xin 2009b:349.*

Y. 2011:22). Unlike the highly formulaic representations of Mount Kunlun, the mountains appearing on this carved brick are hills with steep slopes. On the top of the hill on the right side of the picture the Queen Mother is seated, wearing her signature *sheng* 勝 hairpin and accompanied by the fox and the rabbit (Zhou et al. 1985:Plate 87). It is their proximity to the Queen Mother and her entourage that makes these seemingly common hills Mount Kunlun. A similar example is seen on another carved brick found in Xinzheng 新鄭, Henan Province, also dated to the Han (Li 2000:53, Figure 13; Wang Y. 2011:23). This image shows the profile of the Queen Mother of the West without her iconic hairpin (Henan 1983:98). She can be recognized only because of the rabbit in front of her. Thus the hill that the Queen Mother is seated on can be identified as another representation of Mount Kunlun.

Figure 17.5. Triangle-shaped mountains. Ink-squeeze rubbing of a pictorial stone relief from a tomb discovered at Gounan 溝南, village of Weishandao 微山島, Weishan 微山 County, Shandong Province 山東. Western Han Dynasty. *From Zhongguo 2000b:46.*

Indeed, the triangular symbols seen in the above two examples seem to be a bit too abstract to represent mountains. This is probably why tree and animal motifs were added by the artisans—to make the abstract triangles unmistakably look like a mountainous setting. After all, trees, mountains, and animals are indeed necessary motifs to present a scene of natural wilderness. This we can clearly see in some later works, even when the artistic representation of mountains became more realistic and recognizable. The designs on the walls of a tomb dated to the Sixteen Kingdoms period excavated at Dingjiazha 丁家閘 in Jiuquan 酒泉, Gansu Province, serve as a good example (Jin and Luo 2009:174). Under the motifs of dragons, horses, clouds, spiritual deer, nine-tailed foxes, three-footed crows, the Queen Mother of the West, and the King Father of the East that occupy the upper parts of the walls, there are rows of triangular mountains on the lower parts of each and every wall. With shaded tips and zigzagging slope lines, the layers of mountains and hills are easily recognizable. The motifs of trees, birds, and animals are rendered either on the tips of or between the mountains. Together all the elements—mountains, trees, birds, and animals—form a vivid setting of raw nature at the bottom part of each and every wall (Zheng 2002:50–54).

An alternative way to represent realistic mountains was to use curved lines. The mountain symbols made of curved lines, however steep, are sharply differentiated from the triangular symbols. For example, on the lower part of the back wall of Tomb 1 excavated at Haotan 郝灘 of Dingbian 定邊 County, Shaanxi Province, dated to the Xin 新 (8–23 CE) or the Eastern Han (25–220 CE), the mountains in a hunting scene are drawn with connected blue arcs (Figure 17.6). Goats, sheep, deer, and tigers are running in the mountains. A hunter wearing red is chasing his prey. Riding a horse while shooting at the already wounded animal ahead, the rider on a horse only partially appears in the scene, as if just coming round the side of one of the mountains.

Another typical example of this kind is often seen in battle scenes, generally called *Hu Han jiaozhan* 胡漢交戰 (the battle between the Han and Hu barbarian armies), on carved stones or bricks mostly found in the Shandong and Henan areas. On a carved stone depicting a battle between the Han and Hu armies excavated from the town of Guoli 郭里 in Zoucheng 鄒城, Shandong Province, the whole scene includes three parts: the fighting, the chase, and the hiding, arranged from right to left, respectively. The hiding scene consists of multiple layers of mountains represented

Figure 17.6. Mountain motif using curved lines. Detail from a painting in a tomb discovered at the town of Haotan 郝灘 in Dingbian 定邊, Shaanxi Province. From Wang Mang's Xin Dynasty or the Eastern Han Dynasty. *From Xu 2012:60.*

by curves, in which barbarian soldiers wearing peaked caps are lying in ambush (Jin and Xin 2009b:256–57). Similar compositions with barbarian soldiers hidden in mountains represented by curves are also seen on carved stones found at Zoucheng Normal School and in the town of Sangcun 桑村 in Tengzhou 滕州, both in Shandong Province. Unlike the other depictions, the Sangcun example shows three large curves containing multiple connected smaller ones, but they all symbolize mountains with soldiers hidden in them, as is often seen in this kind of battle scene (Jin and Xin 2009a:156–57; 2009b:258–59).

The curves employed to indicate mountains look more realistic in some cases than in others. For example, in the battle scene depicted on a carved brick found in Fanji 樊集 of Xinye 新野 County, Henan Province, the dark dots added on the curves represent protrusions on the mountain slopes. Moreover, to make the representation look more realistic, the curves are intentionally drawn as less regular than in other cases, and tree motifs are seen at the foot of the mountains (Jin and Xin 2009c:604–5).

When the above battle scene changes to a hunting scene, the mountains symbolized by curves function as hiding places for animals instead of barbarian soldiers. Accordingly, the soldiers and the horses in the battle scene become hunters and hounds, respectively, in the hunting scene, while the compositions of both types of the scenes remain the same. Take, for example, the design of a carved brick found at Cuizhuang 崔莊 in Linyi 臨沂, Shandong Province (Jin and Xin 2009c:32–33). In the lower right corner of the composition are symbols of mountains, range upon range. Animals are running into the mountains, chased by a hunting party and its hounds, which occupy most of the scene.

Curves are also used to represent mountains in a herding scene, as seen on the western wall mural of Tomb 1 excavated at Fenghuangshan 鳳凰山 in Etuoke 鄂托克 Banner, Inner Mongolia. Connected thick curves are used to signify mountains, in which we see cows, sheep, trees, and birds. Herders are watching their herds on the tops or the slopes of the mountains. Shades and colors are also used to make the scene look more realistic (Jin and Luo 2009:51).

A combination of triangles and curves is the third way to symbolize mountains. The overall form of a mountain symbol appears as a triangular design, yet its peak point is not as sharp as a strictly defined triangle but is more or less curved. Moreover, the edges of this kind of triangular symbol are also not as straight as those seen in the first two examples in this section. The triangular symbols made in this way look less abstract than triangles and more realistic

than simple curves; they better represent mountains. We can take the design of mountains on a carved brick discovered at Yangzishan 羊子山 in Chengdu 成都, Sichuan Province, as an example (Figure 17.7). Carved in low relief, the mountains are mostly represented by triangular symbols, which look a little irregular. Animals, birds, trees, and grass are seen on the mountains. There are also farmers working in the fields and hunters chasing their prey. More interestingly, in the lower left corner of the picture is the depiction of a scaffolding structure, on which workers are climbing up and down to make salt—a reflection of salt manufacturing in southwestern Han China. A similar composition appears on a carved brick found in Qionglai 邛崍 in Sichuan Province, dated to the Eastern Han (Jin and Xin 2009c:652). Triangular symbols are carved to represent mountains, in which tree and animal motifs are depicted. There is also a hunting scene in which hunters, with their bows taut and arrows at the ready, are chasing their prey. A land tilling scene is also identifiable. The most striking part is on the left side of the composition, where a high scaffolding structure of multiple layers is raised. Workers on the scaffolding are seen lifting barrels of saltwater from the salt well underneath the structure, while on the ground next to the scaffolding we see workers collecting firewood in order to make salt by boiling saltwater under a pavilion-like building (Chen 2008; Falkenhausen 2006b; Flad 2005:249; for comprehensive archaeological studies on ancient salt production in southwestern China, see Li and Falkenhausen 2006, 2010, 2013).

Mountain symbols of the same sort also appear in a hunting scene on a carved stone discovered at Yingzhuang 英莊 in the Wancheng 宛城 district of Nanyang 南陽, Henan Province (Zhongguo 2000c:147). A cluster of mountain peaks occupies the middle left part of the composition. The images of a standing man and a chariot beside him are seen to the left. To the right, a hunter is leading his team, including hounds, to chase the running prey. Whether the standing figure and the hunting scene separated by the mountain symbols are related to each other or not is unknown. It is clear, however, that each mountain symbol takes the shape of a triangle with its peak point considerably rounded.

A more interesting example on a carved stone discovered at Beizhai 北寨 Village of Yinan 沂南 County, Shandong Province, shows how the above three symbols are used together to represent mountains in the same composition. The design depicts a battle scene between the Han army and it powerful neighbors, barbarians wearing their emblematic peaked caps. In the lower left corner of the composition are curved mountain symbols. To their left, we see multiple

Figure 17.7. Mountain and salt well motifs. Pictorial brick from Yangzishan in Chengdu, Sichuan Province. Eastern Han Dynasty. *From Jin and Xin 2009c:630.*

triangular symbols with rounded peak points to represent mountain ranges. A more careful examination reveals layers of triangles with sharp edges, also representing mountain peaks (Jin and Xin 2009a:170–71). Such a composition strongly suggests that its composer was probably well aware of the different ways of representing mountains and peaks during the Han.

In some cases, wavy lines, often accompanied by one or more of the mountain symbols mentioned above, also illustrate mountainous landscape in Han art. The design on a carved stone excavated at Panjiatuan 潘家疃 in the town of Duozhuang 垛莊 in Fei 費 County, Shandong Province, serves as a good example (Zhongguo 2000c:70–71). The design depicts a hunting scene emphasizing a hunting team and a cart fully loaded with captured prey. Mountains are symbolized by a wavy line slanting down from the upper left corner to the lower edge of the composition. Beneath it are more wavy lines representing rolling mountains. In this section of the composition, we also see a triangular symbol appearing in the lower register, together with other symbols, to represent realistic mountain ranges dotted with trees and animals. Another example is seen on a carved brick found at Gaozhuang 高莊 in Xichuan 淅川, Henan Province. The design on this brick includes two registers (Jin and Xin 2009c:619). The images of six identical Neighborhood Heads (*tingzhang* 亭長) are printed side by side on the lower register, while on the upper register, we see three groups of mountain symbols, also identical, each consisting of two signs resembling a camel's two humps, connected by a curved line. In the mountains we see trees, birds, animals, and hunters here and there. Sometimes the wavy lines extend irregularly, as we can see in the presentation of a hunting scene on the mural of a tomb at Dongjiazhuang 董家莊 of Anqiu 安丘, Shandong Province (Anqiuzhen 1991:Plate 42). Combined with one or two other mountain symbols mentioned above, the whole design unambiguously denotes a mountainous landscape. In this case, it constitutes part of the composition typical of a hunting scene often seen in Shandong and Henan area.

The above discussion on mountain symbols reveals the following iconographic features of their creation in Han pictorial art. First, the mountains represented in Han pictorial art include two different types: legendary mountains for immortals to live in and mountains normally seen in the realistic world. The former mostly look more abstract than the latter. The sacred character of the legendary mountains is revealed through the depiction of immortals, feathered men, and strange beings. The various representations of Mount Kunlun serve as a good example in this regard. As we see above, although rendered differently in different regions, Mount Kunlun can always be recognized as a sacred mountain because of the Queen Mother of the West and her entourage. Even in the same region, though some pictorial elements—including the arrangement of the Queen Mother, her entourage, and Mount Kunlun—may differ, the combination of these elements shows considerable consistency, thus enabling the identification of Mount Kunlun.

Secondly, compared with the presentation of mountains in landscape paintings developed later, the depiction of mountains in Han pictorial art is less realistic. Nevertheless, efforts to make the subject matter realistic in Han pictorial art are noticeable. For example, when employing abstract forms such as triangles, curved lines, or a combination of the two to represent mountains, Han artisans intentionally added tree or animal motifs, or both, to reinforce the realistic characteristics of a mountainous area.

The final point I would like to emphasize here, which is connected with the second, is that the representation of mountains can always easily be identified in Han pictorial art. Not only are simple triangles and curved lines sufficient to mark mountainous areas, a combination of triangles and curved or wavy lines also enables unambiguous presentations of mountains in different scenes. Moreover, the construction of agricultural, pastoral, or manufacturing settings as well as hunting and battle scenes, in which mountainous areas are a meaningful part of the pictorial representation, always helps identify the mountains. For example, although wavy lines are used to symbolize both mountains and clouds, in both of which birds and animals are also often seen, the two different kinds of representations can hardly be mistaken for each other.

The *Boshan* Decoration Resembles Not Mountains but Clouds

Now let us compare the above mountain symbols in Han pictorial art with the forms of *boshan* decorations typically seen on *boshan* incense burners to see whether they match. The difference between the two is obvious.

Let us first examine the gilt *boshan* incense burner excavated from Liu Sheng's tomb, a representative vessel of this kind in Erickson's definition. According to the excavation report, "multiple layers of steep peaks are designed to rise and fall on the outside of the cover and the upper body of the incense burner container" (Zhongguo and Hebei 1980a:63). Our examination of the iconographical features of *boshan* incense burners, however, suggests that this kind of reading is misleading. The examples of mountain symbols discussed in the previous section may seem less than complete or comprehensive, yet they cover all the major ways of representing mountains in Han pictorial art that we know about at the present day. We can hardly spot any similarities between these mountain symbols and the design of the cover of the *boshan* incense burner. Looking at a diagram of the unfolded form of the *boshan* cover of the example from Liu Sheng's tomb, we can easily discover what the previously identified mountain symbols really represent (Zhongguo and Hebei 1980a:65). Rather than mountain peaks, the protrusions seen in the *boshan* design unmistakably represent clouds. More specifically they depict a pattern of thick cloud clusters known as *yuntou* 雲頭 in Chinese. The protrusions of the *boshan* design on the Liu Sheng incense burner cover amount to a three-dimensional representation of cloud clusters. This observation is supported by the remaining gilt cloud designs on the surface of the cover and container of the Liu Sheng incense burner. The gilt decoration clearly shows the flow as well as the convergence of clouds. In fact, some of the peak-like protrusions are covered with gilt patterns of clouds, a strong indication leading to the identification of the protrusions as solidified *qi* clouds rather than mountain peaks.

Another representative example is the cover of a *boshan* incense burner found at Mancheng in the tomb of Dou Wan (Figure 17.8). This *boshan* incense burner, like the others, consists of a cover, a container, a stem, and a base. Unlike most other incense burners, however, the stem of this object is cast as a design showing a half-naked man riding a hybrid animal: half turtle and half dragon. Identified as a strong man, the rider extends his left hand and grasps the head of the animal while raising his right to hold the container of the incense burner (Zhongguo and Hebei 1980a:253).

Like the identification of the protrusions on the cover of the Liu Sheng incense burner, the excavation report also considers the protrusions on the cover of the Dou Wan incense burner to be representations of mountain peaks. It mentions cloud motifs yet does not specify how they are differentiated from the mountains. Again, if we unfold the cone-shaped upper part of the *boshan* cover, we immediately realize that the so-called *boshan* design in the plan does not represent mountains at all. The protrusions on the cover of the incense burner from Dou Wan's tomb, like those on the cover of the incense burner from Liu Sheng's, represent cloud clusters.

Figure 17.8. *Boshan* incense burner excavated from Dou Wan's tomb at Mancheng, Hebei Province. Dated to 104 BCE. *After Zhongguo 2006a:173.*

Here it is necessary to discuss the design of animal motifs on the cover of *boshan* incense burners. As noted in the earlier discussion of the representation of mountains in Han pictorial art, to make the symbols unmistakable as a realistic mountainous world, Han artisans drew additional motifs, such as trees, birds, and animals, in the mountains. That said, we cannot infer that every symbol accompanied by birds and animals represents a mountain. As a matter of fact, animal, bird, and tree motifs, as well as hunting scenes, often appear in cloud designs. To this end, let us first examine the decoration on a bronze tube gilded with gold and silver excavated in 1965 in Tomb 122, a large Western Han tomb, at Sanpanshan 三盤山 in Dingxian 定縣, Hebei Province (Figure 17.9).

Inlaid with turquoise rhombuses and round, red agates, the gilded bronze tube, identified as a chariot fitting from Sanpanshan, consists of four heavily ornate parts joined together end to end. Each of these parts is decorated differently and focuses on a different theme. On the uppermost part we see a winged dragon, a winged horse, a bear, a feathered immortal, birds, deer, and, most significantly, the disproportionate figure of an elephant with multiple riders on its back. Vividly depicted, these elements are smartly distributed in appropriate spots in a seemingly crowded scene. A gold inlay, wavy line with several protrusions on its convex tips crosses the surface of this part of the bronze tube from its upper right to its lower left side. Roughly paralleling this long wavy line, similar lines appear in front of and behind the elephant. Animal and bird motifs are designed to fit in at spots along these wavy lines. Some of the animals and birds are seen resting, running, or flying in the convex parts of the wavy lines. The next section depicts a hunting scene. The hunter, riding a galloping horse, is turning around to shoot a roaring tiger behind him. This section, like the previous one, features two gilt wavy lines, along which are drawn deer, ape, ox, goat, and bird motifs, as well as the aforementioned hunting scene. The most noticeable motifs in the third section include a camel ridden by a human figure and a boar being bitten by a tiger. Two gilt lines are clearly seen in this section; one crosses the middle from left to right and divides the scene into upper and the lower parts, where the two major motifs are respectively located. Such motifs as a wolf, fox, bear, bird, and feathered immortal are arranged along the two gilt wavy lines. The most striking motif on the lowermost register of this bronze tube decoration is a big bird identified as a peacock, seen under a gilt wavy line slanting through the scene from its upper right to its lower left side. More gilt wavy lines are observable in this section. Further protrusions at the bottom indicate that they belong to a hidden line. The motif of a boar being bitten by a tiger reappears along with the gigantic peacock in this scene, while other motifs—a bear, deer, ox, pheasant, and feathered immortal—are arranged along these lines.

What is most relevant to our discussion are the gilt wavy lines similarly drawn on each of the four sections mentioned above. They are identified as *yunshan* 雲山, or cloudy mountains, in a catalog introducing this bronze tube to the public for the first time. The designation has been widely adopted by scholars since then. This term, however, is ill defined. It vaguely refers to both clouds and mountains and is interpreted as a description of mountains surrounded by clouds (similar to what we see when discussing the design of the burner from Dou Wan's tomb).

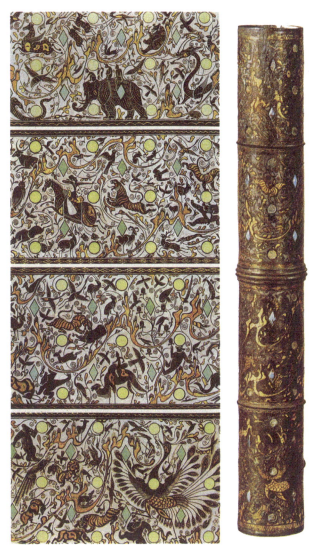

Figure 17.9. Decorated tube with applied gold and silver and its unfolded design. Excavated from Sanpanshan in Ding County, Hebei Province. Western Han Dynasty. *After Zhongguo 2006b:Plate 69.*

I argue that, compared with the ways of making mountain symbols in Han pictorial art examined in the previous section, the gilt wavy lines on the Sanpanshan tube are unlikely to represent mountains; instead, they represent clouds. The protrusions on the convex tips of the wavy lines on each of the four sections of the Sanpanshan bronze tube, like those seen on the covers of the two *boshan* incense burners from the Mancheng tombs, symbolize clusters of thick clouds. From an iconographic perspective, these protrusions, usually accumulating at the convex tips of a wavy line, reflect the thickness and abundance of piled-up clouds. Together with the lines connecting the convex tips, they constitute a complete iconographic representation of clouds.

In addition, it is worth mentioning that not only the gilt wavy lines but also the curly swirly lines extending from the gilt wavy lines, the flowing thin lines, and the fragmentary leaflike patterns that cover the surface of the tube are also symbols of *qi* clouds. They are not plant motifs as previously thought. The curly swirly lines often appear in Han pictorial art known as cloud patterns, as seen on lacquered objects from Han tombs (see, e.g., Hunan and Hunan 2004:133–34, Plates 51 and 54). Also, if examined carefully, the patterns that look like leaves and flowers on the Sanpanshan design turn out to be fragmentary parts of gilt wavy lines or swirly lines or their combination, all signifying flowing *qi* clouds. That is to say, all the motifs of animals, birds, and human figures on the surface of the bronze tube are surrounded by floating clouds.

The design of animals running and birds flying in floating clouds is not rare in Han pictorial art. A best-known example is the design on one of the three nested coffins found in Mawangdui 馬王堆 Tomb 1 in Changsha 長沙, Hunan Province. On the black surface of one of the nested coffins are patterns of floating *qi* clouds surrounding flying feathered figures and motifs of different animals, birds, and snakes. Compared with the design of *qi* clouds on the Sanpanshan bronze tube, the cloud patterns on the Mawangdui coffin look more realistic, especially when delineating the swirly features of the fast-moving *qi* clouds (Jin et al. 2010:132). We also find on the Mawangdui coffin representations of thick cloud clusters and thin air currents, as seen on the Sanpanshan bronze tube (Hunan and Hunan 1973b:18–23, Color Plates 27–31). The cloud patterns on the painted cover of an ink box excavated from a Western Han tomb at Huchang 胡場 of Xihu 西湖 in Yangzhou 揚州, Jiangsu Province, serve as another good example (Jin et al. 2010:198). As shown, big rolling cloud patterns dominate the whole design. The figures of a tiger, a bear, a fox, a goat, and a feathered man riding a galloping horse appear inside the clouds. The design on the lintel of the entrance of an Eastern Han tomb excavated at Mizhi 米脂 in Shaanxi Province is another example (Zhongguo 2000a:45–47). Curved lines with thick *yuntou* designs wind all over the lintel frame. The cloud design contains a skillfully arranged group of birds and animals, including a dragon, a tiger, a deer, and a goat, as well as a feathered immortal, a nine-tailed fox, and a rabbit making elixirs. Similar designs of cloud patterns appear on newly discovered silk and textiles dated to the Han—for example, on a number of fragmentary pieces of textiles excavated from Niya 尼雅 Tomb 1 in Minfeng 民豐 County in Xinjiang (Jin and Zhao 2010:89, 92). Woven cloud patterns with embedded animal motifs, hunting scenes, and Chinese characters are often seen on the textile products. Among these designs, the *yuntou* cloud design on an embroidery with the Chinese characters *qianqiu wandai yi zisun* 千秋萬代宜子孫 (blessing sons and grandsons for thousands of years) is especially relevant, as it is nearly the same as the cloud pattern on the *boshan* incense burner found in Liu Sheng's tomb (Figure 17.10).

Finally, let us examine the gilt incense burner from Maoling (Figure 17.11, left). It comprises a body with a cover and container connected to a heavily decorated circular base by an unusual long stem of the form of a bamboo pole. Measuring 58 cm tall, this incense burner is so far the tallest one found, more than twice the height of the Liu Sheng example. According to the excavation report, the occupant of Maoling Tomb 1 may be one of Western Han emperor Wu's subjects, and the burial items in the pit near the tomb, including the gilt incense burner, were probably crafted during Emperor Wu's reign (r. 141–87 BCE). The inscriptions on the surface of the outer edges of both the burner cover and the circular base state that both parts "were made by the imperial craftsmen in the fourth year and transported to the imperial house in the tenth month of the fifth year" (Xianyang and Maoling 1982:3). If the burner was indeed made in the fourth year of Emperor Wu's reign, we can infer that the Maoling incense burner was manufactured in 138 BCE, which makes it the earliest example of *boshan lu* (Erickson 1992:6).

Although considered the earliest example of *boshan lu*, the Maoling incense burner has its own name inscribed on the outer edges of both the cover and the base: *jinhuang tu zhujie xunlu* 金黃涂竹節熏盧, or a *xunlu* with a gilt bamboo-pole-shaped stem. The character *lu* 爐, as in the term *xianglu* 香爐, is a substitute for its homophone *lu* 盧 (OCM *râ).[5] The term *xunlu* thus denotes a kind of utensil that sends out fragrant smoke provided by a certain burning material. The similarities between the Maoling burner and the two found

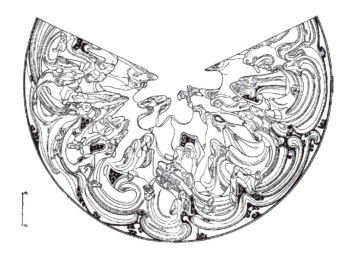

Figure 17.10. Cloud clusters on the *qianqiu wansui yi zisun* embroidery from a tomb discovered at Niya of Minfeng, Xinjiang, compared to cloud patterns on the unfolded design on a gilt *boshan lu* cover from Mancheng Tomb 1. *Created by the author after Jin and Zhao 2010:92; Zhongguo and Hebeisheng 1980a:65.*

Figure 17.11. *Xunlu* with applied gold and silver from Maoling 茂陵 in Shaanxi Province. Early Western Han. *From Zhongguo 2006a:179.*

in Mancheng have prompted speculation that these items may have witnessed interactions between the Western Han imperial family and their high-ranking relatives (Yun 1982). As explained earlier in this section, neither of the covers of those two burners symbolizes mountains or hills. Rather, the form of the Maoling *boshan lu* cover, like that of the two Mancheng incense burners, reflects flowing clouds, possibly in imitation of the smoke swirling out of the holes embedded in the cover. Unlike the Mancheng incense burners, though, the design lacks animals, birds, or immortals hidden in the clouds (Figure 17.11, right).

As a matter of fact, cloud designs are not at all rare on the covers of *boshan* incense burners; nor are they difficult to identify. Take, for instance, the famous *xianglong boshan lu* 降龍博山爐 found in Baoji 寶雞 in 1985 and now housed in the Baoji Museum. The winding clouds on its cover can easily be recognized, but these are taken as a specific decoration known as *boshan feng shi* 博山峰飾, or *boshan* peak decoration in the description of this object (Wang G. 1986:91). A similarly designed *boshan* incense burner appeared previously in the Marchese Taliani de Marchio private collection.[6] The design of its cover also resembles flowing clouds.

Toward a Redefinition and Reinterpretation of *Boshan* Incense Burners

I propose that the feature used to define a *boshan* incense burner is a representation of not mountains but clouds. Accordingly, we need to reconsider Erickson's definition of *boshan lu*. When Erickson takes the mountain-like design on the cover of a *boshan* incense burner to be a representation of realistic mountains, she follows convention to identify the design as an artistic form of legendary mountains in which immortals allegedly dwell. This assumption, as we already know, started at the latest with the Song scholar Lü Dalin and persists to the present. For example, the entry about *boshan lu* in *Zhongguo qingtongqi cidian* 中國青銅器辭典 (*The Dictionary of Chinese Bronze Objects*) touches upon the design of *boshan* covers, the semantic origin of the term *boshan*, and the invention and development of *boshan* incense burners. It reflects the misreading of the *boshan* design in pointing out that *boshan* means "great mountains where legendary immortals live" (Chen 2013:62). It is worth noting how the character *bo* in *boshan* is interpreted. Citing a bronze mirror inscription to strengthen the inference, the entry glosses *bo* as *da* 大 (big) and *boshan* as "big mountains" (Chen 2013:62). A longer version of a similar inscription on the back of a bronze mirror reads as follows:

上大山兮見神人，食玉英兮飲澧泉，駕交龍兮乘浮雲，宜官秩，保子孫。[7]

Climb up big mountains to visit spiritual men, take jade essence and drink sweet spring water, ride dragons floating in the air. [This item] shall bring chances of promotion for office and rank to and protect the sons and grandsons of the user of the mirror.

The inscriptions were meant to bring good fortune to the user of the bronze mirror, wishing him or her longevity, high social status, and familial prosperity. Since the wish for longevity is connected with the idea of immortality, it evokes an aspect of Daoist thinking that may have influenced the making of *boshan* incense burners. In a similar context, the term *dashan* 大山 is sometimes rendered as Huashan 華山, or Mount Hua, which parallels Taishan 泰山, or Mount Tai (see, e.g., Wang G. 2016:85; Wang S. 1987:35). The three characters *da* 大, *tai* 太, and *tai* 泰 are interchangeable in terms of both their sound and their meaning. For this reason, *dashan* is also considered to be Mount Tai. Some scholars further connect the *wangji* 望祭 ritual presented to big mountains and visiting immortals on Mount Tai, concluding that Mount Tai functioned during the Han as the axis mundi closely associated with the Han religious belief of pursuing immortality (Lin 2008:67). Mount Hua is also associated with the idea of pursuing immortality in early Chinese literature. For example, both Lord Zhao 昭 of Qin 秦 (r. 306–251 BCE) and Emperor Wu of Han are protagonists of such tales as playing the *liubo* 六博 game with immortals at the summit of Mount Hua (Ge 2017:296–304; Wang X. 1998:276). In short, based on different sources, the term *boshan* can refer to Mount Tai, Mount Hua, or the sacred mountains in the Eastern Sea. Nevertheless, there is no agreement about exactly where *boshan* is located.

Zhongguo qingtongqi cidian traces the appearance of *boshan* incense burners to the Western Han, a statement consonant with the archaeological discovery of the typical *boshan* incense burners from Maoling and Mancheng. We must admit, however, that the earliest *boshan* incense burners were called *xunlu* instead of *boshan lu* by their makers, according to the inscriptions on the *boshan* incense burner found at Maoling. The *xijing zaji* 西京雜記 (*Miscellaneous Records Regarding the Western Capital City* [of the Western Han]), generally considered a fourth century text, is the earliest source mentioning the term *boshan lu*. It says that in the heyday of Chang'an as the Western Han capital city, a skilled craftsman called Ding Huan 丁緩 was able to "make *boshan* incense burners of nine layers, on which rare birds and strange animals are carved, fully displaying their spiritual, marvelous features, as if they are all alive and can move around."[8] We are not quite sure what exactly the phrase *jiuceng boshan xianglu* 九層博山香鑪 means here, though I tentatively render it as "*boshan* incense burners of nine layers." This phrase could also refer to "incense burners with nine layers of mountainous decoration," if *jiuceng* modifies the term *boshan*, which immediately follows it. Such vagueness results from the ambivalence over the closeness of the terms *boshan* and *xianglu*. If the two form a proper name for a specific incense burner—that is, *boshan* incense burner—then the preceding phrase "nine layers" modifies the noun "incense burner," showing what an ornate item Ding Huan had made and how skillful his craftsmanship was. In other words, *boshan* as a modifier of *incense burner* in this passage does not necessarily refer to mountainous decoration on the cover of the incense burner.

Literary works are often cited in the study of *boshan* incense burners for their vivid descriptions of the form of *boshan lu*. Some of these works indeed use images of hills or mountains to evoke the form of *boshan* incense burners in readers' imaginations, but whether these literary expressions are to be taken in a descriptive or figurative sense remains debatable. One of the two most cited poems preserved in a later anthology and believed to have been written during the Western Han reads as follows:

四坐且莫諠，願聽歌一言，
請說銅鑪器，崔嵬象南山，
上枝似松柏，下根據銅盤，
雕文各異類，離婁自相連，
誰能為此器，公輸與魯班，
朱火然其中，青煙颺其閒，
順風入君懷，四坐莫不歡，
香風難久居，空令蕙草殘。(Ouyang 1999:1222)

Attention, esteemed guests seated in four directions,
I wish you would listen to a song I will sing.
Please allow me to tell you about a burner made of bronze
as lofty as the southern mountains.
Its topmost branches resemble pine and cypress trees';
Its roots below are positioned on a bronze plate.
The carved patterns are each of a different kind;
In openwork the patterns are linked.
Who is capable of creating this burner?
It must be Gongshu Ban of Lu, the carpenter.
Inside the burner vermillion flames rise;
Out of the holes blue smoke flies,
following the winds to fill your embrace.
Thus, of the guests, there is none that isn't elated.
It's difficult to keep the air fragrant for long,
In vain fire of perfumed grass burns down.

The term *boshan lu* is not mentioned in this poem, but it is commonly held that the term *tongluqi* 銅爐器 (a burner made of bronze) is an alternative expression for *boshan* incense burners. Moreover, the line "as lofty as the southern mountain" is understood to describe the mountain-like design of the cover of the incense burner. Nevertheless, reading carefully, we find that this poem starts from a general depiction of this item and then focuses on the decoration of its cover after describing its upper and lower parts in two parallel lines. The depiction ends by describing the flames and smoke that come out of the container of the burner. Based on this understanding, we are confident that the line "as lofty as the southern mountain" illustrates the height of the whole burner rather than the design of the cover, since a detailed description of the cover comes only two lines later. If the term *tongluqi* does refer to a *boshan* incense burner, the depiction of its height may indicate that this incense burner could have resembled the one with the long stem excavated from Maoling. The stem of the incense burner under discussion, though unmentioned in the poetic lines, is regarded metaphorically as the stem of a pine or cypress tree. The burner's upper part, including the cover and container, resembles the top of a tree. Its lower part, the root of a tree, is connected with a plate. The next two lines convey the skillfulness of the craftsmanship of the decoration, mostly focusing on the top of the incense burner, although in some cases its stem and lower part may also be decorated. The next four lines, still focusing on the top of the burner, mention vermillion flames, blue smoke, and the guests' pleasant feelings evoked by the fragrance emanating from the burner, and they clearly picture how it was used. The material used to create the fragrant air mentioned here, as we know from the last line of the poem, was *huicao* 蕙草, another name for *xuncao*, which produces a fragrant smell when it burns.

The other well-known piece mentioned earlier includes several lines of a *ming* 銘 (inscription) attributed to Liu Xiang 劉向 (77–6 BCE). It reads:

嘉此正器，嶄巖若山。
上貫太華，承以銅盤。
中有蘭綺，朱火青煙。(Ouyang 1999:1223)

I laud this upright utensil,
standing lofty and steep like a hill.
Its top pierces Mts. Hua and Tai;
Its root is connected with a bronze plate.
It contains inside orchid grass crisscrossed,
Bringing vermilion flames and blue smoke.

Though it is short, this piece and the poem examined earlier are comparable. According to the above inscription, the term *zhengqi* 正器, like the *tongluqi* mentioned in the previous poem, also refers to an incense burner. The line *zhanyan ruo shan* 嶄巖若山, equivalent to the line *cuiwei xiang nanshan* 崔嵬象南山, also indicates the loftiness of the incense burner. The next two lines are structured like the couplet *shangzhi si songbai, xiagen ju tongpan* 上枝似松柏，下根據銅盤, depicting the upper and lower parts of the incense burner, respectively. Nevertheless, the verb *guan* 貫 (to penetrate or to string together) in the line *shang guan tai hua* 上貫太華 is difficult to understand in this context. Erickson translates this line as "Its top is like Hua Shan" (Erickson 1992:15),[9] yet *guan* does not mean

"to be like," an interpretation most probably influenced by the word *si* 似, used in the previous poem. Richard Mather offers a different translation: "Its top strings together [Mounts] Hua and Tai, [yet they are] contained within a bronze platter" (Erickson 1992:15), an interpretation equally untenable for its obscurity. It seems that not only has Mather confused readers by glossing *guan* as "to string together," but he, like Erickson, has also mistaken the design of the cover for a representation of Mounts Tai and Hua. Both Erickson and Mather consider these two lines as reflecting Liu Xiang's explanation of the design of the *boshan lu* cover, which in their view was associated with people's religious beliefs in venerating sacred mountains (Erickson 1992:15). Without definite textual support to make such a connection, we probably cannot regard the inscriptions of Mounts Tai and Hua as a direct depiction of the design of the *boshan lu* cover, as suggested by both Erickson and Mather.

The term *zhengqi* in the above inscriptions is rendered as *zhengqi* 正氣 in the *Xiangpu* 香譜 (*Manual on Incense*) and *wangqi* 王氣 in the *Xiangsheng* 香乘 (*History about Incense*; Hong 2003, *juanxia* 7:233; Zhou 2003, *juan* 28, 7:575). We can only guess how *qi* 器 in the *Yiwen leiju* 藝文類聚 turned into *qi* 氣 in the *Xiangpu* and *Xiangsheng*, or vice versa, but there is not enough information to determine which *qi* represents the original.[10] The rendering of *qi* 器 as *qi* 氣, however, creates a new context to clarify the connotation of the verb *guan*. The first two lines of the above inscriptions can then be understood as the following: "I laud the proper *qi*, which stands lofty and steep like a hill." It indicates that these two lines describe the form of the *boshan lu* cover that represents *qi* clouds instead of hills or mountains. Only *qi* clouds symbolized by the design on the top of the incense burner can *guan*, or fill, Mounts Hua and Tai. If this is indeed the case, the term *boshan* cannot be a description of the design of the cover of these incense burners. In other words, the term *boshan lu* does not originate from the form of the cover.

Although we must always be aware of the underlying textual conventions that often introduce deliberate distortions and exaggerations in poetic writing, analysis of these two pieces of early poetic writing still prompts us to rethink the definition of a *boshan lu* as referring to the mountain-like design of its cover. It seems that neither of the two pieces mistakes the decoration of the cover of a *boshan* incense burner for a representation of mountains or hills, let alone that of sacred mountains with religious or symbolic meanings. When the character *shan* 山 (mountain) appears in their lines, it functions as a metaphoric vehicle to describe either the appearance of a *boshan* incense burner, exaggerating its height, or the form of solidified *qi* clouds on the cover, if we adopt the version rendering *zhengqi* 正器 as *wangqi* 王氣 or *zhengqi* 正氣 in the inscriptions attributed to Liu Xiang. The iconographic study of the mountain motifs at the beginning of this article clearly demonstrates that the design of the cover of the typical *boshan* incense burner does not represent mountains; nor does early literature show that people of the time equated the term *boshan lu* with the design of the cover. If the term *boshan lu* is not typically a description of the decoration on the cover, the term requires a reinterpretation from a different perspective.

Xuncao and the Function of *Boshan Lu*

When was the term *boshan lu* first used and to what, in fact, does it refer? To answer the first of these questions, we encounter difficulty because the account in the *Xijing zaji* can hardly be dated, even if we can roughly guess the date of the compilation of the whole text. The same reasoning applies to the earliest appearance of the term *boshan lu*. Whether it was used simultaneously with the term *xunlu*, seen in the inscriptions on the Maoling example, is far from clear. If the term *boshan lu* indeed appeared very early, we can nevertheless infer that it initially was not used to describe the design of an incense burner cover. However, if this term came into being at a much later stage to mistakenly describe the design on the covers, it would have done so in a changed context. This kind of change may indicate the termination of the function of this type of utensil in its original context. The change may also reflect the abandonment of the social and religious connotations with which this utensil may have previously been associated. Accordingly, we cannot rely on material such as the *Xijing zaji* to figure out how the term *boshan lu* was originally used and should examine this issue from a different perspective.

Let us assume that the term *boshan lu* is, in fact, associated with mountains or hills. Even so, we are not confident that this term must refer to the form of the cover. In fact, *boshan* was the name of a county in Shandong during the Qing Dynasty (1636–1911). Boshan County was established in Yongzheng's 雍正 reign (1722–1735). There are quite a few hills recorded in the local gazetteer compiled during the Qing, but none of them is named *boshan*, and there is no information whatsoever indicating any connection between *boshan lu* and the name of this county (Wang et al. 1968 [1937]:142–43, 161–76). Based on an account in the "Jiaosi zhi" 郊祀志 chapter of the *Hanshu* 漢書 that mentions "presenting sacrifices to the Eastern Peak of Mt. Tai at Bo," Lin Xiaojuan 林小娟 suspects that the word *boshan* in the term *boshan lu* possibly refers to Mount Tai (Lin 2008:67). Nevertheless, this piece of information is insufficient to make *boshan* the equivalent of Mount Tai. It also sounds a little farfetched for Mount Tai to change its name to Boshan, or Mount Bo, simply because Bo was the place at which Mount Tai was worshiped.

I suggest that the origin of the name *boshan lu* probably has something to do with the function of this kind of object. This hypothesis holds that Boshan was probably the place from which the grass that provided fragrant smoke, or *xiangfeng* 香風 (fragrant air, as described in the early poems), came. In fact, as a specific kind of *xunlu*, *boshan* incense burners were associated with a specific kind of grass from the very beginning, especially when we consider the name of this grass: *xuncao* 熏草. This grass emitted a pleasant smell, described as "fragrant air" in literature, when it was burned inside the upper body of a *boshan* incense burner (Yan and Wang 1989:187–88). According to the *Guangya* 廣雅, *xuncao* is also called *huicao* 蕙草, which "looks like twitch-grass but is fragrant" and for this reason is also named *maoxiang* 茅香, or fragrant twitch-grass. A basket of *maoxiang* was excavated from Mawangdui Tomb 1, dated to the Early Western Han, and it is recorded on a wooden board as *huisi* 蕙笥, a basket containing *huicao*. This basket of *maoxiang* appears in the written record of burial items as *hui yisi* 蕙一笥 (a basket of *huicao*; Hunan and Hunan 1973a:114, 142; 1973b:233). Moreover, archaeologists discovered two ceramic *xunlu* burners from the same tomb—one full of *maoxiang*, the other one containing a number of other kinds of fragrant grass besides *maoxiang* (Hunan and Hunan 1973a:125). All the information suggests that *xuncao*, *maoxiang*, and *huicao* refer to the same kind of grass, burned in an early *xunlu* to produce fragrant air to please its users. This interestingly echoes a line in the poem examined in the previous section: "It's difficult to keep the air fragrant for long. In vain fire of perfumed grass burns down." Thus it is safe to infer that *xunlu*, the other name of *boshan lu*, was closely linked to the grass burned in it from the very beginning of the invention of this type of object.

Based on a record preserved in the *Shanhai jing* 山海經, it seems that *xuncao* was not difficult to find near the Western Han capital city. It says:

又西百二十里，曰浮山，多盼木，枳葉而無傷，木蟲居之。有草焉，名曰熏草，麻葉而方莖，赤華而黑實，臭如蘼蕪，佩之可以已癘。(Guo and Hao 2016:44).

One hundred and twenty *li* further to the west, there is a mountain known as Fushan, on which many *panmu* trees grow. The *panmu* tree leaves resemble those of trifoliate trees and *panmu* trees themselves do not have thorns that hurt people. Wood insects live in the trees. In Fushan there also grows a kind of grass called *xuncao*. Its leaves look like that of hemp, its stalks are squarish, its flowers are red, its fruits look dark. This kind of grass smells like *miwu* and, if worn, can stop the spread of plague.

According to Hao Yixing's 郝懿行 study, on the basis of relevant information from the *Shuijing zhu* 水經註 and the *Yiwen leiju*, the Fushan recorded in the *Shanhai jing* is *Zifushan* 胏浮山, located to the south of Lintong 臨潼 in Shaanxi Province. Hao also identifies the *xuncao* growing in Fushan as *huicao* in another note on a different account in the *Shanhai jing* (Guo and Hao 2016:49–50). More relevant are the similarities between the early pronunciations of the characters *fu* 浮 *bʰjog and *bo* 博 *puak. Both their initials and finals are close enough to each other, respectively, to enable a possible borrowing of the sound of the latter to replace the former.[11] That is to say, when the character *bo* was borrowed to replace *fu*, Fushan became Boshan, famous for its perfumed grass used to produce "fragrant air" in *xunlu* burners during the Western Han. Viewed from this perspective, the name *boshan lu* emphasizes more the *xuncao* grass burned in the object than the form of the object itself. This line of thinking is also in accordance with the word *xunlu* inscribed on the incense burner found near Maoling: the character *xun* indeed refers to *xuncao* grass, which grew in Fushan (read as *boshan*) near the Western Han capital Chang'an 長安.

Conclusion

This study aims to clarify a previous misunderstanding of the term *boshan lu*. Two specific points are worth noting as the results of this study. First, this study challenges the previous view equating the term *boshan* with the depiction of the design of *boshan* incense burners and argues that the designs on the covers of typical Han *boshan* incense burners describe the flow of *qi* clouds. Second, this study suggests that people living in the Han through the Six Dynasties did not take the term *boshan* to be the depiction of the *boshan* designs and that they employed the term *boshan* for a different reason. The term *boshan* as a name for *xunlu* burners probably refers to the place that produced the type of grass burned to provide fragrance. Boshan probably is the same as Fushan, which was associated with *xuncao* grass burned in the *xunlu*, since the pronunciation of *bo* 博 was close to *fu* 浮 in Old Chinese, and that may have led to the replacement of the latter by the character *bo* 博 in writing.

Two additional points can be inferred. One is that the English rendering of the term *boshan lu* appears anachronistic, since we now know from archaeological discoveries that the material used in a *boshan lu* to produce fragrance was not resinous incense but *xuncao* grass, and its name may have directly contributed to the naming of this type of burner. Connected with this point, we may offer an explanation for the question raised at the beginning of this article, about why many burners without mountain designs on their covers are also referred to as *boshan lu*. If the term *boshan* is merely associated with the fragrant grass burned in the burner, the design on its cover is not necessarily an important feature linked to the name of this type of object.

This study also makes clear from an art historical point of view that although there are different ways of representing both mountains and clouds in Han pictorial art, the two are nevertheless unambiguously distinguished and cannot be equated one with the other. The depiction of clouds is characterized by the thickness of *yuntou*, rolling wisps of clouds, and the flow of *qi*, while the mountain designs feature overlapping triangles or curved arcs. The distinction in the artistic representations of these two different kinds of motifs is especially well observed when both appear simultaneously in the same artwork.

Though the representations of both mountains and clouds can be interpreted from a religious perspective to express auspiciousness or the pursuit of immortality (Wu 1984), they are different artistic elements within the same religious background and deserve to be interpreted differently. Now we understand that the designs previously considered to be mountains are actually cloud motifs. As a design on a daily utensil, the cloud motif can be regarded as a representation of the "fragrant air" emitted from the upper body of a *boshan lu*—that is, solidified *qi*. It could also reflect people's religious beliefs during the Han in terms of pursuing immortality by creating a miniature version of an imaginary world of immortals surrounded by clouds.

It is worth noting that different identifications of the same motif may lead to fairly different interpretations. Take, for example, the symbols on the *dixing tu* 地形圖 (typological map) and *zhujun tu* 駐軍圖 (garrison map) excavated from Mawangdui Tomb 3, dated to the early Western Han. The closed, shaded lines on the *dixing tu* and the winding lines with shaded triangular signs in the concave side and connected shaded circles on the convex side on the *zhujun tu* have long been considered depictions of mountains. Thus they were thought to accurately convey actual geographical information on the southern Changsha Princedom and its neighboring state Southern Yue 越. However, a rethinking of these symbols from the perspective of the Warring States and Han iconographical representations of clouds finds that the two kinds of symbols previously considered to be mountains turn out to be cloud symbols (Zhang 2016). This discovery requires a reconsideration of the manufacture and function of these two maps as well as the possible religious meaning they reflect, instead of a historical geographical exploration of the mapped information. As Professor Lothar von Falkenhausen convincingly argued in regard to the reliability of bronze inscriptions as historical records in a review article (Falkenhausen 1993), we shall not take the term and form of *boshan* incense burners at face value. It is always necessary to take into consideration the complex nature of the subject matter and to remain cautious before turning it into evidence.

Admittedly, the reidentification of the design on the *boshan lu* covers merely serves as a necessary step to further exploration of how the term *boshan* was related to *xunlu* burners in the early development of this type of object. My assumption that the term *boshan* refers to the place or places where the specific kind of grass used in *xunlu* burners grew aims to answer this question. Although my assumption awaits further verification, it is my hope that correction of a long unchallenged misunderstanding about the *boshan* design will lead us closer to the truth.

Acknowledgments

Several of my teachers and friends offered generous help at different stages of writing this article. Among them I am especially grateful to Professors Lothar von Falkenhausen, Li Ling, and Wu Hung for their critiques and suggestions, and to my friends Rowan Flad, Anke Hein, Bryan Miller, and Florence Hodous for their comments and relentless editing. I am also thankful to the UCLA Center for Chinese Studies, the UCLA Young Research Library, and the Chiang Ching-kuo Foundation for providing the funds for traveling and for facilitating the workshop and symposium at which I presented the main idea of this article. I also thank the institute I am currently working for: this project is supported by the Fundamental Research Funds for the Central Universities and the Research Funds of Renmin University of China.

Notes

1. The material used to produce a pleasant smell in the earliest *boshan lu* is a grass called *xun* 薰 or *hui* 蕙 in literary sources.
2. This seems to be a generalization widely accepted by scholars. For a more detailed discussion, see Wang Yan 2011.
3. Wu Hung discusses in depth the representation of Mount Kunlun using three-peaked and mushroom-shaped symbols in his work; see Wu 1989:117–26. Sun Ji 孫機, a scholar devoted to the study of Han material culture, strongly disagrees with Wu Hung about considering the peak designs on the sides of coffins excavated from Mawangdui Tomb 1 to be symbols of Mount Kunlun (Sun 2015:195–97).
4. The place where the Queen Mother of the West lives changes in different sections of the *Shan hai jing* 山海經, one of the few early Chinese texts containing accounts of early Chinese mythology. It is in the "Dahuang xi jing" 大荒西經 section that Mount Kunlun is connected with the Queen Mother of the West, a human but beast-like figure wearing a *sheng* 胜 hairpin, later viewed as the most characteristic symbol for identifying the Queen Mother. For relevant information on the Queen Mother and Mount Kunlun, see Yuan 2014:45, 244, 258).
5. For the phonetic reconstruction of *lu* 盧, see Schuessler 2007:364. The character *lu* 爐 indeed appears in the term *xunlu* 熏爐 on an incense burner found in Changsha, Human Province; see Shan 1966:185.
6. See Qiannian qizhen: *Boshan lu* 千年奇珍：博山爐, https://www.sohu.com/a/316751774_100087519, accessed March 9, 2020.
7. See Wang Ganghuai 2016:85. For similar inscriptions on bronze mirrors, see also Wang Shilun 1987:67.
8. See Liu Xin 劉歆 et al. 2012:15. The authorship of this work is still debated, and scholars cannot agree on whether it was written by Liu Xin (50 BCE–23 CE) or Ge Hong (284–364 CE). Whoever wrote it, it seems that the term *boshan* appeared much later than the term *xunlu*, as far as the available information can clarify the issue.
9. Erickson's full translation of the inscriptions goes as follows: "I value this perfect utensil, lofty and steep as a mountain!/Its top is like Hua Shan yet its foot is a bronze plate./It contains rare perfumes, red flames, and green smoke."
10. It is possible that *wangqi* 王氣 was mistaken for *zhengqi* 正氣, which was then rendered as *zhengqi* 正器, as seen in the *Yiwen leiju*. The opposite could also

have happened, with *zhengqi* 正器 becoming *zhengqi* 正氣 and then *wangqi* 王氣.

11 The initial and final of the character *fu* belong to *bing* 並 and *you* 幽, while those of the character *bo* belong to *bang* 幫 and *yu* 魚 or *duo* 鐸. The initials *bing* and *bang* are close enough that one could replace the other, and the sounds of the finals *you* and *yu* were interchangeable in ancient Chinese.

References

Anqiuxian Wenhuaju 安丘縣文化局 and Anqiuxian Wenhuaguan 安丘縣文化館
1991 *Anqiu Dongjiazhuang Han huaxiangshi mu* 安丘董家莊漢畫像石墓. Jinan: Jinan Chubanshe.

Chen Peifen 陳佩芬
2013 *Zhongguo qingtongqi cidian* 中國青銅器辭典. Shanghai: Shanghai cishu Chubanshe.

Chen Pochan
2008 Technical Changes in the Salt Production from the Neolithic Period to the Han Dynasty at Zhongba. In *Sel, eau et forêt D'hier à aujourd'hui*, edited by Olivier Weller, Alexa Dufraisse, and Pierre Pétrequin, pp. 143–61. Presses universitaires de Franche-Comté, Besançon.

De Luca, Federico
2019 Thymiateria e Monete. *Monete Antiche* 107:16–29.

Erickson, Susan N.
1992 *Boshanlu*: Mountain Censers of the Western Han Period: A Typological and Iconological Analysis. *Archives of Asian Art* 45:6–28.
1996–1997 The Freer Gallery of Art *Boshanlu*: Answers to A. G. Wenley's Questions. *Oriental Art* 42(4):27–38.

Falkenhausen, Lothar von
1993 Issues in Western Zhou Studies (Review article on Sources of Western Zhou History, by Edward L. Shaughnessy, and Western Zhou Ritual Bronzes from the Arthur M. Sackler Collections, by Jessica Rawson). *Early China* 18:139–226.
2004 Mortuary Behavior in Pre-Imperial Qin: A Religious Interpretation. In *Chinese Religion and Society*, Vol. 1, edited by John Lagerway, pp. 109–72. Hong Kong: Chinese University Press.
2006a *Chinese Society in the Age of Confucius (1000–250 BC): The Archaeological Evidence*. Los Angeles: Cotsen Institute of Archaeology Press.
2006b The Salt of Ba: Reflection on the Role of the "Peripheries" in the Production Systems of Bronze Age China. *Arts Asiatiques* 61:45–56.
2017 The Problem of Human Representation in Pre-Imperial China. In *Bilder der Macht: Das griechische Porträt und seine Verwendung in der antiken Welt*, edited by Dietrich Boschung and François Queyrel, pp. 377–401. Paderborn: W. Fink.

Flad, Rowan K.
2005 Evaluating Fish and Meat Salting at Prehistoric Zhongba, China. *Journal of Field Archaeology* 30(3):231–53.

Ge Hong 葛洪
2017 *Shenxian zhuan* 神仙傳. Beijing: Zhonghua Shuju.

Guo Pu 郭璞 and Hao Yixing 郝懿行
2016 *Shanhai jing jianshu* 山海經箋疏. Beijing: Zhongguo Zhigong Chubanshe.

Hebeisheng Bowuguan 河北省博物館 and Wenwu Guanlichu 文物管理處, eds.
1980 *Hebeisheng wenwu xuanji* 河北省文物選集. Beijing: Wenwu Chubanshe.

Henan Gudai Yishu Yanjiuhui 河南古代藝術研究會, ed.
1983 *Mixian Han huaxiangzhuan* 密縣漢畫像磚. Zhengzhou: Zhongzhou Guji Chubanshe.

Hong Chu 洪芻
2003 *Xiangpu* 香譜 (Qinding Siku quanshu·zibu 欽定四庫全書·子部). In *Wenyuange siku quanshu*, Vol. 844 文淵閣四庫全書第八四四冊. Shanghai: Shanghai Guji Chubanshe.

Hunansheng Bowuguan 湖南省博物館 and Hunansheng Wenwu Kaogu Yanjiusuo 湖南省文物考古研究所
1973a *Mawangdui yi hao Han mu*, Vol. 1 長沙馬王堆一號漢墓（上集）. Beijing: Wenwu Chubanshe.
1973b *Changsha Mawangdui yi hao Han mu*, Vol. 2 長沙馬王堆一號漢墓（下集）. Beijing: Wenwu Chubanshe.
2004 *Changsha Mawangdui er, san hao Han mu*, Vol. 1, *Tianye kaogu fajue baogao* 長沙馬王堆二、三號漢墓 第一卷：田野考古發掘報告. Beijing: Wenwu Chubanshe.

Jin Weinuo 金維諾, Chen Zhenyu 陳振裕, Jiang Yingchun 蔣迎春, and Hu Desheng 胡德生
2010 *Zhongguo meishu quanji: Qiqi jiaju*, Vol. 1 中國美術全集·漆器家具一. Hefei: Huangshan Shushe.

Jin Weinuo 金維諾 and Luo Shiping 羅世平, eds.
2009 *Zhongguo meishu quanji: Mushi bihua 1* 中國美術全集·墓室壁畫一. Hefei: Huangshan Shushe.

Jin Weinuo 金維諾 and Xin Lixiang 信立祥, eds.
2009a *Zhongguo meishu quanji: Huaxiangshi huaxiangzhuan 1* 中國美術全集·畫像石畫像磚一. Hefei: Huangshan Shushe.
2009b *Zhongguo meishu quanji:· Huaxiangshi huaxiangzhuan 2* 中國美術全集·畫像石畫像磚二. Hefei: Huangshan Shushe.
2009c *Zhongguo meishu quanji: Huaxiangshi huaxiangzhuan 3* 中國美術全集·畫像石畫像磚三. Hefei: Huangshan Shushe.

Jin Weinuo 金維諾 and Zhao Feng 趙豐
2010 *Zhongguo meishu quanji: Fangzhi pin*, Vol. 1 中國美術全集·紡織品一. Hefei: Huangshan Shushe.

Laufer, Berthold
1909 *Chinese Pottery of the Han Dynasty*. Leiden: Brill.

Li Shuicheng 李水城 and Lothar von Falkenhausen 羅泰, eds.
2006 *Zhongguo yanye kaogu (Di yi ji): Changjiang shangyou gudai yanye yu jingguan kaogu de chubu yanjiu* 中國鹽業考古 (第一集): 長江上游古代鹽業與景觀考古的初步研究 [Salt Archaeology in China, Vol. 1, Ancient Salt Production and Landscape Archaeology in the Upper Yangzi Basin: Preliminary Studies]. Beijing: Kexue cubanshe.
2010 *Zhongguo yanye kaogu (Di er ji): Guoji yanye kaogu yanjiu* 中國鹽業考古 (第二集): 國際鹽業考古研究 [Salt Archaeology in China, Vol. 2, International Research on Salt Archaeology]. Beijing: Kexue cubanshe.
2013 *Zhongguo yanye kaogu (Di san ji): Changjiang shangyou gudai yanye yu Zhongba yizhi de kaogu yanjiu* 中國鹽業考古 (第三集): 長江上游古代鹽業與中壩遺址的考古研究 [Salt Archaeology in China, Vol. 3, Archaeological Research on Ancient Salt Production in the Upper Yangzi River Region and at the Site of Zhongba]. Beijing: Kexue cubanshe.

Li Song 李凇
2000 *Lun Handai yishu zhong de Xiwangmu tuxiang* 論漢代藝術中的西王母圖像. Changsha: Hunan Jiaoyu Chubanshe.

Lian Chunhai 練春海
2013 Boshan shi yuanliu kao 博山飾源流考. In *Qi Lu wenwu*, Vol. 2 齊魯文物 (第二輯), edited by Shandong Bowuguan 山東博物館, pp. 123–32. Beijing: Kexue Chubanshe.
2014 *Qiwu tuxiang yu Handai Xinyang* 器物圖像與漢代信仰. Beijing: Sanlian Shudian.

Lin Xiaojuan 林小娟
2008 Boshan lu kao 博山爐考. *Sichuan wenwu* 四川文物3:65–67.

Liu Xin 劉歆 et al.
2012 *Xijing zaji (wai wuzhong)* 西京雜記（外五種）. Shanghai: Shanghai Guji Chubanshe.

Lü Dalin 呂大臨 et al.
2016 *Kaogu tu (Wai wuzhong)* 考古圖（外五種）. Shanghai: Shanghai Shudian Chubanshe.

Ouyang Xun 歐陽詢
1999 *Yiwen leiju* 藝文類聚. Shanghai: Shanghai Guji Chubanshe.

Rawson, Jessica
2006 The Chinese Hill Censer, *Boshanlu*: A Note on Origins, Influences, and Meanings. *Arts Asiatiques* 61:75–86.
2013 Yiyu meihuo: Han diguo jiqi beifang linju 異域魅惑：漢帝國及其北方鄰國. In *Gudai muzang meishu yanjiu*, Vol. 2 古代墓葬美術研究 (第二輯), edited by Wu Hung 巫鴻, pp. 55–71. Changsha: Hunan Meishu Chubanshe.

Ruan Jingjing 阮晶京
2012 Boshan lu de lishi: Yi liang Han Wei Jin Nanbeichao cailiao wei zhongxin 博山爐的歷史：以兩漢魏晉南北朝材料為中心. Master's thesis, School of Humanities, Central Academy of Fine Arts, Beijing.

Schuessler, Axel
2007 *ABC Etymological Dictionary of Old Chinese*. Honolulu: University of Hawai'i Press.

Shan Xianjin 單先進
1966 Changsha Tangjialing Xihan mu qingli baogao 長沙湯家嶺西漢墓清理報告. *Kaogu* 考古 4:181–88.

Shanghai Shudian Chubanshe 上海書店出版社, ed.
2012 *Qinding siku quanshu: Xiqing gujian* 欽定四庫全書·西清古鑒. Shanghai: Shanghai Shudian Chubanshe.

Sun Ji 孫機
2008 *Handai wuzhi wenhua ziliao tushuo* 漢代物質文化資料圖說. Shanghai: Shanghai Guji Chubanshe.
2015 Xian fan you ming zhijian: Han huaxiang shi yu "da xiang qi sheng" 仙凡幽明之間：漢畫像石與"大象其生." In *Yangguan ji: Gu wenwu de xinshang yu jianbie* 仰觀集：古文物的欣賞與鑒別. Beijing: Wenwu Chubanshe.

Tokyo Geijutsu Daigaku 東京芸術大学
1978 *Tokyo Geijutsu Daigaku Zōhin Zuroku* 東京芸術大学蔵品図録. Tokyo: Tokyo Geijutsu Daigaku.

Wang Ganghuai 王剛懷
2016   Mang shi mingwen jing 莽式銘文鏡. In *Zhishui ji* 止水集. Shanghai: Shanghai Guji Chubanshe.

Wang Guizhi 王桂芝
1986   Han xianglong boshan lu 漢降龍博山爐. *Wenbo* 文博 2:91, Plate 3.

Wang Long 王龍
2013   Shandong diqu Handai boshan lu yanjiu 山東地區漢代博山爐研究. Master's thesis, School of History and Culture, Shandong University, Jinan.

Wang Niansun 王念孫
2000   *Guangya shuzheng* 廣雅疏證. Nanjing: Fenghuang Chubanshe.

Wang Shilun 王士倫
1987   *Zhejiang chutu tongjing* 浙江出土銅鏡. Beijing: Wenwu Chubanshe.

Wang Xianqian 王先謙
1998   *Han Feizi jijie* 韓非子集解. Beijing: Zhonghua Shuju.

Wang Yan 王燕
2011   Handai yishu zhong de xianshan tuxiang yanjiu 漢代藝術中的仙山圖像研究. Master's thesis, China Central Academy of Fine Arts, Beijing.

Wang Yingui 王蔭桂, Zhang Xinceng 張新曾, Fu Shen 富申, and Tian Shilin 田士麟
1968 [1937] *Xuxiu Boshan Xian zhi* 續修博山縣志. Taibei: Chengwen Chubanshe.

Wenley, Archibald G.
1948–1949 The Question of the Po-Shan-Hsiang-Lu. *Archives of the Chinese Art Society of America* 3:5–12.

Wu Hung
1984   A Sanpan Shan Chariot Ornament and the Xiangrui Design in Western Han Art. *Archives of Asian Art* 37:38–59.
1989   *The Wu Liang Shrine: The Ideology of Early Chinese Pictorial Art*. Stanford, CA: Stanford University Press.

Xianyang Diqu Wenguanhui 咸陽地區文管會 and Maoling Bowuguan 茂陵博物館
1982   Shaanxi Maoling yihao wumingzhong yikao congzangkeng de fajue 陝西茂陵一號無名冢一號從葬坑的發掘. *Wenwu* 文物 9:1–17, Plates 1–4.

Xu Guangji 徐光冀, ed.
2012   *Zhongguo chutu bihua quanji 6 Shaanxi*, Vol. 1 中國出土壁畫全集6陝西（上）. Beijing: Kexue Chubanshe.

Yan Shigu 顏師古 and Wang Yinglin 王應麟
1989   Jijiu pian 急就篇. In *Shi You* 史遊, *Jijiu pian* 急就篇, pp. 187–88. Changsha: Yuelu Shushe.

Yang Hong 楊泓
1991   Tong boshan lu 銅博山爐. In *Wenwu congtan* 文物叢談, edited by Sun Ji 孫機 and Yang Hong 楊泓, pp. 66–70. Beijing: Wenwu Chubanshe.

Yang Zhishui 揚之水
2004   Liang Song xianglu yuanliu 兩宋香爐源流. *Zhongguo dianji yu wenhua* 中國典籍與文化 2004(1):46–69.

Yuan Ke 袁珂
2014   *Shanhai jing jiaozhu* 山海經校註. Beijing: Beijing Lianhe Chuban Gongsi.

Yun Anzhi 貟安志
1982   Tan "Xinyangjia" Tongqi 談"信陽家"銅器. *Wenwu* 文物 9:18–20.

Zhang Hanmo
2016   Mapped Territory Floating in the Clouds: A Reinterpretation of the Mawangdui Maps in Their Art and Religious Contexts. *Artibus Asiae* 76(2):147–96.

Zheng Yan 鄭岩
2002   *Wei Jin Nanbeichao bihua mu yanjiu* 魏晉南北朝壁畫墓研究. Beijing: Wenwu Chubanshe.

Zheng Luanming 鄭灤明
2000. Dingzhou Sanpanshan Han mu cuo jinyin qingtong che santing wenshi neirong fenxi 定州三盤山漢墓錯金銀青銅車傘鋌紋飾內容分析. *Wenwu Chunqiu* 文物春秋 3:43–48.

Zhongguo Huaxiangshi Quanji Bianji Weiyuanhui 中國畫像石全集編輯委員會
2000a *Zhongguo huaxiangshi quanji 5 Shaanxi, Shanxi Han huaxiangshi* 中國畫像石全集 5 陝西、山西山東漢畫像石. Jinan: Shandong Meishu Chubanshe; Zhengzhou: Henan Meishu Chubanshe.
2000b *Zhongguo huaxiangshi quanji 2 Shandong Han huaxiangshi* 中國畫像石全集2山東漢畫像石. Jinan: Shandong Meishu Chubanshe; Zhengzhou: Henan Meishu Chubanshe.
2000c *Zhongguo huaxiangshi quanji 6 Shandong huaxiangshi* 中國畫像石全集 6 山東漢畫像石. Jinan: Shandong Meishu Chubanshe; Zhengzhou: Henan Meishu Chubanshe.

Zhongguo Meishu Quanji Bianji Weiyuanhui 中國美術全集編輯委員會
2006a *Zhongguo meishu quanji Gongyi meishu bian Qingtongqi*, Vol. 2 中國美術全集·工藝美術編 青銅器（下）Beijing: Renmin Meishu Chunanshe.

2006b   *Zhongguo meishu quanji: Huihua bian Yuanshi shehui zhi Nanbeichao huihua* 中國美術全集·繪畫編 原始社會至南北朝繪畫. Beijing: Renmin Meishu Chubanshe.

Zhongguo Shehui Kexueyuan Kaogu Yanjiusuo 中國社會科學院考古研究所 and Hebeisheng Wenwu Guanlichu 河北省文物管理處

1980a   *Mancheng Han mu fajue baogao*, Vol. 1 滿城漢墓發掘報告（上）. Beijing: Wenwu Chubanshe.

1980b   *Mancheng Han mu fajue baogao*, Vol. 2 滿城漢墓發掘報告（下）. Beijing: Wenwu Chubanshe.

Zhou Dao 周到, Lü Pin 呂品, and Tang Wenxing 湯文興, eds.

1985   *Henan Handai huaxiangzhuan* 河南漢代畫像磚. Shanghai: Shanghai Renmin Meishu Chubanshe.

Zhou Jiazhou 周嘉冑

2003   *Xiangsheng* 香乘 (Qinding siku quanshu·zibu 欽定四庫全書·子部). In *Wenyuange siku quanshu*, Vol. 844 文淵閣四庫全書第八四四冊. Shanghai: Shanghai Guji Chubanshe.

Chapter 18

"What Was the Nicest Thing You Ever Found?"
An Essay on the Meaning of Objects

Hans Barnard

Now that my esteemed colleague and dear friend Lothar von Falkenhausen has turned 60, only a few months before me, the time has come for me to reflect on our discipline. As an archaeologist I have been involved in projects in several countries, ranging from Armenia and Chile to Tunisia and Yemen, but never China. It would therefore not be prudent for me to address its rich archaeology and history, especially within the framework of the volume in hand. Instead, I would like to discuss another subject on which Lothar has written (Falkenhausen 2013, 2015, 2017, 2018)—one that reflects his interest in antiquarianism and the different meanings of objects to anthropological archaeologists and collectors in the widest sense of that word.

More than once I have been asked by strangers, students, and sometimes even colleagues what my favorite or most important find was during my many years of fieldwork as an archaeologist. On such occasions I find it difficult to explain why I struggle to find an answer to this seemingly obvious and innocuous question, partly because a genuine response may sound counterintuitive or even pedantic. Here I elaborate on my reservations evoked by this recurring question, before attempting a response at the very end of this chapter (Figure 18.1).

Archaeologists have an ambiguous relationship with objects. Archaeology can be defined as the study of human development, behavior, and history as inferred from their material remains. The discipline is thus solidly based upon and almost entirely dependent on objects. Individual objects, however, have little to no meaning outside their contexts, their relations to one another, and the environments in which they were found. As a scholarly enterprise, archaeology is not at all about finding things, which would be treasure hunting or looting. Rather it is about finding things out (Nigra et al. 2015).

Archaeological research is facilitated by the fact that all objects created and used by humans intricately complement functionality with meaning (Bennett 2010; De Muijnck 2013; Gosden and Marshall 1999; Hodder 2012; Ingold 2013; Malafouris 2013; Siefkes 2012). Using the game of chess as a model for the world, Ferdinand de Saussure (1959 [1916]:110) wrote, "Take a knight, for instance. By itself is it an element in the game? Certainly not, for by its material make-up—outside its square and the other conditions of the game—it means nothing to the player; it becomes a real, concrete element only when endowed with value and wedded to it." Ernest Dichter (2002 [1960]:97–98) arrived at the same conclusion when developing modern marketing and advertisement strategies: "In 1959 [I had in my] library over twelve hundred studies concerning the phenomenology, the psychology of such diverse objects as cars, soap, toothpaste . . . furniture, silverware, and doilies. Literally each one of these studies and others not listed show again and again that products are not inanimate objects, that to separate or neglect them as objects of scientific analysis is a major oversight on the part of the social scientist."

Figure 18.1. Map of sites mentioned in the text. 1. Bamiyan; 2. Mosul; 3. Heliopolis; 4. Eleon; 5. Oxford; 6. Chapel Hill.
Created by Bryan K. Miller.

This oversight was much later most famously addressed by Alfred Gell (1998) and others (Figure 18.2). John Urry (2007:45) eloquently summarized the notion: "The powers of 'humans' are always augmented by various material worlds, of clothing, tools, objects, paths, buildings. . . . Human life we might say is never just human."

That the intimate relationship between humans and their material environment has considerable time-depth is noted by Raymond Tallis (2003:234): "The extraordinary stability of tools such as hand-axes over time (1.5 million years) and over space (Europe, Africa, Asia) could not have been an accident, nor due solely to inertia. . . . When manufacturing tools, the toolmaker would be making a sign as well as an instrument, and he would want his sign to say the same things as had the tools made by his predecessors." Gregory Bateson (2000 [1972]:318) argued that this relationship is intimate to an extent that obscures the boundary between the object and its user: "Consider a blind man with a stick. Where does the blind man's self begin? At the tip of the stick? At the handle of the stick? Or at some point halfway up the stick?" An observation echoed by Andy Clark and David Chalmers (1998:18): "Most of us already accept that the self outstrips the boundaries of consciousness . . . . once the hegemony of skin and skull is usurped, we may be able to see ourselves more truly as creatures of the world," as well as by Kirk Woolford and Stuart Dunn (2014:125): "Tools may extend human's existing action and perception capabilities. Tools are treated as functional extensions of the user. . . . The boundaries between bodies, tools, and the environment are fluid and dependent upon relationships more than materials."

In his essay *Regrets sur ma vieille robe de chambre*, French philosopher Denis Diderot (1713–1784) described how his room was once chaotic and happy but now elegant yet grim (McCracken 1988:118–29; Tunstall and Scott 2016). He attributed this change to his purchase of a new dressing gown. This prompted an almost subconscious effort to match the room with the gown and consequently a number of other purchases and modifications. The final result was a complete transformation of the room and also, more importantly, a fundamental change in one's mood while residing in it.

From an archaeological point of view, all this means that a careful study of objects can reveal a myriad of information about their human producers and users. Such studies do not just focus on raw materials and production techniques but also address function and use (wear and tear, molecular residues), taphonomy and diagenesis, and the inferred value and associated social status of the object. The resulting data is confronted with information about the context in which the object was found, as well as data on other objects from the same context and similar objects from different contexts. This often results in meaningful and reliable statements about the (relative and absolute) age of the object as well as its context and, more broadly, about the cultural affiliation, social stratification, and stage of technological development of the associated human society at the time.

Some Practical Issues Associated with Objects

Objects are central to archaeological research, but at the same time they are associated with significant issues, resulting in the ambiguous relation between objects and archaeologists mentioned above. Some of these issues are of a practical, others a more fundamental nature. As soon as an object is excavated or otherwise retrieved, issues of ownership manifest themselves. Ownership is claimed and often disputed among the excavators, the owner of the land or site, the local community, and the local, regional, and national authorities. Other parties that get involved may include descendent communities and international organizations considering selected objects as world heritage. Such

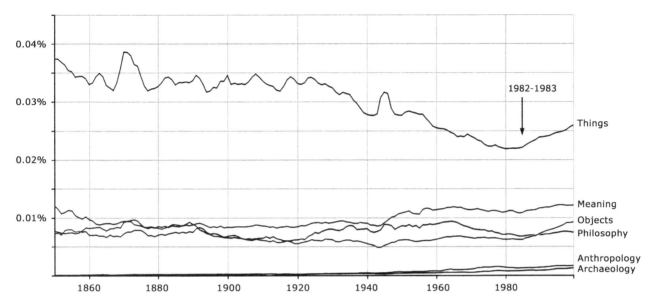

Figure 18.2. Google Ngram, created in July 2019, showing the occurrence of the words *thing(s)*, *meaning*, *object(s)*, *philosophy*, *anthropology*, and *archaeology* in a very large number of books published in English between 1850 and 2000. Note the significant rise in the use of both *thing(s)* and *object(s)* starting in the early 1980s. *Created by the author.*

disputes most often escalate with objects that are inherently valuable, such as those made of precious metals or those attractive to museums and private collectors, or with objects that appear historically, art historically, or culturally significant, such as those bearing inscriptions (Silverman 2011). The ongoing diplomatic and public debates on the rightful ownership and location of the Elgin or Parthenon Marbles—originally from the Acropolis in Athens, Greece, and currently in the Duveen Gallery of the British Museum (London)—and the bust of Nefertiti—found in the workshop of sculptor Thutmose in Amarna, Egypt, and currently on display in the Neues Museum (Berlin)—may serve as paradigms for such disputes (Cuno 2014; Ikram 2011; Kynourgiopoulou 2011; Murphy 2016; O'Connell and DePaul 2005; Woodhouse and Pepin 2017), but they are only two of many similar discussions (Silverman 2011).

Ownership also comes with responsibilities, including first of all appropriate storage. Archaeological objects need to be housed, labeled, and stored in ways that protect them from damage and theft while remaining accessible for study and display. This may be trivial for a few items with limited intrinsic value, but it swiftly becomes a burden for the entire yield of even a small archaeological project or items of great value or significance. The storage space will quickly fill up with fragments of pottery, stone, and other items, which have to be boxed, labeled, and guarded. Additional issues are associated with objects that may be acutely affected by their removal from the matrices in which they were preserved, such as those made of organic materials and those with human remains. Over time, the storage environment will influence almost all materials and alter them in a variety of ways. This brings with it the necessity to preserve, conserve, and possibly even restore some or all of the objects in storage—efforts that can be very time-consuming and costly indeed.

Such practical problems may be challenging but are not insurmountable, and most archaeological projects eventually arrive at a solution. This can be a more or less sophisticated form of joint ownership or stewardship, or a more pragmatic solution in which some excavated objects are reburied after study, others are stored on site—for comparison and future study or sampling—and the remainder are surrendered to the local, regional, or national authorities, who have significantly larger resources and incentives to address issues of storage, preservation, and presentation. Where feasible and legally possible, a small selection of objects may be taken by the excavators for detailed, specialized study or sampling for specific analysis. A single solution that addresses most issues is reburying the items in a place and matrix similar to those in which they were found (Barnard et al. 2016). This allows for the affordable and relatively safe storage of large numbers of objects but obviously at the same time removes them from view and easy access for additional study.

More Fundamental Issues Associated with Objects

Apart from the responsibly to preserve, conserve, and restore objects, de facto ownership of objects also creates opportunities to amend their meaning, form, or function, as well as to move, decommission, or even destroy them. By creating ephemeral or auto-destructive art, several modern artists have pointed out that not all objets d'art necessarily need to be preserved. In October 2018 the painting *Girl with Balloon* by the enigmatic artist Banksy was sold at Sotheby's in London. Directly after its sale, the picture was destroyed by a shredding mechanism hidden in its frame. The event was subsequently named *Love Is in the Bin* by the artist. Comparable artistic statements have been made by Christo (Christo Vladimirov Javacheff), Piero Manzoni, and Richard Long (Ingold 2007:39–71; 2011:19–32).

Instances of iconoclasm and *damnatio memoriae*, both intended to alter history retroactively, are attested throughout human history and invariably involve modifying or destroying material objects. One well-documented ancient case is the removal of the name of the god Amun from ancient Egyptian monuments by Pharaoh Amenhotep IV (Kemp 2012; Reeves 2001), who reigned ca. 1350–1335 BCE and around the fifth year of his rule took the name Akhenaten (Loyal to Aten). In many places he had the name Amun replaced with Aten. After his death and the restoration of the power of the priests of Amun, the name and image of Akhenaten were in turn destroyed where possible and the name of Amun was restored in many places. These changes are now accepted as noteworthy elements of affected objects that were preserved into modern times, while the passion and emotions related to them have faded with the passage of time. For his contemporaries, however, Akhenaten was probably a brutal dictator who forcefully tried to impose his own idiosyncratic religion, social order, and artistic style (Kemp 2012; Reeves 2001), more like Kim Il-sung or Mu'ammar Gaddafi than Mohandas Gandhi or Nelson Mandela. Removing his image from history seems comparable to toppling statues of Josef Stalin after the lifting of the Iron Curtain. At that time many had forgotten that similar events had taken place only half a century earlier, when troops from Nazi Germany invaded the Soviet Union. From the perspective of the objects, these events are equally destructive, and the imagery from the 1940s and the 1990s appears remarkably similar. How to evaluate such actions, their direct results, and their long-term effects depends on our opinions and judgments. This gets increasingly difficult when worldviews are equally vocal, such as political and public discussions concerning the position of Confederate statues in the U.S. Southeast or the fate of the tomb of Francisco Franco in the Valley of the Fallen, near Madrid, Spain (Beetham 2016; Crumbaugh 2011; Ferrándiz 2019; Forest and Johnson 2019; Fuentes Vega 2017; Hepworth 2014; Hite 2008; Morgan 2018; Silverman 2011; Winberry 2015).

The rage and fury that accompany the destruction of hated symbols, however, appear to bridge time and space. The footage of civil rights activists toppling and destroying *The Boys Who Wore Gray* (Durham, North Carolina) and *Silent Sam* (Chapel Hill, North Carolina) in August 2017 and 2018, respectively, looks identical to video images released in February 2015 by Islamic extremists documenting their destruction of artifacts in the Mosul Museum in northern Iraq, across the river Tigris from the ancient city of Nineveh. The latter caused outrage in Europe and the United States, fueled by concerns for the destruction of world heritage and also by anti-Islamic sentiments and the availability of modern media, which was unavailable when Nineveh was raised to the ground in 612 BCE by an informal coalition of its former vassal states.

The statue of King Uthal (Figure 18.3), which was heavily damaged during these actions, became a symbol of the destruction at Mosul after the digital files necessary to print a three-dimensional copy of the statue were widely circulated. Along with those of other destroyed objects, this file was created by Morehshin Allahyari. Printed versions were on display in February and March 2016 in Trinity Square Video (Toronto, Canada) as well as from March to September 2018 in Museo Egizio (Turin, Italy). The head and body of the more than life-size statue of King Uthal were found in 1951 during excavation of the Temple of Baalshamin in Hatra, one of several trading centers in the desert south of Mosul during the first century CE. Being affiliated with the Parthian Empire, Hatra was unsuccessfully attacked by the Romans at least twice and was ultimately destroyed by the Sasanian Empire in 240 CE. It was likely at this time that the statue was first damaged, although it could still be identified when uncovered in modern times by an inscription in Aramaic on its pedestal: "The image of king Uthal, the merciful, noble-minded servant of God, blessed by God" (Fukai 1960).

Little is known about the city of Hatra and King Uthal, but one wonders about the accuracy of the inscription on this statue and if Uthal, in his ascent to power and his reign, was indeed a better man than Akhenaten, Josef Stalin, or Francisco Franco. Maybe he was or maybe he deserved his statue to be destroyed and his memory forgotten, like those of Akhenaten or the Confederate soldiers. Either way, at least twice the decision was made to restore his likeness, once by physically reuniting the recovered stone fragments and a second time digitally after the previously restored object was destroyed by those believing it to be a heretic idol (Thompson 2018). The fragments of the statues of Confederate soldiers

The image of king Uthal, the merciful, noble-minded servant of God, blessed by God.

Figure 18.3. Two statues of King Uthal of Hatra. On the left is a reconstructed life-size stone statue found in 1951 in the Temple of Baalshamin. On the right is a printed plastic model, with embedded electronic components, of the ancient and twice-destroyed stone statue. *Adapted by the author from Fukai 1960:142, Plate 2, and Thompson 2018:49, Figure 3.*

destroyed by those convinced that they represented an objectionable philosophy were instead removed from their original locations and stored away from public access or view. Scientific and scholarly enterprises should obviously not be without reflection on humanistic values and ethical norms, but it is difficult for archaeologists to comment on matters concerning such mutilation or restoration of objects. We study objects as they come down to us through time, with all the marks and scars that history bestowed upon them. Much relevant information is actually in such blemishes, rather than on surfaces that are unscathed and pristine.

The issue becomes even more complex if it remains unclear what should be considered the original, pristine state of an object. The Buddhas of Bamiyan, for instance, were statues of Buddha carved around 510–550 CE into a sandstone cliff in the Bamiyan Valley, in modern Central Afghanistan. The two largest statues, 35 and 50 m tall, were cut out of the living rock, with details modeled in mud mixed with straw, in places supported by wooden frames, and subsequently coated with stucco and painted. The statues and surrounding monuments were part of a trail of Buddhist monasteries along the Silk Road, connecting markets and societies in China with those in India and Europe (Higuchi and Barnes 1995). They functioned as an active religious site until the arrival of Islam in the seventh century CE. Apart from neglect, the statues also suffered active attempts at destruction, fueled by the Islamic prohibition of religious imagery. Significant damage was inflicted by the Mughal emperor Muhi-ud-Din Muhammad in the seventeenth century, by the Persian king Nader Shah Afshar in the eighteenth century, and by the emir of Afghanistan Abdel-Rahman Khan in the nineteenth century. The statues were finally destroyed in March 2001 by the Taliban government of Afghanistan on orders from the mullah Mohammed Omar.

Given that the damage inflicted forms an integral part of the history of the statues and is in line with the current religious beliefs in the region, rather than those of more than 1,000 years ago, the question whether or not the Buddhas of Bamiyan should be restored does not invoke a straightforward answer. If ultimately the choice is made to do so, it remains to be decided which stage in the history of the objects is to be aimed for. If this is the stage just before their final destruction, restoration will necessarily have to include replicating the damage done by time and previous attacks. Alternatively, the decision could be to restore the statues to look as they appeared after just being completed. However, this would deny them their history and raise the question of why not to paint and dress most other ancient stone statues, including the Elgin or Parthenon Marbles. This would go against all modern aesthetic sentiments and most certainly raise considerable resistance. It could also be decided to reconstruct the cliff face to appear as it did before those adhering to the Buddhist faith carved their religious imagery into a sandstone cliff that had been standing for several hundred thousand years. At the time the statues were constructed, objections were likely raised by NIMBYs, those with different religious convictions, or environmentalists *avant la lettre*.

Every decision to create, modify, decommission, restore, or destroy any object is necessarily consciously or subconsciously based upon more or less ephemeral opinions, religious beliefs, or political convictions and at the same time influences those who deliberate their choices and actions. The actual choices made and actions taken are what archaeologists ultimately study and reflect upon. This places us in a difficult position to partake in the discussions leading up to them. One option to approach this quandary is to create digital, virtual reality reconstructions of objects and sites (Denker 2017), allowing users to travel through space and time to appreciate their various iterations. This at the same time renders the actual state of preservation and physical location of an object irrelevant. Obviously, these issues are of importance and must be resolved by custodians of the objects, but archaeologists should probably recuse themselves from this discussion. Throughout this section, statues have featured prominently, as they are among the most evocative examples of anthropogenic objects, but the same issues concern all objects, as they all become intertwined with humans and endowed with meaning, as briefly discussed above.

These issues were eloquently summarized by Willem-Alexander, king of the Netherlands, in a recorded speech explaining why the newly restored Golden Coach would remain retired for the foreseeable future.[1] Between 1903 and 2015 this coach was used during the yearly opening of the parliamentary session. Its side panels were painted by Nicolaas van der Waay (1855–1936), the one on the left showing tribute being brought from the Dutch colonies at the time. The king stated:

> Our history contains much to be proud of. At the same time, it also offers learning material for recognizing mistakes and avoiding them in the future. We cannot rewrite the past. We can try to come to terms with it together. This also applies to the colonial past. There is no point in condemning and disqualifying what has happened through the lens of our time. Simply banning historical objects and symbols is certainly not a solution either. Instead, it takes a concerted effort that goes deeper and lasts longer. An effort that unites us rather than divides us. . . . Listening to and understanding each other are essential conditions for achieving reconciliation and taking away pain in people's souls. I know that we can do it, even if it is a long and difficult road.

Two types of objects associated with additional issues are human remains and texts, which until very recently had an element of materiality, as they were inscribed onto supports such as bone, metal (coins), paper, papyrus, parchment (vellum), plaster, pottery (ostraca), or stone. Human remains should be considered subjects rather than objects (Fletcher et al. 2014; Hahn and Weis 2013; Kilmister 2003) and are thus excluded from this discussion (Brubaker and Cooper 2000; Fowler 2004; Jones 2005; Kim and Steadman 2014; Rakita et al. 2005). The problematic nature of ancient textual information written on or inscribed into ancient objects is generally recognized (Barnard 2013; Bietak 1979; Cooper and Barnard 2017; Lewis 1998; Lightfoot 1995; Papadopoulos 1999; Rosen 2006; Van de Velde 1992; Vermeule 1996; Wendrich et al. 2006; Wobst 1978). The issues can be summarized by the observation that until recently, texts were almost exclusively written by and for a small literate elite. Our written historical sources inevitably reflect their priorities, views, and interpretations of events, as well as their implicit prejudices and biases, especially because usually no efforts were made to avoid opinions and aim for objectivity; rather efforts were made to reinforce specific opinions or even introduce them in accepted history. Furthermore, even as literacy now includes a much larger section of humanity, our inclination to take written information at face value remains almost irresistible. A further discussion of these two specific classes of objects is well beyond the scope of this chapter.

The Role of Museums

Museums are institutions that store, preserve, restore, study, and display objects of cultural, historic, artistic, or scientific significance. There are many types of museums, but the primary function of all of them is to preserve memories and create narratives. These can be directly associated with the objects, or objects can be used as illustration or sources of inspiration for them. Some museums focus on a single event, a single person, or a specific class of objects. Other focus on the long-term history of a region, a people, a natural phenomenon, or a selected human enterprise. Not all museums have or claim to have ownership of the objects in their care. Some are less concerned with the objects themselves and more concerned with their functions or meanings. Among the results of their activities is that museums purposefully or reluctantly create a sense of community and engrain existing narratives.

The original museum (House of the Muses) was founded around 280 BCE by Ptolemy I (Soter) and Ptolemy II (Philadelphus) in Alexandria, Egypt. It comprised the famous Library of Alexandria, lecture and banquet halls, living quarters for scholars, and gardens. This institution was thus more like a university than a museum. Collections of natural and cultural objects, however, had been compiled and displayed for personal or public enjoyment and education centuries earlier (Fowler 2003). As early as the sixth century BCE, Princess Ennigaldi-Nanna, a daughter of the Babylonian king Nabonidus, is said to have maintained a small museum in Ur, complete with clay labels for the objects on display (Gartner 2016:15). Even earlier and firmer evidence is the fossil of an Eocene sea urchin found between 1903 and 1906 in the Temple of Heliopolis (Cairo, Egypt). This object was inscribed with the text "Found to the south of *Ik* [an unidentified place near Gebel Ahmar, about 100 km south of Heliopolis] by the god's father [a priestly title] *Tjanefer*" (Karlshausen and De Putter 2017). It was likely collected during the Ramesside period (ca. 1550–1350 BCE) and was probably on display in the temple as a rare and remarkable object (Figure 18.4). Today, around 3,500 years later, it serves the same function in the Museo Egizio, more than 2,500 km. away. Greek and Roman temples likewise often contained exotic curiosities, which were usually retained when these temples were converted into Christian churches. That was the case with at least six ancient Egyptian obelisks in Rome. And in early medieval cities like Baghdad and Cairo, scientific instruments and manuscripts accumulated, often as tribute or part of the spoils of war.

Found to the south of Ik by the god's father Tjanefer.

Figure 18.4. Inscribed fossil of a mid-Eocene sea urchin *(Echinolampas africanus),* likely collected and inscribed during the Ramesside period (ca. 1550–1350 BCE) and found at the beginning of the twentieth century in the Temple of Heliopolis (Cairo). Museo Egizio S. 2761. *Adapted by the author from Karlshausen and De Putter 2017.*

The forceful or otherwise ethically questionable appropriation of objects of significant intrinsic, aesthetic, or cultural value is attested throughout human history. The Hebrew Bible refers to several such events. An example from 1 Kings 14:25–26: "And it came to pass in the fifth year of king Rehoboam, that Shishak, king of Egypt [likely Shoshenq I, ca. 940–925 BCE], came up against Jerusalem. And he took away the treasures of the house of the Lord, and the treasures of the king's house; he even took away all: and he took away all the shields of gold which Solomon had made" (King James Version). This is repeated almost verbatim in 2 Chronicles 12:9. The Arch of Titus, erected near the Roman Forum in the first century CE by Emperor Domitian, depicts a similar event: the transportation of valuable objects from Jerusalem to Rome in 70 CE by the victorious troops of Titus, the brother of Domitian. One of the objects depicted is the menorah—a large, golden, seven-branched candelabrum—from the Jewish Second Temple.

According to Josephus (*The Jewish War* 7.158–62), the menorah was among the objects shown to the public during the triumphal procession along the Appian Way and through Rome, after which it was put on display in the Temple of Peace. Centuries later, Procopius (*History of the Wars* IV; ix:5–9) seems to tells us that the menorah was carried through the streets of Constantinople in 533 CE, during the triumphal procession of General Belisarius after his successful campaign against Carthage, and was ultimately returned to Jerusalem, albeit to the Christian rather than the Jewish community there. If this interpretation of the account of Procopius is correct, it is most likely that the menorah was taken from the Temple of Peace when Rome was sacked by the Vandals in 455 CE and brought to their capital, Carthage. The fact that the object was not melted down by its successive owners indicates that it was taken from Jerusalem to Rome, Carthage, and Constantinople for its meaning rather than for the value of the gold from which it was made.

In 1204 Constantinople, the capital of the Byzantine Empire, was in turn plundered and heavily damaged during the Fourth Crusade. The decision of Christian crusaders to attack what was at the time the most important Christian city in the world is remarkable and immediately created controversy. Many ancient and early medieval works of art as well as important relics were taken to Italy, including bronze horses from the Hippodrome that are now in the Basilica of Saint Mark in Venice. In 1797 Napoleon had these bronze horses moved from Venice to Paris, from whence they were returned in 1815. In 1453 the rising Ottoman Sultanate conquered Constantinople, the city previously known as Byzantium and afterward increasingly referred to as Istanbul. Six years later, its conqueror, Sultan Mehmed II, started construction of a new palace, now known as Topkapi Palace but originally called Yeni Saray (New Palace). One of the buildings of the palace complex is the Conqueror's Kiosk, designated to house the imperial treasury. Over time this treasury expanded into a vast collection of jewelry, works of art, and other objects, many of which were taken from newly conquered parts of the expanding Ottoman Empire. After the collapse of the empire in 1923, the palace was transformed into a public museum, of which the treasury in the Conqueror's Kiosk is one of the main attractions.

Modern museums, whimsically and not entirely accurately named after the Ptolemaic institution in Classical Alexandria, grew out of *Wunderkammern* and cabinets of curiosities established by the increasingly wealthy aristocrats and merchants of sixteenth and seventeenth century Europe. These exhibits comprised large collections of ancient, archaeological, biological, ethnographic, geological, historic, paleontological, precious, and religious objects, as well as works of art and often lavishly illustrated books (Genoways and Andrei 2016 [2006]; Impey and MacGregor 2018 [1985]). Apart from the human craving to surround oneself with objects and show these off to one's peers, collecting at the time was partly inspired by the discovery of the antiquity of both the natural world and humanity at, for instance, Pompeii, Stonehenge, Industria (a first to fourth century Roman site near Monteu da Po in northern Italy), and later Egypt, following the campaign of Napoleon (1799–1801) and the subsequent publication of *Description de l'Égypte* (1809–1822). The collections provided social status for their owners and served as relatively safe investments. The European practice was quickly replicated in North America and was greatly stimulated by a growing scientific curiosity and the colonial enterprise, which provided access to a plethora of rich, exotic, and fascinating sources. Similar developments took place in other parts of the world (Schnapp 1996 [1993]), probably best documented in China (Falkenhausen 2013, 2015), and can currently be seen in oil-rich Gulf states, several of which house expanding collections of precious objects in impressive buildings such as the Louvre Abu Dhabi and the Museum of Islamic Art in Doha. During the nineteenth century, European museums developed into institutions serving national interests. They celebrated the nation-state, justified its colonial projects, and maintained a narrative of cultural and ethnic superiority (Carbonell 2012).

Elias Ashmole (1617–1692) was an English medical doctor, politician, scholar, and founding fellow of the Royal

Society. During his life he collected numerous natural and cultural artifacts, as well as a large library with volumes on alchemy, astrology, astronomy, botany, history, law, and numismatics. Around 1662 Ashmole acquired the objects and library collected by John Tradescant and his son, also named John, that had been on public display in a complex called The Ark in southern London. Although this transaction was disputed in court, Ashmole donated the collection, together with most of his own, to the University of Oxford on the condition that it would be made available to the public in a suitable, newly constructed building (Swann 2001). The resulting Ashmolean Museum opened in 1683 and is often considered to be the first modern museum.

Similar institutions were subsequently founded all over Europe and later in the United States. Teylers Museum, for instance, opened in 1784 in the city of Haarlem, the Netherlands. Pieter Teyler van der Hulst (1702–1778) was a cloth merchant and banker of Scottish descent living in Haarlem and a collector of art, books, and curiosities. In his last will, he bequeathed his collection and most of his fortune to the city of Haarlem to create a foundation comprising two societies: one to study religion and a second to promote drawing, history, numismatics, physics, and poetry. The executors of the will decided to construct a center for study and education that would house Teyler's library and artifacts, serve as a meeting place for scholars, and allow the general public to peruse the collection for education and enjoyment (MacGregor 2008).

James Smithson (Jacques-Louis Macie; 1765–1829) was an English chemist and mineralogist, born in France as the illegitimate child of Hugh Percy (Hugh Smithson, duke of Northumberland) and Elizabeth Hungerford Keate Macie. During his life he traveled extensively throughout Europe and published numerous articles through the Royal Society. He did not marry or have children and later in life inherited half his mother's fortune, with the remainder going to his half brother. In his last will, Smithson left his fortune to the son of his half brother, on the condition that he would change his name from Henry James Dickenson into Henry James Hungerford. He furthermore stipulated that "in the case of the death of my said nephew without leaving a child or children . . . I then bequeath the whole of my property . . . to the United States of America, to found at Washington, under the name of the Smithsonian Institution, an establishment for the increase and diffusion of knowledge among men." When Hungerford died in 1835, unmarried and without children, Smithson posthumously became the patron of the Smithsonian Institution, even though he was not a collector of artifacts and had never visited Washington, DC, or the United States (Ewing 2007). In 1904 Alexander Graham Bell, at the time a regent of the Smithsonian Institution, traveled to the cemetery of Sampierdarena, near Genoa, Italy, to oversee exhumation of the remains of Smithson and their transport to Washington. They now rest in a mortuary chapel within the Smithsonian Institution.

Collecting and museums thus have a checkered background, yet there are growing numbers of frequently visited and well-respected museums in almost every country in the world. There is obviously a deep human desire to surround oneself with attractive and interesting objects, a desire that escalates with increasing wealth and especially increasing power. There is also an element of inertia: owners are reluctant to give up their property; objects can be difficult to move, for a variety of reasons; and those vying for ownership may be reluctant or unable to enforce their claims or may disagree on a course of action. Furthermore, modern museums are not dominated by private individuals but have moved into the realm of the general public to become institutions of research and education, while the sense of community and the narratives they create are still widely appreciated. Next to the nationalist forces that celebrated the state and its colonial projects, nascent museums were also strongly influenced by Renaissance curiosity—severing the reliance on ancient written sources and instead stimulating personal observations and experiments—and the humanism of the Enlightenment, propagating education and the spread of knowledge to improve the life and fate of all humans. This made them not just into symbols of colonialism but also prominent features in the development of the modern natural sciences—including anthropology, archaeology, biology, ethnography, geology, paleontology, and taxonomy—and indirectly also the Industrial Revolution.

The Smithsonian Institution developed into one of the largest, wealthiest, and most visited museum complexes in the world, while the museums founded by Elias Ashmole and Pieter Teyler also thrived, as did many similar institutions. As individuals, Ashmole, Teyler, and Smithson were obviously not free from vanity, collector's fever, and the desire to improve their social status. They may well have subscribed to ideas of the aptness of colonialism and European cultural and ethnic superiority, which were widespread in their days. They appear, however, primarily driven by humanistic ideals of enlightening humanity by education and the spread of knowledge. Their ideas may have been hijacked by ignoble forces, but ultimately the worthy elements of their legacies seem to have prevailed (Anderson 2012; Carbonell 2012; Genoways 2006). This is another pertinent factor contributing to the worldwide success of modern museums. The sometimes-heard opinion that museums are objectionable colonial institutions is thus not entirely without merit but at the same time is a gross oversimplification of a more complex reality.

The fact that the forceful collecting of objects and the ensuing appropriation of the seized material culture occurred throughout time and territories does in no way justify them but does make clear that the European Enlightenment cannot solely be held responsible for these phenomena. Obviously, the effects of the Enlightenment facilitated the ongoing Columbian exchange (1500–1700) and transatlantic slave trade (1502–1859) and laid the groundwork for the Holocaust (1941–1945) and the atomic bombs that destroyed Hiroshima (August 6, 1945) and Nagasaki (August 9, 1945), among many other deplorable events, resulting in the irretrievable loss of non-European languages, cultures, and knowledge. On the other hand, it gave rise to contemporary science and technology, including industrial production techniques for food and increasingly complex objects, expedient transportation, and modern medicine, education, and communication technology.

Jean-Jacques Rousseau (1712–1778), one of the main actors within the Enlightenment, wrote in his *Du contrat social; ou Principes du droit politique* (1762), "Man is born free, yet everywhere he is in chains," while the U.S. Declaration of Independence (1776) states, "We hold these truths to be self-evident, that all men are created equal, that they are endowed by their creator with certain unalienable rights, that among these are life, liberty and the pursuit of happiness." It is noteworthy that for many who did not grow up with the values of the Enlightenment, through heritage or colonialism, these truths may appear counterintuitive rather than self-evident (Henrich 2020:398–407). In December 1839, Pope Gregory XVI issued papal bull *In supremo apostolates*, in which the Roman Catholic Church resolutely denounces slavery and the slave trade—a position visualized in the powerful and initially controversial painting *Slavers Throwing Overboard the Dead and Dying—Typhoon Coming On* (1840) by J. M. William Turner (1775–1851), now on display in the Museum of Fine Arts in Boston.

The effects of the exclusion of women and non-European peoples, cultures, and knowledge were most acutely felt and opposed in the sciences. In 1903 Marie Skłodowska Curie (1867–1934) was the first woman to be awarded a Nobel Prize. She subsequently became one of only four scholars to receive two Nobel Prizes and the only person to be awarded prizes in different sciences (physics in 1903 and chemistry in 1911). In 1913 Rabindranath Tagore (1861–1941) was the first laureate of non-European decent when he was awarded the Nobel Prize in Literature, while in 1930 Chandrashekhara Venkata Raman (1888–1970) was the first laureate of non-European descent in the sciences when he received the Nobel Prize in Physics. Martin Luther King (1929–1968), Nobel Peace Prize laureate in 1964, eloquently summarized the importance of equality in his "Letter from Birmingham Jail" of April 16, 1963—"We are caught in an inescapable network of mutuality, tied in a single garment of destiny. Whatever affects one directly, affects all indirectly"—as well as in his speech on the steps of the Lincoln Memorial during the March on Washington for Jobs and Freedom (August 28, 1963): "I have a dream that my four little children will one day live in a nation where they will not be judged by the color of their skin, but by the content of their character." The above examples may serve to show that the Enlightenment as a philosophical movement inherently opposes the exclusion of people and ideas—an opposition that undeniably until recently was not voiced sufficiently persuasively, partly to protect real or imagined economic interests.

The Archaeological Perspective

From an archaeological point of view, the gathering of information is generally considered of far greater importance than the objects themselves. As I remarked at the beginning, archaeology is not about finding things but about finding things out. In contrast with the common and understandable emphasis on objects of value and splendor, relatively simple and plain objects, such as potsherds and charred seeds, often have a greater impact on archaeological research than hoards of gold or unique artistic masterpieces. Sometimes objects need to be damaged or even destroyed to extract the maximum of information, obviously after all data that can reasonably be gathered from the intact object has been obtained and recorded. Examples range from the preparation of fresh breaks or microscopic slides of pottery or wood to establish the source of the raw materials to the extraction of organic molecules for chemical analysis to establish the age, use, or composition of an object.

By placing too much emphasis on objects rather than on the information they may convey, archaeologists may appear to be in competition with treasure hunters, looters, legal or illegal antiquities dealers, private collectors, and museums. It may be difficult for archaeologists to disregard completely the attraction of objects of great beauty, significance, or value, but it is essential for them to keep reminding the general public, and at times also themselves, that they are more interested in data than in the objects that contain them. In this context it is important to remember that the antiquities trade is not driven by poor farmers who need extra income to feed their starving children but is instead run by well-organized criminal organizations using the same networks as dealers in illegal drugs and arms. Archaeologists regularly get threatened, harmed, and even killed in the struggle over the ownership of archaeological items, while eminent as well as less important sites get looted and destroyed on an almost daily basis. The primary fuel for such violence and destruction is ultimately provided by those willing and able to pay significant sums of money for ancient artifacts. Only by strictly concentrating on archaeological data rather than more or less valuable objects can the archaeological community hammer home its message against collector's fever. This message is concisely and comprehensively summarized in a campfire song attributed to British archaeologist James L. Starkey (1895–1938):

> Not for the greed of gold,
> Not for the hope of fame,
> Nor for a lasting heritage,
> Not for a far-flung name.
> Rather for making history,
> And for some lore of old.
> This is our aim and object,
> Not for the greed of gold.[2]

The Value of Negative Data

In this final section I provide a response to the question formulated at the very beginning, hoping that after the above, my choice will appear genuine and not pedantic or counterintuitive. Almost all analysis of archaeological materials aims to add to the already known properties of an object—such as its context, purpose, form, and style—rather than provide a single data point. At times, however, little to no relevant data can be extracted from an object or a sample thereof. This can be disappointing and frustrating for the researcher, but from the perspective of research, this can be as important as the accurate and definitive identification of an informative compound.

There is reluctance among researchers and editors to publish unsatisfactory outcomes and negative data, leading to a bias toward positive results in the scholarly record (Easterbrook et al. 1991; Matosin et al. 2014; *Nature* 2017; Schooler 2011), although prime exceptions exist (O'Hare 2011), such as the blank page published by Dennis Upper (1974) in the *Journal of Applied Behavior Analysis*. Despite rare examples, it is desirable that the publication of failures and negative results becomes customary and accepted within the scientific literature, especially in articles focusing on archaeological research. The publication of research that failed or otherwise did not lead to positive results will prevent other researchers going down the same avenue and instead allow them to spend their time, funding, and energy exploring techniques and methods that at first sight may appear less promising. It will furthermore provide a more accurate reflection of academic research and provide scholars with academic credit related to their efforts rather than the luck of conspicuous findings, given the fact that the collection of negative data often takes almost equal amounts of time, effort, and funding compared to research considered fruitful.

Sometimes an overzealous care for objects can be the source of negative data. Many museums and collectors deny sincere researchers access to the materials in their possession. This can especially form a barrier for junior scholars and anyone suggesting to subject objects to experimental, invasive, or destructive analysis. Some reluctance is certainly warranted, but too much has a serious impact on scholarship, as it considerably limits the development of new interpretations and insights. Instead, it results in the control and perseverance of existing narratives. One example of such protectionism is the registration of the Nebra Sky Disk as a trademark by the German state Saxony-Anhalt. The Nebra Sky Disk is an ancient bronze disk with attached pieces of gold that are generally interpreted to represent the sun (or a full moon), a crescent moon, a cluster of stars, and three more enigmatic objects. The disk was found by treasure hunters in 1999 in the Ziegelroda Forest, west of Leipzig, Germany, and appeared to be associated with the Bronze Age Únětice culture, dating to around 1600 BCE. In 2013 it was included in the UNESCO Memory of the World Register as one of the most important archaeological finds of the twentieth century. Despite the facts that the disk is around 3,600 years old and is considered world heritage, the state of Saxony-Anhalt succeeded in two court cases, through which it ensured its copyright over all images of the disk, thus preventing anyone in the scholarly community from using them. This may be a particularly glaring case of obstruction, but many individuals and institutions jealously safeguard their objects and associated narratives in a surprisingly similar fashion.

Now I can finally formulate an answer to the question about what I consider my favorite or most important find. What I would like to show here is not an image of a beautiful, unique, or otherwise remarkable object, and not even an image of an object at all, but rather the total-ion-current chromatogram of organic residues extracted from the ceramic matrix of a fragment of an ancient Greek unpainted angular kylix (Figure 18.5). To obtain this image, the potsherd had to be ground into a fine powder, after its relevant properties had been appropriately recorded and studied. The organic residues attached to the ceramic matrix were

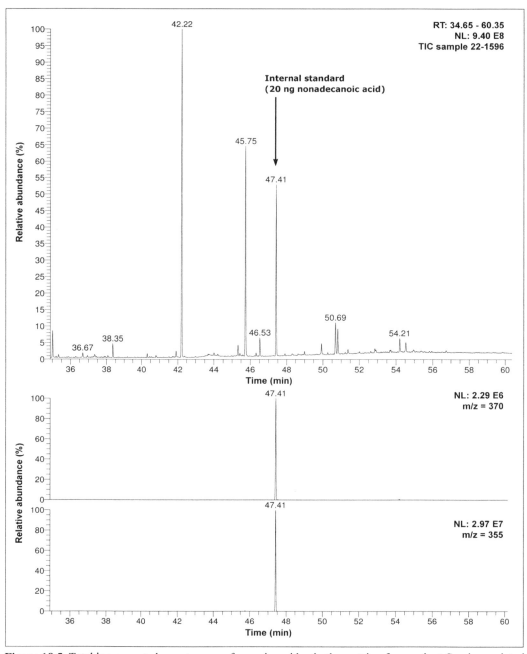

Figure 18.5. Total ion current chromatogram of organic residue in the matrix of an ancient Greek unpainted angular kylix. The two traces at the bottom, of fragments with masses of 370 and 355 Da, respectively, verify the presence of nonadeconoic acid in the sample, to which it was added as an internal standard.
Created by the author.

then dissolved into a mixture of chloroform and methanol. The resulting solution was subsequently chemically treated to increase the thermostability of its component organic molecules, which were finally analyzed by mass spectrometry following gas chromatography. This is a well-established method in archaeological research to analyze organic residue preserved in an ancient vessel and to comment on its former contents or use (Barnard et al. 2007; Eerkens 2005; Evershed 2008; Nigra et al. 2015).

At first glance, this chromatogram appears informative. Closer inspection reveals that the peak occurring 42.22 minutes after injection of the sample represents hexadecanoic (palmitic) acid, the peak at 45.75 minutes octadecanoic (stearic) acid, and the peak at 47.41 minutes

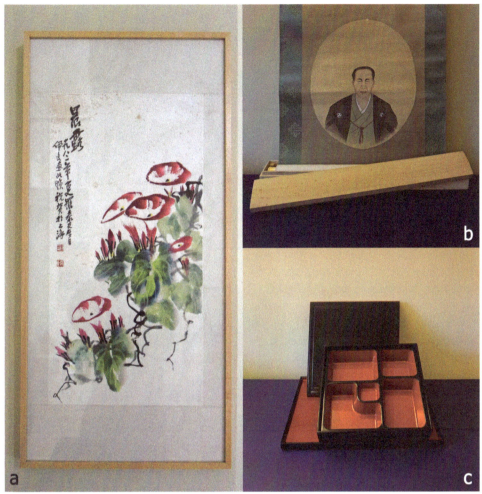

Figure 18.6. Three gifts from Lothar to the author: a: 金佩良 (Jin Peiliang), painting of flowers flanked by Chinese calligraphy (watercolor and ink on paper in a wood and glass frame, 47 × 96 cm), presented as a housewarming gift (September 2015); b: scroll with portrait of an unidentified man, possibly a poet (printed on textile and paper, in a wooden box, 55 × 191 cm), presented on the occasion of Lothar's sixtieth birthday (June 2019); c: bento box (red and black plastic with imitation wood texture, 28 × 37 × 8 cm), presented on the occasion of the author's sixtieth birthday (November 2019). *Photos by the author.*

nonadecanoic acid. These are long-chain, saturated fatty acids containing 16, 18, and 19 carbon atoms, respectively. With the latter, nonadecanoic acid, 20 ng was added to the sample to serve as an internal standard, check the sample preparation and analysis procedures, and quantify the final results. The small amount that may have been present in the ancient residue in the vessel—odd-numbered fatty acids are relatively rare in nature—will have been masked by this added amount. Palmitic and stearic acid are very common fatty acids, which are not specific to their sources and are frequently found to be modern contaminants in ancient samples. This chromatogram therefore shows only the internal standard, added to the sample and indicating that its analysis was successful, and two fatty acids that are either uninformative or modern contaminants. Most likely, the unpainted angular kylix from which the sherd originated did not preserve any organic residues. This may be due to the former contents of the vessel not being of a sufficient organic nature but rather water or some other material low in organic matter, or to taphonomic processes after the vessel was discarded, most likely microbiological organisms digesting any organic remains.

We can now add to the properties of the excavated sherd that the kylix from which it originated probably did not preserve an organic residue, either because it never contained organic materials or because the residue was lost over time. In combination with additional information from other potsherds as well as from the site and its wider context, inferences can now be made about, for instance, the local preservation conditions and the viability of research into organic materials in these circumstances. If other potsherds from similar contexts appear to preserve organic residues, it may be warranted to conclude that the kylix was used for materials low in organic matter, such as water or wine. For such reasoning, it is vital that information is not examined in isolation but rather investigated in a holistic fashion and confronted with as much other properties of the materials as possible (Barnard et al. 2007; Nigra et al. 2015).

The image is presented here as my favorite as it adequately illustrates the main points of my argument above. Once archaeological objects have yielded the information that can reasonably be expected from them, they can be removed from the archaeological realm in the narrow sense of that term, for instance into a museum or a storeroom, or be reburied or destroyed, as was the potsherd yielding the data presented above. Furthermore, certainly within archaeological research, data should be investigated in a holistic fashion, including negative data and even failed research projects. Finally, by emphasizing our search for knowledge and demeaning our appreciation for objects, we can contribute to the preservation of archaeological sites and objects generally deemed worthy of protection.

Coda

The significance of objects and ownership was nicely illustrated by Lothar when he, contrary to Western conventions, handed out presents at the conclusion of the formal dinner celebrating his completion of five cycles of the 12-year East Asian zodiac (Flad et al. 2019). From the large number of books and objets d'art that he had collected over the course of these 60 years, he had selected those whose biographies he thought would be enriched by transferring ownership from himself to one of his guests. For each guest, the received present was obviously imbued with meaning by this procedure and will provide a powerful aide-mémoire toward its donor as well as the event (Barnard, in press). I gratefully and impassionedly added my present to the other objects I had gotten from Lothar (Figure 18.6). May we both live to be 120.

Acknowledgments

I would like to express my sincere thanks to Caroline Arbuckle MacLeod and our students at the Institute for Field Research field school Museology and Egyptian Material Culture in Museo Egizio, Turin (Italy), for their inspiring discussions, and I thank Vanessa Muros for her comments on a previous version of the text. Special thanks are due to Peter Biehl, Ran Boytner, Kym Faull, Efrain Kristal, and Steve Rosen for their support and to Willeke Wendrich for her unwavering encouragement.

Notes

1. "Dutch King: Golden Coach Remains in Coach House Due to Colonial Past," Royal TV, January 13, 2022, https://www.youtube.com/watch?v=W9vWfWS9RPc. Text and translation from the original Dutch by the Royal House of Orange-Nassau.
2. Ros Henry, "James Leslie Starkey," Palestine Exploration Fund, 2022, https://www.pef.org.uk/about/history/james-leslie-starkey.

References

Anderson, Gail, ed.
2012 *Reinventing the Museum: The Evolving Conversation on the Paradigm Shift.* 2nd ed. Plymouth, UK: AltaMira Press.

Barnard, Hans
2012 The Curse of Courtesy. *Backdirt: Annual Review of the Cotsen Institute of Archaeology* 2012:148–50.
2013 The Hinterland of Qasr Ibrim. In *Qasr Ibrim, between Egypt and Africa: Studies in Cultural Exchange: NINO Symposium, Leiden, 11–12 December 2009*, edited by Jacques van der Vliet, Joost L. Hagen, Carolien van Zoest, and Leo E. van de Peut, pp. 83–103. Egyptologische Uitgaven 26. Leiden: Nederlands Instituut voor het Nabije Oosten and Peeters.
In press A Second Exercise in Autovocality: The Archaeology of My Living. In *Archaeology Outside the Box*, edited by Hans Barnard. Los Angeles: Cotsen Institute of Archaeology Press.

Barnard, Hans, Stanley H. Ambrose, Dana E. Beehr, Marcus F. Forster, Rheta E. Lanehart, Mary E. Malainey, Robert E. Parr, Micala Rider, Caroline Solazzo, and Robert M. Yohe II
2007 Mixed Results of Seven Methods for Organic Residue Analysis Applied to One Vessel with the Residue of a Known Foodstuff. *Journal of Archaeological Science* 34:28–37.

Barnard, Hans, Willeke Z. Wendrich, Alexandra Winkels, Jolanda E. M. F. Bos, Bethany L. Simpson, and René T. J. Cappers
2016 The Preservation of Exposed Mudbrick Architecture in Karanis (Kom Aushim), Egypt. *Journal of Field Archaeology* 41:84–100.

Bateson, Gregory
2000 [1972] *Steps to an Ecology of Mind: Collected Essays in Anthropology, Psychiatry, Evolution, and Epistemology.* Foreword by Mary C. Bateson. Chicago: University of Chicago Press.

Beetham, Sarah
2016 From Spray Cans to Minivans: Contesting the Legacy of Confederate Soldier Monuments in the Era of "Black Lives Matter." *Public Art Dialogue* 6(1):9–33.

Bennett, Jane
2010 *Vibrant Matter: A Political Ecology of Things.* Durham, NC: Duke University Press.

Bietak, Manfred
1979 Review Article: The Present State of Egyptian Archaeology. *Journal of Egyptian Archaeology* 65:156–60.

Brubaker, Rogers, and Frederick Cooper
2000 Beyond "'Identity." *Theory and Society* 29:1–47.

Carbonell, Bettina M., ed.
2012 *Museum Studies: An Anthology of Contexts.* 2nd ed. Chichester: John Wiley and Sons.

Clark, Andy, and David Chalmers
1998 The Extended Mind. *Analysis* 58(1):7–19.

Cooper, Julien, and Hans Barnard
2017 New Insights on the Inscription on a Painted Pan-Grave Bucranium, Grave 3252 at Cemetery 3100/3200, Mostagedda (Middle Egypt). *African Archaeological Review* 34:363–76.

Crumbaugh, Justin
2011 Afterlife and Bare Life: The Valley of the Fallen as a Paradigm of Government. *Journal of Spanish Cultural Studies* 12(4):419–38.

Cuno, James
2014 The Case Against Repatriating Museum Artifacts. *Foreign Affairs* 93(6):119–29.

De Muijnck, Wim
2103 The Meaning of Lives and the Meaning of Things. *Journal of Happiness Studies: An Interdisciplinary Forum on Subjective Well-Being* 14:1291–1307.

Denker, Ahmet
2017 Palmyra as It Once Was: 3D Virtual Reconstruction and Visualization of an Irreplaceable Lost Treasure. *International Archives of the Photogrammetry, Remote Sensing and Spatial Information Sciences* 42(5/W1):565–72.

Dichter, Ernest
2002 [1960] *The Strategy of Desire.* Introduction by Arthur A. Berger. New Brunswick, NJ: Transaction Publishers.

Easterbrook, Philippa J., Ramana Gopalan, Jesse A. Berlin, and David R. Matthews
1991 Publication Bias in Clinical Research. *Lancet* 337:867–72.

Eerkens, Jelmer E.
2005 GC-MS Analysis and Fatty Acid Ratios of Archaeological Potsherds from the Western Great Basin of North America. *Archaeometry* 47:83–102.

Evershed, Richard P.
2008 Organic Residue Analysis in Archaeology: The Archaeological Biomarker Revolution. *Archaeometry* 50:895–924.

Ewing, Heather
2007 *The Lost World of James Smithson: Science, Revolution, and the Birth of the Smithsonian.* New York: Bloomsbury USA.

Falkenhausen, Lothar von
2013 Antiquarianism in East Asia: A Preliminary Overview. In *World Antiquarianism: Comparative Perspectives*, edited by Alain Schnapp, Lothar von Falkenhausen, Peter N. Miller, and Tim Murray, pp. 35–66. Los Angeles: Getty Research Institute.
2015 Antiquarianism in China and Europe: Reflections on Momigliano. In *Cross-cultural Studies: China and the World: A Festschrift in Honor of Professor Zhang Longxi*, edited by Suoqiao Qian, pp. 127–51. Leiden: Brill.
2017 The Study of East Asian Art History in Europe: Some Observations on Its Early Stages. In *Bridging Times and Spaces: Papers in Ancient Near Eastern, Mediterranean and Armenian Studies Honouring Gregory E. Areshian on the Occasion of his Sixty-fifth Birthday,* edited by Pavel S. Avetisyan and Yervand H. Grekyan, pp. 89–102. Oxford: Archaeopress.
2018 Four German Art Historians in Republican China. In *Unmasking Ideology in Imperial and Colonial Archaeology: Vocabulary, Symbols, and Legacy*, edited by Bonnie Effros and Guolong Lai, pp. 299–353. Los Angeles: Cotsen Institute of Archaeology Press.

Ferrándiz, Francisco
2019 Unburials, Generals, and Phantom Militarism: Engaging with the Spanish Civil War Legacy. *Current Anthropology* 60(S19):S62–S76.

Flad, Rowan, Anke Hein, and Bryan Miller
2019 Five Cycles of Lothar: Generations Gather to Honor the Sixtieth Birthday of Professor von Falkenhausen. *Backdirt: Annual Review of the Cotsen Institute of Archaeology* 2019:116–20.

Fletcher, Alexandra, Daniel Antoine, and J. D. Hill, eds.
2014 *Regarding the Dead: Human Remains in the British Museum.* London: British Museum.

Forest, Benjamin, and Juliet Johnson
2019 Confederate Monuments and the Problem of Forgetting. *Cultural Geographies* 26(1):127–31.

Fowler, Chris
2004 *The Archaeology of Personhood: An Anthropological Approach.* London: Routledge.

Fowler, Don D.
2003 A Natural History of Man: Reflections on Anthropology, Museums, and Science. *Fieldiana Anthropology*, n.s., 36:11–21.

Fuentes Vega, Alicia
2017 The Politics of Memory, Tourism and Dictatorship: Revisiting Franco's Valley of the Fallen. *Journal of Tourism History* 9(1):70–91.

Fukai, Shinji
1960 The Artifacts of Hatra and Parthian Art. *East and West* 11:135–81.

Gartner, Richard
2016 *Metadata.* Cham: Springer.

Gell, Alfred A. F.
1998 *Art and Agency: An Anthropological Theory.* Oxford: Clarendon Press.

Genoways, Hugh H., ed.
2006 *Museum Philosophy for the Twenty-first Century.* Lanham, MD: AltaMira Press.

Genoways, Hugh H., and Mary A. Andrei, eds.
2016 [2006] *Museum Origins: Readings in Early Museum History and Philosophy.* Rev. ed. London: Routledge.

Gosden, Chris, and Yvonne Marshall
1999 The Cultural Biography of Objects. *World Archaeology* 31(2):169–78.

Hahn, Hans Peter, and Hadas Weis, eds.
2013 *Mobility, Meaning and Transformations of Things: Shifting Contexts of Material Culture through Time and Space.* Oxford: Oxbow Books.

Henrich, Joseph
2020 *The WEIRDest People in the World: How the West Became Psychologically Peculiar and Particularly Prosperous.* New York: Farrar, Straus and Giroux.

Hepworth, Andrea
2014 Site of Memory and Dismemory: The Valley of the Fallen in Spain. *Journal of Genocide Research* 16(4):463–85.

Higuchi, Takayasu, and Gina Barnes
1995 Bamiyan: Buddhist Cave Temples in Afghanistan. *World Archaeology* 27:282–302.

Hite, Katherine
2008 The Valley of The Fallen: Tales from the Crypt. *Forum for Modern Language Studies* 44(2):110–27.

Hodder, Ian
2012 *Entangled: An Archaeology of the Relationships between Humans and Things.* Chichester: John Wiley and Sons.

Ikram, Salima
2011 Collecting and Repatriating Egypt's Past: Toward a New Nationalism. In *Contested Cultural Heritage: Religion, Nationalism, Erasure, and Exclusion in a Global World*, edited by Helaine Silverman, pp. 141–54. New York: Springer.

Impey, Oliver, and Arthur MacGregor, eds.
2018 [1985] *The Origins of Museums: The Cabinet of Curiosities in Sixteenth- and Seventeenth-Century Europe.* Rev. ed. Oxford: Ashmolean Museum.

Ingold, Tim
2007 *Lines: A Brief History.* London: Routledge.
2011 *Being Alive: Essays on Movement, Knowledge and Description.* London: Routledge.
2013 *Making: Anthropology, Archaeology, Art and Architecture.* London: Routledge.

Jones, Andrew
2005 Lives in Fragments? Personhood and the European Neolithic. *Journal of Social Archaeology* 5:193–224.

Karlshausen, Christina, and Thierry De Putter
2017 Un oursin pour le dieu: L'oursin de Tjanefer (Turin Suppl. 2761), *Rivista del Museo Egizio*, http://doi.org/10.29353/rime.2017.1068.

Kemp, Barry J.
2012 *The City of Akhenaten and Nefertiti: Amarna and Its People.* London: Thames and Hudson.

Kilmister, Hugh
2003 Visitor Perceptions of Ancient Egyptian Human Remains in Three United Kingdom Museums. *Papers from the Institute of Archaeology* 14:57–69.

Kim, Jieun, and Dawnie W. Steadman
2014 A Review of Codes of Ethics in the United States and Ethical Dilemmas Surrounding the Native American Graves Protection and Repatriation Act (NAGPRA). *Korean Journal of Physical Anthropology* 27:47–63.

Kynourgiopoulou, Vasiliki
2011 National Identity Interrupted: The Mutilation of

the Parthenon Marbles and the Greek Claim for Repatriation. In *Contested Cultural Heritage: Religion, Nationalism, Erasure, and Exclusion in a Global World*, edited by Helaine Silverman, pp. 155–70. New York: Springer.

Lewis, E. Douglas
1998 The Tyranny of the Text: Oral Tradition and the Power of Writing in Sikka and Tana "Ai, Flores." *Bijdragen tot de Taal-, Land- en Volkenkunde* 154:457–77.

Lightfoot, Kent G.
1995 Culture Contact Studies: Redefining the Relationship between Prehistoric and Historical Archaeology. *American Antiquity* 60:199–217.

MacGregor, Arthur
2008 *Curiosity and Enlightenment: Collectors and Collections from the Sixteenth to the Nineteenth Century.* New Haven, CT: Yale University Press.

Malafouris, Lambros
2013 *How Things Shape the Mind: A Theory of Material Engagement.* Cambridge, MA: MIT Press.

Matosin, Natalie, Elisabeth Frank, Martin Engel, Jeremy S. Lum, and Kelly A. Newell
2014 Negativity Towards Negative Results: A Discussion of the Disconnect between Scientific Worth and Scientific Culture. *Disease Models and Mechanisms* 7:171–73.

McCracken, Grant
1988 *Culture and Consumption: New Approaches to the Symbolic Character of Consumer Goods and Activities.* Bloomington: Indiana University Press.

Morgan, David
2018 Soldier Statues and Empty Pedestals: Public Memory in the Wake of the Confederacy. *Material Religion* 14(1):153–57.

Murphy, Bernice L., ed.
2016 *Museums, Ethics and Cultural Heritage.* Abingdon: Routledge

Nature, ed.
2017 Rewarding Negative Results Keeps Science on Track. *Nature* 551:414.

Nigra, Benjamin T., Kym F. Faull, and Hans Barnard
2015 Analytical Chemistry in Archaeological Research. *Analytical Chemistry* 87:3–18.

O'Connell, Mary Ellen, and Sara DePaul
2005 Report on the Conference Imperialism, Art and Restitution. *International Journal of Cultural Property* 12(4):487–90.

O'Hara, Bob
2011 Negative Results Are Published. *Nature* 471:448–49.

Papadopoulos, John K.
1999 Archaeology, Myth-History and the Tyranny of the Text: Chalkidike, Torone and Thucydides. *Oxford Journal of Archaeology* 18:377–94.

Rakita, Gordon F. M., Jane E. Buikstra, Lane Anderson Beck, and Sloan R. Williams, eds.
2005 *Interacting with the Death: Perspectives on Mortuary Archaeology of the New Millennium.* Gainesville: University of Florida Press.

Reeves, Nicholas
2001 *Akhenaten: Egypt's False Prophet.* London: Thames and Hudson.

Rosen, Steven A.
2006 The Tyranny of Texts: A Rebellion Against the Primacy of Written Documents in Defining Archaeological Agendas. In *"I Will Speak the Riddles of Ancient Times": Archaeological and Historical Studies in Honor of Amihai Mazar on the Occasion of His Sixtieth Birthday*, Vol. 2, edited by Aren M. Maier and Pierre de Miroschedji, pp. 879–93. Winona Lake, IN: Eisenbrauns.

Saussure, Ferdinand de
1959 [1916] *Course in General Linguistics.* Edited by Charles Bally and Albert Sechehaye in cooperation with Albert Redilinger. Translated by Wade Baskin. New York: Philosophical Library.

Schnapp, Alain
1996 [1993] *The Discovery of the Past: The Origins of Archaeology.* Translated by Ian Kinnes and Gillian Varndell. London: British Museum Press.

Schooler, Jonathan
2011 Unpublished Results Hide the Decline Effect. *Nature* 470:437.

Siefkes, Martin
2012 The Semantics of Artefacts: How We Give Meaning to the Things We Produce and Use. *Image: Zeitschrift für Interdisziplinäre Bildwissenschaft* 16:61–91.

Silverman, Helaine, ed.
2011 *Contested Cultural Heritage: Religion, Nationalism, Erasure, and Exclusion in a Global World.* New York: Springer.

Swann, Marjorie
2001 *Curiosities and Texts: The Culture of Collecting in Early Modern England.* Philadelphia: University of Pennsylvania Press.

Tallis, Raymond
2003   *The Hand: A Philosophical Inquiry into Human Being.* Edinburgh: Edinburgh University Press.

Taniguchi, Yoko
2017   Do Archaeological and Conservation Sciences Save Cultural Heritage? Cultural Identity and Reviving Values after Demolishment. In *Ancient West Asian Civilization: Geoenvironment and Society in the Pre-Islamic Middle East*, edited by Akira Tsuneki, Shigeo Yamada, and Ken-ichiro Hisada, pp. 179–97. Cham: Springer.

Thompson, Erin L.
2018   Recreating the Past in Our Own Image: Contemporary Artists' Reactions to the Digitization of Threatened Cultural Heritage Sites in the Middle East. *Future Anterior* 15(1):44–56.

Tunstall, Kate, and Katie Scott
2016   Denis Diderot, Regrets on Parting with My Old Dressing Gown. Translated by Kate Tunstall and Katie Scott. *Oxford Art Journal* 39:175–84.

Upper, Dennis
1974   The Unsuccessful Self-treatment of a Case of "Writer's Block." *Journal of Applied Behavior Analysis* 7:497.

Urry, John
2007   *Mobilities.* Cambridge: Polity Press.

Van de Velde, Piet
1992   Archaeology Is Archaeology and Philology Is Philology and Never the Twain Shall Meet? *Bulletin Antieke Beschaving* 67:183–89.

Vermeule, Emily T.
1996   Archaeology and Philology: The Dirt and the Word. *Transactions of the American Philological Association* 126:1–10.

Wendrich, Willeke Z., Roger S. Bagnall, René T. J. Cappers, James A. Harrell, Steven E. Sidebotham, and Roberta S. Tomber
2006   Berenike Crossroads: The Integration of Information. In *Excavating Asian History: Interdisciplinary Studies in Archaeology and History,* edited by Norman Yoffee and Bradley L. Crowell, pp. 15–66. Tucson: University of Arizona Press.

Winberry, John J.
2015   "Lest We Forget": The Confederate Monument and the Southern Townscape. *Southeastern Geographer* 55(1):19–31.

Wobst, H. Martin
1978   The Archaeo-ethnography of Hunter-Gatherers or the Tyranny of the Ethnographic Record in Archaeology. *American Antiquity* 43:303–9.

Woodhouse, John, and Sarah Pepin
2017   *The Parthenon Sculptures.* House of Commons Briefing Paper 02075. London: House of Commons.

Woolford, Kirk, and Stuart Dunn
2014   Micro Mobilities and Affordances of Past Places. In *Past Mobilities: Archaeological Approaches to Movement and Mobility*, edited by Jim Leary, pp. 113–28. Franham: Ashgate.

Epilogue
The Number 60 and the Beginning of Everything

Willeke Wendrich

Honoring Lothar includes remembering the many contributions he has written in honor of others (Falkenhausen 2003, 2004, 2005, 2006, 2014a, 2014b, 2017; Falkenhausen et al. 2003) and his appreciative overview of the work of colleagues in his often-cited article in *Antiquity* on the history of the field (Falkenhausen 1993). When I received the invitation to give a brief introduction to a symposium in honor of Lothar's sixtieth birthday—as director of the Cotsen Institute of Archaeology—my first reaction as an Egyptologist and archaeologist working in northeastern Africa was one of surprise. Lothar was not retiring, and one would not expect such an honor to be bestowed upon someone in the strength of his life, well before the more traditional retirement age of either 65 or 70. After all, 60 is the new 40. Then it occurred to me that the number 60 might be of Chinese, rather than German, American, or academic significance. A quick online search indeed revealed the significance of the sexagenary in China, ancient and modern. Although birthdays are usually not celebrated there, reaching the ripe old age of 60 is considered worthy of celebration not just because of demographics but especially because 60 denotes the first completion of the life cycle, fulfilling five cycles—associated with the elements metal, fire, water, earth, and wood—of 12 animal-assigned years (rat, ox, tiger, rabbit, dragon, snake, horse, sheep, monkey, rooster, dog, and pig). Life indeed begins at 60.

I further learned that Emperor Kangxi's sixtieth birthday in 1714 was a grand affair, which was recorded in a monumental work. A copy in the Library of Congress shows the various elements of the celebrations, including a long procession. From all over China, people aged 65 and older were invited to court for a banquet, and the emperor not only received magnificent presents, but he also gave gifts to his honored guests (Shen 2014). The chronicle of the events comprised 120 chapters (*juan* 卷) and 40 volumes, a massive enterprise that took three years to complete. Our contribution to honor Lothar is very modest in comparison (even though it took about the same amount of time).

Lothar fulfilled his first cycle of life and longevity, when both the elemental sign and the animal zodiac were the same as in his birth year. The emperor's sixtieth birthday was named *wanshou jie* (萬壽節, 10,000 longevity festival). Both the number 60 and the number 10,000 represent fullness. Even today, numbers carry positive or negative meanings, as outlined in a blog in the *China Daily* (Kemp 2015). These meanings are mostly based on similarities in sound between words for the numbers and lucky or unlucky terms in Cantonese—for instance, *four* 四 (*sì*) and *death* 死 (*sǐ*); *eight* 八 (*bā* or *fā*) and *prosperity* 發財 (*fācái*); *nine* 九 (*jiǔ*) and *long-lasting* 久 (*jiǔ*). Although often characterized as superstition, the belief in the power of these numbers is such that they have a detectable economic influence (Hirshleifer et al. 2016; Woo 1993).

The perceived fullness of the numbers 60 and 10,000 is derived from the multiplication of two auspicious numbers. Especially the significance of the number 9, with its association to the concept of long-lasting, drew my attention. In ancient Egypt, the number 9 occurs often in writings and art, with a meaning of completeness or fullness. Egyptian has singular and plural forms of nouns and also dual forms. In the sequence 1, 2, 3, the third number can also stand for many. Multiplying "many" by "many" results in "everything." Thus 3 × 3 results in 9 but also means completeness. Apart from 3 and 9, other numbers that are conspicuous are 2, which features widely as duality; 4 (often in relation to the four cardinal points); 8 (as a double 4 but also the penultimate: 9 − 1 = 8); and 5 (as 4 + 1). And then there is 30, which is the number of years of rule at which a king needed to prove his vitality by running a course. It was a celebration for which a complete architectural scenery was built but was also a test, and after the first such *heb-sed*, they in principle seem to have taken place every three years until the king passed away and his successor came to the throne (Martin 1984).

Ancient Egyptian written language and drawing are closely connected, because the hieroglyphic signs are also depictions of objects. Word play and sign play with numbers and the way they are represented therefore occur both in texts and in imagery. Below I outline several examples of the use of numbers in religious and political contexts. It should be remembered, however, that the meaning of dualities, trinities, and other number combinations varied through time and were context-dependent. Ancient Egyptian culture appears to change little over the thousands of years of its existence, but that is a mere illusion. An important reason for the seeming continuity is the ancient Egyptian reverence for ancestors and earlier generations. The continuing references to the past are aided by the long-lasting visual language on temple walls and well-preserved papyrus libraries. Even apparent associations and references to earlier texts and symbols were reinterpreted and fitted into the needs of the present (Wendrich 2010).

Two

Duality is the main organizing principle in ancient Egyptian thought, "a mental structuring device the Egyptians lived by, expressing, implicitly or explicitly, a vision of the world and its functioning" (Servajean 2008:4). The number 2 can represent opposites, complements, or both, and in many cases there is a parallelism of dualities that together shape the organization of the world.

The world outside of Egypt was referenced in art by very stereotypical depictions of two of its neighbors: Nubia and Southwest Asia. This combined depiction of Nubians and Southwest Asians is a duality that stands for all foreign lands, typified by the two that Egypt, in different periods throughout history, was either threatened by or sought to subdue. They are depicted in stereotypical fashion—Nubians as dark skinned with curly hair and earrings, and Southwest Asians as bearded with yellow skin—and are often paired with geographic dualities as enemies of the south and the north. They are depicted tied back to back on the soles of Pharaoh Tutankhamun's sandals (ca. 1330 BCE), to be literally trodden on with every step the king takes (Figure E.2).

Another duality is found in Egyptian funerary art, where there are many examples of double statues depicting husband and wife, especially in the royal sphere. Other double statues depict the king and a god, two gods, or, rarely, two brothers (Vasiljević 2008). The Egyptian polytheistic pantheon was also organized in pairs. Tables E.1–E.3 outline gendered dualities and south–north and positive–negative opposites. These pairs do not line up beyond the

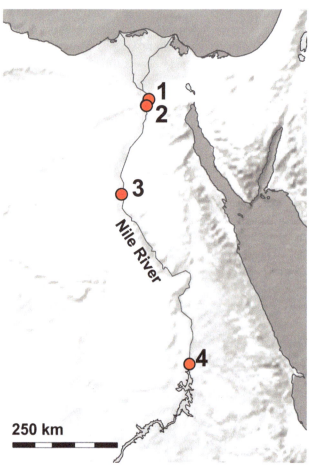

Figure E.1. Map of places mentioned in the text.
1. Heliopolis; 2. Memphis; 3. Hermopolis; 4. Elephantine.
Created by Bryan K. Miller.

Figure E.2. Leather sandals found in the tomb of Pharaoh Tutankhamun, depicting subdued prisoners from Southwest Asia and Nubia, as well as the nine bows, to be downtrodden by the king. *Photo via Art Resource.*

counterparts in a particular context. The god Seth, for instance, occurs in all three tables: as a male god opposite Nephthys, as a god of Upper Egypt opposite Horus of Lower Egypt, and as the negative counterpart of Horus of Egypt as god of the desert, storm winds, violence, and foreign lands (Velde 1967).

The gendered dualities are mostly divine beings in the creation myths of Iunu (Heliopolis) and Khemenu (Hermopolis). They form part of a group of eight or nine gods at the beginning of time. The earliest known mentions of these divine pairs can be found in oblique references in the funerary context of the Fifth Dynasty pyramids, ca. 2465–2323 BCE (Allen 2005). The divinities are mentioned as protectors of the deceased king, and references are made to a preexisting corpus of texts and a rich oral history that has not been preserved. Papyri dating around 1,300 years later (ca. 1160 BCE) provide a more cohesive narrative that may have been similar to the one the Pyramid Texts make reference to (Gardiner 1931). A caveat: we know from the rubrics on papyri, texts written with red ink that contain titles and commentary, that the priests who copied the texts felt the need to add explanations and in some cases reinterpretations of the earlier texts (Wendrich 2014). This makes it quite likely that the early oral history was not identical and may well have differed fundamentally from the later texts.

Table E.1. Examples of gendered dualities

Male	Female
Shu (air/sneeze)	Tefnut (moisture/spit)
Geb (earth)	Nut (sky)
Osiris	Isis
Seth	Nephthys
Nun (primordial water)	Naunet (female component of Nun)
Heh (infinity)	Hauhet (female component of Heh)
Kek (darkness)	Kauket (female component of Kekuy)
Amun (hidden)	Amaunet (female component of Amun)
Hathor	Horus
Khnum	Heket
Atum	Djeretef (his hand)
Male	**Male**
Seth	Horus
Ra (day)	Osiris (night, underworld)
Female	**Female**
Isis	Nephthys

Table E.2. Examples of geographic dualities

South	North
Upper Egypt (Nile valley)	Lower Egypt (Nile delta)
Nekhbet (vulture goddess)	Wadjit (cobra goddess)
Nekheb and Nekhen (Elkab and Hierakonpolis)	Pe and Dep (two hills at Tell el-Farain/Buto)
Nubet	Mesen
Seth	Horus
Lily	Papyrus
White Crown (*hedjet*)	Red Crown (*deshret*)
nesut (sedge?)	*biti* (bee)?
Nubians (enemies in the south)	Southwest Asians (enemies in the north)

Table E.3. Examples of complementary dualities

Positive	Negative
ma'at (order, justice)	*isfet* (chaos)
kemet (black land, Nile valley and delta)	*deshret* (red land, desert)
Horus	Seth
Pharaoh	foreigners and "rebels"
Egypt	foreign lands
entet (that which is)	*iutet* (that which is not)
day sky	night sky

The geographic dichotomy of Upper and Lower Egypt is in many ways a reference to narratives of the creation of Egypt rather than the world as a whole (Figure E.3). The famous predynastic Narmer Palette shows King Narmer (ca. 3000 BCE) on one side wearing a red crown, on the other a white crown (Figure E.4). Based on this depiction and the mythical "Contendings of Horus and Seth," as outlined in the Chester Beatty Papyrus, kept in the British Museum (Gardiner 1931), interpretations of state formation have long adhered to a very schematic and dualistic interpretation. A king of Upper Egypt (Seth) fought a king in Lower Egypt (Horus), who was the legitimate heir of the throne of Osiris. Seth, the strong brother of Osiris, usurped the throne. Part of the early Egyptological understanding of the myth was based on the visual language of duality that was adopted in Egypt as part of the royal canon and continually reproduced, albeit with changes in expression, context, and likely also meaning over time. Depicted often in the royal sphere, for instance on the base of the throne of Pharaoh Senusret II (ca. 1880 BCE), are the two gods tying the papyrus and the lily around the hieroglyph for "to unite." Sometimes the two stereotypical enemies of Egypt are depicted underneath their feet. The geographic duality is expressed but also solved in the action of (re)unification of the two lands under one king.

Table E.3 lists concepts that have positive and negative connotations but are not absolutely good or evil. The two sides of the balance are complementary. The totality of the cosmos is described by the opposite concepts of *entet* and *iutet*. Being only exists in relation to not being; order only exists in balance with chaos. The sun god Ra travels by day through the sky, over the world of the living, and at night through the underworld, where the dead dwell. The night sky is a dangerous place but a necessary counterpart of the day. It is the task of the king to uphold *ma'at* and dispel *isfet*, but both exist in this world. Especially the role of the god Seth is interesting and has changed over time (Velde 1967). As the red-haired god of thunder, violence, and power, he shares many aspects with the Levantine god Ba'al. He is associated with the desert but was especially venerated in the delta, the region from which the kings of the Nineteenth and Twentieth Dynasties hailed (ca. 1290–1175 BCE); many of them were named Sety or "he of Seth." It was not until the Late period (ca. 712–332 BCE) that Seth becomes the equivalent of evil, perhaps under influence of monotheistic or Zoroastrian traditions.

Figure E.3. Dichotomy of a landscape. The desert (red land) and the fertile earth (black land) stand out clearly on a satellite image, as does the distinction between Upper Egypt (the Nile valley) and Lower Egypt (the Nile delta).
Created by the author based on Google Earth. Data source: SIo, NOAA, US Navy, NGA, GEBCO. Image source: Landsat/Copernicus.

Three

In the language and writing system of ancient Egypt, there are separate forms for singular, dual, and plural, as there are in other Semitic languages. The plural is written with three strokes, which represent 3 or any larger number. The number 3 (*khemet*) therefore is considered to mean all, fullness, or completeness, in contrast with the completion or opposition of the dual. The number 3 is used to comprise all the enemies of Egypt, symbolized by the inhabitants to the west (Libya), the east (Southwest Asia), and the south (Nubia). As with the dualism of north and south, Asians and Nubians, these three population groups are depicted in a stereotypical manner, with Libyans usually being characterized by a large feathery plume in the hair. All foreigners are depicted as wearing brightly colored clothing, in contrast with the white linen garments of Egyptians.

In funerary statuary, triads usually represent a family of a wife, husband, and son. Triads in the religious sphere are found in art, temple dedications, and religious textual references and consist of combinations of three gods or goddesses, two gods or divine representations, and the divine ruler. The Old Kingdom valley temple of Pharaoh Menkaure (ca. 2490–2475 BCE) contained life-size statues of the king flanked by two of his wives and several triads of the king with the goddess Hathor and a smaller female figure crowned with a standard-mounted symbol. These triads symbolized the unity of Hathor, Horus-king, and different nomes (provinces) of Egypt (Velde 1971).

Figure E.4. The Narmer Palette (ca. 3000 BCE). One side shows King Narmer smiting an enemy while wearing the white crown. The other side shows King Narmer wearing the red crown, preceded by standard bearers.
Photographer or photographers unknown. Public domain via Wikimedia Commons, https://commons.wikimedia.org/wiki/File:Narmer_Palette.jpg.

Table E.4. Examples of triads

Male	Female	Male Child
Osiris	Isis	Horus
Amun	Mut	Khonsu
Ptah	Sakhmet	Nefertem
Montu	Rattawy	Harpre
Horus	Hathor	Harsomtus Ihi
Atum	Bastet	Horhekenu
Male	**Female**	**Female**
Khnum	Satet	Anuket
King	Isis	Nephthys
Male	**Male**	**Male**
Horus of Bak	Horus of Miam	Horus of Buhen
Amun-Ra	Ra-Harakhte	Ptah
Ra	Tatenen/Ptah	Amun
Ptah	Sokar	Osiris
Khepri	Ra	Atum

The organization of divine beings in triads is mostly an expression of completeness, such as the three forms of Horus venerated in the small temple at Abu Simbel (Table E.4). On the political border of Egypt and Nubia, these three gods of important localities in Nubia represent the complete Nubian pantheon (Desroches-Noblecourt and Kuentz 1968). The large temple at Abu Simbel, fronted by four enormous statues of Pharaoh Ramses II (ca. 1290–1224 BCE) carved out of the living rock, is dedicated to three gods (Amun-Ra, Ra-Harakhte, and Ptah) and the king himself. In the Opet temple at Karnak we see that one god, Thoth, is characterized by a triad of other gods as pars pro toto. He is "The heart of Ra, the tongue of Tatenen and the throat of the Hidden of name." The organization in threes of different divine beings or aspects has been characterized by Egyptologists as one way to explicate multiplicity, while other organizational trinities create unity from multiplicity (Hornung 1971; Velde 1971). Examples of the latter are the unification of Khepri; the sunrise in the form of a dung beetle pushing the sun over the horizon; Ra, the sun in the sky; and Atum, the sun at sunset. United in one name are Ptah-Sokar-Osiris as a divine power related to the underworld, particularly in the Memphis region.

Te Velde (1971) points out that most triads consist of male–female–male child, linked to specific temples and regions. He states that "in triads containing the binary opposition of male and female, the way from plurality to unity is obstructed." (Velde 1971:80).

Four

Where 2 and 3 have many examples, the number 4 (*fedu*) seems mostly linked to the four cardinal points and to celestial phenomena such as the four stars that surround the belt of Orion or the four stars of the Big Dipper (Ursa Major). These two sets of four stars are connected to the four sons of Horus. These are the protectors of the liver, lungs, stomach, and intestines of the deceased. During the late Eighteenth Dynasty, this was expressed by providing the four canopic jars (Figure E.5), which held the innards of the mummified deceased, with the heads of these gods in the shape of a human, a baboon, a jackal, and a falcon (Mathieu 2008). The mothers of these four sons similarly form a protective cadre around the dead. This is most clearly expressed in a physical manner in the golden shrine of Pharaoh Tutankhamun, surrounding a calcite shrine on a sledge that contains the four canopic jars. The goddesses are depicted as statues in wood on the straight edges of the golden shrine and are carved out of stone, stretching their arms protectively around the corners of the calcite canopic box. The heads of the canopic jars in this case depict the likeness of Tutankhamun four times, rather than the four sons of Horus.

The four sons of Horus protect the deceased as they protect the god Osiris, and this is reflected in the night sky. Two constellations, one in the north and one in the south, symbolize this situation. The four stars of the Big Dipper are the four sons of Horus, who surround Osiris, who is invisible in the middle. They are part of the circumpolar stars

Figure E.5. Tutankhamun's canopic chest with four canopic jars, protected by four goddesses. *Adapted by the author from a photo by Ovedc, under Creative Commons Attribution-Share Alike 4.0 International, https://upload.wikimedia.org/wikipedia/commons/e/e8/By_ovedc_-_Egyptian_Museum_%28Cairo%29_-_217.jpg.*

Table E.5. Organization in fours

Shu	Tefnut	Geb	Nut
Osiris	Isis	Seth	Nephthys
Nun	Heh	Kek	Amun
Naunet	Hauhet	Kauket	Amaunet
Imsety (human)	Hapy (baboon, ibis)	Duamutef (jackal)	Qebehsenuf (falcon)
Isis	Nephthys	Neith	Serket
South	North	East	West
liver	lungs	stomach	intestines

on the Egyptian firmament, stars that never set but instead circle above the horizon of the night sky and are therefore strong symbols of eternal life. The southern sky is where the constellation of Orion is visible in the summer, when the Nile River brings its life-giving floodwaters to Egypt. The four stars surrounding the belt of Orion are the four sons of Horus. Osiris, the god of the underworld, rebirth, rejuvenation, and growth, is represented by the three stars in the middle (Mathieu 2008).

There are also four legs of the celestial cow, the pillars of heaven. There are four protective funerary bricks enclosing the burial chamber. The number 4 is 2 × 2, a doubling of a duality featuring the same gods but in a different meaningful configuration. The large temple in Abu Simbel is dedicated to 4, in the form of a triad plus the king: Amun-Ra, Ra-Horakhte, Ptah, and Ramesses II. The fundamental organization of duality and triad, therefore, is recognizable in all other numerical organizations: 4, 5, 7, 8, and 9.

Five

The number 5 (*diju*) is a combination of 4 and 1, 3 and 2, or 1, 2, and 2—for instance, Atum as creator of Shu, Tefnut, Geb, and Nut or Horus as a child of Osiris and Isis but also their siblings Seth and Nephthys.

Seven

Similarly, 7 (*sefekhu*) is a combination of 3 and 4 or 3, 2, and 2. The two astronomical constellations mentioned above consist of four plus three stars. This is recognized, for instance in chapter 17 of the Book of the Dead, where it is written that the four children of Horus are complemented by the three gods Maaitef, Kherybaqef, and Horus-Khentyirty, placed among the circumpolar stars by Anubis to protect the tomb of Osiris (Mathieu 2008).

Eight

The number 8 (*khemen*) represents the duality of four, the group of gods that is known from its Greek translation as the Ogdoad of Hermopolis but that in Egyptian was called the *khemenyu* of Khemenu. They are primordial gods that represent water, darkness, the infinite, and the hidden one in male and female form (Table E.1). The representation of these quite abstract elements of creation is often equally abstract (Figure E.6). The main god of Hermopolis was Thoth, the god who writes and records.

Nine

When multiplicity is multiplied, when 3 is multiplied by 3, the result is completeness. The number 9 (*pesedj*) stands for everything that can be counted, for fullness. The enemies of Egypt that threaten chaos can be expressed as a duality, as a trinity, or as the nine bows (Figure E.2): nine unnamed enemies that encompass all possible threats to the Egyptian balance as maintained by the king (Wildung 1982).

The ninefold of the most important gods of Iunu is usually indicated in Greek as the Ennead. These are the gods of the well-known cosmogony of Heliopolis. Atum, the first god, creates Shu, male god of the air, and Tefnut, goddess of moisture, after which sexual reproduction is possible. They have Geb, god of the earth, and Nut, goddess of the sky. It is Shu who lifts Nut up to span over Geb. The next generation consists of four gods: Isis, Osiris, Seth, and Nephthys. These are the nine gods, but then the Ennead often comprises additional gods, such as Horus, child of Isis and Osiris. The Ennead is one, plus four twosomes. The Ogdoad is four twosomes plus one (Thoth; Brunner 1982).

Figure E.6. The Ogdoad, from the Book of the Dead of Anhai (Twentieth Dynasty, ca. 1196–1070 BCE). British Museum, EA10472. *Reproduced from https://digi.ub.uni-heidelberg.de/diglit/budge1899/0101 (Budge 1899), public domain.*

One

The most powerful number, however, is 1 (*wa*), and the most powerful of the gods are those who existed before the world was created (Derchain 1980). The gods One, of which there are more than one, are at the beginning of creation. They include the goddess Nun, the primordial water, who existed before even the gods were born and who continues to exist. One is also Atum, the creator god, who is depicted in the act of auto-fellatio. He masturbates with his hand, swallows the semen, and creates the first gods by spitting and sneezing (Bickel 1994; Orriols-Llonch 2015). In the Coffin Texts (Spell II, 161A), Atum identifies himself: "I am the male and the female." Similarly, the goddess Neith is considered the father of the fathers and the mother of the mothers. Creative power is also attributed to animals that seemingly "create themselves," such as the turtle and the dung beetle—species that lay eggs but do not brood. One is also Ra, the sun god, who leads the gods in the world and the underworld during the day and night. One is the king of Egypt, the one who unites the two lands of Egypt and who keeps the balance. One is also Aten, the sun disk in the time of Pharaoh Akhenaten (ca. 1353–1336 BCE). Sometimes considered the first monotheistic religion, Atenism is better characterized as monolatry, the veneration of one god over others (Hornung 1971:233). Every One, however, is also part of a dual ordering of the world—balancing day and night, male and female, Upper and Lower Egypt, the desert and the Nile valley, chaos and order, and ultimately existence and nonexistence.

Conclusion

What we can glean of the symbolism of numbers in ancient Egypt is mostly related to organizing the world and especially the divine. Authors writing in the mid-twentieth century often emphasized that the plurality of divinities in ancient Egypt represented a unity, while some of the triads are actually thought to represent trinities (Hornung 1971; Velde 1971). It is impossible to draw conclusions on the symbolism or meaning of numbers that are valid for the entirety of Egyptian history and the full complexity of regional, educational, and social differences. Some efforts to downplay the plurality may derive from a modern wish to see ancient Egyptian religion as a predecessor or inspiration for monotheism. Similarly, the distinction between "high culture," "temple cult," and "popular religion" in our understanding of this ancient culture seems to downplay the fact that Egyptian religion was inherently polytheistic and multivalent. What is clear, though, is that we need to look at the evidence in its temporal, spatial, and social context.

We have ample evidence for a priesthood that was impelled to explain and reinterpret much older texts and did so explicitly by outlining the commentary in red ink. This means that the meaning of textual traditions changed, even if they were presented and perhaps perceived as ongoing and immutable. Especially in the Hellenistic period, we can discern attempts to explain and harmonize seemingly contradictory traditions. Global worship of a very select number of gods, mostly Isis and Osiris in the Hellenized form of Serapis, developed from the fifth century BCE onward, in the same region and period as monotheistic Judaism and Christianity. We need to always keep in mind that these religions developed in a similar cultural and intellectual milieu but have come to us through a strong Greek and later Roman lens.

In the numbers game, every count seems to have meaning, but in Egypt certainly duality and triad are the most important organizing principles. Above all, however, stands the number 1: the beginning of all, the origin. It does not mean being alone but being the first, a unique being, the creator, the start of everything. Similarly, I think of Lothar as the one, unique in many ways: he is the father of a school of thought, the creator of a group of scholars who went on to form and build the next generations of Chinese archaeologists. Yet he is a duality with his spouse, Yan Xing.

References

Allen, James P., ed.
2005   *The Ancient Egyptian Pyramid Texts*. Writings from the Ancient World 23. Atlanta: Society of Biblical Literature.

Bickel, Susanne
1994   *La Cosmogonie* Égyptienne *Avant Le Nouvel Empire*. Orbis Biblicus et Orientalis 134. Freiburg: Universitätsverlag; Göttingen: Vandenhoeck & Ruprecht.

Brunner, Helmut
1982   Neunheit. In *Lexikon Der* Ägyptologie, Vol. 4, edited by Wolfgang Helck and Wolfhart Westendorf, pp. 473–79. Wiesbaden: Otto Harrassowitz Verlag.

Budge, Ernest Alfred Thompson Wallis
1899   The Book of the Dead: Facsimiles of the Papyri of Hunefer, Anhai, Kerāsher and Netchemet ; with Supplementary Text from the Papyrus of Nu with Transcripts, Etc. *Heidelberg Historic Literature—Digitized*, https://doi.org/10.11588/diglit.18905.

Derchain, Philippe
1980 Kosmogonie. In *Lexikon Der* Ägyptologie, Vol. 3, edited by Wolfgang Helck and Wolfhart Westendorf, pp. 747–56. Wiesbaden: Otto Harrassowitz Verlag.

Desroches-Noblecourt, Christine, and Charles Kuentz
1968 *Le Petit Temple d'Abou Simbel*. Cairo: Centre de documentation et d'etude sur l'ancienne Egypte.

Falkenhausen, Lothar von
1993 On the Historiographical Orientation of Chinese Archaeology. *Antiquity* 67(257):839–49.
2003 Richard Casper Rudolph (21 May 1909–9 April 2003). *Journal of Asian Studies* 62(3):1031–33.
2004 Yu Weichao (1933–2003). *Artibus Asiae* 64(2):295–312.
2005 Hayashi Minao (1925–2006). *Artibus Asiae* 65(2):359–67.
2006 Zou Heng (1926–2005). *Artibus Asiae* 66:181–94.
2014a Magdalene von Dewall (8. V. 1927–1. I. 2014), in Memoriam. *Mannheimer Geschichtsblätter* 27:153–55.
2014b The Life and Work of Tong Enzheng. In *The Crescent-Shaped Cultural-Communication Belt: Tong Enzheng's Model in Retrospect*, edited by Anke M. Hein, pp. 18–48. Oxford: Oxbow Books.
2017 David Keightley (1932–2017): A Short Tribute. *Early China* 40:8–9.

Falkenhausen, Lothar von, Robert E. Murowchick, and Chenghwa Tsang
2003 Kwang-Chih Chang (1931–2001). *American Anthropologist* 105(2):481–84.

Gardiner, Alan H.
1931 *The Library of A. Chester Beatty; Description of a Hieratic Papyrus with a Mythological Story, Love-Songs, and Other Miscellaneous Texts.* Chester Beatty Papyri 1. London: Oxford University Press and E. Walker.

Hirshleifer, David, Ming Jian, and Huai Zhang
2016 Superstition and Financial Decision Making. *Management Science* 64(1):235–52.

Hornung, Erik
1971 *Der Eine Und Die Vielen:* Ägyptische *Gottesvorstellungen.* Darmstadt: Wissenschaftliche Buchgesellschaft.

Kemp, Yunus
2015 When Driving Is about Luck and Death. *China Daily, Africa Weekly*, September 25, 2015, http://bbs.chinadaily.com.cn/blog-1353795-17000.html.

Martin, Karl
1984 Sedfest. In *Lexikon Der* Ägyptologie, edited by Wolfgang Helck and Wolfhart Westendorf, 5:782–90. Wiesbaden: Otto Harrassowitz Verlag.

Mathieu, Bernard
2008 Les Enfants d'Horus, théologie et astronomie. *Enquêtes dans les Textes des Pyramides* 1:10.

Orriols-Llonch, M.
2015 Semen Ingestion and Oral Sex in Ancient Egyptian Texts. In *Proceedings of the Tenth International Congress of Egyptologists, University of the Aegean, Rhodes, 22–29 May 2008*, edited by N. Lazaridis, pp. 839–48. Orientalia Lovaniensia Analecta 241. Leuven: Peeters

Servajean, F.
2008 Duality. In *UCLA Encyclopedia of Egyptology*, edited by Jacco Dieleman and Willeke Wendrich, pp. 1–5. Los Angeles: UCLA, https://escholarship.org/uc/item/95b9b2db.

Shen, Chen
2014 Gifts of Boundless Longevity: Celebrating Imperial Birthdays in the Forbidden City. *Orientations* 45(4):76–85.

Vasiljević, Vera
2008 Embracing His Double: Niankhkhnum and Khnumhotep. *Studien Zur Altägyptischen Kultur* 37:363–72, https://www.jstor.org/stable/27751355.

Velde, H. te
1967 *Seth, God of Confusion: A Study of His Role in Egyptian Mythology and Religion*. Probleme Der Ægyptologie 6. Leiden: E. J. Brill.
1971 Some Remarks on the Structure of Egyptian Divine Triads. *Journal of Egyptian Archaeology* 57:80–86, https://doi.org/10.2307/3855945.

Wendrich, Willeke
2010 Epilogue: Eternal Egypt Deconstructed. In *Egyptian Archaeology*, edited by Willeke Wendrich, pp. 274–78. Oxford: Wiley-Blackwell.
2014 Antiquarianism in Egypt. The Importance of Re. In *World Antiquarianism: Comparative Perspectives*, edited by Alain Schnapp, 140–58. Los Angeles: Getty Research Institute.

Wildung, Dietrich
1982 Neunbogen. In *Lexikon Der* Ägyptologie, Vol. 4, edited by Wolfgang Helck and Wolfhart Westendorf, pp. 472–73. Wiesbaden: Otto Harrassowitz Verlag.

Woo, Chi Keung
1993 Vanity, Superstition and Auction Price. *Economics Letters* 44(4):389–95, https://doi.org/10.1016/0165-1765(94)90109-0.

Afterword

Lothar von Falkenhausen

As an inveterate contributor to Festschriften over the years (see Table A.1), having edited or coedited two myself (Falkenhausen 2010; Murowchick et al. 1999–2001), and having pronounced myself on the Festschrift genre in print (Falkenhausen 2009), I may well be under suspicion of angling to get one for myself. If so, I would have done better to remain in Germany. In the United States, where I have been based for my entire career, Festschriften are a rare occurrence. My own experience may demonstrate this: only two of the 19 Festschriften to which I have contributed until now were published in the United States, as against 11 in Europe and six in China. On the other hand, it is true that a number of my senior colleagues on the UCLA faculty have in fact had Festschriften dedicated to them (Table A.2). Quite a few of these were actually published overseas. But the Cotsen Institute of Archaeology Press has published one (Heyn and Steinsapir 2016) and has also published a Festschrift for at least one non-UCLA luminary (Miller and Abadi 2003). The present volume is thus not without local precedent.

Even so, when I first learned of the plan to publish the papers from the unforgettable symposium—a word that in this case truly lived up to its dual meaning: "conference" and "party"—with which my students, colleagues, and friends honored me on my sixtieth birthday, I was genuinely surprised, I tried to persuade those involved to desist. For it is common knowledge that American publishers hate Festschriften, bibliographers find them annoying, and promotion committees do not count them for tenure. Hence I have often advised my students that wasting their energies on contributing to Festschriften—let alone editing them—would be detrimental to their careers. But coming from someone with my record, this warning obviously did not carry much credibility: it must have come across as a case of "Do as I say, not as I do"—the quintessential mark of a bad teacher! Seen in this light, the present volume is a testimony of my pedagogical failures—of my inability to be a proper role model. All I can do now is hope that the quality of the contents will be sufficient to redeem both me and, more importantly, the contributors in the eyes of the reading public. In assessing this, of course I cannot be objective, but I think there is such a chance. Thus I shall now shamefacedly admit that I am tremendously pleased and grateful.

Coincidentally, the number of chapters in the book (counting the substantial epilogue as a chapter) is the same as that of my own contributions to various Festschriften, listed in Table A.1. Their dedicatees make up a distinguished roster of teachers, mentors, respected senior colleagues, former fellow students, and friends. In writing this afterword for my own Festschrift, I am now joining that group. I do so with some trepidation. For I cannot help remembering why my late teacher K. C. Chang strenuously opposed the project of a Festschrift in his honor: one of his teachers, Gao Quxun 高去尋 (1909–1991), for whom he had coedited a Festschrift (Song Wenxun et al. 1991),

Table A.1. Dedicatees of Festschriften to which Lothar von Falkenhausen has contributed

Areshian, Gregory (1949–2020): Falkenhausen 2017b
Chang, Kwang-chih 張光直 (1931–2001): Falkenhausen 2001
Dien, Albert E. (b. 1927): Sun Shouling 2007
Diény, Jean-Pierre (1927–2014): Falkenhausen 1999
Emmerich, Reinhard (b. 1954): Falkenhausen forthcoming a
Gao Ming 高明 (1926–2018): Luo Tai 2006
Höllmann, Thomas O. (b. 1952): Falkenhausen 2017a
Kalinowski, Marc (b. 1946): Falkenhausen forthcoming b
Keightley, David N. (1932–2017): Falkenhausen 1995
Kuczera, Stanisław (1928–2020): Falkenhausen 2013b
Lackner, Michael (b. 1953): Falkenhausen 2018
Ledderose, Lothar (b. 1942): Falkenhausen 2010
Li Ling 李零 (b. 1948): Falkenhausen 2021
Pirazzoli-t'Serstevens, Michèle (1934–2018): Falkenhausen 2006
Rawson, Jessica (b. 1943): Falkenhausen 2013a
Xu Pingfang 徐萍芳 (1930–2011): Luo Tai 2012
Yan Wenming 嚴文明 (b. 1931): Luo Tai forthcoming
Zhang Longxi 張隆溪 (b. 1946): Falkenhausen 2015
Zou Heng 鄒衡 (1927–2005): Falkenhausen 2003

had died before it came out, and Chang superstitiously feared that he too would not live to see his own Festschrift in print. He relented only when he sensed that his end was near; he even took the highly unusual step of contributing the final chapter—a precedent I am now following. Alas, he turned out to be partly right: of the three volumes of his Festschrift (Murowchick et al. 1999–2001), the third, which contained my contribution (Falkenhausen 2001) as well as his own, did not appear until after he passed away. Otherwise, however, the data in Table A.1 give no substance to this kind of foreboding. More than half of the dedicatees listed—10—are alive at the time of this writing. For the remaining nine, a comparison of the publication dates of their Festschriften with their death dates reveals that seven of them survived the publication, four by more than a decade, and aside from the regrettable case of K. C. Chang's third volume, the only other exception is one that was conceived as a memorial volume from the outset. Likewise, among the 24 items referenced in Table A.2, only three were published posthumously, and for six of the 11 dedicatees who are deceased, death came more than 10 years after their Festschrift publication date.

Even so, the publication of a Festschrift in one's honor is apt to remind one of one's mortality. As I write this, the time of my retirement has been decided on, and I must start to wind down my career. My most consequential effort in this connection has been the transfer of my personal library to the Getty Research Institute, which was first announced at the occasion of my sixtieth birthday symposium and took place in the fall of 2019. Three years later, my former books are still boxed up in some remote warehouse. But once properly accessioned, they will hopefully serve as a lasting resource for future researchers—more impactful, I think, than the aggregate of all my publications. Another, less tangible thing I am leaving to posterity is the transmission of what I have learned from my teachers, augmented by what I have been able to find out on my own, to scholars of the next generation, who in turn are adding to it (and also, no doubt, subtracting from it) as they are handing it further down the line. It is this process that is documented—albeit in a symbolic and unsystematic fashion—in the present volume. Writing this afterword gives me an opportunity to acknowledge, with the utmost gratitude, that in my three decades at UCLA I have learned much more from

Table A.2. Partial list of UCLA professors in archaeology and related fields who are dedicatees of Festschriften

Brown, Robert L. (b. 1944): DeCaroli and Lavy 2019
Buccellati, Giorgio (b. 1937), and Marilyn Kelly-Buccellati (b. 1939): Valentini and Guarducci 2019
Chambers, Mortimer H. (1927–2020): Mellor and Tritle 1999
Downey, Susan B. (b. 1938): Heyn and Steinsapir 2016
Gimbutas, Marija (1921–1994): Skomal and Polomé 1987
Heim, Michael H. (1943–2012): Cravens et al. 2008
Ivanov, Vyacheslav Vs. (1929–2017): Nikolaeva 2010
Jamison, Stephanie W. (b. 1948): Gunkel et al. 2016
Lao Gan 勞榦 (1907–2003): Lao Zhenyi Xiansheng Bazhi Rongqing Lunwenji Bianjiweiyuanhui 1986
McCallum, Donald F. (1939–2013): Fowler et al. 2014
Meighan, Clement F. (1925–1997): Dillon and Boxt 2005; Johnson 2005
Murphy, Franklin D. (1916–1994): Buccellati and Speroni 1981
Otto-Dorn, Katharina (1908–1999): Daneshvari 1981
Pedretti, Carlo (1928–2018): Moffatt and Taglialagamba 2016
Posnansky, Merrick (b. 1931): Goucher et al. 1993
Preziosi, Donald (b. 1941): Armstrong and Emerling 2016
Puhvel, Jaan (b. 1932): Disterheft et al. 1997; Greppen and Polomé 1997
Rudolph, Richard C. (1909–2003): Busch and Müller 1979–1980
Schopen, Gregory (b. 1947): Clarke and Boucher forthcoming
Vine, Brent H. (b. ?): Gunkel et al. 2018
Von Grunebaum, Gustave E. (1909–1972): Tikku 1971
Watkins, Calvert (1933–2013): Jasanoff et al. 1998

my students than they could have possibly learned from me. They have already, each in their own way, overtaken me. Their contributions to this volume attest this: even if I had done the research, I could not have written any of them myself; I lack the methodological mettle. That, in my opinion, is a positive sign, indicating substantial progress.

Rather than trying to seek coherence where patently there is none, I have no compunctions about declaring the very disparate nature of the volume's contents to be one of its main strengths. Indeed, the multifariousness of its contents exemplifies what I consider to be best pedagogical practices. It has never been my intention to found an intellectually coherent "UCLA School" of East Asian archaeology or to mold students in my own image. This would not only have been impossible; it would also arguably have been unethical. Instead I have considered it my main task to seize upon each individual student's own interests and to create an academic environment where students can optimally unfold their talents while striving to adhere to the highest standards of scholarship. Such an approach to teaching requires coordination with a large number of people, both at UCLA and elsewhere, for it amounts to a triangulation involving the professor, the student, and UCLA's entire institutional infrastructure, as well as ever-changing outside opportunities that may present themselves. Since no one teacher, no matter how accommodating, can be a fit for every single student who comes along, I have experienced my share of painful disappointments. But in the fortunately quite numerous instances where things did work out, those in whose PhD training in East Asian archaeology at UCLA I have been involved have emerged as unique and distinctive scholar personalities. This fact is abundantly attested by their contributions to the present book, each of which conveys a sense of its author's individuality. To me, that is precisely what makes each chapter precious on its own and the volume as a whole worth reading. I hope that the wider readership will share in these sentiments. The credit for this outcome accrues not to me but to UCLA and to those many people who, at all levels, shape our university's unique learning environment.

Festschriften document both intellectual and social ties. Thus they are useful sources for historical research. Based on the publications referenced in Tables A.1 and A.2, for instance, one could trace networks comprising hundreds if not thousands of scholars, and the closer analysis of these networks would reveal plentiful interesting conjunctures. To give just one example, my own network as documented in Table A.1 extends far beyond my own field of research. Honorees of Festschriften to which I have contributed include archaeologists, art historians, ethnologists, historians, paleographers, sinologists, and scholars of literature, each with their own extensive circles of colleagues. This interdisciplinary diversity reflects, no doubt, my own eclectic scholarly interests, but it also carries some significance in relation to my decades-long efforts to establish the hitherto marginal field of East Asian archaeology more firmly in Euro-American academia. Such an undertaking requires bridge-building across multiple different scholarly and institutional cultures. Hence I found it advisable to take advantage of as many opportunities as I could fit in to embed my research in wider discourses—for example, through participation in a great variety of conferences or indeed by contributing to a far-flung roster of Festschriften. Thanks to the solid growth of the field during recent decades, the next generation may find this less urgent. The present volume, for all its disparity, is overwhelmingly concerned with archaeological issues, and the cast of contributors consists for the most part of archaeologists. This goes some way to demonstrate that East Asian archaeology in the West is beginning to come into its own as a circumscribed academic subdiscipline, with a critical mass of stakeholders to participate in its internal discussions. While this is, in principle, a good thing, one still hopes that the interdisciplinary and inter-institutional connections that have enriched the field so far will continue to be actively maintained.

As I come to the end, it is time to give thanks. Beyond my UCLA-centric networks, the contributors to this volume include three old friends who have grown into eminent scholars: Li Shuicheng from my Peking University days, Miyamoto Kazuo from my time at Kyōto, and Alain Thote, whom I first met in Beijing in 1979 and who has since repeatedly hosted me in Paris. It is I who should be contributing to their Festschriften rather than they to mine. I am all the more grateful that they have cheerfully condescended to join a more junior crowd of contributors and, by their presence, enhanced the intellectual heft of this volume. I would also like to single out for special thanks my dear UCLA colleagues Willeke Wendrich and Hans Barnard for their stimulating papers and for their support of the publication of the book. To each of the other contributors as well, I am profoundly grateful for the great efforts they have made to share their exciting research herein. Thanks are due in particular to the editors, Anke Hein, Rowan Flad, and Bryan Miller, for dealing with the tedious nitty-gritty that editorial work inevitably entails. I am grateful as well to Li Min for his organizational and fund-raising efforts, to the Luce Foundation for contributing to the publication funds through its Institutional Enhancement Grant to UCLA, and to Randi Danforth at the Cotsen Institute of Archaeology Press for their careful and efficient editorial coordination. Finally, I would like to acknowledge all those who spoke at the symposium but who for various reasons are not represented in the volume—Gao Jiangtao, Enno Giele, Burglind Jungmann, Lai Guolong, Li Ling, once more Li Min, Meng Fanzhi, Miao Zhe, Pak Yangjin, Rhi Juhyung, David Schaberg, Adam D. Smith, Wang Mingke, Wu Hung, Yan Yunxiang, Zhang Li (Li Jaang), and Zhang Liangren—and the many colleagues, students, and friends who contributed to the success of the symposium by their attendance. I hope that this volume, besides giving me enormous pleasure, will be of some use to a wide readership.

Ixelles, February 11, 2022
L. v. F.

References

Armstrong, Philip, and Jae Emerling, eds.
2016   A Tribute to Donald Preziosi. Special issue, *Journal of Art Historiography* 15.

Buccellati, Giorgio, and Charles Speroni, eds.
1981   *The Shape of the Past: Studies in Honor of Franklin D. Murphy*. Los Angeles: Institute of Archaeology and Office of the Chancellor, UCLA.

Busch, Heinrich, and Wilhelm K. Müller, eds.
1979–1980 Special issue dedicated to Richard C. Rudolph, *Monumenta Serica* 34.

Clarke, Shayne, and Daniel Boucher, eds.
Forthcoming *Festschrift in Honor of Gregory Schopen*.

Cravens, Craig, Masako U. Fidler, and Susan C. Kresin, eds.
2008   *Between Texts, Languages and Cultures: A Festschrift for Michael Henry Heim*. Bloomington, IN: Slavica Publishers.

Daneshvari, Abbas, ed.
1981 *Essays in Islamic Art and Architecture in Honor of Katharina Otto-Dorn.* Malibu: Undena Publications.

DeCaroli, Robert, and Paul A. Lavy, eds.
2019 *Across the South of Asia: A Volume in Honor of Prof. Robert L. Brown.* New Delhi: D. K. Printworld.

Dillon, Brian D., and Matthew A. Boxt, eds.
2005 *Archaeology without Limits: Papers in Honor of Clement W. Meighan.* Lancaster, CA: Labyrinthos.

Disterheft, Dorothy, Martin E. Huld, and John A. C. Greppen, eds.
1997 Studies in Honor of Jaan Puhvel, Part 1, Ancient Languages and Philology. Special issue, *Journal of Indo-European Studies* 20. Washington, DC: Institute for the Study of Man.

Falkenhausen, Lothar von
1995 Reflections on the Political Rôle of Spirit Mediums in Early China: The Wu Officials in the Zhou li. Festschrift for Professor David N. Keightley, *Early China* 20:279–300.
1999 Late Western Zhou Taste. Festschrift for Professor Jean-Pierre Diény, *Études chinoises* 18(1–2):143–78.
2001 The Use and Significance of Ritual Bronzes in the Lingnan Region during the Eastern Zhou Period. Festschrift in Honor of K. C. Chang, *Journal of East Asian Archaeology* 3(1–2):193–236
2003 The Bronzes from Xiasi and Their Owners. Festschrift for Professor Zou Heng, *Kaoguxue yanjiu* 考古學研究 5(2):755–86.
2006 The Salt of Ba: Reflections on the Role of the "Peripheries" in the Production Systems of Bronze Age China. Festschrift for Professor Michèle Pirazzoli-t'Serstevens, edited by Alain Thote, *Arts Asiatiques* 61:45–56.
2009 Sidelights on the State of Sinology in Germany: Two Recent Festschriften with a Focus on Early and Early Imperial China. *China Review International* 16(1):33–65.
2010 From Action to Image in Early Chinese Art. Festschrift for Professor Lothar Ledderose, edited by Lothar von Falkenhausen, *Cahiers d'Extrême-Asie* 17:51–91.
2013a Neolithic Reminiscences in Shang Art. Festschrift for Professor Dame Jessica Rawson, *Orientations* 44(1):44–50.
2013b Archaeology and the Chinese Lineage. In *Sinologi mira k Iubileiu Stanislava Kučery* [The Sinologists of the World at the Jubilee of Stanisław Kuczera], pp. 119–37. Učënye zapiski Otdela Kitaia 11. Moscow: Institut Vostokovedeniia Rossiskoĭ Akademii Nauk.
2015 Antiquarianism in China and Europe: Reflections on Momigliano. In *Cross-cultural Studies: China and the World, a Festschrift in Honor of Professor Zhang Longxi*, edited by Qian Suoqiao, pp. 127–51. Leiden: E. J. Brill.
2017a Communication with the Divine Sphere in Ancient China. In *Über den Alltag hinaus: Festschrift für Thomas O. Höllmann zum 65. Geburtstag*, edited by Armin Selbitschka and Shing Müller, pp. 19–29. Wiesbaden: Harrassowitz.
2017b The Study of East Asian Art History in Europe: Some Observations on Its Early Stages. In *Bridging Times and Spaces: Festschrift for Gregory E. Areshian on the Occasion of His Sixty-fifth Birthday*, edited by Pavel S. Aretisyan and Yervand H. Grekyan, pp. 89–102. Oxford: Archaeopress.
2018 The Earliest Chinese Bells in Light of New Archaeological Discoveries. In *Reading the Signs: Philology, History, Prognostication, Festschrift for Michael Lackner*, edited by Iwo Amelung and Joachim Kurtz, pp. 42–69. Munich: Iudicium Verlag.
2021 Questions about Cai Jixiang. In *Zhongguo zaoqi shushu, yishu yu wenhua jiaoliu: Li Ling xiansheng qizhi huadan qingshou lunwenji* 中國早期數術、藝術與文化交流：李零先生七秩華誕慶壽論文集 [Occult Arts, Art History, and Cultural Exchange in Early China: A Festschrift in Honor of Professor Li Ling on the Occasion of His Seventieth Birthday], Vol. 2, edited by Miao Zhe 繆哲, Lai Guolong 來國龍, and Zhang Yulin 張鈺霖, pp. 653–95. Zhejiang University Journal of Art History and Archaeology 2. Hangzhou: Zhejiang Daxue Chubanshe.

Forthcoming a "Suspended Music" in Early Imperial China: A Reconsideration. In *Festschrift for Professor Reinhard Emmerich*, edited by Enno Giele et al.

Forthcoming b Ritual Change in Late Bronze Age China: Musical Dimensions. In *Festschrift for Professor Marc Kalinowski*, edited by Marianne Bujard et al.

Falkenhausen, Lothar von, ed.
2010 *Studies of Chinese Art History in Honor of Professor Lothar Ledderose*. Cahiers d'Extrême-Asie 17. Paris: École Française d'Extrême-Orient.

Fowler, Sherry, Chari Pradel, and Yui Suzuki, eds.
2014 *Daring Japanese Art History: Studies in Japanese and Korean Art History in Honor of Donald Frederick McCallum (1939–2013)*. Special issue, *Artibus Asiae* 74(1).

Goucher, Candice L., David W. Phillipson, and David L. Schoenbrun, eds.
1993 *Papers in Honor of Merrick Posnansky*. Special issue, *African Archaeological Review* 11.

Greppen, John A. C., and Edgard C. Polomé, eds.
1997 *Studies in Honor of Jaan Puhvel, Part 2, Mythology and Religion*. *Journal of Indo-European Studies* 21. Washington, DC: Institute for the Study of Man.

Gunkel, Dieter, Stephanie W. Jamison, Angelo O. Mercado, and Kazuhiko Yoshida, eds.
2018 *Vina Diem Celebrant: Studies in Linguistics and Philology in Honor of Brent Vine*. Ann Arbor, MI: Beech Stave Press.

Gunkel, Dieter, Joshua T. Katz, Brent H. Vine, and Michael L. Weiss, eds.
2016 *Sahasram Ati Srajas: Indo-Iranian and Indo-European Studies in Honor of Stephanie W. Jamison*. Ann Arbor, MI: Beech Stave Press.

Heyn, Maura K., and Ann Irving Steinsapir, eds.
2016 *Icon, Cult and Context: Sacred Spaces and Objects in the Classical World*. Festschrift for Professor Susan B. Downey. Los Angeles: Cotsen Institute of Archaeology Press.

Jasanoff, Jay H., H. Craig Melchert, and Lisi Oliver, eds.
1998 *Mir Curad: Studies Presented to Calvert Watkins*. Innsbrucker Beiträge zur Sprachwissenschaft 92. Innsbruck: Institut für Sprachwissenschaft der Universität Innsbruck.

Johnson, Keith L., ed.
2005 *Onward and Upward! Papers in Honor of Clement W. Meighan*. Chico, CA: Stansbury Publishing.

Lao Zhenyi Xiansheng Bazhi Rongqing Lunwenji Bianjiweiyuanhui 勞貞一先生八秩榮慶論文集編輯委員會, ed.
1986 *Lao Zhenyi xiansheng bazhi rongqing lunwenji* 勞貞一先生八秩榮慶論文集 [Collected Essays in Celebration of Professor Lao Zhenyi's [= Lao Gan's] Eightieth Birthday]. Taipei: Taiwan Shangwu Yinshuguan.

Luo Tai 羅泰 (Lothar von Falkenhausen)
2006 Xi Zhou tongqi mingwen de xingzhi 西周銅器銘文的性質 [The Nature of Western Zhou Bronze Inscriptions]. Translated by Lai Guolong 來國龍. Festschrift for Professor Gao Ming, *Kaoguxue yanjiu* 考古學研究 6:343–74.

2012 Zhongguo zaoqi wenming zhong "chengshi" de fazhan jieduan 中國早期文明中'城市'的發展階段 [Stages of Development of "Cities" in Early Chinese Civilization]. Translated by Xu Hong 許宏. In *Xu Pingfang xiansheng jinian wenji* 徐蘋芳先生紀念文集 [Collected Studies in Memory of Professor Xu Pingfang], Vol. 2, edited by Xu Hong 許宏, pp. 13–32. Shanghai: Shanghai Guji Chubanshe.

Forthcoming Youguan Zhongguo kaoguxue zhong tieqishidai wenti de ruogan sikao 有關中國考古學中鐵器時代問題的若干思考 [Some Thoughts on the Iron Age Problem in Chinese Archaeology]. Translated by Li Min 李旻. In *Qingzhu Yan Wenming xiansheng jiushisui lunwenji* 慶祝嚴文明先生九十歲論文集 [Festschrift for Professor Yan Wenming in Celebration of His Ninetieth Birthday].

Mellor, Ronald, and Lawrence Tritle, eds.
1999 *Text and Tradition: Studies in Greek History and Historiography*. Claremont, CA: Regina Books.

Miller, Naomi F., and Kamyar Abadi, eds.
2003 *Yeki Bud, Yeki Nabud: Essays on the Archaeology of Iran in Honor of William M. Sumner*. Los Angeles: Cotsen Institute of Archaeology Press.

Moffatt, Constance, and Sara Taglialagamba, eds.
2016 *Illuminating Leonardo: A Festschrift for Carlo Pedretti Celebrating His 70 Years of Scholarship (1944–2014)*. Leonardo Studies 1. Leiden: E. J. Brill.

Murowchick, Robert E., Lothar von Falkenhausen, Tsang Cheng-hwa, and Robin D. S. Yates, eds.
1999–2001 Festschrift in Honor of K. C. Chang, *Journal of East Asian Archaeology* 1(1–4), 2(1–2), 3(1–2). Leiden: E. J. Brill.

Nikolaeva, Tat'ĭana Mihaĭlovna, ed.
2010 *Issledovaniĭa po lingvistike i semiotike: Sbornik stateĭ k ĭubileĭu Vyachesláva Vsévolodovica Ivánova* [Explorations across Linguistics

and Semiotics: Collection of Studies on the Jubilee of Vyacheslav Vsevolodovich Ivanov]. Moscow: Institut Slavĭanovedenĭĭa Rossiĭskoy Akademii Nauk.

Skomal, Susan Nacev, and Edgar C. Polomé, eds.
1987 *Proto-Indo-European: The Archaeology of a Linguistic Problem, Essays in Honor of Marija Gimbutas*. Washington, DC: Institute for the Study of Man.

Song Wenxun 宋文薰, Li Yiyuan 李亦園, Xu Zhuoyun 許倬雲, and Zhang Guangzhi 張光直, eds.
1991 *Kaogu yu lishi wenhua: Qingzhu Gao Quxun xiansheng bashi dashou lunwenji* 考古與歷史文化: 慶祝高去尋先生八十大壽論文集 [Archaeology and Historical Cultures: Collected Studies in Celebration of Professor Gao Quxun's Eightieth Birthday]. Taipei: Zhengzhong Shuju.

Sun Shouling
2007 Why I Reprinted the Final Portion of the *Vimalakirtinirdesasutra* Using Movable Type Made of Clay. Translated by Adam D. Smith. Annotated and edited by Lothar von Falkenhausen. Essays in Honor of Professor Albert E. Dien, *Early Medieval China* 13–14:233–63.

Tikku, Girdhari L.
1971 *Islam and Its Cultural Divergence: Studies in Honor of Gustave E. von Grunebaum*. Urbana: University of Illinois Press.

Valentini, Stefano, and Guido Guarducci, eds.
2019 *Between Syria and the Highlands: Studies in Honor of Giorgio Buccellati and Marilyn Kelly-Buccellati*. Studies on the Ancient Near East and the Mediterranean 3. Rome: Arbor Sapientiae.

Index

Note: Figures and tables are indicated by page numbers in *bold italic.*

abnegation, 188, *189*
Abu Simbel, 360–361
adornment objects, 47–50, *49*. *See also* arm ornament; bracelet; earring
adze, 228, 233
agriculture, 17, *64,* 73, 181, 203–204, 206–207, 233–234, *234,* 235
Ak-Alakh, *36,* 45
animal objects, gold, 45–46. *See also* figurines
animals
    abnegation of, 188, *189*
    oracle bones from, 152
    sacrifice of, 181–191, *182–187, 189*
antelope, 152
Anyang, 169–170, 208, 256
Anyi Xiaguan, 37
arm ornament, 210
arrow, 63, *64*
arrowhead, *128,* 232
Ashaonao, *265*
awl
    bone, in Donghuishan cemetery, *20, 29*
    metal, in Donghuishan cemetery, *28*
axe, *64, 128,* 137, 228, 233

axle cap, 41, 52n7, 53n15
Ayutthaya, *284,* 285–286, 288

Bactria, 50, 302
Baiyuan, *242, 244*
Bamiyan, *338,* 341–342
Bangkok, *284,* 285
Banshan culture, 209, *209,* 210
Baodun, *262,* 264, 266–268, 272–273, 275n1
Baoji, *36,* 42–43, 170, 178, *314,* 327
barley, 17, 206, 208–209
Bat Trang, *284,* 286
bead, *20, 28, 31,* 47–48, 50–51, 53n21, 96n9, 122, 131, 185, 251
beaker, 47, *128,* 131–132, 137
Beifangtan, *169, 173*
Beikangcun, *36,* 42
Beishan, *127*
Beizhai, 321
Beizhao, *169, 176–177,* 236
bell, *128,* 135–136, 138, 167–179, *169–173, 175–177,* 248, 251
Bencharong porcelain, 283–284, *284–287,* 285–288, 290
beverage container, 37, *38–39*
boar tusk, in Donghuishan cemetery, *28*
bone awl, in Donghuishan cemetery, *20*
bone needle, in Donghuishan cemetery, *30*
bone ornament, in Donghuishan cemetery, *28*

bone spreader, in Donghuishan cemetery, *20, 30*
boshan incense burner, 8, 313–332, *314–315, 318–320, 322, 324–327*
bovid, 152–153, *153, 156–159,* 160, 264
bow plate, *186*
Boxi, *263*
bracelet, *28,* 46, 48, 53n21, 123, *128,* 137
bridle, 42, 186, *186*
bronze, 37–42, *38–39,* 63, *128,* 210–213, 248, 255, 271–272, 325
Bronze Age, 15–25, *18–24,* 62, 71, 110, 113, 115, 123–124, 149–150, 183, 210, 236, 241, 264, 267, 275, 347
bronze mettalurgy, 6, 204, 210, 225–237, *226–228, 231, 234*
Buddhas of Bamiyan, 341–342
burial goods, 18, *20, 22–23, 28–33, 64,* 89–90, 210–212, 252. *See also* cemetery
burial goods industry, 90–91
burial rites, secondary, 16–17
Burkhan Tolgoi, *182*
Butuo, *129*

Cangbaobao, *110,* 112–114, 267
Cangpingcun, *265*
Canton, *284*
Caowangcheng, *228*
Caowangzui, 236, 237n2
caprines, 152–153, *153–154,* 160, 162–163
carnelian, in jewelry, 48–50, *49*
carpines, 152
cattle, 152, *154, 159,* 162, *184,* 189, 208
cauldron
    animal deposits in, 190
    bronze, *128,* 137, *185,* 186
    ceramic, 247, 253
    iron, *65*
    steppe-type, 42
cemetery. *See also* burial goods
    Daodunzi, 182
    at Derestui, 182
    at Donghuishan, 15–25, *18–24, 28–33*
    at Iksan Yŏngdŭng-dong, *66*
    at Ivolga, 182
    at Majiayuan, 51–52
    Renshengcun, *110,* 113–114
    Rujiazhuang, 178
    at Salkhityn Am, 182
    Shombuuzyun-Belchir, *185,* 185–188, *186*
    Sifangtang, *231,* 234–235
    Takhiltyn-Khotgor, 185–188, *187*
    at Xingyuan, 92
    Xiongnu, *182,* 183, *184*
    Yejiashan, 175, 178
    of Yu, 47
    Zhuyangou, 178
ceramics, 7, 42, 62, 75, 92, 110, 122–124, 131–133, 138, 153, 208, 210, 233, 236, 241–256, 264, 273–274, 283, 288. *See also* pottery
    at Baodun, *266*
    in Donghuishan cemetery, 18, *28–33*
    at Erlitou, 243, *243,* 245
    in European hoards, 123
    figurines, 90–91, 94
    in intentional deposits, 127–136, *128–130, 132–134*
    Mahan, 63, *64*
    at Nanwa, 245–248, *247*
    Paekche, 63
    porcelain, 283–290, *284–287, 289*
    production, *234*
    at Sanxingdui, 110, 112
    in Xichang Dayangdui, *130*
chaînes opératoire, 126–127, 200–201
Chalcoithic, 161
Chang'an, 82, *83, 85,* 90, 94, 95n2, *314*
Changxing, *169, 173*
Chapel Hill, *338,* 340
chariot fitting, 42
chariot ornament, 46
Chengcun, *36,* 43
Chenru Houbeishan, *231*
chime, *nao,* 169–170, *170–172*
Chinhan, 60
Chŏllanam-do, 70
Chŏnbuk, 67, 73
chopsticks, 185, *187,* 188, 287
Ch'uk-dong, 73
Chuxiong Wanjiaba, 136
Cirebon, 283, *284,* 288–290
clay flute, in Donghuishan cemetery, *32*
cocoon-shaped *hu* vessel, *38,* 40
coin, 96n9, *128,* 138–140, 299, 305, 342
Cô Loa Citadel, 134
community, 6–7, 261–275
cong tube, 268, 271, 274
contact, 6–7, 42, 48, 50, 60–61, 73, 210, 213, 242
copper mining and smelting, 225–237, *226–228, 231, 234*
cowrie shell, in Donghuishan cemetery, *20*
craft technology, *209,* 209–213, *211*
Cuizhuang, 321
culture, 2, 4, 8, 25, 35, 40, 43, 45, 50–52, 59, 61–63, 67, 70, 72, 74–75, 81, 201–202, 210–211, 214n7, 242, 262, 264, 272, 284, 289–290, 346

Cuoli, *242, 244*
Cuo of Zhongshan, 37, *39*
cup, 37, 40, 52n3, *128,* 130

Dadiwan, 205, *205, 265*
Dadiwan culture, 209
dagger
    iron, 42–43, *44*
    jade, 268
dagger-axes, iron, 43, *44*
Dahekou, *169, 171, 176–177,* 178
Dahezhuang, *150,* 162
Dalupu, 226, *228,* 230, 232–233, *234*
Daodunzi, 182, *182*
Daquan Caowan, *231*
Dashuidang, *265*
Dasikong, *171*
Dayak, 16
Dayangdui, *127,* 131–132, *132,* 136–138
Dayangzhou, *169, 173*
Daye-Yangxin, 226, *227*
Dazasi, *265*
Dechang, *129*
deer, 45, 152, 208, 264
Dengjiapo, *83*
Derstui, 182, *182*
Dian culture, 51, 135–136, 138
Dingbian, *314*
Dingjiazha, *314,* 320
ding tripod, 37, *38–39,* 247
Dingxian, *314*
disk, perforated, in Donghuishan cemetery, *28, 30, 33*
Disk of Nebra, 123, 347
distance, 203–204
domesticated plants, 205–207
Dongganggou, *242, 244*
Donghuishan, 15–25, *18–24, 28–33, 150, 153,* 205
Dongjiazhuang, 322
Dongmagou, *242*
Dongxiafeng culture, 241
Dongxiang, *265*
Dongzhaoyu, *83*
Dongzhuang, *242, 244*
Dou Wan tomb, 323, *324,* 324–325
dragon-shaped object, 251, *252*
drum, 127, *128,* 133–134, *134,* 135, 138–139
duality, 356–358, *357–358*
dui
    egg-shaped, *38,* 40
    with inlaid decoration, *38,* 40

Dunhuang, *298*
Dunhuang Limes, 298

Early Bronze Age, 17, 117, 150
Early Iron Age, 63, 71
ear ornament, 210
earring
    in Donghuishan cemetery, *20, 28, 33*
    gold turqoise, Susa, *49*
economy, defined, 2
egg-shaped vessel, *38,* 40
Ejin River Transfer Zone (ERTZ), 204–205
Elam, *36,* 48, *49*
Eleon, *338*
Elephantine, *356*
Endere, *298*
Erligang, 268
Erlitou, 169, *169,* 170, 225, *242–243,* 242–256, *244, 246, 249–250,* 268
Erlitou culture, 241
ERTZ. *See* Ejin River Transfer Zone (ERTZ)
Etuoke, *314,* 321
Ewangcheng, *228,* 236, 237n2
exchange, 3, 6–7, 35, 41, 43, 50–51, 114, 124, 139–140, 152, 210–211, 241–242, 255, 261, 272, 275, 300, 306, 346

Falkenhausen, Lothar von, 1–2, 8–9, 35, 45, 50–51, 59, 81, 107, 121, 149, 163, 167–168, 174, 181, 199, 213, 225, 241, 256, 261, 284, 297, 300–301, 313, 332, 337, *349,* 355, 363, 365–368
Fangchijie, 269, *269–270,* 272
Fanji, 321
Fenghuangshan, 321
Fenjiwan, 137
Fenshuiling, *36, 39*
figurines, 82–90, *83–87, 270,* 274
Filippovka, *36,* 45–46
fish, *184,* 264
flute, clay, in Donghuishan cemetery, *32*
Fujiamen, *150,* 153, *154,* 161, *265*
funerals
    excessive, 89–94
    socioeconomic dimensions of, 16–17
funerary goods. *See* burial goods

Fuqintai Xiaoqu, *269*
Gāndhārī language, 297–298
Ganggangwa, *205,* 207, 210–211
Gansu, 41–42, 51
Gaokan, *265*

Gaopian, 113
Gaoshan, *265,* 266, 275n1
Gaozhuang, 322
Ghana, 16–17
goat, 153, *153, 184,* 189, 207–208
gold, Xi Wrong, 45–46
gold belt plaque, 47–48, *49,* 53n19
gold decoration, on iron objects, 43–45, *44*
gold earring, in Donghuishan cemetery, *33*
gold jewley, at Majiayuan, 48–50, *49*
Gounan, *319*
grave goods. *See* burial goods
Gualin, *83*
Guangyuan, *265*
Gudunzi, 266
Guiyuanqiao, 264
Guizhou, 135
Guodu, *83*
Guojiabao, 137
Guojiatan, *83*
Guojiazhuang, *171*
Guoli, 320

halberd, *128,* 137
hammer, 228
Hamp'yŏng Sunch'on, 73
Hanjiawan, *83*
Hansŏng, 63
Hanzhong, *226*
Haotan, 320, *320*
hatchet, 42
Hatra, 340–341, *341*
hat-shaped object, ceramic, 251, *251*
Haxiu, *263, 265*
headgear, *65,* 73
Hekoucun, *128,* 137
Heliopolis, *338,* 343, *343, 356,* 357, 362
Henglanshan, *265*
Hermopolis, *356–357,* 362
Hetaozhuang, 207
hoards
    in European archaeology, 122–124
    intentional deposits, *127–130,* 127–137, *132–134*
    Sanxingdui, 95n3, 107–117, *110–112*
hoe, 137
Hongshan culture, 210, 314
horse, 51, *184, 186,* 188–189, 208, 355
Houma, *36,* 37, *39,* 41
house, 246, 266, 272
Huangcui, *169, 171*

Huangmasai, *169, 173*
Huangniangniangtai, *150,* 152–153, *153–154,* 160, 163, *205,* 211
Huaping, *129*
Huayuanzhuang, *169, 171*
Huchang, 325
Huidong, *129*
Huili, *129,* 134, 137
Huili 1994, *128*
Huili Guoyuan, *128, 134*
Huili Hekoucun, *128,* 137
Huili Luoluochong, *128,* 133, *134*
Huili Yimen Xiacunxiang, *128,* 137
Huili Zhuanchangba, *128, 134*
Huizui, *242, 244*
Huizuiwa, *150, 156,* 160, *162, 205,* 208
human remains, 16, 18–19, 22, *22,* 23–24, *24,* 24–25, 160, 339, 342
Huoshiliang, *205,* 207, 210–211
hu vessel
    beverage container, 37, *38–39*
    coccon-shaped, *38,* 40

ibex, 43, 45, 152
identity, 1, 4, 6, 8, 15, 42, 60, 62, 68, 70, 72, 74, 125, 210, 261–262, 274, 289–290, 304
Iksan Yŏngdŭng-dong cemetery, *66*
I'lmovaya pad', *183*
incense burner, 8, 313–332, *314–315, 318–320, 322, 324–327*
ingot, 63, *64,* 231–232, 234–236
innovation, 202–203, 213
intentional deposits, *127–130,* 127–137, *132–134*
interaction, 6–7, 242–245
Iraq, 48. *See also* Mosul
iron, Xi Wrong, 42–45, *44*
Iron Age, 59, *61,* 63, 67, 70–72, 75, 123
Ivolga, 182, *182*

jade, 210, 214n7, 248, 268, 271, 274
Jade Gate, 298
jar, 63, *64–65,* 67, 127, *266,* 272, *273*
jar burial, *69*
Jartai Pass, *205,* 212
jewelry, gold, at Majiayuan, 48–50, *49*
Jiangweicheng, *263*
Jianjia, *83*
Jianshanshai, *265*
Jingdezhen, 283, *284,* 285–286, 288
Jinsha, *108,* 268–269, *269,* 270, *270,* 271, 274
Jinshengcun, *36,* 37, *44*

Jinyang Munagou, *128,* 137
Jiujiang-Ruichang, 226, *227*

Karadong, *298*
Karak-dong, 67
Kaya, 67, 73, 75n1
Kayue culture, 209, *209*
Kele culture, 135
Kelermes, *36*
Keshengzhuang II culture, 209, *209*
Kexitai, 230, *231*
Khanoum, *298*
Kharoṣṭhī Buddha, 301, *301–302,* 306–307
Kiangsi ware, 286
kiln, 90–91, 247, 255, 270
knife. *See also* dagger
    bronze, *128*
    in Donghuishan cemetery, *20, 28, 31–33*
    steppe type, 42
Koch'ang Namsan-ni, 73
Konglongcun, *263, 265*
Korainic language, 298
Krorayinese language, 306
Kucha, *298*
Kurgan 1, 46
kylix, 347–348, *348*
Kyŏnggi, 63, 67, 70–71

Lainumthong ware, 285
Lajia, *150, 156, 161,* 207
Lanyuan, 270–271
Laoguantai culture, *209*
Late Bronze Age, 63, *64,* 71
Late Machang, 17
Late Neolithic, 117, 210, 314
Late Western Zhou Ritual Reform, 167–168, 178–179
Liangchengzhen, 243
Liangdaicun, *169, 176*
Liangshan, *128,* 137–140
Liangzhu, 271
Lijiashan, 134
Lijiaya, 41
linchpin, 41
Linjia, *205,* 210, *265*
Lintan, *265*
Lintao, *265*
Lintong, 42, *44, 314*
Liulige, *36, 39,* 40
Liuping, *36,* 42, 48
Liurongshan, *169,* 172, *173*

Liu Sheng tomb, 45, 315, *315,* 323, 326
Lizhou, *265*
Lo-Dagga, 16–17
Longshan cultures, 268
Longtan, 137
longxingqi, 251, *252*
Los Infieles, 226
Loulan, *298*
Lujianao, 230, *231*
Luoluochong, *127,* 133–134
Luonan xinqu Tangmu, *83*
Luoyang, 82, *83, 85,* 86–87, 92, 94, 95n2–95n3, 298, *298,* 300, 303
Lusi, *242,* 244

Machang culture, 209, *209,* 210–211
Mahan mortuary, 59–75, *60–61, 64–66, 68–69, 71*
Majiayao culture, 153, *154,* 161–162, 209, *209,* 263, 272
Majiayuan, 35–52, *36, 38–39, 44, 49*
Malacca, 283, *284*
Maliucun, 127n2, 132, 136, 138
Mancheng, *36,* 45, *314,* 316, 325
Mangcheng, 275n1, 314, 323, 327
Manila, 283, *284,* 288–290
Maocaoshan Dongpo, *231*
Maojiaping, *36, 39,* 41
Maoling, 313–314, *314,* 316, 326, *327*
Maoqinggou, *36,* 42
Maoshan, *231*
margins, 199–204
Mari, 50
Masjid Sunan Gunung Jati, 288
Matengkong, *83*
Mathurā, *298*
Mawangdui, 51, 325, 330–331, 332n3
Maxianshan, *211*
meaning, objects and, 7–8, 337–350, *338–339, 341, 343, 348–349*
meat-stewing tripod, 37, *38–39*
Medan, *284*
Mehan Garden, 288
Meigu, *129*
Meishan, *242,* 244
Meiyuan, 271
Memphis, *356*
metal awl, in Donghuishan cemetery, *28*
metal earring, in Donghuishan cemetery, *20, 28*
metal knife, in Donghuishan cemetery, *20, 28, 31–33*
metallurgy, 6, 17, 42, 46, 51, 75, 134, 152, 204, 210–211, 225–237

Mianning, *129*
Mianning Xiaogoudi, 131
Mianyang, *265*
Middle Springs and Autumns Ritual Restructuring, 167, 179
millet, 206, 270
Minhe, *154*
mining, 225–237, *226–228*, *231*, *234*
Minjiang Xiaoqu, *269*
Minshan Fandian, 272
mirror, 41–42, 211
Miyi, *129*
Mizhi, *314*
Mogou, *150*, *156*, 160, *161*, *205*
mortuary, Mahan, 59–75, *60–61*, *64–66*, *68–69*, *71*
mortuary rites, 87–89
Mosul, *338*, 340
mountain motifs, *318–320*, 318–323, *322*
Moutuo, *36*, 51, 261, 274
Moutuo Tomb 1, 35, 50
museums, *343*, 343–346

Najiaping, *265*
Nan Dongqiao, *231*
Nanwa, 241–243, *242*, 243–244, *244–245*, 245–248, *246–247*, 254–255
Nanyang, *314*
Nanzhai, *242*, 244
nao bell, 172–174, *173*. *See also* bell
nao chime, 169–170, *170–172*
Narmer Palette, 358, *359*
Nebra, 123
Nebra Sky Disk, 123, 347
needle
 in Donghuishan cemetery, *30*
Neolithic, 123, 149, 161, 209–210, 243, 263–264
net sinker, 248
New Archaeology, 167
New Materialism, 201
Ngadju-Dayak, 16
Niangniangzhai, *242*, *244*
Ninglang, 139
Ninglang Cunyi, *128*, 137
Niya, *298*, 304, *314*, *326*
Niyaa, 325
Nonya ware, 286, 291n6
Nyonya ware, 286

objects, meaning and, 7–8, 337–350, *338–339*, *341*, *343*, *348–349*
oracle bone, 268, 272

burn marks in, 150–153, *155*, *157*, *159*, 160, 163
case study, 152–163, *153–159*, *161–162*
chronology with, 153
domestication and, *207*, 208
taxa in, 152, 160
terminology, *151*, 151–152
use of, 149
Oxford, *338*, 345

Paekche, 59, 63, *65*, 67, 73, 75n1, 75n5
painted pottery, *20*, 206, 209–210, 262–263
Palembang, *284*
Panjiatuan, 322
Panlongcheng, *226*, 236
Pazyryk, *36*, 45–46, 50
Pekalongan, *284*
Penang, 283, *284*
pendant, box-shaped, 48, 53n21
Peranakan porcelain, 283–284, *284*, *287*, 290
Phu Chanh, 134
Phu Lon, 225
Pi, 272
pig, 152–153, *153–155*, *157*, *159*, 160, 162, *184*
Pi Xian Gucheng, 267, 275n1
plants, domesticated, 205–207
plaque
 bronze, 211–212
 gold belt, 47–48, *49*, 53n19
Pleistocene, 206
pointed-bottomed vessel, 272, *273*
porcelain, 283–290, *284–287*, *289*
Poryŏng, 71
pot, 247–248, 253
pottery, 7, 18, *20*, *28–33*, 41, 63, *64–65*, 90–91, *111*, 133, 170, 206, 209–210, 212, 249, 262–273, 339, 342, 346. *See also* ceramics
Prohear, 135
proto-Silk Road, 204–209, *205*, *207*, *209*, *211*
Puducun, *169*, *176*
Puge, *129*
Puge Wadaluo, 127, *128*, 132–133, *133*, 136, 138
Puge Xiaoxingchang, 136
Pungdŏng-ni, 73
Pyŏnhan, 60, 71

Qianjiazhou, *169*, *173*
Qianzhangda, *169*, *171*
Qijia culture, 150, 153, *154*, *158*, 161–163, 209, *209*, 210–212, 264, 271
Qijiaping, *150*, *156*, *161*, *205*, 208

Qijiazhuang East, *171*
Qilipu, *242, 244*
Qimugou, *127,* 130–132, 136
Qinan, *265*
Qingguanshan, 267
Qingshan Xiaoqu, *231*
Qinweijia, *150*
Qinweijia culture, 162
Qionglai, 321
Qujiang, *83*

rabbit, *184*
Renhe, *129*
Renshengcun cemetery, *110,* 113–114
rice, 207, 214n6, 264, 266, 270, 272
ring, gold wire, 45
rites of passage, 16
ritual
    defined, 2
    sacrifice and, 5–6
ritual economy, 2–4
    Donghushan cemetry from perspective of, 17–24, *18–24*
    Mahan mortuary archaeology, 59–75, *60–61, 64–66, 68–69, 71*
ritual vessel, 37–41, *38–39,* 243, *243,* 247–248, 251, 254
Rujiazhuang, *36,* 47, *169,* 178
Ruoergai, *265*

sacrifice, 5–6
    abnegation and, 188, *189*
    animal, 181–191, *182–187, 189*
    objects as, 114–116
sacrificial pits, 109, 112–115, 117. *See also* hoards
Salkhityn Am, 182, *182*
Samhan, 61–62
sandal, *357*
Sanhe Huayuan, 270
Sanpanshan, 324–325, *325*
Sanxingdui, *108, 110,* 121, *262, 265,* 268–270, *270,* 271–273
Sanxingdui hoards, 95n3, 107–117, *110–112*
Scythians, 45
secondary burial, 16–17
Shaanxi, 268, 274
Sha'er, *265*
Shajing culture, 209, *209*
Shangdong, 268
Shanghai, *284*
Shanghai ware, 286
Shangtapo, *83*
Shangwang, *36,* 46, 48

Shanma culture, 209, *209*
Shanxi, 268
Shaochai, *242, 244*
Shawudu, *263, 265*
Shaxi, 270
sheep, 153, *153,* 162, *184,* 189, 207–208
shell, in Donghuishan cemetery, *20*
Shenna, *150, 156, 158, 161*
Shichengshan, *150, 156*
Shidao, *242, 244*
Shi'erqiao culture, 110, *262,* 268–269, *269,* 270, 272–273
Shijiahe, 268
Shilipu, *83*
Shimao, *205,* 212
Shimenkou, *265*
Shipan, *319*
Shizhaishan, 134–135
Shizhaocun, 162, 207, *265*
Shizishan, *265*
Shombuuzyn-Belchir, *182, 185–186*
Shombuuzyun-Belchir, 185–188
Shuanghe, *265,* 275n1
Siba culture, 17, 153, *154,* 162, 209, *209,* 211
sickle, *64–65*
Sifangtang cemetery, *231,* 234–235
Silk Road, 204, 341
Silla, 59, 62, 67, 73, 75n1
silver decoration, on iron objects, 43–45, *44*
Singapore, 283, *284*
Siwa, 41
Siwa culture, 209, *209*
Sixiachuan, *265*
skull, 4, 17, 22–23, 25, 183, 186, 338
smelting, 225–237, *226–228, 231, 234*
social inequality, 15–25
socioeconomic dimensions
    of Buddhist image making, 306–308
    of funerals, 16–17
sociotechnical systems, 202
Sŏkch'ŏn-dong, 67
Songpan, *265*
Songshan, *318*
Sŏsan, 71
spade, 228, 233
spear, *64*
spearhead
    bronze, *128,* 137
    iron, *65,* 137
spindle whorl, *20, 28–31, 33, 128,* 133
spreader, bone, in Donghuishan cemetery, *29–30*

steamer, 40, 247, 253
stirrup, *65*
stone knife, in Donghuishan cemetery, *20, 28, 30, 32–33*
storage vessel, 254
subsistence technology, 205–209, *207*
Suizhou, 175
Sunan Gunung Jati tomb, 288, *289*
Sunqitun, *242, 244*
Susa, *36,* 48, *49*
sword
   bronze, *128,* 137
   iron, 42–43, *64–65*

Ta'erpo, *36*
Taiqinggong, *169, 171*
Takhiltyn-Khotgor, *182,* 185–188, *187*
Taosi, 162, *205*
technology, 6–7, 199–204, 213
Tello, 48
Tengzhou, *314*
textile production, 233, *234*
Thrace, 50
Three Star Mound, 110
Tianma-Qucun, *169, 176–177*
Tianshui, *265*
tiwah, 16
Tocharian language, 304, 308n1
Tolstaia Moguila, *36*
Tolstaya Mogila, 48
tomb
   barrow, 63, *64–66, 67–68, 68–69,* 70–72, *71*
   coffin, *64, 69*
   ditches surrounding, 72
   Dou Wan, 323, *324,* 324–325
   Fenghuangshan, 321
   Gounan, *319*
   Haotan, 320, *320*
   Huchang, 325
   jar burial, *69*
   Liu Sheng, 45, 315, *315,* 323, 326
   at Mahan, 59–75, *60–61, 64–66, 68–69, 71*
   at Majiayuan, *38–39,* 43, *44,* 45–48, *49*
   Maoling, 326
   Mawangdui, 325, 330–331, 332n3
   mounded, 60, 63, *64,* 67–68, *68–69,* 70–72, *71*
   multiple-burial practices, 72–74
   Niya, 325, *326*
   pit, 18, 22, *28–33,* 63, *64–65, 69*
   Sanpanshan, 324, *325*
   at Sifangtang cemetery, 234–235

Sunan Gunung Jati, 288, *289*
terminology, *69*
Tutankhamun, *357, 361*
Tongling-Nanling, 226, *227*
Tonglüshan, 225, *226,* 226–228, *227–228,* 229–231, *231,* 232–236
Tongshankou, *228,* 230
Tongxincun, *36, 44*
tray, wood, *187,* 188
tripod, 37, *38–39,* 40–41, 247, 253
tube, 268, 271, 274, 325
Tumen, *83*
turquoise, 48–50, *49,* 51, 53n21, 210–211, 214n7, 250–251
Tutankhamun tomb, *357, 361*
Tuzangshan, *231*

Únětice culture, 347
Unyang-dong, 71

vat, *266*
volute, 46

walled settlement, 264–267, *265*
Wangjiatang, *231*
Wangwa, *36, 38,* 40–41, 52n5, 52n7
Wardak-Stupa, 304, 306
Wat Arun, 285, *286*
Weihai, 170
Weishan, *314, 319*
Weishan Dao, 319
Wenjiang, 272
wheat, 17, 204, 206, 208–210
Wolonggang, 319
Wulijie, *228,* 236, 237n2
Wushan, *154*
Wuwei, *154, 156,* 211
Wuya Bulintang, *231*

Xiacunxiang, *128,* 137
Xiajiashan, *169, 173*
Xi'an, 42, 82, 86–87, 298, *298,* 300, 304, 316
Xianglushan, *228,* 230, 233
Xiangyun Jiancum, 135
Xi'an Kharoṣṭhī Inscription, *297–302,* 297–308
Xianyang, *36,* 37, *39,* 314
Xiaotuanshan, 137
Xiaotun, 169, *171*
Xiaqiyuan culture, 253
Xichang, *129*
Xichang Bahe, 132

Xichang Dayangdui, *128, 130,* 136, 138
Xichang Maliucun, *128,* 132, *133*
Xichang Qimugou, *128*
Xichang Tianwangshan, 133
Xichang Yingpanshan, *128*
Xichengyi, *205,* 209, 211
Xichengyi culture, 17, 209, *209*
Xichuan, *314*
Xide, *129*
Xiemajian, *265*
Xiezidi, 226, *228,* 230, 232–234, *234*
Xindian culture, 153, *156,* 162, 208–209, *209*
Xindu, 272
Xingan, 172
Xinye, *314*
Xinyicun, *262,* 268–269, *269,* 271, 274
Xinzhai, *242, 244*
Xinzheng, 319
Xiongjialong, *231*
Xiongnu, *182,* 183
Xi Rong, 35–52, *36, 38–39, 44, 49*
Xishanping, 162, *265*
Xiyacun, *242, 244*

yak, 152
Yanbulak culture, 209, *209*
Yandian, *129, 265,* 275n1
Yangguang Didai, 266, 270
Yanglang culture, 42
yan grain steamer, 37, 40–42, 247, 253
Yangshao culture, 209, *209,* 263
Yangzishan, *314,* 321, *322*
Yanjiayuanzi, 112–114
Yanshi Xingyuan, *83*
Yanyinshanjiao, 230, 232–233
Yanyin Shanjiao, *231*
Yanyuan, *129,* 139
Yanyuan "Gong'anju," *128*
Yanyuan Laolongtou, 135
Yejiashan, *169,* 175, *176,* 226
Yenongqiujing, *265*
Yicheng, 178
Yimencun, *36,* 45
Yimen Xiacunxiang, 137

Yingpanshan, *127,* 130–132, 136, 138, *262,* 263, *263,* 264, 272–273, *273,* 274
Yingzhuang, 321
Yinxu, 5, 169, *169,* 170, 208, 256, 268
Yinxu Xiqu, *171*
Yongjing, *154*
Yŏngnam, 70, 72–73
Yŏngsan, 63, *64–65,* 67–68, 72–74
Yongsheng, 139
Yongsheng Duizi, 131
Yongsheng Laoying, *128,* 139
Yongsheng Longtan, *128*
Yongsheng Yangjiaqing, *128*
yongzhon bell, 174–178, *175–177.*
   See also bell
Yoshinogari, 70
Yuanmou Dadunzi, 131
Yucun, *242, 244*
Yueliangwan, *110,* 112–113, 267, 269
Yueliangwan locus, 112
Yuexi, *129*
Yufu, 275n1
Yutucun, *265*

Zaojiashu, *242, 244*
Zaomiao, *39*
Zhangjiapo, *169, 176–177, 265*
Zhaojue, *129,* 133, 137–139
Zhaojue Sikaixiang, *128,* 138–139
Zhengyao, *242, 244*
Zhengzhou, 225, *226,* 236, *244–245, 314,* 318
Zhi-gui, 172
Zhihuijie, 269, *269,* 272, 274
Zhongzipu, *265*
Zhongzui, *231*
Zhoujiazhuang, 162
Zhuanchangba, *127,* 133, 135–136
Zhuge Fen, *84, 86–87*
Zhuoni, *265*
Zhuyuangou, *169,* 170, *171, 176–177,* 178
Zizhu, 275n1
Zongri, 264
Zongri culture, 209, 264
Zoucheng, *314,* 320–321

UCLA COTSEN INSTITUTE OF ARCHAEOLOGY PRESS
Ideas, Debates, and Perspectives

Volume 1 — *Settlement, Subsistence and Social Complexity: Essays Honoring the Legacy of Jeffrey R. Parsons,* edited by Richard E. Blanton

Volume 2 — *Chinese Society in the Age of Confucius (1000–250 BC): The Archaeological Evidence,* by Lothar von Falkenhausen

Volume 3 — *Settlement and Society: Essays Dedicated to Robert McCormick Adams,* edited by Elizabeth C. Stone

Volume 4 — *Blood and Beauty: Organized Violence in the Art and Archaeology of Mesoamerica and Central America,* edited by Heather Orr and Rex Koontz

Volume 5 — *Information and Its Role in Hunter-Gatherer Bands,* edited by Robert Whallon, William A. Lovis, and Robert K. Hitchcock

Volume 6 — *Classic Maya Political Ecology: Resource Management, Class Histories, and Political Change in Northwestern Belize,* edited by Jon C. Lohse

Volume 7 — *Empires & Diversity: On the Crossroads of Archaeology, Anthropology, & History,* edited by Gregory E. Areshian

Volume 8 — *Unmasking Ideology in Imperial and Colonial Archaeology,* edited by Bonnie Effros and Guolong Lai